Lecture Notes in Computer Science   12229

Formal Methods

Subline of Lectures Notes in Computer Science

More information about this series at http://www.springer.com/series/7408

Ritchie Lee · Susmit Jha · Anastasia Mavridou ·
Dimitra Giannakopoulou (Eds.)

NASA
Formal Methods

12th International Symposium, NFM 2020
Moffett Field, CA, USA, May 11–15, 2020
Proceedings

 Springer

Editors
Ritchie Lee 🆔
NASA Ames Research Center
Moffett Field, CA, USA

Susmit Jha 🆔
SRI International
Menlo Park, CA, USA

Anastasia Mavridou 🆔
KBR Inc., NASA Ames Research Center
Moffett Field, CA, USA

Dimitra Giannakopoulou
NASA Ames Research Center
Moffett Field, CA, USA

ISSN 0302-9743 ISSN 1611-3349 (electronic)
Lecture Notes in Computer Science
ISBN 978-3-030-55753-9 ISBN 978-3-030-55754-6 (eBook)
https://doi.org/10.1007/978-3-030-55754-6

LNCS Sublibrary: SL2 – Programming and Software Engineering

This Springer imprint is published by the registered company Springer Nature Switzerland AG
The registered company address is: Gewerbestrasse 11, 6330 Cham, Switzerland

Preface

The sustained improvement in hardware performance, the rapid progress in software-based control, and the emergence of artificial intelligence with near-human performance have accelerated the adoption of cyber-physical systems and, in particular, autonomous or semi-autonomous systems. An immense increase in system complexity has accompanied this acceleration in adoption. The traditional abstraction layers have been broken by the rise in new enabling technologies such as hardware acceleration and big-data-driven models, as well as unique application needs such as energy efficiency, human-in-the-loop systems, and resilient distributed computing. These factors have widened the gap between what can be designed with acceptable average behavior and what can be analyzed for their worst-case behavior.

NASA and the aerospace industry are at the frontier of the effort to tame the growing complexity of systems with the development of formal analysis approaches to ensure system safety and certification. In recent years, new challenges have emerged for system specification, development, verification, and the need for system-wide fault detection, diagnosis, and prognostics. Systems such as autonomous on-board software for Unmanned Aerial Systems (UAS) and UAS Traffic Management (UTM) require rethinking traditional approaches to assurance. The NASA Formal Methods Symposium (NFM) is a forum to foster collaboration between theoreticians and practitioners from NASA, academia, and the industry to address these challenges. The goal is to facilitate the development of advanced techniques that address specification, design, verification, validation, and certification requirements. These techniques will facilitate the responsible adoption of these complex systems in mission-critical and safety-critical applications in aerospace as well as other industries such as automobiles, robotics, and medical equipment.

NFM is an annual event organized by the NFM Steering Committee, comprised of researchers spanning several NASA centers. The series began in 1990 as the Langley Formal Methods Workshop (LFM) at NASA Langley and later became the NASA Formal Methods Symposium starting in 2009 when it became an annual NASA-wide event. The symposium is hosted by a different NASA center each year. This year, NFM was hosted and organized by the NASA Ames Research Center.

This volume contains the papers presented at the 12th NASA Formal Methods Symposium (NFM 2020) held during May 11–15, 2020. The symposium was originally planned to be held physically at NASA Ames. However, due to the travel restrictions and shelter-in-place orders arising from COVID-19, the symposium was shifted to be completely online this year. The convenience of participating in a virtual event brought a record number of registrations. This year, we had 857 registered participants from 48 different countries around the world.

The main program contained two categories of papers: (1) regular papers, presenting fully developed work and complete results and (2) short papers, presenting tools or experience reports on applications of formal methods to real systems. We encouraged, but did not require, that papers be accompanied by publicly-available artifacts.

We received 80 abstract submissions, which ultimately resulted in 62 paper submissions. The symposium accepted a total of 25 papers (20 regular, 5 short) to be presented, resulting in an overall acceptance rate of 40.3% (39.2% regular, 45.4% short). The papers were reviewed by an international Program Committee of 44 members from a mix of academia, government, and industry. All submissions went through a rigorous single-blind reviewing process overseen by the Program Committee chairs. Each submission was reviewed by at least three reviewers.

The main program also featured six invited talks covering all aspects of safety-critical systems. Professor Byron Cook from Amazon Web Services and University College London gave a keynote talk on formal methods for cloud services. Professor David Dill from Facebook Calibra and Stanford University gave a keynote talk about formal methods for blockchain. Dana Schulze from the National Transportation Safety Board (NTSB) gave a keynote talk about transportation accidents and safety. Professor Sanjit Seshia from UC Berkeley gave a keynote talk on formal methods for autonomous and cyberphysical systems. Dr. Vandi Verma from NASA JPL gave a keynote talk about Mars 2020 rover and challenges. Finally, Léonard Bouygues from Google Loon gave a keynote talk about safety and high-altitude balloon networks. The main program also included a special session introducing the SAE G-34/EUROCAE WG-114 Working Group, which is a standards development committee for AI certification.

In addition to the main program, the symposium also had two affiliated workshops: Workshop on AI Safety and Workshop on Formal Methods for Cryptographic Proofs.

We gratefully thank the authors for submitting and presenting their work at NFM 2020. We thank the invited speakers, Steering Committee, session chairs, Program Committee and external reviewers, and support staff, all of whom have contributed to make the virtual symposium successful. Finally, we thank our sponsor UTRC and everyone who attended NFM this year. The NFM 2020 website can be found at https://ti.arc.nasa.gov/events/nfm-2020/.

May 2020

Ritchie Lee
Susmit Jha
Anastasia Mavridou
Dimitra Giannakopoulou

The original version of the book was revised: a forgotten volume editor was added. The correction to the book is available at https://doi.org/10.1007/978-3-030-55754-6_26

Organization

General Chairs

Dimitra Giannakopoulou   NASA Ames Research Center, USA
Anastasia Mavridou   NASA Ames Research Center and KBR, USA

Program Committee Chairs

Ritchie Lee   NASA Ames Research Center, USA
Susmit Jha   SRI International, USA

Steering Committee

Julia Badger   NASA Johnson, USA
Aaron Dutle   NASA Langley, USA
Klaus Havelund   NASA JPL, USA
Michael R. Lowry   NASA Ames, USA
Kristin Y. Rozier   Iowa State University, USA
Johann Schumann   NASA Ames and KBR, USA

Program Committee

Aaron Dutle   NASA Langley, USA
Ahmed Irfan   Stanford University, USA
Alessandro Cimatti   Fondazione Bruno Kessler (FBK), Italy
Alwyn Goodloe   NASA Langley, USA
Arie Gurfinkel   University of Waterloo, Canada
Arnaud Venet   Facebook, USA
Ashlie Hocking   Dependable Computing, USA
Brian Jalaian   Army Research Laboratory, USA
Catherine Dubois   ENSIIE, France
Cesar Munoz   NASA Langley, USA
Christoph Torens   German Aerospace Center (DLR), Germany
Constance Heitmeyer   Naval Research Laboratory, USA
Corina Pasareanu   NASA Ames and Carnegie Mellon University, USA
Cormac Flanagan   UC Santa Cruz, USA
Cristina Seceleanu   Malardalen University, Sweden
Daniel Genin   Johns Hopkins University APL, USA
Erika Ábrahám   RWTH Aachen University, Germany
Ewen Denney   NASA Ames and KBR, USA
Falk Howar   Dortmund University, Germany
Huafeng Yu   Boeing, USA

J. Aaron Pendergrass	Johns Hopkins University APL, USA
Jean-Baptiste Jeannin	University of Michigan, USA
Johann Schumann	NASA Ames and KBR, USA
Klaus Haveland	NASA JPL, USA
Konrad Slind	Rockwell Collins, USA
Kristin Rozier	Iowa State University, USA
Laura Kovacs	TU Wien, Austria
Laura Titolo	NASA Langley and NIA, USA
Marielle Stoelinga	University of Twente and Radboud University, The Netherlands
Michael Lowry	NASA Ames, USA
Michael Whalen	Amazon Web Services, USA
Natasha Neogi	NASA Langley, USA
S. Ramesh	General Motors, USA
Shaun McWherter	NASA Armstrong, USA
Simon Bliudze	Inria, France
Stavros Tripakis	Northeastern University, USA
Stefan Mitsch	Carnegie Mellon University, USA
Stefania Gnesi	ISTI, Italy
Steven Drager	Air Force Research Laboratory, USA
Taylor Johnson	Vanderbilt University, USA
Ufuk Topcu	The University of Texas at Austin, USA
Virginie Wiels	ONERA, France
Willem Visser	Stellenbosch University, South Africa
Xiaoqing Jin	Apple, USA

Additional Reviewers

Peter Backeman	Rom Langerak
Davide Basile	Nham Le
Steven Carr	Makai Mann
Esther Conrad	Omer Nguena Timo
Thao Dang	Melkior Ornik
Jyotirmoy Deshmukh	Ivan Perez
Florian Faissole	Arnau Prat i Sala
Alessandro Fantechi	Swarn Priya
Lu Feng	John Rushby
Predrag Filipovikj	Sebastian Schirmer
Jie Fu	Stefan Schupp
Georgios Giantamidis	Maximilian Schwenger
Stephen Giguere	Tanner Slagel
Rong Gu	Hari Govind Vediramana Krishnan
Arnd Hartmanns	Abhinav Verma
Fabian Immler	Haoze Wu
Brian Kempa	Djurre van der Wal

Abstracts of Invited Talks

Automated Reasoning at Amazon

Byron Cook

Amazon Web Services, University College London
b.cook@cs.ucl.ac.uk

Abstract. This talk will discuss the development and use of formal verification tools within Amazon Web Services (AWS) to increase the assurance of its cloud infrastructure and to help customers help themselves build correct cloud-based systems. I will also discuss some open challenges that could inspire future research in the community.

Biography

Byron Cook is Professor of Computer Science at University College London (UCL) and Senior Principal Scientist at Amazon. Byron's interests include computer/network security, program analysis/verification, programming languages, theorem proving, logic, hardware design, operating systems, and biological systems.

A Formal Verifier for the Libra Blockchain Move Language

David Dill

Facebook Inc., Stanford University
dill@cs.stanford.edu

Abstract. The Libra blockchain, which was initiated last year by Facebook, includes a novel programming language called Move for implementing smart contracts. We plan for the Libra blockchain to host massive amounts of assets, and all transactions are mediated by Move programs, and smart contracts on other blockchains have had devastating bugs resulting in major losses of assets, so we consider the correctness of Move programs to be critical. The Move language is designed to be as safe as we can make it, and it is accompanied by a formal specification and automatic verification tool, called the Move Prover. Our aspiration is that every Move program will be thoroughly specified and verified before being deployed on the blockchain.

Biography

David L. Dill is a Lead Researcher at Facebook, working on the Libra blockchain project. He is also Donald E. Knuth Professor, Emeritus, in the School of Engineering at Stanford University. He was on the faculty in the Department of Computer Science at Stanford from 1987 until going emeritus in 2017, and starting his current position at Facebook in 2018. Prof. Dill's research interests include formal verification of software, hardware, and protocols, with a focus on automated techniques, as well as voting technology and computational biology. He is an IEEE Fellow, an ACM Fellow, a member of the National Academy of Engineering, and the American Academy of Arts and Sciences. He received an EFF Pioneer Award for his work in voting technology and is the founder of VerifiedVoting.org.

Improving Design Assurance Through Accident/Incident Lessons Learned

Dana Schulze

National Transportation Safety Board (NTSB)
dana.schulze@ntsb.gov

Abstract. The NTSB has investigated or participated in the investigation of numerous accidents and incidents involving the failure of complex aircraft systems. While accidents involving these types of failures are quite rare, their occurrence offers lessons learned for the design and certification communities. Findings in several cases suggest that these malfunctions are not typically the result of software production deficiencies but rather system or software requirements deficiencies. Case studies involving two NTSB investigations will be discussed and used to introduce the broader set of design issues that accident and incident investigations have revealed, which could be useful in understanding the improvements needed in design assurance methods and their implementation to improve complex system certification outcomes.

Biography

Dana Schulze, Director of the Office of Aviation Safety, has been with the National Transportation Safety Board since 2002. She began her career with the Safety Board as an Aircraft System Safety Engineer in the Aviation Engineering Division and served as a Group Chairman and investigator on numerous major domestic and international airline accident investigations, including Alaska Airlines flight 261, Pinnacle Airlines flight 3701, and American Airlines flight 587. In 2006, Ms. Schulze became Chief of the Aviation Engineering Division, which is responsible for investigating the airworthiness of aircraft involved in major aviation accidents and serious incidents. Ms. Schulze later served as the Chief of the Major Investigations Division where she oversaw more than a dozen major airline accident investigations, including the investigation of US Airways flight 1549 in Weehawken, New Jersey, and Colgan Air flight 3407 in Clarence Center, New York, and subsequently as Deputy Director, leading the organization's execution of air carrier investigations and safety initiatives as well as the development of emergent programs for unmanned aircraft systems and commercial space accident investigation. In 2018, she was named the Acting Director of the Office of Aviation Safety and moved into the Director role in 2019. Prior to joining the NTSB, Ms. Schulze worked in the commercial aerospace industry in staff engineering and engineering management roles related to design, system safety, reliability, and quality. She received her Bachelor of Science degree in Space Sciences and Mechanical Engineering from the Florida Institute of Technology and Master of Science degree in Mechanical Engineering from the State University of New York.

Ms. Schulze is also a recipient of the Distinguished Presidential Rank Award, which recognizes a select group of career members of the United States Government Senior Executive Service (SES) for sustained extraordinary accomplishments on a national or international level.

Verified Artificial Intelligence and Autonomy

Sanjit Seshia

UC Berkeley
sseshia@berkeley.edu

Abstract. Verified artificial intelligence (AI) is the goal of designing AI-based systems that have strong, verified assurances of correctness with respect to mathematically-specified requirements. This goal is particularly important for autonomous and semi-autonomous systems. In this talk, I will consider Verified AI from a formal methods perspective and with a special focus on autonomy. I will describe the challenges for and recent progress towards attaining Verified AI, with examples from the domain of intelligent cyber-physical systems, with a particular focus on autonomous vehicles and aerospace systems.

Biography

Sanjit A. Seshia is a Professor in the Department of Electrical Engineering and Computer Sciences at the University of California, Berkeley. He received a Masters and PhD in Computer Science from Carnegie Mellon University, and a Bachelor in Computer Science and Engineering from the Indian Institute of Technology, Bombay. His research interests are in formal methods for dependable and secure computing, with a current focus on the areas of cyber-physical systems, computer security, machine learning, and robotics. He has made pioneering contributions to the areas of satisfiability modulo theories (SMT), SMT-based verification, and inductive program synthesis. He is co-author of a widely-used textbook on embedded, cyber-physical systems and has led the development of technologies for cyber-physical systems education based on formal methods. His awards and honors include a Presidential Early Career Award for Scientists and Engineers (PECASE), an Alfred P. Sloan Research Fellowship, the Frederick Emmons Terman Award for contributions to electrical engineering and computer science education, the Donald O. Pederson Best Paper Award for the IEEE Transactions on CAD, and the IEEE Technical Committee on Cyber-Physical Systems (TCCPS) Mid-Career Award. He is a Fellow of the IEEE.

Operable NASA Robots on Mars and Beyond

Vandi Verma

NASA Jet Propulsion Laboratory (JPL)
vandana.verma@jpl.nasa.gov

Abstract. The talk will provide an overview of Mars rovers and the challenges with developing operable space robots.

Biography

Vandi Verma leads the Operable Robotics group in the Mobility and Robotic Systems Section at NASA Jet Propulsion Laboratory. She has developed software for and operated multiple rovers on Mars and has worked on research rovers deployed in the Arctic, Antarctic, and the Atacama. Vandi's interests include space robotics, autonomy, and operability. She is currently working on robotic arm and sample caching algorithms, flight software for the Mars 2020 Perseverance rover, and is the software architect for the Europa Lander advanced autonomy prototype. She has a PhD in Robotics from Carnegie Mellon University.

Evolving Airspace Regulations and Systems to Enable Large Scale, Highly Automated Operations in the Stratosphere

Léonard Bouygues

Google Loon
leonardb@loon.com

Abstract. Loon is a network of stratospheric vehicles that provide connectivity to thousands of people living in underserved regions around the world. With over 350k flight hours in 2019 and over one million flight hours total, it is the world's first large-scale automated fleet of unmanned vehicles.

Aviation regulations, concepts of operations, and aviation systems need to evolve to enable new technologies like Loon. Loon is partnering with regulators, the entire community of stratospheric operators, and research organizations to cooperatively evolve this airspace. 1) Develop collaborative traffic management concepts that are necessary to handle the unique vehicle performance characteristics and the dynamic ecosystem. 2) Develop new risk and performance-based safety frameworks needed to ensure a safe environment in which technologies and designs can evolve rapidly. 3) Develop new validation methods for modern software development techniques and a rapidly evolving software ecosystem. 4) Propose adaptations to roles and responsibilities of humans in the context of large-scale automated systems.

Biography

Léonard is currently Head of Aviation Strategy at Loon. Loon is a network of high-altitude balloons that provide telecommunications access to unserved and underserved populations. It is the first large-scale automated fleet of unmanned vehicles and has already surpassed one million flight hours.

In this role, Léonard is responsible for the development of innovative aviation concepts. He currently leads industry players in the development of the "Collaborative Traffic Management in the Stratosphere" CONOPs. He is also a key contributing author of the initial paper that he presented at Drone Enable 2019. Additionally, Léonard is currently working in partnerships with NASA, MITRE, academia, and research organizations to evolve safety frameworks within FAA's safety continuum, in particular for in-time safety management, risk budgeting, and human-automation teaming for the supervision of large autonomous fleets.

After joining Loon in 2015, Léonard led Loon's Flight Operations from 2017–2019. In this position, he built and managed the company's Operation Control Center, enabling Loon to supervise a fleet of hundreds of autonomous vehicles. In this effort,

Léonard's team also developed technology for live risk computation of Loon operations.

Léonard started at Google's European headquarters as an Analytical Lead, before joining the Mountain View office to work as a Product Lead in the advertising division. Léonard holds a Master's in Aeronautical Engineering from Imperial College London, a Master of Science in Management of Technology and Innovation form MIT, and a Master of Science in management from HEC Paris.

Contents

Validation and Solvers

Solvers and Program Analysis

Verification and Timed Systems

Autonomy and Other Applications

Hybrid and Cyber-Physical Systems

Learning and Formal Synthesis

From Passive to Active:
Learning Timed Automata Efficiently

Bernhard K. Aichernig[1], Andrea Pferscher[1(✉)], and Martin Tappler[1,2]

[1] Institute of Software Technology, Graz University of Technology, Graz, Austria
{aichernig,andrea.pferscher,martin.tappler}@ist.tugraz.at
[2] Schaffhausen Institute of Technology, Schaffhausen, Switzerland
mt@sit.org

Abstract. Model-based testing is a promising technique for quality
assurance. In practice, however, a model is not always present. Hence,
model learning techniques attain increasing interest. Still, many learning
approaches can only learn relatively simple types of models and advanced
properties like time are ignored in many cases. In this paper we present
an active model learning technique for timed automata. For this, we build
upon an existing passive learning technique for real-timed systems. Our
goal is to efficiently learn a timed system while simultaneously minimizing the set of training data. For evaluation we compared our active to
the passive learning technique based on 43 timed systems with up to 20
locations and multiple clock variables. The results of 18 060 experiments
show that we require only 100 timed traces to adequately learn a timed
system. The new approach is up to 755 times faster.

Keywords: Active automata learning · Genetic programming · Timed
automata · Model learning · Model inference

1 Introduction

Modeling of systems is an increasingly important area in computer science. The
reason for the popularity is that models help to create a common understanding
of — often complex — systems. Additionally, models are a useful tool to verify a
system, where the verification of models includes well-proven formal techniques
like model checking. However, during software development processes there is
usually little time to create or maintain system models. Furthermore, creating a
model can be a complex process. According to Peled et al. [22] we may face the
problem that we have no insight into the system under test (SUT), e.g., using
third party components. One promising solution for this problem is to learn
system models completely automatically instead of creating them manually.

In automata learning we distinguish between passive and active learning. The
former learns based on provided observations of the system, whereas the latter
generates learning data by querying the system on demand. Already in the 1980s
Angluin [7] proposed L^*, which still presents a base for many active learning

© Springer Nature Switzerland AG 2020
R. Lee et al. (Eds.): NFM 2020, LNCS 12229, pp. 3–21, 2020.
https://doi.org/10.1007/978-3-030-55754-6_1

approaches. The basic principle of active learning is to ask questions about the SUT. Using the obtained answers, active learning interactively refines the learned model until the model conforms to the SUT. In passive learning algorithms we use given observation data, e.g. execution traces (logs). However, passive learning requires a large number of system traces to create an adequate model of the SUT. The reason is that the given observations must be representative, i.e. they need to adequately cover the SUT. Active learning overcomes this problem by selecting required tests on demand. Nevertheless, the number of asked questions (tests) can be high. Thus, Walkinshaw et al. [32] proposed that learning based on heuristics combined with model-based testing [29] can be a promising solution.

Automata learning provides a convenient technique to model systems. However, many approaches focus on comparatively simple representation schemes, e.g., Mealy machines. The problem is that such representation schemes can hardly describe complex system properties like time. For this, Alur and Dill [5] introduced timed automata (TA) which are a modeling technique to represent timed behavior of real-time systems. TA are labeled transition system (LTS) that are equipped with clock variables that represent time values. Constraints on time values define the behavior of the TA. However, learning general TA can be a challenging task, since their state space is infinitely large and they do not have canonical forms [13]. Therefore, many learning approaches assume discrete time or can only capture a restricted timed behavior.

Similar to our passive learning algorithm [27] we learn general input-output TA. For this, we assume real-valued clock variables and distinguish between input and output actions. Our assumed type of TA conforms to the one that is used in the model-checker UPPAAL [9]. However, to ensure testability we assume that our TA are deterministic, input-enabled and output urgent. Regarding determinism, we also assume that our TA have isolated outputs, i.e. only one output action can be enabled at a single point in time.

Due to real-valued clock variables the state space is infinite. Hence, the TA have no canonical form, which makes deterministic learning techniques, like L^*, not useful. To overcome this problem we use a metaheuristic search algorithm to learn TA. It is based on genetic programming (GP). GP [16] is a machine learning technique that uses the principle of evolution and natural selection. Over several generations a population develops. During the evolution only the fittest individuals survive and build a new population using crossover and mutation. In our approach the population consists of TA. We evolve the population via syntactic changes until no further improvement regarding fitness can be made and then output the fittest individual of the population as a candidate solution. The fact that TA have a very simple syntax and that GP is based on syntactic manipulation, qualify it as a strong candidate for learning TA.

In this work we propose active model learning for TA. Our proposed technique builds upon our passive learning procedure [27]. We use GP to build TA based on a set of timed traces. These timed traces are actively generated by asking questions about the SUT. Using conformance testing, we check whether the proposed solution generated by GP behaves equally to the SUT. In the case of non-conformance, we extend our test data by counterexamples showing non-conformance between the proposed solution and the SUT. With these extended data we learn a new TA. We repeat this process until we find a conforming TA.

In Sect. 2 we discuss the required background. Section 3 introduces our active learning technique for TA via GP. In Sect. 4 we provide a tool that demonstrates this technique. Section 5 discusses the comprehensive evaluation. Finally, Sect. 6 concludes this paper.

2 Preliminaries

2.1 Timed Automata

Timed automata (TA) are labeled transition systems (LTSs) that are equipped with real-valued variables. These variables store time values and, therefore, represent real-time clocks. The clock values increase when time elapses. TA consist of locations which are connected via edges that are labeled with input and output actions. The behavior of a TA is defined via clock constraints, which are denoted as guards. Let $\mathcal{C}$ be a finite set of clocks where each clock is a real-valued variable c_i with $i \in \mathbb{N}_0$. We denote the set of guards over $\mathcal{C}$ as $\mathcal{G}(\mathcal{C})$. Guards are a conjunction of the formulas $c_i \oplus k$, with $c_i \in \mathcal{C}$, $\oplus \in \{>, \geq, \leq, <\}$, and $k \in \mathbb{N}$.

We write Σ for the set of input and output action symbols, where $\Sigma_I \subseteq \Sigma$ includes all input actions and $\Sigma_O \subseteq \Sigma$ all output actions, and $\Sigma_I \cap \Sigma_O = \emptyset$. An input action is postfixed with a question mark "?" and an output action with an exclamation mark "!".

A TA over $(\mathcal{C}, \Sigma)$ is a triple $\langle L, l_0, E \rangle$, with the set of locations L, the initial location l_0, and the set of edges $E \subseteq L \times \Sigma \times \mathcal{G}(\mathcal{C}) \times 2^{\mathcal{C}} \times L$. Further, let $2^{\mathcal{C}}$ be the power set of $\mathcal{C}$. We write $l \xrightarrow{g,a,r} l'$ for an edge $(l, g, a, r, l') \in E$ with $g \in \mathcal{G}(\mathcal{C})$, $a \in \Sigma$, and the clock resets $r \in 2^{\mathcal{C}}$. In the event of a clock reset each clock in the set r is set to zero.

A clock valuation $\nu \in \mathbb{R}_{\geq 0}^{\mathcal{C}}$ is a mapping $\nu : \mathcal{C} \to \mathbb{R}_{\geq 0}$ that assigns a value to each clock. Further, we denote $\mathbf{0}_{\mathcal{C}}$ as the assignment of zero to each clock. An increase of ν denotes the progress of time. We write $\nu + d$ for an increase of time by a delay $d \in \mathbb{R}_{\geq 0}$ where $(\nu + d)(c_i) = \nu(c_i) + d$. If the clock valuation ν satisfies a guard $g \in \mathcal{G}(\mathcal{C})$ we write $\nu \models g$. Let $\nu[r]$ denote a reset, where every clock $c_i \in r$ is reset to zero, i.e. $\nu[r](c_i) = 0$, and every $c_j \in \mathcal{C} \setminus r, \nu[r](c_j) = \nu(c_j)$.

The semantics of a TA $\mathcal{T}$ is defined as a timed transition system (TTS) $[\![\mathcal{T}]\!] = \langle Q, q_0, \Sigma, T \rangle$ with the set of states $Q \subseteq L \times \mathbb{R}_{\geq 0}^{\mathcal{C}}$, the initial state q_0, and the transitions $T \subseteq Q \times (\Sigma \cup \mathbb{R}_{\geq 0}) \times Q$. A state $q \in Q$ is as a pair (l, ν), where the initial state q_0 of a TTS is $(l_0, \mathbf{0}_{\mathcal{C}})$. Furthermore, in a TTS we distinguish timed and discrete transitions. A timed transition $(l, \nu) \xrightarrow{d} (l, \nu + d)$ is performed on a delay $d \in \mathbb{R}_{\geq 0}$ without changing the location. A discrete transition $(l, \nu) \xrightarrow{a} (l', \nu[r])$ is performed on an action $a \in \Sigma$ and may lead to a location change and clock resets when taking an edge $l \xrightarrow{g,a,r} l'$ where $\nu \models g$ holds.

Figure 1 shows a TA of a smart light switch inspired by an example of Hessel et al. [15]. This TA has five locations and one clock variable c_0. We can either *press* or *release* the switch. Depending on how long the switch is pressed we observe either (1) nothing on a release before five time units, (2) *touch* on the release after five time units, or (3) *starthold* after ten time units pressing the button.

To ensure that the learning of TA is tractable, we make assumptions on the semantic level of TA. Our assumptions are originally proposed by Springintveld et al. [26] and then adapted by Hessel et al. [15] and in our previous work [27]. Given a TTS with $a \in \Sigma$, $o, o' \in \Sigma_O$, and $d \in \mathbb{R}_{\geq 0}$, we assume $\forall q \in Q$:

1. *Determinism:* if $\exists q', q'' \in Q : q \xrightarrow{a} q'$, $q \xrightarrow{a} q''$ then $q' = q''$,
2. *Input Enabledness:* $\forall i \in \Sigma_I : \exists q' \in Q : q \xrightarrow{i} q'$,
3. *Output Urgency:* if $\exists q' : q \xrightarrow{o} q' \in Q$ then $\nexists q'' \in Q : q \xrightarrow{d} q''$,
4. *Isolated Outputs:* if $\exists q', q'' \in Q : q \xrightarrow{o} q' \wedge q \xrightarrow{o'} q''$ then $o = o'$ and $q' = q''$.

To establish testability, we assume deterministic and input enabled TA. Input enabledness ensures that all inputs contribute to valid tests, since every input behaviour is defined in all states. Note that in illustrations of TA, e.g. Fig. 1, we hide inputs on self-loops for clearness.

We model urgent outputs as eager actions [11]. They limit the sojourn time in a location since they are executed immediately after they are enabled. For this, we introduce the following semantic extension: A timed transition $(l, \nu) \xrightarrow{d} (l, \nu + d)$ is possible iff $\forall d' \in \mathbb{R}_{\geq 0}, d' < d : \nu + d' \models \neg \bigvee_{g \in G_O} g$ with $G_O = \{g | \exists l', o, r : l \xrightarrow{g, o, r} l', o \in \Sigma_O\}$. Other definitions of TA add location invariants to limit the sojourn time in locations.

To test TA, we use test sequences.

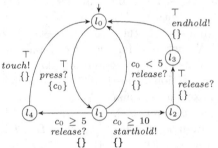

Fig. 1. The illustrated TA represents a smart light switch adapted from the example of Hessel et al. [15].

A test sequence *ts* is an ascendingly ordered sequence of time stamps t_j and inputs i_j. Formally, $ts = t_0 \cdot i_0 \cdots t_m \cdot i_m \in (\mathbb{R}_{\geq 0} \times \Sigma_I)^*$ with $\forall j \in \{0, \ldots, m - 1\} : t_j \leq t_{j+1}$. Let *tt* denote a timed trace that represents the execution of a test sequence on a TA. A timed trace includes all inputs of a test sequence as well as the observed outputs with their corresponding time stamps, i.e. $tt = t_0 \cdot a_0 \cdots t_{n-1} \cdot a_{n-1} \in (\mathbb{R}_{\geq 0} \times \Sigma)^*$ with $\forall i \in \{0, \ldots, n - 1\} : t_i \leq t_{i+1}$. A timed trace *tt* consists of pairs $\langle t_i, a_i \rangle$ of time stamps $t_i \in \mathbb{R}_{\geq 0}$ and actions $a_i \in \Sigma$. Let $|tt|$ denote the size of *tt*, i.e. the number of elements. Aichernig et al. [3] denote a run in a TTS $[\![\mathcal{T}]\!]$ as an alternating sequence of delay and discrete transitions in form of

$$(l_0, \nu_0) \xrightarrow{d_0} (l_0, \nu_0 + d_0) \xrightarrow{a_0} (l_1, \nu_1) \xrightarrow{d_1} (l_1, \nu_1 + d_1) \xrightarrow{a_1} \cdots$$

The run induces a timed trace $tt = t_0 \cdot a_0 \cdots t_i \cdot a_i \cdots t_{n-1} \cdot a_{n-1}$ with all previous delays $d_0 \cdots d_j, j < i$ summed up to the time stamp $t_i \in \mathbb{R}_{\geq 0}$. One possible observable timed trace in the smart light switch, depicted in Fig. 1, is e.g.:

$$10.8 \cdot press? \cdot 18.4 \cdot release? \cdot 18.4 \cdot touch! \cdot 20.6 \cdot release? \cdots$$

2.2 Genetic Programming

Genetic programming (GP) [16] is developed on the basis of genetic algorithms. Genetic algorithms are metaheuristic search-based algorithms that use the principles of natural selection and the evolutionary process to find a candidate solution. Using these principles, GP provides a tool to automatically generate programs without explicitly programming them. In GP, a set of programs represents the population and a program in a population is called individual. After creating an initial population, the population is evaluated, where each individual of the population receives a fitness value. Fitness is calculated using a domain-specific fitness function and measures how well an individual solves its given task. Based on the principle of natural selection the fittest individuals build a new population. Following operations exist to build a new population:

- *Reproduction:* An individual is copied unmodified.
- *Crossover:* Properties of two individuals are merged.
- *Mutation:* Properties of one individual are changed.

In addition, GP comprises different design concepts. One of these concepts is *subpopulations and migration*, which is based on the idea that several populations develop simultaneously and individuals of one population can migrate to the other populations. Another design concept is *elitism*, where the fittest individuals are always copied to the next generation. Elitism helps to avoid destroying already well-conforming solutions. The generation of a new population is repeated until no further fitness improvements can be made or the maximum number of generations is reached.

2.3 Genetic Programming for Timed Automata

In previous work [27] we described a passive learning algorithm of TA. We introduce GP as a promising solution to learn timed systems. Figure 2 depicts the basic procedure of our passive learning algorithm for TA based on GP.

The learning process is based on test data provided in the form of timed traces. All used traces are generated beforehand. Independently, an initial

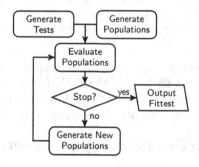

Fig. 2. Basic procedure of our passive learning algorithm [27]. The algorithm learns TA via GP based on provided timed traces.

population is randomly generated using the provided alphabet of the system under test (SUT). Afterwards, the individuals of this population are evaluated. For this, a fitness function for TA is defined. This fitness function is based on the number of passing tests and further properties, e.g., size of the generated TA and non-deterministic properties of the learned TA.

The GP procedure terminates if either the maximum number of generations is reached or a solution is found that passes all test sequences and no further fitness improvements can be observed. In this case, the procedure outputs the fittest TA of the population. We refer to the fittest TA as our hypothesis $\mathcal{H}$ of the SUT.

If the termination criterion is not satisfied, a new population is generated. The used principles to generate a new population are basically crossover and mutation. Furthermore, two populations, a global and a local population, are evolved simultaneously. The global population develops based on all timed traces and the local population only uses the timed traces that fail on the fittest individual of the global population. Crossover between the two populations is used to correct the failing behavior in the global population. In addition, the concept of elitism is applied. Further details about the used mutations and the applied fitness function can be found in [27].

2.4 Active Automata Learning

An active automata learning algorithm learns a model of the SUT by asking questions about the system. Approaches based on Angluin's L^* [7] require, however, an equivalence oracle, which is, according to Berg et al. [10] the bottleneck of active learning. Similarly, Walkinshaw et al. [32] point out that asking a large number of questions to build an adequate model is not useful. Therefore, Walkinshaw et al. introduce an iterative refinement technique that uses heuristics to learn an LTS and model-based testing to generate tests for conformance checking. The following steps are performed to learn a system:

1. Infer an initial LTS from a provided set of execution traces
2. Generate tests from the LTS using a model-based tester
3. Execute the tests on the SUT and check if the tests fail
4. If no failing test is found: **stop** and output the learned LTS
5. Otherwise add the tests to the learning set and learn a new LTS then return to Step 2

Using this approach we consider a learned LTS erroneous if a test generated from the LTS fails on the SUT. In this case, the iterative refinement approach starts again by adding the failing test case to the test suite and inferring a new hypothesis. This process is repeated until a conforming hypothesis is learned.

3 Active Learning via Genetic Programming

3.1 Basic Procedure

The basic procedure of our active learning algorithm is based on the iterative refinement approach proposed by Walkinshaw et al. [32] which we introduced in

Sect. 2.4. Figure 3 illustrates our basic procedure. Our active learning algorithm starts with an initial set of randomly generated timed traces, e.g. monitored execution traces. These randomly generated traces build our initial test data and based on these test data we learn our initial hypothesis. The creation of the initial hypothesis is done via genetic programming (GP) as introduced in Sect. 2.3. Our hypothesis is always the fittest individual of the GP procedure.

Afterwards, we check if the hypothesis conforms to the SUT via model-based testing. We define a conforming behavior between SUT and hypothesis by trace equivalence, i.e. the conformance relation is satisfied if two timed systems produce the same timed traces. Related to Tretmans' [28] implementation relation, we write $\mathcal{H}$ **conforms to** $\mathcal{I}$ if the hypothesis

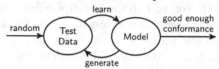

Fig. 3. In recurring order, we learn a model and extend our test data by counterexamples to conformance until we find a conforming model.

$\mathcal{H}$ conforms to the SUT $\mathcal{I}$. Let $Traces(\llbracket\mathcal{T}\rrbracket)$ be a function that performs all possible runs in a TTS $\llbracket\mathcal{T}\rrbracket$ starting at the initial state q_0. The function returns the corresponding timed traces of all runs. We use $Traces(\llbracket\mathcal{T}\rrbracket)$ to define the following conformance relation for the hypothesis $\mathcal{H}$ and the SUT $\mathcal{I}$:

$$\mathcal{H} \textbf{ conforms to } \mathcal{I} \iff Traces(\llbracket\mathcal{H}\rrbracket) = Traces(\llbracket\mathcal{I}\rrbracket). \tag{1}$$

We use $\mathcal{H}$ **passes** tt to denote that a timed trace tt produced by executing the corresponding test sequence ts on $\mathcal{H}$ is equal to the trace produced by $\mathcal{I}$. Respectively, $\mathcal{H}$ **fails** tt if the timed traces are different. Note that here we perform black-box testing on the SUT $\mathcal{I}$. We execute a test sequence, which is a sequence of inputs with timestamps, and observe a timed trace produced by $\mathcal{I}$. This means that we do not require knowledge about the internal structure of $\mathcal{I}$. Similar to the approach of Walkinshaw et al., we try to find a counterexample that contradicts the conformance relation. If we find a counterexample to equivalence between hypothesis and SUT, i.e. $\mathcal{H}$ **fails** tt, we add this trace to our test data. Based on this updated test data we relearn a new hypothesis via GP.

Considering real-valued timed systems the number of possible traces is infinite. During testing, we sample a finite amount of traces to find counterexamples to language equivalence. Conformance Relation 1 combined with a hypothesis $\mathcal{H}$ serves as an oracle for testing. However, the conformance relation is not directly applicable for learning, as we learn from our test data, a finite set of sampled traces. Therefore, we restrict the conformance relation for learning to this finite set of traces, requiring hypothesis and SUT to agree on those traces.

We always start the GP procedure with the last population of the previous procedure, if there is one. Like in our passive approach, the GP procedure either terminates if a solution is found or the maximum number of generations is reached. The parameter $g_{\mathrm{max_{active}}}$ limits the number of generations of the GP procedure in each iteration in the active learning algorithm. Again, our hypothesis is the fittest timed automaton of the GP procedure.

After creating a new hypothesis, we repeat our conformance check on the newly learned TA. However, the maximum number of overall performed generations in all iterations of the active learning is limited by g_{max}. The active learning either terminates if our test data contain no counterexamples to conformance between the hypothesis and the SUT and no further counterexamples can be found, or the maximum number of generations is reached.

In contrast to the iterative refinement approach proposed by Walkinshaw et al. [32], we only add test data that reveal non-conformance between the hypothesis and the SUT, i.e. failing timed traces. The reason for that is the underlying fitness function, which calculates the fitness value based on the number of passing and failing timed traces. We want to achieve that learning the behavior corresponding to the failing timed traces pays off. Adding passing timed traces decreases the relative weight of the failing timed traces. Additionally, we increase the weight by adding multiple failing timed traces simultaneously. Therefore, implementing the failing timed traces increases the fitness value in the GP process. If the fitness value increases significantly, it is more likely that the individuals that implement the failing timed traces survive. As a result, adding several failing timed traces increases the probability to find a better hypothesis.

3.2   Timed Trace Selection for Learning

For the timed trace selection we use a model-based testing approach to find counterexamples to conformance between the hypothesis and the SUT. Figure 4 illustrates our proposed testing procedure.

The timed traces are generated by randomly walking through the hypothesis. This random walk is explained in more detail in the next section. After we generated a timed trace, we execute the test sequence of the timed trace on the SUT. The timed trace generated by the SUT is then compared with the trace of the hypothesis. Let $\text{CMP}(tt, tt')$ denote a function that compares two timed traces $tt, tt' \in (\mathbb{R}_{\geq 0} \times \Sigma)^*$, where $tt = t_0 \cdot a_0, \cdots, t_{m-1} \cdot a_{m-1}$ and $tt' = t'_0 \cdot a'_0, \cdots, t'_{n-1} \cdot a'_{n-1}$ with $n, m \in \mathbb{N}$. We compare the elements of the traces one by one until the end of the shorter trace is reached. The function returns $|tt'|$ if the traces are equal. Otherwise,

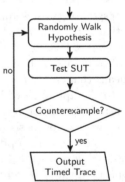

Fig. 4. We select timed traces that reveal a different behavior.

the function returns the index i of the first element where t_i or a_i are different. We can formalize the function by:

$$\text{CMP}(tt, tt') = \begin{cases} \min\{i \mid \exists\, t_i a_i \in tt, t'_i a'_i \in tt' : t_i \neq t'_i \lor a_i \neq a'_i\} & \text{if } \exists\, i \\ |tt'| & \text{otherwise} \end{cases}$$

Let $tt_{\mathcal{H}}$ be a timed trace that is observable during a random walk through the hypothesis and $tt_{\mathcal{I}}$ be the timed trace that can be observed when executing the test sequence of $tt_{\mathcal{H}}$ on the SUT. If $\text{CMP}(tt_{\mathcal{H}}, tt_{\mathcal{I}}) = |tt_{\mathcal{H}}|$ then $\mathcal{H}$ **passes** $tt_{\mathcal{I}}$. Otherwise, $\mathcal{H}$ **fails** $tt_{\mathcal{I}}$, i.e. we found a counterexample. In this case, we process the timed trace $tt_{\mathcal{I}}$ and add it to our test data.

Since executing a prefix of a timed trace is faster than executing the whole trace, counterexample processing reduces the trace length. More concretely, we reduce the length of the timed trace to the smallest length that reveals a difference between the SUT and the hypothesis. This value is equal to the index returned by $\text{CMP}(tt_{\mathcal{H}}, tt_{\mathcal{I}})$. Furthermore, we check if the timed traces contain at least one output. Our goal is to avoid timed traces without outputs, since our TA are input-enabled. Using timed traces with no outputs would reward trivial automata structures. If we find a counterexample that contains only inputs, we try to extend the timed trace until we find an output. The processed counterexample is then added to the test data.

The procedure in Fig. 4 is repeated until a counterexample is found, but at the maximum n_{attempts} times. After selecting n_{fail} counterexamples, we start a new GP procedure based on our extended test data.

3.3   Timed Trace Generation

We generate timed traces for the previously introduced model-based testing approach. Aichernig and Tappler [4] showed that random walks through automata are effective in test-based learning of Mealy machines. Here, we perform a random walk on the semantic level of the timed transition system (TTS) of the hypothesis. Figure 5 illustrates the steps of the random walk. The output of a random walk is a timed trace $tt_{\mathcal{H}} \in (\mathbb{R}_{\geq 0} \times \Sigma)^*$.

The procedure starts with the initialization of the required variables. For a random walk through a TTS we always start at the initial state $q_0 = (l_0, \mathbf{0}_{\mathcal{C}})$. Additionally, we store the overall elapsed time using the variable $t \in \mathbb{R}_{\geq 0}$. The initial value of t is always zero. The random walk terminates once the generated timed trace has the length of the parameter $n_{\text{len}} \in \mathbb{N}$.

Whenever we extend a timed trace, we first check if any output is enabled. Since we assume that outputs are urgent we have to take edges with enabled outputs. In this case we add all urgent outputs and the current value of t to $tt_{\mathcal{H}}$.

Since our hypothesis is created with GP, we may observe non-deterministic behavior during our random walk. We assume isolated outputs, i.e. only one output in the current state can be enabled concurrently. If more than one output is enabled, we randomly select one of the enabled outputs. Later in the GP procedure, the fitness function penalizes the non-deterministic behavior. For details on the fitness function see [27].

Another problem due to the generation via GP is that the TA may produce an infinite amount of outputs without time elapsing. In the literature, this behavior is denoted as Zeno behavior [8]. We assume that a Zeno behavior does not occur in the SUT and penalize this misbehavior in a hypothesis by adding timed traces that reveal infinite output loops. If the same state is visited in a sequence of enabled outputs twice we stop the random walk. After observing such an infinite output sequence we add a randomly chosen input, to show that this input is not possible and return immediately the timed trace $tt_{\mathcal{H}}$.

If no infinite output sequence is detected, we select an outgoing edge in the current location. For this we have to make two decisions: (1) performing a non-changing input and (2) selecting a delay from the constants of the edges.

A non-changing input is an input where the execution of this input neither causes a location change nor a clock reset. We can perform such inputs since our TA are input-enabled. The goal of performing non-changing inputs is to explore new behavior that is not yet captured in our hypothesis. The probability to perform such a non-changing input is defined by the parameter p_{input}. In later iterations of our active learning approach we focus more on testing the already explored behavior. Therefore, we decrease the probability p_{input} in each iteration of the active learning algorithm by a constant.

The second decision to make is the selection of a delay. In random walks we either delay the system by a randomly chosen delay or by a constant that is present in the guards of the outgoing edges of the current location. The probability to perform a delay based on a guard constant is defined by the parameter p_{trans}. This delay selection method selects uniformly at random one constant of the guards of the outgoing edges. This method provides the opportunity to check whether the learned delays are correct. The random delays are selected in accordance with a provided set of relevant constants of the SUT. Like non-changing inputs, selecting random delays helps to explore undefined behavior.

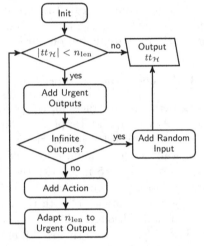

Fig. 5. In the random walk we follow edges of the TA and save the delays and actions in a timed trace.

After selecting a delay $d \in \mathbb{R}_{\geq 0}$, we increase the clock valuation ν to $\nu + d$ and select an action. If we do not perform a non-changing input, we check whether outgoing edges are enabled. If there is a guard g such that $g \models \nu$ holds, we add the action of this edge and $t + d$ to our timed trace. Outputs may be triggered earlier due to the assumed output urgency, where we adapt d to the occurrence of the output action.

As a last step of our random walk, we check again if an output is enabled and if $|tt_{\mathcal{H}}| = n_{len}$. If both are true, we increase n_{len} and we can add the output in the next iteration. If $|tt_{\mathcal{H}}| = n_{len}$ and no output is present, we return $tt_{\mathcal{H}}$.

4   Implementation

For the active learning approach, we extended our existing tool [27] which is a graphical demonstrator of the passive learning procedure. The tool [24] now demonstrates the passive and the active learning algorithm for 43 different examples, which are also discussed in Sect. 5. The predefined parameter setup conforms to the one used in our case studies. However, all parameters are configurable. **The tool is available online** [24] including a short user manual.

5   Case Studies

In our case studies we evaluated 43 different timed systems including three examples from the industry and 40 randomly generated timed systems. The aim of these case studies is to check whether the proposed active technique can learn timed systems adequately. Furthermore, we compare the results of the active with our previously introduced passive learning algorithm [27]. In the remainder of this section we distinguish between *learning set* and *validation set*[1]. Former denotes the test data that are used by the learning algorithm to learn the timed automaton (TA) and latter is used to evaluate the final learned TA.

For the following case studies, we address following research question: **Can our active learning technique improve the existing passive technique regarding performance?** For this we measure performance based on the following three criteria: (1) number of passing tests, (2) test-execution time and (3) runtime.

Passing Tests. For the measurement of passing tests, we generate a validation set which consists of 2 000 randomly generated timed traces. For this, we uniformly select delays and inputs from the input alphabet of the SUT. These randomly generated test sequences are then simulated on the SUT. The length of the generated timed traces is geometrically distributed. The evaluation in our previous work [27] shows that 2 000 randomly generated timed traces are sufficient to represent the behavior of all considered

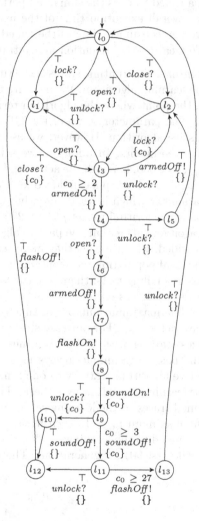

Fig. 6. A learned TA of the car alarm system (CAS) which we adapted from Aichernig et al. [2,3].

erated timed traces are sufficient to represent the behavior of all considered

---

[1] In machine learning these sets are often denoted as training and test set.

systems. Furthermore, a manual analysis of the learned TA showed that they were generally observationally equivalent to the SUTs. Here, we state the percent of passed timed traces. Hence, 100% indicates that all 2 000 timed traces passed.

Test-Execution Time. Since we learn timed systems the test execution depends on time. In practice, we prefer tests that take less time. The test-execution time of a timed trace is the sum of all performed delays. In these case studies we state the overall execution time of the used learning set. This execution time is the average consumed time of the timed traces multiplied by the learning set size. We measure the execution in arbitrary time units.

Runtime. The runtime states the actual required time, given in minutes (min), by the learning algorithm. We measure the runtime from the start of the algorithm to the point where the algorithm terminates and outputs a final solution.

The parameter setup of the GP procedure is akin to our evaluation of the passive algorithm. However, we use the same population size $n_{pop} = 2\,000$ for all experiments. In addition, we set the maximum number of generations to $g_{max} = 2\,000$, i.e. both the active and the passive algorithm use at most g_{max} generations to develop a candidate solution. The crossover probability p_{cr} is the only parameter which is set differently for the active and passive algorithm. For the passive algorithm we set $p_{cr} = 0.25$ and for the active algorithm $p_{cr} = 0.05$. The reason for this is that the passive algorithm learns from a large number of traces provided, which means that more tests are failing at the beginning. Therefore, the local population may contain more advanced solutions. The active algorithm has less failing tests, therefore, the local population contains less knowledge and crossover is less useful.

The maximum number of timed traces in the learning set is defined by the parameter n_{test}. For our case studies, we use 21 different maximum learning set sizes starting with 50 and continue with 100 to 2 000 using a step size of 100. The passive technique always uses a training set with n_{test} timed traces. The active algorithm starts with one randomly generated timed trace, which is used for learning the initial hypothesis. Then the active algorithm only adds as many timed traces to the learning set as required to find a confirming solution, but at the maximum n_{test}. In each iteration of the active algorithm n_{fail} timed traces are added to the learning set. We assume that it is useful to add all timed traces in the first 90% of generations. Therefore, we define n_{fail} as follows:

$$n_{fail} = \left\lceil \frac{n_{test}}{\frac{g_{max}}{g_{max_{active}}} \cdot 0.9} \right\rceil \tag{2}$$

For the active algorithm, we set $p_{input} = 0.9$ and reduced this probability in each iteration of the active approach by 0.1. Furthermore, $g_{max_{active}} = 100$, $n_{attempts} = 2000$ and $p_{trans} = 0.5$. To make the active and the passive algorithm comparable, we used learning sets where the average lengths of the timed traces are almost equal. For these case studies we achieve this by setting the maximum timed trace length n_{len} to 40. For other systems, this parameter could be set

Table 1. Results of the active and passive learning algorithm.

Quartile		Passing tests (%)			Test-execution time (time units $\cdot 10^3$)			Runtime (min)		
		1st	2nd	3rd	1st	2nd	3rd	1st	2nd	3rd
Light	Active		100		6.3	10.6	15.7	1.5	1.8	4.0
	Passive		72.7		31.0	62.1	92.6	344.1	1360.1	1505.8
CAS	Active		100		39.0	71.9	103.0	43.4	53.4	64.8
	Passive		100		87.8	173.5	261.4	95.4	145.0	208.3
PC	Active		100		15.5	31.5	40.2	37.9	57.1	93.1
	Passive	93.8	99.8	100.0	23.7	47.5	71.9	378.1	642.8	996.1
C10/1	Active		100		9.4	17.6	24.2	5.0	8.0	9.4
	Passive		100		28.2	56.9	85.1	9.9	25.0	35.5
C15/1	Active		100		23.9	38.5	51.7	43.2	55.3	72.6
	Passive	99.6	99.8	99.9	28.5	57.7	86.4	259.0	570.9	712.4
C10/2	Active		100		13.2	27.0	39.7	52.1	82.7	134.5
	Passive	99.8	99.9	99.9	22.3	44.9	66.8	183.0	372.6	630.4
C20/1	Active		100		23.4	44.0	66.4	96.7	146.2	179.4
	Passive	99.8	99.9	99.9	29.8	59.8	88.7	278.3	470.7	572.5

according to an estimation of the system size or could be replaced by a stopping probability for the trace generation.

The 43 timed systems include three examples from the industry and 40 randomly generated TA which serve as SUTs. The examples from the industry include a smart light switch (Light) [15], which is depicted in Fig. 1. The other two examples from the industry are more complex. The first one is from the automotive industry and represents a car alarm system (CAS). Figure 6 depicts a learned TA of the CAS. In the literature, this example is used for various different case studies on testing [2,3]. The third industrial example is a particle counter (PC) [1], that counts particles in exhaust gases. A correct TA of the PC includes one clock and 16 locations. The 40 randomly generated TA can be categorized into four categories C10/1, C15/1, C10/2 and C20/1 according to their number of locations (first number) and clock variables (second number). Each category consists of ten different timed systems. The automata in the categories with 10 locations have four distinct inputs and four distinct outputs. The automata from the other categories have five distinct inputs and outputs. All timed automata of these case studies can be found online [24].

Overall we performed 18 060 experiments (43 timed systems × 21 training set sizes × 10 repetitions × 2 learning algorithms). Due to this large number of experiments, we had to distribute the experiments on different systems including cloud services. Since cloud services use virtual CPUs the runtime values may differ on other setups. However, we assume the trend of the results is independent from the underlying setup.

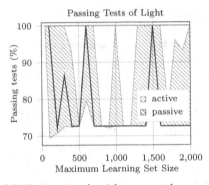

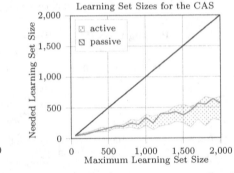

(a) The passive algorithm cannot learn an adequate model due to a local maximum in the fitness function. This problem is not observable in our active algorithm.

(b) The active algorithm can learn adequately with only a fraction of the maximum learning set size. The values are increasing due to Eq. 2.

Fig. 7. Comparison of the active and passive learning algorithm based on passing learning and validation set sizes.

Table 1 shows the results of our evaluation. These values represent the first, second (median), third quartile of the median results of all learning set sizes. For the randomly generated timed systems we use the median results over all ten different timed systems in one category. If all three values are equal, we state only one number.

In our research question we asked if our active technique can achieve improvements compared to the passive technique. The following results regarding (1) passing tests, (2) test-execution time and (3) runtime can be observed:

Passing Tests. Table 1 shows the active algorithm passes all tests, whereas the passive algorithm does not reach 100% for all examples. If we have a closer look at the evaluation data, we see that the median percentage of passed tests is always 100% for learning sizes starting at 100 timed traces. Hence, our active technique can learn timed systems sufficiently with a learning set consisting of 100 timed traces. In addition, Table 1 shows that the passive technique cannot correctly learn the Light example. We used the same example from our previous evaluation [27], but increased the maximum clock constant c_{max} from 12 to 20. Consequently, the passive algorithm seems to have problems to learn adequately when an imprecise largest clock constant is provided.

Figure 7a gives a more detailed overview of the passing tests results of the Light example for all learning set sizes. The x-axis states the maximum learning set size, which is the actual learning set size of the passive approach but can be lower in the active approach. On the y-axis we find the number of passing tests in percent. The solid lines indicate the median values and the surrounding areas in the corresponding color the range between the first and the third quartile. We see that the median percentage of passing tests fluctuates for the passive algorithm. The median percentage of passing tests is for the passively learned Light only

72.7%. We assume that this behavior is due to a local maximum in the fitness function. Performing further mutations seems to decrease the fitness value and, therefore, the population does not develop properly. We do not observe such a behavior using the active algorithm. A reason for that might be the continuous improvement of the learning set. In the active technique more failing timed traces are added and, therefore, mutations more likely increase the fitness value.

Test-execution time. We can also decrease the overall test-execution time of the used learning sets. This improvement was mainly achieved due to the fact that the active algorithm requires less timed traces to learn the TA. Consequently, an adequate TA can be learned with a smaller learning set containing timed traces that better reflect the behavior of the SUT. Figure 7b depicts the needed training set size for the CAS and shows that the active algorithm passes all tests with significantly smaller learning set size compared to the passive algorithm. However, due to Eq. 2,

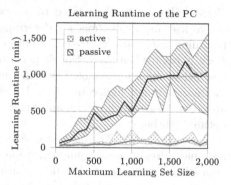

Fig. 8. The active algorithm has a more stable runtime than the passive algorithm and can be decreased significantly.

we use more timed traces for a larger n_{test}. We selected the CAS because both the active and the passive algorithm achieved 100% passing tests.

Runtime. The results in Table 1 show significant improvements in the runtime. The median runtime to actively learn the Light example is only 1.8 min, whereas the passive algorithm requires 1360.1 min. However, for this example the passive technique cannot learn the TA correctly and, therefore, searches for a solution until the maximum number of generations is reached. Overall the median runtime of the active algorithm is at least 2.7 and up to 755 times faster than the passive algorithm. Figure 8 shows the runtime for learning the PC in more detail. We see that even the third quartile of the active algorithm's runtime is significantly lower than the runtime in the first quartile of the passive learning algorithm.

Further experiments and a more detailed description of the found results are presented in the Master's thesis of Pferscher [23].

6   Conclusion

Summary. In this paper we presented an active learning algorithm for timed automata (TA) using model-based testing and genetic programming (GP). For this, we combined our previously introduced passive learning algorithm [27] and the iterative refinement approach of Walkinshaw et al. [32]. We proposed a test data generator for TA which generates timed traces based on a random walk through TA that also considers undefined behavior of the currently tested model.

In a comprehensive evaluation – including 18 060 experiments – we found that the active approach performs more efficiently than the passive approach. Since we need fewer timed traces than the passive approach we could also decrease the median execution time of the test suite by a factor of up to 5.8. In addition, the active approach is up to 755 times faster. The tool and the analyzed timed systems are available for download [24].

Related Work. Closely related to our work Grinchtein et al. [13,14] proposed active learning algorithms for deterministic-event recording automata. Event-recording automata [6] are TA where every action has its own clock and the clock is reset when the action is performed. Such a modeling approach can be insufficient for input enabled systems. Furthermore, the approaches seem to be impractical due to high complexity. Lin et al. [17] also proposed an active learning approach for event-recording automata. However, in their setup they assume an optimal teacher.

Verwer et al. [30] uses state-merging to learn deterministic real-time automata. Real-time automata [12] have only one clock which is reset in every transition. Furthermore, they do not distinguish between input and output. Verwer et al. [31] extended their approach to learn probabilistic real-time automata. Mediouni et al. [20] proposed an improvement of the extended approach. Mao et al. [18] learn continuous-time labeled Markov chains via state-merging. In this approach the sojourn time spent in a state is defined by an exponential function. More general assumptions about the timed behavior are considered by de Matos Pedro et al. [19]. In their work they learn generalized semi-Markov processes generated by stochastic TA. Since all of these approaches rely on state-merging the learned model is only as good as the provided set of samples. Pastore et al. [21] extended the passive learning algorithm *k-Tail* to learn nested timed sequences. However, they can only model a timed behavior that can be described by a start and end point. Soto et al. [25] proposed an algorithm to synthesize linear hybrid automata. Similar to our technique they start with an initial model which they improve further by new execution samples. In contrast to our algorithm, which is based on equivalence testing, they build a model using membership testing.

Future Work. One may use other tools, e.g. UPPAAL [9], to model-check the learned TA. The results of the model checker can then be used for learning. Additionally, many systems do not have the assumed strict limitations on the timing of outputs. Softening the assumptions on output urgency would immensely increase the applicability of the proposed learning technique. Another not yet covered behavior of systems is uncertainty. Learning stochastic timed automata would be an interesting field for future work.

Acknowledgments. The work has been carried out as part of the TU Graz LEAD project "Dependable Internet of Things in Adverse Environments". We also want to thank the anonymous reviewers for their insightful comments and suggestions.

References

1. Aichernig, B.K., et al.: Model-based mutation testing of an industrial measurement device. In: Seidl, M., Tillmann, N. (eds.) TAP 2014. LNCS, vol. 8570, pp. 1–19. Springer, Cham (2014). https://doi.org/10.1007/978-3-319-09099-3_1
2. Aichernig, B.K., Brandl, H., Jöbstl, E., Krenn, W.: UML in action: a two-layered interpretation for testing. ACM SIGSOFT Softw. Eng. Notes **36**(1), 1–8 (2011). https://doi.org/10.1145/1921532.1921559
3. Aichernig, B.K., Lorber, F., Ničković, D.: Time for mutants — model-based mutation testing with timed automata. In: Veanes, M., Viganò, L. (eds.) TAP 2013. LNCS, vol. 7942, pp. 20–38. Springer, Heidelberg (2013). https://doi.org/10.1007/978-3-642-38916-0_2
4. Aichernig, B.K., Tappler, M.: Learning from faults: mutation testing in active automata learning. In: Barrett, C., Davies, M., Kahsai, T. (eds.) NFM 2017. LNCS, vol. 10227, pp. 19–34. Springer, Cham (2017). https://doi.org/10.1007/978-3-319-57288-8_2
5. Alur, R., Dill, D.L.: A theory of timed automata. Theor. Comput. Sci. **126**(2), 183–235 (1994). https://doi.org/10.1016/0304-3975(94)90010-8
6. Alur, R., Fix, L., Henzinger, T.A.: Event-clock automata: a determinizable class of timed automata. Theor. Comput. Sci. **211**(1–2), 253–273 (1999). https://doi.org/10.1016/S0304-3975(97)00173-4
7. Angluin, D.: Learning regular sets from queries and counterexamples. Inf. Comput. **75**(2), 87–106 (1987). https://doi.org/10.1016/0890-5401(87)90052-6
8. Asarin, E., Maler, O., Pnueli, A., Sifakis, J.: Controller synthesis for timed automata. IFAC Proc. **31**(18), 447–452 (1998). https://doi.org/10.1016/S1474-6670(17)42032-5, http://www.sciencedirect.com/science/article/pii/S1474667017420325, Special issue on the 5th IFAC Conference on System Structure and Control 1998 (SSC 1998), Nantes, France, 8–10 July
9. Behrmann, G., David, A., Larsen, K.G.: A tutorial on UPPAAL. In: Bernardo, M., Corradini, F. (eds.) SFM-RT 2004. LNCS, vol. 3185, pp. 200–236. Springer, Heidelberg (2004). https://doi.org/10.1007/978-3-540-30080-9_7
10. Berg, T., Grinchtein, O., Jonsson, B., Leucker, M., Raffelt, H., Steffen, B.: On the correspondence between conformance testing and regular inference. In: Cerioli, M. (ed.) FASE 2005. LNCS, vol. 3442, pp. 175–189. Springer, Heidelberg (2005). https://doi.org/10.1007/978-3-540-31984-9_14
11. Bornot, S., Sifakis, J., Tripakis, S.: Modeling urgency in timed systems. In: de Roever, W.-P., Langmaack, H., Pnueli, A. (eds.) COMPOS 1997. LNCS, vol. 1536, pp. 103–129. Springer, Heidelberg (1998). https://doi.org/10.1007/3-540-49213-5_5
12. Dima, C.: Real-time automata. J. Autom. Lang. Comb. **6**(1), 3–23 (2001). https://doi.org/10.25596/jalc-2001-003
13. Grinchtein, O., Jonsson, B., Leucker, M.: Learning of event-recording automata. Theor. Comput. Sci. **411**(47), 4029–4054 (2010). https://doi.org/10.1016/j.tcs.2010.07.008
14. Grinchtein, O., Jonsson, B., Pettersson, P.: Inference of event-recording automata using timed decision trees. In: Baier, C., Hermanns, H. (eds.) CONCUR 2006. LNCS, vol. 4137, pp. 435–449. Springer, Heidelberg (2006). https://doi.org/10.1007/11817949_29

15. Hessel, A., Larsen, K.G., Nielsen, B., Pettersson, P., Skou, A.: Time-optimal real-time test case generation using UPPAAL. In: Petrenko, A., Ulrich, A. (eds.) FATES 2003. LNCS, vol. 2931, pp. 114–130. Springer, Heidelberg (2004). https://doi.org/10.1007/978-3-540-24617-6_9

16. Koza, J.R.: Genetic Programming: On the Programming of Computers by Means of Natural Selection. Complex Adaptive Systems. MIT Press (1993). ISBN 978-0-262-11170-6

17. Lin, S.-W., André, É., Dong, J.S., Sun, J., Liu, Y.: An efficient algorithm for learning event-recording automata. In: Bultan, T., Hsiung, P.-A. (eds.) ATVA 2011. LNCS, vol. 6996, pp. 463–472. Springer, Heidelberg (2011). https://doi.org/10.1007/978-3-642-24372-1_35

18. Mao, H., Chen, Y., Jaeger, M., Nielsen, T.D., Larsen, K.G., Nielsen, B.: Learning deterministic probabilistic automata from a model checking perspective. Mach. Learn. 105(2), 255–299 (2016). https://doi.org/10.1007/s10994-016-5565-9

19. de Matos Pedro, A., Crocker, P.A., de Sousa, S.M.: Learning stochastic timed automata from sample executions. In: Margaria, T., Steffen, B. (eds.) ISoLA 2012. LNCS, vol. 7609, pp. 508–523. Springer, Heidelberg (2012). https://doi.org/10.1007/978-3-642-34026-0_38

20. Mediouni, B.L., Nouri, A., Bozga, M., Bensalem, S.: Improved learning for stochastic timed models by state-merging algorithms. In: Barrett, C., Davies, M., Kahsai, T. (eds.) NFM 2017. LNCS, vol. 10227, pp. 178–193. Springer, Cham (2017). https://doi.org/10.1007/978-3-319-57288-8_13

21. Pastore, F., Micucci, D., Mariani, L.: Timed k-tail: automatic inference of timed automata. In: 2017 IEEE International Conference on Software Testing, Verification and Validation, ICST 2017, Tokyo, Japan, 13–17 March 2017, pp. 401–411. IEEE Computer Society (2017). https://doi.org/10.1109/ICST.2017.43, http://ieeexplore.ieee.org/xpl/mostRecentIssue.jsp?punumber=7922464

22. Peled, D.A., Vardi, M.Y., Yannakakis, M.: Black box checking. J. Autom. Lang. Comb. 7(2), 225–246 (2002). https://doi.org/10.25596/jalc-2002-225

23. Pferscher, A.: Active model learning of timed automata via genetic programming. Master's thesis, Graz University of Technology, Graz, Austria (2019). https://diglib.tugraz.at/active-model-learning-of-timed-automata-via-genetic-programming-2019

24. Pferscher, A., Tappler, M.: Supplemental materials for "From passive to active: learning timed automata efficiently" (2020). https://doi.org/10.6084/m9.figshare.9976211.v1, https://figshare.com/articles/Supplemental_Materials_for_From_Passive_to_Active_Learning_Timed_Automata_Efficiently_/9976211/1

25. García Soto, M., Henzinger, T.A., Schilling, C., Zeleznik, L.: Membership-based synthesis of linear hybrid automata. In: Dillig, I., Tasiran, S. (eds.) CAV 2019. LNCS, vol. 11561, pp. 297–314. Springer, Cham (2019). https://doi.org/10.1007/978-3-030-25540-4_16

26. Springintveld, J., Vaandrager, F.W., D'Argenio, P.R.: Testing timed automata. Theor. Comput. Sci. 254(1–2), 225–257 (2001). https://doi.org/10.1016/S0304-3975(99)00134-6

27. Tappler, M., Aichernig, B.K., Larsen, K.G., Lorber, F.: Time to learn – learning timed automata from tests. In: André, É., Stoelinga, M. (eds.) FORMATS 2019. LNCS, vol. 11750, pp. 216–235. Springer, Cham (2019). https://doi.org/10.1007/978-3-030-29662-9_13

28. Tretmans, J.: Model based testing with labelled transition systems. In: Hierons, R.M., Bowen, J.P., Harman, M. (eds.) Formal Methods and Testing. LNCS, vol. 4949, pp. 1–38. Springer, Heidelberg (2008). https://doi.org/10.1007/978-3-540-78917-8_1

29. Utting, M., Pretschner, A., Legeard, B.: A taxonomy of model-based testing approaches. Softw. Test. Verification Reliab. **22**(5), 297–312 (2012). https://doi.org/10.1002/stvr.456

30. Verwer, S., de Weerdt, M., Witteveen, C.: An algorithm for learning real-time automata. In: Benelearn 2007: Proceedings of the Annual Machine Learning Conference of Belgium and the Netherlands, Amsterdam, The Netherlands, 14–15 May 2007, pp. 128–135 (2007)

31. Verwer, S., de Weerdt, M., Witteveen, C.: A likelihood-ratio test for identifying probabilistic deterministic real-time automata from positive data. In: Sempere, J.M., García, P. (eds.) ICGI 2010. LNCS (LNAI), vol. 6339, pp. 203–216. Springer, Heidelberg (2010). https://doi.org/10.1007/978-3-642-15488-1_17

32. Walkinshaw, N., Derrick, J., Guo, Q.: Iterative refinement of reverse-engineered models by model-based testing. In: Cavalcanti, A., Dams, D.R. (eds.) FM 2009. LNCS, vol. 5850, pp. 305–320. Springer, Heidelberg (2009). https://doi.org/10.1007/978-3-642-05089-3_20

Generating Correct-by-Construction Distributed Implementations from Formal Maude Designs

Si Liu[1(✉)], Atul Sandur[2], José Meseguer[2], Peter Csaba Ölveczky[3], and Qi Wang[2]

[1] ETH Zürich, Zürich, Switzerland
si.liu@inf.ethz.ch
[2] University of Illinois, Urbana-Champaign, Champaign, USA
[3] University of Oslo, Oslo, Norway

Abstract. Developing a reliable distributed system meeting desired performance requirements is a hard and labor-intensive task. Formal specification and analysis of a system *design* can yield correct designs as well as reliable performance predictions. In this paper we present a correct-by-construction automatic transformation mapping such a verified formal specification of a system design in Maude to a *distributed implementation* satisfying the same safety and liveness properties. Two case studies applying this transformation to state-of-the-art distributed transaction systems show that high-quality implementations with acceptable performance and meeting performance predictions can be automatically generated. In this way, formal models of distributed systems analyzed within the same formal framework for both *logical* and *performance* properties are automatically transformed into correct-by-construction implementations for which similar performance trends can be shown.

1 Introduction

Designing and implementing high-performance distributed systems are complex tasks. Cloud-based systems, which typically rely on widely distributed data storage for scalability, availability, and disaster tolerance, have further increased this complexity. For example, the communication needed to maintain strong consistency across sites may incur unacceptable latencies, so that designers must balance consistency and performance. Both *performance* and *functional correctness* are therefore important system requirements that should be analyzed.

Formal methods have been advocated to develop and analyze high-level models of distributed system designs. However, today's distributed systems present a number of challenges to formal methods: (i) the complexity and heterogeneity of such systems require a flexible and expressive formal framework [32]; (ii) the correctness properties that these systems must satisfy can be quite complex, and there is a desire in industry for *automatic* verification methods [32]; and (iii) both *correctness* and *performance* are, as mentioned, crucial requirements.

One formal framework that has shown promise in meeting the challenges (i)–(iii) is Maude [10], a high-performance formal framework for executable specification, verification, and programming of concurrent systems based on rewriting

R. Lee et al. (Eds.): NFM 2020, LNCS 12229, pp. 22–40, 2020.
https://doi.org/10.1007/978-3-030-55754-6_2

logic [8,28,29]. Maude meets challenge (i) by being based on a general and expressive, yet simple and intuitive, formalism. Regarding challenge (ii), Maude provides a range of automatic model checking methods, including reachability analysis and LTL and LTLR temporal logic model checking [2,10], which allows us to express and analyze complex properties (see, e.g., [25]). For challenge (iii), the PVESTA [1] *statistical model checker* can be used to statistically predict the performance of a design specified in Maude.

These features have made possible the use of Maude to model and analyze both the correctness and performance of high-level designs of a wide range of systems [29]. To cite just one area, Maude has been used to formally model and analyze, often for the first time, state-of-the-art industrial and academic cloud-based transaction systems such as Apache Cassandra [18], ZooKeeper [19], Google's Megastore [4], P-Store [35], RAMP [3], and Walter [38]; and to design the entirely new system ROLA [22] (see [7,23,24,33]). Furthermore, model-based performance predictions using PVESTA have shown good correspondence with experimental evaluation of implementations of Cassandra, RAMP, and Walter.

In this way, we can develop mature designs satisfying given correctness criteria and having good predicted performance. However, this still leaves open the problem of how to pass from a *verified system design* to a *correct-by-construction distributed implementation*. This is the problem this paper solves.

Since Maude provides TCP/IP sockets as external objects which can interact with standard Maude objects by message passing [10], a Maude object system can be deployed as a *distributed system* across several machines. The goal of this paper is to *fully automate* the passage from an object-based Maude design M to a distributed Maude implementation $D(M)$, and to *prove* that M and an abstract model $D_0(M)$, which hides the details of $D(M)$'s TCP/IP-based network communication, are *stuttering bisimilar* [27,30] and therefore satisfy the same CTL^* properties for any formulas not using the "next" operator. Therefore, both *safety* and *liveness* properties are preserved by the transformation. Since both the formal specification and its distributed implementation are given in Maude, proving correctness of the generated code is quite straight-forward. This is in contrast to code generation frameworks that generate code in languages, such as C or Java, that are different from the formal specification language, and where proving correctness of the generated code is hard and typically not done.

We have developed a prototype that automates the $M \mapsto D(M)$ transformation, and have evaluated its effectiveness on two case studies. In the first one we compare the distributed Maude implementation $D(M)$ automatically generated from the Maude specification M of the NO_WAIT transaction protocol with a state-of-the-art conventional C++ implementation of NO_WAIT. In the second case study we compare the Maude design M of the new distributed transaction system ROLA with its *first ever* distributed implementation $D(M)$.

Main Contributions: (i) the formal definition of the $M \mapsto D(M)$ transformation; (ii) the proof that for any actor-like Maude specification M the system $D_0(M)$ and M are stuttering bisimilar; (iii) a "proof-of-concept" implementation of the $M \mapsto D(M)$ transformation allowing us to generate, deploy, and evaluate correct-by-construction implementations of state-of-the-art system designs, and allowing interaction of such implementations with *foreign objects* (see Sect. 3.3) such as the YCSB workload generator [12]; (iv) two case studies using state-of-the-art distributed transaction systems evaluating the implementations obtained by the $M \mapsto D(M)$ transformation with respect to: (a) the statistical-model-checking-based performance predictions for M; and (b) a conventional high-performance C++ implementation. To the best of our knowledge, this is the first time that formal models of distributed systems analyzed within the same formal framework for *both* logical and performance properties are automatically transformed into logically correct-by-construction implementations for which similar performance trends can be shown.

2   Preliminaries

Rewriting Logic and Maude. Maude [10] is a rewriting-logic-based executable formal specification language and high-performance analysis tool for distributed systems. Formal analysis methods include: simulation, reachability analysis, LTL model checking, theorem proving [34,37], and, for performance estimation purposes, statistical model checking with the PVeStA tool [1].

A Maude module specifies a *rewrite theory* $(\Sigma, E \cup B, R)$, where:

- Σ is an algebraic *signature*; i.e., a set of *sorts*, *subsorts*, and *function symbols*.
- $(\Sigma, E \cup B)$ is a *membership equational logic theory* specifying the system's data types, with E a set of conditional equations and membership axioms, and B a set of equational axioms such as associativity, commutativity, and identity, so that equational deduction is performed *modulo* the axioms B.
- R is a collection of *labeled conditional rewrite rules* $[l] : t \longrightarrow t'$ **if** *cond*, specifying the system's local transitions.

We summarize the syntax of Maude and refer to [10] for details. Operators are introduced with the **op** keyword: **op** $f : s_1 \ldots s_n$ -> s and can have user-definable syntax. Equations and rewrite rules are introduced with, respectively, keywords **eq**, or **ceq** for conditional equations, and **rl** and **crl**. The mathematical variables in such statements are declared with the keywords **var** and **vars**.

A *class* declaration **class** $C \mid att_1 : s_1, \ldots, att_n : s_n$ declares a class C of objects with attributes att_1 to att_n of sorts s_1 to s_n. An *object* of class C is represented as a term < $o : C \mid att_1 : val_1, \ldots, att_n : val_n$ >, where o, of sort Oid, is the object's *identifier*, and where val_1 to val_n are the current values of the attributes att_1 to att_n. A *message* is a term of sort Msg. A system state is modeled as a term of the sort Configuration, and has the structure of a *multiset* made up of objects and messages. The dynamic behavior of a system is axiomatized by specifying its transition patterns as rewrite rules. For example, the rule

```
rl [1] :  m(O,w)   < O : C | a1 : x, a2 : O', a3 : z >    =>
                   < O : C | a1 : x + w, a2 : O', a3 : z >   m'(O',x) .
```

defines a family of transitions in which a message m(O, w) is read and consumed by an object O of class C, whose attribute a1 is changed to x + w, and a new message m'(O',x) is generated. Attributes whose values do not change and do not affect the next state, such as a3 and a2, need not be mentioned in a rule.

Sockets in Maude. Maude's erewrite command supports rewriting with external objects (that do not reside in the configuration) when the "portal" object <> is present in the configuration. Objects in a Maude process, here called a *session*, can communicate with *external objects* in the *same session* by message passing. One such external object is Maude's built-in *socket manager* object, with name socketManager, that supports communicating through TCP sockets with other *remote Maude objects* in other Maude sessions, as well as with *remote foreign objects* (see Sect. 3.3) in other processes. Some of the messages defining the interface between a Maude process and Maude's socket manager are the following: A message send(*socketName*, *myOid*, *string*) asks Maude to send *string* through the socket *socketName*, and receive(*socketName*, *myOid*) solicits data through a socket. When some data (*string*) is received through a socket, the socket manager sends the message received(*myOid*, *socketName*, *string*).

Stuttering Bisimulations. A *Kripke structure* $\mathcal{A}$ on a set *AP* of *atomic propositions* is a 4-tuple $\mathcal{A} = (A, \rightarrow_{\mathcal{A}}, a_0, L_{\mathcal{A}})$ where A is a set of *states*, $\rightarrow_{\mathcal{A}} \subseteq A \times A$ is the *total transition relation on states*, $a_0 \in A$ is the *initial state*, and $L_{\mathcal{A}}$, called the *labeling function*, is a function $L_{\mathcal{A}} : A \rightarrow \mathcal{P}(AP)$ assigning to each state $a \in A$ the set of atomic state predicates $L_{\mathcal{A}}(a)$ true in state a. A *path* π in $\mathcal{A}$ is function $\pi : \mathbb{N} \rightarrow A$ such that $\pi(0) = a_0$ and $\forall n \in \mathbb{N}\ \pi(n) \rightarrow_{\mathcal{A}} \pi(n+1)$.

Definition 1. *[30] Given Kripke structures* $\mathcal{A} = (A, \rightarrow_{\mathcal{A}}, a_0, L_{\mathcal{A}})$ *and* $\mathcal{B} = (B, \rightarrow_{\mathcal{B}}, b_0, L_{\mathcal{B}})$, *a stuttering bisimulation map, denoted* $h : \mathcal{A} \rightarrow \mathcal{B}$, *is a function* $h : A \rightarrow B$ *such that: (1) given any path* π *in* $\mathcal{A}$ *there is a path* ρ *in* $\mathcal{B}$ *and a strictly monotonic function* $\kappa : \mathbb{N} \rightarrow \mathbb{N}$ *such that: (i) for each* $n \in \mathbb{N}$ *and each* i, $\kappa(n) \leq i < \kappa(n+1)$, *(ii)* $h(\pi(\kappa(n))) = h(\pi(\kappa(i))) = \rho(n)$, *and (iii)* $L_{\mathcal{A}}(\pi(\kappa(n))) = L_{\mathcal{A}}(\pi(i)) = L_{\mathcal{B}}(\rho(n))$. *And (2) given any path* ρ *in* $\mathcal{B}$ *there is a path* π *in* $\mathcal{A}$ *and a strictly monotonic function* $\kappa : \mathbb{N} \rightarrow \mathbb{N}$ *satisfying (i)–(iii)*.

The key property of a stuttering bisimulation map $h : \mathcal{A} \rightarrow \mathcal{B}$ is that all formulas $\varphi \in CTL^* \setminus \bigcirc$ satisfied by $\mathcal{B}$ are also satisfied by $\mathcal{A}$, and vice versa, where $CTL^* \setminus \bigcirc$ denotes the subset of the CTL^* temporal logic not involving the "next" operator $\bigcirc$ (for more on CTL^* and its LTL sublogic, see [9]):

Theorem 1. *[30] (Implementation Correctness). If* $h : \mathcal{A} \rightarrow \mathcal{B}$ *is a stuttering bisimulation map, for each* $\varphi \in CTL^* \setminus \bigcirc$ *we have:* $\mathcal{B} \models \varphi \Leftrightarrow \mathcal{A} \models \varphi$.

We can associate to a rewrite theory $\mathcal{R} = (\Sigma, E, R)$ and an initial state $init \in T_{\Sigma/E}$ a corresponding *Kripke structure* $\mathcal{K}(\mathcal{R}, init) = (Reach(init), \longrightarrow^{\bullet}_{R/E}, init, L)$ where $Reach(init)$ is the set of all states $[u] \in T_{\Sigma/E}$ reachable from $init$, $\longrightarrow^{\bullet}_{R/E}$ is the (totalization of) the one-step rewrite relation $\longrightarrow_{R/E}$, and L maps each reachable state $[u]$ to the set $L([u]) = \{p \in AP \mid u \models p =_E true\}$.

3   The D Transformation

We define the transformation $M \mapsto D(M)$, mapping a Maude model M of a distributed system to a distributed Maude program $D(M)$ deployed on different machines. Multiple concurrent Maude sessions may run on the same machine.

The transformation D takes as input:

- an object-oriented Maude module M defining an actor system (see below);
- an initial state init of sort Configuration, which is a set of objects

$$< o_1 : C_1 \mid atts_1 > \quad \ldots \quad < o_n : C_n \mid atts_n > \qquad \text{with distinct names } o_i;$$

- a *distribution information* function $di : \{o_1, \ldots, o_n\} \rightarrow \text{String} \times \mathbb{N}$ assigning to each (top-level) object o_j in init a pair (ip, i), where ip is the IP address of the machine in which o_j resides, and i is a session number.

The transformation D then gives us:

- A Maude program $M_{D_{di}}$ that runs on each distributed Maude session; and
- an initial state $\text{init}_{D_{di}}(ip, i)$ for each Maude session (ip, i).

   Notation. We write $M_{D_{di}}$ for $D(M, \text{init}, di)$.

   The object-oriented module M should model an "actor" system, so that its rewrite rules must have the form

$$(\text{to } o \text{ from } o' : mc) \ < o : C \mid \ldots > \ \Rightarrow \ < o : C \mid \ldots > \ msgs \ [\text{if} \ \ldots] \qquad (\dagger)$$

or

$$< o : C \mid \ldots > \ \Rightarrow \ < o : C \mid \ldots > \ msgs \ [\text{if} \ \ldots] \qquad (\ddagger)$$

where $msgs$ is a term of sort Configuration which, applying the equations in the module, reduces to a multiset of *messages*

$$(\text{to } o_1 \text{ from } o\theta : mc_1) \quad \ldots \quad (\text{to } o_k \text{ from } o\theta : mc_k)$$

for $k \geq 0$, where θ is the substitution used when applying the rule. In such a message, mc_i is the message content (or payload) of the message being sent to the object named o_i from the object named $o\theta$.

3.1   The $M \mapsto M_{D_{di}}$ Transformation

The main idea for defining the distributed Maude program $M_{D_{di}}$ is to add middleware for communication between Maude sessions and with external objects. This is done by adding to *each* Maude session a *communication mediator* object that takes care of communication with non-local objects, as illustrated in Fig. 1.

This mediator object opens and maintains sockets for communication between objects; there is in general one socket for each pair of objects that communicate remotely (across machine/session boundaries). Objects in the same Maude session communicate without using the mediator.

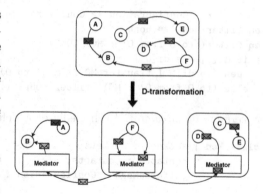

The only modification of the rewrite rules in M is that a message addressed to a *remote* object is "redirected" to the local mediator, which (i) establishes the required socket between the pair of objects if not already established; (ii) transforms the original message into a string with an "end-of-message" marker; and (iii) sends the resulting string through the appropriate socket.

Fig. 1. Visualization of the D-Transformation

For receiving, the mediator object receives external messages through sockets associated to "its" objects. Since TCP sockets do not preserve message boundaries, the mediator has to buffer the messages received in each socket. When the buffered string contains the "end-of-message" string, the mediator extracts the string representing the message, transforms it to a message, and leaves the message (having a local addressee) in the local configuration.

The distributed program $M_{D_{di}}$ consists of:

- A constant `di` of sort `Map{Oid,Pair{String,Nat}}` which specifies *di* as a map from `Oid` to `Pair{String,Nat}` using an equation `eq di = ....`
- The module *filter*(M), which transforms M as described below.
- Declarations and rewrite rules defining the mediator objects and their behaviors (which import the `SOCKET` module).

The Module filter(M). The only change made by *filter*(M) to the rewrite rules in M is that any message `(to o' from o : mc)` generated by a rule in M is replaced by a message `(to di(o') transfer mc from o to o')` if o' and o reside in different Maude sessions. Formally, this is done by adding an object identifier `< ip ; session >` for each mediator object, adding a message constructor

`op to_transfer_from_to_ : Oid MsgContent Oid Oid -> Msg [ctor] .`

and changing each rewrite rule in M of the form (†) to

`(to o from o' : mc) < o : C | ... > => < o : C | ... > filter(`*msgs*`) [if ...]`

(and similar with rules of the form (‡)), where `filter` redirects the messages going to remote objects to the mediator and leaves the other messages unchanged[1]:

---

[1] We do not show variable declarations in this paper, but follow the convention that variables are written in (all) capital letters.

```
op filter : Configuration -> Configuration .
eq filter(none) = none .
eq filter((to O from O' : MC) CONF)
= if di[O] =/= di[O']
  then (to di[O'] transfer MC from O' to O)  filter(CONF)
  else (to O from O' : MC)  filter(CONF) fi .
```

Specifying the Mediator. Each mediator is defined as an object of class

```
class Med | sockets : Sockets,
            contacts : Contacts,
            bufferedMsgs : Configuration .
```

– sockets values are terms $[socket_1, str_1]$ ... $[socket_k, str_k]$, denoting that the string str_j has been received through socket $socket_j$ (and then buffered) since the last time a message was extracted from this buffer;
– contacts is a set of triples < $localObjId$, $socket$, $remoteObjId$ >, denoting the socket used to communicate between two objects; and
– bufferedMsgs contains the outgoing messages when the appropriate sockets have not yet been established.

We refer to https://github.com/siliunobi/d-transformation for a complete specification of the mediator object, where most of the rewrite rules deal with establishing Maude sockets along the lines explained in [10, Chapter 11]. In this paper we just show the following two rewrite rules for the mediator.

```
rl [sendRemote] :
   (to O transfer MC from O' to O'')
   < O : Med | contacts : CONTACTS ; < O', SOCKET, O'' > >
 =>
   < O : Med | >
   send(SOCKET, O', msg2string(to O'' from O' : MC) + "[msep]") .
```

In this rule, the mediator is tasked with transferring the message content MC from the local object O' to the remote object O''. The rule uses Maude's built-in message send to send the message through the socket SOCKET, which has already been established between O' and O''. Since sockets transport strings, the function msg2string is used to transform the message into a string; the end-of-message separator "[msep]" is then appended to the string.

The following rule applies when a configuration receives a message received(S, SKT, DATA), denoting that a string DATA has been received through socket SKT. The mediator adds DATA to the string STR that it has buffered for socket SKT:

```
rl [receiveData] :
   received(S, SKT, DATA)
   < O : Med | sockets : SKTS [SKT, STR] >
 =>
   < O : Med | sockets : SKTS [SKT, STR + DATA] >
   receive(SKT, S) .
```

See our report [26] for the rule where the mediator extracts a message from a socket and adds it to the local configuration. Objects in the same Maude session communicate without going through sockets or mediators.

The Module $M_{D_{di}}$. To summarize, the distributed Maude program $M_{D_{di}}$ executed at each local host consists of the definition of *di* and the union of the module *filter*(*M*) and the mediator specification:

```
mod M_{D_di} is including filter(M) + MEDIATOR .    eq di = ... .    endm
```

3.2 Distributed Initial States

The initial state $\text{init}_{D_{di}}(ip, n)$ at Maude session (ip, n) is a configuration with:

- the objects in init mapped to (ip, n) by *di*;
- one mediator object

    `< <ip ; n> : Med | sockets : empty, contacts : empty, bufferedMsgs : none >`

- one occurrence of the built-in "portal" object <> denoting that we rewrite with external objects, such as Maude's built-in socket manager; and
- for each top-level (non-mediator) object *o* in the configuration, a message

    `createServerTcpSocket(socketManager, o, port#, 5)`

3.3 Communicating with Foreign Objects

A socket-based distributed Maude object system can easily be extended to *interact with objects foreign to it* with no changes to the existing rewrite rules: only the new messages and rules defining the interaction with new foreign objects—databases, web sites, display devices, and so on—need to be specified.

Suppose that C is a class of Maude objects that needs to communicate with foreign objects. All we need are three things: (a) a *signature* of messages sent by objects in C to such foreign object and by foreign objects to objects in C; (b) *rewrite rules* for the objects of class C specifying how messages to foreign objects are generated and how objects of class C react to messages sent by foreign objects; and (c) a *wrapper* encapsulating a foreign object that can transform the *string representation* of a message from a C object into an internal command to the foreign object, and a reply from the foreign object into the *string representation* of a message to a C object. In this work we have used the steps (a)–(c) to allow communication between a YCSB [12] foreign object and standard Maude objects to carry out system evaluations on realistic workloads.

3.4 Deployment

We have built a simple Python-based prototype that automates the process of deploying and running the distributed Maude model on distributed machines. The tool takes as input the IP addresses of the distributed machines and the number of Maude sessions on each machine.

We have run distributed Maude deployments to perform large-scale experiments on distributed transaction systems. To experiment with realistic workloads, we have connected our distributed implementation to the well-known YCSB workload generator [12] as explained in Sect. 3.3. Our tool also invokes the workload generator to initialize and to load data into the database, and to generate transactions for the different Maude instances to execute.

To measure the performance of our distributed implementation, we have added a "log" attribute to each mediator object that records relevant data during the distributed execution. A Python script then inspects and aggregates these logs after execution to compute the overall performance metric of the system.

4 Correctness Preservation

Our goal is to obtain a distributed implementation of a Maude specification that is correct by construction: If the original Maude model M, with initial state init, satisfies a CTL^* temporal logic property ϕ that does not contain the "next" operator $\bigcirc$, then ϕ should also hold in the distributed implementation $M_{D_{di}}$ when started with corresponding distributed initial state(s), and vice versa.

Since $M_{D_{di}}$ uses TCP/IP socket objects for communication between different Maude sessions, a full proof of correctness of the $M \mapsto M_{D_{di}}$ transformation would require modeling the TCP/IP protocol and its associated network failure model, which is beyond the scope of this paper. Instead, we use the approach followed in other proofs of correctness of distributed systems obtained by transformation from formal specifications, e.g., [36,40], where network communication is abstracted away. Therefore, we present below a proof of correctness which uses an intermediate formal model $D_0(M, \text{init}, di)$ which abstracts away the network communication details by providing a high-level abstraction of it.

4.1 The Model $D_0(M, \text{init}, di)$

The rewrite theory $D_0(M, \text{init}, di)$ is essentially as $M_{D_{di}}$, except that it abstracts away the establishment of the appropriate sockets, and models the effect of socket communication in rewriting logic at a higher level of abstraction. The model $D_0(M, \text{init}, di)$ therefore simplifies $M_{D_{di}}$ as follows.

Concerning the *mediator* class:

- Since we no longer have explicit sockets, the contacts attribute of Med is no longer needed.
- Since we assume that the sockets have been successfully established, the attribute bufferedMsgs, used to buffer outgoing messages that could not yet be transmitted since some socket was not established, is not needed.

- Since we abstract away the fact that TCP sockets do not preserve message boundaries, we do not need to buffer messages at the receiving end, and therefore the attribute sockets is no longer needed.

The mediator class therefore no longer needs any attributes, and is declared as follows in $D_0(M, \text{init}, di)$:   class Med .

The *rewrite rules* in $D_0(M, \text{init}, di)$ differ from those in $M_{D_{di}}$ as follows:

- Since we abstract from the establishment of sockets, the rules in $M_{D_{di}}$ dealing with this issue (not shown in this paper) are omitted from $D_0(M, \text{init}, di)$.
- The rule sendRemote in $M_{D_{di}}$ is replaced by the rule

```
rl [sendRemote] :
   (to O transfer MC from O' to O'')   < O : Med | >
   =>
   < O : Med | >   transfer(di[O''], O, msg2string(to O'' from O' : MC)) .
```

where a "transfer" message models socket communication.
- When a mediator receives such a transfer message (modeling socket communication), it transforms the received string into a message, which is then released into the configuration. Rules receiveData and extractRemoteMsg in $M_{D_{di}}$ are therefore replaced by the following rewrite rule in $D_0(M, \text{init}, di)$:

```
crl [receiveRemoteMsg] :
   transfer(O, O', STRING)   < O : Med | >
   =>
   < O : Med | >   string2msg(STRING) .
```

Initial States. The initial state in $D_0(M, \text{init}, di)$ corresponding to the state init in M is just init with an additional mediator object < < ip ; n > : Med | > for each $(ip, n) \in image(di)$. We call this initial state init_{D_0}.

4.2 $D_0(M, \text{init}, di)$ and M are Stuttering Bisimilar

We show that the Kripke structures $\mathcal{K}(D_0(M, \text{init}, di), \text{init}_{D_0})$ and $\mathcal{K}(M, \text{init})$ are stuttering bisimilar for their respective labeling functions $L \circ h$ and L.

We define the map $h : Reach(\text{init}_{D_0}) \rightarrow Reach(\text{init})$ as follows:

```
eq h(none) = none .
eq h(< O : Med | >  CONF) = h(CONF) .
ceq h(< O : C | >  CONF) = < O : C | >  h(CONF) if C =/= Med .
eq h((to O transfer MC from O' to O'') CONF)
 = (to O'' from O' : MC) h(CONF) .
eq h((transfer(O,O',STRING)) CONF) = string2msg(STRING) h(CONF) .
eq h((to O from O' : MC) CONF) = (to O from O' : MC) h(CONF) .
```

That is, h maps a configuration in $D_0(M, \text{init}, di)$ to a similar configuration in M with the following modifications: (i) the mediator objects are forgotten, and (ii) the three intermediate messages involved in transferring a message content mc from o to a remote o' are all mapped to the message (to o' from o : mc).

Theorem 2. *h is a stuttering bisimulation map*

$$h : \mathcal{K}(D_0(M, \textit{init}, \textit{di}), \textit{init}_{D_0}) \rightarrow \mathcal{K}(M, \textit{init})$$

with corresponding labeling functions $L \circ h$ and L.

The proof of Theorem 2 is given in our longer report [26]. The following main correctness-preservation result follows immediately from Theorems 1 and 2:

Theorem 3. *Given a rewrite theory M specifying a distributed system and an initial state* **init** *as described in Sect. 3, a distribution information function di mapping the top-level objects in* **init** *to different machines/Maude sessions, a labeling function L over a set AP of atomic propositions, and a CTL^* formula φ over AP not containing the "next" operator, then*

$$\mathcal{K}(M, \textit{init}) \models \varphi \text{ if and only if } \mathcal{K}(D_0(M, \textit{init}, \textit{di}), \textit{init}_{D_0}) \models \varphi$$

for the labeling function $L \circ h$ in $\mathcal{K}(D_0(M, \textit{init}, \textit{di}), \textit{init}_{D_0})$.

5   Prototype and Experiments

We have implemented, in around 300 LOC, a "proof-of-concept" prototype of the D transformation that automatically transforms a Maude model of a distributed system into a distributed Maude implementation. We have applied our prototype to the Maude specification of: (i) a lock-based distributed transaction protocol which has been implemented in C++ and evaluated in [16]; and (ii) the ROLA transaction system design. ROLA [22] is a new design whose correctness and performance have been analyzed using Maude and PVESTA, but which has never been implemented. Using our prototype and the Maude specification of ROLA we obtain the first distributed implementation of ROLA *for free*.

We have subjected our two distributed Maude implementations so obtained to realistic workloads generated by YCSB to answer to the following questions:

Q1: Are the performance evaluations obtained for the distributed Maude implementations consistent with conventional distributed implementations of the same designs (if available) and with the model-based performance predictions obtained by statistical model checking of the original Maude designs?

Q2: How does the performance of a distributed Maude implementation automatically generated by our unoptimized prototype compare with that of a state-of-the-art distributed implementation in C++ of the same design?

Answers to Q1 cannot be an agreement between the performance *values predicted* by statistically model checking a Maude model and the *values measured* in an experimental evaluation. This is impossible because: (i) measured values depend on the experimental platform used; (ii) the probability distributions used in statistical model checking are only approximations of the expected behavior; and (iii) the sizes of initial states used in statistical model checking and in experimental evaluations are typically quite different, due to feasibility restrictions placed by statistical model checking. Therefore, the desired consistency between the performance predicted by statistically model checking a model and the performance obtained by experimentally evaluating an implementation is an agreement between predicted and measured *trends*: If, e.g., throughput increases as a function of the proportion of read transactions, then consistency means that it should do so along curves that are *similar* up to a change of scale.

5.1 Experimental Setup

Implementation-Based Evaluation. We evaluated the two case studies using the Yahoo! Cloud Serving Benchmark (YCSB) [12], which is the open standard for performance evaluation of data stores. We used the built-in C++ implementation of YCSB in [16] in our first case study. For ROLA, we used a variant of the original Java implementation of YCSB adapted to transaction systems [3]. We deployed the two systems on a cluster of d430 Emulab machines, with ping time between machines approximately 0.13 ms. In both cases, we considered 5 partitions (of the database) on 5 machines, and client processes split across another 5 separate machines; we considered the same mix of read-only, write-only, and read-write transactions, with each transaction accessing up to 8 keys. We used Zipfian distribution for key accesses with parametric skew factor *theta*.

Statistical Model Checking (SMC). By running Monte-Carlo simulations from a given initial state, SMC estimates the expected value of an expression up to a user-specified level of confidence. We probabilistically generated initial states so that each PVeStA simulation starts from a different state. To mimic the real-world network environment, we used lognormal distribution for message delays [5]. We used 10 machines of the above type to perform statistical model checking with PVESTA. The confidence level for all our statistical experiments is 95%.

Standard Model Checking. We used the CAT tool [25] for model checking consistency properties of our Maude models. The analysis was performed with all initial states up to 4 transactions, 2 keys, 2 clients, and 2 servers.

5.2 Case Study I: Lock-Based Distributed Transactions

NO_WAIT [13] is a strict two-phase-locking-based distributed transaction system with two-phase commit (2PC) as its atomic commitment protocol, and has been implemented in the Deneva framework [16] using C++. We formally specified NO_WAIT in Maude, and then automatically generated the corresponding distributed Maude implementation. We used the C++ implementation in [16] in our experiments with NO_WAIT. Our Maude model of NO_WAIT has around 600 LOC, whereas the C++ implementation in [16] has approximately 12K LOC.

We performed two sets of experiments (Lock_A and Lock_B in Fig. 2), focusing on the effect of varying the contention in the system. For each set of experiments, we plot the results of statistical model checking of our Maude model, and of measurements of the distributed Maude and C++ implementations.

Regarding Q1, in Lock_A we vary the contention by tuning the skew *theta*, and compare two workloads, with 50% and 100% update transactions. In Lock_B we analyze the throughput as a function of the percentage of read-only transactions with skew *theta* = 0.5, and focus on the impact of transaction sizes (number of operations in a transaction). All three plots in each experiment show similar trends for the model- and implementation-based evaluations. That is, our distributed Maude implementation-based evaluation not only agrees with statistical predictions, but also with state-of-the-art implementation-based results.

Regarding Q2, our distributed system achieves lower peak throughput, by a factor of 6, than the C++ implementation. Some reasons for this lower performance are: (i) our tool is an unoptimized prototype, whereas the C++ implementation of NO_WAIT is optimized for performance (e.g., the socket library *nanomsg* provides a fast and scalable networking layer); and (ii) the $M \mapsto D(M)$ transformation allows adding any benchmarking tool as a *foreign object*, which is flexible but adds an extra layer of communication, whereas YCSB and the protocol clients are directly integrated in the C++ implementation.

We have also used the CAT tool [25] to model check our Maude model of NO_WAIT against 6 consistency properties, without finding any violation. If our trusted code base executes correctly, Theorem 3 ensures that our distributed Maude implementation of NO_WAIT satisfies the same consistency properties for the corresponding initial states.

5.3   Case Study II: The ROLA Transaction System

ROLA [22] is a recent distributed transaction protocol design that guarantees read atomicity (RA) and prevents lost updates (PLU). In [22], ROLA was formalized in Maude, model checked for the above consistency properties, and statistical model checking performance estimation showed that ROLA outperforms well-known distributed transaction system designs guaranteeing RA and PLU. However, up to now there was no distributed implementation of ROLA. Using our tool and the Maude specification of ROLA in [22] (which consists of approximately 850 LOC), we obtain such a correct-by-construction distributed implementation *for free*.

We have performed statistical model checking of the Maude specification, and have run our distributed Maude implementation on YCSB-generated workloads, on two groups of experiments (see Fig. 3). In ROLA_A we increase the amount of reads, and compare throughput with various partitions of the entire database (5 partitions against 3 partitions). In ROLA_B we plot throughput as a function of the number of concurrent clients, and focus on the effect of increasing the amount of contention (95% reads against 50% reads). Both plots in each experiment agree reasonably well.

All consistency properties model checked in [22] are preserved (Theorem 3) assuming correct execution of the trusted code base.

All system models, property specifications, and distributed Maude implementations are available at https://github.com/siliunobi/d-transformation.

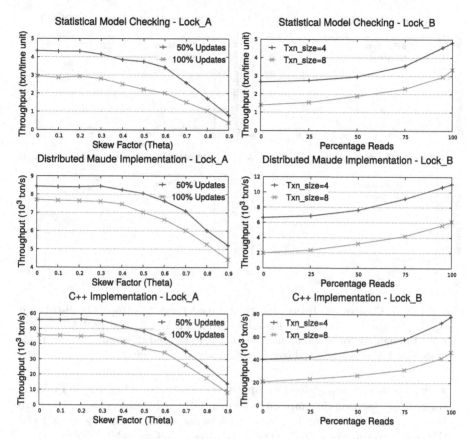

Fig. 2. NO_WAIT: Throughput obtained from statistical model checking (top), distributed Maude implementation (middle), and C++ implementation (bottom). Experiments Lock_A (left) and Lock_B (right) measure throughput for different ratios of updates and transaction sizes when varying skew factors and ratios of reads, resp.

6   Related Work

Our work is related to various formal frameworks for specification, verification, and implementation of distributed systems that try to reduce the *formality gap* [41] between the formal specification of a distributed system's *design* and its *implementation*. They can be roughly classified in three categories (only some example frameworks in each category are discussed):

1. Generating Imperative Implementation from Formal Models. Formal frameworks such as those in, e.g., [14,15,39], offer the possibility of generating distributed Java or C implementations from formal models.

2. Specification, Verification, and Proof of Imperative Implementation. A good example of state-of-the art recent work in this category is the IronFleet frame-

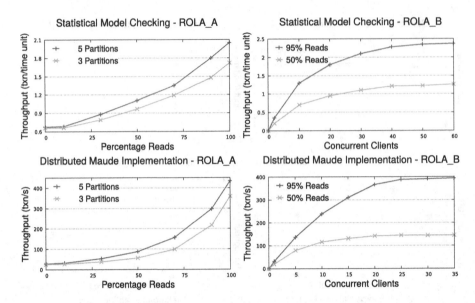

Fig. 3. ROLA: Comparison between statistical model checking (top) and distributed Maude implementation (bottom). Experiments ROLA_A (left) and ROLA_B (right) measure throughput for different number of partitions and different ratios of reads when varying ratios of reads and concurrent clients, respectively.

work [17]. Distributed systems are specified in a mixture of Lamport's TLA and Hoare logic assertions for imperative sequential code in Leino's Dafny language [20]. They are then formally verified with various tools, including Z3 [31] and the Dafny prover. Dafny code is then compiled into C# code.

3. Specification, Verification, and Transformation into Correct Distributed Implementation. Work in this category has for the most part been based on constructive logical frameworks such as Nuprl [11] and Coq [6]. In particular: (i) the *Event-ML* framework begins with an Event-ML specification and the desired properties both expressed in Nuprl and extracts a GPM program implementation; (ii) the *Verdi* framework [40] begins with a distributed system design and a set of safety properties, both specified in Coq; after desired properties are verified in Coq, the OCaml code of a correct implementation is extracted and deployed using a trusted shim; (iii) the *Chapar* framework [21] is specialized to extract correct-by-construction implementations of key-value stores in OCaml from formal specifications of such stores and of their consistency properties expressed and verified in Coq; and (iv) the *Disel* modular framework [36] specifies both distributed system designs and their desired properties in Coq, uses Coq to prove the desired properties, and extracts correct-by construction OCaml code.

Comparison with the Maude Framework. To the best of our knowledge, none of the above frameworks provide support for prediction of performance properties by statistical model checking, whereas Maude does so through PVeSta. In contrast to related work in category (1), where the correctness of the generated Java or C code is not proved (e.g., [15]), we prove the correctness of the generated distributed implementation. A possible exception is the effort in [14,39] which "argues the correctness" of their compilation from I/O automata to Java by modeling the compiled code as I/O automata. They also assume correctness of data type implementations, and only claim preservation of safety properties, whereas we also prove preservation of liveness properties. The main difference with the IronFleet framework in category (2) is that imperative programs are a problematic, low level choice for expressing formal design specifications. Furthermore, system properties can be considerably harder to prove at that level. Regarding frameworks in category (3), our work within the Maude framework shares with them the possibility of generating correct-by-construction distributed implementations from designs and of verifying such designs using theorem proving [34,37], but also adds the possibility of rapid exploration of different design alternatives by testing and by automatic model checking analysis, and the prediction of system performance before implementation. The point is that beginning with a human-intensive theorem proving verification effort may be both premature and costly. Instead, in Maude, designs can be analyzed and improved by fully automated methods *before* a mature design is fully verified by theorem proving.

7 Conclusions

We have presented and implemented a "proof-of-concept" prototype of the D transformation taking a Maude model M of a distributed system design and automatically generating the distributed Maude implementation $D(M)$. We have proved that M and a model $D_0(M)$ of $D(M)$ abstracting network communication details are *stuttering bisimilar* and therefore satisfy the same safety and liveness properties. We have applied our method to automatically obtain distributed implementations of two state-of-the-art distributed transaction system designs—and have executed them on YCSB workloads. We have also compared the performance of $D(M)$ and a high-performance conventional C++ implementation, which outperforms our prototype by a factor of six. This work shows that it is possible to automatically generate reasonable, but not yet optimal, correct-by-construction distributed implementations from very high level and easy to understand executable formal specifications of state-of-the-art system designs which are much shorter (a factor of 20 for the C++ implementation of NO_WAIT) than conventional implementations.

Our Maude implementation of the $M \mapsto D(M)$ transformation is a proof-of-concept prototype with ample room for improvement. The obvious next step is to arrive at an efficient Maude implementation of the $M \mapsto D(M)$ transformation.

Acknowledgments. We thank the anonymous reviewers for helpful comments on a previous version of this paper. This work has been partially supported by NRL under contract N00173-17-1-G002, and the National Science Foundation under grant NSF CCF 16-17401.

References

1. AlTurki, M., Meseguer, J.: PVESTA: a parallel statistical model checking and quantitative analysis tool. In: Corradini, A., Klin, B., Cîrstea, C. (eds.) CALCO 2011. LNCS, vol. 6859, pp. 386–392. Springer, Heidelberg (2011). https://doi.org/10.1007/978-3-642-22944-2_28

2. Bae, K., Meseguer, J.: Model checking linear temporal logic of rewriting formulas under localized fairness. Sci. Comput. Program. **99**, 193–234 (2015)

3. Bailis, P., Fekete, A., Ghodsi, A., Hellerstein, J.M., Stoica, I.: Scalable atomic visibility with RAMP transactions. ACM Trans. Database Syst. **41**(3), 15:1–15:45 (2016)

4. Baker, J., et al.: Megastore: providing scalable, highly available storage for interactive services. In: CIDR 2011, pp. 223–234 (2011)

5. Benson, T., Akella, A., Maltz, D.A.: Network traffic characteristics of data centers in the wild. In: IMC 2010, pp. 267–280. ACM (2010)

6. Bertot, Y., Castéran, P.: Interactive Theorem Proving and Program Development - Coq'Art: The Calculus of Inductive Constructions. Springer, Heidelberg (2004). https://doi.org/10.1007/978-3-662-07964-5

7. Bobba, R., et al.: Survivability: design, formal modeling, and validation of cloud storage systems using Maude. In: Assured Cloud Computing, chap. 2, pp. 10–48. Wiley-IEEE Computer Society Press (2018)

8. Bruni, R., Meseguer, J.: Semantic foundations for generalized rewrite theories. Theor. Comput. Sci. **360**(1–3), 386–414 (2006)

9. Clarke, E.M., Grumberg, O., Peled, D.A.: Model Checking. MIT Press, Cambridge (2001)

10. Clavel, M., et al.: All About Maude. LNCS, vol. 4350. Springer, Heidelberg (2007). https://doi.org/10.1007/978-3-540-71999-1

11. Constable, R.L.: Implementing Mathematics with the Nuprl Proof Development System. Prentice Hall, Englewood Cliffs (1987)

12. Cooper, B.F., Silberstein, A., Tam, E., Ramakrishnan, R., Sears, R.: Benchmarking cloud serving systems with YCSB. In: SOCC 2010, pp. 143–154. ACM (2010)

13. Eswaran, K.P., Gray, J.N., Lorie, R.A., Traiger, I.L.: The notions of consistency and predicate locks in a database system. Commun. ACM **19**(11), 624–633 (1976)

14. Georgiou, C., Lynch, N.A., Mavrommatis, P., Tauber, J.A.: Automated implementation of complex distributed algorithms specified in the IOA language. STTT **11**(2), 153–171 (2009)

15. Haberl, W.: Code generation and system integration of distributed automotive applications. Ph.D. thesis, Technical University Munich (2011)

16. Harding, R., Van Aken, D., Pavlo, A., Stonebraker, M.: An evaluation of distributed concurrency control. Proc. VLDB Endow. **10**(5), 553–564 (2017)

17. Hawblitzel, C., et al.: IronFleet: proving safety and liveness of practical distributed systems. Commun. ACM **60**(7), 83–92 (2017)

18. Hewitt, E.: Cassandra: The Definitive Guide. O'Reilly Media, Sebastopol (2010)

19. Hunt, P., Konar, M., Junqueira, F.P., Reed, B.: Zookeeper: wait-free coordination for internet-scale systems. In: USENIX ATC 2010. USENIX Association (2010)

20. Leino, K.R.M.: Dafny: an automatic program verifier for functional correctness. In: Clarke, E.M., Voronkov, A. (eds.) LPAR 2010. LNCS (LNAI), vol. 6355, pp. 348–370. Springer, Heidelberg (2010). https://doi.org/10.1007/978-3-642-17511-4_20

21. Lesani, M., Bell, C.J., Chlipala, A.: Chapar: certified causally consistent distributed key-value stores. In: POPL 2016, pp. 357–370. ACM (2016)

22. Liu, S., Ölveczky, P.C., Santhanam, K., Wang, Q., Gupta, I., Meseguer, J.: ROLA: a new distributed transaction protocol and its formal analysis. In: Russo, A., Schürr, A. (eds.) FASE 2018. LNCS, vol. 10802, pp. 77–93. Springer, Cham (2018). https://doi.org/10.1007/978-3-319-89363-1_5

23. Liu, S., Ölveczky, P.C., Wang, Q., Gupta, I., Meseguer, J.: Read atomic transactions with prevention of lost updates: ROLA and its formal analysis. Formal Asp. Comput. **31**(5), 503–540 (2019)

24. Liu, S., Ölveczky, P.C., Wang, Q., Meseguer, J.: Formal modeling and analysis of the Walter transactional data store. In: Rusu, V. (ed.) WRLA 2018. LNCS, vol. 11152, pp. 136–152. Springer, Cham (2018). https://doi.org/10.1007/978-3-319-99840-4_8

25. Liu, S., Ölveczky, P.C., Zhang, M., Wang, Q., Meseguer, J.: Automatic analysis of consistency properties of distributed transaction systems in Maude. In: Vojnar, T., Zhang, L. (eds.) TACAS 2019. LNCS, vol. 11428, pp. 40–57. Springer, Cham (2019). https://doi.org/10.1007/978-3-030-17465-1_3

26. Liu, S., Sandur, A., Meseguer, J., Ölveczky, P.C., Wang, Q.: Generating correct-by-construction distributed implementations from formal Maude designs. Technical report, Department of Computer Science, University of Illinois at Urbana-Champaign (2019). http://hdl.handle.net/2142/106018

27. Manolios, P.: A compositional theory of refinement for branching time. In: Geist, D., Tronci, E. (eds.) CHARME 2003. LNCS, vol. 2860, pp. 304–318. Springer, Heidelberg (2003). https://doi.org/10.1007/978-3-540-39724-3_28

28. Meseguer, J.: Conditional rewriting logic as a unified model of concurrency. Theor. Comput. Sci. **96**(1), 73–155 (1992)

29. Meseguer, J.: Twenty years of rewriting logic. J. Algebr. Log. Program. **81**, 721–781 (2012)

30. Meseguer, J., Palomino, M., Martí-Oliet, N.: Algebraic simulations. J. Log. Algebr. Program. **79**(2), 103–143 (2010)

31. de Moura, L., Bjørner, N.: Z3: an efficient SMT solver. In: Ramakrishnan, C.R., Rehof, J. (eds.) TACAS 2008. LNCS, vol. 4963, pp. 337–340. Springer, Heidelberg (2008). https://doi.org/10.1007/978-3-540-78800-3_24

32. Newcombe, C., Rath, T., Zhang, F., Munteanu, B., Brooker, M., Deardeuff, M.: How Amazon Web Services uses formal methods. Commun. ACM **58**(4), 66–73 (2015)

33. Ölveczky, P.C.: Formalizing and validating the P-Store replicated data store in Maude. In: James, P., Roggenbach, M. (eds.) WADT 2016. LNCS, vol. 10644, pp. 189–207. Springer, Cham (2017). https://doi.org/10.1007/978-3-319-72044-9_13

34. Rocha, C., Meseguer, J.: Proving safety properties of rewrite theories. In: Corradini, A., Klin, B., Cîrstea, C. (eds.) CALCO 2011. LNCS, vol. 6859, pp. 314–328. Springer, Heidelberg (2011). https://doi.org/10.1007/978-3-642-22944-2_22

35. Schiper, N., Sutra, P., Pedone, F.: P-store: genuine partial replication in wide area networks. In: SRDS 2010, pp. 214–224. IEEE Computer Society (2010)

36. Sergey, I., Wilcox, J.R., Tatlock, Z.: Programming and proving with distributed protocols. PACMPL **2**(POPL), 28:1–28:30 (2018)

37. Skeirik, S., Stefanescu, A., Meseguer, J.: A constructor-based reachability logic for rewrite theories. In: Fioravanti, F., Gallagher, J.P. (eds.) LOPSTR 2017. LNCS, vol. 10855, pp. 201–217. Springer, Cham (2018). https://doi.org/10.1007/978-3-319-94460-9_12

38. Sovran, Y., Power, R., Aguilera, M.K., Li, J.: Transactional storage for geo-replicated systems. In: SOSP 2011, pp. 385–400. ACM (2011)

39. Tauber, J.A.: Verifiable compilation of I/O automata without global synchronization. Ph.D. thesis, Massachusetts Institute of Technology (2005)
40. Wilcox, J.R., et al.: Verdi: a framework for implementing and formally verifying distributed systems. In: PLDI 2015, pp. 357–368. ACM (2015)
41. Woos, D., Wilcox, J.R., Anton, S., Tatlock, Z., Ernst, M.D., Anderson, T.E.: Planning for change in a formal verification of the Raft consensus protocol. In: CPP 2016, pp. 154–165. ACM (2016)

Parameter Synthesis and Robustness
Analysis of Rule-Based Models

Matej Troják[✉], David Šafránek, Lukrécia Mertová, and Luboš Brim

Systems Biology Laboratory, Masaryk University, Brno, Czech Republic
xtrojak@fi.muni.cz

Abstract. We introduce the Quantitative Biochemical Space Language, a rule-based language for a compact modelling of probabilistic behaviour of complex parameter-dependent biological systems. Application of rules is governed by an associated parametrised rate function, expressing partially known information about the behaviour of the modelled system. The parameter values influence the behaviour of the model. We propose a formal verification-based method for the synthesis of parameter values (parameter synthesis) which ensure the behaviour of the modelled system satisfies a given PCTL property. In addition, we demonstrate how this method can be used for robustness analysis.

1 Introduction

In systems biology, models of biological processes have to reflect several levels of abstraction adapted accordingly to the known information. At every level, the system has to be described rigorously in a formal language to avoid misunderstood and ambiguous interpretations.

Rule-based languages represent an intuitive and convenient modelling tool for biologists because the dynamics of biochemical systems is typically determined by the underlying causal rules. Existing rule-based languages focus on specific features such as structures binding [15,19], regulatory interactions [41], modularity [39], or spatial aspects [24]. However, a challenge is to combine suitable levels of abstraction (ranging from qualitative to quantitative aspects) with the compactness of the description while not compromising human readability. To that end, we have introduced Biochemical Space Language (BCSL) [42], a high-level rule-based language that combines several features of rule-based frameworks in a single formalism.

BCSL design stems from a long-time practical experience with describing biochemical processes rigorously but still in a way that is understandable by the users (biologists in this case). The central goal is to describe the biochemistry of a given process at the mechanistic level, in our words, to build the so-called biochemical space of the given process. Biochemical space plays a central role in the platform we are developing for modelling, specification, and analysis of biological processes [43]. In this context, the rule-based description in BCSL serves

This work has been supported by the Czech Science Foundation grant 18-00178S.

R. Lee et al. (Eds.): NFM 2020, LNCS 12229, pp. 41–59, 2020.
https://doi.org/10.1007/978-3-030-55754-6_3

as a bridge between the explicit biological knowledge and mathematical models that typically encrypt the information in non-trivial chains of approximations. It is worth noting that rule-based description of (bio)chemical processes is the essence of chemistry and hence the rule-based view is natural to systems modellers [38]. BCSL has been successfully used in the international consortium for cyanobacteria modelling and analysis [43].

Apparently, by building the biochemical space in a rule-based language, we obtain an executable alternative to the existing mathematical models [20]. In particular, the long-term goal is to use the biochemical space as an integrated model of the given biological problem. To fulfil this goal, the language has to support *quantitative aspects* of the rules, e.g., the rate of performing the rule. Such quantitative aspects have been addressed in Kappa [15], BNGL [19], and BIOCHAM [11], a more general framework has been introduced in Chromar [24], and in the process-algebraic approach of BioPEPA [13]. However, quantitative aspects have not yet been addressed in BCSL. Due to the specific level of abstraction considered in BCSL, it is not possible to directly adapt the solutions employed in above-mentioned languages.

In this paper, we introduce the *quantitative BCSL* (qBCSL) by extending BCSL with quantitative dynamical aspects. This is realised by associating rules with parametrised *rate functions* of the current state of the system dynamics. The intended meaning is to quantify the rate of the particular interaction. A model with rate-assigned rules gives rise to probabilistic semantics which is expressed by means of parametric Markov Chains (pMC) [16,33] representing the family of Discrete Time Markov Chains (DTMC) for all admissible settings of parameters (*parametrisations*) appearing in rate functions. Based on the tool Storm [18] we establish a framework for (exact) *parameter synthesis* of qBCSL models with respect to PCTL [23] properties. Technically, the method computes a rational function that assigns the probability of satisfying a given property to each parametrisation. Note that the stochastic semantics of a rule-based model is traditionally formalised as a Continuous Time Markov Chain (CTMC) [21]. However, the scalability of existing exact methods [2,10] is limited to small models, other available methods are just simulation-based, thus providing only approximative results. Following the idea of using approximate models with discrete-time semantics [3], we consider the DTMC that provides efficient methods to analyse exact probability of PCTL properties.

In addition, we provide an approach for *global robustness analysis* of qBCSL models with respect to a given parameter perturbation and a PCTL formula. Global robustness characterises the mean validity of a formula over all parameter values in the given perturbation set [5,12]. The entire framework is implemented in the open source tool eBCSgen[1] and demonstrated on a biological case study.

The primary contribution of this paper is in bringing the exact parameter synthesis into the field of rule-based models with stochastic semantics. The uniqueness of our solution is not only in the level of abstraction qBCSL provides but also in the fact that we directly interpret rule-based models by means

---

[1] https://github.com/sybila/eBCSgen.

of DTMCs to support formal analysis. Such a setting allows to apply efficient parameter synthesis techniques [16,17,22] to rule-based models.

1.1 Related Work

In qBCSL, objects are projected into multisets that represent the model states. The stochastic multiset rewriting (SMR) was used in [3] to encode expressive process calculi such as π-calculus. In [4], SMR was used as a base for parametrised mass-action reaction-based models encoded by means of interval Markov Chains (iMC) where parameters range over closed intervals. Given the fixed structure of mass-action kinetics and intervals of kinetic parameters values, they compute lower and upper bounds for reachability probability. In our case, we support rational parametrised kinetic functions and employ parameter synthesis techniques giving a symbolic function representing the exact parameter sets.

Methods for parameter synthesis of pMCs have been introduced with symbolic computation of reachability properties through state elimination [16,22,27], recently improved by parameter lifting [40] and fraction-free Gaussian elimination [26]. Here we employ these techniques as implemented in Storm tool.

An alternative approach to the analysis of complex stochastic models under parameter uncertainty is based on statistical methods [1,8,9,35]. There are only a few works that bridge the rule-based framework to such techniques. In [34], a statistical parameter sampling method is employed to analyse unknown parameters in BNGL models represented by means of CTMCs where the rate function is limited to mass action kinetics. The work [28] employs statistical model checking for parameter synthesis of CTMCs. The recent work [30] combines statistical model checking with machine learning techniques to calibration (estimation) of parameters in order to maximise the probability of satisfying a given specification. In [6], the authors adapt simulation-based and moment-based methods. In general, statistical techniques do not give an exact symbolic representation of satisfying parameter sets.

2 Preliminaries

Throughout this section, we consider a given set of atomic propositions AP. *Discrete Time Markov Chain* (DTMC) is a tuple $(\mathcal{S}, s_0, \rho, L)$ where $\mathcal{S}$ is the set of *states*, $s_0 \in \mathcal{S}$ is the *initial state*, $\rho : \mathcal{S} \times \mathcal{S} \rightarrow [0,1]$ is the *transition probability matrix*, where for all $s \in \mathcal{S}$ we require that $\sum_{s' \in \mathcal{S}} \rho(s, s') = 1$, and $L : \mathcal{S} \rightarrow 2^{\text{AP}}$ is a *labelling function* which gives the atomic propositions that are true in a state.

The matrix entry $\rho(s, s')$ gives the probability of making a transition from s to s'. The probability of following a finite path $s_0 s_1 \ldots s_n$ is $\rho(s_0, s_1) \cdot \rho(s_1, s_2) \cdot \ldots \cdot \rho(s_{n-1}, s_n)$. These probabilities for finite paths give rise to a unique probability measure $\mathbf{Pr}_s$ on the set $Path_s$ of infinite paths starting in state s defined on the sets of paths having a finite common prefix, such that

$$\mathbf{Pr}(\{\omega \mid \omega = ss_1 \ldots s_n.\omega'\}) = \rho(s, s_1) \cdot \rho(s_1, s_2) \cdot \ldots \cdot \rho(s_{n-1}, s_n).$$

The logic PCTL [23] is a probabilistic variant of CTL where the existential and the universal quantification over paths in CTL is replaced with a *probabilistic operator* $\Pi_{\bowtie\varrho}(\cdot)$, where $\bowtie \in \{\leq, <, >, \geq\}$ and $\varrho \in [0,1]$ is the *probability threshold*, that can be applied to a path formula. The formal syntax of PCTL formulae is given by the following grammar:

$$\phi ::= \mathsf{True} \mid a \in \mathsf{AP} \mid \phi \wedge \phi \mid \neg\phi \mid \Pi_{\bowtie\mathsf{n}}(\psi)$$
$$\psi ::= \mathbf{X}\phi \mid \phi\mathbf{U}\phi$$

The semantics of PCTL is the same as that of CTL [14] for the fragment where they both coincide. The semantics of the probabilistic operator is:

$$s \models \Pi_{\bowtie\mathsf{n}}(\psi) \quad \text{iff} \quad \mathbf{Pr}_s(\{\omega \in Paths \mid \omega \models \psi\}) \bowtie \mathsf{n}$$

meaning that the probability measure of the set of paths satisfying ψ is calculated and compared to the threshold n, yielding true or false.

The standard qualitative model checking algorithm proceeds in the same way as for CTL, by induction on ϕ. In [16], a symbolic approach was proposed. It is based on derivation of a finite state automaton (FSA) $\mathcal{A} = (\mathcal{S}, \Sigma, \delta, \mathcal{S}_f)$ from given DTMC. $\mathcal{S}$ is the same set of states as in the DTMC, the alphabet Σ consists of the strictly positive entries of the probability matrix, the set of final states $\mathcal{S}_f$ and the transition function δ depend on the path formula under consideration.

The regular language $\mathcal{L}(\mathcal{A}, s)$ recognized by $\mathcal{A}$ with an initial state $s \in \mathcal{S}$, corresponds to the (possibly infinite) set Ω of finite paths from s to some final state in $\mathcal{S}_f$, following only transitions allowed by δ.

A regular expression r over an alphabet Σ is computed using the state-elimination algorithm [25]. The evaluation val(r) of the regular expression can be done by replacing union by addition, concatenation by multiplication, and star by the limit of a geometric series (for the formal definition, see [16]).

The evaluation of a regular expression r computed for a language $\mathcal{L}(\mathcal{A}, s)$ is the probability measure in s of the set of paths with prefixes in Ω:

$$\mathsf{val}(r) = \mathbf{Pr}_s(\{\omega \in Paths \mid \exists k \geq 0.\omega(k) \in \mathcal{S}_f \wedge \forall l < k, \exists a \in \Sigma.\omega(l+1) \in \delta(\omega(l), a)\})$$

The model checking problem can be then solved for a state s by evaluating a regular expression r equivalent to the language recognized by the automaton with the initial state s, i.e. $s \models \Pi_{\bowtie\mathsf{n}}(\psi)$ iff val(r) $\bowtie$ n.

We can also directly specify properties which evaluate to a numerical value – the result of *quantitative model checking*. This is achieved by replacing the probability bound from Π operator with '=?'. Note that this is only allowed when the Π in question is the outermost operator of the property. The evaluation is then given as $\Pi_{=?}(\psi) = \mathbf{Pr}_s(\{\omega \in Paths \mid \omega \models \psi\})$ which means it can be computed using the symbolic approach as $\Pi_{=?}(\psi) = \mathsf{val}(r)$.

3   Quantitative Biochemical Space Language

In this section, we define quantitative Biochemical Space Language (qBCSL) with quantitative aspects, as an extension of BCSL [42]. The quantitative aspects enable to reason about the *rate* of interactions to occur. All the definitions are demonstrated in a simple example in Sect. 3.1.

Let $\mathbb{N}_T$, $\mathbb{N}_A$, $\mathbb{N}_c$, and $\mathbb{N}_\delta$ be mutually exclusive finite sets of agent, atom, compartment, and feature names, respectively. The *syntax* of the qBCSL objects is given by the following grammar:

multiset	$M ::= \emptyset \mid T \mid M, M$	atomic name	$\eta ::= x \in \mathbb{N}_A$
agent	$T ::= \mu_c^\lambda(\gamma)$	agent name	$\mu ::= x \in \mathbb{N}_T$
composition	$\gamma ::= \emptyset \mid A, \gamma$	feature	$\delta ::= x \in \mathbb{N}_\delta$
atom	$A ::= \eta\{\delta\}$	compartment	$c ::= x \in \mathbb{N}_c$
		complex ID	$\lambda ::= x \in \mathbb{N}$

We restrict ourselves only to finite expressions and require that an atomic name occurs at most once in a composition.

We denote by $\mathbb{M}$ the set of all multisets. We assume the *structural congruence* $\equiv$ to be the least congruence on multisets satisfying axioms $M_1, M_2 \equiv M_2, M_1$ and $M, \emptyset \equiv M$, where M_1, M_2 represents the union of multisets M_1 and M_2. Additionally, we assume a similar relation $\equiv_\gamma$ on compositions defined as the least congruence satisfying axioms $A, \gamma \equiv_\gamma \gamma, A$ and $\emptyset, \gamma \equiv_\gamma \gamma$.

The structural congruence $\equiv$ (resp. $\equiv_\gamma$) allows us to formally define the algebraic multiset operations $\in, \subseteq, \subset, \cup, \cap$ and $\setminus$ on qBCSL terms. For example, $T \in \mathbb{M}$ corresponds to $\exists M' \in \mathbb{M}.M \equiv T, M'$ and $M \subseteq M'$ corresponds to $\exists M'' \in \mathbb{M}.M' \equiv M, M''$. Moreover, by $M(T)$ we denote the number of occurrences of agent T in the multiset M and by $M(M')$ the number of occurrences of multiset M' in the multiset M, which is at least one in the case $M \subseteq M'$ (formally, it is defined as minimal $M(T)$ for all $T \in M'$).

We denote by Λ the set of all complex IDs of a multiset M. Two multisets are *equal*, $M_1 = M_2$, if there exists a bijective function $h : \Lambda_1 \to \Lambda_2$ such that $M_1^h \equiv M_2$ where M_1^h denotes M_1 with every occurrence of a complex ID λ replaced by $h(\lambda)$.

Agent signature $\sigma_T : \mathbb{N}_T \to 2^{\mathbb{N}_A}$ is a function from an agent name to a set of atomic names. Set of possible agent signatures is denoted as Σ_T. *Atomic signature* $\sigma_A : \mathbb{N}_A \to 2^{\mathbb{N}_\delta}$ is a function from an atomic name to a non-empty set of feature names. Set of possible agent signatures is denoted as Σ_A.

Let $\mathbb{V}_c$ and $\mathbb{V}_\lambda$ be mutually exclusive finite sets of the compartment and complex variables, respectively. Additionally, let $\mathbb{V}_\delta = \mathbb{N}_\delta \cup \{\varepsilon\}$ be a set of feature names extended by a special symbol ε. *Pattern* P is defined according to the same grammar as multisets with the following modifications:

feature	$\delta ::= s \in \mathbb{V}_\delta$
compartment	$c ::= v \in \mathbb{V}_c \cup \mathbb{N}_c$
complex ID	$\lambda ::= l \in \mathbb{V}_\lambda$

We denote by $\mathcal{P}$ the set of all patterns and with $\mathcal{P}_\perp$ we denote the set of all patterns restricted to $\delta \in \mathbb{N}_\delta$ and $c \in \mathbb{N}_c$. Note that the congruence relation defined on multisets does *not* hold in case of patterns. A pattern is *well-formed* if the atoms are alphanumerically sorted with respect to their names.

An *instantiation* is a function $\mathcal{I} : \mathbb{V}_\delta \cup \mathbb{V}_c \cup \mathbb{V}_\lambda \to \mathbb{N}_\delta \cup \mathbb{N}_c \cup \mathbb{N}$ such that $\mathcal{I}(s) \in \mathbb{N}_\delta$, $\mathcal{I}(v) \in \mathbb{N}_c$, and $\mathcal{I}(l) \in \mathbb{N}$ for $s \in \mathbb{V}_\delta$, $v \in \mathbb{V}_c$, and $l \in \mathbb{V}_\lambda$, respectively. We denote by Γ the set of all instantiations.

Given an atomic signature σ_A and a pattern $P \in \mathcal{P}$, with $\mathcal{I}(P)$ we denote the multiset obtained by replacing each occurrence of a term ν appearing in P with the corresponding instantiation $\mathcal{I}(\nu)$ respecting the signature σ_A. Particularly, the signature σ_A restricts instantiation of each feature ε to one of the feature names defined for the appropriate atomic name. Please note that the same term repeating on separate positions in the pattern can be instantiated to different values.

Given two finite patterns $P = T_1, T_2, \ldots, T_n$ and $P' = T'_1, T'_2, \ldots, T'_m$, instantiations $\mathcal{I}, \mathcal{I}' \in \Gamma$ are *consistent* with respect to the given patterns P, P', written $\mathcal{I}(P) \Delta \mathcal{I}'(P')$, if $\forall i \in [1, \min(m, n)]$ the following conditions hold:

1. $\lambda(T_i) = \lambda(T'_i) \Rightarrow \lambda(\mathcal{I}(T_i)) = \lambda(\mathcal{I}'(T'_i))$
2. $c(T_i) = c(T'_i) \Rightarrow c(\mathcal{I}(T_i)) = c(\mathcal{I}'(T'_i))$
3. $A_k(T_i) = A_k(T'_i) \Rightarrow A_k(\mathcal{I}(T_i)) = A_k(\mathcal{I}'(T'_i))$

where $\lambda(T)$ denotes the complex ID λ of the agent T, $c(T)$ denotes compartment c of the agent T, and $A_k(T)$ denotes the atom from the composition γ of agent T on a position k.

Pattern expansion is a function $\langle \_ \rangle : \mathcal{P} \times \Sigma_T \to \mathcal{P}$ which extends a given pattern P to a pattern $\langle P \rangle$ such that every occurrence of a composition γ of an agent T is extended by atoms whose names are not yet present in γ and are defined in the given signature $\sigma_T \in \Sigma_T$. These newly added atoms have assigned feature ε and are inserted to the composition in such way that they preserve the alphanumerical order.

Let $\mathbb{V}$ be a set of parameters. For each parameter v, a domain of admissible positive values is assigned, denoted by $\mathcal{D}(v) \in 2^{\mathbb{R}^+}$. In the following, we define the grammar for the algebraic rational *rate expression* f:

rate expression	$f ::= \frac{g}{g} \mid g$
polynomial expression	$g ::= c \mid v \mid [\, t \,] \mid g + g \mid g \times g \mid g^n$

where $c \in \mathbb{R}$ is a *constant*, $v \in \mathbb{V}$ is a *parameter*, $n \in \mathbb{N}$ is an *exponent*, and $t \in \mathcal{P}$ is a *pattern* such that all agents have the same complex ID λ.

We denote by $\mathbb{F}$ the set of all rate expressions and with $\mathbb{F}_v$ rate expressions without the patterns (note that $\mathbb{F}_v \subseteq \mathbb{F}$). For the sake of readability, we allow additional simplifications (e.g. parentheses) which can always be converted to a form given by the provided grammar.

Multiset evaluation $\mathbb{F} \times \mathbb{M} \to \mathbb{F}_v$ of a rate expression f on a multiset M, written f(M), is a rate expression $f' \in \mathbb{F}_v$ such that each pattern $[\, t \,]$ is replaced by an integer $\sum_{\mathcal{I} \in \Gamma} M(\mathcal{I}\langle t \rangle)$ expressing the sum of all possible instantiations of the pattern. Note that number of possible instantiations Γ is finite with respect to the set of all complex IDs Λ of multiset M.

Rewrite rule R is a triple $(P_l, P_r, f) \in \mathcal{P} \times \mathcal{P} \times \mathbb{F}$, usually written as $P_l \xrightarrow{f} P_r$. It describes a structural change of a multiset defined by the difference between left-hand and right-hand side patterns, associated with the rate expression f.

A qBCSL *model* $\mathcal{M}$ is a tuple $(\mathcal{R}, \sigma_T, \sigma_A, M_0, V)$ such that $\mathcal{R}$ is a finite set of rewrite rules, $\sigma_T \in \Sigma_T$ is an agent signature, $\sigma_A \in \Sigma_A$ is an atomic signature, $M_0 \in \mathbb{M}$ is an initial multiset, and $V \in \mathbb{V}$ is a set of parameters.

3.1 Example

We provide an example consisting of a fragment of photosynthesis processes of cyanobacteria. Note that this fragment is not accurate and its purpose is to demonstrate all the formal aspects of the language only.

Let $ps_{tlm}^1(p700\{n\}, a\{n\}, achl\{*\})$ denote an *agent* – photosystem of cyanobacteria – in thylakoid membrane compartment (tlm) with three active domains represented as atoms: photosystem reaction center p700, primary acceptor of photosystem a (both in neutral state n), and chlorophyll antenna achl in excited state *.

Next, let us have an *agent signature* $\sigma_T = \{ps \rightarrow \{p700, a, achl\}\}$, which defines allowed set of atoms for the photosystem. Note that each atomic name defined in the agent signature for an agent has to be used in its composition. An *atomic signature* $\sigma_A = \{p700 \rightarrow \{n, +\}, a \rightarrow \{n, -\}, achl \rightarrow \{n, *, +\}\}$ defines allowed states for reaction center p700, acceptor a, and antenna achl.

We can use a *pattern* $P = ps_{tlm}^x(p700\{n\}, a\{\varepsilon\})$ to describe the photosystem such that its affiliation to a particular complex is not given, only identified by a variable x. The state of p700 is specified as neutral while for the acceptor a it is unknown (denoted with ε). Additionally, note that not every atom from the signature has to be specified (achl is omitted), which is the key aspect for compactness of the rule-based approach.

Such pattern can be *instantiated* by function $\mathcal{I} = \{x \rightarrow 1, \varepsilon \rightarrow -\}$ which assigns to each unspecified element of a pattern a particular value. Applying the instantiation on the pattern P, we obtain $\mathcal{I}(P) = ps_{tlm}^1(p700\{n\}, a\{-\})$.

However, the achl atom is missing in the composition. For this purpose, the *pattern expansion* is defined, which, when applied on a pattern, creates the expanded pattern $\langle P \rangle = ps_{tlm}^x(p700\{n\}, a\{\varepsilon_1\}, achl\{\varepsilon_2\})$. Given the instantiation function $\mathcal{I} = \{x \rightarrow 1, \varepsilon_1 \rightarrow -, \varepsilon_2 \rightarrow +\}$, the instantiation of expanded pattern is $\mathcal{I}\langle P \rangle = ps_{tlm}^1(p700\{n\}, a\{-\}, achl\{+\})$.

$$ps_{tlm}^x(p700\{n\}, achl\{+\}) \xrightarrow{k_1 \times [ps_{tlm}^x(p700\{n\}, achl\{+\})]} ps_{tlm}^x(p700\{+\}, achl\{n\}) \quad (1)$$

The *rule* 1 represents a reduction of oxidized primary electron donor in photosystem. It describes a change of states of p700 and achl regardless of the state of acceptor a. Complex variable x ensures that the complex ID of the agent does not change. The rate expression is dependent on the number of occurrences of the pattern in a given multiset and a parameter $k_1 \in [5, 10]$ representing admissible values for *mass action* law constant.

$$\mathsf{ps}^{\mathsf{x}}_{\mathsf{tlm}}(\emptyset), \mathsf{ps}^{\mathsf{y}}_{\mathsf{tlm}}(\emptyset) \xrightarrow{k_2 \times [\mathsf{ps}^{\mathsf{x}}_{\mathsf{tlm}}(\emptyset)] \times ([\mathsf{ps}^{\mathsf{y}}_{\mathsf{tlm}}(\emptyset)]-1)} \mathsf{ps}^{\mathsf{x}}_{\mathsf{tlm}}(\emptyset), \mathsf{ps}^{\mathsf{x}}_{\mathsf{tlm}}(\emptyset) \qquad (2)$$

The rule 2 describes a formation of a complex from two ps agents. The formation is independent of the particular conformation of compositions of the agents (represented by $\emptyset$). Similar to the previous rule, the rate is dependent on the number of occurrences and a parameter $k_2 \in [0, 2]$ representing admissible values for mass action law constant.

3.2 Semantics

The semantics for the qBCSL is given in two steps – (1) we construct a parametric Quantitative Labelled Transition System (pQLTS) by transitive *rewriting* of multisets with rules such that nodes represent multisets, transitions applied rules, and quantitative labels evaluated rate expressions; and (2) we create parametric DTMC (pMC) from pQLTS such that labels of outgoing edges for each state are normalised to probability functions of parameters.

Let $\mathcal{M} = (\mathcal{R}, \sigma_\mathsf{T}, \sigma_\mathsf{A}, \mathsf{M}_0, \mathsf{V})$ be a qBCSL model. The *rewriting* of the multisets is given by labelled transition relation $\mathsf{M}_1 \xrightarrow{f'} \mathsf{M}_2$ with $f' \in \mathbb{F}_\mathsf{v}$ and $\mathsf{M}_1, \mathsf{M}_2 \in \mathbb{M}$ satisfying the following inference rule:

$$\frac{\begin{array}{cc} R : \mathsf{P}_l \xrightarrow{f} \mathsf{P}_r & \mathsf{M}_s = \mathsf{M}_t \\ \exists\, \mathcal{I}, \mathcal{I}' \in \Gamma.\ \mathcal{I}\langle \mathsf{P}_l \rangle = \mathsf{M}_l \wedge \mathcal{I}'\langle \mathsf{P}_r \rangle = \mathsf{M}_r \\ \mathcal{I}\langle \mathsf{P}_l \rangle \Delta \mathcal{I}'\langle \mathsf{P}_r \rangle \\ \mathsf{Unique}(\mathsf{M}_s; \mathsf{M}_l) \wedge \mathsf{Unique}(\mathsf{M}_t; \mathsf{M}_r) \end{array}}{\mathsf{M}_s, \mathsf{M}_l \xrightarrow{f(\mathsf{M}_s, \mathsf{M}_l)} \mathsf{M}_t, \mathsf{M}_r}$$

It is possible to consider multiset rewriting which is context-free in terms of complex manipulations. It enables so-called *side effects* – modifications beyond the scope of the rule (e.g. synthesis of a new agent with an already existing complex ID). In order to avoid these side effects, we define predicate $\mathsf{Unique}(\mathsf{M}_1; \mathsf{M}_2)$ which holds if $\forall (\mathsf{T}_1, \mathsf{T}_2) \in \mathsf{M}_1 \times \mathsf{M}_2.\lambda(\mathsf{T}_1) \neq \lambda(\mathsf{T}_2)$ for some $\mathsf{M}_1, \mathsf{M}_2 \in \mathbb{M}$. This predicate is used in conditions of inference rule of labelled transition relation, which ensures that if the rule is modifying a complex, it is modifying it as a whole and if the rule is creating a new complex, it has a unique identifier across the newly created multiset. An indirect consequence of disabled side effects is that the number of encoded particular agents of a model is finite.

We define *parametric Quantitative Labelled Transition System* pQLTS as a triple $(\mathcal{S}, \mathcal{L}, \mapsto)$ where each transition corresponds to the application of a rewrite rule. For a model, it is obtained by transitive closure of inference rule starting from M_0. The label $\ell \in \mathcal{L}$ of a transition is an evaluated rate expression of the applied rule. We denote by $\ell(s, s')$ the label of transition $t(s, s') \in \mapsto$.

Parametric Markov chain pMC is a tuple $(\mathcal{S}, s_0, \rho', \mathsf{V}, L)$ where $\mathcal{S}$ is a finite set of *states*, $s_0 \in \mathcal{S}$ is the *initial state*, $\rho' : \mathcal{S} \times \mathcal{S} \to \mathbb{F}_\mathsf{v}$ is the *parametric transition probability matrix*, V is a finite set of parameters, and $L : \mathcal{S} \to 2^{\mathsf{AP}}$ is a labelling function which gives the atomic propositions that are true in a state.

We consider a given set of atomic propositions AP which are expressions over the set of patterns $\mathcal{P}_\perp$ of type $[a] \bowtie n$ where $a \in \mathcal{P}_\perp$, $\bowtie \in \{\leq, <, >, \geq\}$, and $n \in \mathbb{N}$. Moreover, Boolean combinations of such expressions are also allowed.

We define the *probabilistic semantics* of a qBCSL model using a translation from its pQLTS into a pMC. We have to calculate, for each states s and s' of pQLTS, the probability of moving from s to s', by exploiting rate functions. We define a function $\vartheta : \mathcal{S} \to \mathbb{F}_V$ where

$$\vartheta(s) = \sum_{s' \in \mathcal{S}} \ell(s, s') \qquad (3)$$

such that by default if $t(s, s') \not\mapsto$ then $\ell(s, s') = 0$.

We derive a pMC $(\mathcal{S}, s_0, \rho', V)$ from a pQLTS $(\mathcal{S}, \mathcal{L}, \mapsto)$ by computing *parametric transition probability matrix* $\rho' : \mathcal{S} \times \mathcal{S} \to \mathbb{F}_V$ such that $\forall s, s' \in \mathcal{S}.s \neq s'$ holds that if $\vartheta(s) = 0$ then $\rho'(s, s') = 0$ and $\rho'(s, s) = 1$; $\rho'(s, s') = \ell(s, s')/\vartheta(s)$ otherwise. Moreover, V is set of all parameters used in the rate expression in $\mathcal{L}$.

Given the set of parameters V and a domain $\mathcal{D}(v)$ for each parameter $v \in V$, the *parameter space* $\boldsymbol{P}$ induced by the set of parameters V is defined as the Cartesian product of individual parameter domains $\boldsymbol{P} = \times_{v \in V} \mathcal{D}(v)$. A *parametrisation* $p \in \boldsymbol{P}$ is a $|V|$-tuple holding a single value for each parameter, i.e. $p = (v_{1_p}, \ldots, v_{|V|_p})$, assuming an arbitrary ordering on parameters.

For a pMC C, the set of DMTCs induced by the parameter space $\boldsymbol{P}$ is defined as $\mathcal{C} = \{C_p \mid p \in \boldsymbol{P}\}$. For each C_p, all parameters in the probability matrix are instantiated to respective components of p. A DTMC C_p is *well-defined* iff $\rho(s, s') \in [0, 1]$ for all $s, s' \in \mathcal{S}$ and $\sum_{s' \in \mathcal{S}} \rho(s, s') = 1$ for all $s \in \mathcal{S}$. For every pMC C we assume the set $\mathcal{C}$ contains only well-defined DTMCs.

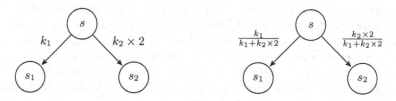

Fig. 1. *(left)* A state s of pQLTS with all its outgoing edges, labelled with appropriate multiset evaluation of rate function – state s_1 was created by applying the rule 1 and s_2 by applying the rule 2. *(right)* A pMC constructed from the pQLTS on the right such that the labels of both its outgoing edges are computed as the appropriate label from pQLTS divided by the sum of all outgoing labels, which is $k_1 + k_2 \times 2$. This, in general, ensures the sum of all labels of outgoing edges for a state is always 1.

3.3 Example (Continued)

Let $M = \mathsf{ps}^1_{\mathsf{tlm}}(\mathsf{p700}\{n\}, a\{-\}, \mathsf{achl}\{+\}), \mathsf{ps}^2_{\mathsf{tlm}}(\mathsf{p700}\{n\}, a\{n\}, \mathsf{achl}\{*\})$ be a multiset consisting of two ps agents differing in the state of their atoms a and achl, and their complex ID. We show how application of two rules from the previous example modify the multiset M.

Applying the rule 1 changes states of the first ps agent and creates a multiset $M_1 = ps^1_{tlm}(p700\{+\}, a\{-\}, achl\{n\}), ps^2_{tlm}(p700\{n\}, a\{n\}, achl\{*\})$. The label of the transition is multiset evaluation of rate function, $f(M)$, which is $k_1 \times 1$. $([ps^x_{tlm}(p700\{n\}, achl\{+\})] = 1)$.

Applying the rule 2 forms a complex from both agents and creates a multiset $M_2 = ps^1_{tlm}(p700\{n\}, a\{-\}, achl\{+\}), ps^1_{tlm}(p700\{n\}, a\{n\}, achl\{*\})$. The label of the transition is multiset evaluation of rate function, $f(M)$, which is $k_2 \times 2 \times 1$. $([ps^x_{tlm}(\emptyset)] = 2, [ps^y_{tlm}(\emptyset)] = 2)$. Please note the instantiation of variables in rate functions is independent on the instantiation of left-hand side of the rule.

Both applications give rise to a simple pQLTS, from which a pMC can be constructed (Fig. 1).

4   Model Analysis

We now provide algorithms for parameter synthesis and robustness problems for qBCSL models. Both algorithms are done semi-symbolically.

4.1   Parameter Synthesis

Given a qBCSL model $\mathcal{M} = (\mathcal{R}, \sigma_T, \sigma_A, M_0, V)$ and a PCTL formula ϕ, the *problem of parameter synthesis* is to compute a partitioning of parameter space into three disjoint subsets: TRUE – the model satisfies the property, FALSE – the model does *not* satisfy the property, and UNKNOWN – the result is not known. We solve this problem in three steps – (1) we construct pQLTS for the given qBCSL model by transitive closure of inference rule starting from initial state; (2) we derive a pMC from the pQLTS by computing parametric transition probability matrix as a normalisation of the label for all outgoing edges for every state; (3) we apply a method introduced in [16] and elaborated in [22], which is very similar to the model checking of DTMC outlined in preliminaries.

The Finite State Automaton for a pMC and a path formula is derived as in the non-parametric case. The regular expression is also evaluated recursively. Operators of union, concatenation, and star on regular expressions, are replaced by addition, multiplication, and inversion for *rational functions* respectively. Thus, by evaluating the corresponding regular expression, we obtain an algebraic expression of the probability measure of the sets of paths satisfying a path formula, as a rational function of parametrisations. We can use the result to check whether the system satisfies a formula for different values of the parameters, without having to model check the system for any given parametrisation.

This method is applicable to formulas without nested probabilistic operators only, but this does not represent a strong restriction in practice because such formulas are usually not needed to specify the properties of interest.

The computed rational function is used in parameter space exploration. An SMT solver (e.g., Z3) can be used to determine whether there exists a parametrisation inside the candidate region of the parameter space whose corresponding instantiated DTMC exceeds a given threshold on the probability.

The general approach is to maintain a set UNKNOWN of regions for which the result is still unknown. Initially, it is represented as the whole parameter space P. Then, it takes a region out of this set and tries to decide its value. The answer can be definite, i.e. either the region satisfies the formula ϕ and is added to set TRUE or it does not satisfy the formula ϕ is added to set FALSE; or the answer is uncertain and the region is split into smaller subregions. This can be recursively executed until the required precision is met (e.g., coverage of the decided area, a boundary in recursion depth).

For a PCTL formula ϕ, we additionally consider a set of atomic propositions AP' such that the expressions of type [a] ⋈ n are extended to a $\in \mathcal{P}$. These formulae allow to reason about patterns which is very natural in the rule-based setting. The semantics of the expression is:

$$s \models [a] \bowtie n \quad \text{iff} \quad \sum_{\mathcal{I} \in \Gamma} s(\mathcal{I}\langle a\rangle) \bowtie n$$

In order to use the instantiation, the signatures are required. These are available in the qBCSL model.

We have implemented our approach in the prototype tool eBCSgen, which can generate explicit pMC straightforwardly represented as a PRISM model [32]. The only issue is the presence of patterns allowed in atomic propositions of the PCTL property. Since a pattern basically compactly represents all possible instantiated agents (resp. multisets), it can be expressed as a sum of these agents. To that end, we introduce *formulas* which encode the sum in the PRISM model. Once defined, properties operating with their identifier (in our case the pattern itself) are valid.

Then, we employ Storm, which for a PRISM model, PCTL formula, and given parameter space returns the partitioning of the space to required areas (using storm − pars). In addition, the tool uses parameter lifting optimisation [40], which improves the state-elimination approach. We apply a simple visualisation to show the result of partitioning graphically.

4.2 Robustness Analysis

The *problem of global robustness* [31] of a system s is defined as

$$R_{a,P}^s = \int_P \psi(p) D_a^s(p) dp$$

where a is the property of the system under scrutiny, P is the set of all perturbations, $\psi(p)$ is the probability of the perturbation p, *local robustness* $D_a^s(p)$ is a measure stating how much the property a is preserved in perturbation p. The local robustness returns for each *parameterisation* $p \in P$ the quantitative model checking result for the respective DTMC (built for the parameterisation p) and the given property a.

We solve this problem for given qBCSL model $\mathcal{M}$ and a PCTL property ϕ (with the outermost operator $\Pi_{=?}$). We construct pMC from the model followed by algorithm from [16] to compute the rational function f. Function f can be directly used for evaluation of the local robustness.

We consider the parameter space $\boldsymbol{P}$ as the set of all perturbations. Since each parameterisation $p \in \boldsymbol{P}$ has uniform probability, computing $\psi(p)$ is straightforward – it is inversely proportional to the volume of the entire parameter space. Considering all the assumptions, the robustness for the qBCSL model $\mathcal{M}$ and a property ϕ is computed as $R^{\mathcal{M}}_{\phi,\boldsymbol{P}} = \int_{\boldsymbol{P}} \frac{1}{|\boldsymbol{P}|} f(p)dp$.

We have used Storm to obtain the rational function f and package `scipy` [29] to compute the definite integral of the function in the assumed parameter space. Moreover, since it is possible some discontinuities are present in the function f, we first analyse them using package `sympy` [36] and then integrate without these particular points.

$$\text{KaiC}^{x}_{\text{cyt}}(\text{S}\{\text{u}\}), \text{KaiC}^{x}_{\text{cyt}}(\text{S}\{\text{u}\}) \xrightarrow{\frac{\text{kcat}_1 \times [\text{KaiA2}^{y}_{\text{cyt}}(\emptyset)])}{(\text{Km}+[\text{KaiC}^{x}_{\text{cyt}}(\text{S}\{\text{u}\}),\text{KaiC}^{x}_{\text{cyt}}(\text{S}\{\text{u}\})])}} \text{KaiC}^{x}_{\text{cyt}}(\text{S}\{\text{p}\}), \text{KaiC}^{x}_{\text{cyt}}(\text{S}\{\text{p}\})$$

$$\text{KaiC}^{x}_{\text{cyt}}(\text{T}\{\text{u}\}), \text{KaiC}^{x}_{\text{cyt}}(\text{T}\{\text{u}\}) \xrightarrow{\frac{\text{kcat}_3 \times [\text{KaiB4}^{y}_{\text{cyt}}(\text{act}\{\text{a}\}),\text{KaiA2}^{y}_{\text{cyt}}(\emptyset)])}{(\text{Km}+[\text{KaiC}^{x}_{\text{cyt}}(\text{T}\{\text{u}\}),\text{KaiC}^{x}_{\text{cyt}}(\text{T}\{\text{u}\})])}} \text{KaiC}^{x}_{\text{cyt}}(\text{T}\{\text{p}\}), \text{KaiC}^{x}_{\text{cyt}}(\text{T}\{\text{p}\})$$

$$\text{KaiC}^{x}_{\text{cyt}}(\text{S}\{\text{p}\}), \text{KaiC}^{x}_{\text{cyt}}(\text{S}\{\text{p}\}) \xrightarrow{\frac{\text{kcat}_2 \times [\text{KaiA2}^{y}_{\text{cyt}}(\emptyset)])}{(\text{Km}+[\text{KaiC}^{x}_{\text{cyt}}(\text{S}\{\text{p}\}),\text{KaiC}^{x}_{\text{cyt}}(\text{S}\{\text{p}\})])}} \text{KaiC}^{x}_{\text{cyt}}(\text{S}\{\text{u}\}), \text{KaiC}^{x}_{\text{cyt}}(\text{S}\{\text{u}\})$$

$$\text{KaiC}^{x}_{\text{cyt}}(\text{T}\{\text{p}\}), \text{KaiC}^{x}_{\text{cyt}}(\text{T}\{\text{p}\}) \xrightarrow{\frac{\text{kcat}_4 \times [\text{KaiB4}^{y}_{\text{cyt}}(\text{act}\{\text{a}\}),\text{KaiA2}^{y}_{\text{cyt}}(\emptyset)])}{(\text{Km}+[\text{KaiC}^{x}_{\text{cyt}}(\text{T}\{\text{p}\}),\text{KaiC}^{x}_{\text{cyt}}(\text{T}\{\text{p}\})])}} \text{KaiC}^{x}_{\text{cyt}}(\text{T}\{\text{u}\}), \text{KaiC}^{x}_{\text{cyt}}(\text{T}\{\text{u}\})$$

$$\text{KaiB4}^{x}_{\text{cyt}}(\text{act}\{\text{i}\}) \xrightarrow{\frac{\text{kcat}_{\text{b2}} \times [\text{KaiB4}^{x}_{\text{cyt}}(\text{act}\{\text{i}\})]}{\text{Km}_{\text{b2}}+[\text{KaiB4}^{x}_{\text{cyt}}(\text{act}\{\text{i}\})]}} \text{KaiB4}^{x}_{\text{cyt}}(\text{act}\{\text{a}\})$$

$$\text{KaiB4}^{x}_{\text{cyt}}(\text{act}\{\text{a}\}) \xrightarrow{\frac{\text{kcat}_{\text{b1}} \times [\text{KaiB4}^{x}_{\text{cyt}}(\text{act}\{\text{a}\})]}{\text{Km}_{\text{b1}}+[\text{KaiB4}^{x}_{\text{cyt}}(\text{act}\{\text{a}\})]}} \text{KaiB4}^{x}_{\text{cyt}}(\text{act}\{\text{i}\})$$

$$\text{KaiC}^{x}_{\text{cyt}}(\emptyset), \text{KaiC}^{y}_{\text{cyt}}(\emptyset) \xrightarrow{\text{k}_{\text{dimer}} \times [\text{KaiC}^{x}_{\text{cyt}}(\emptyset)] \times ([\text{KaiC}^{y}_{\text{cyt}}(\emptyset)]-1)} \text{KaiC}^{x}_{\text{cyt}}(\emptyset), \text{KaiC}^{x}_{\text{cyt}}(\emptyset)$$

$$\text{KaiC}^{x}_{\text{cyt}}(\emptyset), \text{KaiC}^{x}_{\text{cyt}}(\emptyset) \xrightarrow{\text{k}_{\text{dimer}} \times [\text{KaiC}^{x}_{\text{cyt}}(\emptyset),\text{KaiC}^{x}_{\text{cyt}}(\emptyset)]} \text{KaiC}^{x}_{\text{cyt}}(\emptyset), \text{KaiC}^{y}_{\text{cyt}}(\emptyset)$$

Fig. 2. Rules of simplified Miyoshi et al. model. The first four rules are responsible for the change of phosphorylation level of KaiC dimers. The rate functions of these rules represent enzymatic laws and are dependent on current numbers of KaiA dimers and KaiB tetramers. The next two rules change the activity level of KaiB4 complex and the last two rules form and disassembly the KaiC dimer. The particular values of known constants are $\text{Km} = 0.602$, $\text{Km}_{\text{b1}} = 2.423$, $\text{kcat}_{\text{b1}} = 0.602$, $\text{k}_{\text{dimer}} = 1.77$, $\text{Km}_{\text{b2}} = 66.75$, and $\text{kcat}_{\text{b2}} = 0.346$. The exact meaning of individual constants and parameters is described in [37]

5 Case Study

In this section, we demonstrate our contribution on a case study[2] from the biological domain. Miyoshi et al. [37] ODE model describes circadian rhythms in cyanobacteria. We have adopted this model to our rule-based formalism with several simplifications in order to avoid combinatorial explosion.

The core of the circadian rhythms model is formed by three main proteins – KaiA, KaiB, and KaiC. The protein KaiC has two phosphorylation sites (S – serine and T – threonine), both of them can be either phosphorylated or unphosphorylated. Two KaiC proteins can form a homo-dimer.

1. **Phosphorylation experiment**
   (a) *initial state*:
   $$\mathsf{KaiC}^1_{\mathsf{cyt}}(\mathsf{S}\{\mathsf{u}\},\mathsf{T}\{\mathsf{u}\}), \mathsf{KaiC}^2_{\mathsf{cyt}}(\mathsf{S}\{\mathsf{u}\},\mathsf{T}\{\mathsf{u}\}), \mathsf{KaiB4}^3_{\mathsf{cyt}}(\mathsf{act}\{\mathsf{a}\}), \mathsf{KaiA2}^4_{\mathsf{cyt}}(\emptyset)$$
   (b) *property of interest*:
   $$\Pi_{\geq 0.99}(\mathsf{True}\ \mathbf{U}\ [\mathsf{KaiC}^x_{\mathsf{cyt}}(\mathsf{S}\{\mathsf{p}\},\mathsf{T}\{\mathsf{p}\}), \mathsf{KaiC}^x_{\mathsf{cyt}}(\mathsf{S}\{\mathsf{p}\},\mathsf{T}\{\mathsf{p}\})] > 0)$$
   (c) *parameters*:

$\mathsf{kcat}_1 \in [0,1]$	$\mathsf{kcat}_2 = 0.539$	$\mathsf{k}_{\mathsf{enz}} = 8.756 \times 10^{-4}$
$\mathsf{kcat}_3 \in [0,2]$	$\mathsf{kcat}_4 = 0.89$	

   (d) *additional rule* for construction of KaiA dimer and KaiB4 tetramer complex:
   $$\mathsf{KaiB4}^x_{\mathsf{cyt}}(\emptyset), \mathsf{KaiA2}^y_{\mathsf{cyt}}(\emptyset) \xrightarrow{\ \mathsf{k}_{\mathsf{enz}} \times [\mathsf{KaiB4}^x_{\mathsf{cyt}}(\emptyset)] \times [\mathsf{KaiA2}^y_{\mathsf{cyt}}(\emptyset)]\ } \mathsf{KaiB4}^x_{\mathsf{cyt}}(\emptyset), \mathsf{KaiA2}^x_{\mathsf{cyt}}(\emptyset)$$

2. **Dephosphorylation experiment**
   (a) *initial state*:
   $$\mathsf{KaiC}^1_{\mathsf{cyt}}(\mathsf{S}\{\mathsf{p}\},\mathsf{T}\{\mathsf{p}\}), \mathsf{KaiC}^2_{\mathsf{cyt}}(\mathsf{S}\{\mathsf{p}\},\mathsf{T}\{\mathsf{p}\}), \mathsf{KaiB4}^3_{\mathsf{cyt}}(\mathsf{act}\{\mathsf{a}\}), \mathsf{KaiA2}^3_{\mathsf{cyt}}(\emptyset)$$
   (b) *property of interest*:
   $$\Pi_{\geq 0.99}(\mathsf{True}\ \mathbf{U}\ [\mathsf{KaiC}^x_{\mathsf{cyt}}(\mathsf{S}\{\mathsf{u}\},\mathsf{T}\{\mathsf{u}\}), \mathsf{KaiC}^x_{\mathsf{cyt}}(\mathsf{S}\{\mathsf{u}\},\mathsf{T}\{\mathsf{u}\})] > 0)$$
   (c) *parameters*:

$\mathsf{kcat}_1 = 0.539$	$\mathsf{kcat}_2 \in [0,1]$	$\mathsf{k}_{\mathsf{enz}} = 8.756 \times 10^{-4}$
$\mathsf{kcat}_3 = 1.079$	$\mathsf{kcat}_4 \in [0,2]$	

   (d) *additional rule* for disassembly of KaiA dimer and KaiB4 tetramer complex:
   $$\mathsf{KaiB4}^x_{\mathsf{cyt}}(\emptyset), \mathsf{KaiA2}^x_{\mathsf{cyt}}(\emptyset) \xrightarrow{\ \mathsf{k}_{\mathsf{enz}} \times [\mathsf{KaiB4}^x_{\mathsf{cyt}}(\emptyset), \mathsf{KaiA2}^x_{\mathsf{cyt}}(\emptyset)]\ } \mathsf{KaiB4}^x_{\mathsf{cyt}}(\emptyset), \mathsf{KaiA2}^y_{\mathsf{cyt}}(\emptyset)$$

Fig. 3. Two setups of the Miyoshi model in qBCSL. The goal of the experiment (1) is to find parametrisation such that the model reaches the fully phosphorylated level of KaiC dimer. The model is extended by a rule for the construction of complex possibly disabling the phosphorylation. The experiment (2) is focused on dephosphorylation of KaiC dimer enabled by an additional rule for the enzymatic complex disassembly.

Protein KaiA can also form a homo-dimer and act as a kinase for phosphorylation of KaiC dimers. Since the KaiA dimer cannot undergo any modification, we model it as a single agent. Protein KaiB can form a homo-tetramer, which

---

[2] An additional case study targeting a tumour growth is available in Appendix A.

can be either active or inactive as a whole. For this reason and, again, for the simplicity, we model it as a single agent.

The KaiA dimer has a positive enzymatic effect on the phosphorylation of KaiC dimers. On the other hand, active KaiB tetramer then serves as an inhibitor of KaiC dimer phosphorylation, i.e. it enhances its dephosphorylation. This is done such that it forms a complex with KaiA dimer and inhibits its phosphorylation efforts.

The rules of the model are available in Fig. 2. The mechanism of phosphorylation and activation causes the model to have an oscillatory behaviour. For our simplified case, we investigate whether the probability of reaching the phosphorylated KaiC dimer followed by reaching the unphosphorylated dimer is close to one.

We assume two different experiments both having different initial conditions, one additional rule for manipulation of KaiA and KaiB interaction, different unknown parameters, and finally a different property of interest. Both experiments are specified in Fig. 3. The first experiment expresses conditions with unphosphorylated KaiC dimer and property of reaching the phosphorylated KaiC dimer. For the second experiment, it is the other way around. The probability for both properties should be close to one since the oscillation should always be present.

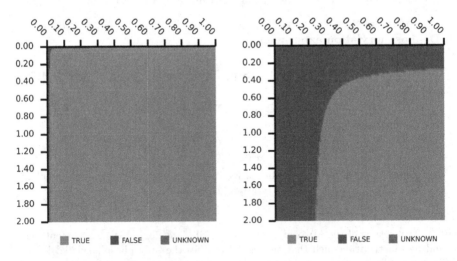

Fig. 4. Visualisation of results of parameter synthesis for the Miyoshi model. The *left* picture depicts the results for the phosphorylation experiment (Fig. 3, 1). The horizontal axis represents values of the parameter $kcat_1 \in [0, 1]$ and the vertical axis represents values of the parameter $kcat_3 \in [0, 2]$. The *right* picture depicts the results for the dephosphorylation experiment (Fig. 3, 2). The horizontal axis represents values of the parameter $kcat_2 \in [0, 1]$ and the vertical axis represents values of the parameter $kcat_4 \in [0, 2]$.

In Fig. 4, there is a visualisation of parameter synthesis for both cases. The results of the first experiment show that the property is almost always satisfied except for some marginal cases when the parameter values are close to zero. This fact is in agreement with the global robustness degree, which is approximately 0.995. In the second experiment, the property was satisfied in a smaller fraction of parameter space, caused by different initial conditions and the additional rule. However, this difference is very insignificant, which confirms the robustness degree with a value of approximately 0.98. These results confirm that the behaviour of the model is very robust to perturbation of parameters directly responsible for phosphorylation activity, thus showing the oscillatory behaviour is very persistent.

6   Conclusions

First, we have defined a quantitative version of the Biochemical Space Language (qBCSL). The language allows us to specify parametrised quantitative aspects (rates) of the dynamics of individual rules, resulting in probabilistic behaviour of models considered in discrete time. Second, we have encoded the semantics of qBCSL models by means of parametric Markov Chains. That enables applications of existing symbolic parameter synthesis methods. Finally, we have shown how to (exactly) compute robustness of a given property with respect to a given parameter perturbation. Bridging the efficient parameter synthesis methods with rule-based modelling is an important step towards application of formal methods in biological domain [7,10]. To that end, we have demonstrated our approach on a case study from the biological domain.

The main challenge to be faced in future is the scalability. Rule-based models can expand in large state spaces making thus the construction of the pQLTS (and pMC) infeasible. In particular, we want to find ways allowing to avoid enumeration of the pMC, e.g., by employing on-the-fly and static analysis approaches.

A   Tumour Growth

Tumour growth is based on *mitosis* (i.e. cell division). The cell cycle is the process between two mitoses and it consists of four phases: the resting phase G_1, the DNA replication phase S, the resting phase G_2, and the mitosis phase M in which the cells segregate the duplicated sets of chromosomes between daughter cells. The three phases G_1, S, and G_2 constitute the pre-mitotic phase, also called *interphase*.

We have adopted the model of tumour growth [44] to our language. It considers two populations of tumour cells: those in interphase and those in mitosis. We represent the tumour cell as an agent T. The current phase is expressed with an atom phase in its composition, which can have two different states – i for interphase and m for mitosis. For simplicity, we omit the compartment from the rules since it does not change and plays no important role in this model.

$$T^x(\text{phase}\{i\}) \xrightarrow{a_1 \times [T^x(\text{phase}\{i\})]} T^x(\text{phase}\{m\})$$

$$T^x(\text{phase}\{m\}) \xrightarrow{a_2 \times [T^x(\text{phase}\{m\})]} T^y(\text{phase}\{i\}), T^z(\text{phase}\{i\})$$

$$T^x(\text{phase}\{i\}) \xrightarrow{d_1 \times [T^x(\text{phase}\{i\})]} \emptyset$$

$$T^x(\text{phase}\{m\}) \xrightarrow{d_2 \times [T^x(\text{phase}\{m\})]} \emptyset$$

Fig. 5. Rules of the tumour growth model. The first rule describes the change of the phase of a cell from interphase to mitosis. The second rule describes the duplication of the cell to two daughter cells. Note that both start in interphase. The last two rules describe the death of cells in both possible states.

The rules of the model are available in Fig. 5. Note that this model is a demonstration where all rules are *reaction-based*, i.e. they do not describe an abstract rule, only modification of concrete agents.

Given rate functions of rules are parametrised. Parameters a_1 and a_2 are present in rules responsible for change of phase and cell division, while parameters d_1 and d_2 are in the rules where the cell *disappears* or *dies*. The values $a_2 = 0.5$ and $d_1 = 0.3$ are constant the other two parameters are given by admissible ranges: $a_1 \in [0;3]$ and for $d_2 \in [0.001;0.5]$.

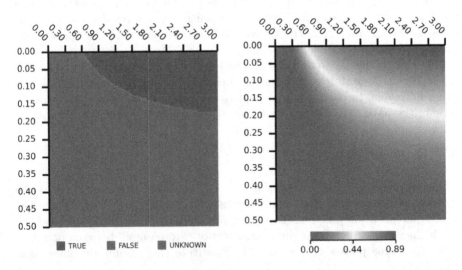

Fig. 6. Visualisation of results of parameter synthesis (*left*) and quantitative model checking using sampling (*right*) for property ϕ for tumour growth model. The horizontal axis represents values of the parameter $a_1 \in [0,3]$ and the vertical axis represents values of the parameter $d_2 \in [0.001, 0.5]$. The probability threshold 0.5 from the property ϕ is visible in both sampling (approximately the yellow line) and parameter synthesis (the grey line). It shows that the parameter synthesis method gives us a very precise result and is in agreement with quantitative model checking. (Color figure online)

For the *initial state*, we assume a single agent $T^1(\text{phase}\{i\})$. Please note that the model gives rise to infinite pMC since the second rule can *generate* additional agents. To obtain a finite abstract probabilistic model, we have heuristically limited the number of states of the model. Particularly, we generate all the states having the number of individuals of both species less or equal to 5 and we introduce a special abstract state which represents all the other states, which limits the size of possible state space to 6^2. This approximation is incorrect only in cases when one wants to reach a state which is represented by the special state.

We are interested in property whether the population of tumour cells will reach almost its maximum with the probability higher than 0.5, meaning that the growth is not random but has rather tendency to grow without limitations. This property can be expressed as $\phi = \Pi_{\geq 0.5}(\text{True U } T^j(\emptyset) > 8)$. In Fig. 6, there is a visualisation of parameter synthesis. The results show that the higher values of the parameter a_1 (cell division) and the lower values of the parameter d_2 increase the probability of property satisfaction. This result is quite expected, because both parameters directly influence cell division (a_1) and degradation (d_2) of cells. We have also computed the global robustness degree of the property, which is approximately 0.24. It can be interpreted as 24% of parameter space satisfies the property $\text{True U } T^j(\emptyset) > 8$.

References

1. Backenköhler, M., Bortolussi, L., Wolf, V.: Moment-based parameter estimation for stochastic reaction networks in equilibrium. TCBB **15**(4), 1180–1192 (2018)
2. Baier, C., Haverkort, B., Hermanns, H., Katoen, J.P.: Model-checking algorithms for continuous-time Markov chains. IEEE Trans. Softw. Eng. **29**(6), 524–541 (2003)
3. Barbuti, R., Caravagna, G., Maggiolo-Schettini, A., Milazzo, P.: An intermediate language for the stochastic simulation of biological systems. TCS **410**(33–34), 3085–3109 (2009)
4. Barbuti, R., Levi, F., Milazzo, P., Scatena, G.: Probabilistic model checking of biological systems with uncertain kinetic rates. TCS **419**, 2–16 (2012)
5. Bartocci, E., Bortolussi, L., Nenzi, L., Sanguinetti, G.: On the robustness of temporal properties for stochastic models. arXiv preprint arXiv:1309.0866 (2013)
6. Bock, C., Bortolussi, L., Krüger, T., Mikeev, L., Wolf, V.: Model-based whole-genome analysis of DNA methylation fidelity. In: Abate, A., Šafránek, D. (eds.) HSB 2015. LNCS, vol. 9271, pp. 141–155. Springer, Cham (2015). https://doi.org/10.1007/978-3-319-26916-0_8
7. Bonzanni, N., Feenstra, K.A., Fokkink, W., Krepska, E.: What can formal methods bring to systems biology? In: Cavalcanti, A., Dams, D.R. (eds.) FM 2009. LNCS, vol. 5850, pp. 16–22. Springer, Heidelberg (2009). https://doi.org/10.1007/978-3-642-05089-3_2
8. Bortolussi, L., Milios, D., Sanguinetti, G.: Smoothed model checking for uncertain continuous-time Markov chains. Inform. Comput. **247**, 235–253 (2016)
9. Bortolussi, L., Silvetti, S.: Bayesian statistical parameter synthesis for linear temporal properties of stochastic models. In: Beyer, D., Huisman, M. (eds.) TACAS 2018. LNCS, vol. 10806, pp. 396–413. Springer, Cham (2018). https://doi.org/10.1007/978-3-319-89963-3_23

10. Brim, L., Češka, M., Šafránek, D.: Model checking of biological systems. In: Bernardo, M., de Vink, E., Di Pierro, A., Wiklicky, H. (eds.) SFM 2013. LNCS, vol. 7938, pp. 63–112. Springer, Heidelberg (2013). https://doi.org/10.1007/978-3-642-38874-3_3

11. Calzone, L., Fages, F., Soliman, S.: BIOCHAM: an environment for modeling biological systems and formalizing experimental knowledge. Bioinformatics **22**(14), 1805–1807 (2006)

12. Česka, M., Šafránek, D., Dražan, S., Brim, L.: Robustness analysis of stochastic biochemical systems. PLoS ONE **9**(4), e94553 (2014)

13. Ciocchetta, F., Hillston, J.: Bio-PEPA: an extension of the process algebra PEPA for biochemical networks. ENTCS **194**(3), 103–117 (2008)

14. Clarke, E.M., Emerson, E.A., Sistla, A.P.: Automatic verification of finite-state concurrent systems using temporal logic specifications. ACM Trans. Program. Lang. Syst. (TOPLAS) **8**(2), 244–263 (1986)

15. Danos, V., Laneve, C.: Formal molecular biology. Theor. Comput. Sci. **325**(1), 69–110 (2004)

16. Daws, C.: Symbolic and parametric model checking of discrete-time Markov chains. In: Liu, Z., Araki, K. (eds.) ICTAC 2004. LNCS, vol. 3407, pp. 280–294. Springer, Heidelberg (2005). https://doi.org/10.1007/978-3-540-31862-0_21

17. Dehnert, C., et al.: PROPhESY: A PRObabilistic ParamEter SYnthesis tool. In: Kroening, D., Păsăreanu, C.S. (eds.) CAV 2015. LNCS, vol. 9206, pp. 214–231. Springer, Cham (2015). https://doi.org/10.1007/978-3-319-21690-4_13

18. Dehnert, C., Junges, S., Katoen, J.-P., Volk, M.: A storm is coming: a modern probabilistic model checker. In: Majumdar, R., Kunčak, V. (eds.) CAV 2017. LNCS, vol. 10427, pp. 592–600. Springer, Cham (2017). https://doi.org/10.1007/978-3-319-63390-9_31

19. Faeder, J.R., Blinov, M.L., Hlavacek, W.S., et al.: Rule-based modeling of biochemical systems with BioNetGen. Methods Mol. Biol. **500**, 113–167 (2009)

20. Fisher, J., Henzinger, T.A.: Executable cell biology. Nat. Biotechnol. **25**(11), 1239 (2007)

21. Gillespie, D.T.: Exact stochastic simulation of coupled chemical reactions. J. Phys. Chem. **81**(25), 2340–2361 (1977)

22. Hahn, E.M., Hermanns, H., Zhang, L.: Probabilistic reachability for parametric Markov models. STTT **13**(1), 3–19 (2011)

23. Hasson, H., Jonsson, B.: A logic for reasoning about time and probability. FAOC **6**, 512–535 (1994)

24. Honorato-Zimmer, R., Millar, A.J., Plotkin, G.D., Zardilis, A.: Chromar, a rule-based language of parameterised objects. TCS **335**, 49–66 (2017)

25. Hopcroft, J.E.: Introduction to Automata Theory, Languages, and Computation. Pearson Education India (2008)

26. Hutschenreiter, L., Baier, C., Klein, J.: Parametric Markov chains: PCTL complexity and fraction-free Gaussian elimination. arXiv preprint arXiv:1709.02093 (2017)

27. Jansen, N., et al.: Accelerating parametric probabilistic verification. In: Norman, G., Sanders, W. (eds.) QEST 2014. LNCS, vol. 8657, pp. 404–420. Springer, Cham (2014). https://doi.org/10.1007/978-3-319-10696-0_31

28. Jha, S.K., Clarke, E.M., Langmead, C.J., Legay, A., Platzer, A., Zuliani, P.: A Bayesian approach to model checking biological systems. In: Degano, P., Gorrieri, R. (eds.) CMSB 2009. LNCS, vol. 5688, pp. 218–234. Springer, Heidelberg (2009). https://doi.org/10.1007/978-3-642-03845-7_15

29. Jones, E., Oliphant, T., Peterson, P., et al.: SciPy: open source scientific tools for Python (2001). http://www.scipy.org/
30. Khalid, A., Jha, S.K.: Calibration of rule-based stochastic biochemical models using statistical model checking. In: 2018 IEEE BIBM, pp. 179–184 (2018)
31. Kitano, H.: Towards a theory of biological robustness. Mol. Syst. Biol. **3**(1), 137 (2007)
32. Kwiatkowska, M., Norman, G., Parker, D.: Quantitative analysis with the probabilistic model checker PRISM. ENTCS **153**(2), 5–31 (2006)
33. Lanotte, R., Maggiolo-Schettini, A., Troina, A.: Parametric probabilistic transition systems for system design and analysis. FAOC **19**(1), 93–109 (2007)
34. Liu, B., Faeder, J.R.: Parameter estimation of rule-based models using statistical model checking. In: 2016 IEEE BIBM, pp. 1453–1459. IEEE (2016)
35. Lück, A., Wolf, V.: Generalized method of moments for estimating parameters of stochastic reaction networks. BMC Syst. Biol. **10**(1), 98 (2016)
36. Meurer, A., et al.: SymPy: symbolic computing in Python. PeerJ Comput. Sci. **3**, e103 (2017)
37. Miyoshi, F., Nakayama, Y., Kaizu, K., Iwasaki, H., Tomita, M.: A mathematical model for the Kai-protein-based chemical oscillator and clock gene expression rhythms in cyanobacteria. J. Biol. Rhythms **22**(1), 69–80 (2007)
38. Nedbal, L., Červený, J., Schmidt, H.: Scaling and integration of kinetic models of photosynthesis: towards comprehensive e-photosynthesis. In: Laisk, A., Nedbal, L., Govindjee (eds.) Photosynthesis in Silico. AIPH, pp. 17–29. Springer, Dordrecht (2009). https://doi.org/10.1007/978-1-4020-9237-4_2
39. Pedersen, M., Phillips, A., Plotkin, G.D.: A high-level language for rule-based modelling. PLoS ONE **10**, 1–26 (2015)
40. Quatmann, T., Dehnert, C., Jansen, N., Junges, S., Katoen, J.-P.: Parameter synthesis for markov models: faster than ever. In: Artho, C., Legay, A., Peled, D. (eds.) ATVA 2016. LNCS, vol. 9938, pp. 50–67. Springer, Cham (2016). https://doi.org/10.1007/978-3-319-46520-3_4
41. Romers, J.C., Krantz, M.: rxncon 2.0: a language for executable molecular systems biology. bioRxiv (2017)
42. Troják, M., Šafránek, D., Brim, L.: Executable biochemical space for specification and analysis of biochemical systems. In: SASB (2018, to appear)
43. Troják, M., Šafránek, D., Hrabec, J., Šalagovič, J., Romanovská, F., Červený, J.: E-Cyanobacterium.org: a web-based platform for systems biology of cyanobacteria. In: Bartocci, E., Lio, P., Paoletti, N. (eds.) CMSB 2016. LNCS, vol. 9859, pp. 316–322. Springer, Cham (2016). https://doi.org/10.1007/978-3-319-45177-0_20
44. Villasana, M., Radunskaya, A.: A delay differential equation model for tumor growth. J. Math. Biol. **47**(3), 270–294 (2003)

Formal Methods for DNNs

PaRoT: A Practical Framework for Robust Deep Neural Network Training

Edward W. Ayers[1], Francisco Eiras[2], Majd Hawasly[2], and Iain Whiteside[2(✉)]

[1] DPMMS, Cambridge University, Cambridge, UK
e.w.ayers@maths.cam.ac.uk
[2] FiveAI, 20 Cambridge Place, Cambridge, UK
{francisco.eiras,majd.hawasly,iain.whiteside}@five.ai

Abstract. Deep Neural Networks (DNNs) are finding important applications in safety-critical systems such as Autonomous Vehicles (AVs), where perceiving the environment correctly and robustly is necessary for safe operation. Raising unique challenges for assurance due to their black-box nature, DNNs pose a fundamental problem for regulatory acceptance of these types of systems. Robust training—training to minimize excessive sensitivity to small changes in input—has emerged as one promising technique to address this challenge. However, existing robust training tools are inconvenient to use or apply to existing codebases and models: they typically only support a small subset of model elements and require users to extensively rewrite the training code. In this paper we introduce a novel framework, *PaRoT*, developed on the popular TensorFlow platform, that greatly reduces the barrier to entry. Our framework enables robust training to be performed on existing DNNs without rewrites to the model. We demonstrate that our framework's performance is comparable to prior art, and exemplify its ease of use on off-the-shelf, trained models and its testing capabilities on a real-world industrial application: a traffic light detection network.

1 Introduction

Deep Neural Networks (DNNs) are finding important applications in safety-critical systems, such as Autonomous Vehicles (AVs), where perceiving a complex environment correctly and robustly is necessary for safe operation [4,11,17]. The challenge of assuring these so-called *AI-enabled systems* is well-known [22] and has attracted the attention of researchers and research bodies, e.g., DARPA [9]. Existing standards and techniques—such as the ubiquitous 'V' model—lean heavily on the existence of a clear specification to verify against [32]. Unfortunately, the very nature of deep learning—where the specification is implicit in the training data—poses a fundamental problem for regulatory acceptance of these systems in a safety-critical domain.

One of the most troubling features of DNNs is their 'intriguing' susceptibility to *adversarial examples*: imperceptible perturbations in the input space that

© Springer Nature Switzerland AG 2020
R. Lee et al. (Eds.): NFM 2020, LNCS 12229, pp. 63–84, 2020.
https://doi.org/10.1007/978-3-030-55754-6_4

(a)   (b)   (c)

(d)

Fig. 1. *Traffic Light Detection Network*: (a) an image from the test set in which the traffic light is identified correctly; (b) an adversarial example: a subtly modified version of the original image, identified using *PaRoT*; (c) norm of the difference between the original image and the adversarial images; (d) the inference result on the adversarial example, with a confidence heatmap on the left and bounding boxes of the identified traffic lights on the right.

cause a large change in the output space. For example, causing an object detection network to misclassify an image [35]. Figure 1 shows an adversarial example on a traffic light detector.

The formal verification community has responded to this provocation with gusto [3,5,13,16,19,20]. Exacerbating the verification challenge is the indirect nature of any 'fixes' that can be applied to failure of post-hoc formal verification for a DNN: typically an augmentation to the training set. Unlike with traditional software, fixes to DNNs can feel very much like playing a game of whack-a-mole.

The emerging *robust training* paradigm, which integrates the verification process directly into the training scheme, is, in our view, the most promising approach towards formally verified neural networks. The goal of robust training is to minimize a so-called worst-case adversarial loss. Formally, let $N_\theta : \mathbb{R}^p \to \mathbb{R}^q$ be a neural network with p input features and q outputs, parameterized with weights θ. Let $\mathcal{B}_\epsilon(x)$ be an ℓ_∞-ball of radius ϵ around an input point $x \in \mathbb{R}^p$. For a given loss function $\mathcal{L}$, we can define the *worst-case adversarial loss* $\mathcal{L}_{N_\theta}$ at a point x as:

$$\mathcal{L}_{N_\theta}(x, y) := \max_{\tilde{x} \in \mathcal{B}_\epsilon(x)} \mathcal{L}(N_\theta(\tilde{x}), y) \tag{1}$$

In general, one may replace the ball $\mathcal{B}_\epsilon(x)$ with some parameterized set $\pi_\epsilon(x)$. For a set of labelled training data $\{(x_i, y_i)\}_{i=1}^n$, robust training can be formulated as a saddle-point problem:

$$\min_{\theta} \max_{i} \mathcal{L}_{N_\theta}(x_i, y_i) \tag{2}$$

Finding the worst-case adversarial loss for a given example is computationally expensive in general. In practice, most approaches approximate the worst-case adversarial loss in one way or another [27,41,42]. In recent years, robust training has progressed from single layer, dense networks to moderate—though not yet state-of-the-art—sized Convolutional Neural Networks (CNNs). This has brought these techniques within the realm of various DNNs used within the reference AV stack being built by Five AI. In our bid to understand the practicalities of robust training, we found that existing tools are inconvenient to use or apply to existing models: they typically only support a small subset of model elements and require users to re-specify the models in a specialized language, which can mean extensive rewrites to the training code.

To tackle these problems, we introduce a framework in this paper, called *Practical Robust Training (PaRoT)*[1], developed on the popular TensorFlow platform [1]. Our framework allows robust training—using differentiable abstract interpretation [27]—to be performed on arbitrary DNNs without any rewrites of the model. In *PaRoT*, one can start a robust model training for a popular convolutional neural network with a minimal amount of code, as we demonstrate in Listing 1.2. We have, for example, used *PaRoT* to robustly train the traffic light detection network seen in Fig. 1.

Contributions. The main contribution of this paper is a practical framework, *PaRoT*, built in the Tensorflow platform [1]. In particular,

– Our tool can automatically apply abstract interpretation on an existing model definition. Thus, it can be used to verify robustness on existing DNNs without having to change the model code, allowing for seamless adoption with existing codebases.
– Our framework implements a broad set of robustness properties that go beyond the usual ϵ-ball, and provides a clean interface for specifying custom properties.
– We improve upon the abstract interpretation techniques used by Mirman *et al.* [27]. In particular, we refine several abstract transformers for activation functions.

Structure of Paper. In Sect. 2 we introduce the requisite background in robust training with abstract interpretation. In Sect. 3 we describe the architecture and functionality of the *PaRoT* framework and evaluate its performance in Sect. 4. In Sect. 5 we place our work more broadly in the field of formal verification of DNNs. Finally, in Sect. 6, we conclude and present future directions for this framework and paradigm.

---

[1] The framework is available at https://github.com/fiveai/parot

2   Background

We build on the robust training approach of DiffAI, introduced by Mirman *et al.* [27], where the inner maximization of Eq. 2 is approximated using abstract interpretation. In this section, we sketch the mathematical prerequisites to our framework.

2.1   Abstract Interpretation

Abstract interpretation is a general theory for approximating infinite sets of behaviours with a finite representation [7,8]. In the present study, this corresponds to convex approximations of a non-convex adversarial polytope.

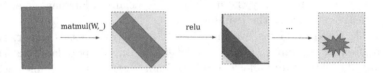

Fig. 2. An illustration of abstract domains. The dotted grey box corresponds to a domain object, and the blue shape is the true set that the domain object seeks to approximate. (Color figure online)

The two basic constructs in abstract interpretation are the *abstract domain* and the *abstract transformer*. Intuitively, an abstract domain gives a finite (approximate) representation of the (potentially infinite) concrete space, while an abstract transformer provides an over-approximation of the behaviour of a function. Formally, an abstract domain is a set $\mathcal{D}$ (the *domain*) and a pair of maps $\alpha : \mathcal{P}(\mathbb{R}^p) \to \mathcal{D}$ and $\gamma : \mathcal{D} \to \mathcal{P}(\mathbb{R}^p)$, called the *abstraction* and *concretization* maps, respectively. $\mathcal{P}(X)$ is the powerset of X. The abstraction function is defined such that $U \subseteq \gamma(\alpha(U))$ for all $U \subseteq \mathbb{R}^p$.

Additionally, an abstract domain is equipped with a mapping from a fixed set of primitive functions $\mathcal{F}$ to *abstract transformers* in $\mathcal{D}$ such that each $f : \mathbb{R}^p \to \mathbb{R}^q$ in $\mathcal{F}$ is mapped to a function $\mathcal{D}(f) : \mathcal{D} \to \mathcal{D}'$. For each element in the concrete space, z, transformers must obey the following *soundness relation*:

$$f[\gamma(z)] \subseteq \gamma(\mathcal{D}(f)(z)) \tag{3}$$

This ensures that transformers produce new abstract elements whose concretization overapproximates the image of the function. Since transformers compose, we may transform any composite function $f = f_1 \circ f_2 \circ \cdots \circ f_n : \mathbb{R}^p \to \mathbb{R}^q$ where $f_i \in \mathcal{F}$. Figure 2 illustrates graphically the abstract domains and transformers for a single layer of a DNN. We can construct a composite transformer $\mathcal{D}(N)$ that represents that network, and write the sound approximation for an ϵ-ball around a point x as:

$$\gamma(\mathcal{D}(N)[\alpha(\mathcal{B}_\epsilon(x))]). \tag{4}$$

2.2 Abstract Domains for DNNs

We consider three abstract domain types: BOX, ZONOTOPE and HYBRIDZONO-
TOPE:

- BOX, represented by $i = \langle \mathbf{c}, \mathbf{b} \rangle$. A BOX domain is a p-dimensional axis-aligned
  box, parameterized by its center $\mathbf{c} \in \mathbb{R}^p$ and a positive vector $\mathbf{b} \in \mathbb{R}^p_{>0}$
  containing the half-widths of the box. Figure 2 illustrates the concept of the
  BOX domain.
- ZONOTOPE, represented by $z = \langle \mathbf{c}, \mathbf{E} \rangle$. For dimension p, a ZONOTOPE is
  parameterized by a center point $\mathbf{c} \in \mathbb{R}^p$ as well as a matrix $\mathbf{E} \in \mathbb{R}^{p \times e}$ for
  some fixed dimension e. The set $z \subseteq \mathbb{R}^p$ is the $\mathbf{E}$ image of an e-dimensional
  hypercube, centerd at $\mathbf{c}$. The concretization is given by:

$$\gamma(z) := \{ \mathbf{c} + \mathbf{E}\,\mathbf{v} \; : \; |\mathbf{v}_i| \le 1, \; i \in \{1, \ldots, e\} \} \tag{5}$$

The key feature of a ZONOTOPE domain is that transformers exist for affine
functions—such as the matrix multiplications associated with transition functions of DNNs—that do not increase the approximation error.

- HYBRIDZONOTOPE, represented by $h = \langle \mathbf{c}, \mathbf{b}, \mathbf{E} \rangle$. One problem with the
  ZONOTOPE domain is that computation can be expensive compared to a BOX
  domain. The HYBRIDZONOTOPE solves this problem with the inclusion of an
  extra positive vector $\mathbf{b} \in \mathbb{R}^p_{>0}$, with a concretization:

$$\gamma(h) := \{ \mathbf{c} + \mathbf{E}\,\mathbf{v} + \mathrm{diag}(\mathbf{b})\,\mathbf{w} \mid |\mathbf{v}_i| \le 1, \; |\mathbf{w}_j| \le 1,$$
$$i, \in \{1, \ldots, e\}, \; j \in \{1, \ldots, p\} \}. \tag{6}$$

Note that these definitions mean that BOX and ZONOTOPE are both subsets
of HYBRIDZONOTOPE. In the HYBRIDZONOTOPE domain, it is possible to con-
vert $\mathbf{b}$ values to $\mathbf{E}$ values and vice-versa through *correlation* and *decorrelation*,
as noted in [28].

2.3 Hybrid Zonotope Transformers for DNNs

It is straightforward to show that exact transformers can be constructed for
matrix multiplication [27]. In contrast, accurate modeling of piecewise linear activation functions, such as $\mathrm{relu}(x) := \max(x, 0)$, necessarily introduce an approximation. Here we generalize the work in [34] to find optimal hybrid zonotopes
for a given activation function. Since activations are one-dimensional (1D) and
act on each dimension separately, we may consider just the problem in 1D. For
a given function $f : \mathbb{R} \to \mathbb{R}$ and input bounds $\underline{x}$, $\overline{x}$, the challenge is to find a
parallelogram containing the graph of f restricted to $[\underline{x}, \overline{x}]$ that has minimal
area, as shown in Fig. 3 below.

In the first instance, we consider an activation function f which is convex or
concave. If $\overline{x} = \underline{x}$, we can treat the transformer as acting on a point. Otherwise,
we compute the slope of the parallelogram:

$$\mu := \frac{f(\overline{x}) - f(\underline{x})}{\overline{x} - \underline{x}}$$

We provide an *extremum function* $x_f(\mu)$ for the given f. Assuming a convex function:

$$x_f(\mu) = \underset{x \in \mathbb{R}}{\operatorname{argmin}}(f(x) - \mu x) \tag{7}$$

If f is concave, replace argmin with argmax. Since f is convex/concave, this $x_f(\mu)$ will always be in the interval $[\underline{x}, \overline{x}]$ or otherwise $f(x) - \mu x$ is zero everywhere in $[\underline{x}, \overline{x}]$. For many of the activation functions we care about, it is simple to find these extremum functions. For example, $x_{\text{relu}}(\mu) = 0$ and $x_{\text{exp}}(\mu) = \ln \mu$. Then, one can compute:

$$e := x_f(\mu) \cdot \mu - \frac{f(\underline{x}) \cdot \overline{x} + \underline{x} \cdot f(\overline{x})}{\overline{x} - \underline{x}} \tag{8}$$

which may be interpreted as the height of the resulting zonotope parallelogram. From this we may compute the center of the parallelogram in the y direction:

$$c_y := \frac{1}{2}(f(\overline{x}) + f(\underline{x}) - e) \tag{9}$$

Finally we compute the new 1D hybrid zonotope:

$$D(f)\langle c_x, b_x, \mathbf{E}_x \rangle = \langle c_y, \ \mu b_x + \frac{e}{2}, \ \mu \mathbf{E} \rangle \tag{10}$$

To extend this approach to nonconvex functions, such as sigmoid, we instead need to find a pair of extrema $x_f(\mu)$, $\overline{x_f}(\mu)$ which may in general depend on the interval bounds $[\underline{x}, \overline{x}]$. In the case of sigmoid, one can show that these are minus the natural logarithm of the solutions $Y_\pm$ to the quadratic equation $\mu + (2\mu - 1)Y + \mu Y^2 = 0$. Figure 3 shows zonotope transformers for relu and sigmoid activation functions.

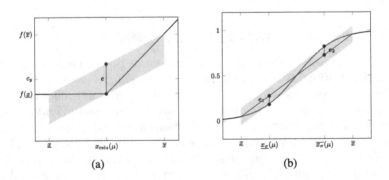

(a)   (b)

Fig. 3. Constructing zonotope transformers for relu and sigmoid activation functions.

2.4   Robust Training

To train with an abstract domain on a model N, from each training datum $(\mathbf{x}, \mathbf{y})$ we compute a prediction value $N(\mathbf{x})$ and a transformed domain object $\mathcal{D}(N)(\mathcal{B}_\epsilon(\mathbf{x}))$ of the domain representation of an ℓ_∞-ball $\mathcal{B}_\epsilon(\mathbf{x})$ around the input $\mathbf{x}$ for some fixed perturbation radius ϵ. An axis-aligned bounding box is drawn around the resulting output domain object, and the vertex v furthest away from the true target $\mathbf{y}$ is chosen. We construct a combined loss $\mathcal{L}_{\text{comb}}$ with the standard loss, the adversarial loss, a mixing factor $\lambda \in \mathbb{R}_{\geq 0}$, and a regularization term $\xi(N)$:

$$\mathcal{L}_{\text{comb}}(\mathbf{x}, \mathbf{y}) := \mathcal{L}(N(\mathbf{x}), \mathbf{y}) + \lambda \mathcal{L}(\operatorname*{argmax}_{\mathbf{v} \in \mathcal{D}(N)(\mathbf{x})} \|\mathbf{v} - \mathbf{y}\|_2, \mathbf{y}) + \xi(N) \qquad (11)$$

3   PaRoT System Description

In this section, we detail how *PaRoT* can be used for robust training and testing. The main overview of the system is presented in Fig. 4. The training aspects of the framework can be divided into *domains* (in the module `parot.domains`), which correspond to the ones identified in Sect. 2.2[1], and *properties* (in the module `parot.properties`) corresponding to the types of adversaries we are trying to robustify against. Section 3.2 presents the built-in properties available in *PaRoT*. As our system uses the TensorFlow platform, we first introduce some terminology.

TensorFlow [1] is a deep learning platform that enables the user to build a *computation graph* representing their neural network model and training scheme. This computation graph is a directed, acyclic graph whose nodes are *tensors*—a generalization of matrices to potentially higher dimensions—and whose edges are called *ops* and consist of a list of input and output tensors. An output tensor can be the input tensor for arbitrarily many ops. To illustrate, the left-hand side of Fig. 5 shows the computation graph constructed for a single dense layer of a neural network. The ops MatMul (matrix multiplication), BiasAdd (adding a bias to a value), and ReLU (rectified linear unit operation) form those required to represent this example layer.   Once a computation graph has been created, TensorFlow compiles it, allowing *PaRoT* to use this graph to automatically derive abstract transformers for a given model, as described in Sect. 3.1. This enables a user to use an existing model and immediately start robust training without needing code rewrites. It should be noted that the models supported by *PaRoT* must use only the operations supported by the framework in the selected domain. A list of the operations is available in Appendix 6.

---

[1] With the exception of the ZONOTOPE domain, which is not implemented in *PaRoT*.

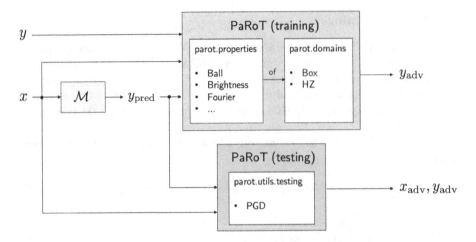

Fig. 4. *PaRoT* overview. Robust training is enabled by a property and an abstraction domain which can be chosen from those supported by *PaRoT* or extended with a custom domain. Given an input and a model prediction, *PaRoT* creates a domain object for the input based on the specified property, and it automatically transforms the operations associated with the model (see Sect. 3.1). At testing time, *PaRoT* provides auxiliary utilities.

3.1   Automatic Transformer Generation

In order to transform a computation graph G from a given input tensor $\mathbf{x}$ to an output tensor $\mathbf{z}$, we find the subgraph $S_{\mathbf{x},\mathbf{z}}$ of G whose vertices are the $\mathbf{y}$s such that there exist paths $\mathbf{x} \rightsquigarrow \mathbf{y}$ and $\mathbf{y} \rightsquigarrow \mathbf{z}$. This can be easily extended to multiple inputs and outputs. This subgraph $S_{\mathbf{x},\mathbf{z}}$ is found through a graph traversal algorithm backtracking from $\mathbf{z}$, which also produces a pair of adjacency maps C and M. C maps a tensor to a set of ops which consume it, while M maps an op f to the indices of the output tensors of the op in G. Once $S_{\mathbf{x},\mathbf{z}}$ is constructed, the transformation process can begin. The output of the process is a dictionary $\mathcal{T}$ which maps p-dimensional tensors to domain objects D (or the constant None). $\mathcal{T}$ is constructed by iteratively exploring $S_{\mathbf{x},\mathbf{z}}$ starting at $\mathbf{x}$. The complete transformation algorithm is given in Algorithm 1.

Algorithm 1: Automatic graph transformation algorithm

Data: A subgraph $S_{x,z}$, initial domain object $D \in \mathcal{D}$
Result: A transformed domain object $Z \in \mathcal{D}$

1 front $\leftarrow [x]$;
2 $\mathcal{T} \leftarrow \{x \mapsto D\}$;
3 **while** *front* $\neq \emptyset$ **do**
4     $s \leftarrow$ pop front;
5   **for** $f \leftarrow$ *consumers of* s *in* $S_{x,z}$ **do**
6        $s_1, \cdots, s_n \leftarrow$ the inputs of f in G;
7   **if** $\exists\, i\colon s_i \in S_{x,z} \wedge s_i \notin \mathcal{T}$ **then**
8 | continue;   *// wait for other inputs to be transformed*
9   **end**
10   **for** $1 \leq i \leq n$ **do**
11   **if** $s_i \notin \mathcal{T} \vee \mathcal{T}(s_i) = $ None **then**
12 | $S_i \leftarrow s_i$;
13   **else**
14 | $S_i \leftarrow \mathcal{T}(s_i)$;
15   **end**
16   **end**
17       $T_1, \cdots, T_m \leftarrow \mathcal{D}(f)(S_1, \cdots, S_n)$;
18   **for** $1 \leq j \leq m$ **do**
19          $t_j \leftarrow j$th output of f;
20          $\mathcal{T}(t_j) \leftarrow T_j$;
21   push j to front;
22   **end**
23   **end**
24 **end**
25 **return** $\mathcal{T}(z)$;

When transforming ops, various challenges arise. For example, a transformer $\mathcal{D}(f)$ can accept inputs that are not domain objects but instead just tensors. This occurs, for example, when a constant tensor needs to be added to a domain object. The acyclic graph structure makes this transformation non-trivial. The first issue arises when an operation consumes two or more domain objects. This happens in reticulated model architectures e.g., SkipNet from [40].

To illustrate the challenges of transforming ops, take two tensors x, y, consider the transformed computation graph for their addition $x + y$ where both x and y have abstract domains to be transformed. To transform $+$ for the Box domain, this entails merely adding the cs and bs of x and y. However, for HYBRIDZONOTOPE, the manner with which the merging should take place depends on how the E matrices were constructed. If x and y are both derived from the same starting zonotope, then their E matrices will both be referencing the same parameterization. In this case the E matrices for x and y can be added. However, if they originate from different starting zonotopes, then their e dimensions may not match up, and in this case they need to be *concatenated* along the e dimension:

$$\langle c_x, b_x, E_x \rangle + \langle c_y, b_y, E_y \rangle := \langle c_x + c_y, b_x + b_y, [E_x, E_y] \rangle \qquad (12)$$

Similar considerations must be made for, e.g., the `Concat` op which concatenates two tensors along a given dimension.

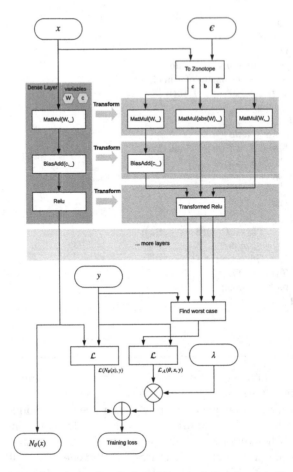

Fig. 5. An example computation graph for robust training showing the original (blue) and generated (green) computation graph on a dense layer. (Color figure online)

Another complication in extending transformers to computation graphs arises with ops which do not output a transformed domain object. The most prominent example of this is the `Shape` op which returns the dimensions of a tensor. We support these operations by allowing the domain implementer to return `None` instead of a domain object, flagging that the transformer algorithm should use the un-transformed output.

With these two considerations in mind, we have a procedure for transforming arbitrary TensorFlow graphs composed from a set of atomic transformers.

Figure 5 illustrates computing the transformed graph of the nodes on the left-hand side which represent the ops of a dense layer. Each green group on the right-hand side is the generated transformer computation graph of the corresponding f in the domain HYBRIDZONOTOPE, i.e.,, the result of calling $\mathcal{D}(f)$ for the op. Note that the variables from the original layer are shared with the transformed ops.

```
 1 from parot.domains import Box
 2 from parot.properties import Property
 3
 4 class NewProperty(Property):
 5     # define the supported domains of this property
 6     SUPPORTED_DOMAINS = [Box]
 7
 8     def __init__(self, param)
 9         # replace the initializer to accept desired parameters
10         pass
11
12     def generate_property(self, domain, input_tensor):
13         # implement the property here; safely assume domain is one
14         # of the types in NewProperty.SUPPORTED_DOMAINS
15         pass
16
17 # use the property on a tensor
18 x_box = NewProperty(param_instance).of(Box, x)
```

Listing 1.1. Implementing custom properties with *PaRoT*.

3.2   Robustness Properties

In this section, we describe several built-in robustness properties that can be trained with in *PaRoT*, and an interface for specifying custom properties.

Built-in Properties. Let $\mathbb{1}_s$ denote a tensor with shape s with all elements being ones. All the following supported properties are centered on a training input x with shape s.

- **BallDemoted**: the ℓ_∞-norm ball adversarial attack represented as an axis-aligned Box where $\mathbf{b} = \epsilon \cdot \mathbb{1}_s$.
- **BallPromoted**: another ℓ_∞-norm ball adversarial attack represented in the $\mathbf{E}$ matrix of the HYBRIDZONOTOPE as $\mathbf{E} = \epsilon \cdot \mathrm{diag}(\mathbb{1}_s)$
- **Brightness**: a simple property with a single column in $\mathbf{E}$ where all pixels may have a constant added to them. That is, $\mathbf{E} = \epsilon \cdot \mathbb{1}_{...s,1}$.
- **UniformChannel**: similar to **Brightness** except that each channel of the image is allowed to vary independently.
- **Fourier**: for a 2D image x, each column of $\mathbf{E}$ is a plane wave. That is, each column of $\mathbf{E}$ is an image $I : H \times W \to \mathbb{R}$:

$$I(i,j) = \epsilon \cdot \kappa \left(i\frac{2\pi n}{H} + j\frac{2\pi m}{W} \right),$$

for $\kappa \in \{\sin, \cos\}$, $n \in \{-N, ..., N\} \subset \mathbb{Z}$ and $m \in \{-M, ..., M\} \subset \mathbb{Z}$. Our motivation to investigate this property is to study the robustness to perturbations that we might observe in real data collected in the field. For example, in the case of detecting traffic lights, we can investigate whether it is possible to attack the network using only low frequencies (to model markings or distortions on a physical traffic light). An example of an adversarial example obtained through the `Fourier` on `MNIST` [24] is shown in Fig. 6.

Custom Properties. Defining a custom property in *PaRoT* is as simple as implementing a child class of `Property`, as presented in Listing 1.1.

3.3   Robust Training Using *PaRoT*

Integrating our framework in a codebase can easily be done with minimal changes to the existing code, as exemplified in Listing 1.2. Given a training dataset with inputs `x` and groundtruth outputs `y` in tensor form, as well as the predictions of the model for the inputs, `y_pred`, we create a domain object using a BOX abstraction around the inputs and transform the resulting computation graph. Then, a combined loss function can be created and passed to the desired optimizer for robust training.

4   Experiments

We evaluate *PaRoT* quantitatively to demonstrate performance, and qualitatively to validate its ease of use. We first show that our performance is comparable to the results obtained by DiffAI [27]. We then exemplify the ease of use on pre-trained models and finish with qualitative examples demonstrating a *PaRoT* robustness property. Throughout these experiments, we use the terms 'standard', 'regular' and 'baseline' interchangeably to describe a training process that solely uses a sparse cross-entropy loss.

In quantitative experiments, we make use of three metrics to measure performance:

- **Test Error**: percentage of misclassified examples in the testing set; the complement of classification accuracy.
- Test error under a **PGD** attack: a test based on the state-of-the-art Projected Gradient Descent attack first presented in [26] and used in [27]. PGD finds an adversarial example by following the gradient of the loss function inside an ϵ-ball around the actual test example on the input side. Thus, the reported values correspond to a lower bound on the percentage of the misclassified examples in the testing set that are susceptible to an attack of this type.
- Test error under a HYBRIDZONOTOPE attack **Verify**: similar to the `hSwitch` upper bound metric in [27], this metric uses the adversarial example discovered by the HYBRIDZONOTOPE on the output side, as in (11). Thus, the reported values correspond to an upper bound of the percentage of verifiably-susceptible examples in the testing set under this attack.

4.1 DiffAI Comparison

To validate the results of our framework, we ran robust training experiments similar to those in [27] of the Box and HYBRIDZONOTOPE domains for MNIST [24] and CIFAR10 [23]. The architecture of the networks used is as defined in [27] and is also presented in Appendix 6. We similarly augment the loss with an adversarial term with weight $\lambda = 0.1$ and an $L2$ regularization constant of 0.01. The learning rate and ϵ used are 10^{-3} and 0.1 for MNIST, and 10^{-4} and 0.007 for CIFAR10, respectively. We run all experiments for 100 epochs using the Adam optimizer [21]. The results are in Table 1.

As the table shows, our framework achieves comparable results to those obtained in [27]. In all cases, introducing an adversarial training method leads to a minor drop in accuracy—an expected outcome when optimizing for a combined loss function with a finite capacity [18,37]. In terms of Box training, we observe, as expected, a slight increase in PGD and a strong increase in the number of verifiably-safe examples. For a HYBRIDZONOTOPE training when compared to the baseline, we notice that the number of examples susceptible to a PGD attack grows slightly while, in general, the number of verifiable cases improves significantly. Overall, these results are similar and in many cases improve upon the ones in [27] with minor exceptions that can be justified by implementation differences and stochasticity in weight initialization.

4.2 Re-training Models

In this experiment, we showcase the ease of use of *PaRoT* using a pre-trained network. We train a network with two convolutional layers and two dense layers, following the architecture of ConvSmall (see [27]), on the MNIST dataset using a standard loss for 200 epochs (learning rate of 10^{-3}) and save it to a TensorFlow checkpoint file. We proceed to load this checkpoint's graph, and, using *PaRoT*'s Box abstract domain, add an adversarial term to the loss function, which we then use to further train the loaded model for 100 epochs. The results of the process are presented in Table 2. Re-training achieves similar accuracy, while improving significantly the PGD and verification metrics. It should be noted that at no point in the re-training process did we have to re-define the model or state the required operations, one of the main advantages of our framework.

4.3 Custom Robustness Properties: Case Study

As described in Sect. 3.2, *PaRoT* includes a variety of built-in robustness properties on 2D images for HYBRIDZONOTOPE. In this section, we showcase the identification of adversarial examples based on the Fourier property. Figure 6 exemplifies an attack on a regularly trained network following the architecture of ConvMed (see [27]). The Fourier robustness property is motivated by the observation that a typical adversarial attack will include high frequency components which may be filtered away or rendered irrelevant by the variability in the real-world input image. It is interesting to ask whether adversarial examples exist only consisting of frequencies at roughly the scale of the original image.

Table 1. *Quantitative Comparison*: results of running our framework on the same datasets, architectures and parameters as in [27]. In the experiments run, we used $\epsilon = 0.1$ for MNIST and 0.007 for CIFAR10.

Dataset	Model	Train method	Test Error %	PGD %	Verify %
MNIST	FFNN	Baseline	1.8	3.2	100.0
		Box	3.2	4.2	30.6
		HYBRIDZONOTOPE	3.2	4.0	30.2
	ConvSmall	Baseline	1.4	2.4	100.0
		Box	2.0	2.4	12.8
		HYBRIDZONOTOPE	1.8	2.4	91.8
	ConvMed	Baseline	1.8	2.2	100.0
		Box	1.8	2.2	13.6
		HYBRIDZONOTOPE	2.4	2.6	88.6
	ConvBig	Baseline	0.6	1.2	100.0
		Box	1.2	1.4	14.0
		HYBRIDZONOTOPE	1.8	2.0	74.2
	ConvSuper	Baseline	0.6	1.0	100.0
		Box	1.0	1.2	12.2
		HYBRIDZONOTOPE	1.0	1.6	72.4
	Skip	Baseline	0.6	0.8	100.0
		Box	1.0	1.8	11.0
		HYBRIDZONOTOPE	0.8	1.6	10.0
CIFAR10	FFNN	Baseline	45.8	45.8	100.0
		Box	50.4	50.4	76.2
		HYBRIDZONOTOPE	48.8	48.8	75.8
	ConvSmall	Baseline	33.3	33.4	100.0
		Box	36.2	36.2	72.0
		HYBRIDZONOTOPE	38.6	38.6	96.2
	ConvMed	Baseline	34.6	34.6	100.00
		Box	35.8	35.8	69.6
		HYBRIDZONOTOPE	34.4	34.6	96.4
	ConvBig	Baseline	35.4	35.6	100.0
		Box	36.0	36.0	71.2
		HYBRIDZONOTOPE	38.0	38.0	99.4
	ConvSuper	Baseline	34.4	35.2	100.0
		Box	33.6	34.2	100.0
		HYBRIDZONOTOPE	35.3	35.4	98.6
	Skip	Baseline	34.0	34.6	100.0
		Box	40.0	39.8	73.2
		HYBRIDZONOTOPE	39.4	39.6	74.0

Table 2. *Re-training Models*: comparison between the original network trained only with standard loss and a re-trained network using an adversarial loss term.

Model	Test error %	PGD %	Verify %
Original	1.70	2.30	100.00
Re-trained (Box)	2.88	1.47	14.80

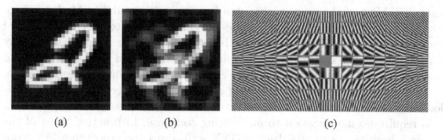

| (a) | (b) | (c) |

Fig. 6. *Fourier Attack*: example of a `Fourier` attack on an image of the MNIST dataset (a) an image that under regular training is correctly identified as a 2 (b) an adversarial example identified using *PaRoT* and a `Fourier` attack which leads the network trained with a standard loss function to identify as a 3. (c) is a grid of thumbnails of the available Fourier terms that were added to (a).

In this scenario, the network correctly identifies the Figure 6a as a 2, yet is stumped by the adversarially generated image of Fig. 6b (using the Fourier terms presented in Fig. 6c), mistakenly identifying it as a 3. After training with HYBRIDZONOTOPE with $\lambda = 0.1$ and $\epsilon = 0.01$ for 200 epochs for this robustness property, the model correctly identifies this specific example as a 2.

5   Related Work

We consider three main areas of related work: early, *heuristic* approaches to training more robust networks; *formal verification tools* that typically operate on fully trained networks; and several other representative *robust training* approaches.

Heuristic Approaches. Early art in adversarial robustness in the deep learning community broadly tackled the problem with heuristic techniques: with architecture and training scheme modifications [6,14,38,44]. These techniques have shown quite impressive results, and real progress has been made to training more inherently robust networks. However, it has been shown that these networks often remain susceptible to simple attacks [29,30]. This game of cat and mouse has led to ever more sophisticated attack and defense, e.g., [2,10,12,15,26,36,43]. In terms of their usability, however, many of these early approaches are comparable to ours. A lot of the techniques involve modifications to the training scheme rather than the network architecture itself. As has been shown, this is broadly similar to how robust training can be applied within our framework. The main limitation of these approaches is that they do not provide guarantees for robustness and, as ever, the bad guys tend to be one step ahead.

Formal Verification. Formal verification techniques provide guarantees on the robustness of a DNN at individual data-points [3, 13, 16, 19, 20], and, in at least one case for a small single-layer network, across the entirety of the input space [31]. Most of the work in this area focuses on Satisfiability Modulo Theories (SMT), reachability or optimization-based approaches to provide sound and complete guarantees on a per-example basis [25]. It has been shown that many of these techniques can be viewed as flavours of a unified Branch-and-Bound framework [5]. Through this lens, one can see the scalability challenges as an artifact of the combinatorial branching associated with piecewise-linear activation functions such as ReLUs. Similar to our framework, these formal verification tools require no modification to an existing codebase. In practice, most of the tooling is limited to a small subset of DNN activations and layer types (e.g., convolutional networks are often not supported) limiting their utility in practice. Furthermore, the intractability of these approaches, as detailed in [25], detracts their use in many of the larger networks we study in this paper. Lastly, as has been previously noted, these approaches do not offer systematic improvements at scale, i.e., the verification or falsification of each point needs to be considered iteratively in the training process.

Verifiably Robust Training. Our work falls within a *verifiably robust training* approach. We omit any theoretical comparison of the approaches, which is well described in [27]. Our system is most closely similar to DiffAI [27]. However, it distinguishes itself in the way the abstract transformers are generated from existing models: DiffAI requires that the user specify their model using specialized classes. This makes their library difficult to use with pre-existing models, since it requires rewriting the models to fit within the DiffAI framework. Our framework, on the other hand, can take an existing TensorFlow graph [1] representing a model and transform it automatically without having to rewrite any model code, as shown in Sect. 3. This makes it more practical to use within an existing pipeline, as it decouples the maintenance of the model from the verified robustness procedure, allowing for faster development and testing. We observe that *PaRoT* achieves similar performance to DiffAI and in a similar total training times to those reported in [27] for the same GPU configuration (Nvidia GeForce GTX 1080 Ti).

In [39], the introduced framework, MixTrain, reaches better accuracy and a higher percentage of verifiably-safe examples when compared to [27]. Similarly, comparing the results presented in [39] with ours, we conclude that MixTrain outperforms the ones obtained in Sect. 4. However, it should be noted that some of techniques that MixTrain uses to achieve this improvement can be replicated easily when using our framework. For example, while in Listing 1.2 we defined the loss function as in [27] for the sake of simplicity, our framework allows for flexible definitions, including the dynamic loss function defined per epoch in [39].

Other works in this area involve convex relaxation techniques such as the ones presented in [33], or dual optimization techniques as in [42]. In terms of accuracy and adversarial robustness, further studies need to be carried out to compare our work to [33] and [42]. Despite this, the implementation of both [33] and [42] requires the re-writing of the models to adapt to the method's requirements, which, as in the case of [27], constitutes a set back to integration efforts in production software stacks.

6   Conclusion and Future Work

In this paper we introduce *PaRoT*, a novel framework for verifiable robust training that can be used directly on existing codebases and requires minimal code changes. We believe that this is the first practical framework for robust training that supports the vast majority of operations required for most large-scale models. Our work further contributes to the community with the introduction of new abstract transformers, novel formal robustness properties, and a framework for adding user-defined properties to robust training. We plan to build upon this framework in several directions:

- We wish to investigate more natural training schemes that, for example, use the robust loss more effectively and adapt the robustness property through the training cycle. Similarly, we plan to explore how we could provide features such as the stochastic robust approximation techniques from [39] for better performance.
- We also want to perform a theoretical study of abstract domains and training techniques that scale better with larger DNN widths and lengths; a fundamental problem of most of the methods presented in Sect. 5 [25]. It can be seen in Table 1, for example, that HYBRIDZONOTOPEs did not perform as well as would be expected on larger networks, and an in-depth analysis could help shed some light on the cause of this phenomenon.
- We wish to introduce an API for users to easily add and test their own op transformers, so that the framework can easily be extended to work on model code with currently unsupported ops. Currently supported ops may be viewed in Appendix 6.
- Finally, we would like to conduct a comprehensive ablation study that includes many of the alternatives mentioned in Sect. 5 to further understand the comparative performance of our framework.

Appendix A Implemented TensorFlow Operations and Keras Layers

Table 3 lists the currently implemented TensorFlow operations in *PaRoT*, while Table 4 shows the implemented Keras layers. Other Keras layers might be supported depending on the implementation in terms of TensorFlow operations.

Table 3. TensorFlow operations implemented in *PaRoT*

Operation type	Box	HybridZonotope
Abs		✓
Add	✓	✓
BiasAdd	✓	✓
ConcatV2	✓	✓ (only between HZ and tf.Tensor)
Conv2D	✓	✓ (the second input should be tf.Tensor)
Exp		✓
GreaterEqual	✓	✓
Log		✓
Log1p		✓
MatMul	✓	✓ (only first input HZ)
Maximum		✓
MaxPool	✓	✓ (only for 'keras.MaxPool2D(2))
Mean		✓
Minimum		✓
Mul	✓	✓
Neg	✓	✓
OnesLike	✓	✓
Pack	✓	
RealDiv	✓	✓
Relu	✓	✓
Reshape	✓	✓
Select		✓ (first input not HZ)
Shape	✓	✓
Sigmoid	✓	✓
Softmax	✓	✓
StridedSlice	✓	✓
Sub	✓	✓
Sum		✓
Transpose	✓	✓
ZerosLike	✓	✓

Appendix B Network architectures

We follow the design of [27]. For convolutional layers $c \times w \times h$ [s] is for channels, kernel width, kernel height and stride, respectively.

FFNN. Five fully-connected layers, 100-node each, with ReLU.

Table 4. Keras layers supported by *PaRoT* out of the box

Layer	Box	HYBRIDZONOTOPE
Concatenate	✓	✓
Conv2D	✓	✓
Dense('relu')	✓	✓
Dense('sigmoid')	✓	✓
Dense('softmax')	✓	✓
Flatten	✓	✓
MaxPooling2D	✓	✓

ConvSmall. Two convolutional layers with no padding ($16 \times 4 \times 4$ [2], $32 \times 4 \times 4$ [2]), followed by a 100-node fully-connected layer.

ConvMed. Two convolutional layers with padding of 1 ($16 \times 4 \times 4$ [2], $32 \times 4 \times 4$ [2]), followed by a 100-node fully-connected layer.

ConvBig. Four convolutional layers with padding of 1 ($32 \times 3 \times 3$ [1], $32 \times 4 \times 4$ [2], $64 \times 3 \times 3$ [1], $64 \times 4 \times 4$ [2]), followed by a 512-node fully-connected layer, ReLU, and a 512-node fully-connected layer.

ConvSuper. Four convolutional layers with no padding ($32 \times 3 \times 3$ [1] , $32 \times 4 \times 4$ [1], $64 \times 3 \times 3$ [1], $64 \times 4 \times 4$ [1]), followed by a 512-node fully-connected layer, ReLU, and a 512-node fully-connected layer.

Skip. A concatenation of two covolutional networks followed by ReLU, 200-node fully-connected network, and ReLU. The two networks are:

- Three convolutional layers ($16 \times 3 \times 3$ [1], $16 \times 3 \times 3$ [1], $32 \times 3 \times 3$ [1]), followed by a 200-node fully-connected layer
- Two convolutional layers ($32 \times 4 \times 4$ [1], $32 \times 4 \times 4$ [1]) followed by a 200-node fully-connected layer.

References

1. Abadi, M., et al.: TensorFlow: a system for large-scale machine learning. In: 12th {USENIX} Symposium on Operating Systems Design and Implementation ({OSDI} 2016), pp. 265–283 (2016)
2. Akhtar, N., Mian, A.S.: Threat of adversarial attacks on deep learning in computer vision: a survey. IEEE Access **6**, 14410–14430 (2018)
3. Akintunde, M., Lomuscio, A., Maganti, L., Pirovano, E.: Reachability analysis for neural agent-environment systems. In: Principles of Knowledge Representation and Reasoning: Proceedings of the Sixteenth International Conference, KR 2018, Tempe, Arizona, 30 October–2 November 2018, pp. 184–193 (2018)

4. Bojarski, M., et al.: End to end learning for self-driving cars. CoRR abs/1604.07316 (2016)

5. Bunel, R., Turkaslan, I., Torr, P.H.S., Kohli, P., Mudigonda, P.K.: A unified view of piecewise linear neural network verification. In: Advances in Neural Information Processing Systems 31: Annual Conference on Neural Information Processing Systems 2018, NeurIPS 2018, 3–8 December 2018, Montréal, Canada, pp. 4795–4804 (2018)

6. Cissé, M., Bojanowski, P., Grave, E., Dauphin, Y.N., Usunier, N.: Parseval networks: improving robustness to adversarial examples. In: Proceedings of the 34th International Conference on Machine Learning, ICML 2017, Sydney, NSW, Australia, 6–11 August 2017, pp. 854–863 (2017)

7. Cousot, P., Cousot, R.: Abstract interpretation: a unified lattice model for static analysis of programs by construction or approximation of fixpoints. In: Proceedings of the 4th ACM SIGACT-SIGPLAN symposium on Principles of Programming Languages, pp. 238–252. ACM (1977)

8. Cousot, P., Cousot, R.: Abstract interpretation frameworks. J. Log. Comput. **2**(4), 511–547 (1992)

9. Defense Advanced Research Projects Agency: Assured Autonomy. https://www.darpa.mil/program/assured-autonomy

10. Dong, Y., et al.: Boosting adversarial attacks with momentum. In: 2018 IEEE Conference on Computer Vision and Pattern Recognition, CVPR 2018, Salt Lake City, UT, USA, 18–22 June 2018, pp. 9185–9193 (2018)

11. Goodfellow, I., Bengio, Y., Courville, A.: Deep Learning. The MIT Press (2016)

12. Goodfellow, I.J., Shlens, J., Szegedy, C.: Explaining and harnessing adversarial examples. In: 3rd International Conference on Learning Representations, ICLR 2015, Conference Track Proceedings, San Diego, CA, USA, 7–9 May 2015 (2015)

13. Gopinath, D., Wang, K., Zhang, M., Pasareanu, C.S., Khurshid, S.: Symbolic execution for deep neural networks. CoRR abs/1807.10439 (2018)

14. Gu, S., Rigazio, L.: Towards deep neural network architectures robust to adversarial examples. In: 3rd International Conference on Learning Representations, ICLR 2015, Workshop Track Proceedings, San Diego, CA, USA, 7–9 May 2015 (2015)

15. Huang, R., Xu, B., Schuurmans, D., Szepesvári, C.: Learning with a strong adversary. CoRR abs/1511.03034 (2015). http://arxiv.org/abs/1511.03034

16. Huang, X., Kwiatkowska, M., Wang, S., Wu, M.: Safety verification of deep neural networks. In: Majumdar, R., Kunčak, V. (eds.) CAV 2017. LNCS, vol. 10426, pp. 3–29. Springer, Cham (2017). https://doi.org/10.1007/978-3-319-63387-9_1

17. Janai, J., Güney, F., Behl, A., Geiger, A.: Computer vision for autonomous vehicles: problems, datasets and state-of-the-art. CoRR abs/1704.05519 (2017)

18. Jetley, S., Lord, N.A., Torr, P.H.: With friends like these, who needs adversaries? In: Proceedings of the 32nd International Conference on Neural Information Processing Systems, NIPS 2018, pp. 10772–10782. Curran Associates Inc., USA (2018)

19. Katz, G., Barrett, C., Dill, D.L., Julian, K., Kochenderfer, M.J.: Reluplex: an efficient SMT solver for verifying deep neural networks. In: Majumdar, R., Kunčak, V. (eds.) CAV 2017. LNCS, vol. 10426, pp. 97–117. Springer, Cham (2017). https://doi.org/10.1007/978-3-319-63387-9_5

20. Katz, G., Katz, G., et al.: The Marabou framework for verification and analysis of deep neural networks. In: Dillig, I., Tasiran, S. (eds.) CAV 2019. LNCS, vol. 11561, pp. 443–452. Springer, Cham (2019). https://doi.org/10.1007/978-3-030-25540-4_26

21. Kingma, D.P., Ba, J.: Adam: a method for stochastic optimization. arXiv preprint arXiv:1412.6980 (2014)

22. Koopman, P., Wagner, M.: Challenges in autonomous vehicle testing and validation (2016)
23. Krizhevsky, A., et al.: Learning multiple layers of features from tiny images. Technical report, Citeseer (2009)
24. LeCun, Y., Bottou, L., Bengio, Y., Haffner, P., et al.: Gradient-based learning applied to document recognition. Proc. IEEE **86**(11), 2278–2324 (1998)
25. Liu, C., Arnon, T., Lazarus, C., Barrett, C., Kochenderfer, M.J.: Algorithms for verifying deep neural networks. arXiv preprint arXiv:1903.06758 (2019)
26. Madry, A., Makelov, A., Schmidt, L., Tsipras, D., Vladu, A.: Towards deep learning models resistant to adversarial attacks. In: 6th International Conference on Learning Representations, ICLR 2018, Vancouver, BC, Canada, 30 April–3 May 2018, Conference Track Proceedings (2018)
27. Mirman, M., Gehr, T., Vechev, M.: Differentiable abstract interpretation for provably robust neural networks. In: Dy, J., Krause, A. (eds.) Proceedings of the 35th International Conference on Machine Learning. Proceedings of Machine Learning Research, Stockholmsmässan, Stockholm, Sweden, 10–15 July 2018, vol. 80, pp. 3578–3586. PMLR (2018)
28. Mirman, M., Singh, G., Vechev, M.T.: A provable defense for deep residual networks. CoRR abs/1903.12519 (2019)
29. Moosavi-Dezfooli, S., Fawzi, A., Fawzi, O., Frossard, P.: Universal adversarial perturbations. In: 2017 IEEE Conference on Computer Vision and Pattern Recognition (CVPR), pp. 86–94, July 2017. https://doi.org/10.1109/CVPR.2017.17
30. Papernot, N., McDaniel, P., Jha, S., Fredrikson, M., Celik, Z.B., Swami, A.: The limitations of deep learning in adversarial settings. In: 2016 IEEE European Symposium on Security and Privacy (EuroS P), pp. 372–387, March 2016
31. Raghunathan, A., Steinhardt, J., Liang, P.: Certified defenses against adversarial examples. In: 6th International Conference on Learning Representations, Conference Track Proceedings, ICLR 2018, Vancouver, BC, Canada, 30 April–3 May 2018 (2018)
32. Salay, R., Czarnecki, K.: Using machine learning safely in automotive software: an assessment and adaption of software process requirements in ISO 26262. CoRR abs/1808.01614 (2018)
33. Salman, H., Yang, G., Zhang, H., Hsieh, C.J., Zhang, P.: A convex relaxation barrier to tight robustness verification of neural networks. arXiv preprint arXiv:1902.08722 (2019)
34. Singh, G., Gehr, T., Mirman, M., Püschel, M., Vechev, M.: Fast and effective robustness certification. In: Advances in Neural Information Processing Systems, pp. 10802–10813 (2018)
35. Szegedy, C., et al.: Intriguing properties of neural networks. In: 2nd International Conference on Learning Representations, ICLR 2014, Conference Track Proceedings, Banff, AB, Canada, 14–16 April 2014 (2014)
36. Tramèr, F., Kurakin, A., Papernot, N., Goodfellow, I.J., Boneh, D., McDaniel, P.D.: Ensemble adversarial training: Attacks and defenses. In: 6th International Conference on Learning Representations, ICLR 2018, Conference Track Proceedings, Vancouver, BC, Canada, 30 April–3 May 2018 (2018)
37. Tsipras, D., Santurkar, S., Engstrom, L., Turner, A., Madry, A.: Robustness may be at odds with accuracy. In: 7th International Conference on Learning Representations, ICLR 2019, New Orleans, LA, USA, 6–9 May 2019 (2019)

38. Wang, B., Gao, J., Qi, Y.: A theoretical framework for robustness of (deep) classifiers against adversarial samples. In: 5th International Conference on Learning Representations, ICLR 2017, Workshop Track Proceedings, Toulon, France, 24–26 April 2017 (2017)
39. Wang, S., Chen, Y., Abdou, A., Jana, S.: MixTrain: scalable training of formally robust neural networks. arXiv preprint arXiv:1811.02625 (2018)
40. Wang, X., Yu, F., Dou, Z.-Y., Darrell, T., Gonzalez, J.E.: SkipNet: learning dynamic routing in convolutional networks. In: Ferrari, V., Hebert, M., Sminchisescu, C., Weiss, Y. (eds.) ECCV 2018. LNCS, vol. 11217, pp. 420–436. Springer, Cham (2018). https://doi.org/10.1007/978-3-030-01261-8_25
41. Wong, E., Kolter, J.Z.: Provable defenses against adversarial examples via the convex outer adversarial polytope. In: Proceedings of the 35th International Conference on Machine Learning, ICML 2018, Stockholmsmässan, Stockholm, Sweden, 10–15 July 2018, pp. 5283–5292 (2018)
42. Wong, E., Schmidt, F., Metzen, J.H., Kolter, J.Z.: Scaling provable adversarial defenses. In: Advances in Neural Information Processing Systems, pp. 8400–8409 (2018)
43. Yuan, X., He, P., Zhu, Q., Li, X.: Adversarial examples: attacks and defenses for deep learning. IEEE Trans. Neural Netw. Learn. Syst. **30**(9), 2805–2824 (2019)
44. Zheng, S., Song, Y., Leung, T., Goodfellow, I.: Improving the robustness of deep neural networks via stability training. In: 2016 IEEE Conference on Computer Vision and Pattern Recognition (CVPR), pp. 4480–4488, June 2016

Simplifying Neural Networks Using Formal Verification

Sumathi Gokulanathan[1], Alexander Feldsher[1], Adi Malca[1], Clark Barrett[2], and Guy Katz[1(✉)]

[1] The Hebrew University of Jerusalem, Jerusalem, Israel
{sumathi.giokolanat,feld,adimalca,guykatz}@cs.huji.ac.il
[2] Stanford University, Stanford, USA
barrett@cs.stanford.edu

Abstract. Deep neural network (DNN) verification is an emerging field, with diverse verification engines quickly becoming available. Demonstrating the effectiveness of these engines on real-world DNNs is an important step towards their wider adoption. We present a tool that can leverage existing verification engines in performing a novel application: neural network simplification, through the reduction of the size of a DNN without harming its accuracy. We report on the work-flow of the simplification process, and demonstrate its potential significance and applicability on a family of real-world DNNs for aircraft collision avoidance, whose sizes we were able to reduce by as much as 10%.

Keywords: Deep neural networks · Simplification · Verification · Marabou

1 Introduction

Deep neural networks (*DNNs*) are revolutionizing the way complex software is produced, obtaining unprecedented results in domains such as image recognition [28], natural language processing [5], and game playing [27]. There is now even a trend of using DNNs as controllers in autonomous cars and unmanned aircraft [2,18]. With DNNs becoming prevalent, it is highly important to develop automatic techniques to assist in creating, maintaining and adjusting them.

As DNNs are used in tackling increasingly complex tasks, their sizes (i.e., number of neurons) are also increasing—to a point where modern DNNs can have millions of neurons [13]. DNN size is thus becoming a liability, as deploying larger networks takes up more space, increases energy consumption, and prolongs response times. Network size can even become a limiting factor in situations where system resources are scarce. For example, consider the ACAS Xu airborne collision avoidance system for unmanned aircraft, which is currently being developed by the Federal Aviation Administration [18]. This is a highly safety-critical system, for which a DNN-based implementation is being considered [18]. Because this system will be mounted on actual drones with limited

© Springer Nature Switzerland AG 2020
R. Lee et al. (Eds.): NFM 2020, LNCS 12229, pp. 85–93, 2020.
https://doi.org/10.1007/978-3-030-55754-6_5

memory, efforts are being made to reduce the sizes of the ACAS Xu DNNs as much as possible, without harming their accuracy [17,18].

Most work to date on DNN simplification uses various heuristics, and does not provide formal guarantees about the simplified network's resemblance to the original. A common approach is to start with a large network, and reduce its size by removing some of its components (i.e., neurons and edges) [12,15]. The parts to be removed from the network are determined heuristically, and network accuracy may be harmed, sometimes requiring additional training after the simplification process has been performed [12].

Here, we propose a novel simplification technique that harnesses recent advances in DNN verification (e.g., [9,19,32]). Using verification queries, we propose to identify components of the network that *never affect its output*. These components can be safely removed, creating a smaller network that is completely equivalent to the original. We empirically demonstrate that many such removable components exist in networks of interest.

We implement our technique in a proof-of-concept tool, called *NNSimplify*. The tool uses the following work-flow: (i) it performs lightweight simulations to identify parts of the DNN that are candidates for removal; (ii) it invokes an underlying verification engine to dispatch queries that determine which of those parts can indeed be removed without affecting the network's outputs; and (iii) it constructs the simplified network, which is equivalent to the original. A major benefit of the proposed verification-based simplification is that it does not require any retraining of the simplified network, which may be expensive.

Our implementation of NNSimplify (available online [10]) can use existing DNN verification tools as a backend. For the evaluation reported here, we used the recently published Marabou framework [21] as the underlying verification engine. We evaluated our approach on the ACAS Xu family of DNNs for airborne collision avoidance [18], and were able to reduce the sizes of these DNNs by up to 10%—a highly significant reduction for systems where resources are scarce.

The rest of the paper is organized as follows. In Sect. 2, we provide a brief background on DNNs and their verification and simplification. Next, we describe our verification-based approach to simplification in Sect. 3, followed by an evaluation in Sect. 4. We then conclude in Sect. 5.

2   Background: DNNs, Verification and Simplification

DNNs are comprised of an input layer, an output layer, and multiple hidden layers in between. A layer is comprised of multiple nodes (neurons), each connected to nodes from the preceding layer using a predetermined set of weights (see Fig. 1). By assigning values to inputs and then feeding them forward through the network, values for each layer can be computed from the values of the previous layer, finally resulting in values for the outputs.

As DNNs are increasingly used in safety-critical applications (e.g., [2,18]), there is a surge of interest in verification methods that can provide formal guarantees about DNN behavior. A DNN verification query consists of a neural network and a property to be checked; and it results in either a formal guarantee

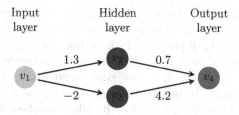

Fig. 1. A small neural network with 2 hidden nodes in one hidden layer. Weights are denoted over the edges. Hidden node values are typically determined by computing a weighted sum according to the weights, and then applying a non-linear activation function to the result.

that the network satisfies the property, or a concrete input for which the property is violated (a counter-example). Verification queries can encode various properties about DNNs; e.g., that slight perturbations to a network's inputs do not affect its output, and that it is thus robust to *adversarial perturbations* [1,4,30].

Recently, there has been significant progress on DNN verification tools that can dispatch such queries (see a recent survey [24]). Some of the proposed approaches for DNN verification include the use of specialized SMT solvers [14,19,21], the use of LP and MILP solvers [7,31], symbolic interval propagation [32], abstract interpretation [9], and many others (e.g., [3,6,8,25,26]). This new technology has been applied in a variety of contexts, such as collision avoidance [19], adversarial robustness [11,14,20], hybrid systems [29], and computer networks [22]. Although DNN verification technology is improving rapidly, scalability remains a major limitation of existing approaches. It has been shown that a common variant of the DNN verification problem is NP-complete, and becomes exponentially harder as the network size increases [19,23].

In recent years, enormous DNNs have been appearing in order to tackle increasingly complex tasks—to a point where DNN size is becoming a liability, because large networks take longer to train and even to evaluate when deployed. Techniques for neural network minimization and simplification have thus started to emerge: typically, these take an initial, large network, and reduce its size by removing some of its components [12]. The pruning phase involves the removal of edges from the network. The selection of which edges to remove is done heuristically, often by selecting edges that have very small weights, because these edges are less likely to significantly affect the network's outputs. If all edges connecting a node to the preceding layer or to the succeeding layer are removed, then the node itself can be removed. After the pruning phase, the reduced network is retrained [12,15].

3   Simplification Using Verification

Despite the demonstrated usefulness of pruning-based DNN simplification [12, 15], heuristic-based approaches might miss removable edges, if these edges do not have particularly small weights. However, such edges can be identified using verification. For example, consider the network shown in Fig. 2. As all edge weights have identical magnitudes, none of them would be pruned by a heuristic-based approach. However, using a verification engine, it is possible to check the property: "does there exist an input for which v_4 takes a non-zero value?". If the verification tool answers "no", as is the case for the network in Fig. 2 (because $v_4 = v_2 - v_3$ and $v_2 = v_3$), then we are guaranteed that v_4 is always assigned 0, regardless of the input. In turn, this means that v_4 can never affect nodes in subsequent layers. In this case, v_4 and all its edges can be safely removed from the network (rendering the network's output constant). Due to the soundness of the verification process, we are guaranteed that the simplified DNN is completely equivalent to the original DNN, and thus no retraining is required.

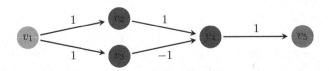

Fig. 2. Using verification, we can discover that node v_4 can safely be removed from the network.

Using verification to identify nodes that are always assigned 0 for every possible input, and can thus be removed, is the core of our technique. However, because verification is costly, posing this query for every node of the DNN might take a long time. To mitigate this difficulty, we propose the following work-flow:

1. Use lightweight simulations to identify nodes that are candidates for removal. Initially, all hidden nodes are such candidates. We then evaluate the network for random input values, and remove from the list of candidates any hidden node that is assigned a non-zero value for some input. With each simulation, the number of candidates for removal decreases.
2. For each remaining candidate node v, we create a separate verification query stating that $v \neq 0$, and use the underlying verification engine to dispatch it. If we get an UNSAT answer, we mark node v for removal. The candidates are explored in a layer-by-layer order, which allows us to only examine a part of the DNN for every query. For example, when addressing a candidate in layer #2, we do not encode layers #3 and on as part of our verification query, as a node's assignment can only be affected by nodes in preceding layers. Because verifying smaller networks is generally easier, this layer-by-layer approach accelerates the process as a whole. In addition, this process naturally lends itself to parallelization, by running each verification query on a separate machine.
3. Finally, we construct the simplified network, in which the nodes marked for removal and all their incoming and outgoing edges are deleted. We can also remove any nodes that subsequently become irrelevant due to the removal of all of their incoming or outgoing edges (e.g., for the DNN in Fig. 2, after removing v_4 we can also remove v_2 and v_3, as neither has any remaining outgoing edges).

We note that our technique can be extended to simplify DNNs in additional ways, by using different verification queries. For example, it can identify separate nodes that are always assigned identical, non-zero values (duplicates) and unify them, thus reducing the overall number of nodes. It can also identify and remove nodes that can be expressed as linear combinations of other nodes.

4   Evaluation

Our proof-of-concept implementation of the approach, called NNSimplify, is comprised of three Python modules, one for performing each of the aforementioned steps. The tool is general, in two ways: (1) it can be applied to simplify any DNN, regardless of its application domain; and (2) it can use any DNN verification engine as a backend, benefiting from any future improvement in verification technology. For our experiments we used the Marabou [21] verification engine. In practice, it is required that the DNN in question be supported by the backend verification engine—for example, some engines may not support certain network topologies. Additionally, the DNN needs to be provided in a format supported by NNSimplify; currently, the tool supports the NNet format [16], and we plan to extend it to additional formats. The tool, additional documentation, and all the benchmarks reported in this section are available online [10].

We evaluated NNSimplify on the ACAS Xu family of DNNs for airborne collision avoidance [18]. This set contains 45 DNNs, each with 5 input neurons, 5 output neurons, and 300 hidden neurons spread across 6 hidden layers. The ACAS Xu networks are fully connected, and use the ReLU activation function in each of their hidden nodes—and are thus supported by Marabou.

For each of the 45 ACAS Xu DNNs, we ran the first Python module of NNSimplify (random simulations), resulting in a list of candidate nodes for removal. For each DNN we performed 20000 simulations, and this narrowed down the list of nodes that are candidates for removal to about 7% of all hidden nodes (see Fig. 3). The simulations were performed on points sampled uniformly at random, although other distributions could of course be used.

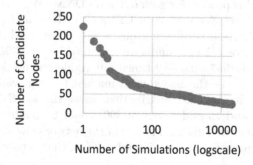

Fig. 3. Using simulation to identify nodes that are candidates for removal, on one ACAS Xu network.

Next, for each candidate for removal we ran the second Python module, which takes as input a DNN and a node v that is a candidate for removal. This module constructs a temporary, smaller DNN, where the candidate node v is the only output node (subsequent layers are omitted). These temporary DNNs were then passed to the underlying verification engine, with the query $v \neq 0$. Here, we encountered the following issue: the Marabou framework, like many linear-programming based tools, does not provide a way to directly specify that $v \neq 0$, but rather only to state that $v \geq \varepsilon$ for some $\varepsilon > 0$ (we assume all hidden nodes are, by definition, never negative, which is the case for the ACAS Xu DNNs). We experimented with various values of ε (see Fig. 4), and concluded that the choice of ε has very little effect on the outcome of the experiment—i.e., nodes tend to either be obsolete, or take on large values. The set of removed nodes was almost identical in all experiments, with minor differences due to different queries timing out for different values of ε.

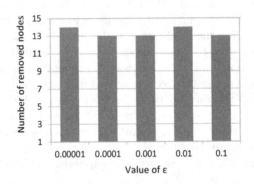

Fig. 4. Number of removed nodes as a function of the value of ε, on one of the ACAS Xu networks.

Finally, we ran the third Python module that uses the results of the previous steps to construct the simplified network.

We performed this process for each of the 45 DNNs. We ran the experiments on machines with Intel Xeon E5-2670 CPUs (2.60GHz) and 8GB of memory, and used $\varepsilon = 0.01$. Each verification query was given a 4-h timeout. Out of 1069 verification queries (1 per candidate node), 535 were UNSAT (node marked for removal), 15 were SAT, and 519 timed out (node not marked for removal). Thus, on average, 4% of the nodes were marked for removal (535 nodes out of 13500). Figure 5 depicts their distribution across the 45 DNNs. In most networks, between 11 and 15 nodes (out of 300) could be removed; but for a few networks, this number was higher. For one of the networks we discovered 29 neurons that could be removed—approximately 10% of that network's total number of neurons.

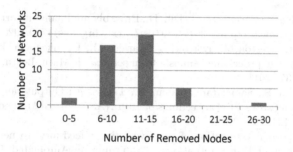

Fig. 5. Total number of removed nodes in the ACAS Xu networks.

5   Conclusion

DNN verification is an emerging field, and we are just now beginning to tap its potential in assisting engineers in DNN development. We presented here the NNSimplify tool, which uses black-box verification engines to simplify neural networks. We demonstrated that this approach can lead to a substantial reduction in DNN size. Although our experiments show that the tool is already applicable to real-world DNNs, its scalability is limited by the scalability of its underlying verification engine; but as the scalability of verification technology improves, that limitation will diminish. In the future, we plan to extend this work along several axes. First, we intend to explore additional verification queries, which would allow to simplify DNNs in more sophisticated ways—for example by revealing that some neurons can be expressed as linear combinations of other neurons, or that some neurons are always assigned identical values and can be merged. In addition, we plan to investigate more aggressive simplification steps, which may change the DNN's output, while using verification to ensure that these changes remain within acceptable bounds. Finally, we intend to apply the technique to additional real-world DNNs and case studies.

Acknowledgements. This project was partially supported by grants from the Binational Science Foundation (2017662), the Israel Science Foundation (683/18), and the National Science Foundation (1814369).

References

1. Bastani, O., Ioannou, Y., Lampropoulos, L., Vytiniotis, D., Nori, A., Criminisi, A.: Measuring neural net robustness with constraints. In: Proceedings of 30th Conference on Neural Information Processing Systems (NIPS) (2016)
2. Bojarski, M., et al.: End to end learning for self-driving cars. Technical report (2016). http://arxiv.org/abs/1604.07316
3. Bunel, R., Turkaslan, I., Torr, P.H., Kohli, P., Kumar, M.P.: Piecewise linear neural network verification: a comparative study. Technical report (2017). https://arxiv.org/abs/1711.00455v1

4. Carlini, N., Katz, G., Barrett, C., Dill, D.: Provably minimally-distorted adversarial examples. Technical report (2017). https://arxiv.org/abs/1709.10207
5. Collobert, R., Weston, J., Bottou, L., Karlen, M., Kavukcuoglu, K., Kuksa, P.: Natural language processing (almost) from scratch. J. Mach. Learn. Res. (JMLR) **12**, 2493–2537 (2011)
6. Dutta, S., Jha, S., Sanakaranarayanan, S., Tiwari, A.: Output range analysis for deep neural networks. In: Proceedings of 10th NASA Formal Methods Symposium (NFM), pp. 121–138 (2018)
7. Ehlers, R.: Formal verification of piece-wise linear feed-forward neural networks. In: Proceedings of 15th International Symposium on Automated Technology for Verification and Analysis (ATVA), pp. 269–286 (2017)
8. Elboher, Y., Gottschlich, J., Katz, G.: An abstraction-based framework for neural network verification. Technical report (2019). http://arxiv.org/abs/1910.14574
9. Gehr, T., Mirman, M., Drachsler-Cohen, D., Tsankov, P., Chaudhuri, S., Vechev, M.: AI2: safety and robustness certification of neural networks with abstract interpretation. In: Proceedings of 39th IEEE Symposium on Security and Privacy (S&P) (2018)
10. Gokulanathan, S., Feldsher, A., Malca, A., Barrett, C., Katz, G.: The NNSimplify Code (2020). https://drive.google.com/open?id=19TbPS7P9fo-2tRXo8ENnggLY1LxxPCd1
11. Gopinath, D., Katz, G., Păsăreanu, C., Barrett, C.: DeepSafe: a data-driven approach for checking adversarial robustness in neural networks. In: Proceedings of 16th International Symposium on Automated Technology for Verification and Analysis (ATVA), pp. 3–19 (2018)
12. Han, S., Mao, H., Dally, W.: Deep compression: compressing deep neural networks with pruning, trained quantization and Huffman coding. Technical report (2015). http://arxiv.org/abs/1510.00149
13. Howard, A., et al.: MobileNets: efficient convolutional neural networks for mobile vision applications. Technical report (2017). http://arxiv.org/abs/1704.04861
14. Huang, X., Kwiatkowska, M., Wang, S., Wu, M.: Safety verification of deep neural networks. In: Majumdar, R., Kunčak, V. (eds.) CAV 2017. LNCS, vol. 10426, pp. 3–29. Springer, Cham (2017). https://doi.org/10.1007/978-3-319-63387-9_1
15. Iandola, F.N., Han, S., Moskewicz, M.W., Ashraf, K., Dally, W.J., Keutzer, K.: SqueezeNet: AlexNet-level accuracy with 50x fewer parameters and <0.5 MB model size. Technical report (2016). http://arxiv.org/abs/1602.07360
16. Julian, K.: NNet Format (2018). https://github.com/sisl/NNet
17. Julian, K., Kochenderfer, M., Owen, M.: Deep neural network compression for aircraft collision avoidance systems. J. Guid. Control Dyn. **42**(3), 598–608 (2019)
18. Julian, K.D., Lopez, J., Brush, J.S., Owen, M.P., Kochenderfer, M.J.: Policy compression for aircraft collision avoidance systems. In: Proceedings of 35th Digital Avionics Systems Conference (DASC), pp. 1–10 (2016)
19. Katz, G., Barrett, C., Dill, D., Julian, K., Kochenderfer, M.: Reluplex: an efficient SMT solver for verifying deep neural networks. In Proceedings of 29th International Conference on Computer Aided Verification (CAV), pp. 97–117 (2017)
20. Katz, G., Barrett, C., Dill, D., Julian, K., Kochenderfer, M.: Towards proving the adversarial robustness of deep neural networks. In: Proceedings of 1st Workshop on Formal Verification of Autonomous Vehicles (FVAV), pp. 19–26 (2017)
21. Katz, G., et al.: The Marabou framework for verification and analysis of deep neural networks. In: Proceedings of 31st International Conference on Computer Aided Verification (CAV), pp. 443–452 (2019)

22. Kazak, Y., Barrett, C., Katz, G., Schapira, M.: Verifying deep-RL-driven systems. In: Proceedings of 1st ACM SIGCOMM Workshop on Network Meets AI & ML (NetAI), pp. 83–89 (2019)
23. Kuper, L., Katz, G., Gottschlich, J., Julian, K., Barrett, C., Kochenderfer, M.: Toward scalable verification for safety-critical deep networks. Technical report (2018). https://arxiv.org/abs/1801.05950
24. Liu, C., Arnon, T., Lazarus, C., Barrett, C., Kochenderfer, M.: Algorithms for verifying deep neural networks. Technical report (2019). http://arxiv.org/abs/1903.06758
25. Lomuscio, A., Maganti, L.: An approach to reachability analysis for feed-forward ReLU neural networks. Technical report (2017). http://arxiv.org/abs/1706.07351
26. Narodytska, N., Kasiviswanathan, S., Ryzhyk, L., Sagiv, M., Walsh, T.: Verifying properties of binarized deep neural networks. Technical report (2017). http://arxiv.org/abs/1709.06662
27. Silver, D., et al.: Mastering the game of Go with deep neural networks and tree search. Nature **529**(7587), 484–489 (2016)
28. Simonyan, K., Zisserman, A.: Very deep convolutional networks for large-scale image recognition. Technical report (2014). http://arxiv.org/abs/1409.1556
29. Sun, X., Khedr, H., Shoukry, Y.: Formal verification of neural network controlled autonomous systems. In: Proceedings of 22nd ACM International Conference on Hybrid Systems: Computation and Control (HSCC), pp. 147–156 (2019)
30. Szegedy, C., et al.: Intriguing properties of neural networks. Technical report (2013). http://arxiv.org/abs/1312.6199
31. Tjeng, V., Xiao, K., Tedrake, R.: Evaluating robustness of neural networks with mixed integer programming. In: Proceedings of 7th International Conference on Learning Representations (ICLR) (2019)
32. Wang, S., Pei, K., Whitehouse, J., Yang, J., Jana, S.: Formal security analysis of neural networks using symbolic intervals. Technical report (2018). http://arxiv.org/abs/1804.10829

High Assurance Systems

Neural Simplex Architecture

Dung T. Phan[1]([⊠]), Radu Grosu[2], Nils Jansen[3], Nicola Paoletti[4],
Scott A. Smolka[1], and Scott D. Stoller[1]

[1] Department of Computer Science, Stony Brook University, Stony Brook, NY, USA
`dphan@cs.stonybrook.edu`
[2] Department of Computer Engineering, Technische Universität Wien,
Vienna, Austria
[3] Department of Software Science, Radboud University, Nijmegen, The Netherlands
[4] Department of Computer Science, Royal Holloway, University of London,
London, UK

Abstract. We present the *Neural Simplex Architecture* (NSA), a new
approach to runtime assurance that provides safety guarantees for neural controllers (obtained e.g. using reinforcement learning) of autonomous
and other complex systems without unduly sacrificing performance. NSA
is inspired by the Simplex control architecture of Sha et al., but with
some significant differences. In the traditional approach, the advanced
controller (AC) is treated as a black box; when the decision module
switches control to the baseline controller (BC), the BC remains in control forever. There is relatively little work on switching control back to
the AC, and there are no techniques for correcting the AC's behavior
after it generates a potentially unsafe control input that causes a failover
to the BC. Our NSA addresses both of these limitations. NSA not only
provides safety assurances in the presence of a possibly unsafe neural
controller, but can also improve the safety of such a controller in an
online setting via retraining, without overly degrading its performance.
To demonstrate NSA's benefits, we have conducted several significant
case studies in the continuous control domain. These include a target-
seeking ground rover navigating an obstacle field, and a neural controller
for an artificial pancreas system.

Keywords: Runtime assurance · Simplex architecture · Online
retraining · Reverse switching · Safe reinforcement learning

1 Introduction

Deep neural networks (DNNs) in combination with *reinforcement learning* (RL)
are increasingly being used to train powerful *AI agents*. Such agents have
achieved unprecedented success in strategy games, including defeating the world
champion in Go [30] and surpassing state-of-the-art chess and shogi engines [29].
For these agents, safety is not an issue: when a game-playing agent makes a
mistake, the worst-case scenario is losing a game. The same cannot be said for

© Springer Nature Switzerland AG 2020
R. Lee et al. (Eds.): NFM 2020, LNCS 12229, pp. 97–114, 2020.
https://doi.org/10.1007/978-3-030-55754-6_6

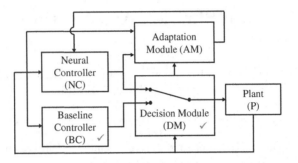

Fig. 1. The Neural Simplex Architecture. The green check marks indicate pre-certified components. (Color figure online)

AI agents that control autonomous and other complex systems. A mistake by an AI controller may cause physical damage to the controlled system and its environment, including humans.

In this paper, we present the *Neural Simplex Architecture* (NSA), a new approach to runtime assurance that provides safety guarantees for AI controllers, including neural controllers, of autonomous and other complex systems without unduly sacrificing performance. NSA is inspired by Sha et al.'s Simplex control architecture [26,28], where a pre-certified *decision module* (DM) switches control from a high-performance but unverified (hence potentially unsafe) *advanced controller* (AC) to a verified-safe *baseline controller* (BC) if the AC produces an *unrecoverable action*; i.e., an action that would lead the system within one time step to a state from which the BC is not guaranteed to preserve safety.

In the traditional Simplex approach, the AC is treated as a black box, and after the DM switches control to the BC, the BC remains in control forever. There is, however, relatively little work on switching control back to the AC [10,18,34], and there are no techniques to correct the AC after it generates an unrecoverable control input.

NSA, illustrated in Fig. 1, addresses both of these limitations. The high-performance *Neural Controller* (NC) is a deep neural network (DNN) that given a plant state (or raw sensor readings), produces a control input for the plant. NSA's use of an NC, as opposed to the black-box AC found in traditional Simplex, allows for online retraining of the NC's DNN. Such retraining is performed by NSA's *Adaptation Module* (AM) using RL techniques. For systems with large state spaces, it may be difficult to achieve thorough coverage during initial training of the NC. Online retraining has the advantage of focusing the learning on areas of the state space that are relevant to the actual system behavior, i.e., regions of the state space the system actually visits.

The AM seeks to eliminate unrecoverable actions from the NC's behavior, without unduly degrading its performance, and in some cases actually improving its performance. While the BC is in control of the plant, the NC runs in shadow mode and is actively retrained by the AM. The DM can subsequently switch control back to the NC with high confidence that it will not repeat the same mistakes, permitting the mission to continue under the auspices of the high-performance NC. Note that because NSA preserves the basic principles of Simplex architecture, it guarantees that the safety of the plant is never violated.

NSA addresses the problem of *safe reinforcement learning* (SRL) [15,38]. In particular, when the learning agent (the NC) produces an unrecoverable action, the AM uses that action as a training sample (but does not execute it), with a large negative reward. A comparison with related approaches to SRL is provided in Sect. 6.

We conducted an extensive evaluation of NSA on several significant example systems, including a target-seeking rover navigating through an obstacle field, and a neural controller for an artificial pancreas. Our results on these case studies conclusively demonstrate NSA's benefits.

In summary, the main contributions of this paper are the following:

- We introduce the Neural Simplex Architecture, a new approach to runtime assurance that provides safety guarantees for neural controllers.
- We address two limitations of the traditional Simplex approach, namely lack of established guidelines for switching control back to the AC so that mission completion can be attained; and lack of techniques for correcting the AC's behavior after a failover to the BC, so that reverse switching makes sense in the first place.
- We provide a key insight into safe reinforcement learning (by demonstrating the utility of potentially unsafe training samples, when appropriately and significantly penalized), along with a thorough evaluation of the NSA approach on two significant case studies.

2   Background

Simplex Architecture. The main components of the Simplex architecture (AC, BC, DM) were introduced above. The BC is certified to guarantee the safety of the plant only if it takes over control while the plant's state is within a *recoverable region* $\mathcal{R}_{BC}$. For example, consider the BC for a ground rover that simply applies maximum deceleration a_{max}. The braking distance to stop the rover from a velocity v is therefore $d_{br}(v) = v^2/(2 \cdot a_{max})$. The BC can be certified to prevent the rover from colliding with an obstacle if it takes over control in a state where $d_{br}(v)$ is less than the minimum distance d_{min} to any obstacle. The set of such states is the recoverable region of this BC.

A control input is called *recoverable* if it keeps the plant inside $\mathcal{R}_{BC}$ within the next time step. Otherwise, the control input is called *unrecoverable*. The DM switches control to the BC when the AC produces an unrecoverable control input. The DM's *switching condition* determines whether a control input is unrecoverable. We also refer to it as the *forward switching condition* (FSC) to distinguish it from the condition for *reverse switching*, a new feature of NSA.

Techniques to determine the FSC include: (i) shrink $\mathcal{R}_{BC}$ by an amount equal to a time step times the maximum gradient of the state with respect to the control input; then classify any control input as unrecoverable if the current state is outside this smaller region; (ii) simulate a model of the plant for one time step if the model is deterministic and check whether the plant strays from $\mathcal{R}_{BC}$; (iii) compute a set of states reachable within one time step and determine whether the reachable set contains states outside $\mathcal{R}_{BC}$.

Reinforcement Learning. Reinforcement learning [32] deals with the problem of how an *agent* learns which sequence of *actions* to take in a given *environment* such that a cumulative *reward* is maximized. At each time step t, the agent receives observation s_t (the environment state) and reward r_t from the environment and takes action a_t. The environment receives action a_t and emits observation s_{t+1} and reward r_{t+1} in response. In the control of autonomous systems, the agent represents the controller, the environment represents the plant, and the state and action spaces are typically continuous.

The goal of RL is to learn a *policy* $\pi(a\,|\,s)$, i.e., a way of choosing an action a having observed s, that maximizes the expected *return* from the initial state, where the return at time t is defined as the discounted sum of future rewards from t (following policy π): $R_t = \sum_{k=t}^{\infty} \gamma^{k-t} r_{k+1}$; here $\gamma \in [0, 1]$ is a discount factor. For this purpose, RL algorithms typically involve estimating the action-value function $Q^\pi(s, a) = \mathbb{E}[R_t \mid s_t = s, a]$, i.e., the expected return for selecting action a in state s and then always following policy π; and the state-value function $V^\pi(s) = \mathbb{E}[R_t \mid s_t = s]$, i.e., the expected return starting from s and following π.

While early RL algorithms were designed for discrete state and action spaces, recent *deep RL* algorithms, such as TRPO [25], DDPG [19], A3C [21], and ACER [36], have emerged as promising solutions for RL-based control problems in continuous domains. These algorithms leverage the expressiveness of deep neural networks (DNNs) to represent policies and value functions.

3   Neural Simplex Architecture

In this section, we discuss the main components of NSA, namely the neural controller (NC), the adaptation module (AM), and the reverse switching logic. These components in particular are not found in the Simplex control architecture.

The dynamics of the plant, i.e., the system under control, is given by $s_{t+1} = f(s_t, a_t)$, where $s_t \in \mathcal{S}$ is the state of the plant at time t, $\mathcal{S} \subseteq \mathbb{R}^n$ is the real-valued state space, f is a possibly nonlinear function, and $a_t \in \mathcal{A}$ is the control input to the plant at time t, with $\mathcal{A} \subseteq \mathbb{R}^m$ the action space. This equation specifies a deterministic dynamics, even though our approach equally supports nondeterministic ($s_{t+1} \in f_{nd}(s_t, a_t)$) and stochastic ($s_{t+1} \sim f_{st}(s \mid s_t, a_t)$) plant dynamics. We assume full observability, i.e., that the BC and NC have access to the full state of the system s_t.[1]

We denote with $\mathrm{DM}_t \in \{\mathrm{NC}, \mathrm{BC}\}$ the state of the decision module at time t: $\mathrm{DM}_t = \mathrm{NC}$ ($\mathrm{DM}_t = \mathrm{BC}$) indicates that the neural (baseline) controller is in

---

[1] In case of partial observability, the full state can typically be reconstructed from sequences of past states and actions, but this process is error-prone.

control. Let a_t^{NC} and a_t^{BC} denote the action computed by the NC and the BC, respectively. The final action a_t performed by the NSA agent depends on the DM state: $a_t = a_t^{NC}$ if $DM_t = NC$, $a_t = a_t^{BC}$ if $DM_t = BC$.

Let β be the BC's control law, i.e., $a_t^{BC} = \beta(s_t)$. For a set of unsafe states $\mathcal{U} \subseteq \mathcal{S}$, the *recoverable region* is the largest set $\mathcal{R}_{BC}$ such that $s \in \mathcal{R}_{BC} \Rightarrow f(s, \beta(s)) \in \mathcal{R}_{BC}$ and $\mathcal{R}_{BC} \cap \mathcal{U} = \emptyset$. For $s \in \mathcal{S}$, $a \in \mathcal{A}$, the forward switching condition must satisfy $f(s, a) \notin \mathcal{R}_{BC} \Rightarrow FSC(s, a)$.

The Neural Controller. The NC is represented by a DNN-based policy π_{θ_t}, where θ_t are the current DNN parameters. The policy maps the current state into a proposed action $a_t^{NC} = \pi_{\theta_t}(s_t)$. We stress the time dependency of the parameters because adaptation and retraining of the policy is a key feature of NSA. As for the dynamics f, our approach supports stochastic policies $(a_t^{NC} \sim \pi(a \mid s_t, \theta_t))$.

The NC can be obtained using any RL algorithm. We used DDPG with the safe learning strategy of penalizing unrecoverable actions, as discussed in Sect. 4. DDPG is attractive as it works with deterministic policies, and allows uncorrelated samples to be added to the pool of samples for training or retraining. The latter property is important because it allows us to collect disconnected samples of what the NC would do while the plant is under the BC's control, and to use these samples for online retraining of the NC.

Adaptation and Retraining. The AM is used to retrain the NC in an online manner while the BC is in control of the plant (due to NC-to-BC failover). The main purpose of this retraining is to make the NC less likely to trigger the FSC, thereby allowing it to remain in control for longer periods of time, thereby improving overall system performance.

Techniques that we consider for online retraining of the NC include supervised learning and reinforcement learning. In supervised learning, state-action pairs of the form (s, a) are required for training purposes. The training algorithm uses these examples to teach the NC safe behavior. The control inputs produced by the BC can be used as training samples, although this will train the NC to imitate BC's behavior, which may lead to a loss in performance.

We therefore prefer SRL for online retraining, with a reward function that penalizes unrecoverable actions and rewards recoverable, high-performing ones. The reward function for retraining can be designed as follows.

$$r(s, a, s') = \begin{cases} r_{unrecov}, & \text{if } FSC(s, a) \\ r_{perf}(s, a, s'), & \text{otherwise} \end{cases} \tag{1}$$

where $r_{perf}(s, a, s')$ is a performance-related reward function, and $r_{unrecov}$ is a negative number used to penalize unrecoverable actions. The benefits of this approach to SRL are discussed in Sect. 4.

The AM retrains the NC at each time step the BC is in control by maintaining a pool of retraining samples of the form (s_t, a_t^{NC}, s', r'), where a_t^{NC} is the NC-proposed action, $s' = f(s_t, a_t^{NC})$ is the state that the system would evolve to if the NC was in control, and $r' = r(s, a_t^{NC}, s')$ is the corresponding reward. I.e., samples are obtained by running the NC in shadow mode: when BC is in control, the AM obtains a retraining sample by running a simulation of the system for one time step and applying a_t^{NC}, while the actual system evolves according to the BC action a_t^{BC}.

The AM updates the NC's parameters θ_t as follows:

$$\theta_t = \begin{cases} \text{RL}(\theta_{t-1}, (s_t, a_t^{NC}, s', r')), & \text{if } \text{DM}_t = \text{BC} \\ \theta_{t-1}, & \text{otherwise} \end{cases}$$

where RL is the deep RL algorithm chosen for NC adaptation. Note that as soon as the DM switches control to the BC after the NC has produced an unrecoverable action (see also the Switching Logic paragraph below), a corresponding retraining sample for the NC's action is added to the pool.

We evaluated a number of variants of this procedure by making different choices along the following dimensions.

1. Start retraining with an empty pool of samples or with the pool created during the initial training of the NC.
2. Add (or do not add) exploration noise to NC's action when collecting a sample. With exploration noise, the resulting action is $a_t^{NC} + \nu_t$, where ν_t is a random noise term. Note that we consider noise only when NC is running in shadow mode (BC in control), as directly using noisy actions to control the plant would degrade performance.
3. Collect retraining samples only while BC is in control or at every time step. In both cases, the action in each training sample is the action output by NC (or a noisy version of it); we never use BC's action in a training sample. Also, in both cases, the retraining algorithm for updating the NC is run only while the BC is in control.

We found that reusing the pool of training samples (DDPG's so-called experience replay buffer) from initial training of the NC helps evolve the policy in a more stable way, as retraining samples gradually replace initial training samples in the sample pool. Another benefit of reusing the initial training pool is that the NC can be immediately retrained without having to wait for enough samples to be collected online. We found that adding exploration noise to NC's actions in retraining samples, and collecting retraining samples at every time step, both increase the benefit of retraining. This is because these two strategies provide more diverse samples and thereby help achieve more thorough exploration of the state-action space.

Switching Logic. NSA includes *reverse switching* from the BC to the retrained NC. An additional benefit of well-designed reverse switching is that it lessens the burden on the BC to achieve performance objectives, leading to a simpler BC design that focuses mainly on safety. Control of the plant is returned to the NC when the reverse switching condition (RSC) is true in the current state. We can summarize NSA's switching logic by describing the evolution of the DM state

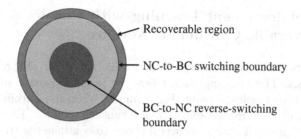

Fig. 2. Switching boundaries. The blue region is a subset of the orange area, which in turn is a subset of the green region. (Color figure online)

DM_t. NSA begins with the NC in control, i.e., $DM_t = NC$ for $t \leq 0$. For $t > 0$, the DM state is given by:

$$DM_t = \begin{cases} BC, & \text{if } DM_{t-1} = NC \text{ and FSC } (s_t, a_t^{NC}) \\ NC, & \text{if } DM_{t-1} = BC \text{ and RSC } (s_t) \\ DM_{t-1}, & \text{otherwise} \end{cases}$$

To ensure safety when returning control to the NC, the FSC must not hold if the RSC is satisfied, i.e., $RSC(s) \Rightarrow \neg FSC(s, a)$, for all $s \in \mathcal{S}, a \in \mathcal{A}$.

We seek to develop reverse switching logic that returns control to NC when it is safe to do so and which avoids frequent back-and-forth switching between the BC and NC. We propose two such approaches. One is to reverse-switch if a forward switch will not occur in the near future. This can be checked by simulating the composition of the NC and plant for T time steps, and reverse-switching if the FSC does not hold within this time horizon.[2] Formally, $RSC(s_t) = \bigwedge_{t'=t}^{t+T} \neg FSC(s'_{t'}, \pi_{\theta_t}(s'_{t'}))$, where $s'_t = s_t$ and $s'_{t'+1} = f(s'_{t'}, \pi_{\theta_t}(s'_{t'}))$. This approach, used in our inverted pendulum and artificial pancreas case studies, prevents frequent switching.

A simpler approach is to reverse-switch if the current plant state is sufficiently far from the NC-to-BC switching boundary; see Fig. 2. Formally, $RSC(s_t) = \sup\{d(s_t, s') \mid s' \in \mathcal{S}, FSC(s', \pi_{\theta_t}(s'))\} > \epsilon$, where d is a metric on $\mathbb{R}^n$ and $\epsilon \in \mathbb{R}^+$ is the desired distance. This approach is used in our rover case study.

We emphasize that the choice of RSC does not affect safety and is application-dependent. Note that both of our approaches construct an RSC that is stricter than a straight complement of the FSC. This helps avoid excessive switching. In our experiments, we empirically observed that the system behavior was not very sensitive to the exact value of T or ϵ; so choosing acceptable values for them is not difficult.

---

[2] For nondeterministic (stochastic) systems, a (probabilistic) model checker can be used instead of a simulator, but this approach may be computationally expensive.

4   Safe Reinforcement Learning with Penalized Unrecoverable Continuous Actions

We evaluate the use of two policy-gradient algorithms for safe reinforcement learning in NSA. The first approach filters the learning agent's unrecoverable actions before they reach the plant. For example, when the learning agent, i.e., the NC, produces an unrecoverable action, a runtime monitor [13] or a preemptive shield [3] replaces it with a recoverable one to continue the trajectory. The recoverable action is also passed to the RL algorithm to update the agent and training continues with the rest of the trajectory.

In the second approach, when the learning agent produces an unrecoverable action, we assign a penalty (negative reward) to the action, use it as a training sample, and then use recoverable actions to safely terminate the trajectory (but not to train the agent). Safely terminating the trajectory is important in cases where for example the live system is used for training. We call this approach *safe reinforcement learning with penalized unrecoverable continuous actions* (SRL-PUA). By "continuous" here we mean real-valued action spaces, as in [9]. Other SRL approaches such as [2] use discrete actions.

To compare the two approaches, we used the DDPG and TRPO algorithms to train neural controllers for an inverted pendulum (IP) control system. Details about our IP case study, including the reward function and the BC used to generate recoverable actions, can be found in [24].

We used the implementations of DDPG and TRPO in rllab [11]. For TRPO, we trained two DNNs, one for the mean and the other for the standard deviation of a Gaussian policy. Both DNNs have two fully connected hidden layers of 32 neurons each and one output layer. The hidden layers use the `tanh` activation function, and the output layer is linear. For DDPG, we trained a DNN that computes the action directly from the state. The DNN has two fully connected hidden layers of 32 neurons each and one output layer. The hidden layers use the `ReLU` activation function, and the output layer uses `tanh`. We followed the choice of activation functions in the examples accompanying rllab.

For each algorithm, we ran two training experiments. In one experiment, we reproduce the filtering approach; i.e., we replace an unrecoverable action produced by the learning agent with the BC's recoverable action, use the latter as the training sample, and continue the trajectory. We call this training method SRL-BC. In the other experiment, we evaluate the SRL-PUA approach. Note that both algorithms explore different trajectories by resetting the system to a random initial state whenever the current trajectory is terminated. We set the maximum trajectory length to 500 time steps, meaning that a trajectory is terminated when it exceeds 500 time steps.

We trained the DDPG and TRPO agents on a total of one million time steps. After training, we evaluated all trained policies on the same set of 1,000 random initial states. During evaluation, if an agent produces an unrecoverable action, the trajectory is terminated. The results are shown in Table 1. For both algorithms, the policies trained with recoverable actions (the SRL-BC approach) produce unrecoverable actions in all test trajectories, while the SRL-PUA approach, where the policies are trained with penalties for unrecoverable actions, does not produce any such actions. As such, the latter policies achieve superior returns and trajectory lengths (they are able to safely control the system the entire time).

In the above experiments, we replaced unrecoverable actions with actions generated by a deterministic BC, whereas the monitoring [13] and preemptive shielding [2] approaches allow unrecoverable actions to be replaced with random recoverable ones, an approach we refer to as SRL-RND. To show that our conclusions are independent of this difference, we ran one more experiment with each learning algorithm, in which we replaced each unrecoverable action with an action selected by randomly generating actions until a recoverable one is found. The results, shown in Table 2, once again demonstrate that training with only recoverable actions is ineffective. Compared to filtering-based approaches (SRL-BC in Table 1 and SRL-RND in Table 2), the SRL-PUA approach yields a 25- to 775-fold improvement in the average return.

Table 1. Policy performance comparison. **SRL-BC**: policy trained with BC's actions replacing unrecoverable ones. **SRL-PUA**: policy trained with penalized unsafe actions. **Unrec Trajs**: # trajectories terminated due to an unrecoverable action. **Comp Trajs**: # trajectories that reach the limit of 500 time steps. **Avg. Return** and **Avg. Length**: average return and trajectory length over 1,000 trajectories.

	TRPO		DDPG	
	SRL-BC	**SRL-PUA**	**SRL-BC**	**SRL-PUA**
Unrec Trajs	1,000	0	1,000	0
Comp Trajs	0	1,000	0	1,000
Avg. Return	112.53	4,603.97	61.52	4,596.04
Avg. Length	15.15	500	14.56	500

Table 2. Policy performance comparison. **SRL-RND**: policy trained with random recoverable actions replacing unrecoverable ones.

	TRPO		DDPG	
	SRL-RND	**SRL-PUA**	**SRL-RND**	**SRL-PUA**
Unrec Trajs	1,000	0	1,000	0
Comp Trajs	0	1,000	0	1,000
Avg. Return	183.36	4,603.97	5.93	4,596.04
Avg. Length	1.93	500	14	500

5   Case Studies

An additional case study, the Inverted Pendulum, along with further details about the case studies presented in this section can be found in [24].

5.1   Rover Navigation

We consider the problem of navigating a rover to a predetermined target location while avoiding collisions with static obstacles. The rover is a circular disk of radius r. It has a maximum speed v_{max} and a maximum acceleration a_{max}. The maximum braking time is therefore $t_{br\_max} = v_{max}/a_{max}$, and the maximum braking distance is $d_{br\_max} = v_{max}^2/(2 \cdot a_{max})$. The control inputs are the accelerations a_x and a_y in the x and y directions, respectively. The system uses discrete-time control with a time step of dt.

The rover has n distance sensors whose detection range is l_{max}. The sensors are placed evenly around the perimeter of the rover; i.e., the center lines of sight of two adjacent sensors form an angle of $2\pi/n$. The rover can only move forwards, so its orientation is the same as its heading angle. The state vector for the rover is $[x, y, \theta, v, l_1, l_2, ..., l_n]$, where (x, y) is the position, θ is the heading angle, v is the velocity, and the l_i's are the sensor readings.

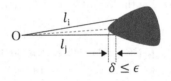

Fig. 3. Illustration of assumptions about obstacle shapes.

We assume the sensors have a small angular field-of-view so that each sensor reading reflects the distance from the rover to an obstacle along the sensor's center line of sight. If a sensor does not detect an obstacle, its reading is l_{max}.

We also assume that when the sensor readings of two adjacent sensors s_i and s_j are l_i and l_j, respectively, then the (conservative) minimum distance to any obstacle point located in the cone formed by the center lines of sight of s_i and s_j is $\min\{l_i, l_j\} - \epsilon$. Here, ϵ is a constant that limits by how much an obstacle can protrude into the blind spot between s_i and s_j's lines of sight; see Fig. 3.

A state s of the rover is *recoverable* if starting from s, the baseline controller (BC) can brake to a stop at least distance d_{safe} from any obstacle. Let the braking distance in state s be $d_{br}(s) = v^2/(2 \cdot a_{max})$, where v is the rover's speed in s. Then s is recoverable if the minimum sensor reading l_{min} in state s is at least $d_{safe} + d_{br}(s) + \epsilon$.

The FSC holds when the control input u_{NC} proposed by the NC will put the rover in an unrecoverable state in the next time step. We check this condition by simulating the rover for one time step with u_{NC} as the control input, and by then determining if $l_{min} < d_{safe} + d_{br}(s) + \epsilon$.

The RSC is $l_{min} \geq m \cdot v_{max} \cdot dt + d_{safe} + d_{br\_max} + \epsilon$, ensuring that the FSC does not hold for the next $m - 1$ time steps. Parameter m can be chosen to reduce excessive back-and-forth switching between the NC and BC.

The BC performs the following steps: 1) Apply the maximum braking power a_{max} until the rover stops. 2) Randomly pick a safe heading angle θ based on the current position and sensor readings. 3) Rotate the rover until its heading angle is θ. 4) Move with heading angle θ until either the FSC becomes true (this is checked after each time step by the BC itself), in which case the BC is re-started at Step 1, or the RSC becomes true (this is checked by the DM), in which case the NC takes over.

Experimental Results. Parameter values used: $r = 0.1\,\text{m}$, $v_{max} = 0.8\,\text{m/s}$, $a_{max} = 1.6\,\text{m/s}^2$, $l_{max} = 2\,\text{m}$, $n = 32$, $d_{safe} = 0.2\,\text{m}$, $\epsilon = 0.01\,\text{m}$, $m = 5$, $dt = 0.1\,\text{s}$. The target is a circular disk at location $(0,0)$ with a radius of 0.1m. The obstacle field, which is fixed during training and testing, consists of 12 circular obstacles with a minimum radius of 0.25m. Rover initial position (x_0, y_0) is randomized in the area $[-5, 5] \times [-5, 5]$.[3] We assume that the sensor field-of-view is at least $7.25°$, thereby satisfying the assumption that an obstacle does not protrude more than ϵ into the blind spot between adjacent sensors. See also Fig. 3. The NC is a DNN with two ReLU hidden layers, each of size 64, and a tanh output layer. We used the DDPG algorithm for both initial training and online retraining of the NC. For initial training, we ran DDPG for 5 million time steps. The reward function for initial training and online retraining is:

$$r(s, a, s') = \begin{cases} -20,000, & \text{if FSC}(s, a) \\ 10,000, & \text{if DT}(s) \leq 0.2 \\ -1 - 20 \cdot \text{DT}(s), & \text{otherwise} \end{cases} \tag{2}$$

where $\text{FSC}(s, a)$ is the forward switching condition and $\text{DT}(s)$ is the center-to-center distance from the rover to the target in state s. The rover is considered to have reached the target if $\text{DT}(s) \leq 0.2$, as, recall, the target is a circular disk with radius of $0.1\,\text{m}$ and the radius r of the rover is 0.1m. If the action a triggers the forward switching logic, it is penalized by assigning it a negative reward of -20,000. If a causes the rover to reach the target, it receives a positive reward of 10,000. All other actions are penalized by an amount proportional to the distance to the target, encouraging the agent to reach the target quickly.

Our experiments with online retraining use the same DDPG settings as in initial training, except that we initialize the AM's pool of retraining samples with the pool created by initial training, instead of an empty pool. The pool created by initial training contains one million samples; this is the maximum pool size,

---

[3] Although the obstacles are fixed, the NC still generalizes well (but not perfectly) to random obstacle fields not seen during training, as shown in this video https://youtu.be/ICT8D1unilw.

which is a parameter of the algorithm. When creating retraining samples, the AM adds Gaussian noise to the NC's actions. The NC's actions are collected (added to the pool) at every time step, regardless of which controller is in control; thus, the AM also collects samples of what the NC would do while the BC is in control.

We ran the NSA instance starting from 10,000 random initial states. Out of 10,000 trajectories, forward switching occurred in 456 of them. Of these 456 trajectories, the BC was in control for a total of 70,974 time steps. This means there were 70,974 ($\sim$71K) retraining updates to the NC. To evaluate the benefits of online retraining, we compared the performance of the NC after initial training and after 20K, 50K, and 71 K online updates. We evaluated the performance of each of these controllers (by itself, without NSA) by running it from the same set of 1,000 random initial states.

The results in Table 3 show that after 71 K retraining updates, the NC outperforms the initially trained version on every metric. Table 3 also shows that the NC's performance increases with the number of retraining updates, thus demonstrating that NSA's online retraining not only improves the safety of the NC, but also its performance.

Table 3. Benefits of online retraining ($\sim$71K NC updates in total) for ground rover navigation. **IT**: results for initially trained NC. **20K RT**, **50K RT**, **71K RT**: results for NC after 20K, 50K, 71K retraining updates. All controllers evaluated on same set of 1,000 random initial states. **FSCs**: # trajectories in which FSC becomes true. **Timeouts**: # trajectories that reach the limit of 500 time steps without reaching target or having FSC become true. **Targets**: # trajectories that reach the target. **Avg. Ret.** and **Avg. Len.**: average return and average trajectory length over all 1,000 trajectories.

	IT	20K RT	50K RT	71K RT
FSCs	100	79	43	8
Timeouts	35	49	50	22
Targets	865	872	907	970
Avg. Ret.	−9,137.3	−9,968.8	−5,314.6	−684.0
Avg. Len.	138.67	142.29	156.13	146.56

We resumed initial training to see if this would produce similar improvements. Specifically, we continued the initial training for an additional 71K, 1M, and 3M samples. The results, included in [24], show that extending the initial training slowly improves both the safety and performance of the NC but requires substantially more updates. 71K retraining updates provide significantly more benefits than even 3M additional samples of initial training.

5.2 Artificial Pancreas

The artificial pancreas (AP) is used to control blood glucose (BG) levels in Type 1 diabetes patients through automated delivery of insulin. We use the linear plant model of [6] to describe the physiological state of the patient. The main state variable of interest is G, which is the difference between the reference BG (7.8 mmol/L) and the patient's BG. The control action, i.e., the insulin input, is denoted by u. Further details of this model, including its ODE dynamics, can be found in [24].

The AP should maintain BG levels within the safe range of 4 to 11 mmol/L. In particular, it should avoid hypoglycemia (i.e., BG levels below the safe range), which can lead to severe health consequences. Hypoglycemia occurs when the controller overshoots the insulin dose. Insulin control is uniquely challenging because the controller cannot take a corrective action to counteract an excessive dose; its most extreme safety measure is to turn off the insulin pump. Hence, the baseline controller for the AP sets $u = 0$.

We intentionally under-train the initial NC so that it exhibits low performance and produces unrecoverable actions. Low-performing AP controllers may arise in practice for several reasons, e.g., when the training-time model parameters do not match the current real-life patient parameters.

The reward function r is designed to penalize deviations from the reference BG level, as captured by state variable G. We assign a positive reward when G is close to zero (within ± 1), and we penalize larger deviations with a $5\times$ factor for mild hyperglycemia ($1 < G \leq 3.2$), a $7\times$ factor for mild hypoglycemia ($-3.8 \leq G < -1$), $9\times$ for strong hyperglycemia ($G > 3.2$), and $20\times$ for strong hypoglycemia ($G < -3.8$). The other constants are chosen to avoid jump discontinuities in the reward function.

$$
r(s, u, s') = \begin{cases}
10 - |G'|, & \text{if } |G'| \leq 1 \\
14 - 5 \cdot |G'|, & \text{if } 1 < G' \leq 3.2 \\
26.8 - 9 \cdot |G'|, & \text{if } G' > 3.2 \\
16 - 7 \cdot |G'|, & \text{if } -3.8 \leq G' < -1 \\
65.4 - 20 \cdot |G'| & \text{otherwise}
\end{cases}
$$

where G' is the value of G in state s'.

An AP plant state s is *recoverable* if under the control of the BC, a state where $G' < -3.8$ cannot be reached starting from s. This condition can be checked by simulation. The FSC holds when the NC's action leads to an unrecoverable state in the next time step. For reverse switching, we return control to the NC if the FSC does not hold within time $T = 10$ from the current state.

Experimental Results. To produce an under-trained NC, we used 107,000 time steps of initial training. We ran NSA on the under-trained controller on 10,000 trajectories, each starting from a random initial state. Among the first 400 trajectories, 250 led to forward switching and hence retraining. The retraining was very effective, as forward switching did not occur after the first 400 trajectories.

As in the other case studies we conducted, we then evaluated the benefits of retraining by comparing the performance of the initially trained NC and the retrained NC on trajectories starting from the same set of 1,000 random initial states. The results are given in Table 4. Retraining greatly improves the safety of the NC: the initially trained controller reaches an unrecoverable state in all 1,000 of these trajectories, while the retrained controller never does. The retrained controller's performance is also significantly enhanced, with an average return 2.9 times that of the initial controller.

Table 4. Benefits of retraining for the AP case study. There were 61 updates to the NC. Row labels are as per Table 1.

	Initially trained	Retrained
Unrecov Trajs	1,000	0
Complete Trajs	0	1,000
Avg. Return	824	2,402
Avg. Length	217	500

6 Related Work

The original Simplex architecture did not consider reverse switching. In [26, 27], when the AC produces an unrecoverable action, it is disabled until it is manually re-enabled. It is briefly mentioned in [18] that reverse switching should be performed only when the FSC is false, and that a stricter RSC might be needed to prevent frequent switching, but the paper does not pursue this idea further. A more general approach to reverse switching, which uses reachability analysis to determine if the plant is safe in the next two time steps irrespective of the controller, is presented in [10]. This approach results in more conservative reverse switching conditions, as it does not take the behavior of the AC into account, unlike one of the approaches we propose. The idea of reverse switching when the AC's outputs are stabilized is briefly mentioned in [34].

Regarding approaches to safe reinforcement learning (SRL), we refer the reader to two recent comprehensive literature reviews [15, 38]. Bootstrapping of policies that are known to be safe in certain environments is employed in [31], while [16] restricts exploration to a portion of the state space close to an optimal, pre-computed policy.

In [3], the authors synthesize a *shield* (a.k.a. *post-posed shield*) from a temporal-logic safety specification based on knowledge of the system dynamics. The shield monitors and corrects an agent's actions to ensure safety. This approach targets systems with finite state and action spaces. Suitable finite-state abstractions are needed for infinite-state systems. In [5], the shield-based approach is extended to stochastic systems. In contrast, NSA's policy-gradient-based approach is directly applicable to systems with infinite state spaces and continuous action spaces.

In [13], the authors use formally verified runtime monitors in the RL training phase to constrain the actions taken by the learning agent to a set of safe actions.

The idea of using the learned policy together with a known-safe fallback policy in the deployed system is mentioned, but further details are not provided. In contrast, we discuss in detail how the NSA approach guarantees runtime safety and how SRL is is used for online retraining of the NC. In [14], a verification-preserving procedure is proposed for learning updates to the environment model when SRL is used and the exact model is not initially known. The approach to SRL is mainly taken from [13], so again the learned policy is not guaranteed safe. Note that the SRL approach of [13,14] allows the training algorithm to speculate when the plant model is deviating from reality.

Other approaches to SRL incorporate formal methods to constrain the SRL exploration process. These include the use of (probabilistic) temporal logic [17,20,37], ergodicity-based notions of safety [22], and providing probably approximately correct (PAC) guarantees [12]. All of these techniques work on finite state spaces.

In [8], the authors use Lyapunov functions in the framework of constrained Markov decision processes to guarantee policy safety during training. They focus on policy-iteration and Q-learning for discrete state and action problems. Their approach is currently not applicable to policy-gradient algorithms, such as the DDPG algorithm used in our experiments, nor continuous state/action problems. Lyapuanov functions are also used in [4] for SRL, but it likewise cannot be used for policy-gradient algorithms.

In [33], the authors propose Reward Constrained Policy Optimization (RCPO), where a per-state weighted penalty term is added to the reward function. Such weights are updated during training. RCPO is shown to almost surely converge to a solution, but does not address the problem of guaranteeing safety during training. In contrast, we penalize unrecoverable actions and safely terminate the current trajectory to ensure plant safety.

In [1], the authors present the Constrained Policy Optimization algorithm for constrained MDPs, which guarantees safe exploration during training. CPO only ensures approximate satisfaction of constraints and provides an upper bound on the cost associated with constraint violations. In [23], the authors use control barrier functions (CBFs) for SRL. Whenever the learning agent produces an unsafe action, it is minimally perturbed to preserve safety. In contrast, in NSA, when the NC proposes an unsafe action, the BC takes over and the NC is retrained by the AM. CBFs are also used in [7].

Similar to the shield-based method, a safety layer is inserted between the policy and the plant in [9]. Like the CBF approach, the safety layer uses quadratic programming to minimally perturb the action to ensure safety. There are, however, no formal guarantees of safety because of the data-driven linearization of the constraint function.

7   Conclusions

We have presented the Neural Simplex Architecture for assuring the runtime safety of systems with neural controllers. NSA features an adaptation module that retrains the NC in an online fashion, seeking to eliminate its faulty behavior without unduly sacrificing performance. NSA's reverse switching capability allows control of the plant to be returned to the NC after a failover to BC, thereby allowing NC's performance benefits to come back into play. We have demonstrated the utility of NSA on three significant case studies in the continuous control domain.

As future work, we plan to investigate methods for establishing statistical bounds on the degree of improvement that online retraining yields in terms of safety and performance of the NC. We also plan to incorporate techniques from the L1Simplex architecture [35] to deal with deviations of the plant model's behavior from the actual behavior.

Acknowledgments. We thank the anonymous reviewers for their helpful comments. This material is based upon work supported in part by NSF grants CCF-191822, CPS-1446832, IIS-1447549, CNS-1445770, and CCF-1414078, FWF-NFN RiSE Award, and ONR grant N00014-15-1-2208. Any opinions, findings, and conclusions or recommendations expressed in this material are those of the author(s) and do not necessarily reflect the views of these organizations.

References

1. Achiam, J., Held, D., Tamar, A., Abbeel, P.: Constrained policy optimization. In: International Conference on Machine Learning, pp. 22–31 (2017)
2. Alshiekh, M., Bloem, R., Ehlers, R., Könighofer, B., Niekum, S., Topcu, U.: Safe reinforcement learning via shielding. arXiv preprint arXiv:1708.08611 (2017)
3. Alshiekh, M., Bloem, R., Ehlers, R., Könighofer, B., Niekum, S., Topcu, U.: Safe reinforcement learning via shielding. In: AAAI (2018). https://www.aaai.org/ocs/index.php/AAAI/AAAI18/paper/view/17211
4. Berkenkamp, F., Turchetta, M., Schoellig, A., Krause, A.: Safe model-based reinforcement learning with stability guarantees. In: Advances in Neural Information Processing Systems, pp. 908–918 (2017)
5. Bouton, M., Karlsson, J., Nakhaei, A., Fujimura, K., Kochenderfer, M.J., Tumova, J.: Reinforcement learning with probabilistic guarantees for autonomous driving. CoRR abs/1904.07189 (2019)
6. Chen, H., Paoletti, N., Smolka, S.A., Lin, S.: Committed moving horizon estimation for meal detection and estimation in type 1 diabetes. In: American Control Conference (ACC 2019), pp. 4765–4772 (2019)
7. Cheng, R., Orosz, G., Murray, R.M., Burdick, J.W.: End-to-end safe reinforcement learning through barrier functions for safety-critical continuous control tasks. AAAI (2019)
8. Chow, Y., Nachum, O., Duenez-Guzman, E., Ghavamzadeh, M.: A Lyapunov-based approach to safe reinforcement learning. In: Advances in Neural Information Processing Systems, pp. 8103–8112 (2018)
9. Dalal, G., Dvijotham, K., Vecerik, M., Hester, T., Paduraru, C., Tassa, Y.: Safe exploration in continuous action spaces. arXiv e-prints (2018)
10. Desai, A., Ghosh, S., Seshia, S.A., Shankar, N., Tiwari, A.: A runtime assurance framework for programming safe robotics systems. In: IEEE/IFIP International Conference on Dependable Systems and Networks (DSN) (2019)

11. Duan, Y., Chen, X., Houthooft, R., Schulman, J., Abbeel, P.: Benchmarking deep reinforcement learning for continuous control. In: Proceedings of the 33rd International Conference on Machine Learning ICML 2016, vol. 48, pp. 1329–1338 (2016). http://dl.acm.org/citation.cfm?id=3045390.3045531

12. Fu, J., Topcu, U.: Probably approximately correct MDP learning and control with temporal logic constraints. In: 2014 Robotics: Science and Systems Conference (2014)

13. Fulton, N., Platzer, A.: Safe reinforcement learning via formal methods. In: AAAI 2018 (2018)

14. Fulton, N., Platzer, A.: Verifiably safe off-model reinforcement learning. In: Vojnar, T., Zhang, L. (eds.) TACAS 2019. LNCS, vol. 11427, pp. 413–430. Springer, Cham (2019). https://doi.org/10.1007/978-3-030-17462-0_28

15. García, J., Fernández, F.: A comprehensive survey on safe reinforcement learning. J. Mach. Learn. Res. **16**(1), 1437–1480 (2015). http://dl.acm.org/citation.cfm?id=2789272.2886795

16. García, J., Fernández, F.: Probabilistic policy reuse for safe reinforcement learning. ACM Trans. Auton. Adapt. Syst. (TAAS) **13**(3), 14 (2019)

17. Hasanbeig, M., Abate, A., Kroening, D.: Logically-correct reinforcement learning. CoRR abs/1801.08099 (2018)

18. Johnson, T., Bak, S., Caccamo, M., Sha, L.: Real-time reachability for verified Simplex design. ACM Trans. Embed. Comput. Syst. **15**(2), 26:1–26:27 (2016). https://doi.org/10.1145/2723871, http://doi.acm.org/10.1145/2723871

19. Lillicrap, T., et al.: Continuous control with deep reinforcement learning. arXiv preprint arXiv:1509.02971 (2015)

20. Mason, G., Calinescu, R., Kudenko, D., Banks, A.: Assured reinforcement learning with formally verified abstract policies. In: ICAART, no. 2, pp. 105–117. SciTePress (2017)

21. Mnih, V., et al.: Asynchronous methods for deep reinforcement learning. In: ICML, pp. 1928–1937 (2016)

22. Moldovan, T.M., Abbeel, P.: Safe exploration in Markov decision processes. In: ICML. icml.cc/Omnipress (2012)

23. Ohnishi, M., Wang, L., Notomista, G., Egerstedt, M.: Barrier-certified adaptive reinforcement learning with applications to Brushbot navigation. IEEE Trans. Robot. 1–20 (2019). https://doi.org/10.1109/TRO.2019.2920206

24. Phan, D., Paoletti, N., Grosu, R., Jansen, N., Smolka, S.A., Stoller, S.D.: Neural simplex architecture. arXiv preprint arXiv:1908.00528 (2019)

25. Schulman, J., Levine, S., Abbeel, P., Jordan, M., Moritz, P.: Trust region policy optimization. In: ICML, pp. 1889–1897 (2015)

26. Seto, D., Krogh, B., Sha, L., Chutinan, A.: The Simplex architecture for safe online control system upgrades. In: Proceedings of 1998 American Control Conference, vol. 6, pp. 3504–3508 (1998). https://doi.org/10.1109/ACC.1998.703255

27. Seto, D., Sha, L., Compton, N.: A case study on analytical analysis of the inverted pendulum real-time control system (1999)

28. Sha, L.: Using simplicity to control complexity. IEEE Softw. **18**(4), 20–28 (2001). https://doi.org/10.1109/MS.2001.936213

29. Silver, D., Hubert, T., Schrittwieser, J., et al.: Mastering chess and shogi by self-play with a general reinforcement learning algorithm. arXiv preprint arXiv:1712.01815 (2017)

30. Silver, D., Schrittwieser, J., Simonyan, K., et al.: Mastering the game of Go without human knowledge. Nature **550**(7676), 354 (2017)

31. Simão, T.D., Spaan, M.T.J.: Safe policy improvement with baseline bootstrapping in factored environments. In: AAAI, pp. 4967–4974. AAAI Press (2019)

32. Sutton, R., Barto, A.: Reinforcement Learning: An Introduction. MIT Press, Cambridge (1998)

33. Tessler, C., Mankowitz, D.J., Mannor, S.: Reward constrained policy optimization. arXiv e-prints (2018)

34. Vivekanandan, P., Garcia, G., Yun, H., Keshmiri, S.: A Simplex architecture for intelligent and safe unmanned aerial vehicles. In: 2016 IEEE 22nd International Conference on Embedded and Real-Time Computing Systems and Applications (RTCSA), pp. 69–75 (2016). https://doi.org/10.1109/RTCSA.2016.17

35. Wang, X., Hovakimyan, N., Sha, L.: L1Simplex: fault-tolerant control of cyber-physical systems. In: 2013 ACM/IEEE International Conference on Cyber-Physical Systems (ICCPS), pp. 41–50 (2013)

36. Wang, Z., et al.: Sample efficient actor-critic with experience replay. arXiv preprint arXiv:1611.01224 (2016)

37. Wen, M., Ehlers, R., Topcu, U.: Correct-by-synthesis reinforcement learning with temporal logic constraints. In: IROS, pp. 4983–4990. IEEE Computer Society Press (2015)

38. Xiang, W., et al.: Verification for machine learning, autonomy, and neural networks survey. arXiv e-prints (2018)

Strengthening Deterministic Policies for POMDPs

Leonore Winterer[1]([⊠]), Ralf Wimmer[1,2], Nils Jansen[3], and Bernd Becker[1]

[1] Albert-Ludwigs-Universität Freiburg, Freiburg im Breisgau, Germany
{winterel,wimmer,becker}@informatik.uni-freiburg.de
[2] Concept Engineering GmbH, Freiburg im Breisgau, Germany
[3] Radboud University, Nijmegen, The Netherlands
n.jansen@science.ru.nl

Abstract. The synthesis problem for partially observable Markov decision processes (POMDPs) is to compute a policy that satisfies a given specification. Such policies have to take the full execution history of a POMDP into account, rendering the problem undecidable in general. A common approach is to use a limited amount of memory and randomize over potential choices. Yet, this problem is still NP-hard and often computationally intractable in practice. A restricted problem is to use neither history nor randomization, yielding policies that are called stationary and deterministic. Previous approaches to compute such policies employ mixed-integer linear programming (MILP). We provide a novel MILP encoding that supports sophisticated specifications in the form of temporal logic constraints. It is able to handle an arbitrary number of such specifications. Yet, randomization and memory are often mandatory to achieve satisfactory policies. First, we extend our encoding to deliver a restricted class of randomized policies. Second, based on the results of the original MILP, we employ a preprocessing of the POMDP to encompass memory-based decisions. The advantages of our approach over state-of-the-art POMDP solvers lie (1) in the flexibility to strengthen simple deterministic policies without losing computational tractability and (2) in the ability to enforce the provable satisfaction of arbitrarily many specifications. The latter point allows to take trade-offs between performance and safety aspects of typical POMDP examples into account. We show the effectiveness of our method on a broad range of benchmarks.

1 Introduction

Partially observable Markov decision processes (POMDPs) are a formal model for planning under uncertainty in partially observable environments [23,37]. POMDPs adequately model a number of real-world applications, see for instance [33,43]. While an agent operates in a scenario modeled by a POMDP, it receives *observations* and tries to infer the likelihood of the system being in a certain state, the belief state. Together with a belief update function, the space of all belief states forms a (uncountably infinite) *belief MDP* [5,26,35].

© Springer Nature Switzerland AG 2020
R. Lee et al. (Eds.): NFM 2020, LNCS 12229, pp. 115–132, 2020.
https://doi.org/10.1007/978-3-030-55754-6_7

Consider the following simple example [11] as sketched in Fig. 1. A space shuttle has to transport goods between two stations, while docking at these stations is subject to failure with certain probabilities. The perception of the shuttle is limited in the sense that it will only see the stations if it is directly facing them. If not, it can only see empty space and has to infer from the history which of the stations is the next one to deliver goods to.

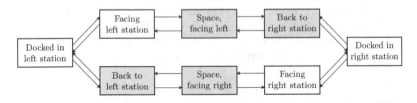

Fig. 1. The space shuttle benchmark – yellow states share an observation. Transitions have been simplified for clarity. (Color figure online)

Traditional POMDP problems typically comprise the computation of a policy that maximizes a cumulative reward over a finite horizon. However, the application may require that the agent's behavior obeys more complicated specifications. For example, temporal logics (e.g., LTL [31]) describe task properties like reachability or liveness that cannot be expressed using reward functions [25]. For the aforementioned space shuttle, maximizing the reward corresponds to maximizing the number of succesful deliveries. Additional specifications may for instance require the shuttle to only navigate in empty space for a limited number of steps.

Policy synthesis for POMDPs is hard. For infinite- or indefinite-horizon problems, computing an optimal policy is undecidable [26]. Optimal action choices depend on the whole history of observations and actions, and thus require an infinite amount of memory. When restricting the specifications to maximizing accumulated rewards over a finite horizon and also limiting the available memory, computing an optimal policy is PSPACE-complete [29]. This problem is, practically, intractable even for small instances [27]. When policies are restricted to be *memoryless*, finding an optimal policy within this set is still NP-hard [39]. For the more general LTL specifications, synthesis of policies with limited memory is even EXPTIME-complete [8].

State-of-the-art. The aforementioned hardness and intractability of the computation of exact solutions for the POMDP problems discussed earlier triggered several feasible approaches. Notably, there are approximate [20], point-based [30], or Monte-Carlo-based [36] methods. Yet, none of these approaches provides guarantees for temporal logic specifications. The tool PRISM-pomdp [28] actually provides guarantees by approximating the belief space into a fully observable belief MDP, but is restricted to small examples. Other techniques, such as those employing an incremental satisfiability modulo theory (SMT) solver over a bounded belief space [40] or a simulation over sets of belief models [18], are

also restricted to small examples. [42] employs a game-based abstraction approach to efficiently solve problems with specific properties. In [22], finite-state
controllers for POMDPs are computed using parameter synthesis for Markov
chains [19,21] by applying convex optimization techniques [12,13]. Another work
employs machine learning techniques together with formal verification to achieve
sound but not optimal solutions [7].

Our Approach. The problem we consider in this paper is to compute a policy for
a POMDP that provably satisfies one or more specifications such as temporal
logic constraints and expected (discounted) reward properties. First, we restrict
ourselves to a simple class of policies which are both memoryless and do not
randomize over action choices, that is, they are *deterministic*. A natural approach
encodes this problem as a mixed-integer linear program (MILP) [34]. We extend
previous approaches [2,24] to account for multiple specifications and provide a
particular encoding for temporal logic constraints. The advantage is that these
MILPs yield simple, small, and easy-to-analyze policies which can be computed
by efficient state-of-the-art tools like Gurobi [17].

However, policies that incorporate randomization over choices often trade
off the necessity of memory-based decisions [1,10], and randomization may be
needed for multiple objectives [3,15]. To preserve the advantages of MILP solving, we propose *static randomization*. We augment the MILP encoding in the
following way. In addition to deterministic choices, the policy may to select an
arbitrary but fixed distribution over all possible actions. As we will demonstrate
in this paper, often any distribution is sufficient as long as randomization is
possible.

Yet, for certain problems a notion of (at least finite) memory is required. As
a third step to strengthen deterministic policies, we perform a preprocessing of
the POMDP regarding previous computations for purely deterministic policies.
At states where the choices are bad according to the specifications, we perform a
technique we call *observation and state splitting* which essentially encodes finite
memory into the state space of the POMDP. Intuitively, we enable a policy to
distinguish states that previously shared an observation.

Summarized, we provide three contributions. First, we enable the computation of deterministic polices that provably adhere to multiple specifications.
Second, we augment the underlying MILP to account for randomization using
fixed distributions over actions. Third, we introduce a novel POMDP preprocessing which encodes finite memory into critical states. We showcase the feasibility
and competitiveness of our approach by a thorough experimental evaluation on
well-known case studies.

2   Preliminaries

For a finite or countably infinite set X, $\mu \colon X \to [0,1]$ with $\sum_{x \in X} \mu(x) = 1$
denotes a *probability distribution* over X; the set of all probability distributions
over X is $Dist(X)$. A partial function $f \colon X \nrightarrow Y$ is a function $f \colon X' \to Y$ for
some subset $X' = \mathrm{dom}(f) \subset X$.

Definition 1 (Markov Decision Process). *A Markov Decision Process (MDP) is a tuple* $M = (S, s_{init}, Act, P, R)$ *where* S *is a finite set of* states, $s_{init} \in S$ *the* initial state, Act *a finite set of* actions, $P: S \times Act \nrightarrow Dist(S)$ *a (partial) probabilistic transition function, and* $R: S \times Act \rightarrow \mathbb{R}$ *a reward function that assigns to every tuple* $(s, \alpha) \in \mathrm{dom}(P)$ *a real-valued reward.*

The set of actions that are enabled in s is $Act(s) = \{\alpha \in Act \mid (s, \alpha) \in \mathrm{dom}(P)\}$.

A partially observable Markov decision process (*POMDP*) [23] models restricted knowledge of the current state of an MDP.

Definition 2 (POMDP). *A partially observable Markov decision process (POMDP) is a tuple* $D = (M, \mathcal{O}, \lambda)$ *such that* $M = (S, s_{init}, Act, P, R)$ *is the underlying MDP of* D, $\mathcal{O}$ *a finite set of* observations, *and* $\lambda: S \rightarrow \mathcal{O}$ *the* observation function.

Note that in our definition of a POMDP each state has exactly one observation. Sometimes a more general definition of POMDPs is used, in which the observation function depends not only on the current state, but also on the previous action, and returns not a fixed observation, but a probability distribution over the possible observations. However, there is a polynomial reduction from this general case to the one we use in this work [9].

Definition 3 (Path). *A sequence* $\pi = s_0 \alpha_0 s_1 \alpha_1 \ldots$ *with* $s_i \in S$, $\alpha_i \in Act$ *and* $P(s_i, \alpha_i)(s_{i+1}) > 0$ *for all* $i \geq 0$ *is called a* path. *Paths can be finite (ending in a state) or infinite. The set of finite paths is* Paths_{fin} *and the set of infinite paths* Paths_{inf}. *For a finite path* π, *we denote by* $last(\pi)$ *the final state of* π.

Definition 4 (Observation Sequence). *If* $\pi = s_0 \alpha_0 s_1 \alpha_1 \ldots s_{n-1} \alpha_{n-1} s_n$ *is a finite path, then* $\theta := \lambda(\pi) := \lambda(s_0) \alpha_0 \lambda(s_1) \alpha_1 \ldots \lambda(s_{n-1}) \alpha_{n-1} \lambda(s_n)$ *is called the* observation sequence *of* π.

Before a probability space over paths of (PO)MDPs can be defined, the nondeterminism needs to be resolved. This resolution is done by an entity called a policy that determines the next action to execute:

Definition 5 (Policy). *A policy for a POMDP* D *is a function* $\sigma: \mathsf{Paths}_{fin} \rightarrow Dist(Act)$ *such that* $\sigma(s_0 \ldots s_n)(\alpha) > 0$ *implies* $\alpha \in Act(s_n)$. *We denote the set of all possible policies for a POMDP* D *with* Σ_D.

A policy is observation-based *if* $\sigma(\pi) = \sigma(\pi')$ *holds for all* π, π' *with* $\lambda(\pi) = \lambda(\pi')$. *A policy is* σ stationary *if* $\sigma(\pi) = \sigma(\pi')$ *holds whenever* $last(\pi) = last(\pi')$. *The set of all stationary policies for a POMDP* D *is* Σ_D^{stat}. *Policies that are not stationary, are called* history-dependent. *A policy is* deterministic *if* $\sigma(\pi)(\alpha) \in \{0, 1\}$ *for all* π *and* α. *Policies that are not deterministic are called* randomized.

Stationary observation-based policies are typically regarded as functions $\sigma: \mathcal{O} \rightarrow Dist(Act)$ (randomized policy) or $\sigma: \mathcal{O} \rightarrow Act$ (deterministic policy). As a policy resolves all nondeterminism and partial observability, it turns a (PO)MDP into a discrete-time Markov chain (DTMC), which is a purely stochastic process.

Definition 6 (Induced DTMC). *Let* D *be a POMDP as defined above with reward function* R *and* $\sigma\colon \mathsf{Paths}_{fin} \to Dist(Act)$ *a policy. The induced DTMC is a tuple* $\mathsf{D}_\sigma = (\mathsf{Paths}_{fin}, s_{init}, P')$ *such that* $P'(\pi, \pi') = \sigma(\pi)(\alpha) \cdot P(last(\pi), \alpha, s)$ *if* $\pi' = \pi\alpha s$, *and* $P'(\pi, \pi') = 0$ *otherwise. The induced reward function* $R'\colon \mathsf{Paths}_{fin} \to \mathbb{R}$ *is defined as* $R'(\pi) = \sum_{\alpha \in Act(last(\pi))} \sigma(\pi)(\alpha) \cdot R(last(\pi), \alpha)$.

In the following we consider the computation of observation-based policies for POMDPs. The goal is to find a policy such that the induced DTMC satisfies a given specification. For the scope of this paper, we focus on *reachability* and *expected discounted reward* specifications and combinations thereof. Note that general LTL properties for probabilistic systems can be reduced to reachability [4].

Definition 7 (Reachability). *Let* $\mathsf{C} = (S, s_{init}, P)$ *be a DTMC and* $T \subseteq S$ *a set of target states. The probability to reach a state in* T *from* s *is the unique solution of the following linear equation system:*

$$
x_s = \begin{cases} 1 & \text{if } s \in T, \\ 0 & \text{if there is no path from } s \text{ to } T, \\ \sum_{s' \in \text{succ}(s)} P(s, s') \cdot x_{s'} & \text{otherwise.} \end{cases}
$$

Definition 8 (Expected discounted rewards). *For a discount factor* $\beta \in (0,1)$ *and a DTMC* $\mathsf{C} = (S, s_{init}, P)$, *the* expected discounted reward *of a state state* s *is the unique solution of the following linear equation system:*

$$
r_s = R(s) + \beta \cdot \sum_{s' \in \text{succ}(s)} P(s, s') \cdot r_{s'} \qquad \text{for each } s \in S.
$$

Recall that the problem to determine a policy that optimizes expected rewards or probabilities is undecidable [26] in general.

3 Solving POMDPs as MILPs

While several sophisticated algorithms exist to compute policies for POMDPs, a simple, small, and easy-to-analyze policy can be obtained by encoding the POMDP into a *Mixed Integer Linear Program* (MILP), which can be solved with linear optimization tools like *Gurobi* [17]. As a central advantage of the MILP formulations, it is straightforward to support multiple specifications simultaniously. For instance, one can maximize the discounted reward under the condition that the probability of reaching a target state is above a given bound and the discounted cost below another threshold.

3.1 Maximum Reachability Probabilities

Let $\mathsf{D} = (\mathsf{M}, \mathcal{O}, \lambda)$ be a POMDP and $T \subseteq S$ a set of target states. We assume that the states in T have been made absorbing and that M contains only states from which T is reachable under at least one possible policy. All other states can be removed from the POMDP. We define the following MILP:

$$\text{maximize:} \quad p_{s_{\text{init}}} \tag{1a}$$

$$\text{subject to:}$$

$$\forall s \in S \setminus T: \quad \sum_{\alpha \in Act(s)} \sigma_{\lambda(s),\alpha} = 1 \tag{1b}$$

$$\forall s \in T: \quad p_s = 1 \tag{1c}$$

$$\forall s \in S \setminus T \; \forall \alpha \in Act(s): \quad p_s \le (1 - \sigma_{\lambda(s),\alpha}) + \sum_{s' \in \text{succ}(s,\alpha)} P(s,\alpha,s') \cdot p_{s'} \tag{1d}$$

$$\forall (s,\alpha) \in Act^{\text{pr}} \; \forall s' \in \text{succ}(s,\alpha): \quad r_s < r_{s'} + 1 - t_{s,s'} \tag{2a}$$

$$\forall (s,\alpha) \in Act^{\text{pr}}: \quad p_s \le 1 - \sigma_{\lambda(s),\alpha} + \sum_{s' \in \text{succ}(s,\alpha)} t_{s,s'} \tag{2b}$$

The variables $p_s \in [0,1]$ store the probability to reach a target state from s under the chosen policy. We maximize this probability for the initial state s_{init} (1a). The variables $\sigma_{z,\alpha}$ for $z \in \mathcal{O}$ and $\alpha \in Act$ encode the policy. $\sigma_{\lambda(s),\alpha} = 1$ implies that the policy chooses action α in all states with observation $\lambda(s)$ – as we are computing stationary deterministic policies, $\sigma_{\lambda(s),\alpha} \in \{0,1\}$ for all $s \in S$ and $\alpha \in Act(s)$. Thus, (1b) ensures that for each observation exactly one action is selected. (1c) ensures that target states are assigned a probability of 1. For non-target states $s \in S \setminus T$, (1d) recursively defines the probability p_s: for actions that are not chosen, i.e., $\sigma_{\lambda(s),\alpha} = 0$, the inequality is always satisfied, as it can be simplified to $p_s \le 1 + \epsilon$ with $\epsilon \ge 0$. If $\sigma_{\lambda(s),\alpha} = 1$, the probability is defined as the sum of the probability in each of the successors of the current state, multiplied with the probability to proceed to this successor when taking the current action. Maximizing the value of p_s ensures that this constraint is satisfied by equality. If the target states are reachable from all states under all possible policies, (1a)–(1d) are sufficient. We add (2a) and (2b) to avoid computing invalid values under policies that make the targets unreachable from some states: we define the problematic states S^{pr} as the set of states that can only reach the target states under some policies, and compute them using standard graph algorithms. The problematic actions are then given by $Act^{\text{pr}} = \{(s,\alpha) \in S \times Act \mid \alpha \in Act(s) \wedge \text{succ}(s,\alpha) \subseteq S^{\text{pr}}\}$. We then introduce a ranking over the problematic states: each $s \in S^{\text{pr}}$ is assigned a value $r_s \in [0,1]$. Next, we try to assign a transition to a successor state of s by setting $t_{s,s'} = 1$ such that the value of the rank increases along the transition, i.e., $r_{s'} > r_s$. If this is not the case, (2a) enforces $t_{s,s'} = 0$. If the target state cannot be reached under the current policy, i.e., $t_{s,s'} = 0$ for all successors of s, (2b) ensures that $p_s = 0$. This technique is inspired by the reachability constraints from [41] that are used to compute counterexamples for MDPs [14]. An alternative formulation of reachability constraints using flow constraints can be found in [38].

3.2   Maximum Expected Discounted Rewards

Let $D = (M, \mathcal{O}, \lambda)$ be a POMDP. For a discount factor $\beta \in (0, 1)$ and an upper bound on the maximum discounted expected reward $v^*_{\max}$, we can built the MILP as follows:

$$\text{maximize:} \quad v_{s_{\text{init}}} \tag{3a}$$

$$\text{subject to:}$$

$$\forall s \in S: \quad \sum_{\alpha \in Act(s)} \sigma_{\lambda(s),\alpha} = 1 \tag{3b}$$

$$\forall s \in S \;\forall \alpha \in Act(s): \quad v_s \leq v^*_{\max} \cdot (1 - \sigma_{\lambda(s),\alpha}) + r(s, \alpha)$$
$$+ \beta \cdot \sum_{s' \in \text{succ}(s,\alpha)} P(s, \alpha, s') \cdot v_{s'} \tag{3c}$$

The MILP for maximum discounted reward is analogous to the formulation for maximum reachability, with the following differences: The real-valued variables $v_s \in \mathbb{R}$ for each $s \in S$ store the maximum discounted expected reward corresponding to the selected policy.

As v_s can have values >1, in (3c), we need an upper bound $v^*_{\max}$ on the maximum expected reward. One possibility is setting $v^*_{\max}$ to the maximum expected discounted reward of the underlying MDP M, which serves as an upper bound on the reward that can be achieved in D. An alternative is using $v^*_{\max} := \frac{1}{1-\beta} \cdot \max_{s,\alpha} R(s, \alpha)$. Since we no longer have any target states, the expected reward is computed for an infinite run of D under the selected policy. $0 < \beta < 1$ guarantees that the expected reward converges to a finite number. Thus, we don't need the reachability constraints we introduced in Sect. 3.1. This simplification makes the MILP considerably smaller and more efficient to solve.

3.3   Randomization

Stationary, deterministic policies can be restrictive in many use cases. However, while randomization might often be necessary, sometimes the actual probability distribution does not matter. In Fig. 2, any stationary deterministic policy can reach the blue state with probability of at most 0.5. However, assigning any distribution with $\sigma_{\text{yellow},\alpha} > 0$ and $\sigma_{\text{yellow},\beta} > 0$ leads to a probability of 1.

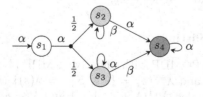

Fig. 2. Simple example that needs arbitrary randomization for maximum reachability of s_4. (Color figure online)

In order to achieve this effect, we allow (besides deterministic choices) a randomized choice with an arbitrary, but fixed distribution over the enabled actions. This can be done by introducing an additional action $u \notin Act$ that is enabled in the set $S' \subseteq S$ of states with (1) a non-unique observation and (2) more than one enabled action. We replace the underlying MDP M by $M' = (S, s_{\text{init}}, Act_u, P_u)$ such that $Act_u := Act \cup \{u\}$ and P_u as follows: P_u coincides with P in states $S \setminus S'$ and whenever $\alpha \neq u$. For instance, consider a state $s \in S'$ where we want to achieve a uniform distribution over all actions. We set $P_u(s, u, s') = \frac{1}{|Act(s)|} \cdot \sum_{\alpha \in Act(s)} P(s, \alpha, s')$ for $s' \in S$.

Any finite set of distributions can be supported that way. We suggest three modes of randomization, as illustrated in Fig. 3: *Pure* (no randomization), *Light* (adding one uniform distribution the enabled actions for each state) and *Heavy* (adding a uniform distribution for each non-empty subset of enabled actions.

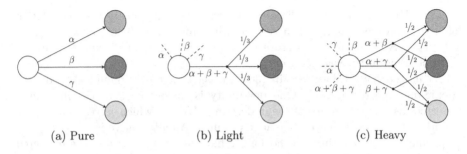

(a) Pure   (b) Light   (c) Heavy

Fig. 3. A POMDP without, with light, and with heavy static randomization

4   Splitting Observations and States

Finding an optimal stationary policy is a much easier problem than optimizing over all (history-dependent) policies, but the quality of stationary policies can be arbitrarily worse than the quality of a general optimal policy. We attempt to preprocess POMDPs in a way that implicitly adds history locally by encoding previous observations into the states – thus, making stationary policies computed on the augmented POMDP more powerful. In order to do so, we introduce *observation splitting* and *state splitting*.

4.1   Observation Splitting

Let $D = (M, \mathcal{O}, \lambda)$ be a POMDP with underlying MDP $M = (S, s_{\text{init}}, Act, P, R)$, $z \in \mathcal{O}$ an observation, and $\lambda^{-1}(z) = \{s \in S \mid z = \lambda(s)\}$ the set of states with observation z. W. l. o. g., let $|\lambda^{-1}(\lambda(s_{\text{init}}))| = 1$ and $P(s, s_{\text{init}}) = 0$ for all $s \in S$. An existing POMDP can easily be modified to conform with these requirements.

Definition 9 (Pre-observations). *For $s \in S$, the pre-observations of s are defined as* $pred_D(s) = \{(z, \alpha) \in \mathcal{O} \times Act \mid \exists s' \in S \colon z = \lambda(s') \wedge P(s', \alpha, s) > 0\}$.

Assume that s, s' are the only states with observation $z = \lambda(s) = \lambda(s')$ and that the pre-observations of s are disjoint from the pre-observations of s'. A history-dependent policy can easily distinguish the two states by remembering the previous observation and action, but a stationary policy can not. Observation splitting assigns distinct observations to the two states. While a memoryless policy on the original POMDP has to make the same decision in s and s', it can make different decisions on the modified system. Therefore, a memoryless policy on the modified system typically corresponds to a history-dependent policy on the original POMDP. Note that this operation does not increase the number of states or transitions.

An observation z can be split if we can partition $\lambda^{-1}(z)$ into two disjoint subsets A and B such that $\left(\bigcup_{s \in A} pred_D(s)\right) \cap \left(\bigcup_{s \in B} pred_D(s)\right) = \emptyset$, i.e., when z is observed, we can distinguish states in A from states in B if the observation in the predecessor state as well as the last chosen action are known. This information can be encoded into the POMDP by assigning distinct observations to the states in A and the states in B. Formally, we get the POMDP $D' = (M, \mathcal{O}', \lambda')$ with

$$\mathcal{O}' = (\mathcal{O} \setminus \{z\}) \,\dot\cup\, \{z_A, z_B\} \text{ and } \lambda'(s) = \begin{cases} \lambda(s) & \text{if } s \notin A \,\dot\cup\, B, \\ z_A & \text{if } s \in A, \\ z_B & \text{if } s \in B. \end{cases}$$

Theorem 1. *Let D' be the POMDP we obtain by splitting some observation z of POMDP D into new observations z_A and z_B. Then:*

1. $\{D_\sigma \mid \sigma \in \Sigma_D\} = \{D'_\sigma \mid \sigma \in \Sigma_{D'}\}$, *and*
2. $\{D_\sigma \mid \sigma \in \Sigma_D^{stat}\} \subseteq \{D'_\sigma \mid \sigma \in \Sigma_{D'}^{stat}\}$.

If we consider the set of all policies, observation splitting does not make a difference as we can obtain the same induced DTMCs before and after observation splitting. However, if we only consider stationary policies, we get more freedom and can choose among a larger set of induced DTMCs.

Proof. Let D be a POMDP and D' result from D by splitting observation z. Let, for $i = 1, 2$, $\pi_i = s_0^i \alpha_0^i s_1^i \alpha_1^i \ldots s_n^i \in \text{Paths}_{fin}$ be two finite paths in D, and π_i' be the corresponding paths in D'. It is easy to see that $\lambda'(\pi_1') = \lambda'(\pi_2')$ iff $\lambda(\pi_1) = \lambda(\pi_2)$. That means, for each policy in D there is a corresponding policy in D' that makes the same decisions and vice versa.

Additionally, for all states s_1, s_2 of D and D', we have $\lambda(s_1) \neq \lambda(s_2) \Rightarrow \lambda'(s_1) \neq \lambda'(s_2)$. Therefore a stationary policy that can make different choices in s_1 and s_2 in D can make different choices in D' as well. $\square$

4.2 State Splitting

Often, observation splitting is not applicable to a given POMDP. We define state splitting for refining the POMDP to enable observation splitting: In Fig. 4, all states that have the same color share an observation (i.e., $\lambda(s_1) = \lambda(s_2) = \lambda(s_3)$). We have $\mathrm{pred}_D(s_2) = \mathrm{pred}_D(s_1) \cup \mathrm{pred}_D(s_3)$, so the three states cannot be split into disjoint sets by means of their pre-observations and thus, observation splitting cannot be applied. However, by creating two copies s_2^1 and s_2^2, the pre-observations of s_2^1 and s_1 on the one hand and s_2^2 and s_3 on the other hand become disjoint, thus enabling observation splitting on the yellow observation.

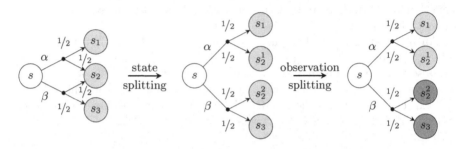

Fig. 4. Applying state splitting and observation splitting to a POMDP. The observations are given by the color of the states. (Color figure online)

Formally, we can split a state $s \in S$ in a POMDP $D = (M, \mathcal{O}, \lambda)$ whenever $|\mathrm{pred}_D(s)| > 1$. Again, we assume that $\mathrm{pred}_D(s_{\mathrm{init}}) = \emptyset$. We obtain a modified POMDP $D' = (M', \mathcal{O}', \lambda')$ with

- $S' := (S \setminus \{s\}) \mathrel{\dot\cup} \{(s, z, \alpha) \mid (z, \alpha) \in \mathrm{pred}_D(s)\}$;

- for all $t \in S'$ we set: $\lambda'(t) := \lambda(s)$ if $t = (s, z, \alpha)$ for some $z \in \mathcal{O}$ and $\alpha \in Act$, and $\lambda'(t) := \lambda(t)$ otherwise;
- for all $t, t' \in S'$, $\beta \in Act$:

$$
P'(t, \beta, t') := \begin{cases}
P(t, \beta, t') & \text{if } t, t' \in S \setminus \{s\}, \\
P(s, \beta, s) & \text{if } t = (s, z, \alpha) \text{ and } t' = (s, z, \beta) \\
& \qquad \text{for some } z \in \mathcal{O} \text{ and } \alpha \in Act, \\
P(t, \beta, s) & \text{if } t \in S \setminus \{s\} \text{ and } t' = (s, \lambda(t), \beta), \\
P(s, \beta, t') & \text{if } t = (s, z, \alpha) \text{ for some } z \in \mathcal{O} \\
& \qquad \text{and } \alpha \in Act \text{ and } t' \in S \setminus \{s\}, \\
0 & \text{otherwise};
\end{cases}
$$

- for all $t \in S'$ and $\beta \in Act(t)$ we set: $R'(t, \beta) := R(s, \beta)$ if $t = (s, z, \alpha)$ for some $z \in \mathcal{O}$ and $\alpha \in Act$, and $R'(t, \beta) := R(t, \beta)$ otherwise.

Algorithm 1: Splitting Heuristic

Input: POMDP D
oldResult ← 0;
splitObservations(D);
newResult ← computeMILP(D);
while *newResult > oldResult* **do**
  oldResult ← newResult;
  splitGroup ← computeSplitGroup(D, oldResult);
  splitStates(D, splitGroup);
  splitObservations(D);
  newResult ← computeMILP(D);

Theorem 2. *Let* D *be a POMDP and let* D' *result from* D *by splitting a state* s *of* D. *Then* D *and* D' *are bisimilar.*

After extending the definition of bisimulation to POMDPs, this can be proven by defining an equivalence relation between s and the states (s, z, α) produced by splitting it.

It is well known [16] that bisimilar systems satisfy (among others) the same LTL and PCTL properties, including reachability and discounted expected rewards.

5   Implementation

We implemented both MILP formulations described in Sect. 3 and use the commercial solver Gurobi [17] to solve them. From our experience, Gurobi often finds a feasible solution, which satisfies all constraints, quickly, but then spends a lot of time trying to improve this initial solution or prove its optimality. However, even this initial solution is often already close to the optimum. Thus, we have implemented a *time limit* mode, in which the solver tries to optimize the result for a predefined number of seconds after the first solution is found.

We implemented the MILPs with three different levels of randomization as in Sect. 3.3, and observation and state splitting as in Sect. 4.

State splitting by itself only increases the size of the state space and yields a bisimilar system. Therefore it only makes sense to apply state splitting when it enables observation splitting, which in turn increases the power of stationary policies. However, it is not clear beforehand which states to split. So as a rule of thumb, we want to determine a small subset of states whose splitting enables a large number of observation splits.

Splitting Heuristic. We suggest a splitting heuristic that uses previous results of the MILP to iteratively refine the POMDP by selecting states for splitting, see Algorithm 1 for an outline. First, we apply observation splitting on the original POMDP and compute the optimal stationary policy in that POMDP to get a baseline for the following optimization. Then, we use this solution to determine a set of states for splitting. Similar to what policy iteration for MDPs [32] does, we check if locally changing a selected action would result in an improvement. σ^* is the current policy and v_s^* the corresponding value of state s. We choose

$$\sigma'(s) :\in \operatorname*{argmax}_{\alpha \in Act(s)} \sum_{s' \in S} P(s, \alpha, s') \cdot v_{s'}^*,$$

preferring $\sigma'(s) = \sigma^*(s)$ where possible.

Whenever $\sigma'(s) \neq \sigma^*(s)$ holds, then being able to distinguish s from the other states with the same observation would lead to an improvement. Therefore s is added to the set *splitGroup*. State splitting is applied to all states in *splitGroup*. Afterwards we apply observation splitting as long as it modifies the POMDP, and solve the MILP for the modified POMDP. We repeat this procedure, until no further improvements can be made.

In case of multiple specifications, it can happen that the initial MILP is infeasible on the original POMDP. In this case we apply Algorithm 1 to optimize the first constraint until it is satisfied. Then we optimize the second one under the condition that the first constraint is satisfied, etc. In the end, we either obtain a policy that satisfies all constraints, or at some point we cannot satisfy one of the specifications. This can have two reasons: either the POMDP does not satisfy the specification or state plus observation splitting are not powerful enough to yield a POMDP on which a stationary policy satisfies the constraints. Note that a complete method does not exist due to the undecidability of the problem.

6   Experiments

Experimental Setup. All experiments were run on a machine with a 3.3 GHz Intel® Xeon® E5-2643 CPU and 64 GB RAM, running Ubuntu 16.04.

We consider seven benchmarks from two different sources. The *4 × 4grid_avoid* was taken from the PRISM-pomdp model checker[1] and is a maximum reachability probability grid world (with one absorbing "bad" state that needs to be avoided). The other benchmarks were adopted from the POMDP page[2] and slightly modified to fit our definitions. *1d*, *4 × 4.95*, *cheese.95*, *minihall2*, and *parr95.95* are grid worlds in which a reward is issued for reaching certain states. *shuttle.95* describes a space shuttle delivering cargo between two space stations, and a reward is issued for every successful delivery (see Fig. 1).

For two of the benchmarks, we added secondary constraints to demonstrate the effectiveness of our approach to multi-objective model checking. On 4 × 4grid_avoid, we added a cost of 1 for each step in the grid (except for the self loops in the goal and bad state). We require the reachability probability to be at least 0.25, and minimize the (un-discounted) expected reward. Note that

---

[1] http://www.prismmodelchecker.org/files/rts-poptas/.
[2] http://www.pomdp.org/examples/.

computing un-discounted reward is sound in this case, as we asure the computation of a valid policy by the reachability contraints as seen in Sect. 3.1 and a sink state is eventually reached with probability 1. On cheese.95, we added a new state – each time the goal state is reached, there is a choice to continue back into the maze, or to transit to a rewardless sink state. We then declared one state of the grid "bad" and required that the probability to reach this state is at most 0.5, while still maximizing the total expected discounted reward.

We run our MILP implementation using Gurobi 8.1 to solve all benchmarks. To improve runtimes, we used time limits of 5, 10, 30, and 60 s for the optimization part of each solver call (see Sect. 5). We also let the optimization run to termination (with a total time limit of 7200 s) to get an assessment of the quality of the solutions that were found.

For comparison, we also ran the maximum expected reward benchmarks with the explicit point based POMDP solvers *SARSOP* [6] and *solvePOMDP*[3]. The results for the maximum reachability probability benchmark (4 × 4grid_avoid) were compared against PRISM-pomdp. All solvers were run using standard parameters. We did not find any solver that could handle the type of multi-objective model checking we implemented for 4 × 4.95 and cheese.95.

Table 1. Results for different benchmarks, timeouts, and implementations

Benchmark	TO	Pure	Light	Heavy	Pure + H	Light + H	Heavy + H	SARSOP	solvePOMDP	PRISM-pomdp
1d	5 s	**0.61/0.1s**	**0.65/0.1s**	**0.65/0.1s**	**0.83/0.1s**	**0.83/0.7s**	**0.83/0.1s**	0.95/0.003s	0.95/1.3s	—
	10 s									
	30 s									
	60 s									
4×4.95	5 s	**0.22/0.1s**	**0.41/0.4s**	3.0/0.7s	**0.22/0.5s**	3.55/34.3s	**3.0/4.0s**	3.55/0.05s	3.55/20.5s	—
	10 s					3.55/71.6s				
	30 s					**3.55/209.2s**				
	60 s									
4×4grid_avoid	5 s	**0.21/0.1s**	**0.3/0.2s**	0.85/0.1s	**0.21/0.2s**	0.88/3.3s	0.93/9.3s	—	—	0.96/346.9s
	10 s									
	30 s									
	60 s									
4×4grid_avoid (p≥0.25, MinR)	5 s	UNSAT/0.1s	13.63/0.1s	4.4/0.2s	UNSAT/0.1s	3.43/2.8s	4.40/17.2s*	—	—	
	10 s						4.40/34.8s*			
	30 s						4.21/112.3s*			
	60 s						3.95/456.5s*			
cheese.95	5 s	0.62/0.6s	1.2/1.6s	1.84/19s*	3.31/35.3s	1.2/16.7s	1.84/34.7s*	3.40/0.03s	3.40/13.7s	—
	10 s			1.84/37.7s*	3.31/72.7s	2.06/71.7s	1.84/70.3s*			
	30 s			1.84/113.7s*	3.34/226.2s*	2.1/222.8s*	1.84/217s*			
	60 s			**1.84/162.5s**	3.34/454.3s*	2.1/452s*	1.84/382.4s*			
cheese.95 (p≤0.5, MaxR)	5 s	0.40/0.8s	0.45/1.9s	0.47/19.1s*	**0.40/0.8s**	0.50/39.8s	0.47/36.4s*	—	—	—
	10 s			0.47/37.5s*		0.50/77.7s	0.47/73.3s*			
	30 s			0.47/116.2s*		0.50/232.2s	0.47/229.3s*			
	60 s			**0.47/148.7s**		0.51/464.6s*	0.47/370.8s*			
mini-hall2	5 s	**2.43/0.4s**	**2.43/12s**	2.43/18.1s	2.5/20.1s	2.43/29.5s*	2.43/33.6s	2.71/0.04s	2.71/33.8s	—
	10 s			2.43/37.2s	2.58/38.2s*	2.43/46.3s*	2.43/71.2s			
	30 s			2.46/114.2s	2.43/114.2s	2.43/121.5s*	2.46/213s			
	60 s			**2.51/228s**	2.58/227.9s*	2.43/235s*	2.51/434.9s*			
parr95.95	5 s	**6.0/0.2s**	**6.0/0.2s**	**6.0/0.2s**	6.84/0.5s	6.84/0.5s	6.84/0.7s	6.84/0.02s	6.84/8.1s	—
	10 s									
	30 s									
	60 s									
shuttle.95	5 s	**18.0/0.2s**	**18.0/0.4s**	**18.0/1.0s**	31.25/36.8s*	31.25/34.1s*	18.63/18.3s	31.25/0.05s	31.25/804s	—
	10 s				31.25/74.6s	31.25/71.1s*	22.8/67.3s			
	30 s				31.25/226s*	31.25/223.2s*	31.25/217.3s*			
	60 s				31.25/452s*	31.25/451.5s*	31.25/443.6s*			

---

[3] https://www.erwinwalraven.nl/solvepomdp/.

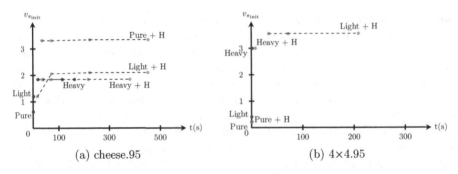

(a) cheese.95   (b) 4×4.95

Fig. 5. Probability and runtime of the different MILP approaches for different grid world benchmarks (Color figure onlie)

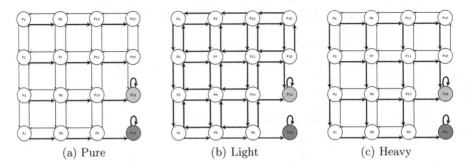

(a) Pure   (b) Light   (c) Heavy

Fig. 6. Policies computed for the 4×4grid_avoid benchmark with different randomization modes (Color figure online)

Results. Table 1 summarizes our experimental results. The first column has the name of the benchmark – for each benchmark, there are four lines representing the four different timeouts used, as specified in the second column ("TO"). Each entry shows both the result (maximum expected discounted reward or maximum reachability probability) for the initial state of the POMDP, and the run time. For each randomization mode (Pure, Light, Heavy) we show both the result of a single MILP call as well as the result of the state splitting heuristic introduced in Sect. 5, indicated by "+H" in the column name. For the "+H" column, the solve time comprises all calls to the solver as well as the time used for splitting states and observations.

Entries printed in **bold** had the same result and runtime as the optimal solution without timeouts, i.e., they were not influenced by the timeouts. In these cases, we omit the entries for higher timeouts, as they had the same values.

For entries marked with an star (∗), the result is either the same as the optimal solution or (for the columns using the splitting heuristic) the same/better than the last iteration that could be solved optimally within two hours. Additionally, the results for cheese.95 and 4×4.95 are also visualized in Fig. 5 – the blue dots represent the results for Pure, Light and Heavy randomization modes without state splitting, while the red dots represent the results when applying the splitting heuristic. Data points that have been produced on the same mode, but using different timeouts, are connected by a dashed line.

Figure 6 shows the polices computed by the MILP using different randomization modes for the 4×4grid_avoid benchmark.

Evaluation. Solving the MILP just once and without any randomization is fast, but doesn't yield a very good result in most cases. However, already the "Light" randomization can improve the result significantly, in same cases up to a factor of 2, without significantly increasing the computation time. Adding the full "Heavy" randomization yields a further improvement in the result – most noticeably for the 4×4.95 benchmark, where the result is improved by factor 7 – but it can also significantly increase the run time of the solver.

While some benchmarks, like 4×4.95 and 4×4grid_avoid, profit immensely from adding randomization, others, like 1d, have an immediate benefit when using preprocessing. parr95.95 and shuttle.95 even achieve the same results as the reference solvers when applying the state splitting heuristic, while randomization had no effect on the results at all. In general, deterministig, history dependend policies are more powerful than stationary, randomized ones and with arbitrary history, randomization can be simulated – e.g., taking an action every second time a state is visited.

All benchmarks can achieve results that are very close to those of the reference solvers. In terms of run time, our approach is slower than SARSOP, but highly outperforms solvePOMDP and PRISM-pomdp.

As can be seen in Fig. 5a, when using different timeouts, the intermediary solution Gurobi returns before fully optimizing the result is already very close to the optimum in many cases. Interestingly, for the mini-hall2 benchmark and the "Pure + H" combination, a timeout of 10 s even yields a better result than a 30 s timeout: the less-optimized result after 10 s causes the heuristic to trigger additional state splits that the benchmark ultimately benefits from.

The same cause can result in the values getting worse when more randomization is added, as seen with the 4×4.95 benchmark. The heuristic picks different states to split, resulting in a higher value for the maximum expected discounted reward in the Light + H case than the Heavy + H approach. However, these additional split states also lead to a higher run time.

For the 4×4grid_avoid benchmark with multi objective model checking, we get UNSAT for the two entries using no randomization, since the required level of reachability probability can not be achieved.

The effects randomization has on a policy are shown in Fig. 6. All sub-figures depict the 4×4grid_avoid benchmark, a grid world with one absorbing goal state (blue) and an absorbing bad state (red). All of the white states share an observation and have four possible actions, although we omit the self-loops that occur when trying to move outside of the grid. The arrows corresponding to actions chosen under the current policy are drawn **bold**. The system randomly starts in one of the white states. The policy without randomization always chooses to move right – only s_1, s_5 and s_9 can reach the goal state. The policy computed with "Light" randomization enables all actions for all states – now each state has the possibility to reach the goal state, but the probability to get to the bad state is still higher. Only with "Heavy" randomization can the bad state be avoided with a higher probability – each state has equal probability to move down and right, getting the best chance to reach the goal in the lower right corner. All sub-figures depict the 4×4grid_avoid benchmark, a grid world with one absorbing goal state (blue) and an absorbing bad state (red).

7   Conclusion

We introduced a MILP formulation to optimize both reachability probabilities and expected discounted rewards in POMDPs. We used these MILPs to compute optimal stationary deterministic policies and employed the concept of static randomization. Furthermore, we introduced state and observation splitting as preprocessing for a POMDP to locally add history to the otherwise stationary policies. Since blindly splitting states leads to a significant growth of the state space, we proposed a heuristic that iteratively improves solutions by splitting carefully selected states. We show the approaches are competitive to state-of-the-art POMDP solvers, and that MILP formulations for rewards and reachability can easily be combined to find policies that satisfy an arbitrary number of specifications at the same time.

References

1. Amato, C., Bernstein, D.S., Zilberstein, S.: Optimizing fixed-size stochastic controllers for POMDPs and decentralized POMDPs. Auton. Agent. Multi-Agent Syst. **21**(3), 293–320 (2010). https://doi.org/10.1007/s10458-009-9103-z
2. Aras, R., Dutech, A., Charpillet, F.: Mixed integer linear programming for exact finite-horizon planning in decentralized POMDPs. In: ICAPS, pp. 18–25. AAAI (2007). http://www.aaai.org/Library/ICAPS/2007/icaps07-003.php
3. Baier, C., Dubslaff, C., Klüppelholz, S.: Trade-off analysis meets probabilistic model checking. In: CSL-LICS, pp. 1:1–1:10. ACM (2014). https://doi.org/10.1145/2603088.2603089
4. Baier, C., Katoen, J.P.: Principles of Model Checking. MIT Press, Cambridge (2008)
5. Braziunas, D.: POMDP Solution Methods. University of Toronto (2003)
6. Brock, O., Trinkle, J., Ramos, F.: SARSOP: Efficient point-based POMDP planning by approximating optimally reachable belief spaces. In: Robotics: Science and Systems IV. MIT Press (2009). https://doi.org/10.15607/RSS.2008.IV.009
7. Carr, S., Jansen, N., Wimmer, R., Serban, A.C., Becker, B., Topcu, U.: Counterexample-guided strategy improvement for POMDPs using recurrent neural networks. In: IJCAI, pp. 5532–5539. ijcai.org (2019)
8. Chatterjee, K., Chmelík, M., Gupta, R., Kanodia, A.: Qualitative analysis of POMDPs with temporal logic specifications for robotics applications. In: ICRA, pp. 325–330 (2015). https://doi.org/10.1109/ICRA.2015.7139019

9. Chatterjee, K., Chmelík, M., Gupta, R., Kanodia, A.: Optimal cost almost-sure reachability in POMDPs. Artif. Intell. **234**, 26–48 (2016). https://doi.org/10.1016/j.artint.2016.01.007

10. Chatterjee, K., De Alfaro, L., Henzinger, T.A.: Trading memory for randomness. In: QEST. IEEE (2004). https://doi.org/10.1109/QEST.2004.1348035

11. Chrisman, L.: Reinforcement learning with perceptual aliasing: the perceptual distinctions approach. In: AAAI, pp. 183–188. AAAI Press/The MIT Press (1992)

12. Cubuktepe, M., Jansen, N., Junges, S., Katoen, J.-P., Papusha, I., Poonawala, H.A., Topcu, U.: Sequential convex programming for the efficient verification of parametric MDPs. In: Legay, A., Margaria, T. (eds.) TACAS 2017. LNCS, vol. 10206, pp. 133–150. Springer, Heidelberg (2017). https://doi.org/10.1007/978-3-662-54580-5_8

13. Cubuktepe, M., Jansen, N., Junges, S., Katoen, J.-P., Topcu, U.: Synthesis in pMDPs: a tale of 1001 parameters. In: Lahiri, S.K., Wang, C. (eds.) ATVA 2018. LNCS, vol. 11138, pp. 160–176. Springer, Cham (2018). https://doi.org/10.1007/978-3-030-01090-4_10

14. Dehnert, C., Jansen, N., Wimmer, R., Ábrahám, E., Katoen, J.-P.: Fast debugging of PRISM models. In: Cassez, F., Raskin, J.-F. (eds.) ATVA 2014. LNCS, vol. 8837, pp. 146–162. Springer, Cham (2014). https://doi.org/10.1007/978-3-319-11936-6_11

15. Etessami, K., Kwiatkowska, M.Z., Vardi, M.Y., Yannakakis, M.: Multi-objective model checking of Markov decision processes. Logical Methods Comput. Sci. **4**(4) (2008). https://doi.org/10.2168/LMCS-4(4:8)2008

16. Givan, R., Dean, T.L., Greig, M.: Equivalence notions and model minimization in Markov decision processes. Artif. Intell. **147**(1–2), 163–223 (2003)

17. Gurobi Optimization, LLC: Gurobi optimizer reference manual (2019). http://www.gurobi.com

18. Haesaert, S., Nilsson, P., Vasile, C.I., Thakker, R., Agha-mohammadi, A., Ames, A.D., Murray, R.M.: Temporal logic control of POMDPs via label-based stochastic simulation relations. IFAC-PapersOnLine **51**(16), 271–276 (2018). In: ADHS

19. Hahn, E.M., Hermanns, H., Zhang, L.: Probabilistic reachability for parametric Markov models. Softw. Tools Technol. Transfer **13**(1), 3–19 (2010)

20. Hauskrecht, M.: Value-function approximations for partially observable Markov decision processes. J. Artif. Intell. Res. **13**, 33–94 (2000)

21. Junges, S., et al.: Parameter synthesis for Markov models. CoRR abs/1903.07993 (2019)

22. Junges, S., Jansen, N., Wimmer, R., Quatmann, T., Winterer, L., Katoen, J., Becker, B.: Finite-state controllers of POMDPs using parameter synthesis. In: UAI, pp. 519–529. AUAI Press (2018)

23. Kaelbling, L.P., Littman, M.L., Cassandra, A.R.: Planning and acting in partially observable stochastic domains. Artif. Intell. **101**(1), 99–134 (1998)

24. Kumar, A., Mostafa, H., Zilberstein, S.: Dual formulations for optimizing Dec-POMDP controllers. In: ICAPS, pp. 202–210. AAAI Press (2016)

25. Littman, M.L., Topcu, U., Fu, J., Isbell, C., Wen, M., MacGlashan, J.: Environment-independent task specifications via GLTL. arXiv preprint 1704.04341 (2017)

26. Madani, O., Hanks, S., Condon, A.: On the undecidability of probabilistic planning and infinite-horizon partially observable Markov decision problems. In: AAAI, pp. 541–548. AAAI Press (1999)

27. Meuleau, N., Peshkin, L., Kim, K.E., Kaelbling, L.P.: Learning finite-state controllers for partially observable environments. In: UAI, pp. 427–436. Morgan Kaufmann (1999)
28. Norman, G., Parker, D., Zou, X.: Verification and control of partially observable probabilistic systems. Real-Time Syst. **53**(3), 354–402 (2017)
29. Papadimitriou, C.H., Tsitsiklis, J.N.: The complexity of Markov decision processes. Math. Oper. Res. **12**(3), 441–450 (1987)
30. Pineau, J., Gordon, G., Thrun, S.: Point-based value iteration: an anytime algorithm for POMDPs. In: IJCAI, pp. 1025–1032. Morgan Kaufmann (2003)
31. Pnueli, A.: The temporal logic of programs. In: FOCS, pp. 46–57. IEEE Computer Society (1977). https://doi.org/10.1109/SFCS.1977.32
32. Puterman, M.L.: Markov Decision Processes: Discrete Stochastic Dynamic Programming. Wiley Series in Probability and Statistics, Wiley-Interscience (2005)
33. Russell, S.J., Norvig, P.: Artificial Intelligence - A Modern Approach (3. internat. ed.). Pearson Education (2010)
34. Schrijver, A.: Theory of Linear and Integer Programming. Wiley, Hoboken (1999)
35. Shani, G., Pineau, J., Kaplow, R.: A survey of point-based POMDP solvers. Auton. Agents Multi-Agent Syst. **27**(1), 1–51 (2013)
36. Silver, D., Veness, J.: Monte-carlo planning in large pomdps. In: Lafferty, J.D., Williams, C.K.I., Shawe-Taylor, J., Zemel, R.S., Culotta, A. (eds.) NIPS, pp. 2164–2172. Curran Associates, Inc. (2010)
37. Thrun, S., Burgard, W., Fox, D.: Probabilistic Robotics. The MIT Press, Cambridge (2005)
38. Velasquez, A.: Steady-state policy synthesis for verifiable control. In: Kraus, S. (ed.) IJCAI, pp. 5653–5661. ijcai.org (2019). https://doi.org/10.24963/ijcai.2019/784
39. Vlassis, N., Littman, M.L., Barber, D.: On the computational complexity of stochastic controller optimization in POMDPs. ACM Trans. Comput. Theory **4**(4), 12:1–12:8 (2012). https://doi.org/10.1145/2382559.2382563
40. Wang, Y., Chaudhuri, S., Kavraki, L.E.: Bounded policy synthesis for POMDPs with safe-reachability objectives. In: AAMAS, pp. 238–246. Int'l Foundation for Autonomous Agents and Multiagent Systems Richland, SC, USA/ACM (2018)
41. Wimmer, R., Jansen, N., Ábrahám, E., Katoen, J.P., Becker, B.: Minimal counterexamples for linear-time probabilistic verification. Theor. Comput. Sci. **549**, 61–100 (2014). https://doi.org/10.1016/j.tcs.2014.06.020
42. Winterer, L., et al.: Motion planning under partial observability using game-based abstraction. In: CDC, pp. 2201–2208. IEEE (2017)
43. Wongpiromsarn, T., Frazzoli, E.: Control of probabilistic systems under dynamic, partially known environments with temporal logic specifications. In: CDC, pp. 7644–7651. IEEE (2012)

Benchmarking Software Model Checkers on Automotive Code

Lukas Westhofen[1], Philipp Berger[2(✉)], and Joost-Pieter Katoen[2]

[1] OFFIS e.V, Oldenburg, Germany
lukas.westhofen@offis.de
[2] RWTH Aachen University, Aachen, Germany
{berger,katoen}@cs.rwth-aachen.de

Abstract. This paper reports on our experiences with verifying automotive C code by state-of-the-art open source software model checkers. The embedded C code is automatically generated from Simulink open-loop controller models. Its diverse features (decision logic, floating-point and pointer arithmetic, rate limiters and state-flow systems) and the extensive use of floating-point variables make verifying the code highly challenging. Our study reveals large discrepancies in coverage—which is at most only 20% of all requirements—and tool strength compared to results from the main annual software verification competition. A hand-crafted, simple extension of the verifier CBMC with k-induction delivers results on 63% of the requirements while the proprietary BTC EmbeddedValidator covers 80% and obtains bounded verification results for most of the remaining requirements.

1 Introduction

Software Model Checking. Software model checking is an active field of research. Whereas model checking algorithms initially focused on verifying models, various dedicated techniques have been developed in the last two decades to enable model checking of program code. This includes e.g., predicate abstraction, abstract interpretation, bounded model checking, counterexample-guided abstraction refinement (CEGAR) and automata-based techniques. Combined with the enormous advancements of SAT and SMT-techniques [1], nowadays program code can be directly verified by powerful tools. Companies like Microsoft, Facebook, Amazon, and ARM check software on a daily basis using in-house model checkers. The enormous variety of code verification techniques and tools has initiated a number of software verification competitions such as RERS, VerifyThis, and SV-COMP. For software model checking, the annual SV-COMP competition is most relevant. Launched with 9 participating tools in 2012, it gained popularity over the years with more than 40 competitors in 2019 [2]. It runs off-line in a controlled manner, and has several categories. Competitions like SV-COMP have established standards in input and output format, and evaluation criteria. Software model checkers are ranked based on the verification results, earning points for correct results while being punished for wrong outcomes. A more recent

© Springer Nature Switzerland AG 2020
R. Lee et al. (Eds.): NFM 2020, LNCS 12229, pp. 133–150, 2020.
https://doi.org/10.1007/978-3-030-55754-6_8

development is the usage of witnesses to validate verification results. Results are provided in so-called quantile plots indicating the required verification time versus the cumulative score over the benchmarks.

Aims of this Paper. This paper focuses on: *how do the SV-COMP competitors perform on automotive code?* and *how do these tools compare to proprietary tools that are tailored to such code?* The objective of this paper is to benchmark a rich set of participating tools in SV-COMP using two case studies from a major car manufacturer taken from [3]. In contrast to the SV-COMP, where a diverse set of open-source verification tasks ranging from small academic examples over concurrent programs up to software systems are submitted by research and development groups, we focus on an industrial grade automotive code base. To the best of our knowledge, such an evaluation has not been made before. While a set of two case studies is certainly a small benchmark in comparison, the size of the two case studies (of about 1400 and 2500 lines of embedded C code respectively), its diverse features (decision logic, floating-point arithmetic, pointer dereferencing, rate limiters, bitwise operations and state-flow systems), the rich set of (179) requirements, and the availability of verification results obtained by the proprietary software model checker BTC EmbeddedValidator, make it an interesting starting point to validate and compare various open-source software model checkers on an automotive code base.

Approach. We selected 11 software model checkers from the SV-COMP 2019 [2], based on (a) the aforementioned characteristics of the two automotive case studies, (b) the requirements that mostly are safety properties, and (c) the availability of a license that enables an academic evaluation. In addition, we considered a simple hand-crafted extension of CBMC [4] with k-induction that is tailored to the control-flow characteristics of the two benchmarks. We conducted two main experiments. The first experiment runs the 12 software model checkers on the 179 requirements, 99% of which are invariants, and *focuses on comparing the coverage of the tools (how many requirements could be verified or refuted), and their verification time.* The second experiment *benchmarks the open-source code verifiers against the proprietary verifier BTC EmbeddedValidator*[1].

Our Main Findings. The main results of this paper are:

- The SV-COMP competitors are able to obtain results for at most 20% of all requirements. Various competitors covered between 0 and 5% only.
- A hand-crafted, simple extension of CBMC with k-induction covers 63%.
- BTC EmbeddedValidator covers 80% and obtains bounded verification results for 85% of the remaining requirements.

Our results show that there is a lot of untapped optimization potential for making existing open source software model checkers more appealing and applicable to automotive code. Suitable benchmark candidates are currently too closely

---

[1] https://www.btc-es.de/en/products/btc-embeddedplatform/.

guarded by industry to be really driving scientific development. Therefore, the message of this paper is to emphasize the need for a synchronization between the industrial and scientific software verification communities.

2 Preliminaries

2.1 The Automotive Benchmarks

Benchmark Description. Both case studies involve auto-generated code of two R&D prototype Simulink models from Ford Motor Company: the next-gen *Driveline State Request* (DSR) feature and the next-gen *E-Clutch Control* (ECC) feature. The DSR and ECC features implement the decision logic for opening and closing the driveline and calculating the desired clutch torque and corresponding engine control torque of the vehicle, respectively. The case studies are described in detail in [3]. Unfortunately, because of non-disclosure agreements, we cannot make the benchmarks publicly available; instead we give a detailed characterization of the used code in the following.

Code Characteristics. From the Simulink models, generated by a few thousand blocks, around 1,400 and 2,500 source lines of C code were extracted for DSR and ECC. Both code bases have a cyclomatic complexity of over 200 program paths. The cyclomatic complexity is a common software metric indicating the number of linearly independent paths through a program's code. Table 1 presents the metrics collected on both case studies.

Constants are used to account for configurability, i.e. they represent parameters of the model that can be changed for different types of applications. The configurable state-space consists of 77 and 274 constants, for DSR and ECC respec-

Table 1. Code metrics of the benchmarks.

Metric	DSR	ECC
Complexity		
Source lines of code	1,354	2,517
Cyclomatic complexity	213	268
Global constants	*77*	*274*
char	12	8
char[]	[12,32] 2	0
float	35	77
float[]	[6-12] 9	[2-7] 4
float*	1	1
void*	18	184
Global variables	*273*	*775*
char	199	595
char[]	[16-32] 3	0
float	46	110
float[]	[4-10] 25	[2-4] 70
Operations	*5232*	*10096*
Addition/subtraction	133	346
Multiplication/division	52	253
Bit-wise operations	65	191
Pointer dereferences	83	180

tively. Most of them are of type `float`, sometimes in a fixed-length array, as indicated by the square brackets. Their size range is also given in square brackets. Additionally, both case studies contain pointers to constant data (e.g. `const void*`).

With a couple of hundred variables, *globals are heavily employed*. They are used for exchanging data with other compilation units. Here, the `char` type is most prevalent, taking up around three quarters of the variable count. `float` variables make up the remaining quarter.

The number of operations in the call graph are around $5,000$ and $10,000$ for DSR and ECC. While *linear arithmetic* is most prominent, we also observe a large amount of *multiplication* and *division* operations, possibly on non-constant variables. Challenges for software verifiers rise along with the complexity of operators used. Pointer and floating-point arithmetic, as well as bit-wise operations impose challenges. These case studies employ a variety of *bit-wise operations* such as `>>`, `&`, and `|`, mainly on 32-bit variables. Such operators can force the underlying solvers to model the variable bit by bit. A noticeable amount of *pointer dereferences*, namely 180 and 83 occurrences, is present in the programs.

Requirement Characteristics. The requirements originate from internal and informal documents of the car manufacturer and have been formalized by hand. As described in [3], obtaining an unambiguous formal requirement specification can be a substantial task. All differences between the formalization in [3] and this work in number of properties stem from different splitting of the properties. For the DSR case study, from 42 functional requirements we extracted 105 properties, consisting of 103 invariants and two bounded-response properties. For the ECC case study, from 74 functional requirements we extracted 71 invariants and three bounded-response properties.

Invariant properties are assertions that are supposed to hold for all reachable states. Bounded-response properties request that a certain assertion holds within a given number of computational steps whenever a given, second assertion holds.

2.2 The Software Model Checkers

In order to analyze the performance of open-source verifiers on our specific use case of embedded automotive C code from Simulink models, we selected a suitable subset of C verifiers based on the following criteria:

1. Has matured enough to compete in the SV-COMP 2019 [2] in the *ReachSafety* and *SoftwareSystems* category.
2. Has a license that allows an academic evaluation.

Based on these criteria, we selected the verifiers: 2LS, CBMC, CPAChecker, DepthK, ESBMC, PeSCo, SMACK, Symbiotic, UltimateAutomizer, UltimateKojak, and UltimateTaipan. The study was conducted in March 2019. We used the latest stable versions of each tool to that date. We also included CBMC+k (described in Sect. 2.3), a variant of CBMC that enables k-induction as a proof generation technique on top of CBMC. Let us briefly introduce the selected open-source verifiers.

CBMC 5.11 [5]. The *C Bounded Model Checker* is a matured bounded model checker for C programs. CBMC takes a pre-specified bound up to which the program loops are unrolled. The resulting transition system is encoded symbolically, and finally passed to an SAT-solver. For a given bound k, this formula over the program states is created in the following manner, where I is the initial condition, T the transition relation, s_i a state and P the property:

$$BMC_k(s_0, \ldots, s_k) = I(s_0) \wedge \left(\bigwedge_{i=0}^{k-1} T(s_i, s_{i+1}) \right) \wedge \left(\bigvee_{i=0}^{k} \neg P(s_i) \right) \quad (1)$$

ESBMC 6.0.0 [6]. The *Efficient SMT-based Bounded Model Checker* was forked off of a 2008 version of CBMC and has been replacing original framework parts ever since. One of its goals is to directly translate to SMT-theories instead of relying on SAT-solvers. It furthermore supports k-induction. Here, a generalized mathematical induction is applied to program loops, where a "look-back" of k steps is allowed for the induction hypothesis. The verification task can be specified as a formula over the program states:

$$IND_k(s_0, \ldots, s_k) = \left(\bigwedge_{i=0}^{k-1} T(s_i, s_{i+1}) \right) \wedge \left(\bigwedge_{i=0}^{k-1} P(s_i) \right) \wedge \neg P(s_k) \quad (2)$$

2LS 0.7.0 [7]. This is another fork of CBMC that expands from bounded model checking to a multitude of verification approaches. It interprets program analysis as a problem of solving a second-order logic instance. This leads to a variety of concepts that 2LS can employ, including (incremental) bounded model checking, k-induction, k-induction k-invariants, and abstract interpretation.

CPAChecker 1.8.0 [8]. The *Configurable Program Analysis Checker* provides a framework for implementing a rich set of analysis and verification techniques. By employing an abstract analysis algorithm, it implements concrete approaches such as predicate abstraction [9], value analysis [10], and k-induction [11].

PeSCo 1.7 [12]. PeSCo is a recent fork of CPAChecker which exploits *machine learning* to effectively select a fitting configuration for the given verification task.

DepthK 3.1 [13]. DepthK uses *k-induction on top of ESBMC* combined with an *invariant-strengthening* approach. It supports the iterative proof process by inferring possibly over-approximating invariants over polyhedral constraints.

SMACK 1.9.3 [14]. Rather than being a verifier by itself, SMACK translates from the LLVM intermediate representation (IR) into the *Boogie* [15] intermediate verification language (IVL). Corral, the default verification back end, employs bounded model checking with a goal-directed search algorithm.

Symbiotic 6.0.3 [16]. Symbiotic applies program instrumentation, *static slicing* and symbolic execution to identify counterexamples. Internally, it uses a patched KLEE version for symbolic execution and witness generation.

UltimateAutomizer 91b1670e [17]. This tool implements a trace-abstraction based on *automata* in a CEGAR fashion. Its development is based on the Ultimate framework which provides access to program representation, code transformations, and SMT-solvers. It applies a CEGAR scheme until an error automaton with sufficient abstraction is found.

UltimateKojak 91b1670e [18]. As part of the Ultimate tool chain, UltimateKojak uses CEGAR with *interpolation* over multiple program paths.

UltimateTaipan 91b1670e [19]. Similar to UltimateAutomizer, UltimateTaipan employs automata-based trace abstraction and CEGAR. It uses a fixed-point iteration to refine error paths until a sufficient precision is reached.

2.3 A Simple, Tailored Variant of CBMC

The SV-COMP verifiers are complemented by a simple, hand-crafted extension of the bounded model checker CBMC (version 5.11) with k-induction. Our implementation is tailored to the two case studies, in particular to programs with one main outermost control loop. Our prime motivation to consider this variant is to show the effect of a simple, almost trivial, tweak of a bounded model checker. The main goal of k-induction is harvesting the power of efficient bounded model checkers such as CBMC for proof generation. In this way, verifiers that natively only support bug hunting but have matured over time, can be elevated.

```
extern void __VERIFIER_error();          extern void __VERIFIER_error();
                                         extern void __VERIFIER_assume(int);
int main() {                             int main() {
  initialize();                            initialize();
                                           set_loop_variables_nondet();
                                           unsigned int i = 0;
  while(1) {                                while(1) {
                               ⤳             __VERIFIER_assume(property());
                                             i++;
    step();                                  step();
    if(!property())                          if(i == k && !property())
      __VERIFIER_error();                      __VERIFIER_error();
  }                                        }
}                                        }
```

Fig. 1. The transformation that is applied in the k-th induction step.

Our implementation CBMC+k is realized by a straightforward code transformation [20], see Fig. 1. It creates a new program representing the induction step such that all input variables are set non-deterministically on entering the loop. It then runs the back-end verifier on both the base step – i.e. the input file – and the induction step. If the base step returns a counterexample, the tool reports *False*. In case the induction step returns no counterexample for iteration k and the base case has also reached k, it reports *True*. Our two case studies do not require the forward case in [20], thus simplifying the implementation.

CBMC+k has *severe restrictions on its input code*. It is targeted to embedded C programs containing one (unbounded) main loop with a strictly bounded loop body. The property has to be checked at the very end of every loop iteration. Although there exist transformations from general programs to one-loop programs, we decided to skip this step as our case studies do not exhibit nested unbounded loops. Evidently, CBMC+k inherits the capabilities (and deficiencies) of its back-end verifier, specifically its ability to handle large state spaces.

CBMC+k should thus not be considered a generic, widely applicable extension of CBMC with k-induction. Our prime motivation to consider this variant is to show the effect of a simple, almost trivial, tweak on a bounded model checker. We have taken CBMC for this variant as it performed very well in identifying counterexamples, an important trait for k-induction.

The CBMC+k implementation is made publicly available at https://github.com/moves-rwth/cbmc-with-kInduction.

2.4   Experimental Setup

All experiments were performed on a machine with 192 GB RAM and two Intel Xeon Platinum 8160 processors, each containing 24 cores at 2.1 GHz. Our benchmark script executed ten benchmarks in parallel, giving each execution four CPU cores with a memory limit of 18 GB and a CPU-time limit of two hours. Further details can be found in the Appendix. Every verification was followed by two witness validation runs of CPAChecker and Ultimate. Conforming to the regulations of the SV-COMP 2019, the time limit for a correctness witness was two hours, whereas a violation witness had to complete within 12 min. We collected the data points:

- the result; either *True*, *False* or *Unknown*,
- why no definite answer was given, e.g. *Timeout*, *Memout* or *Verifier bug*,
- the used CPU-time, in seconds,
- the peak memory usage, in MB,
- if measurable, the time spent by a SAT solver, in seconds,
- if measurable, the reached depth in a BMC or k-induction setting, and
- the witness validation results; either *Correct* (validation result = original result), *Invalid* (unparseable witness) or *Unknown* (resource exhaustion, or validation result $\neq$ original result).

To keep the results comparable and the competition fair, we used the default configurations that the tool maintainers chose for the SV-COMP 2019 reachability tasks. The exact settings can be found in the Appendix. CBMC was invoked with increasing values of k by a wrapper script similar to the one employed in the SV-COMP 2019. For the Ultimate tool chain, a bit-precise memory model was applied[2] to the Boogie translator configuration. The witness validation processes for CPAChecker and Ultimate were set up as in SV-COMP 2019 with scaled run times where necessary. Due to the aforementioned confidentiality reasons, we cannot disclose the extracted benchmark data and verifier outputs.

---

[2] by adding `Memory model=HoenickeLindenmann_Original`.

3   Comparing the Open-Source Verifiers

Coverage. Figure 2 shows the verification results of running the open-source verifiers on the two case studies, omitting the results of the witness validation.

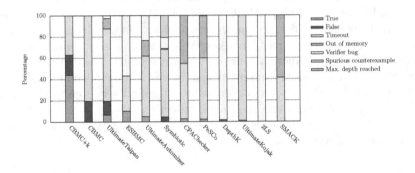

Fig. 2. The overall result distribution for each software model checker, in percent.

CBMC+k is able to verify about 63% of the verification tasks; CBMC and UltimateTaipan cover roughly 20%. ESBMC delivers results on 10% of the requirements. The remaining verifiers reach a coverage of at most 5%. The majority of the verifiers is either able to identify counterexamples or produce proofs, but seldom both. 2LS and SMACK cannot return a single definite result. The only successful witness validation was a proof of PeSCo validated by CPAChecker, indicated by *True (Correct)*. CBMC delivered invalid witnesses on all tasks, leading it to fail the witness validation process.

Figure 2 also indicates the reasons for *Unknown* answers. We observe that *time- and memory-outs prevail*, but a large number of verifiers exhibit *erroneous behavior*. A detailed description of the latter issues is given in Sect. 5.

To get insight into which requirements are covered by which software model checker, Fig. 3 depicts two Venn diagrams indicating the subsets of all 179 verification tasks. Each area represents the set of verification tasks on which a verifier returned a definite result. Those areas are further divided into overlapping sub-areas, where a number indicates the size of this set. For reasons of clarity, we included only the top five verifiers for the respective case study, based on the number of definite answers. For both case studies, there is not one verifier which covers all requirements covered by the other verifiers. For DSR, CBMC+k covers all but one definite results of the remaining verifiers. In this case, CBMC was able to identify a counterexample close to the timeout. CBMC+k exhausts its resources on this requirement as the inductive case occupies a part of the available computation time. For ECC, UltimateTaipan, ESBMC, and CBMC+k together cover the set of all definite results. Note that some verifiers—e.g. UltimateTaipan and ESBMC—perform rather well on one case study, but lose most of their coverage on the other. In most of such cases, this is due to erroneous behavior of the verifier manifesting on just one of the two case studies.

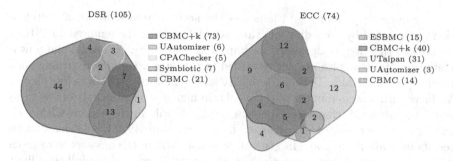

Fig. 3. Venn diagrams indicating the requirement coverage (i.e., a definite result was issued) by the top-five verifiers for case study DSR (left) and ECC (right).

We believe that the substantial difference in verifier coverage for the two case studies, as seen in Fig. 3, is the result of structural differences in the benchmark code. While the overall control-flow structure (closed loop, step-based input to output propagation) is the same for DSR and ECC, the difference in overall size and the higher number of global constants, pointers and floating-point variables make ECC imposing different challenges. Even a small increase in code size can lead to verifiers not even getting through costly initial preparatory steps, that, if completed, might have quickly been followed by a result.

Quantile Plot. As standard in SV-COMP, a quantile plot for the results on both case studies together is depicted in Fig. 4. Note the log-log scale. To this end, a score is assigned to each verification run according to the SV-COMP[3] scheme in Table 2.

Table 2. The employed scoring scheme for the quantile plots as adopted from SV-COMP.

Verification result	*False*			*True*		
Validation result	✓	?	✗	✓	?	✗
Score	+1	±0	±0	+2	+1	±0

The score depends on the results of the witness validation which can either be validated (verification and validation result coincide, indicated by ✓), not validated (resource exhaustion or verification and validation result differ, ?) or invalid (unparseable witness, ✗). In absence of expected verification results, no punishments for wrong answers are given. In Sect. 4, we compare the verification results against those obtained by the commercial verifier BTC EmbeddedValidator.

---

[3] https://sv-comp.sosy-lab.org/2019/rules.php#scores.

The quantile plot in Fig. 4 indicates the accumulated score for all verification runs, sorted by ascending run time (x-axis), against the required CPU-time (y-axis). A (log, log) scale is used for improved readability. As invalid and unvalidated counterexamples are not rewarded in this score, verifiers returning such results – 2LS, CBMC, DepthK, SMACK and Symbiotic – obtain a zero score. Verifiers with a large number of proofs obtain higher scores. As only one witness could be validated, this aspect plays a negligible role in the scores. CBMC+k exhibits a higher score than other verifiers; runner-up ESBMC obtains various results only after one hour. In general, 50% and 90% of the answers were given within seven and 75 min, respectively. Only few verifiers used the full time limit of two hours: The Ultimate verifiers and CBMC+k obtained many results within an hour.

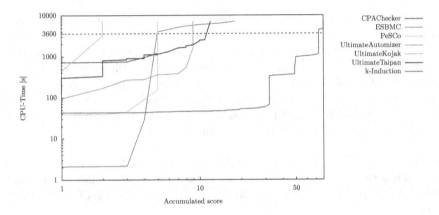

Fig. 4. The quantile (log, log) plot for all verifiers except the tools 2LS, CBMC, DepthK, SMACK and Symbiotic (as they reach a zero score).

4   Benchmarking Against BTC EmbeddedValidator

To compare the results of open-source software verifiers to a commercial tool, we additionally ran the verification tasks using BTC EmbeddedValidator (BTC for short).[4] The main purpose of this examination is the establishment of a reference point. This reference can subsequently be used as a foundation to interpret the applicability of the open-source verifiers to the industrial case studies.

BTC EmbeddedValidator is part of BTC EmbeddedPlatform, a commercial model-checking tool developed for industrial applications. It is, among others, heavily optimized for industrial embedded software—such as the benchmarks

---

[4] Similar results were provided in [3]. We have used a more recent version of BTC EmbeddedValidator and considered 179 rather than 112 requirements, as requirements were split differently.

considered in this paper—and unsurprisingly performs very well on the ECC and DSR case studies. This focus is also a weak point: It can not or not easily deal with memory allocation and many standard library headers usually not present in the targeted embedded code, making it unsuitable for a direct comparison on established SV-COMP benchmarks. Requirements can be specified directly using a pattern-based approach, see [21,22]. BTC EmbeddedValidator employs several back-end tools for verification: CBMC[5], iSAT3, AutoFXP, SMIBMC, and VIS. Code transformation, static analysis, and detection of spurious, i.e., incorrect, counterexamples are done as part of the verification.

We used BTC EmbeddedPlatform 2.3p1 under Windows 7 with 4 GB RAM and an Intel i7-6700HQ with a timeout of two hours. While this setup is using a smaller CPU and less RAM than our experiment in Sect. 3 and is therefore incomparable, it is important to stress that we use the results of BTC only for deciding the baseline truth and do not depend on the performance (see also Sect. 4.2).

4.1   BTC EmbeddedValidator Verification Results

Table 3 states the result distribution for both case studies, in percent of the 105 and 74 verification tasks, respectively.

Table 3. Verification results of BTC EmbeddedValidator on both case studies, in percent of the 105 and 74 verification tasks.

Case study	DSR (105)			ECC (74)		
Result	*True*	*False*	*Unknown*	*True*	*False*	*Unknown*
Percentage	56.2%	21.9%	21.9%	55.4%	27.0%	17.6%

BTC did not return a result on 21.9% of the DSR tasks; 91% of which were due to reaching only bounded correctness, but no unbounded proof. BTC timed out on the remaining 9%. Of the 17.6% *Unknown* answers for ECC, 92% are bounded proofs, and 8% timed out. In comparison to the open-source verifiers, BTC takes first place in both case studies when considering the overall number of definite answers. As witness output is not available in BTC and wall clock times were measured, we cannot integrate BTC fairly into our scoring system, and thus refrain from calculating a quantile plot score. Although we were not able to determine exact CPU-times from BTC due to tool limitations, a wall clock time was collected. The average wall clock time of BTC on tasks where definite answers were returned amounts to $17 \pm 4\,\text{s}$ on DSR and $308 \pm 1109\,\text{s}$ on ECC. Figure 5 shows the results for all 143 verification tasks on which BTC returned a definite result. It also indicates conflicts, i.e. different outcomes than BTC EmbeddedValidator.

---

[5] A different, custom version than used in SV-COMP 2019.

4.2 Scores Assuming Correct Results by BTC EmbeddedValidator

In absence of the true verification results, let us assume the results of BTC EmbeddedValidator as a "ground truth". As this is a mature industrial tool developed over many years specifically for such industrial cases considered here, we believe that this is a reasonable assumption. For this, we restrict the verification tasks to those on which BTC returns a definite answer. We are aware of the fact that this is debatable, but given the very low number of verification results by BTC EmbeddedValidator that could be shown by other tools to be invalidated (as depicted later), this gives a quite good impression. We would like to point out that we are not interested in either shaming or praising specific tools, we simply are trying to provide a look at the "big picture" with respect to model checking certain types of industrial embedded code. Our assumption of using BTC EmbeddedValidator as a ground truth does certainly not imply the validity of all its results. But, considering the purpose of this section, it represents a sufficiently precise reference point for a comparison. We update the quantile plots to *now punish wrong results* (i.e., results in conflict with BTC) by −16 *and* −32 *points for wrong violation and proof results*, respectively, as in the SV-COMP. The resulting plots are given in Fig. 6.

Compared to Fig. 4, the scores of CBMC+k are substantially worse as it has three conflicts with BTC EmbeddedValidator. This is due to the fact that the SV-COMP punishment scheme is bad for verifiers returning many results of which some are wrong. It is almost as good (in terms of the scoring scheme) to not generate any result at all (and thus no "wrong" result). This effect is certainly important when witness validaation is seldom, as it is the case in our setting where only one witness could be validated. CBMC+k produced definite verification results on many of the requirements, and consequently has a higher chance of producing a conflicting result. With conflicts being punished heavily and non-validated answers that are deemed correct not being accounted for much, the accumulated score of a verifier returning many definitive results some of which are wrong has a high chance to score worse than a verifier returning a small number of results. Figure 7 presents updated Venn diagrams when removing all results that are in conflict with BTC.

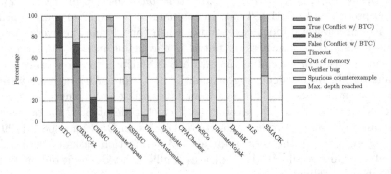

Fig. 5. The verification results for each verifier, in percent of the 143 verification tasks on which BTC returned a definite result. No witness validation results are depicted, as they were previously given in Fig. 2.

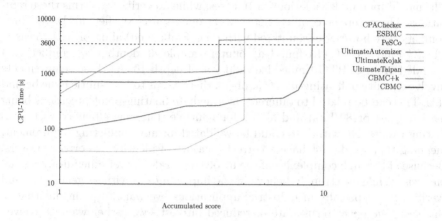

Fig. 6. The quantile plot for each verifier, assuming BTC results as ground truth. The tools 2LS, DepthK, SMACK and Symbiotic have been omitted as they do not reach a score other than zero.

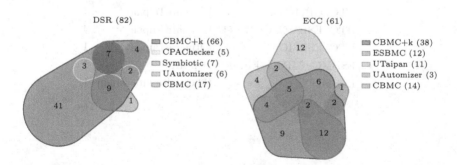

Fig. 7. Venn diagrams indicating the requirement coverage (i.e., a definite result was issued) by the top-five verifiers for case study DSR (left) and ECC (right), assuming BTC results as ground truth.

We did a careful comparison of the verification results of all verifiers. Our findings are summarized in Table 4. For the ECC case study, the verifiers gave contradicting answers for 18 requirements, i.e., about 24% of all requirements. UltimateTaipan finds violations in 16 cases, while no verifier confirms these refutations. There were no conflicts between the open-source verifiers for DSR. Three conflicts were however encountered with BTC EmbeddedValidator. In two cases, CBMC (and CBMC+k) found a counterexample at depth two, conflicting a bounded proof of BTC EmbeddedValidator of depth 10. As these requirements involve equality of floating-point numbers, there seems to be a subtle issue behind this. This can be related to different intermediate floating-point precisions being used (e.g. 64 or 80 bits) and allows for multiple different, albeit correct, conflicting results. No witnesses could be validated for any conflicting requirement, meaning that we do not have a correct measure of identifying correct answers. Because of the high complexity of the involved C code, we refrained from manual analysis. While we strongly believe in the importance of witness generation and -verification, especially in industrial applications, we want to point out that in this case, the exact results are of reduced interest—we rather want to convey the overall big picture of how well the selected open source model checkers are optimized towards real-world industrial applications.

Table 4. The contradicting results observed in DSR and ECC, respectively.

Case study	True	False	Count
DSR	CBMC+k	BTC	1
	BTC	CBMC, CBMC+k	2
			$\sum = 3$
ECC	BTC	UltimateTaipan	7
	BTC, CBMC+k	UltimateTaipan	4
	BTC, ESBMC, CBMC+k	UltimateTaipan	4
	BTC, ESBMC	UltimateTaipan	1
	ESBMC, CBMC+k	DepthK	1
	ESBMC	BTC, UltimateTaipan	1
			$\sum = 18$

5   Encountered Issues

During the course of this work we identified issues and bugs in most of the verifiers. In case we were able to identify a minimal working example, we reported bugs to the developers as noted in the footnotes below. We give a brief description of the occurring issues. Issues encountered with earlier versions of BTC EmbeddedValidator have been described in [3].

CBMC 5.11. We encountered a bug that presented itself on the code outputted by Frama-C [23], which led CBMC to report *spurious counterexamples.* In version 5.11, CBMC did not handle variables that are local to a switch block correctly and always assumed a non-deterministic value for them[6]. This bug has been fixed in subsequent releases. Additionally, when employing CBMC 5.9 or larger for CBMC+k we noticed *a drop in performance for the inductive steps* compared to version 5.8, sometimes resulting in resource exhaustion for the 5.11 version. This behavior was not emerging in the base cases, i.e., it most likely corresponds to the introduced non-deterministic state spaces, although we were not able to identify a specific cause. Lastly, CBMC outputs *witnesses that do not adhere to the format specification*[7].

ESBMC 6.0.0. On DSR, we observed *a verifier bug on 97.1%* of the verification tasks. Here, ESBMC seems to specify a faulty input for its default SMT solver, Boolector. Specifically, it appears to create if-else branching conditions of different sorts. This problem could be avoided e.g. by using Z3.

2LS 0.7.0. We identified a simple program on which 2LS delivers *false negatives*, consisting of two nested loops and a __VERIFIER_error() statement after the inner loop. 2LS reports such a program as safe with its k-induction setting[8]. Apart from this, 2LS did not execute on any verification task. This seems to be due to *a bug in a bit-vector map implementation*, where a size assertion fails.

CPAChecker 1.8.0. C typedefs were not resolved correctly[9]. This bug initially prevented the tool from running on the case studies completely, although *it was quickly fixed by the tool developers.* Furthermore, we found that switch-local variables, similar to CBMC, are not represented internally at all, and thus ignored[10]. As we tried to run CPAChecker with Z3, we were deterred by a bug in the Z3-abstraction of JavaSMT[11].

DepthK 3.1. Due to the bug exhibited by ESBMC (see above), DepthK did not execute on most of the verification tasks. Here, it creates ESBMC instances which immediately fail until DepthK reaches the time out.

SMACK 1.9.3. SMACK did not return a single definite answer, most likely due to the *default loop bound of one.*

Symbiotic 6.0.3. For both case studies, there are some properties for which KLEE prints that it is silently concretizing an expression to value 0 due to floating points, which leads to Symbiotic failing the verification. Additionally, KLEE

---

[6] https://github.com/diffblue/cbmc/issues/3283.

[7] https://github.com/diffblue/cbmc/issues/4418.

[8] https://github.com/diffblue/2ls/issues/123.

[9] https://groups.google.com/forum/#!topic/cpachecker-users/wTqHOedBOb0.

[10] https://groups.google.com/forum/#!topic/cpachecker-users/_bH55x_INOw.

[11] https://groups.google.com/forum/#!topic/cpachecker-users/6wv6fgwHnk4.

extracted some spurious counterexamples that it could not replay. Symbiotic stops the execution thereafter.

UltimateAutomizer 91b1670e. We observed two verification runs where UltimateAutomizer is unable to convert an assertion to an internal function representation. There are 40 ECC verification tasks leading to erroneous behavior. In 38 cases the usage of an unknown **enum** constant leads to program abortion. The remaining two instances are identical to the described bug on DSR.

UltimateTaipan 91b1670e. On DSR and ECC, the same two conversion error instances as for UltimateAutomizer apply.

6 Epilogue

This paper reported on applying 12 software model checkers to two embedded C code case studies from the automotive domain. Although this is a rather limited set of case studies, our findings give some observations that we hope to be insightful for the software verification community. From the fact that the open-source verifiers cover in the best up to 20% of all requirements—about 99% of them being invariants—makes clear that *there seems to be a serious gap between the needs of automotive code verification and open-source software model checker capabilities.* The specific characteristics of the two case studies (many floating-points, pointer dereferencing, bitwise operations etc.) are certainly a decisive factor in this respect. Additionally, the structure of an infinite outer loop (forever processing inputs) with nested finite loops seems to require an tailored k-induction to properly capture behavior, which we believe explains part of the success of CBMC+k and BTC. While both tools are heavily tailored towards special use-cases and are unsuitable for more general programs, we firmly believe these optimizations are worth pursuing and integrating into mainstream open-source verifiers. Admittedly, the fact that our benchmarks are not publicly available is a weak point. More studies like the one in this paper are needed. To that end, *the software model checking community and industrial partners covering various application domains should take up an orchestrated effort to set up a substantial set of industrial benchmarks.* The only way to meet the needs in industry is to be able to apply software model checkers on real industrial software of different domains. Finally, the results of our study (particularly, the score of CBMC+k relative to BTC) suggest *to revisit the scoring scheme of verification competitions such as SV-COMP.* In particular, the punishment of wrong verification results is too severe; it is currently measured in absolute terms (the number of wrong answers), whereas a relative judgment (what is the percentage of wrong answers that a verifier obtained) seems to be more fair.

Acknowledgment. We thank BTC Embedded Systems AG, in particular Tino Teige and Markus Gros, for their support and helpful advice. We are grateful to Md Tawhid Bin Waez and Thomas Rambow (both from Ford Motor Company) for their support on the case studies in an earlier phase and for fruitful discussions on formal verification and Simulink. We thank Dirk Beyer for very useful feedback on an earlier version of the paper.

References

1. Beyer, D., Dangl, M., Wendler, P.: A unifying view on SMT-based software verification. J. Autom. Reason. **60**(3), 299–335 (2018)
2. Beyer, D.: Automatic verification of C and Java programs: SV-COMP 2019. In: Beyer, D., Huisman, M., Kordon, F., Steffen, B. (eds.) TACAS 2019. LNCS, vol. 11429, pp. 133–155. Springer, Cham (2019). https://doi.org/10.1007/978-3-030-17502-3_9
3. Berger, P., Katoen, J.-P., Ábrahám, E., Waez, M.T.B., Rambow, T.: Verifying auto-generated C code from simulink. In: Havelund, K., Peleska, J., Roscoe, B., de Vink, E. (eds.) FM 2018. LNCS, vol. 10951, pp. 312–328. Springer, Cham (2018). https://doi.org/10.1007/978-3-319-95582-7_18
4. Kroening, D., Tautschnig, M.: CBMC – C bounded model checker. In: Ábrahám, E., Havelund, K. (eds.) TACAS 2014. LNCS, vol. 8413, pp. 389–391. Springer, Heidelberg (2014). https://doi.org/10.1007/978-3-642-54862-8_26
5. Clarke, E., Kroening, D., Lerda, F.: A tool for checking ANSI-C programs. In: Jensen, K., Podelski, A. (eds.) TACAS 2004. LNCS, vol. 2988, pp. 168–176. Springer, Heidelberg (2004). https://doi.org/10.1007/978-3-540-24730-2_15
6. Gadelha, M.R., Monteiro, F.R., Morse, J., Cordeiro, L.C., Fischer, B., Nicole, D.A.: ESBMC 5.0: an industrial-strength C model checker. In: 33rd ACM/IEEE International Conference on Automated Software Engineering, pp. 888–891. ACM Press (2018)
7. Schrammel, P., Kroening, D.: 2LS for program analysis. In: Chechik, M., Raskin, J.-F. (eds.) TACAS 2016. LNCS, vol. 9636, pp. 905–907. Springer, Heidelberg (2016). https://doi.org/10.1007/978-3-662-49674-9_56
8. Beyer, D., Henzinger, T.A., Théoduloz, G.: Configurable software verification: concretizing the convergence of model checking and program analysis. In: Damm, W., Hermanns, H. (eds.) CAV 2007. LNCS, vol. 4590, pp. 504–518. Springer, Heidelberg (2007). https://doi.org/10.1007/978-3-540-73368-3_51
9. Beyer, D., Keremoglu, M.E., Wendler, P.: Predicate abstraction with adjustable-block encoding. In: FMCAD, pp. 189–197. IEEE (2010)
10. Beyer, D., Löwe, S.: Explicit-state software model checking based on CEGAR and interpolation. In: Cortellessa, V., Varró, D. (eds.) FASE 2013. LNCS, vol. 7793, pp. 146–162. Springer, Heidelberg (2013). https://doi.org/10.1007/978-3-642-37057-1_11
11. Beyer, D., Dangl, M., Wendler, P.: Boosting k-induction with continuously-refined invariants. In: Kroening, D., Păsăreanu, C.S. (eds.) CAV 2015. LNCS, vol. 9206, pp. 622–640. Springer, Cham (2015). https://doi.org/10.1007/978-3-319-21690-4_42
12. Richter, C., Wehrheim, H.: PeSCo: predicting sequential combinations of verifiers. In: Beyer, D., Huisman, M., Kordon, F., Steffen, B. (eds.) TACAS 2019. LNCS, vol. 11429, pp. 229–233. Springer, Cham (2019). https://doi.org/10.1007/978-3-030-17502-3_19
13. Rocha, W., Rocha, H., Ismail, H., Cordeiro, L., Fischer, B.: DepthK: a k-induction verifier based on invariant inference for C programs. In: Legay, A., Margaria, T. (eds.) TACAS 2017. LNCS, vol. 10206, pp. 360–364. Springer, Heidelberg (2017). https://doi.org/10.1007/978-3-662-54580-5_23

14. Rakamarić, Z., Emmi, M.: SMACK: decoupling source language details from verifier implementations. In: Biere, A., Bloem, R. (eds.) CAV 2014. LNCS, vol. 8559, pp. 106–113. Springer, Cham (2014). https://doi.org/10.1007/978-3-319-08867-9_7

15. Barnett, M., Chang, B.-Y.E., DeLine, R., Jacobs, B., Leino, K.R.M.: Boogie: a modular reusable verifier for object-oriented programs. In: de Boer, F.S., Bonsangue, M.M., Graf, S., de Roever, W.-P. (eds.) FMCO 2005. LNCS, vol. 4111, pp. 364–387. Springer, Heidelberg (2006). https://doi.org/10.1007/11804192_17

16. Chalupa, M., Vitovská, M., Jonáš, M., Slaby, J., Strejček, J.: Symbiotic 4: beyond reachability. In: Legay, A., Margaria, T. (eds.) TACAS 2017. LNCS, vol. 10206, pp. 385–389. Springer, Heidelberg (2017). https://doi.org/10.1007/978-3-662-54580-5_28

17. Heizmann, M., Hoenicke, J., Podelski, A.: Software model checking for people who love automata. In: Sharygina, N., Veith, H. (eds.) CAV 2013. LNCS, vol. 8044, pp. 36–52. Springer, Heidelberg (2013). https://doi.org/10.1007/978-3-642-39799-8_2

18. Ermis, E., Nutz, A., Dietsch, D., Hoenicke, J., Podelski, A.: Ultimate kojak. In: Ábrahám, E., Havelund, K. (eds.) TACAS 2014. LNCS, vol. 8413, pp. 421–423. Springer, Heidelberg (2014). https://doi.org/10.1007/978-3-642-54862-8_36

19. Greitschus, M., et al.: Ultimate Taipan: trace abstraction and abstract interpretation. In: Legay, A., Margaria, T. (eds.) TACAS 2017. LNCS, vol. 10206, pp. 399–403. Springer, Heidelberg (2017). https://doi.org/10.1007/978-3-662-54580-5_31

20. Gadelha, M.Y.R., Ismail, H.I., Cordeiro, L.C.: Handling loops in bounded model checking of C programs via k-induction. STTT **19**(1), 97–114 (2017)

21. Teige, T., Bienmüller, T., Holberg, H.J.: Universal pattern: formalization, testing, coverage, verification, and test case generation for safety-critical requirements. In: MBMV, Albert-Ludwigs-Universität Freiburg (2016). P. 6–9

22. Berger, P., Nellen, J., Katoen, J.-P., Ábrahám, E., Waez, M.T.B., Rambow, T.: Multiple analyses, requirements once. In: Larsen, K.G., Willemse, T. (eds.) FMICS 2019. LNCS, vol. 11687, pp. 59–75. Springer, Cham (2019). https://doi.org/10.1007/978-3-030-27008-7_4

23. Cuoq, P., Kirchner, F., Kosmatov, N., Prevosto, V., Signoles, J., Yakobowski, B.: Frama-C. In: Eleftherakis, G., Hinchey, M., Holcombe, M. (eds.) SEFM 2012. LNCS, vol. 7504, pp. 233–247. Springer, Heidelberg (2012). https://doi.org/10.1007/978-3-642-33826-7_16

Requirement Specification and Testing

Automated Requirements-Based Testing of Black-Box Reactive Systems

Massimo Narizzano[1]([✉]), Luca Pulina[2], Armando Tacchella[1],
and Simone Vuotto[1,2]

[1] DIBRIS, University of Genoa, Viale Causa 13, 16145 Genoa, Italy
{massimo.narizzano,armando.tacchella}@unige.it
[2] Chemistry and Pharmacy Department, University of Sassari,
Via Vienna 2, Sassari, Italy
{lpulina,svuotto}@uniss.it

Abstract. We present a new approach to conformance testing of black-box reactive systems. We consider system specifications written as linear temporal logic formulas to generate tests as sequences of input/output pairs: inputs are extracted from the Büchi automata corresponding to the specifications, and outputs are obtained by feeding the inputs to the systems. Conformance is checked by comparing input/output sequences with automata traces to detect violations of the specifications. We consider several criteria for extracting tests and for stopping generation, and we compare them experimentally using both indicators of coverage and error-detection. The results show that our methodology can generate test suites with good system coverage and error-detection capability.

Keywords: Automated testing and verification · Runtime verification · Black-box conformance testing

1 Introduction

We are concerned with the problem of checking whether a reactive system—which we can execute, but for which we have no internal representation—conforms to a set of requirements provided as temporal logic formulas. This problem arises in a variety of contexts, e.g., when a system is developed by integrating commercial off-the-shelf (COTS) components [20]. In these scenarios, techniques such as model checking [4] or (white-box) model-based testing [28] are ruled out. Also, classical black-box techniques like random testing, equivalence partitioning or boundary analysis [11] either do not take into account the specification or require manual effort to assemble meaningful test suites. Techniques aimed at automated test generation for black-box reactive systems relying on formal models of the specifications have been explored—see, e.g., [5,17–19,26]—and they seem more promising than classical techniques when both efficiency of test generation and effectiveness in covering the specification are considered. Runtime verification [9] techniques can be seen as a form of *oracle-based testing* [10]:

© Springer Nature Switzerland AG 2020
R. Lee et al. (Eds.): NFM 2020, LNCS 12229, pp. 153–169, 2020.
https://doi.org/10.1007/978-3-030-55754-6_9

each test is executed on the system implementation and the test oracle, i.e., the monitor in runtime verification jargon, observes the system and checks whether its executions are behaviors allowed by the specification or not. Following this stream of research, a technique based on the use of monitors as test oracles is proposed in [3]. Their approach can test for safety properties ("something bad will never happen"), but it does not deal with liveness properties ("something good will happen infinitely often"). While liveness properties are not amenable to monitoring on finite executions, their proper subclass of co-safety properties ("something good will happen") consists of formulas that can be monitored on finite traces and that we wish to consider when testing a system for conformance.

Our approach is inspired by [3], but aims to deal with a more general class of properties. Our methodology is based on a visit of the Büchi automaton corresponding to the requirements. The visit starts from the initial state of the automaton and generates a sequence of input values with which the black-box system is fed to obtain a corresponding sequence of output values. We check such input/output sequence against the automaton, i.e., we check whether there exists at least one state in the automaton that can be reached along the sequence. If there is no such state, then the system is not conformant to the requirements and the sequence provides a counterexample. Otherwise, we can continue the generation of the sequence by iterating the above steps until either (i) an acceptance state of the automaton is reached with a sequence of length at least k_{min} or (ii) an acceptance state cannot be reached with a sequence of length at most k_{max}, where k_{min} and k_{max} are two parameters such that $k_{min} < k_{max}$. Multiple tests can be obtained by iterating this procedure until all the reachable transitions have been visited at least once.

We evaluate our approach in three different experimental settings. In the first one we consider benchmarks taken from the LTL Track of the 2018 edition of the Reactive Synthesis Competition (SYNTCOMP 2018)[1] and we compare our approach with the one described in [3]. In the second setting we use the Adaptive Cruise Control (ACC) prototype implemented in [2] and we compare the tests generated by our approach with those generated with a model-based generation strategy. In the third setting we test the model of a robotic arm controller in order to evaluate our approach on a large set of requirements coming from an industry-grade prototype. In the two former settings we use a mix of fault-injection [15] and mutation analysis [1] in order to compare different approaches. In the third setting we inject faults manually. The results we obtained with our experiments show that our approach can outperform the one in [3] by finding more induced faults. Furthermore, generating tests based on the specification can be as effective as approaches based on the system model, discovering almost the same number of faults. Finally, our approach can be effective in finding faults in small-to-medium sized industry-grade systems.

The rest of the paper is structured as follows. In Sect. 2 we present some basic notation and definitions. In Sect. 3 we describe our framework for test case generation of black-box system. Finally, in Sect. 4 we show experimental

---

[1] http://www.syntcomp.org/.

results and we conclude the paper in Sect. 5 with some remarks and an agenda for future work.

2 Preliminaries and Related Work

In this Section we recall the basic concepts used trough the paper. First, we present some basic definitions, followed by syntax and semantics of Linear Temporal Logic (LTL). Then we provide a short introduction to ω-regular grammars and languages and we conclude the section by presenting related work.

2.1 Non Deterministic Büchi Automa

Definition 1 (Non Deterministic Büchi Automata). *A non deterministic Büchi Automata (NBA) $\mathcal{A}$ is a tuple $\mathcal{A} = (Q, \Sigma, \delta, q_0, F)$ where:*

- *Q is a finite set of states,*
- *Σ is an alphabet,*
- *$\delta : Q \times \Sigma \to 2^Q$ is a transition function*
- *$q_0 \in Q$ is the initial state*
- *$F \subseteq Q$ is a set of accept states, called acceptance set.*

Let Σ^ω denote the set of all infinite words over the alphabet Σ.

Definition 2 (Run). *A run for an infinite word $\sigma = A_0 A_1 A_2... \in \Sigma^\omega$ denotes an infinite sequence $\varrho = q_0 q_1 q_2...$ of states in $\mathcal{A}$ such that $q_0 \in Q_0$ and $q_{i+1} = \delta(q_i, A_i)$ for $i \geq 0$, and $\forall A_i,\ A_i \in \Sigma$.*

Notice that each run ϱ in a NBA *induces a corresponding word $\sigma \in \Sigma^\omega$.*

Definition 3 (Accepting run). *A run ϱ is accepting if there exist $q_i \in F$ such that q_i occurs infinitely many times in ϱ.*

Figure 1 (top), shows a NBA where $Q = \{0, 1, 2, 3, 4, 5, 6\}$, $\Sigma = 2^{AP}$, $AP = \{p_0, p_1\}$, $q_0 = 0$, and $F = \{1, 3, 5\}$. Throughout the paper we make use of propositional logic formulae as a shorthand notation for the transitions of NBAs. For instance, a label $a \vee b$ on an edge from a state q to a state p, represents three transitions from q to p: one for the symbol $\{a\}$, one for the symbol $\{b\}$, and one for the symbol $\{a, b\}$.

2.2 LTL Syntax and Semantics

Linear temporal logic (LTL) [25] formulae consist of atomic propositions, Boolean operators, and temporal operators. The syntax of a LTL formula ϕ is given as follows:

$$\phi = \top \mid \bot \mid a \mid \neg \phi_1 \mid \phi_1 \vee \phi_2 \mid \mathcal{X} \phi_1 \mid \phi_1 \mathcal{U} \phi_2 \mid (\phi)$$

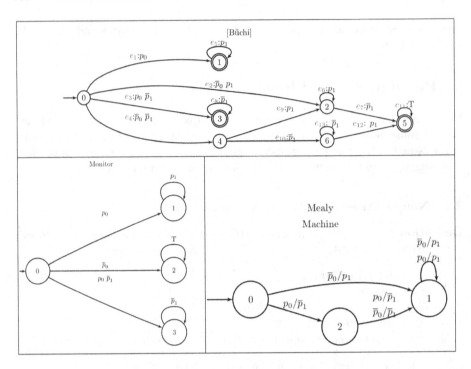

Fig. 1. A state-based Büchi automaton (top), the corresponding monitor (bottom-left) and a Mealy machine (bottom-right). We write $\bar{p}_i$ to denote $\neg p_i$.

where $a \in AP$, ϕ, ϕ_1, ϕ_2 are LTL formulae, $\mathcal{X}$ is the "next" operator and $\mathcal{U}$ is the "until" operator. In the following, unless specified otherwise using parentheses, unary operators have higher precedence than binary operators. We also write $\bar{\phi}$ to denote $\neg\phi$.

Informally, the semantics of an LTL formula ϕ can be defined over the language that contains all infinite words over the alphabet 2^{AP}. More precisely:

Definition 4 (Set of words over 2^{AP}). *Given a set of atomic propositions AP, $(2^{AP})^\omega$ denotes the set of words that arise from the infinite concatenation of symbols from the alphabet (2^{AP}). Each word is defined as $\sigma = A_0 A_1 A_2 \ldots \in (2^{AP})^\omega$, where each A_i is a set over AP, i.e. $A_i \in 2^{AP}$.*

In the following, for $\sigma = A_0 A_1 A_2 \ldots \in (2^{AP})^\omega$, $\sigma[j \ldots] = A_j A_{j+1} \ldots \in (2^{AP})^\omega$ is the suffix of σ starting in the $(j+1)$st symbol A_j.

Definition 5 (LTL semantics over words). *Let ϕ be an LTL formula over the set AP and let $\sigma = A_0 A_1 A_2 \ldots$ be an infinite word over (2^{AP}). We define the relation "$\models$" between σ and ϕ as as the smallest relation with the following properties:*

1. $\sigma \models true$

2. $\sigma \models a$ iff $a \in A_0$
3. $\sigma \models \phi_1 \wedge \phi_2$ iff $\sigma \models \phi_1$ and $\sigma \models \phi_2$
4. $\sigma \models \neg \phi$ iff $\sigma \not\models \phi$
5. $\sigma \models \mathcal{X} \phi$ iff $\sigma[1...] = A_1 A_2 A_3 \models \phi$
6. $\sigma \models \phi_1 \mathcal{U} \phi_2$ iff $\exists j \geq 0$ such that $\sigma[j...] = A_j A_{j+1}... \models \phi_2$ and $\sigma[i...] \models \phi_1$
   $\forall 0 \leq i < j$

We consider other Boolean connectives like "$\wedge$" and "$\rightarrow$" with the usual meaning, while we introduce $\Diamond \phi$ ("eventually") to denote $\top \mathcal{U} \phi$ and $\Box \phi$ ("always") to denote $\neg \Diamond \neg \phi$.

Definition 6 (Accepted Words for a LTL formula). *We also define the set of accepted Words of a LTL formula ϕ as the set containing all the infininte word σ over 2^{AP} that satisfy the property ϕ, i.e.*

$$Words(\phi) = \{\sigma \in 2^{AP} \mid \sigma \models \phi\}$$

Theorem 1 (Constructing an NBAs for an LTL formula [4]). *For any LTL formula ϕ (over AP) there exists an NBA $\mathcal{A}_\phi$ with $Words(\phi) = \mathcal{L}_\omega(\mathcal{A}_\phi)$.*

Example 1. Figure 1 (top), shows a NBA obtained from the formula

$$p_0 \leftrightarrow (\mathcal{X} \Box p_1 \vee \overline{\Diamond p_1})$$

where $AP = \{p_0, p_1\}$. The NBA is obtained using SPOT [13].[2]

Definition 7 (Mealy machine).
A Mealy machine is a tuple $\mathcal{M} = (S, s_0, I, O, \delta)$ where:

- *S is a finite set of states,*
- *$s_0 \in S$ is the start state*
- *I is a set of symbols called input alphabet,*
- *O is a set of symbols called output alphabet,*
- *$\delta : S \times I \rightarrow S \times O$ is a transition function mapping pairs of states and input symbols to the corresponding pairs of states and output symbols*

In other words, a Mealy machine is a finite-state machine whose output values are determined by its current state and the current inputs.

Example 2. Figure 1 (bottom-right) shows a Mealy machine obtained by using STRIX [23] on the formula

$$p_0 \leftrightarrow (\mathcal{X} \Box p_1 \vee \overline{\Diamond p_1})$$

where $S = \{0, 1, 2\}$, $s_0 = 0$, $I = \{p_0\}$ and $O = \{p_1\}$.

---

[2] Using the command line *ltl2tgba -B -f* "p0 <−> (X G p1 | ! F p1)".

2.3 Monitor

A monitor is an automaton supposed to follow the execution of a system and move accordingly. An error is detected when the monitor cannot move, i.e., the system has performed some action, or reached some state that it was not meant to be.

Definition 8 (Monitor). *A monitor $\mathcal{M}$ is a tuple $\mathcal{M} = (Q,\ \Sigma,\ \delta,\ q_0)$ where:*

- *Q is a finite set of states,*
- *Σ is an alphabet,*
- *$\delta : Q \times \Sigma \rightarrow 2^Q$ is a transition function*
- *$q_0 \in Q$ is the initial state*

Example 3. Figure 1 (bottom-left) shows a monitor obtained using SPOT [13][3] for the formula

$$p_0 \leftrightarrow (\mathcal{X}\,\square\,p_1 \vee \overline{\lozenge p_1})$$

where $Q = \{0,\ 1,\ 2,\ 3\}$, $\Sigma = 2^{AP}$, $AP = \{p_0, p_1\}$, and $q_0 = 0$.

2.4 Related Work

The research most closely related to ours is presented in [3] where the authors describe a methodology for online testing of Java classes. Their key technique is to exploit a monitor derived from LTL specifications to check conformance of the system to stated requirements, with a focus on safety properties. In order to compare this mehodology with our approach, we reimplemented the idea presented in [3], making it applicable to any black-box system and not just Java classes. Another work related to ours is presented in [19] where the authors describe a methodology for specification based testing of black-box systems. They assume that the specification of the system is given as a non-blocking input/output timed automaton, and the system itself—whose model need not to be known—is also a timed automaton. The two main differences between their methodology and ours are (*i*) the capability of dealing with real-time requirements and (*ii*) the form of the specification: ours is "declarative", in the form of a set of LTL requirements, whereas theirs is "operational" in the form of an automaton. We thus incur into one additional step, i.e., extracting an automaton from the requirements, after which the two methodologies proceed in a similar way. However, given the different form and expressivity of the requirements, a direct comparison is not easily feasible, and might be even misleading. More recently in [5], another approach based on timed automata to specify input signals constraints has been proposed. Also this approach bears some similarity with ours and with that of [19], but in our opinion it is not directly comparable, at least in the settings that we consider for our experimental analisys.

Other research which is closely related to ours appears in a series of papers [27,29,30] where the authors present a test-case generation methodology that (*i*) translates LTL requirements into Generalized Büchi Automata, (*ii*)

---

[3] Fired with command line *ltl2tgba* -MD -f "p0 <-> (X G p1 | ! F p1)".

builds trap properties from them—using different criteria—and (*iii*) performs model checking of negated trap properties against the system model in order to extract test cases. The main difference with our work is that such methodology relies on a model of the system under testing, a model that must be verified against the system specification. Failing to do so, may generate conflicting tests, i.e., a test which fulfills a requirement, and violates another. To the extent of our knowledge there is no other recent work on formally-grounded methods for requirement based testing, while there is some not-so-recent work mentioning conformance testing to specification, such as, for example [17,18,26]. However, in these works specifications are mostly "operational" in the form, e.g., of finite state machines and thus a direct comparison with our methodology is not possible.

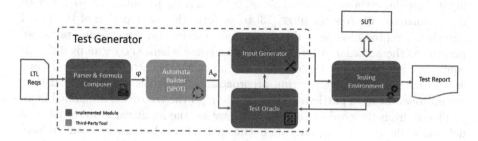

Fig. 2. The main workflow of our approach.

3   Automatic Test Case Generation from LTL Specification

In order to test black-box systems, our approach adopts the workflow presented in Fig. 2. We assume that the specification is composed of a list of LTL formulas, the declaration of the set I of input propositions, and the set O of output propositions such that $I \cup O = AP$ and $I \cap O = \emptyset$. The "Test Generator" pipeline in Fig. 2 has the goal to produce a set of valid tests to execute on the system under test (SUT). The pipeline comprises four components:

- **Parser** reads the input specification, creates the intermediate data structures and builds the conjunction of requirements.
- **Automata Builder** builds a Büchi or equivalent automaton representation of the input specification.
- **Input Generator** chooses which inputs to execute on the SUT.
- **Test Oracle** evaluates the output produced by the SUT and checks if it satisfies the specifications.

Testing Environment is responsible for orchestrating the interaction between the components. It queries Input Generator for new inputs to test and it executes them on the SUT. Testing Environment collects the output and passes it to Test Oracle for evaluation. If the test is complete, Testing Environment stores the final verdict and resets the environment to start a new test. Moreover, the Test Oracle provides to the Input Generator the set of possible states in which the automaton can currently be, given the executed trace. In the following, we present each step of our implementation in more detail.

3.1 Requirements and Automata Processing

The input of the test generator algorithm is a set $R = \{\phi_1, \ldots, \phi_n\}$ of LTL formulas along with the list of input and output variables. The parser reads the input formulas as a conjunction $\Phi = \phi_1 \wedge \cdots \wedge \phi_n$ to build the corresponding automaton. We rely on SPOT [13] to perform the construction of the Büchi automaton represented as a directed graph. Before test generation starts, we preprocess the automaton by expanding the edges where SPOT groups different equivalent assignments to move from one state another, to obtain exactly one assignment for each edge. During preprocessing, variables are omitted if they are not relevant for a particular transition, e.g., if the transition is enabled independently from their value. In such cases, we set the input variables to false by default, while we leave the outputs unchanged. This is because we want to have a fully defined and deterministic input, but we do not want to impose additional constraints that are not specified by the requirements on the outputs. Other choices are possible; for example, one could set the undefined inputs randomly or could copy the value of such variables from previous assignments, if any.

3.2 Test Oracle

The aim of the test oracle is to decide if a trace τ, composed of input and output variables, is correct with respect to the given LTL specification Φ. A more permissive check, often considered for runtime monitoring, consists in verifying that τ is a valid prefix of the language $Words(\Phi)$. This can be done by checking that there exists a run induced by τ on the automaton A_Φ, or, equivalently, using monitors. This kind of check is useful to identify violations of safety properties, but it is ineffective for liveness ones, even for the co-safety subclass. For example, we cannnot detect violations of the formula $\phi = \Diamond a$ with a monitor, because every prefix is valid as long as the proposition a becomes true eventually. In order to solve this issue, a number of different LTL semantics for finite traces have been proposed, such as $FLTL$ [21], $LTL^\mp$ [14], LTL_3 [7] and $LTL\text{-}RV$ [8]. In [6] the authors propose a *counting semantics* making predictions based on the number of steps necessary to witness the satisfaction or violation of a formula. Evaluations under such semantics can range from a 2-valued verdict – namely *True* ($\top$) or *False* ($\bot$) – to a 5-value one; *True* ($\top$), *Presumably True* ($\top_P$), *Inconclusive* (?), *Presumably False* ($\bot_P$) and *False* ($\bot$). The choice of the semantics defines the specific kind of conformance to the specification adopted and implemented by the test oracle. In the following, we rely on the FLTL semantics, formalized below in Definition 9—for a discussion of different semantics, we refer the reader to [8].

Definition 9. *Given a finite word (or trace) τ of length n and an FLTL formula ϕ, $\tau(=\tau,0)$ satisfies ϕ, denoted as $\tau \models \phi$, under the following conditions (s.t. $0 \leq i < n$):*

$\tau, i \models p \in AP$ iff $a \in \tau[i]$
$\tau, i \models \neg\phi$ iff $\tau, i \not\models \phi$
$\tau, i \models \phi_1 \wedge \phi_2$ iff $\tau, i \models \phi_1$ and $\tau, i \models \phi_2$
$\tau, i \models \mathcal{X}\phi$ iff $(i+1 < n)$ and $\tau, i+1 \models \phi$
$\tau, i \models \mathcal{N}\phi$ iff $(i+1 \geq n)$ or $\tau, i+1 \models \phi$
$\tau, i \models \phi_1 \mathcal{U} \phi_2$ iff $\exists i \leq j < n.(\tau, j \models \phi_2 \wedge \forall i \leq m < j.(\tau, m \models \phi_1))$
$\tau, i \models \Diamond\phi$ iff $\exists i \leq j < n.(\tau, j \models \phi)$
$\tau, i \models \Box\phi$ iff $\forall i \leq j < n.(\tau, j \models \phi)$

Regarding the boolean operators, FLTL semantics coincides with the standard LTL semantics on infinite words. However, with temporal operators, such as $\mathcal{X}$ and $\mathcal{U}$, there is a difference concerning the maximum length of the word. In particular, the semantics distinguishes between a strong next operator $\mathcal{X}$, which require a next time step to exists, and a weak version $\mathcal{N}$, which it is always satisfied at the last step of a trace. In our requirements, however, we only make use of the strong variant. In our approach, the FLTL oracle is implemented on an automaton and traces are checked directly on the generated Büchi Automa. We posit that every trace τ ending in an acceptance state q^* of the Automata A_Φ, also satisfies the formula Φ from which the automaton is built.

3.3   Input Generator

The main idea behind the generation of input sequences for testing the SUT consists in exploring different paths of the automaton A_Φ that represents the specification. Given a choice of (i) an exploration strategy to prioritize paths and (ii) a termination condition to end the search, we obtain our algorithm Guided Depth First Search (GDFS) presented in 1. As the name suggests, it is a variant of the classical depth-first search algorithm on directed graphs.

The algorithm takes as input the automaton A_Φ, the interval k_{min} and k_{max}, i.e., the minimum and the maximum length of each trace, the *oracle* object and the environment *env* object. The algorithm starts with the initialization of the *visitCounter* map, that counts how many times an edge has been explored (lines 2–5). Notice that only the outgoing edges from the initial state are initialized, while the other ones are incrementally added during the exploration (lines 11–13). The algorithm terminates when all the edges in *visitCounter* have been visited at least once. At the beginning of each test, the trace τ is initialized to an empty word and the current state s_c is initialized to the initial state of the automaton (lines 7–8). Then the enviroment is reset to start at the initial state (line 9). The test is computed by iteratively choosing an edge (line 14),

---

Algorithm 1. Guided Depth First Search

1: **function** GDFS($A_\Phi, k_{min}, k_{max}, oracle, env$)
2:    $visitCounter \leftarrow$ EMPTYMAP( )
3:    **for** $e \in A_\Phi$.OUTGOINGEDGES($A_\Phi.initState$) **do**
4:       $visitCounter[e] \leftarrow 0$
5:    **end for**
6:    **while** $\exists e \in visitCounter.(visitCounter[e] == 0)$ **do**
7:       $\tau \leftarrow \{\}$
8:       $s_c \leftarrow A_\Phi.initState$
9:       env.RESET( )
10:      **while** $oracle$.VALIDPREFIX(τ) $\wedge |\tau| < k_{max}$ **do**
11:         **for** $e \in A_\Phi$.OUTGOINGEDGES(s_c) $\wedge e \notin visitCounter$ **do**
12:            $visitCounter[e] \leftarrow 0$
13:         **end for**
14:         $e \leftarrow$ SELECTNEXTEDGE($A_\Phi, s_c, visitCounter$)
15:         $i \leftarrow$ GETINPUT(e)
16:         **for** $e \in A_\Phi$.OUTGOINGEDGES(s_c) $\wedge$ GETINPUT(e) $== i$ **do**
17:            $visitCounter[e] \leftarrow visitCounter[e] + 1$
18:         **end for**
19:         $o \leftarrow env$.PERFORMACTION(i)
20:         $s_c \leftarrow$ GETSUCCESSOR($A_\Phi, s_c, i \cup o$)
21:         τ.APPEND($i \cup o$)
22:         **if** $|\tau| \geq k_{min} \wedge s_c \in A_\Phi.acceptanceStates$ **then**
23:            **break**
24:         **end if**
25:      **end while**
26:      $res \leftarrow oracle$.EVALUATE(τ)
27:      env.ADDTEST(τ, res)
28:   **end while**
29: **end function**

---

extracting the input on its label (line 15), executing it on the SUT by means of the *env* object (line 19) and using the output to choose the successor state, if any, and to build the trace τ (lines 20–21). The function selectNextEdge chooses the next state to execute by selecting the edge with less visits so far. In case of multiple edges with the same score, it sorts them with an heuristics that takes into account the distance from the nearest acceptance state and the degree of the target state. Moreover, the *visitCounter* is updated after each choice (lines 16–18) by increasing the counter of all edges leaving s_c that present the input i. This is a small optimization to reduce the number of steps necessary to terminate, because many edges could produce the same input but expect different accepted outputs. From an input point of view, these edges are equivalent, but only one of them will be traversed, depending on the produced output. Termination of a test occurs exactly when one of the following three cases is true: (i) τ is no more a valid prefix of $\mathcal{L}(A_\Phi)$ and therefore the test failed; (ii) the length τ reached the maximum length k_{max}; (iii) the length of τ is greater than k_{min} and the exploration reached an acceptance state. At the end of each test, the oracle gives its final verdict and the result is stored in the *env* object (lines 26–27).

4   Experimental Analysis

We present the results of three experiments[4] involving the framework previously introduced. In the first one, we aim to assess the quality of the generated test suite involving a set of benchmarks borrowed by the LTL Track of the Reactive Synthesis Competition 2018[5] (SYNTCOMP 2018). The second experiment aims to compare the effectiveness of our approach with respect to model-based strategies; in order to do that, we consider the use case of an Adaptive Cruise Control System made available in [2] and we compare our algorithm with state-of-the-art model-based approaches when it comes to spotting erroneous mutants. Finally, our last experiment aims to evaluate the scalability of our approach in a real world use case. So, we consider a set of requirements from the design of an embedded controller for a robotic manipulator used in the context of the EU project CERBERO[6] [22,24]. The experiments described in the following ran on a workstation equipped with an Intel Xeon E31245 @ 3.30 GHz CPU and 32 GB RAM running Lubuntu 18.10 64bits. For all the experiments, we granted a time limit of 600 CPU seconds (10 min) and a memory limit of 30 GBs.

4.1   Syntcomp Benchmarks

The set of benchmarks we consider is the one provided for the LTL Track of the Reactive Synthesis Competition 2018. We first translate the TLSF [16] specifications into equivalent LTL ones accepted by our tool. Note that we do not use SyFCo, a tool for manipulating and transforming TLSF specifications in other existing specification formats for synthesis, because we handle ASSUME formulae in a different way. In particular, SyFCo would translate ASSUME formulae are as a precondition (left-hand side of an implication) and the ASSERT and GUARANTEE formulae aspostconditions (right-hand side of an implication). Therefore, if an ASSUME formula is violated, the system is not required to satisfy the given requirements. This behavior would lead to many useless tests, because whenever an assumption is falsified during the test execution, the specification would be trivially satisfied and no constraint would be enforced on the output. In order to solve this problem, we require the ASSUME part to be satisfied together with the ASSERT and GUARANTEE part, i.e., we replace implication with conjunction. We refer the reader to [16] for more details on the standard translation from TLSF to LTL. We exclude benchmarks whose output assignments appear in the ASSUME part of the specification. This is because, as explained before, we require the assumptions to hold during the execution of the test, but assumptions containing outputs can always be falsified, thus failing

---

[4] All benchmarks are available at https://gitlab.sagelab.it/sage/benchmarks-tests.
[5] http://www.syntcomp.org/.
[6] http://cerbero-h2020.eu.

the test. We sysntesize Mealy machines for the specifications with Strix [23], the winner of the SYNTCOMP 2018 competition, and we exclude benchmarks for which Strix times out in 600 CPU seconds. For each synthesized Mealy machine, we compute 100 mutants randomly applying one of the following rules:

- change the target state of a random transition to a different one;
- flip the output value of a variable on a random transition, namely setting it to *false* if it was *true* and vice-versa.

We apply only one mutation per mutant because the synthesized models are usually small in size and one variation is often enough to expose a violation of the specification. However, some of the resulting mutants may still be correct with respect to the corresponding specification. At the end of this process we have 128 different benchmarks, each of those with 100 mutants. In the experiment, we compare the results obtained with 5 different algorithms. GDFS-1, GDFS-3 and GDFS-5 are the algorithm described in Sect. 3 with k_{min} set to 1, 3 and 5, respectively. For comparison purpose, we also re-implemented, – and generalized to fit our framework – the algorithm presented in [3]. Briefly, the algorithm traverses the monitor automaton of the specification during the test execution, and stops when a coverage criteria is fulfilled. A test is concluded either when an objective is reached or when the maximum length k_{max} of the trace is reached. In [3] two strategies are proposed, namely Random Walk (RW) and Guided Walk (GW) and we implemented and tested both of them. As for the coverage criteria, we implemented what they call *Atomic Proposition Coverage* (APC), i.e., each atomic proposition on each transition of the monitor must be covered. For each algorithm we set k_{max} equal to 100 and we stop the execution as soon as a test fails and the mutant is killed. Notice that 600 CPU seconds are alloted to each benchmark, including automata processing and evaluation of all mutants.

Figure 3 (left) shows the number of mutants killed per benchmark by each algorithm, ranging from 0 to 100. Figure 3 (right) shows the average number of steps executed, namely the sum of the length of each test, averaged over the mutants. In both charts, the abscissa represents the number of benchmarks, while the ordinate shows the number of mutants killed (left) and the number of steps executed (right). Notice that, since the results of RW and GW can vary due to non-deterministic behaviors, we execute the test 3 times and we report the median value as reference for these two algorithms. The results reveal that GDFS-5 clearly outperform all the other algorithms in terms of total amount of mutants killed, and that the number of executed steps is only slightly higher than GDFS-1 and GDFS-3. However, only for two benchmarks all the 100 mutants have been killed. Moreover, in 25 cases it did not kill any mutant, 15 of which due to timeouts. Regarding RW and GW, they both revealed totally ineffective for 73 of the 129 benchmarks, although only 2 timeouts occurred. However, looking at Fig. 3 (right) we notice that in 59 of these benchmarks, the two algorithms did not perform any testing at all. This phenomenon is due to the nature of the benchmarks involved, where the specification only contains liveness properties and the monitor is a single state automaton accepting all prefixes.

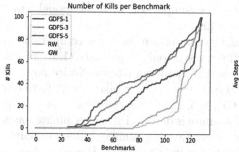
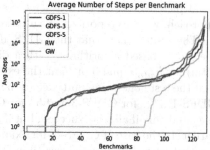

Fig. 3. Total amount of mutants killed (left) and average number of steps (right) computed by the considered algorithms in the set of SYNTCOMP 2018 benchmarks.

Table 1. Experimental results on the ACC use case.

	RC	AC	UFC	GDFS-1	GDFS-3	GDFS-5
Number of test cases	6	7	18	26	4912	2597
Branch coverage (%)	78.3	78.3	86.7	45.0	70.0	71.7
Number of killed mutants	488	488	488	414	480	480
Killed mutants (%)	93.1	93.1	93.1	79.0	91.6	91.6

4.2 Adaptive Cruise Control

In our second experiment we consider the Adaptive Cruise Control (ACC) prototype implemented in [2]. The ACC system adjusts the current velocity of the vehicle towards a target cruise velocity defined by driver. If the vehicle gets too close to the forward vehicle, the ACC system must adjust the current distance between the two and maintain a certain safety distance. Additionally, the driver can intervene by: (1) activating the system via an ACC button; (2) deactivating the system via the ACC button; and (3) deactivating the system by braking or accelerating the car. The authors of [2] also generated test cases from LTL requirements using three different requirements coverage criteria: requirements coverage (RC), antecedent coverage (AC), and unique first cause coverage (UFC). Tests are generated with a model-based generation strategy: trap-properties are built from requirements, and a counterexample is produced with a model checker. The algorithms are evaluated with 524 mutants of the correct implementation.

The goal of the experiment here described is to compare the performance of our algorithm with respect to model-based techniques that make explicit use of a model to generate test cases. We modified slightly the set of requirements, reducing numerical comparisons and enums (available in the NuSMV [12] models used in [2]) to boolean variables. This is a mere syntactic variation to represents LTL formulae in the default syntax as described in Sect. 2.2. The resulting specification is composed of 12 requirements, 6 input and 10 output variables. The results are depicted in Table 1. In order to ease the comparison with the model-based approach, we also report the results from [2].

The results show that the GDFS algorithm performances are comparable to the model-based algorithms, with a difference of only 8 mutants (1.5% of the total) for k_{min} equal 3 or 5, at the expense of many more tests. Notice however that the test generation and execution is still quite small; it takes about 1 s to run GDFS-1, 11 s for GDFS-3 and 5 s for GDFS-5. Moreover, the whole test suite is executed only if all tests succeed, but if a failure is detected it can terminate much earlier. In the case of GDFS-5, for example, the average number of tests executed per mutant is 329, much lower than the test suite size (2597). However, despite the large test suite, GDFS reaches a lower branch coverage than the model-based counterparts, stopping at 71.7%. Also notice that, in this context, with all requirements being safety properties, the RW algorithm described in the previous experiment performs well, achieving similar results to GDFS-5 (although with some variation due to randomness). These results show that the black-box testing with the framework presented in Sect. 3 can be almost as effective as model-based techniques, where more manual work is required to model the system. A final remark on the k_{min} and k_{max} parameters of the GDFS algorithm is in order. As shown in Table 1, k_{min} plays an important role in the test suite size and performance. In our experience, the longer the test, the more the automaton is covered and the less transitions close to the initial state are repeated. Similarly, also k_{max} can influence a test suite size and performance: an excessively small value could lead to some false positive tests, while an excessively large value could produce unnecessarily long tests before declaring them failed. However, the generated test suite depends not only on the algorithm and the specification, but also on the SUT behavior. The optimal values of such parameters is context dependent, and may require some fine tuning.

4.3   Robotic Manipulator

Our last experiment considers a set of requirements from the design of an embedded controller for a robotic manipulator. The controller should direct a properly initialized robotic arm—and related vision system—to look for an object placed in a given position and move to such position in order to grab the object; once grabbed, the object has to be moved and released into the bucket without touching it. The robot must stop also in the case of an unintended collision with other objects or with the robot itself—collisions can be detected using torque estimation from current sensors placed in the joints. Finally, if a general alarm is detected, e.g., by the interaction with a human supervisor, the robot must stop as soon as possible. The manipulator is a 4 degrees-of-freedom Trossen Robotics WidowX arm[7] equipped with a gripper. The design of the embedded controller is part of the activities related to the "Self-Healing System for Planetary Exploration" use case in the context of the EU project CERBERO. In this case the specification is composed of 31 requirements, 3 inputs and 11 outputs. The SUT

---

[7] http://www.trossenrobotics.com/widowxrobotarm.

is implemented as an smv model. With GDFS-5 ($k_{min} = 5$ and $k_{max} = 30$), we obtain 1441 tests and a total of 12867 steps executed in 1171 s. At each step, NuSMV [12] is called in order to determine the evolution of the system. Then, we manually inject faults by removing some constraints in the guards (forcing the system to evolve from one state to another) or by modifying value assignments of some variables. At the end, we obtain 10 different NuSMV faulty models. We show the results of this analysis in Table 2. First, we report that a failed test has been detected in all considered cases. Looking at the Table, we can observe that, for each bugged system, a small number of tests is necessary to discover the failure. Therefore, in most cases, it is not necessary to perform a complete exploration of the automaton and an early stopping strategy can save substantial time when debugging an application.

Table 2. Fault-Injection results on the robotic manipulator use case.

# Injection	# Tests	# Steps	Time(s)
1	1	2	7.64
2	2	14	8.61
3	2	14	8.74
4	1	2	7.75
5	1	7	8.15
6	4	25	8.61
7	56	502	25.23
8	1	3	8.15
9	1	6	7.84
10	2	10	8.17

5   Conclusions

In this paper, we have described a new approach to conformance testing of black-box reactive systems. We evaluated our approach across three different experimental settings. In the first setting we synthesized a set of benchmarks taken from the SYNTCOMP 2018 competition and we showed that our approach is better at finding mutants than (a generalization of) two different algorithms presented in [3]. In the second setting, we showed that our approach compares favorably with state-of-the-art model-based techniques. Finally, in the third setting we tested a controller for a robotic manipulator modeled in SMV and we showed that our approach is able to find some manually injected faults. As future work, we plan to (i) extend the framework with more test oracles and exploration strategies and (ii) increase the input language expressiveness with the addition of numerical constraints. The implementation of our approach is freely available in the SpecPro[8] Java library.

---

[8] https://gitlab.sagelab.it/sage/SpecPro.

Acknowledgments. The research of Luca Pulina and Simone Vuotto is part of the FitOptiVis project funded by the ECSEL Joint Undertaking under grant number H2020-ECSEL-2017-2-783162. The research of Luca Pulina has been also partially funded by the ECSEL JU Project COMP4DRONES and the Sardinian Regional Projects PROSSIMO (POR FESR Sardegna 2014/20-ASSE I).

References

1. Andrews, J.H., Briand, L.C., Labiche, Y., Namin, A.S.: Using mutation analysis for assessing and comparing testing coverage criteria. IEEE Trans. Softw. Eng. **32**(8), 608–624 (2006)
2. Aniculaesei, A., Howar, F., Denecke, P., Rausch, A.: Automated generation of requirements-based test cases for an adaptive cruise control system. In: 2018 IEEE Workshop on Validation, Analysis and Evolution of Software Tests (VST), pp. 11–15. IEEE (2018)
3. Arcaini, P., Gargantini, A., Riccobene, E.: Online testing of LTL properties for java code. In: Bertacco, V., Legay, A. (eds.) HVC 2013. LNCS, vol. 8244, pp. 95–111. Springer, Cham (2013). https://doi.org/10.1007/978-3-319-03077-7_7
4. Baier, C., Katoen, J.P.: Principles of Model Checking. MIT press, Cambridge (2008)
5. Barbot, B., Basset, N., Dang, T.: Generation of signals under temporal constraints for CPS testing. In: Badger, J.M., Rozier, K.Y. (eds.) NFM 2019. LNCS, vol. 11460, pp. 54–70. Springer, Cham (2019). https://doi.org/10.1007/978-3-030-20652-9_4
6. Bartocci, E., Bloem, R., Nickovic, D., Roeck, F.: A counting semantics for monitoring LTL specifications over finite traces. In: Chockler, H., Weissenbacher, G. (eds.) CAV 2018. LNCS, vol. 10981, pp. 547–564. Springer, Cham (2018). https://doi.org/10.1007/978-3-319-96145-3_29
7. Bauer, A., Leucker, M., Schallhart, C.: Monitoring of real-time properties. In: Arun-Kumar, S., Garg, N. (eds.) FSTTCS 2006. LNCS, vol. 4337, pp. 260–272. Springer, Heidelberg (2006). https://doi.org/10.1007/11944836_25
8. Bauer, A., Leucker, M., Schallhart, C.: Comparing LTL semantics for runtime verification. J. Logic Comput. **20**(3), 651–674 (2010)
9. Bauer, A., Leucker, M., Schallhart, C.: Runtime verification for LTL and TLTL. ACM Trans. Softw. Eng. Methodol. (TOSEM) **20**(4), 14 (2011)
10. Bernot, G., Gaudel, M.C., Marre, B.: Software testing based on formal specifications: a theory and a tool. Softw. Eng. J. **6**(6), 387–405 (1991)
11. Burnstein, I.: Practical Software Testing: A Process-oriented Approach. Springer, Heidelberg (2006)
12. Cimatti, A., Clarke, E., Giunchiglia, E., Giunchiglia, F., Pistore, M., Roveri, M., Sebastiani, R., Tacchella, A.: NuSMV 2: an opensource tool for symbolic model checking. In: Brinksma, E., Larsen, K.G. (eds.) CAV 2002. LNCS, vol. 2404, pp. 359–364. Springer, Heidelberg (2002). https://doi.org/10.1007/3-540-45657-0_29
13. Duret-Lutz, A., Lewkowicz, A., Fauchille, A., Michaud, T., Renault, É., Xu, L.: Spot 2.0—a framework for LTL and ω-automata manipulation. In: Artho, C., Legay, A., Peled, D. (eds.) ATVA 2016. LNCS, vol. 9938, pp. 122–129. Springer, Cham (2016). https://doi.org/10.1007/978-3-319-46520-3_8
14. Eisner, C., Fisman, D., Havlicek, J., Lustig, Y., McIsaac, A., Van Campenhout, D.: Reasoning with temporal logic on truncated paths. In: Hunt, W.A., Somenzi, F. (eds.) CAV 2003. LNCS, vol. 2725, pp. 27–39. Springer, Heidelberg (2003). https://doi.org/10.1007/978-3-540-45069-6_3

15. Hsueh, M.C., Tsai, T.K., Iyer, R.K.: Fault injection techniques and tools. Computer **30**(4), 75–82 (1997)

16. Jacobs, S., Klein, F., Schirmer, S.: A high-level LTL synthesis format: Tlsf v1. 1. arXiv preprint arXiv:1604.02284 (2016)

17. Jard, C., Jéron, T.: TGV: theory, principles and algorithms. Int. J. Softw. Tools Technol. Transfer **7**(4), 297–315 (2005)

18. Koch, B., Grabowski, J., Hogrefe, D., Schmitt, M.: Autolink-a tool for automatic test generation from SDL specifications. In: Proceedings. 2nd IEEE Workshop on Industrial Strength Formal Specification Techniques, pp. 114–125. IEEE (1998)

19. Krichen, M., Tripakis, S.: Black-box conformance testing for real-time systems. In: Graf, S., Mounier, L. (eds.) SPIN 2004. LNCS, vol. 2989, pp. 109–126. Springer, Heidelberg (2004). https://doi.org/10.1007/978-3-540-24732-6_8

20. Li, J., Conradi, R., Bunse, C., Torchiano, M., Slyngstad, O.P.N., Morisio, M.: Development with off-the-shelf components: 10 facts. IEEE Softw. **26**(2), 80–87 (2009)

21. Manna, Z., Pnueli, A.: Temporal Verification of Reactive Systems: Safety. Springer, Heidelberg (2012). https://doi.org/10.1007/978-1-4612-4222-2

22. Masin, M., Palumbo, F., Myrhaug, H., de Oliveira Filho, J., Pastena, M., Pelcat, M., Raffo, L., Regazzoni, F., Sanchez, A., Toffetti, A., et al.: Cross-layer design of reconfigurable cyber-physical systems. In: Proceedings of the Conference on Design, Automation & Test in Europe, pp. 740–745. European Design and Automation Association (2017)

23. Luttenberger, M., Meyer, P.J., Sickert, S.: Strix (2018). https://strix.model.in.tum. de/. Accessed 27 June 2019

24. Palumbo, F., et al.: CERBERO: cross-layer model-based framework for multi-objective design of reconfigurable systems in uncertain hybrid environments: Invited paper: CERBERO teams from UniSS, UniCA, IBM research, TASE, INSA-Rennes, UPM, USI, Abinsula, Ambiesense, TNO, S&T, CRF. In: Proceedings of the 16th ACM International Conference on Computing Frontiers, pp. 320–325. ACM (2019)

25. Pnueli, A.: The temporal logic of programs. In: 18th Annual Symposium on Foundations of Computer Science, 1977, pp. 46–57. IEEE (1977)

26. Schmitt, M., Ebner, M., Grabowski, J.: Test generation with autolink and test composer. In: Proceedings of 2nd Workshop of the SDL Forum Society on SDL and MSC-SAM, vol. 2000 (2000)

27. Tan, L., Sokolsky, O., Lee, I.: Specification-based testing with linear temporal logic. In: Conference on Information Reuse and Integration, pp. 483–498 (2004)

28. Utting, M., Legeard, B.: Practical Model-Based Testing: A Tools Approach. Morgan Kaufmann Publishers Inc., San Francisco (2007)

29. Zeng, B., Tan, L.: Test reactive systems with Büchi automata: acceptance condition coverage criteria and performance evaluation. In: 2015 IEEE International Conference on Information Reuse and Integration, pp. 380–387. IEEE (2015)

30. Zeng, B., Tan, L.: Test reactive systems with Büchi-automaton-based temporal requirements. In: Bouabana-Tebibel, T., Rubin, S.H. (eds.) Theoretical Information Reuse and Integration. AISC, vol. 446, pp. 31–57. Springer, Cham (2016). https://doi.org/10.1007/978-3-319-31311-5_2

Formal Verification of Parallel Prefix Sum

Mohsen Safari[1(✉)], Wytse Oortwijn[2], Sebastiaan Joosten[1],
and Marieke Huisman[1]

[1] Formal Methods and Tools, University of Twente, Enschede, The Netherlands
{m.safari,s.j.c.joosten,m.huisman}@utwente.nl
[2] Department of Computer Science, ETH Zurich, Zurich, Switzerland
woortwijn@inf.ethz.ch

Abstract. With the advent of dedicated hardware for multicore programming, parallel algorithms have become omnipresent. For example, various algorithms have been proposed for the parallel computation of a prefix sum in the literature. As the prefix sum is a basic building block for many other multicore algorithms, such as sorting, its correctness is of utmost importance. This means, the algorithm should be functionally correct, and the implementation should be thread and memory safe.

In this paper, we use deductive program verification based on permission-based separation logic, as supported by VerCors, to show correctness of the two most frequently used *parallel* in-place prefix sum algorithms for an *arbitrary array size*. Interestingly, the correctness proof for the second algorithm reuses the auxiliary lemmas that we needed to create the first proof. To the best of our knowledge, this paper is the first *tool-supported* verification of functional correctness of the two parallel in-place prefix sum algorithms which does not make any assumption about the size of the input array.

Keywords: GPU verification · Deductive verification · Separation logic

1 Introduction

With many emerging parallel computing paradigms and architectures, investigating how to parallelize algorithms to optimize performance has become an active research area. General Purpose Graphics Processing Units (GPGPUs) are a promising new parallel architecture, where many threads cooperate together, executing the same instructions, but on different data.

One of the algorithms for which several parallel (GPU-based) implementations have been proposed is the prefix sum algorithm [4,9,15,20]. It takes an array of integers and, for each element, it computes the sum of the previous elements. The prefix sum algorithm is used in many other algorithms, e.g. in radix sort, quick sort, to solve recurrences, and in tridiagonal linear systems; see Blelloch [4]. Blelloch introduced a parallel in-place prefix sum algorithm and Harris [12] adapted it for GPUs. Kogge-Stone [15] proposed a different parallel in-place

© Springer Nature Switzerland AG 2020
R. Lee et al. (Eds.): NFM 2020, LNCS 12229, pp. 170–186, 2020.
https://doi.org/10.1007/978-3-030-55754-6_10

prefix sum algorithm and Horn [13] adapted it for GPUs. These two parallel versions [4,15] are the most used in practice and are available as a primitive operation in many libraries (e.g., AMD APP SDK[1], NVIDIA CUDA SDK[2]).

The GPU-based implementations of these two algorithms are widely used, even as a building block for other algorithms (e.g., sorting). Therefore, the correctness of these algorithms is of utmost importance. This means that the algorithms must be memory and thread safe (i.e. free of data races), *and* that they must be functionally correct, i.e. it actually produces the result we expect. Concretely, in this case functional correctness means that the result must be the prefix sum of the input. In general, proving functional correctness of parallel programs is a difficult task. In particular, proving the functional correctness of these two parallel prefix sum algorithms is challenging for several reasons. First, both algorithms are in-place, i.e. we need to reason about values that are unstable and change during the algorithm. Second, the computational pattern of the algorithms makes it complex to reason about the final result. Therefore, it is a challenge to find suitable properties to relate the internal computation steps in the algorithms to the final result. In particular, in Blelloch's algorithm, there are two independent, but closely related phases with different computation pattern in each phase, which makes the verification harder. As a result, establishing functional correctness of the two algorithms is non-trivial.

For the verification, we use deductive verification, a static approach that does not require running the programs. Intermediate annotations are added to capture the intermediate properties of the program. Then, using a proof system, the annotated code is translated into proof obligations which are discharged to an automated theorem prover; in our case Z3.

To prove memory safety and functional correctness of two parallel prefix sum algorithms, we use VerCors [5], which is a verification tool for reasoning about the correctness of concurrent programs. First, we show how to verify the correctness of Blelloch's algorithm. An important feature of our verification is that it is a non-trivial example of how ghost code[3] helps to reason about in-place algorithms. Second, we show how we can verify a different parallel in-place prefix sum algorithm, Kogge-Stone, using the same approach as the first verification. This demonstrates that the verification setup introduced in this paper (approach, operations and lemma) is not specific to this particular case study and can be used in other verifications. To the best of our knowledge, this is the only *tool-supported* verification of data race-freedom and functional correctness of the two most used *parallel* prefix sum algorithms for any *arbitrary size of input*. Note that none of the existing other approaches to analyse GPU applications is able to verify similar properties. Most approaches are dynamic [11,17–19,21], and only aim to find bugs. Other existing static verification techniques [3,10,14,16] either require a bound on the input size, or they do not fully model all aspects of GPU

---

[1] http://developer.amd.com/tools/heterogeneous-computing/amd-accelerated-parallel-processing-app-sdk.

[2] https://developer.nvidia.com/gpu-computing-sdk.

[3] Ghost code is not part of the algorithm and is used purely for verification purposes.

programming, such as the use of barriers. Furthermore, our work enables the verification of other complicated parallel algorithms, such as stream compaction and radix sort, that are built on top of the prefix sum algorithms.

Contributions. The main contributions of this paper are:

1. We show the parallel prefix sum algorithm by Blelloch is data race-free and functionally correct for any arbitrary size of input, using deductive approach.
2. We show the lemmas used to verify the first algorithm are general enough to prove data race-freedom and functional correctness of a different algorithm, Kogge-Stone, for any arbitrary size of input.

Organization. Section 2 explains the necessary background, i.e., it introduces VerCors, the two prefix sum algorithms verified in this paper, and their encoding in VerCors. Section 3 and Sect. 4 describe how to specify and verify the correctness of the prefix sum algorithms by Blelloch and Kogge-Stone, respectively. Section 5 discusses related work and Sect. 6 concludes the paper.

2 Background

This section briefly describes VerCors and explains both parallel prefix sum algorithms. In particular, it briefly discusses the VerCors verifier and its underlying logic. We describe the prefix sum problem and then we explain the parallel algorithms proposed by Blelloch and Kogge-Stone to solve this problem. In addition, we discuss the pseudocode of the algorithms as we encoded in VerCors.

2.1 VerCors

VerCors is a verifier to specify and verify (concurrent and parallel) programs written in a high-level language such as (subsets of) Java, C, OpenCL, OpenMP and PVL, where PVL is VerCors' internal language for prototyping new features. VerCors can be used to verify memory safety (e.g., race freedom) and functional correctness of programs. The program logic behind VerCors is based on permission-based separation logic [1,7]. Therefore, the programs are annotated with pre/post-conditions in permission-based separation logic [2,8]. Permissions are used to capture which memory locations may be accessed by which threads. Permissions are written as fractional values in the interval $(0, 1]$ (cf. Boyland [8]): any fraction in the interval $(0, 1)$ indicates a read permission, while 1 indicates a write permission. A write permission can be split into multiple read permissions and read permissions can be added up, and transformed into a write permission if they add up to 1. Blom et al. [6] show how to reason about GPU kernels including barriers. We illustrate the logic to verify a GPU kernel by an example.

List. 1. A simple annotated GPU program

```
1    /*@ context_everywhere array != NULL && array.length == size;
2        requires tid != 0 ==> Perm(array[tid-1], read);
3        requires tid == 0 ==> Perm(array[size-1], read);
4        ensures Perm(array[tid], 1);
5        ensures tid != 0 ==> array[tid] == \old(array[tid-1]);
6        ensures tid == 0 ==> array[tid] == \old(array[size-1]); @*/
7    __kernel void rightRotation(int array[], int size) {
8        int temp;
9      int tid = get_global_id(0);  // get the index
10       if (tid != 0) { temp = array[tid-1]; } else { temp = array[size
             -1]; }
11
12       /*@ requires (tid != 0 ==> Perm(array[tid-1], read)) **
13               (tid == 0 ==> Perm(array[size-1], read));
14          ensures Perm(array[tid], 1); @*/
15       barrier(CLK_GLOBAL_MEM_FENCE);
16       array[tid] = temp;
```

Verification Example. List 1 shows a specification of a simple kernel that rotates the elements of an array to the right[4]. To specify permissions, we use predicates $Perm(L, \pi)$ where L is a heap location and π a fractional value in the interval $(0, 1]$[5]. Preconditions and postconditions, keywords 'requires' and 'ensures', respectively (lines 2–6), should hold at the beginning and the end of the function, respectively. The keyword 'context_everywhere' is used as an invariant (line 1) that must hold throughout the function. As preconditions, each thread has read permission to its left neighbor (except thread 0 which has read permission to the last index) in lines 2–3. The postconditions indicate each thread has write permission to its location (line 4) and the result of the function as right rotation of all elements (lines 5–6). Each thread first reads its left location (lines 10). Then it synchronizes in the barrier (line 15). When a thread invokes a barrier, it has to fulfill the barrier preconditions, and then it can assume the barrier postconditions. Additionally, it has to be shown that the barrier only redistributes the resources that are available by the threads upon entering the barrier. In this case, each thread gives up read permission on its left location and obtains write permission on its own location (lines 12–14). After that, each thread writes the value read before to its own location (line 16). Note that, we use && for logical conjunction (line 1) and ** as separating conjunction in separation logic (lines 12–13). Moreover, the keyword \old is used for an expression to refer to the value of that expression before entering a function (lines 5–6). The OpenCL example is translated into the PVL language of VerCors, using two parallel nested blocks. The outer block indicates the number of workgroups and the inner one shows the number of threads per workgroup (see [6] for more details). In this case study, we reason at the level of the PVL

---

[4] We assume there is one workgroup and 'size' threads inside it.

[5] The keywords 'read' and 'write' can also be used instead of fractions in VerCors.

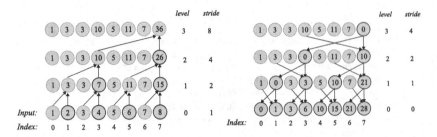

Fig. 1. After the up-sweep phase (left) and the down-sweep phase (right) in Blelloch's algorithm (two arrows coming to a circle indicates summation and one arrow indicates replacement, red color values show the effect of computations and circles with thick border are *indicators* as in Algorithm 1). (Color figure online)

encoding directly, but it is straightforward to adapt this to the verification of the OpenCL kernel.

2.2 Prefix Sum Algorithms

Given an array of integers, the prefix sum of the array is another array with the same size such that each element is the summation of all previous elements. We define an algorithm as an (inclusive) prefix sum if it satisfies the following:

- INPUT: An array *Input* of integers of size N.

- OUTPUT: An array *Output* of size N such that $Output[i] = \sum_{t=0}^{i} Input[t]$ for $0 \leq i < N$.

In the exclusive prefix sum algorithm, where the ith element is excluded from the summation, the output will be:

- OUTPUT: An array *Output* of size N such that $Output[i] = \sum_{t=0}^{i-1} Input[t]$ for $0 \leq i < N$.

Blelloch's Parallel Prefix Sum. Blelloch's algorithm [4] consists of two phases: up-sweep and down-sweep. Figure 1 illustrates both up and down-sweep phases visually, and Algorithm 1 shows the encoding of the in-place algorithm in VerCors. The up-sweep part in the figure corresponds to lines 2–8 of the algorithm and the down-sweep part corresponds to lines 12–23. Therefore, each iteration in the up/down phases in Algorithm 1 (lines 3–8/16–23) correspond to different levels in Fig. 1. We suppose that at the beginning of Algorithm 1, the input and output array have the same values. There is a variable, *stride*, which initially is 1 (line 2) and it is updated in both phases (lines 8 and 23). In the figure, the input values are at level 0 in the up-sweep phase. As we can see, in each iteration of the up-sweep, each pair is summed up at each level. As a result, the last element at the highest level is the summation of the input values. In the

---

Algorithm 1. Blelloch's Prefix Sum Algorithm

```
1:  function EXCLUSIVE_PREFIXSUM(int[] Input, int[] Output, int tid, int N)
2:      int indicator = 2 × tid + 1; int stride = 1;
3:      while stride < N do
4:          if indicator < N && indicator ≥ stride then
5:              Output[indicator] = Output[indicator] + Output[indicator − stride];
6:          Barrier(tid);
7:          indicator = 2 × indicator + 1;
8:          stride = 2 × stride;
9:
10:     Barrier(tid);
11:
12:     indicator = N × tid + N - 1; stride = N / 2;
13:     int temporary;
14:     if indicator < N then
15:         Output[indicator] = 0;
16:     while stride ≥ 1 do
17:         if indicator < N && indicator ≥ stride then
18:             temporary = Output[indicator];
19:             Output[indicator] = Output[indicator] + Output[indicator − stride];
20:             Output[indicator − stride] = temporary;
21:         Barrier(tid);
22:         indicator = (indicator - 1) / 2;
23:         stride = stride / 2;
```

---

down-sweep phase, we first set the last element to 0. Then, we use the partial sums calculated from the up-sweep to compute the prefix sum of the input as indicated at the lowest level in down-sweep. Note that in order to synchronize threads at each level of both phases, a barrier is needed (lines 6 and 21). There is also a barrier between up-sweep and down sweep (line 10). The main purpose of having this barrier is for a specification to redistribute the threads permissions.

Kogge-Stone's Parallel Prefix Sum. In contrast to Blelloch's algorithm, Kogge-Stone's [15] algorithm consists of one phase. Algorithm 2 illustrates the encoding and Fig. 2 illustrates the algorithm visually. The levels in the figure correspond to lines 2–11 of the algorithm. In the figure, the lowest level are the input values. As we can see, at each level, each thread (tid) sums up elements in locations tid and $tid - offset$. Since threads need current values before updating, in the algorithm, we use an auxiliary variable, $temp$, and a barrier (line 7). The threads are synchronized at each level by another barrier (line 10). As a result, at the highest level, where $offset$ exceeds the length of the array, the values are the prefix sum of the values in the input array.

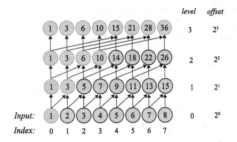

Fig. 2. Kogge-Stone's prefix sum algorithm (two arrows coming to a circle indicates summation and one arrow indicates replacement, red color values show the effect of computations and circles with thick border show *tid ≥ offset* as in Algorithm 2). (Color figure online)

Algorithm 2. Kogge-Stone's Prefix Sum Algorithm

```
 1: function INCLUSIVE_PREFIXSUM(int[] Input, int[] Output, int tid, int N)
 2:     int offset = 1; int temp;
 3:     while offset < N do
 4:         temp = Output[tid];
 5:         if tid ≥ offset then
 6:             temp = Output[tid − offset] + temp;
 7:         Barrier(tid);
 8:         if tid ≥ offset then
 9:             Output[tid] = temp;
10:         Barrier(tid);
11:         offset = 2 × offset;
```

---

3   Verification of Blelloch's Algorithm

In this section, we explain how we verify Blelloch's parallel prefix sum algorithm. We first discuss how to prove data race-freedom and then functional correctness. Instead of presenting the full specification, we explain the main ideas and verification steps by pictures and refer to Appendix A for the crucial annotations[6].

3.1   Data Race-Freedom

To show that the algorithm is data race-free, we need to specify permissions over resources that are shared among threads. Algorithm 1 has two arrays for input and output. Thus, we specify how threads can read or write from these two arrays. In the input array, each thread (*tid*) only needs read access to location *tid*. The situation is more complicated for the output array. Figure 3 visualizes the permission scheme of threads for the output array graphically. The red elements indicate the initial permissions for both phases. In the up-sweep, each

---

[6] The source code is available at https://github.com/Safari1991/Prefixsum.

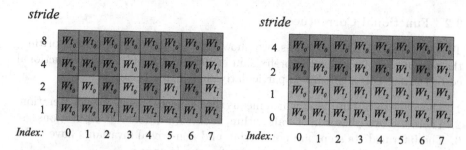

Fig. 3. Permission patterns for array of length 8: (left) up-sweep and (right) down sweep phases of Blelloch's algorithm (Wt_i indicates thread i has write permission, red color indicates initial permissions of active threads, blue shows changes in permission pattern and green shows lost permissions which assigned to thread 0. (Color figure online)

thread needs write access to *indicator* and *indicator − stride* (line 5 in Algorithm 1). Since initially, *indicator* and *stride* are $2 \times tid + 1$ and 1, respectively, we specify write access for each thread to locations $2 \times tid + 1$ and $2 \times tid$, indicated by red color in Fig. 3 (left). Then, in each iteration, *indicator* and *stride* are updated. Therefore, in the barrier of up-sweep (line 6), we change the permissions according to the new values of *indicator* and *stride*, as shown in blue.

Note that, in each iteration some threads lose permissions, since *indicator* exceeds the array length (N). According to this scheme, at the end of up-sweep, no threads have permissions left to access elements of the output array due to *indicator* > N (blue color disappears). However, we need the same pattern of permissions in down-sweep, and in the barrier between up and down sweep (line 10), we cannot invent permissions, but we can only redistribute the current permissions. To solve this, we specify that one random thread (thread 0) collects the lost permissions in each iteration (indicated by green). As we can see, at the end of up-sweep, thread 0 has write permission to all locations in the array.

In the down-sweep phase, Fig. 3 (right), we have the same permission pattern in reverse direction. In down-sweep, thread 0 is the only one whose *indicator* initially is in the bound of the output size (i.e, *indicator* is $N \times tid + N − 1$). Thus, initially, thread 0 has write access to *indicator* and *indicator − stride* (indicated in red). Note that, at the beginning of this phase we update *stride* to $N/2$. Thread 0 also has write permission for the rest of elements (indicated by green color), since we need the permissions to redistribute them in the barrier of down-sweep (line 21). As we can see, when we move down, the permission scheme changes according to *indicator* and *stride*. In the end, each thread (*tid*) has write permission to its own location (*tid*) of the output array. In this way threads can safely compute the prefix sum in parallel.

3.2   Functional Correctness

To verify functional correctness, we show that at the end of this algorithm, the output array contains the prefix sum of the input array. Proving functional correctness of this algorithm is particularly challenging because:

1. The algorithm is in-place; which means the elements change in each iteration.
2. There are two phases in the algorithm, each with different computations.
3. The intermediate steps are non-trivial, and non-trivial invariants have to be proven to conclude that indeed the prefix sum is proven.

To overcome the above challenges, we keep track of the values in each iteration of the algorithm. For this history of values, we use ghost variables (i.e., for each iteration in both phases, we assign the current values of the output array to a ghost variable of type sequence). Moreover, we need to specify invariants that relate the computations in up-sweep and down-sweep. If we look at the only values that change in Fig. 1 (red-colored values), we notice that in up-sweep (left) the sum of those values equals the sum of the values in the input array in each iteration. Further, in the down-sweep (right), the red values at each level are the prefix sum of the red values at the corresponding level in the up-sweep. Therefore, our general strategy to tackle the above challenges is:

1. Define different ghost variables in both up-sweep and down-sweep to keep a history of values.
2. Define mathematical functions to update the ghost variables (according to actual computations) in each iteration of the algorithm.
3. Prove functional correctness over the ghost variables using two invariants:
   – In up-sweep, the sum of values that change in each iteration equals the sum of the values in the input array.
   – In down-sweep, the values that change at each level are the prefix sum of the values that change at the corresponding level in up-sweep.
4. Relate the ghost variables to the actual arrays; i.e., prove that the elements in the ghost variables capture the same elements as in the actual arrays.

Up-Sweep Ghost Variables. We go through the steps above to show functional correctness of the algorithm. First, in the up-sweep phase, we define two ghost variables: one to keep track of all values in each iteration as a full history (f_hist with type sequence of sequences), and one to keep history of the only values that change as a partial history (p_hist with type sequence of sequences). We define two different ghost variables because p_hist is used to show preservation of the above two invariants, while f_hist is used to prove that the ghost variable in down-sweep is capturing the elements in the output array. Initially, these two ghost variables contain the values in the input array.

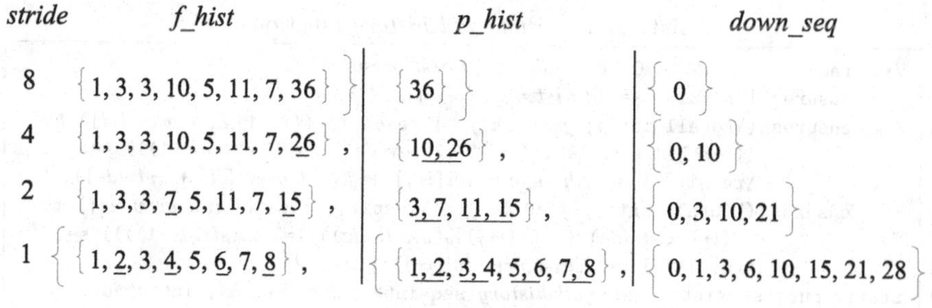

stride	f_hist	p_hist	down_seq
8	$\{1, 3, 3, 10, 5, 11, 7, 36\}$	$\{36\}$	$\{0\}$
4	$\{1, 3, 3, 10, 5, 11, 7, 26\}$,	$\{10, 26\}$,	$\{0, 10\}$
2	$\{1, 3, 3, 7, 5, 11, 7, 15\}$,	$\{3, 7, 11, 15\}$,	$\{0, 3, 10, 21\}$
1	$\{1, 2, 3, 4, 5, 6, 7, 8\}$,	$\{1, 2, 3, 4, 5, 6, 7, 8\}$,	$\{0, 1, 3, 6, 10, 15, 21, 28\}$

Fig. 4. Ghost variables: (left) Building *f_hist* by applying *Build_full_history* to *f_hist_prev_lvl*, blue color indicates how value changes, (middle) Building *p_hist* by applying *Build_partial_history* to *p_hist_prev_lvl*, colors show combination of each pair and (right) creating *down_seq* by applying *p_sum* to *p_hist_lvl*. (Color figure online)

The next step is to define mathematical functions over these ghost variables to update them in the same way as the actual computations do over the actual arrays. To update *f_hist* in each iteration of up-sweep, we must add a new sequence of current values in the output array to the chain of sequences in *f_hist*. Therefore, we define a *Build_full_history* function as shown in List 2. The function takes the previous level in *f_hist*, named as *f_hist_prev_lvl*, the *stride* and an integer i. The integer i, starts from 0 and increases up to the length of *f_hist_prev_lvl*, indicates the location of elements in *f_hist_prev_lvl* to be updated. The *Build_full_history* function goes through all elements and updates the elements if the condition $(i\%(2 \times stride)) == (2 \times stride - 1)$ && $(i \geq stride)$ holds (lines 11–13), otherwise it keeps the elements unchanged (lines 14–15). Note that, this is a recursive function that captures the same computation as in the algorithm, but over the ghost variable. The postconditions (lines 2–8) specify that the result is either the sum of two elements (according to *stride*) if the condition holds (lines 3–5) or unchanged (lines 6–8) otherwise. By applying this function (to *f_hist_prev_lvl*), in each iteration of the algorithm, a full history of values is created like a matrix as sequence of sequences (Fig. 4 (left)). In the figure, the underlined elements show the locations where the condition (in *Build_full_history*) holds and the blue ones show how the values change according to *stride*.

List. 2. The *Build_full_history* function

```
1   /*@ requires stride > 0 && stride < |f_hist_prev_lvl|;
2       ensures |\result| == |f_hist_prev_lvl|-i;
3       ensures (\forall int j; j ≥0 && j <|\result|; ((i <|f_hist_prev_lvl|) &&
4           ((i+j)≥stride) && (((i+j)%(2×stride)) == (2×stride-1))) ==>
5           \result[j] == f_hist_prev_lvl[i+j] + f_hist_prev_lvl[i+j-stride]);
6       ensures (\forall int j; j ≥0 && j <|\result|; ((i <|f_hist_prev_lvl|) &&
7           (((i+j)<stride) || (((i+j)%(2×stride)) != (2×stride-1)))) ==>
8           \result[j] == f_hist_prev_lvl[i+j]); @*/
9   static pure seq<int> Build_full_history(seq<int> f_hist_prev_lvl, int stride,
10      int i) = i <|f_hist_prev_lvl| ? (
11          ((i%(2×stride)) == (2×stride-1) && (i ≥ stride) ?
12          seq<int> {f_hist_prev_lvl[i] + f_hist_prev_lvl[i-stride]} +
13              Build_full_history(f_hist_prev_lvl, stride, i+1) :
14          seq<int> {f_hist_prev_lvl[i]} +
15              Build_full_history(f_hist_prev_lvl, stride, i+1) )) : seq<int> {};
```

To update *p_hist*, which keeps only the values that change during the iterations, we define a *Build_partial_history* function (see List 3). It takes the previous sequence, *p_hist_prev_lvl*, as an argument, and it creates a sequence that contains the values that changed according to the actual computation by summin up each pair of elements (lines 4–5). Note that, the function uses operations **head** and **tail**, where **head** returns the first element of a sequence and **tail** returns a new sequence by eliminating the first element. Figure 4 (middle) shows the result of applying *Build_partial_history* to *p_hist_prev_lvl*.

Down-Sweep Ghost Variables. Next, in down-sweep, we define a ghost variable, *down_seq*, as a sequence to keep the values that change only in the current iteration. In this way, we can show that the values that change in down-sweep are in fact the exclusive prefix sum of the values changed in up sweep in each iteration. To update *down_seq* in each iteration of down-sweep, we define a function, *epsum* (List 4), and we apply it to the corresponding level of *p_hist*, shown as *p_hist_lvl* in the function. The argument i is initially 0. Note that the **intsum** operation sums all elements in a sequence and **take(xs, i)**, returns the i first elements of a sequence **xs**. The *epsum* function calculates the exclusive prefix sum for each element in *p_hist_lvl* and returns it as a sequence to update *down_seq*. As an example, Fig. 4 (right) shows how *down_seq* is updated in each iteration. As we can see, the elements in *down_seq* are the exclusive prefix sum of the elements in *p_hist* at each level. Hence, it is the exclusive prefix sum of the lowest level which is the input array.

stride										p_hist (middle)	lvl	tid/indicator				stride
8	1	3	3	10	5	11	7	36		{36}	3	0/7	1/15	2/23	3/46	8
4	1	3	3	10	5	11	7	26		{10, 26} ,	2	0/3	1/7	2/11	3/15	4
2	1	3	3	7	5	11	7	15		{3, 7, 11, 15} ,	1	0/1	1/3	2/5	3/7	2
1	1	2	3	4	5	6	7	8		{1, 2, 3, 4, 5, 6, 7, 8}	0					1
Index:	0	1	2	3	4	5	6	7								

Fig. 5. Relation between Output (left) and p_hist (middle) according to active threads (grey color) in the table (right): $Output[indicator] == p\_hist[lvl - 1][2 \times tid + 1]$ and $Output[indicator - stride] == p\_hist[lvl - 1][2 \times tid]$ $(lvl > 0)$.

List. 3. The *Build_partial_history* function

```
1   //@ requires |p_hist_prev_lvl| ≥ 0;
2   static pure seq<int> Build_partial_history(seq<int> p_hist_prev_lvl) =
3       1 < |p_hist_prev_lvl| ?
4           seq<int> {head(p_hist_prev_lvl) + head(tail(p_hist_prev_lvl))} +
5           Build_partial_history(tail(tail(p_hist_prev_lvl))) : p_hist_prev_lvl;
```

List. 4. The *epsum* function

```
1   /*@ requires 0 ≤ i && i ≤ |p_hist_lvl|;
2       ensures |\result| == |p_hist_lvl|-i;
3       ensures (\forall int j; j ≥0 && j <|\result|;
4           \result[j] == intsum(take(p_hist_lvl, i+j))); @*/
5   static pure seq<int> epsum(seq<int> p_hist_lvl, int i) =
6       i <|p_hist_lvl| ? seq<int> {intsum(take(p_hist_lvl, i))} + epsum(
7           p_hist_lvl, i+1) :
        seq<int> { };
```

Relating Ghost Variables and Concrete Variables. We proved functional correctness over the ghost variables, but we need to prove it against the actual arrays. Therefore, the last step is to relate them. First of all, It is trivial to relate the levels in *f_hist* to the output array, because of the postconditions in List 2 (lines 2–8), but we should relate the output array and *p_hist*. Figure 5 indicates the relationship between the output array and *p_hist*, according to *tid* and *indicator*, where gray colors (in the table) indicate the active threads in each iteration. The loop of the algorithm starts from level 1. We update the values in the output array according to the current values. Correspondingly, the values are created in *p_hist* according to the previous level. The *indicator* and *stride* are also updated in each iteration. In the output array and *p_hist*, the same colors belong to one thread according to *tid*, *indicator* and *stride*. The invariants that we have in each iteration of up-sweep is $Output[indicator] == p\_hist[lvl - 1][2 \times tid + 1]$ and $Output[indicator - stride] == p\_hist[lvl - 1][2 \times tid]$. To prove them as loop invariants in VerCors, we need some smaller steps and prove a property:

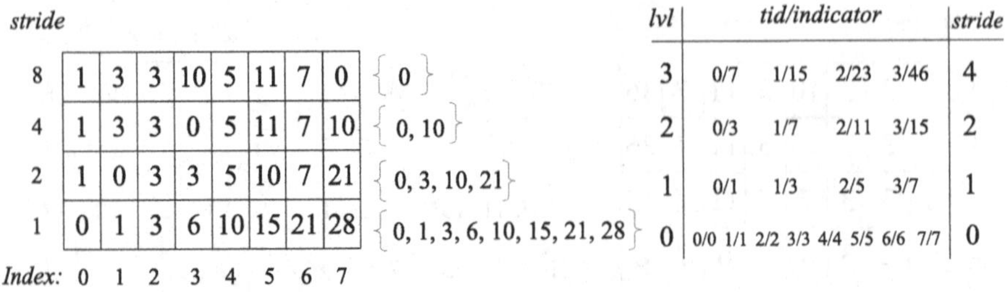

Fig. 6. Relation between the actual array, *Output*, (left) and the ghost variable, *down_seq* (middle) according to active threads (grey color) in the table (right).

Property 1. For any sequence xs:
$\forall i. 0 \le i < |xs| \rightarrow Build\_partial\_history(xs)[i] == xs[2 \times i] + xs[2 \times i + 1]$.

Using this property and the invariants, we can establish the relation between the output array and *p_hist*. The invariants that hold in each iteration of down-sweep is $Output[indicator] == down\_seq[tid]$ and $Output[indicator - stride] == p\_hist[lvl][2 \times tid]$ (see Fig. 6, for an example). Again, the gray colors indicate the active threads and the same colors (in ghost and array) belong to one thread. To prove the invariants in the tool, we first prove these two properties:

Property 2. For any sequence xs:
$\forall i. 0 \le i < |xs|/2 \rightarrow epsum(Build\_partial\_history(xs))[i] == epsum(xs)[2 \times i]$.

Property 3. For any sequence xs:
$\forall i. 0 \le i < |xs|/2 \rightarrow epsum(xs)[2 \times i + 1] == epsum(xs)[2 \times i] + xs[2 \times i]$.

As in up-sweep, by using the invariants, the two properties and several intermediate small steps, we can establish the relation between *down_seq* and the output array. We refer to the implementation for further proof details.

4   Verification of Kogge-Stone's Algorithm

This section explains the verification of Kogge-Stone's parallel prefix sum algorithm. We discuss how to verify this algorithm using the same approach as before. Again, we first discuss data race-freedom and then functional correctness. We only present the main ideas and refer to Appendix B for crucial annotations[7].

4.1   Data Race-Freedom

To verify data race freedom of this algorithm, we need to specify permissions over the output array. Figure 7 shows the permission pattern in each iteration.

---
[7] The source code is available at https://github.com/Safari1991/Prefixsum.

offset	Index: 0	1	2	3	4	5	6	7
8	Rt_0	Rt_1	Rt_2	Rt_3	Rt_4	Rt_5	Rt_6	Rt_7
	Wt_0	Wt_1	Wt_2	Wt_3	Wt_4	Wt_5	Wt_6	Wt_7
4	Rt_0t_4	Rt_1t_5	Rt_2t_6	Rt_3t_7	Rt_4	Rt_5	Rt_6	Rt_7
	Wt_0	Wt_1	Wt_2	Wt_3	Wt_4	Wt_5	Wt_6	Wt_7
2	Rt_0t_2	Rt_1t_3	Rt_2t_4	Rt_3t_5	Rt_4t_6	Rt_5t_7	Rt_6	Rt_7
	Wt_0	Wt_1	Wt_2	Wt_3	Wt_4	Wt_5	Wt_6	Wt_7
1	Rt_0t_1	Rt_1t_2	Rt_2t_3	Rt_3t_4	Rt_4t_5	Rt_5t_6	Rt_6t_7	Rt_7

Fig. 7. Permissions in Kogge-Stone's algorithm; R_{t_i,t_j} indicates read permission by threads i and j, W_{t_i} indicates write permission by thread i, red color shows initial permissions, blue/green show how the permissions change in the first/second barrier. (Color figure online)

As in Algorithm 2, each thread (tid) first needs read permission to locations tid and $tid - offset$ (lines 4 and 6). Since $offset$ initially is 1, each thread (tid) needs read permission to its own (tid) and its left ($tid - 1$) locations as indicated by the red color in Fig. 7. Then, in the first barrier (line 7), each thread gives up read permissions and obtains write permission to its location to store the results of the computation in line 9 (as shown in blue in Fig. 7). Finally, threads reach the second barrier (line 10) and we change the permissions according to the new value of $offset$ for the next iteration. This is indicated in green in the figure. This pattern is repeated by each iteration of the algorithm. At the end of this algorithm, since $offset$ is greater than all $tids$, each thread only has read permission to its own location (tid).

4.2 Functional Correctness

Next, we briefly discuss how to verify functional correctness of the algorithm. The difference between this algorithm and the previous one is that first, Kogge-Stone is an inclusive prefix sum algorithm and second, there is only one phase. Having one phase makes it easier to verify functional correctness, even though this algorithm is in-place as well. We could reuse the functions and operations we defined for the earlier verification. Since this algorithm is for an inclusive prefix sum, first of all, we slightly change the definition of $epsum$ to be an inclusive prefix sum ($ipsum$). The strategy to verify this algorithm is the same as before, i.e., we define a ghost variable to capture the elements in the output array and a function to update this ghost variable in the same way as the actual computation does. Then, we prove functional correctness over this ghost variable by using a suitable property. Finally, we relate the ghost variable to the output array.

As we can see in Fig. 2, in each iteration, the values from index 0 up to index $offset$ are actually the inclusive prefix sum of the input array. We use this property as a loop invariant to show that at the end of the algorithm, we have the prefix sum of the input array. Thus, we define a ghost variable, $temp\_seq$, and we update it inside the loop according to the *partial_prefixsum* function in List 5. This function captures the same computation as in the algorithm. We can see from the postcondition of the function (lines 4–6 in List 5) that if *index* (and the corresponding *tid*) is less than *offset*, then the second `intsum` returns 0, and the first `intsum` returns the prefix sum up to *index*[8]. Thus, in each iteration for *tid* less than *offset* the result will be the prefix sum in *temp_seq*. Therefore, in the end, when *offset* is the length of the input (and output) array, all values in the ghost variable are the prefix sum of the values in the input array.

List. 5. The *partial_prefixsum* function

```
1    /*@ requires |input_seq| ≥ 0 && index ≥ 0 && index ≤ |input_seq|;
2        requires offset > 0 && offset ≤ 2×|input_seq|;
3        ensures |\result| == |input_seq| - index;
4        ensures (\forall int j; 0≤ j && j <|\result|; \result[j] ==
5            intsum(take(input_seq, index+j+1)) -
6            intsum(take(input_seq, index+j+1-offset))); @*/
7    static pure seq<int> partial_prefixsum(seq<int> input_seq, int index,
         int offset) =
8      index < |input_seq| ? seq<int> {intsum(take(input_seq, index+1)) -
9          intsum(take(input_seq, index+1-offset))} +
10         partial_prefixsum(input_seq, index+1, offset) : seq<int> { };
```

As we use *offset* in the function and from the postcondition that we defined, VerCors can infer that in each iteration for *tid* less than *offset*, *temp_seq* and the output array have the same values (specified by a loop invariant). Thus, we conclude that Kogge-Stone's algorithm indeed computes the prefix sum.

5   Related Work

There are a few approaches to reason about GPGPU programs which mostly focus on finding data races. In dynamic approach, programs are instrumented, and then memory accesses are recorded by running them, trying to identify data races (e.g., cuda-memcheck [18], Oclgrind [19] and GRace [21]). This is a simple technique to apply, but since it depends on concrete inputs, it does not guarantee the absence of data races. An improvement over this approach is dynamic symbolic execution where concrete and symbolic (concolic) execution is used, such as GKLEE [17] and KLEE-CL [11]. There are also several static approaches to verify data race-freedom of GPGPU programs. In static approaches, we use logic and theorem provers to guarantee the absence of data races. The key of this approach is using invariants to prove data race-freedom. In addition to VerCors, tools such as PUG [16] and GPUVerify [3] are based on this approach. Except VerCors and VeriFast [14], none of these tools can reason about functional correctness of parallel programs. VeriFast is a verification tool based on static approach to

---

[8] Note that, the *partial_prefixsum* is a recursive function. In lines 4–6, for the final result, *j* is 0 and the parameter of `take` will be *index + 1*, which means the first *index + 1* elements (i.e., starting from 0 it becomes up to element *index*).

prove functional correctness of single-threaded and multithreaded C and Java programs, but not able to reason about GPGPU programs.

The closest related work to our paper is by Chong et al. [10] where they verify data race-freedom and propose a method to verify functional correctness of Blelloch's and Kogge-Stone's algorithm along with two other parallel prefix sum algorithms for all inputs *up to fixed sizes*. They show that if a parallel prefix sum algorithm is proven to be data race-free, then the correctness can be established by generating one test case. Therefore, they use GPUVerify to prove data race-freedom of 4 parallel prefix sum algorithms. Their approach is applicable for any parallel prefix sum algorithm with other operations and types instead of summation and integers. Comparing VerCors to their tool, GPUVerify benefits from more automation, while we need to specify the annotations manually. However, since GPUVerify is based on model-checking approaches, to verify even data race-freedom of GPU programs, the input size must be bounded. As a result, they only show functional correctness for *a fixed input size* (a realistic size for current GPUs). In this paper, we verified data race-freedom and also functional correctness of the two algorithms for *any arbitrary size of input*. We believe that it should be no problem to also prove the other two algorithms.

6   Conclusion

This paper shows how we verify data race-freedom and functional correctness of the two most widely-used parallel prefix sum algorithms, Blelloch's and Kogge-Stone's algorithm, for *an arbitrary input size* by encoding the algorithms into VerCors verifier. Proving functional correctness of Blelloch's algorithm is challenging for multiple reasons. First, the algorithm is in-place. Second, it consists of two independent, but related phases and third, it is non-trivial to relate the computations in both phases to conclude the desired end result (i.e., that it establishes a prefix sum). We overcome these challenges by introducing ghost variables and defining suitable functions that mimic the computations on the ghost variables. Moreover, we prove suitable properties that help us to reason about the algorithm. The verification of Kogge-Stone's algorithm is not as hard as the first one, since there is only one phase and the property that we define is straightforward. We benefit from functions, operations and properties that are defined in the earlier verification and reuse them in the second verification.

As future work, we plan to verify more complicated parallel algorithms that use the prefix sum algorithm internally, such as stream compaction and sorting algorithms. We also would like to investigate how to further automate the process of proof creation. We believe that a substantial part of the required annotations, in particular those related to permissions, can be generated automatically. In addition, we plan to add a CUDA front-end to the tool.

References

1. Amighi, A., Haack, C., Huisman, M., Hurlin, C.: Permission-based separation logic for multithreaded Java programs. LMCS **11**(1), 2–65 (2015)

2. Berdine, J., Calcagno, C., O'Hearn, P.W.: Smallfoot: modular automatic assertion checking with separation logic. In: de Boer, F.S., Bonsangue, M.M., Graf, S., de Roever, W.-P. (eds.) FMCO 2005. LNCS, vol. 4111, pp. 115–137. Springer, Heidelberg (2006). https://doi.org/10.1007/11804192_6
3. Betts, A., Chong, N., Donaldson, A., Qadeer, S., Thomson, P.: GPUVerify: a verifier for GPU kernels. In: OOPSLA, pp. 113–132. ACM (2012)
4. Blelloch, G.E.: Prefix Sums and their Applications, Synthesis of Parallel Algorithms. Morgan Kaufmann Publishers Inc., San Francisco (1993)
5. Blom, S., Darabi, S., Huisman, M., Oortwijn, W.: The VerCors tool set: verification of parallel and concurrent software. In: Polikarpova, N., Schneider, S. (eds.) IFM 2017. LNCS, vol. 10510, pp. 102–110. Springer, Cham (2017). https://doi.org/10.1007/978-3-319-66845-1_7
6. Blom, S., Huisman, M., Mihelčić, M.: Specification and verification of GPGPU programs. Sci. Comput. Program. **95**, 376–388 (2014)
7. Bornat, R., Calcagno, C., O'Hearn, P., Parkinson, M.: Permission accounting in separation logic. In: POPL, pp. 259–270 (2005)
8. Boyland, J.: Checking interference with fractional permissions. In: Cousot, R. (ed.) SAS 2003. LNCS, vol. 2694, pp. 55–72. Springer, Heidelberg (2003). https://doi.org/10.1007/3-540-44898-5_4
9. Brent, R.P., Kung, H.T.: A regular layout for parallel adders. IEEE Trans. Comput. **3**, 260–264 (1982)
10. Chong, N., Donaldson, A.F., Ketema, J.: A sound and complete abstraction for reasoning about parallel prefix sums. In: ACM SIGPLAN Notices, vol. 49, pp. 397–409. ACM (2014)
11. Collingbourne, P., Cadar, C., Kelly, P.H.J.: Symbolic testing of OpenCL code. In: Eder, K., Lourenço, J., Shehory, O. (eds.) HVC 2011. LNCS, vol. 7261, pp. 203–218. Springer, Heidelberg (2012). https://doi.org/10.1007/978-3-642-34188-5_18
12. Harris, M., Sengupta, S., Owens, J.D.: Parallel prefix sum (scan) with CUDA. GPU Gems **3**(39), 851–876 (2007)
13. Horn, D.: Stream reduction operations for GPGPU applications. GPU Gems **2**(36), 573–589 (2005)
14. Jacobs, B., Smans, J., Philippaerts, P., Vogels, F., Penninckx, W., Piessens, F.: VeriFast: a powerful, sound, predictable, fast verifier for C and Java. In: Bobaru, M., Havelund, K., Holzmann, G.J., Joshi, R. (eds.) NFM 2011. LNCS, vol. 6617, pp. 41–55. Springer, Heidelberg (2011). https://doi.org/10.1007/978-3-642-20398-5_4
15. Kogge, P.M., Stone, H.S.: A parallel algorithm for the efficient solution of a general class of recurrence equations. IEEE Trans. Comput. **100**(8), 786–793 (1973)
16. Li, G., Gopalakrishnan, G.: Scalable SMT-based verification of GPU kernel functions. In: SIGSOFT FSE 2010, Santa Fe, NM, USA, pp. 187–196. ACM (2010)
17. Li, G., Li, P., Sawaya, G., Gopalakrishnan, G., Ghosh, I., Rajan, S.P.: GKLEE: concolic verification and test generation for GPUs. In: ACM SIGPLAN Notices, vol. 47, pp. 215–224. ACM (2012)
18. Nvidia: Cuda-memcheck: User manual (version 10) (2019). https://developer.nvidia.com/cuda-memcheck
19. Price, J., McIntosh-Smith, S.: Oclgrind: an extensible OpenCL device simulator. In: Proceedings of the 3rd International Workshop on OpenCL, p. 12. ACM (2015)
20. Sklansky, J.: Conditional-sum addition logic. IRE Trans. Electron. Comput. **2**, 226–231 (1960)
21. Zheng, M., Ravi, V.T., Qin, F., Agrawal, G.: GRace: a low-overhead mechanism for detecting data races in GPU programs. ACM SIGPLAN Not. **46**(8), 135–146 (2011)

Specification Quality Metrics Based on Mutation and Inductive Incremental Model Checking

Vassil Todorov[1,2]([✉]), Safouan Taha[2], and Frédéric Boulanger[2]

[1] Groupe PSA, 78140 Vélizy-Villacoublay, France
[2] Université Paris-Saclay, CNRS, CentraleSupélec, LRI,
91405 Orsay, France
todorov@lri.fr

Abstract. When using formal verification on Simulink or SCADE models, an important question about their certification is how well the specified properties cover the entire model. A method using unsatisfiable cores and inductive model checking called IVC (Inductive Validity Cores) has been recently proposed within modern SMT-based model checkers such as JKind. The IVC algorithm determines a minimal set of model elements necessary to establish a proof and gives back the traceability to the design elements (lines of code) necessary for the proof. These metrics are interesting but are rather coarse grain for certification purposes.

In this paper, we propose to use mutation combined with incremental inductive model checking to give more precision and quality to the traceability process and look inside the lines of code. Our algorithm, based on the result of IVC, mutates the source code to determine which parts inside a line of code have an impact on the properties (killed mutants) and which parts have no impact on the properties (survived mutants). Furthermore, using the incremental feature present in modern SMT-solvers, we observe that mutation can scale up to industrial models. We demonstrate the metrics first on a simple example, then on a complex industrial program and on the JKind benchmark.

Keywords: Formal verification · Model-based mutation · Incremental inductive model checking · Model coverage · Symbolic model checking

1 Introduction

Today, most of the embedded application software in the automotive industry is developed using model-based design tools such as Simulink or SCADE. This paradigm of using a model brings a higher level of abstraction compared to the code and has the possibility to automatically generate the final code. A system designer creates a model by dragging and dropping blocks from a library and simulates its behavior to check if it corresponds to what is expected.

For the development of critical systems, it has been argued that formal proof should be applied to gain higher confidence than with testing only [17, 20, 23].

© Springer Nature Switzerland AG 2020
R. Lee et al. (Eds.): NFM 2020, LNCS 12229, pp. 187–203, 2020.
https://doi.org/10.1007/978-3-030-55754-6_11

Even if these tools can prove formal properties on the model, this feature is not well understood and used by the designers. Actually, specifying properties (based on the requirements specification) within the aforementioned tools is not more complicated than designing the model itself because they are written with the same library blocks as the model. However, there are two main problems: the proof process does not always terminate, and when a property is proved to be valid, no further information is provided about its coverage. For certification of critical software, we should be able to measure quality and exhaustiveness of the proved properties.

For the first problem, we worked on the improvement of the invariant generation used in most of the modern symbolic model checkers and implemented it in JKind [11] to improve the provability of properties involving time. Actually, proving properties involving time is rather challenging when they involve long durations and timers. These properties are generally not inductive and even advanced techniques such as PDR/IC3 [5] are unable to handle them on production models in reasonable time. We proposed an algorithm [26] and a new methodology using physical types (speed, acceleration, etc.), which restricted the number of candidates to only those that made sense and thus outperformed the JKind and Kind2 model checkers.

The second problem is important in the sense that even if the model checker has proved all the properties to be valid, we cannot answer the question about whether our model contains features that are not covered by the properties. Unlike testing, where we can follow the execution trace, the proof process uses the whole model, but many parts of it may not be necessary to prove the properties. This problem has been studied using the following approaches: mutation proof [7, 9, 16, 24] and inductive validity cores [2–4, 12].

The mutation approach shown in Fig. 1 consists in mutating a model for which safety properties were proved valid, and trying to prove the same properties on the mutated models (*mutants*) again. If they are proved to be valid (the mutant has *survived*), the mutant reveals a part of the model that is not covered by the properties. It can also be dead code that will never be accessed. The algorithms used to compute coverage in the aforementioned papers can underapproximate which parts of the model are necessary to prove the properties

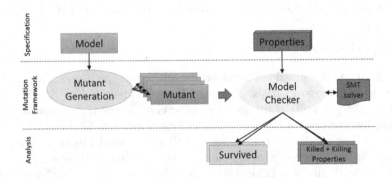

Fig. 1. Mutation proof framework

and tend to be computationally very expensive because there are many mutated models to be verified.

Inductive validity cores (IVCs) represent minimal sets of model elements necessary to construct inductive proofs for the specified properties. The algorithms proposed in the articles cited above are based on the *Unsatisfiable Core* support built into current SMT solvers. They can efficiently generate over-approximated inductive validity cores or exhaustively compute minimal ones. The authors show that calculating IVCs is more efficient than classical state of the art mutation. Calculating IVCs gives the coverage of properties in terms of lines of code of the model, which is more precise than a simple syntactic slicing, but does not look inside the lines of code and therefore does not consider the coverage of elementary operations inside an equation.

In this paper, we propose to go further in the precision of the coverage and zoom into the lines of code. Actually, a property can be covered by a line of code but inside the line there may still be some code that has no impact on the property. We argue that it is inside the lines of code that some subtle bugs can still subsist, and it is useful to uncover them. We use mutation to mutate some operators of the model, and symbolic model checking combined with induction-based techniques (k-induction [25], IC3/PDR [5,10]), and take advantage of the incremental query capabilities of modern SMT solvers. We observed that mutation-based coverage for model checking is no longer out of reach, and this technique scales with our industrial use cases. We implemented this algorithm in the JKind open-source model checker [11], which is based on the Lustre [6] formal language. Lustre is used as base language for SCADE, so we could transform a SCADE model into Lustre. Simulink can also be transformed into Lustre using the CoCoSim framework developed at NASA Ames[1].

2   Preliminaries

In this section, we introduce the architecture of the industrial inductive model checker JKind [11] which is representative of other model checkers such as Kind2 and PKind.

2.1   The JKind Model Checker

JKind is an open-source industrial infinite-state model checker for safety properties. Models and properties are written in Lustre, a synchronous data-flow language, using theories of real and integer arithmetic. JKind uses SMT-solvers (SMTInterpol, Z3, Yices, CVC4, MathSAT) to prove or falsify the properties. It is structured as several parallel *engines* that cooperate to prove properties. Some engines are directly responsible for proving properties, some contribute to that effort by generating invariants, and others are for post-processing proofs or counterexample results. Each engine can be enabled or disabled separately. The architecture of JKind is shown in Fig. 2. At the center of this architecture the **Director** allows any engine to broadcast information (invariants, valid and invalid properties) to the other engines.

---

[1] CoCoSim: https://ti.arc.nasa.gov/tech/rse/research/cocosim.

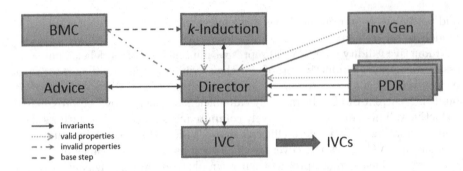

Fig. 2. The JKind model checker architecture

The **Bounded Model Checking (BMC)** engine performs a standard iterative unrolling of the transition relation to find counterexamples or to serve as the base case of k-induction. The BMC engine guarantees that any counterexample it finds is minimal in the number of steps from the initial state. The **k-Induction** engine performs the inductive step of k-induction, possibly using invariants generated by other engines. The **Invariant Generation** engine uses a template-based invariant generation technique [19] using its own k-induction loop. The **Property Directed Reachability (PDR)** engine performs property directed reachability [10] using the implicit abstraction technique [8]. Unlike BMC and k-induction, each property is handled separately by a different PDR sub-engine. The **Advice** engine saves invariants from previous runs of JKind and reuses them for new proofs to decrease the verification time.

A great effort was done in JKind on the post-processing of the results. We can cite the *Smoothing* counterexamples feature based on MaxSat which minimizes the number of changes to input variables. The other important post-processing feature is IVC.

Inductive Validity Cores (IVC). For a proven property, an inductive validity core is a subset of Lustre equations from the input model for which the property still holds [13,15]. An IVC is *minimal* when no equation can be removed without breaking the provability. Depending on the model and property, there may exist several IVCs with different sizes. A *minimum* IVC has the smallest number of equations, and is not necessarily unique. Computing a minimum IVC is more difficult than computing any IVC, because it involves an exhaustive search. The IVC engine uses a heuristic algorithm to efficiently produce minimal IVCs but not minimum ones. As a side-effect, the IVC algorithm also minimizes the set of invariants used to prove a property, and shares this reduced set with other engines (notably the Advice engine).

2.2   IVC Formalizations

In this section we re-use and adapt the formalization of IVC given by Ghassabani et al. in [14] to compare IVC to our mutation proof using similar definitions of coverage.

Models, Requirements and Provability. Given a state space U, a transition system (I, T) consists of an initial state predicate $I : U \rightarrow bool$ and a transition step predicate $T : U \times U \rightarrow bool$. A safety property $P : U \rightarrow bool$ is a state predicate that holds on a transition system (I, T) when it satisfies the following formulas:

$$\forall u. \, I(u) \Rightarrow P(u)$$

$$\forall u, u'. \, P(u) \wedge T(u, u') \Rightarrow P(u')$$

When this is the case, we write $(I, T) \vdash P$.

Coming from the Lustre model that is a set of equations $\{eq_1 \ldots eq_n\}$, the transition relation T has the structure of a top-level conjunction $T = t_1 \wedge \cdots \wedge t_n$ where each t_i is an equality corresponding to eq_i. By further abuse of notation, T is identified with the set of its top-level equalities. When an equation is removed from the Lustre model, an equality t_i is removed from T and the transition relation becomes $T \setminus \{t_i\}$.

Definition 1. Inductive Validity Core (IVC). $S \subseteq T$ for $(I, T) \vdash P$ is an Inductive Validity Core, iff $(I, S) \vdash P \wedge \forall t_i \in S. \, (I, S \setminus \{t_i\}) \nvdash P$.

As defined here, we are only interested in minimal sets that satisfy a property P. Note that given $(I, T) \vdash P$, P always has at least one IVC, which is not necessarily unique. For example, consider 2 boolean variables a and b initialized to true, i.e. $I = a \wedge b$, and assigned true at each step $T = (t_1 : a = true) \wedge (t_2 : b = true)$. If $P = a \vee b$ then both $\{t_1\}$ and $\{t_2\}$ are IVCs. We note $AIVC(P)$ the set of all IVCs of P. Computing the $AIVC$ for each property, one gets a clear picture of all the model elements constrained by the property. The set $AIVC$ for all properties demonstrates a complete mapping from the requirements to the design elements, which is called *complete traceability* [21].

Property and Model Coverage. The article by Ghassabani et al. [14] defines the two following metrics of coverage.

Definition 2. (MAY-COV): $t_i \in T$ is covered by P iff $t_i \in$ MAY-COV(P), where MAY-COV$(P) = \{t_i \mid \exists S \in AIVC(P) \cdot t_i \in S\}$.

Definition 3. (MUST-COV): $t_i \in T$ is covered by P iff $t_i \in$ MUST-COV(P), where MUST-COV$(P) = \{t_i \mid \forall S \in AIVC(P) \cdot t_i \in S\}$.

This categorization of coverage helps to identify the role and relevance of each design element in satisfying a property. MUST-COV specifies the parts of the model that are absolutely necessary for the property satisfaction. Any change to these parts will affect the provability of the property. On the other hand, MAY-COV parts are relevant to the proof but may be modified without affecting the satisfaction of P. The MAY-COV heuristic leads to higher coverage scores, because MUST-COV$(P) \subseteq$ MAY-COV(P).

In JKind, the IVC engine computes one IVC and avoids exploring all possible ones. Therefore, it partially computes the MAY-COV(P) and it does not handle MUST-COV(P).

Mutation. A mutator is a function that mutates any transition predicate T to a set of mutants $\{T_{mut}^1, \ldots, T_{mut}^m\}$, where each mutant T_{mut}^i is obtained by applying a small change to T.

A very simple mutator is the one that simply removes an equality t_i from T, which amounts to removing the corresponding line of code from the Lustre model. In our framework, we call this basic mutator eq_remove (see Sect. 4). The authors of [15] only consider this simple mutator and define the corresponding coverage as follows:

Definition 4. Mutation coverage (MUT-COV) $t_i \in T$ *is covered by property* P *iff* $t_i \in$ MUT-COV(P), *where* MUT-COV$(P) = \{t_i \mid (I, T) \vdash P \wedge (I, T \setminus \{t_i\}) \nvdash P\}$.

An immediate corollary proved in [15] states that if an equation is covered by such a mutation, it is also covered by all IVCs and conversely:

Corollary 1. MUT-COV$(P) =$ MUST-COV(P).

The MUT-COV metrics can be generalized to more advanced mutators. In Sect. 4, we will show how the MUT-COV metrics can be improved to give a very precise coverage inside each t_i detected within MUST-COV or MAY-COV.

3   Model Coverage Techniques

An important question for the certification of safety-critical systems is whether the requirements and tests are covering the implementation. For example, in ISO 26262 [18], which is the functional safety standard for road vehicles, tests are derived from requirements. An argumentation of why the performed tests give sufficient coverage shall be provided. As the critical level increases, a more rigorous method for test coverage (statement, branch, MC/DC) is required. If complete coverage is not achieved, an analysis is performed to decide whether additional tests or/and requirements are needed to increase coverage. DO-178C [22] with its supplement DO-333 (Formal Methods) go further in offering the possibility to use formal methods in replacement of all structural coverage objectives (including heavyweight MC/DC), but arguments showing that coverage is achieved by the formal proof should then be provided, see Table 1.

In this section, we present different techniques for model coverage, going progressively from coarse-grained coverage to fine-grained coverage. We consider the application of these techniques to the domain of inductive symbolic model checking. We propose to use mutation-based proof, taking advantage of the possibility to request SMT solvers in an incremental way, in order to look inside the operators in a way MC/DC does for testing. We show that the performance of this technique is equivalent to IVC and therefore quite faster than state of the art mutation-based methods. To the best of our knowledge, this technique has never been studied. The closest related work on mutation-based proof does not use inductive model checking for software verification nor incremental SMT solving. The work of Chockler et al. [7] presents an algorithm to re-use previously

Table 1. DO-333 accepts replacing MC/DC coverage by formal proof coverage

DO-178C table A-7 objective	DO-333 table FM.A-7 objective
1. Test procedures are correct	FM1. Formal analysis cases and procedures are correct
2. Test results are correct and discrepancies explained	FM2. Formal analysis results are correct and discrepancies explained
3. Test coverage of High Level Requirements (HLRs) is achieved	FM3. Coverage of HLRs is achieved
4. Test coverage of Low Level Requirements (LLRs) is achieved	FM4. Coverage of LLRs is achieved
5. Test coverage of software structure (modified condition/decision coverage) is achieved	FM5 – FM8. Verification coverage of software structure is achieved
6. Test coverage of software structure (decision coverage) is achieved	(A single objective that replaces the four structural coverage objectives in DO-178C)
7. Test coverage of software structure (statement coverage) is achieved	
8. Test coverage of software structure (data coupling and control coupling) is achieved	
9. A verification of additional code, that cannot be traced to source code, is achieved	FM9. Verification of property preservation between source and object code
N/A	FM10. Formal method is correctly defined, justified, and appropriate

computed inductive invariants and counterexamples to identify the parts of a hardware system that are covered by a property. In [9], Claessen presents a coverage analysis based on LTL that gives the possibility to have underconstrained properties. In [16], the authors present an approach to estimate coverage in BMC (Bounded Model Checking). They generate coverage properties for each important signal for hardware verification purposes. Finally, in [24], Sayantan et al. present a method for determining the coverage of a formal LTL specification against a high-level fault model for hardware verification.

3.1   Simple Running Example

We use a simple running example to illustrate the difference between slicing, IVC and mutation proof. Consider the SCADE model shown both graphically and textually in Fig. 3. The property Prop1 we want to prove is the output of an OR block which takes a constant input equal to true and its negation. Obviously this property is always true. The Lustre code is obtained by using the SCADE option "Convert to textual" and we just add the comment on line 11 to tell JKind which output represents our safety property to be proved (invariant that shall always be true).

3.2   Slicing

The backward static slicing (or slicing for short) is a coarse-grained technique that allows to remove the parts of the code that do not affect the properties to

```
 1  node demo () returns (Prop1: bool; d: bool);
 2  var
 3      L1, L2, L3, L4: bool;
 4  let
 5      L1 = L2 or L3;
 6      L2 = true;
 7      L3 = not L2;
 8      L4 = not L1;
 9      Prop1 = L1;
10      d = L4;
11      —%PROPERTY Prop1;
12  tel
```

Fig. 3. A simple running example in Lustre

be proved. It works by simply calculating the dependency graph for the variables used in the properties. Modern inductive model checkers use slicing to reduce the size of the queries sent to the SAT/SMT solver. It is interesting to see how much of the code is removed and to check if we really need this code or if our properties are simply not complete enough. After slicing, d and L4 are removed and we obtain the lines:

```
1      L1 = L2 or L3;
2      L2 = true;
3      L3 = not L2;
4      Prop1 = L1;
```

3.3 Inductive Validity Cores (IVCs)

IVCs are much smaller and more precise than static slicing. For our short example, the IVC engine will either remove the equation of L3 because L1 does not depend on it since L2 is true, or it will keep the equation of L3 and remove the equation of L2 since the equation of L1 is a tautology when we consider the equation of L3. When running IVC on Prop1, it turns out that we obtain the first inductive validity core: {L1, L2}

```
1      L1 = L2 or L3;
2      L2 = true;
```

3.4 A Simple Mutator for Must-Cov: Equation Remover

We want to go further than IVC, so we propose to use a simple mutator called "equation remover" which removes equations one by one and replays the proof process in an incremental way (using the SMT-LIB [1] *pop* and *push* commands). Our equation remover does not affect the properties because we want to mutate only the model and not the specification. If after removing an equation the properties are still proved (surviving mutant), it means that the removed equation has no impact on the proof. If the properties do not hold anymore (killed mutant), this means that the removed equation is essential for the proof. This mutator computes the *minimum* core defined as MUST-COV in Sect. 2, whereas IVC is working in MAY-COV mode. Using this technique, we obtain that only the equation of L1 is essential for any proof of Prop1 :

```
1    L1 = L2 or L3;
```

3.5 Using Other Mutators for Deep Coverage

We propose to add other mutation operators to zoom inside a line of code/e-quation and see what is covered by the properties. We explain these operators in detail in Sect. 4. For the moment, we give an example to see the difference between mutation and IVC. Our example is shown in Fig. 4.

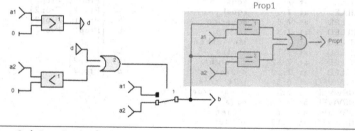

```
1   node demo2 (a1, a2: int)
2     returns (Prop1: bool; b: int);
3   var
4     d: bool;
5   let
6     d = (a1 > 0);
7     b = if d or (a2 < 0) then a1 else a2;
8     Prop1 = (b = a1 or b = a2);
9     —%PROPERTY Prop1;
10  tel;
```

Fig. 4. Example of inlined code and *if-then-else* operator mutations

This model takes two inputs a1 and a2, and depending on whether their value is positive or negative, a1 or a2 is assigned to the output b. We have a property Prop1 specifying that the output b should take the value of a1 or a2. If slicing is applied to this model, it will remove nothing because Prop1 depends statically on the entire model. However, applying IVC tells us that we should only keep b to cover our property Prop1. It is more precise than slicing because d is not necessary to prove that property (b is always equal to a1 or a2).

Now, let us apply some mutations such as: replacing the condition of the *if* statement by *true* or *false*, replacing *or* by *xor*, replacing > by < etc. This leads to 22 possible mutations.

For Prop1 we have 5 mutants killed out of 22. If we want to cover 100% of the code, we need to kill all mutants. To achieve this coverage, we need to strengthen our properties. We add a second property: Prop2 = ((a1 > 0) => b = a1). At this stage IVC covers 100% of the model as d is now necessary to Prop2. However, only 14 mutants are killed out of 22, see Fig. 5. For example, if the condition of the *if* statement at line 7 (Fig. 4) is replaced by *true*, *Prop1* and *Prop2* are proved valid. This means that the condition has no impact on these properties. Let us add a third property: Prop3 = ((a2 < 0) => b = a1). This time, we kill 16 mutants out of 22. Finally, we need a fourth property: Prop4 = (((a1 <= 0) and (a2 >= 0)) => b = a2) to kill all 22 mutants.

```
INDUCTIVE VALIDITY CORE: b, d
+++++++++++++++++++++++++++++++++++++++++++++++++++++
MUTATION:
KILLED      at  6:3      equal_false            by [Prop2]
KILLED      at  6:3      equation_remove        by [Prop2]
KILLED      at  6:3      init_false             by [Prop2]
KILLED      at  6:11     g2l                    by [Prop2]
KILLED      at  6:13     (const int 0 -> 1)     by [Prop2]
KILLED      at  7:3      init_-1                by [Prop1, Prop2]
KILLED      at  7:3      equal_5                by [Prop1, Prop2]
KILLED      at  7:3      equal_-2               by [Prop1, Prop2]
KILLED      at  7:3      equation_remove        by [Prop1, Prop2]
KILLED      at  7:3      init_5                 by [Prop1, Prop2]
KILLED      at  7:7      ifelsethen             by [Prop2]
KILLED      at  7:7      ifelse                 by [Prop2]
KILLED      at  7:12     or2right               by [Prop2]
KILLED      at  7:12     or2xor                 by [Prop2]
SURVIVED    at  6:3      init_true
SURVIVED    at  6:3      equal_true
SURVIVED    at  6:11     g2ge
SURVIVED    at  7:7      ifthen
SURVIVED    at  7:12     or2left
SURVIVED    at  7:19     l2g
SURVIVED    at  7:19     l2le
SURVIVED    at  7:21     (const int 0 -> 1)
```

Fig. 5. IVCs and mutation proof results on *demo2* for properties *Prop1* and *Prop2*

4   From Mutation Testing to Mutation Proof

Mutation testing is used to evaluate the quality of a test suite that is a set of test cases. It consists in modifying the program under test in small ways. Each mutated version of the program is called a *mutant* and test cases are replayed on it to detect whether its behavior is different from the behavior of the original version. This process is called 'killing the mutant'. The more mutants are killed, the better are the test cases. The quality of a test suite is measured as the percentage of killed mutants. Mutants that are left can be killed by specifying additional test cases or justified as equivalent to the original program. *Mutators* are mutation operators used to generate mutants, and they tend to mimic standard programming errors. A mutation builds a mutant by applying a mutator on some position in the code. Taking ideas from mutation testing, we developed a *mutation proof* framework for standard inductive model checking using incremental SMT solving. In this section, we present our mutators and describe our mutation proof algorithm.

4.1 Mutators

Our mutators directly modify the Lustre code. We implemented classical mutators, but more advanced ones may be easily added to our framework. We present our mutators in Table 2.

Table 2. Mutators for deep coverage measurement

Mutator	Description
or2xor	OR is mutated to XOR
xor2implies	XOR is mutated to $\implies$
implies2and	$\implies$ is mutated to AND
and2or	AND is mutated to OR
or2left	$X\ OR\ Y$ is mutated to X
or2right	$X\ OR\ Y$ is mutated to Y
and2left	$X\ AND\ Y$ is mutated to X
and2right	$X\ AND\ Y$ is mutated to Y
rm_not	NOT is removed
eq. 2neq	$=$ is mutated to $\neq$
neq2eq	$\neq$ is mutated to $=$
g2ge	$>$ is mutated to $\geq$
ge2g	$\geq$ is mutated to $>$
l2le	$<$ is mutated to $\leq$
le2l	$\leq$ is mutated to $<$
g2l	$>$ is mutated to $<$
l2g	$<$ is mutated to $>$
ge2le	$\geq$ is mutated to $\leq$
le2ge	$\leq$ is mutated to $\geq$
plus2minus	$+$ is mutated to $-$
minus2plus	$-$ is mutated to $+$
rm_minus	$-$ is removed
ifthen	IF condition is replaced by TRUE
ifelse	IF condition is replaced by FALSE
ifelsethen	THEN and ELSE statements are reversed
ConstantMutator	Constant is replaced by 1
eq_remove	Removes an entire equation/line of code

Our first category of mutators are the *boolean mutators*. For example, the *and2or* mutator transforms a `AND` b into a `OR` b. Then we have *relational mutators* such as *ge2le*, which transforms a $\geq$ operator into $\leq$. We also have some *arithmetic mutators* such as *plus2minus*, which replaces $+$ by $-$. *Branching mutators* act on *if-then-else* statements replacing the condition by TRUE or FALSE or reversing the THEN and ELSE statements. Finally, we have the *constant mutator* that replaces all constants by 1, and the *equation remover mutator* that removes an entire line of code as seen before.

4.2   Our Contribution: Mutation Proof Algorithm

The main contribution of our paper is the mutation proof algorithm that can be applied to modern inductive model checkers. It takes as input the proved properties and the invariants found during the proof process. It uses BMC and k-induction to retry the proof on mutants. Then, it returns a verdict: *KILLED* (proof fails with a counterexample), *SURVIVED* (proof succeeds), or *UNKNOWN* (proof fails with no counterexample). Our quality metrics is the ratio of killed mutants over the total number of mutants. The more mutants are killed, the better is the quality of the specification, because the better is the coverage of the model by the properties in the specification.

Algorithm 1: Mutation proof algorithm

input : M, P
output: *report*

1 Prove $P : \{P_0, P_1 \ldots\}$ on M
2 $Invs \leftarrow$ invariants from the proof of P on M
3 $k_{proof} \leftarrow$ maximum k-depth for proving P on M
4
5 **foreach** *mutation LCM* **do**
6    $M_{mut} \leftarrow MUTATE(M, LCM)$
7   **if** $BMC((M_{mut}, \emptyset, \emptyset), P, k_{proof}) = SAT$ **then**
8      $M_{SAT} \leftarrow getModel()$
9      $report\ +=$ **KILLED**(mut:LCM, KillingProps:$\{P_i \in P \mid M_{SAT} \vDash \neg P_i\}$)
10   **else**
11     $SI \leftarrow FilterInvs(Invs, M_{mut})$
12     $UP \leftarrow \emptyset$
13     $SP \leftarrow P$
14   **while** $KIND((M_{mut}, SI, \emptyset), SP, k_{proof}) = SAT$ **do**
15       $M_{SAT} \leftarrow getModel()$
16       $UP = UP \cup \{P_i \in SP \mid M_{SAT} \vDash \neg P_i\}$
17       $SP = P \setminus UP$
18   **if** $SP = P$ **then**
19       $report\ +=$ **SURVIVED**(mut:LCM)
20   **else**
21   **if** $BMC((M_{mut}, SI, SP), UP, k_{kill}) = SAT$ **then**
22         $M_{SAT} \leftarrow getModel()$
23         $report\ +=$ **KILLED**(mut:LCM, KillingProps:$\{P_i \in UP | M_{SAT} \vDash \neg P_i\}$)
24   **else**
25         $report\ +=$ **UNKNOWN**(mut:LCM, SurvivingProps:SP)

Before describing our algorithm, let us define its variables and functions: P are the specification Properties, M is the original Model, M_{mut} is the current mutated Model (Mutant), LCM represents a mutation in the form Line:Column of code and Mutator, function $MUTATE(M, LCM)$ returns the mutant M_{mut} corresponding to LCM applied to M, KP are the Killing Properties, SI are the Surviving Invariants, SP are the Surviving Properties, UP are the Unknown Properties, k_{kill} is a parameter for maximum k-depth to kill a mutant, functions $BMC((Model, Invariants, ValidProperties), Prop, k)$ and $KIND(\dots)$ run respectively BMC and K-INDuction on a model together with its invariants and its valid properties to check new properties $Prop$ at depth k and answer $UNSAT$ (all $Prop$ are valid) or SAT (some of $Prop$ are not valid). When the answer is SAT, the function $getModel()$ gives the counterexample. Finally, function $FilterInvs(invariants, M_{mut})$ filters the $invariants$ of the original Model M using BMC and k-induction to find the ones that survive the mutation and are still invariants of the current mutant M_{mut}.

Starting from the proof of P on M which requires the generation of invariants $Invs$ and induction at depth k_{proof}, our algorithm applies a mutation LCM at each iteration to obtain a mutant M_{mut} and retries the proof of P on M_{mut}. It runs first BMC at depth k_{proof} to verify whether all properties in P hold on M_{mut} for the first k_{proof} steps. If it is not the case, the mutant M_{mut} is already killed by some properties in P reported within the verdict $KILLED$. When all properties in P hold, which means that the base step is valid, the algorithm will try the k-induction step after filtering the invariants $Invs$ of M to keep only those that are still valid for M_{mut}. When the k-induction step succeeds ($UNSAT$), all properties in SP are k-inductive and survive, otherwise we use the counterexample model to find the properties that are not k-inductive, add them to the unknown properties UP, and we try again the k-induction on the remaining properties $SP \setminus UP$. We add the non k-inductive properties to UP because they can be valid but may require a k-induction of a higher depth. The verdict is $SURVIVED$ when the k-induction succeeds at the first iteration and in this case all properties in P hold for M_{mut} (i.e. $P = SP$ and UP is empty). If UP is not empty, we run again BMC at maximum depth k_{kill} to try to kill the current mutant by any property from UP. If this last attempt to kill M_{mut} fails, we return the verdict $UNKNOWN$.

5   Implementation and Initial Results

5.1   Implementation

We implemented our algorithm on a GitHub fork of JKind[2]. Our algorithm, shown in Fig. 6, runs as a separate engine (module) of JKind and starts at the end of the proof process. It retrieves the invariants and k_{proof} used for proving the properties and returns mutations verdicts.

---

[2] JKind with Mutation on GitHub: https://github.com/v-todorov/jkind.

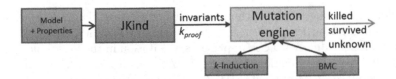

Fig. 6. Mutation engine implementation in JKind

5.2 Optimizations

Our implementation is very efficient because instead of submitting the entire mutated model to the SMT-solver it works in an incremental way, using *pop* and *push* only on the mutated lines. Furthermore, to take maximum advantage of this incremental feature, we group the mutations of the same line of code and run them all on the same SMT-solver instance.

We introduced two major optimizations as parameters in JKind: parallel-Mutants and ivcMutation. Firstly, unlike IVC, which cannot be parallelized, our mutation algorithm can run each mutation proof on a different thread. We group mutations that affect a given line of code. Different groups can be executed in parallel. The second optimization is intended for large models and runs the mutation only over the resulting minimal core produced by IVC. Thus IVC eliminates the unused part of the model, and mutation runs faster based on the results of IVC. The designer should be informed of the unused part in order to be able to write some additional properties about it.

5.3 Initial Results

We used the benchmark of JKind (from GitHub), which provides Lustre files and properties to be proved. We selected 22 example Lustre files with only valid properties, because it is not useful to analyze the coverage of invalid properties. We used a laptop equipped with an Intel Xeon E-2176M CPU and 32GB RAM to run the benchmarks. We applied IVC alone, Mutation with equation removing only, and Mutation with all mutators activated. We activated the *parallelMutants* option to use the 6 cores of our CPU and we did not activate IVC when running Mutation. The results are shown in Fig. 7. On the left, we see the results that compare Mutation with only the equation removing mutator (Mut-Eq) to IVC. We notice that in 82% of the use cases we obtained equal times for calculating IVC and Mut-Eq, in 9% of the cases mutation (Mut-Eq) was faster than IVC and in another 9% it was slower. For Mutation using all mutators (Mut-All), we had same execution times in 59% of the cases, mutation (Mut-All) was faster than IVC in 5% of the cases, and it was slower in 36% of the cases.

The unsat cores given by most SMT solvers are not necessarily minimal, IVC needs some backtracking to reduce them to minimal ones. The IVC implementation in JKind is sequential and requires calculation power. On the other hand, our algorithm runs in parallel and uses incremental SMT solving. Thus, we obtain a greater coverage precision thanks to the mutation, with an equivalent performance most of the time.

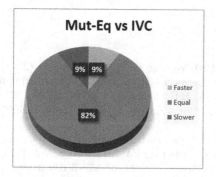 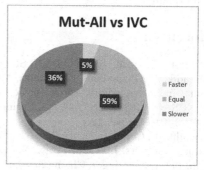

Fig. 7. Comparison between equation remover mutation/full mutation and IVC

5.4 Industrial Use Case Results

We also used a representative industrial use case that is a cruise control function developed in SCADE (1250 lines of Lustre code), with some valid safety properties coming from high level requirements [26]. Using IVC, as well as using mutation with equation removing only, shows that all lines of code were covered and therefore necessary to the specification proof, but when running our mutation proof framework with all mutators activated, we only obtained 39% of killed mutations. This means that we need to strengthen the properties e.g. by adding additional ones to kill the 61% surviving mutations. In particular, we found some interesting mutations of *if-then-else* statements revealing branches that were not covered by the original properties.

6 Conclusions and Future Work

In this paper we proposed a new coverage metrics for evaluating the quality of properties (specification) that are proved valid using model checking on a given model (program). The algorithm we used is particularly efficient unlike classical mutation testing techniques. Its efficiency comes from the fact that instead of submitting each mutant to the SMT solver, we only submit the original model once and we iteratively remove (pop) an equation and push its mutated version to check all mutants. The mutation process can also be run in parallel and thus its performance is almost equivalent to IVC, another heuristic algorithm to find the coverage of the properties on a model. The main advantage of our mutation framework over IVC is that we can look inside the lines of code and see the effect of mutating a constant, a variable or an operator.

As a future work, we will develop a link between invariant generation and mutation proof. It consists in finding parts of the code that are not covered by the automatically generated invariants and highlight them to give an immediate feedback to the designer who will need to strengthen the specification on that particular parts of the code. It will improve the provability of the specification and its quality.

References

1. Barrett, C., et al.: The SMT-LIB Standard: Version 2.0. Technical report (2010)
2. Bendík, J., Ghassabani, E., Whalen, M., Černá, I.: Online enumeration of all minimal inductive validity cores. In: Johnsen, E.B., Schaefer, I. (eds.) SEFM 2018. LNCS, vol. 10886, pp. 189–204. Springer, Cham (2018). https://doi.org/10.1007/978-3-319-92970-5_12
3. Bendík, J., Černá, I., Beneš, N.: Recursive online enumeration of all minimal unsatisfiable subsets. In: Lahiri, S.K., Wang, C. (eds.) ATVA 2018. LNCS, vol. 11138, pp. 143–159. Springer, Cham (2018). https://doi.org/10.1007/978-3-030-01090-4_9
4. Berryhill, R.: Chasing Minimal Inductive Validity Cores in Hardware Model Checking, October 2019
5. Bradley, A.R., Manna, Z.: Property-directed incremental invariant generation. Formal Aspects Comput. **20**, 379–405 (2008). https://doi.org/10.1007/s00165-008-0080-9
6. Caspi, P., Pilaud, D., Halbwachs, N., Plaice, J.A.: LUSTRE: a declarative language for real-time programming. In: POPL '87, pp. 178–188. ACM (1987)
7. Chockler, H., Kupferman, O., Kurshan, R.P., Vardi, M.Y.: A practical approach to coverage in model checking. In: Berry, G., Comon, H., Finkel, A. (eds.) CAV 2001. LNCS, vol. 2102, pp. 66–78. Springer, Heidelberg (2001). https://doi.org/10.1007/3-540-44585-4_7
8. Cimatti, A., Griggio, A., Mover, S., Tonetta, S.: IC3 Modulo Theories via Implicit Predicate Abstraction. CoRR abs/1310.6847 (2013)
9. Claessen, K.: A coverage analysis for safety property lists. In: Formal Methods in Computer Aided Design (FMCAD 2007), pp. 139–145, November 2007
10. Een, N., Mishchenko, A., Brayton, R.: Efficient implementation of property directed reachability In: FMCAD '11, Austin, pp. 125–134 (2011)
11. Gacek, A., Backes, J., Whalen, M., Wagner, L., Ghassabani, E.: The JKIND model checker. In: Chockler, H., Weissenbacher, G. (eds.) CAV 2018. LNCS, vol. 10982, pp. 20–27. Springer, Cham (2018). https://doi.org/10.1007/978-3-319-96142-2_3
12. Ghassabani, E., Whalen, M., Gacek, A., Heimdahl, M.: Inductive validity cores. IEEE Trans. Softw. Eng. 1–1 (2019)
13. Ghassabani, E., Gacek, A., Whalen, M.W.: Efficient generation of inductive validity cores for safety properties. In: Proceedings of the 2016 24th ACM SIGSOFT International Symposium on Foundations of Software Engineering (FSE 2016), pp. 314–325. ACM, New York (2016)
14. Ghassabani, E., Gacek, A., Whalen, M.W., Heimdahl, M.P.E., Wagner, L.: Proof-based coverage metrics for formal verification. In: Proceedings of the 32Nd IEEE/ACM International Conference on Automated Software Engineering, November 2017, Urbana-Champaign, IL, USA, pp. 194–199. ASE: IEEE Press, Piscataway (2017)
15. Ghassabani, E., Whalen, M., Gacek, A.: Efficient generation of all minimal inductive validity cores. In: Proceedings of the 17th Conference on Formal Methods in Computer-Aided Design (FMCAD 2017), Vienna, Austria, pp. 31–38. FMCAD Inc., Austin, November 2017

16. Große, D., Kühne, U., Drechsler, R.: Estimating functional coverage in bounded model checking. In: Proceedings of the Conference on Design, Automation and Test in Europe (DATE 2007), Nice, France, pp. 1176–1181. EDA Consortium, San Jose (2007)

17. Hardin, D., Hiratzka, T.D., Johnson, D.R., Wagner, L., Whalen, M.: Development of security software: a high assurance methodology. In: Breitman, K., Cavalcanti, A. (eds.) ICFEM 2009. LNCS, vol. 5885, pp. 266–285. Springer, Heidelberg (2009). https://doi.org/10.1007/978-3-642-10373-5_14

18. ISO: Road vehicles - Functional safety (2011)

19. Kahsai, T., Garoche, P.-L., Tinelli, C., Whalen, M.: Incremental verification with mode variable invariants in state machines. In: Goodloe, A.E., Person, S. (eds.) NFM 2012. LNCS, vol. 7226, pp. 388–402. Springer, Heidelberg (2012). https://doi.org/10.1007/978-3-642-28891-3_35

20. Miller, S.P., Whalen, M.W., Cofer, D.D.: Software model checking takes off. Commun. ACM **53**(2), 58–64 (2010)

21. Murugesan, A., Whalen, M.W., Ghassabani, E., Heimdahl, M.P.E.: Complete traceability for requirements in satisfaction arguments. In: 2016 IEEE 24th International Requirements Engineering Conference (RE), pp. 359–364 (2016)

22. RTCA DO-178C: Software Considerations in Airborne Systems and Equipment Certification. Washington, DC, December 2011

23. Rushby, J.: Software verification and system assurance. In: 2009 Seventh IEEE International Conference on Software Engineering and Formal Methods, pp. 3–10, November 2009

24. Das, S., et al.: Formal methods for analyzing the completeness of an assertion suite against a high-level fault model. In: 18th International Conference on VLSI Design held jointly with 4th International Conference on Embedded Systems Design, pp. 201–206, January 2005

25. Sheeran, M., Singh, S., Stålmarck, G.: Checking safety properties using induction and a SAT-solver. In: Hunt, W.A., Johnson, S.D. (eds.) FMCAD 2000. LNCS, vol. 1954, pp. 127–144. Springer, Heidelberg (2000). https://doi.org/10.1007/3-540-40922-X_8

26. Todorov, V., Taha, S., Boulanger, F., Hernandez, A.: Improved invariant generation for industrial software model checking of time properties. In: Proceedings of the 19th IEEE International Conference on Software Quality, Reliability, and Security, pp. 334–341. IEEE, Sofia, Bulgaria, October 2019

Validation and Solvers

A Validation Methodology
for OCaml-to-PVS Translation

Xiaoxin An, Amer Tahat[✉], and Binoy Ravindran

Virginia Tech, Blacksburg, VA 24061, USA
{xxan15,antahat,binoy}@vt.edu

Abstract. We present a methodology, called OPEV, to validate the translation between OCaml and PVS, which supports non-executable semantics. This validation occurs by generating large-scale tests for OCaml implementations, generating test lemmas for PVS, and generating proofs that automatically discharge these lemmas. OPEV incorporates an intermediate type system that captures a large subset of OCaml types, employing a variety of rules to generate test cases for each type. To prove the PVS lemmas, we developed automatic proof strategies and discharged the test lemmas using PVS Proof-Lite, a powerful proof scripting utility of the PVS verification system. We demonstrated our approach on two case studies that include two hundred and fifty-nine functions selected from the Sail and Lem libraries. For each function, we generated thousands of test lemmas, all of which are automatically discharged. The methodology contributes to a reliable translation between OCaml and PVS.

Keywords: Translation validation · PVS · OCaml

1 Introduction

Verifying a "translator" that translates a specification written in one language to another language is of fundamental interest in many settings, such as compilers, assemblers, and interpreters. A rigorous methodology that can be used to verify the translation is *refinement proving*. This method requires a translation into a formal verification language to generate a formal certificate. The translated model, whether it was generated manually or mechanically, must comply with the intended meaning of the program being certified for the certificate to be valid. For example, seL4's formal certification used a translation from a subset of C called C_0 into Isabelle/HOL [1]. The conformance relationship was established based on a refinement proof that required significant human effort [2].

However, the validation of translation between different languages is exacerbated when languages at either end of the "translation pipe" have no formal semantics, which is the case in many settings. This precludes establishing a two-way equivalence relationship between the source and the destination languages. In such cases, a testing methodology is perhaps a more effective verification

© Springer Nature Switzerland AG 2020
R. Lee et al. (Eds.): NFM 2020, LNCS 12229, pp. 207–221, 2020.
https://doi.org/10.1007/978-3-030-55754-6_12

strategy to establish equivalence between the two specifications. For example, Lem [3] is a specification language that used to translate mathematically rigorous models of multiple ISAs into different theorem provers and into OCaml. For instance, Lem can be translated to OCaml for emulation of testing as well as to Isabelle/HOL, Coq, HOL4, and other languages. The OCaml translation was validated via predefined tests written in the Lem language [3].

Though translators can be validated by testing [4], this does not have the same level of rigor as refinement proofs and does not require formal semantics for the target languages. Testing requires that both languages are executable. However, some specifications with formal semantics can be either executable or non-executable, and the results of the non-executable specification cannot be directly calculated. For example, in the Prototype Verification System (PVS) [5], PVSio [6], the emulator utility in PVS, can only execute a subset of the functional specifications in PVS. This is a limitation of many theorem provers, not just PVS – their specification languages are designed to state and prove theorems, but not execute. In fact, large subsets of many provers' powerful specifications are non-executable. This downside can be overcome by stating theorems on these specifications that capture the intended behaviors and proving them, mostly interactively – a highly labor-intensive effort. For example, validation of the CompCert compiler [7] involved 100K lines of Coq proof.

Motivated by these concerns, we present a test-and-proof methodology to validate the translation between two different languages with one of them supporting non-executable semantics. Our methodology (Sect. 2), folded into a tool called OPEV (for "OCaml-to-PVS Equivalence Validation"), takes an OCaml program and a corresponding PVS implementation as input. From these inputs, OPEV automatically generates large-scale test cases, which are directly executed on the OCaml program and also used for constructing a large number of test lemmas on the PVS specification. The test lemmas are proved automatically using proof strategies. The results are compared to establish equivalence.

We demonstrate OPEV by using it to validate a manually implemented OCaml-to-PVS translation and a Sail-to-PVS parser (Sect. 3.2) that we manually developed. This parser includes 2,763 LOC and was used to translate 7,542 LOC of Lem code to 10,990 LOC of PVS implementation. OPEV generated and proved 458,247 test lemmas for these two case studies, and detected 11 errors (Sect. 3). The development of OPEV took 3 person-months and the effort to develop and validate the translator took 5 person-months.

This paper's central contribution is the proposed, semi-automatic test-and-proof methodology for validating translators supporting non-executable specifications. In principle, the OPEV methodology can be applied to any pair of target languages where one has non-executable semantics.

2   OPEV: OCaml-to-PVS Equivalence Validation

OPEV's methodology increases the trust in the translated OCaml code into PVS. The translation can be automatic (for a subset of OCaml) or manual.

Moreover, OPEV enables proving auto-generated test cases from the target language OCaml to PVS, where the inputs/ouputs have identical names and arguments.

2.1 OPEV Workflow

Figure 1 shows the OPEV workflow. In OPEV, we have designed an intermediate type system, Subsect. 2.2, to capture the commonality of OCaml and PVS types, which are restricted to a subset of the complete OCaml and PVS types. OPEV parses the PVS and OCaml sources to construct the intermediate type annotations for each function. With these annotations, OPEV generates random test cases for every OCaml and PVS function. OPEV then runs the OCaml test cases to obtain the test results, translates the OCaml test results to PVS, and constructs PVS test lemmas using the PVS test cases and translated results. The test lemmas are directly employed as *test oracles*, which can be automatically verified using manually implemented, generic PVS proof strategies. If the test lemmas are proved to be false, we know that there are mismatches in the OCaml-to-PVS translation. Thus, we investigate the cases and try to detect the reasons. The total codebase of OPEV is 3,783 LOC.

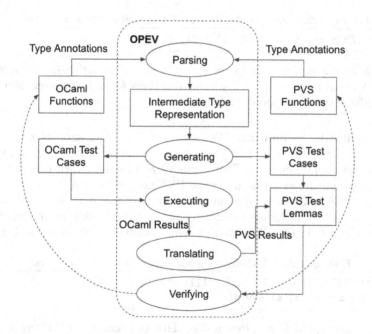

Fig. 1. The OPEV workflow.

Extensibility. OPEV has already incorporated the semantics of a large subset of OCaml and PVS for automatic test-generation. To ensure that OPEV can be extended to incorporate more types in the future, we represent the generated test cases and testing results in the `string` format to circumvent the real type system of OCaml and PVS.

Listing 1.1. A sample PVS reverse function.

```
rev[A:TYPE](l:list[A]) : RECURSIVE list[A] =
CASES l OF
cons(x, xs): append(rev(xs), cons(x, null))
ELSE null
ENDCASES
MEASURE length(l)
```

For example, in Listing 1.1, suppose we randomly generate [1, 6, 8] as the test value for the argument `l` of function `rev`. We then construct a string "let res = rev [1; 6; 8];;" as the OCaml command and delegate it to the OCaml `Toploop` library to execute the command. The result can be fetched from the `res` variable, which has the value [8; 6; 1]. Then OPEV parses the result according to its type and composes a PVS test lemma, such as `th_rev` in Listing 1.2.

Listing 1.2. A sample of OPEV PVS test lemmas for `rev` function.

```
th_rev: LEMMA rev((: 1, 6, 8 :)) = ((: 8, 6, 1 :))
```

The lemma is also written in the string format. This string-format representation allows us to avoid writing various functions for different argument types and simplifies the extension of OPEV.

Non-executable Semantics. We construct PVS test lemmas rather than directly executing the PVS test cases because the semantics of some testing functions are non-executable. That is, in PVS, functions with non-executable semantics cannot be executed using the PVS ground evaluator and PVS built-in strategies. For instance, most functions with set-theoretic semantics in PVS are non-executable, including relational specifications, which are represented as predicates on sets in PVS. For example, the semantics of the function `filter`,

Listing 1.3. A PVS function with non-executable semantics.

```
filter[A:TYPE](p:[A->bool])(s:set[A]):set[A]=
  {x: A | member(x, s) AND p(x)}
```

shown in Listing 1.3, is non-executable. This is because the `filter` function simply describes what kind of elements should be in the result set after the execution of the function but does not specify the steps of how to execute the function in PVS executable syntax. For instance, trying to execute this function directly in PVSio will issue an error message that indicates the `filter` function includes a non ground expression.

2.2 Intermediate Type Classification

To generate tests for OCaml and PVS functions respectively, we have to determine the commonality and difference between the two languages. Therefore, we design an intermediate type system to fill the gap between the type systems of the two languages. Since the types of the two languages cannot be matched with each other one-to-one, we classify the types of the two languages into five different classes and design rules to handle them separately.

OPEV's intermediate type system is categorized into 6 different classes: PEmpty, PBasic, PComplex, PDef, PExt, and PSpec. In this classification, PEmpty represents a dummy type that is used as a placeholder to occupy some blank space in the type notation. The existing OCaml types are then grouped according to the remaining five classes. Namely, basic built-in types such as bool, nat, and int; complex data types such as string, tuple, and list; user-defined types including datatype, record, and others; external library types; and types requiring special treatment such as functional types.

For each intermediate type, we design a generating rule and parsing rule according to the class of the type. Currently, OPEV only handles a subset of the OCaml type system. To extend the current OPEV type system into new types, one has to manually add specialized test generating heuristics in OPEV for the new types.

2.3 Test Generation

Types in the PBasic and PComplex classes have corresponding built-in types in OCaml and PVS. Thus, the test generating rules are simple and straightforward. OPEV generates multiple values for every function argument according to its type and then denotes the values to fit them into OCaml and PVS formats.

For example, for the int type, OPEV randomly generates an integer in a predefined range ($[-10, 10]$ by default). The integer follows a uniform distribution, and the predefined range can be modified by the user. For instance, for the range $[-5, 5]$, the corresponding command is as follows:

```
./opev --range -5 5 library_path
```

For types in the PDef, PExt, and PSpec classes, we develop more intricate and complex rules to generate the test cases. For example, OPEV only generates test cases for concrete types. Thus, for an arbitrary type, we define a rule that each arbitrary type must be instantiated to bool or nat, following the built-in test rules in the Lem source code.

Complex Data Types. For complex data types such as list and string, we set a length parameter that constrains the maximum length of the type element:

```
./opev --length 16 library_path
```

Since these complex data types have corresponding built-in definitions in OCaml and PVS, we do not need to consider the termination problem for some recursively defined data types because we design specific rules for each of these data types.

For example, if the argument type is `list`, OPEV first randomly generates an integer which is the length of the list, constrained by the predefined maximum length parameter. Then OPEV generates elements for the list, following the rules for the list type. The test value for the list is constructed for OCaml and PVS, respectively, following their list representations. For instance, for a list of length n, if the list elements are x_0, x_1, ..., and x_{n-1}, OPEV composes an OCaml list as $[x_0; x_1; ...; x_{n-1}]$ and a PVS list as $(: x_0, x_1, ..., x_{n-1} :)$.

User-Defined Types. In OCaml, developers can apply the `type` keyword to define a new type that represents a `record` or a `datatype`. The newly defined type may have various fields, and each field is denoted with a specific constructor and the corresponding type annotation. OPEV sequentially constructs test-cases for each field of the user-defined type. However, this may cause an infinite loop when there are recursive definitions in the user-defined type; thus, we set a maximum limit of recursive times to prevent infinite construction. Additionally, if the return type is a user-defined type, OPEV requires additional construction rules to directly translate the return results from OCaml to PVS, which means that, if a developer intends to use OPEV to generate tests for a new user-defined type, he/she needs to implement the construction function in the source code of OPEV.

External Types. To automatically generate test cases for the case studies (Sect. 3), we define generation rules for some external types that are used in these libraries. External types are the OCaml types imported from external libraries, which means we do not know the detailed implementations of the interfaces regarding these types. We have to manually design specific mapping functions from the OPEV intermediate type to OCaml external types and PVS types.

For instance, in our case studies, a typical external type is `Nat_big_num.num`, which is introduced in the library file `nums.cma`. This type is employed to handle the situation where there are large integer operations. However, in PVS, there are no limitations on the range of the default `int` and `nat` types. Thus, in PVS, the test cases can be generated following the rules for `int` and `nat`. On the other hand, in OCaml, we introduce a mapping function named `Nat_big_num.of_int`, which converts an integer into a `Nat_big_num.num` number.

Functional Types. The challenge of constructing a functional argument lies in that the function domain and range are potentially infinite. We initially considered applying the methods in Haskell QuickCheck [8] to generate a functional argument; however, the generated function might have different behaviors in OCaml and PVS because they take random generation seeds. Since we have to generate equivalent functions for OCaml and PVS, we designed a comparatively simple method to generate the functional argument.

First, we define multiple functions in PVS with some specific function patterns. Then OPEV randomly selects a predefined function and applies the function name as the PVS argument. Meanwhile, the OCaml argument is the corresponding function name related to the PVS one.

However, if there are no predefined PVS functions for certain patterns or there are no matching OCaml functions, OPEV constructs a LAMBDA expression to take symbolic arguments as the inputs and return a randomly generated constant as the output. This LAMBDA expression directly serves as the PVS argument, and a corresponding fun expression is built as the OCaml argument.

Dependent Types. The generation tactic for a dependent type is to construct the arguments according to its supertype, complying with the constraints of the dependent type. Right now, the supported constraints include arithmetic and comparison operations. Aside from these types of constraints, OPEV will directly generate test cases according to the supertype.

For example, a dependent type in PVS named word is defined as follows. word is a subtype of nat, and the word type is constrained by the constant N. OPEV uses the constraint to set up a new range for the natural number and generate a natural number within the range as a word type argument.

```
word : TYPE = {i: nat | i < exp2(N)}
```

This test construction strategy does not support more complicated constraints than arithmetic and comparison operations, as those would result in some redundant test lemmas that OPEV would reject. Although such test lemmas do not cause any inconsistency for the OCaml and PVS equivalence, they narrow the test coverage for functions with arguments of these dependent types.

2.4   Proof Automation

For each PVS function, OPEV can automatically generate thousands of test lemmas. It is impractical to manually prove all of them. To automate the proof process, we prove 392 general theorems that support fundamental properties of many translated functions, such as the commutativity and associativity of add operations for bit-vectors with the same length, Listing 1.4.

Listing 1.4. A general PVS theorem.

```
minus_eq_plus_neg: LEMMA FORALL (n:nat, m:nat, bv1:bvec[n],
    bv2:bvec[m]): m = n IMPLIES bv1 - bv2 = bv1 +
    add_vec_range[m]((bv2), 1)
```

Then we implement generic PVS strategies using these general theorems according to the patterns of the functions that are being tested.

For example, in Listing 1.4, the theorem named minus_eq_plus_neg proved that the subtraction of two bit-vectors is equivalent to the addition of the first bit-vector and the negation of the second bit-vector. With this theorem, testing regarding bit-vector subtraction operation can be rewritten to addition operation and negation operation.

With the pre-implemented PVS strategies, we then leverage a utility in PVS called Proof-Lite [6] to prove the test lemmas on these functions. The strategies will be able to instantiate these general theorems with concrete numbers as need be in the test lemmas. Moreover, Proof-Lite verifies the test lemmas sequentially. Therefore, we design a memory management algorithm to prove the test lemmas concurrently while efficiently utilizing memory. In the memory management algorithm, OPEV calls multiple processes to verify the test lemmas concurrently, monitors the status of the running machine, and automatically adjusts the number of activated processes according to the memory usage of the machine.

Automatic Proof Strategies. To automatically prove large-scale test lemmas with non-executable semantics in PVS, we implement a set of generic PVS strategies. To construct a generic PVS strategy for different functions, we start from a single test lemma and prove it manually. During the manual proof procedure, we extract a simple PVS strategy for this test lemma pattern. Then we try to prove other tests with different patterns using this PVS strategy. If this strategy does not work, we manually prove the new tests and get new PVS strategies. Then we try to combine the PVS strategies for different test patterns together using branching, backtracking, or feature extracting and summarizing. By repeatedly carrying out this process, we synthesize the unified pattern behind the verification of the test lemmas. We then construct a generic PVS strategy using the unified pattern. (It is possible to automate this proof generation, possibly using SMT solvers; we scope that out as future work.)

For instance, in the basic OCaml-to-PVS translation (Sect. 3.1) library, functions mainly focus on bit-vector operations. The functions in this library involve conversions between natural numbers and their corresponding bit-vector representations. This conversion from natural number to bit-vector in PVS is defined as follows (the source code is in [9]):

```
nat2bv(val: below(exp2(N))): {bv: bvec[N] | bv2nat(bv) = val}
```

The nat2bv function is non-executable since it just declares that it is the inverse function of bv2nat, which defines the conversion from bit-vector to natural number. Meanwhile, most of the functions in the OPEV_Value library call this nat2bv function. Thus, we can exploit the relation between nat2bv and bv2nat to circumvent the execution of nat2bv function, which is non-executable, and to prove test lemmas containing nat2bv function.

For example, the `case-split-strat` strategy, as illustrated in Listing 1.5, applies the injectivity and invariance properties of the `nat2bv` and `bv2nat` functions. This PVS strategy can be grandly applied to test lemmas for functions in the OPEV_Value (Sect. 3.1) library.

Listing 1.5. A generic PVS strategy.

```
(defstep case-split-strat (fname &optional (fnum 1))
  (let ((rewritestr1 (format nil "~a_inj" fname))
        (rewritestr2 (format nil "~a_inv" fname)))
    (branch (case-insert-fname fname fnum)
            ((then (rewrite rewritestr1)(grind)(eval-formula))
             (then (hide 2)(rewrite rewritestr2)(grind)(eval-formula))
             (then (grind)(eval-formula)))))
  "" "")
```

After implementing the generic strategy, we apply Proof-Lite, augmented with our memory management algorithm, and the PVS strategy to prove all the test lemmas generated for the functions in the library. We are able to efficiently prove hundreds of thousands of test lemmas automatically. The statistics are illustrated in Sect. 3.

3 Case Studies

We now illustrate the application of OPEV on two case studies: a manually implemented OCaml-to-PVS translation and a Sail-to-PVS parser. We detected 11 mismatches during the validation of these case studies. Documentation on these errors is available in [10]. The verification was carried out on an AMD Opteron server (2.3 GHz, 64 core, 128 GB).

3.1 Manually Implemented OCaml-to-PVS Translation

OPEV validated a manually implemented PVS library for which the source is a single OCaml file in the Sail source code [11], which supplies Sail with definitions and operations of bits and bit-vectors. Since the translation is done manually, the translated PVS library is error-prone. It is desirable to increase the reliability of the translation.

Table 1 illustrates the statistics for this validation. We verified ~200K test lemmas and found 6 mismatches. An example mismatch: in the implementation of `add_overflow_vec_bit_signed` function in PVS, if the second operand is false, we then assume that there is no overflow and no carry bit for the addition operation. However, in one version of sail_values.ml [11] (commit ce962ff), overflow is set to true. Thus, there is a conflict in the two implementations and the results parsed from the execution of the OCaml function cannot be verified in the PVS test lemmas. OPEV detected this difference in intention as an error.

Table 1. Statistics on validating the OCaml-to-PVS translation.

OCaml source code size	1,488 LOC
PVS destination code size	1,533 LOC
# of validated functions	150
# of manually proved generic lemmas	268
# of auto-generated test lemmas	215,562
# of missmatches found	6

3.2   Sail-to-PVS Parser

The Sail language [12], which is a first-order imperative language, has been used to describe the semantics of ISAs such as x86, ARM, RISC-V, and PowerPC [12]. To facilitate the reasoning on these semantics, we implemented a Sail-to-PVS Parser to expose the semantics of many ISAs and their multitudes of variants – already available in Sail – to the community of PVS users.

The architecture of the parser is shown in Fig. 2. First, we rely on the Sail compiler [11] to automatically translate Sail source code to Lem [13], which was designed to serve as a semantic model that was mathematically rigorous [3] and can be translated to OCaml for emulation of testing as well as to Isabelle/HOL, Coq, HOL4, and other languages. Then we employ the Lem compiler to translate the resulting Lem source code into a typed Abstract Syntax Tree (AST). Both the Sail and Lem compilers are in our trusted computing base. (We argue that trusting these two compilers is reasonable due to their small codebase. Besides, they have undergone intensive unit testing in prior work [13].)

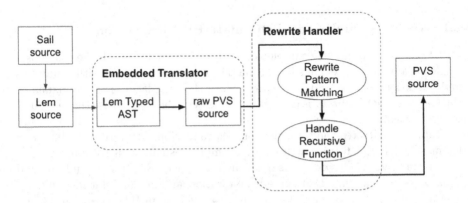

Fig. 2. Architecture of Sail-to-PVS parser.

Our Sail-to-PVS parser takes this typed AST as input and implements two independent parts: an embedded translator and a rewrite handler. The translator is embedded in the Lem source and translates the typed AST into corresponding PVS code using PVS syntax. The Lem type system does not support dependant types and originally was designed to translate Sail specifications into theorem provers that do not support dependant types, such as HOL4 and Isabelle [13]. In addition to this challenge, at this stage, the generated PVS code is challenging and error-prone due to other differences between PVS and Lem specification languages. For example, the method of reasoning about the termination of recursive functions and various formats of pattern matching for different pattern types. To solve the problems, we apply a rewrite handler, written in Python, to adjust the problematic PVS code. The rewrite handler performs two tasks: rewrite the pattern matching to ensure that the PVS code has consistent types and add **measure** functions for all the recursive functions. The total LOC of the Sail-to-PVS parser, including the embedded translator (1,730 lines of OCaml code) and the rewrite handler (1,033 lines of Python code), is 2,763. However, with these modifications Sail-to-PVS parser is still restricted to pure functions of Sail.

An important use case of the Sail-to-PVS parser is program verification at the assembly level (using PVS). For such a use case, it is critically important that the translation is provably correct. We automatically translate a Lem basic library [13] respectively to PVS and OCaml using the Sail-to-PVS parser and Sail's built-in compiler. Although Sail and Lem are executable, the generated PVS code would call some built-in PVS functions, some of which are non-executable; however, all of them are pure. Since the generated OCaml code is within the scope of OPEV's OCaml subset, it enables us to validate the equivalence between the generated OCaml and PVS code using OPEV. If the equivalence is validated, our trust in that the Sail-to-PVS parser carries out similar functionality as the Sail built-in compiler will increase significantly.

We generated small-scale test cases at the beginning, namely 10 test cases for each function, and attempted to prove all the test lemmas by a default PVS strategy called **grind**. For the test lemmas that cannot be proved, we designed the PVS strategies by proving auxiliary lemmas or by combining multiple strategies together according to the steps described in Sect. 2.4. Then we generated large-scale test lemmas and verified them using the corresponding strategies.

Table 2. Statistics on validation of Sail-to-PVS parser.

Lem source code size	7,542 LOC
PVS destination code size	10,990 LOC
# of validated functions	109
# of manually proved generic lemmas	124
# of auto-generated test lemmas	242,685
# of missmatches found	5

Table 2 shows the statistics for the library. OPEV determined multiple unprovable test lemmas in the PVS implementation. In turn, we modified the source code of the Sail-to-PVS parser, which generated the test lemmas reported in the table. Due to the gap between the semantics of the Lem and PVS languages, OPEV detected 5 mismatches. Doing this translation validation is practically impossible to achieve manually without OPEV.

4   Past and Related Work

Significant literature exists on translation validation. In [14], the authors show that the seL4 source code and its binary code have the same behavior. The translation validation relies on *refinement proofs*. A refinement proof is possible here due to formal semantics that was created for both the source and target languages. However, the semantics of OCaml and PVS cannot be mapped to each other one-to-one. Besides, refinement proofs, in general, are labor-expensive due to the significant human intervention required. The seL4 refinement proof [1] took 8 person-years; the seL4 total verification effort [1] is more significant and took ~20 person-years.

CompCert [7,15] uses a *formally verified compiler* to establish the correctness of compilation from a subset of C to PowerPC, ARM, RISC-V, or x86 assembly code. The compilation guarantees that the assembly code executes with the behavior that was designated by the original C program [16]. However, the formal proofs of CompCert did not cover the correctness of the formal specifications of C and assembly [15]. In addition, it took six person-years of effort and involved 100,000 lines of Coq code [7].

In contrast with compiler verification and refinement proofs, OPEV is a lightweight approach for the validation of a translation from a high-level language into a theorem prover using **random testing**. OPEV is therefore significantly less labor-expensive. Additionally, OPEV allows non-executable specifications and proofs for generic theorems after translating the code for further verification.

OPEV also differs from some other test-based light-weight verification techniques. For instance, Haskell's QuickCheck mechanism [8] is designed to aid in the verification of properties of a given function. The tests are randomly generated until either a counterexample is discovered in a given domain or a preset threshold is reached. Likewise, AutoTest for Eiffel [17] checks program annotations based on randomly generated test suites. Similar methods exist for theorem provers. Besides, QuickCheck [18] and Nitpick [19] for Coq and Isabelle/HOL uses random testing [20] to support counterexample discovery for a given conjecture. These mechanisms work well with executable specifications. OPEV differs from these efforts by its focus on validating the translation into a theorem prover and the supporting of non-executable semantics. Additionally, our translation into PVS allows the user to *verify* properties and specified conjectures for the translated functions using PVS's built-in test-generator [21] to assist in proving these properties or reaching a counterexample once applicable. But like the other built-in translations, it is restricted to generated PVS's executable specifications from our tool.

The closest work to OPEV is MINERVA [22], which provides a practical and rigorous general approach to produce high assurance software systems using model animation on mirrored implementations for verified algorithms [22]. However, MINERVA is limited to the executable subset of PVS. OPEV can be viewed as complementary to MINERVA when the specification is not executable.

5 Conclusions

In this paper, we presented a validation methodology, called OPEV, that provides a high assurance on the equivalence between OCaml and PVS specifications. OPEV employs an intermediate type system to capture the commonality of the subset of OCaml and PVS and generate test cases for both OCaml and PVS implementations. The reliability of the validation is ensured by executing large-scale stress tests and automatically proving test lemmas using generic PVS strategies. OPEV tool generated more than three hundred thousand test cases and proofs. We demonstrated the OPEV methodology on two case studies, namely a manual OCaml-to-PVS translation and a Sail-to-PVS parser. OPEV significantly increases our trust in the translations.

Currently, OPEV handles a subset of OCaml types and pure functions. In the future, we aim to extend the functionality of OPEV and incorporate more test generation rules for it. We also intend to increase automation in the proof process of OPEV. These enhancements would allow us to translate multiple mainstream instruction sets (ISA) specifications written in Sail into PVS, a necessary step to reason about the binary code of these architectures in PVS [23]. For instance, the methodology of [23] of lifting ARMv8 binaries into PVS7 based on translating ARM specification language ASL [24] into PVS, is interesting to us to generalize for other architectures. It allows the translation of system binary code of ARMv8 into PVS, based on PVS generic theories, theory parameters, and dependent types, in place of monad theory. Therefore, our work would open the door for more future research to verify the binary code of several mainstream instruction sets based on translating Sail ISAs specifications into the prototype verification system PVS.

Artifacts of the OPEV methodology are open-source and publicly available at: https://ssrg-vt.github.io/Renee/.

Acknowledgements. This material is based upon work supported by the US Office of Naval Research (ONR) under grant N00014-18-1-2665.

References

1. Klein, G., et al.: seL4: formal verification of an OS kernel. In: ACM Symposium on Operating Systems Principles, pp. 207–220. ACM (2009)
2. Greenaway, D., Andronick, J., Klein, G.: Bridging the gap: automatic verified abstraction of C. In: Beringer, L., Felty, A. (eds.) ITP 2012. LNCS, vol. 7406, pp. 99–115. Springer, Heidelberg (2012). https://doi.org/10.1007/978-3-642-32347-8_8

3. Mulligan, D.P., Owens, S., Gray, K.E., Ridge, T., Sewell, P.: Lem: reusable engineering of real-world semantics. SIGPLAN Not. **49**(9), 175–188 (2014). https://doi.org/10.1145/2692915.2628143
4. Conrad, M.: Testing-based translation validation of generated code in the context of IEC 61508. Formal Methods Syst. Des. **35**(3), 389–401 (2009)
5. Owre, S., Rushby, J.M., Shankar, N.: PVS: a prototype verification system. In: Kapur, D. (ed.) CADE 1992. LNCS, vol. 607, pp. 748–752. Springer, Heidelberg (1992). https://doi.org/10.1007/3-540-55602-8_217
6. Munoz, C.: Batch proving and proof scripting in PVS. NIA-NASA Langley, National Institute of Aerospace, Hampton, VA, Report NIA Report (2007–03) (2007)
7. Kästner, D., et al.: Compcert: practical experience on integrating and qualifying a formally verified optimizing compiler. In: ERTS2 2018-Embedded Real Time Software and Systems (2018)
8. Claessen, K., Hughes, J.: Quickcheck: a lightweight tool for random testing of Haskell programs. In: Proceedings of the Fifth ACM SIGPLAN International Conference on Functional Programming (ICFP 2000), pp. 268–279. ACM, New York, NY, USA (2000). https://doi.org/10.1145/351240.351266
9. PVS source code. http://www.csl.sri.com/users/owre/drop/pvs-snapshots/
10. OPEV bug report.OPEVBugReport
11. Sail project. https://github.com/rems-project/sail. Accessed 31 May 2019
12. Gray, K.E., Sewell, P., Pulte, C., Flur, S., Norton-Wright, R.: The sail instruction-set semantics specification language (2017)
13. Lem project. https://github.com/rems-project/lem. Accessed 31 May 2019
14. Sewell, T.A.L., Myreen, M.O., Klein, G.: Translation validation for a verified OS kernel. In: Proceedings of the 34th ACM SIGPLAN Conference on Programming Language Design and Implementation (PLDI 2013), pp. 471–482. Association for Computing Machinery, New York, NY, USA (2013). https://doi.org/10.1145/2491956.2462183
15. Leroy, X., Blazy, S., Kästner, D., Schommer, B., Pister, M., Ferdinand, C.: Compcert-a formally verified optimizing compiler. In: ERTS 2016: Embedded Real Time Software and Systems, 8th European Congress (2016)
16. Kästner, D., Leroy, X., Blazy, S., Schommer, B., Schmidt, M., Ferdinand, C.: Closing the gap-the formally verified optimizing compiler compcert. In: Safety-critical Systems Symposium 2017 (SSS 2017), pp. 163–180. CreateSpace (2017)
17. Ciupa, I., Pretschner, A., Oriol, M., Leitner, A., Meyer, B.: On the number and nature of faults found by random testing. Softw. Test. Verif. Reliab. **21**(1), 3–28 (2011). https://doi.org/10.1002/stvr.415
18. Tanter, É., Tabareau, N.: Gradual certified programming in coq. In: ACM SIGPLAN Notices, vol. 51, pp. 26–40. ACM (2015)
19. Blanchette, J.C., Nipkow, T.: Nitpick: a counterexample generator for higher-order logic based on a relational model finder. In: Kaufmann, M., Paulson, L.C. (eds.) ITP 2010. LNCS, vol. 6172, pp. 131–146. Springer, Heidelberg (2010). https://doi.org/10.1007/978-3-642-14052-5_11
20. Wada, Y., Kusakabe, S.: Performance evaluation of a testing framework using QuickCheck and Hadoop. JIP **20**(2), 340–346 (2012). https://doi.org/10.2197/ipsjjip.20.340
21. Crow, J., Owre, S., Rushby, J., Shankar, N., Stringer-Calvert, D.: Evaluating, testing, and animating PVS specifications, March 2019
22. Narkawicz, A., Munoz, C.A., Dutle, A.M.: The MINERVA software development process (2017)

23. Tahat, A., Joshi, S.P., Goswami, P., Ravindran, B.: Scalable translation validation of unverified legacy OS code. In: 2019 Formal Methods in Computer Aided Design (FMCAD), pp. 1–9 (2019)
24. Trustworthy specifications of Arm v8-A and v8-M system level architecture. In: Proceedings of Formal Methods in Computer-Aided Design (FMCAD 2016), pp. 161–168, October 2016. https://alastairreid.github.io/papers/fmcad2016-trustworthy.pdf

On the Usefulness of Clause Strengthening in Parallel SAT Solving

Vincent Vallade[1(✉)], Ludovic Le Frioux[2], Souheib Baarir[1,3], Julien Sopena[1,4], and Fabrice Kordon[1]

[1] Sorbonne Université, CNRS, LIP6, UMR 7606, Paris, France
vincent.vallade@lip6.fr
[2] LRDE, EPITA, Le Kremlin-Bicêtre, France
[3] Université Paris Nanterre, Nanterre, France
[4] Inria, DELYS Team, Paris, France

Abstract. In the context of parallel SATisfiability solving, this paper presents an implementation and evaluation of a clause strengthening algorithm. The developed component can be easily combined with (virtually) any CDCL-like SAT solver. Our implementation is integrated as a part of Painless, a generic and modular framework for building parallel SAT solvers.

Keywords: Parallel satisfiability · Tool · Strengthening · Clause sharing · Portfolio · Divide-and-conquer

1 Introduction

Modern CDCL SAT solvers [1,12] have been successfully used to solve a wide variety of real-world problems, such as those issued from hardware and software verification [4].

With the omnipresence of many-core machines, these solvers have been adapted to become parallel [3]. In this context, a key feature in the efficiency is information sharing. This is usually implemented as sets of new (learnt) lemmas that are exchanged between the different participants of the parallelization solving strategy (i.e., the underling sequential solvers).

Besides, it is well admitted that the shorter the learnt lemmas the more powerful they are. This explained the proposal of different techniques based on resolution to shorten them [7,8,15,16]. A process known as *strengthening*. Potentially as difficult as the SAT problem itself, the strengthening of those learnt lemmas can benefit from parallelization [17].

This paper presents the implementation and evaluation of a parallel strengthening algorithm inspired from [17]. Our implementation is integrated as a part of Painless [9], a framework for building parallel SAT solvers.

Paper Structure. Section 2 introduces some background. Strengthening is presented in Sect. 3. Its implementation is described in Sect. 4. Some experimental results are depicted in Sect. 5. Section 6 concludes the paper.

© Springer Nature Switzerland AG 2020
R. Lee et al. (Eds.): NFM 2020, LNCS 12229, pp. 222–229, 2020.
https://doi.org/10.1007/978-3-030-55754-6_13

2 Background

This section introduces useful background used in the remaining of this paper.

Boolean Satisfiability. A *propositional variable* is a variable that has two possible values: *true* or *false*. A *literal* is a propositional variable or its negation (NOT). A *clause* is a finite disjunction (OR) of literals. A clause with a unique literal is called *unit clause*. A *conjunctive normal form (CNF) formula* is a finite conjunction (AND) of clauses. In the rest of the paper clauses are represented by the set of their literals, and formulas by the set of their clauses. Let F be a formula, an *assignment* of variables of F is defined as a function $\mathcal{A} : \mathcal{V} \rightarrow \{true, false\}$, where $\mathcal{V}$ is the set of variables of F. A clause is satisfied when at least one of its literals is evaluated to *true*. A formula is satisfied if all its clauses are evaluated to *true*. A formula is said to be SATif there is at least one assignment of its variables that makes it *true*; it is reported to be UNSATotherwise. The Boolean satisfiability (SAT) problem consists in determining if a given formula is SATor UNSAT.

CDCL Algorithm. Conflict-driven clause learning algorithm [14,18] is used in almost all (complete) modern SAT solvers. It enumerates assignments for the given formula. Variables' values are forced using *unit propagation* [5] (*i.e.,*fixing recursively the values of variables in unit clauses). If an empty clause is generated a conflict has been reached. The reasons are studied and a learnt clause is derived and stored. The search backtracks and starts over. If unit propagation does not generate a conflict, a guess is done (branching) to grow up the current assignment. The search ends if a satisfying assignment has been found or if all have been checked without finding solutions.

Let F be a formula, unit propagation can be iteratively applied for a given partial assignment $\mathcal{A}$: `iterativeUnitPropagation`$(F, \mathcal{A})$ produces the set of assignments implied by this operation. $F|_{\mathcal{A}}$ returns the formula simplified by the iterative unit propagations of $\mathcal{A}$ on F.

3 Strengthening Algorithm

The pseudo-code of the strengthening algorithm we implemented in our tool is presented in Algorithm 1. The theoretical basics of this technique are presented in [17]. This section only focuses on the technical details.

Algorithm 1 takes a clause C_{in} as input, and, potentially outputs a reduced size (strengthened) clause, w.r.t. C_{in}, (lines 8 and 14). It considers an empty assignment $\mathcal{A}$ (line 3), the knowledge of all the clauses of the problem F, and it manages its own set of learnt clauses L_R (line 4) empty at the beginning of the program.

To achieve its strengthening task, Algorithm 1 iteratively assigns a false value to each literal of the clause C_{in}, until it reaches a conflict or it assigns successfully all literals of the input clause. Therefore, there are two possible outputs, respectively C_{new} and C_{out}.

Algorithm 1: Strengthening algorithm

---

1 **function** strengthen(C_{in}: *clause*) : *the strengthened clause*
2 | $C_{out} := \emptyset$
3 | $\mathcal{A} := \emptyset$
4 | $F' := F \cup L_R$
5 | **for** $l \in (C_{in} \setminus C_{out})$ s.t. $\neg l \notin$ iterativeUnitPropagation$(F', \mathcal{A})$ **do**
6 | | **if** $\emptyset \in F'|_{\mathcal{A}}$ **then**
7 | | | $(L_R, C_{new}) :=$ analyze$(F', \mathcal{A})$
8 | | | **return** C_{new}
9 | | **end**
10 | | $C_{out} = C_{out} \cup \{l\}$
11 | | $\mathcal{A} = \mathcal{A} \cup \{\neg l\}$
12 | **end**
13 | $L_R = L_R \cup \{C_{out}\}$
14 | **return** C_{out}

At each iteration, Algorithm 1 picks a literal whose complementary is not implied by the current assignment ($\neg l \notin$ iterativeUnitPropagation$(F', \mathcal{A})$). This ensures the stripping of the input clause from all literals that are implied by the rest of the clause. Then, it executes a unit propagation (line 5). If no conflict is discovered, the literal is added to the output clause C_{out} and its negation is added to the set of assignment $\mathcal{A}$ (line 10–11).

When a conflict is reached (line 6), function analyze() is then called (line 7): it executes a sequence of backtracking, unit propagation, and conflict analysis until getting out of the conflict or emptying the set $\mathcal{A}$. During this phase, the algorithm learns new clauses (that are added to L_R). When analyze() reaches a zone without conflict (while assuming $\mathcal{A}$), it generates the clause C_{new} that is returned (line 8). This last is composed of the set of literals: $\{l | \neg l \in \mathcal{A}\} \cup \{k\}$, k being some literal of $C_{out} \notin \mathcal{A}$.

If all the literal of C_{in} are assigned successfully, then the clause C_{out} is added to L_R and then returned (lines 13–14).

4   Implementation

Our implementation is based on Painless [9] which is a framework allowing the implementation of parallel SAT solvers for many-core environments. The main components of Painless are: working organization, clause sharing, and sequential engines. For this work, we focused on the third component and implemented a reducer solver that can be included in all Painless' configurations.[1]

About the Painless Framework. The main idea of the framework is to separate the technical components (*e.g.*, dedicated to concurrent programming

---

[1] This version of Painless can be found at https://github.com/lip6/painless, branch strengthening.

aspects) from those implementing heuristics and optimizations embedded in a parallel SAT solver. Three main components arise when treating parallel SAT solvers: *Sequential Engines, Parallelisation,* and *Sharing.* These form the global architecture of Painless. They can be instantiated independently to produce new complete solvers.

The core element considered here is a sequential SAT solver. This can be any CDCL-like solver. Technically, these engines are operated through a generic *SolverInterface* providing basics of sequential solvers: *solve, add clauses,* etc.

To build a parallel solver using the aforementioned engines, one needs a parallelisation strategy (*e.g.,s* portfolio, divide-and-conquer). In Painless, a strategy is represented by a tree-structure of arbitrary depth. The internal nodes of the tree (*WorkingStrategy*) represent parallelisation strategies, and leaves are core engines operated by a thread (*SequentialWorker*).

In Painless, solvers can export (import) clauses to (from) the others during the resolution process. The sharing of these learnt clauses is dedicated to particular components called *Sharers.* Each *Sharer* is in charge of sets of producers and consumers and its behaviour reduces to a loop of sleeping and exchange phases *w.r.t.*to a given *SharingStrategy.*

Implementing Strengthening. This section presents the implementation of strengthening we included into the Painless framework. The development of such a component has been designed to be easily used in combination with all other mechanisms provided by Painless.

The *Reducer* engine of Fig. 1 implements Algorithm 1. As it can be easily observed, the main component of this algorithm are iterative unit propagation and analysis (based on assumptions) procedures. These are also the usual components provided by any CDCL-like SAT solver.

Therefore, we implemented the strengthening operation as a decorator of *SolverInterface.* This decorator is a *SolverInterface* itself that uses, by delegation, another *SolverInterface* to apply the strengthening (see Fig. 1).

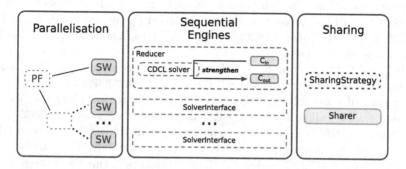

Fig. 1. Parallel strengthening architecture

The CDCL solver needs to be able to solve a formula with a set of assumptions. Assumptions are literals with a predefined value that the solver must accept as immutable. This is how we implemented the loop in Algorithm 1. We give the negation of the learnt clause as assumptions to the solver, which stops the resolution when a conflict is reached or when the solver has branched on all the assumptions. The solver must also be able to express a conflict only in terms of assumptions, i.e. the set of literals returned by the analysis contains only literals present in the initial set of assumptions.

The *Reducer* is always at the root of a portfolio. For example, if one wants to implement a divide-and-conquer solver complemented by a *Reducer*, they must create a portfolio with a *Reducer* and a divide-and-conquer as workers. This is extremely easy to do thanks to the composite nature of Painless' *Parallelisation* engine. The *Reducer* is both a consumer and a producer of the Sharer. It receives clauses, strengthened them and shares them back after.

5   Empirical Study

To assess the performances of the developed component and study its impact in different parallel solvers, we integrated our *Reducer* in several parallelisation strategies. We then conducted a set of experiments to compare the results.

Solvers Description. All parallel solvers we constructed, but one, are based on `P-MCOMSPS` [11]. It implements a portfolio strategy [6] (PF) and uses `MapleCOMSPS` [13] as sequential engine. The solvers differ however by their sharing strategies.

One of the main heuristics used in sharing strategies is the so-called Literal Block Distance (LBD) measure: the LBD of a clause is the number of decision levels represented in that clause. It is fairly admitted that the lower the LBD, the better the clause [1]. In a parallel context, it is useful to share these low LBD clauses.

We therefore derived the following strategies: **AI**, only learnt clauses with an LBD value less or equal than a threshold are shared. This threshold is additively increased if not enough clauses are exchanged [2]; **L**i shares only learnt clauses with an LBD value $\leq i$. Hence, we ended up by developing the solver `P-MCOMSPS-AI`[2], the solver `P-MCOMSPS-L2`[3] and the solver `P-MCOMSPS-L4` (*L4* is a new untested yet strategy).

To complete the picture, we also developed a divide-and-conquer (DC) solver that uses L4 sharing strategy. We call this solver `DC-MCOMSPS-L4` [10].

For each of these solvers, we created its counterpart including the *Reducer* component. We called them by extending their names by -REDUCE (e.g., `P-MCOMSPS-L4-REDUCE`). It is important to note that the we do not use a additional core for the *Reducer*, e.g., if we use 12 cores for `P-MCOMSPS-L4`, we also use 12 cores for `P-MCOMSPS-L4-REDUCE`, one thread performs the strengthening instead of the CDCL algorithm.

---

[2] *AI* is the strategy used by the winner of the parallel track of 2018 SAT competition.

[3] *L2* is the strategy used by the second of the parallel track of 2018 SAT competition.

Table 1. Results of the different solvers on the SAT benchmark 2018

Parallelisation	Solvers	PAR-2	CTI	UNSAT	SAT	SCR(400)
PF	P-MCOMSPS-L4	363h06	26h53	115	165	280
	P-MCOMSPS-L4-REDUCE	342h33	21h47	121	168	289
	P-MCOMSPS-L2	379h32	23h04	108	165	273
	P-MCOMSPS-L2-REDUCE	371h53	20h45	115	163	278
	P-MCOMSPS-AI	356h13	37h10	121	165	286
	P-MCOMSPS-AI-REDUCE	342h36	32h15	125	167	292
DC	DC-MCOMSPS-L4	448h34	17h17	100	146	246
	DC-MCOMSPS-L4-REDUCE	437h44	18h59	103	149	252

Experimental Results. For the evaluation we use the main benchmark of the SAT competition 2018[4] which contains 400 instances. All jobs were run on an Intel Xeon CPUs @ 2.40 GHz and 1.48 TB of RAM. Solvers have been launched with 12 threads, a 150 GB memory limit, and a 5000 s timeout (the timeout is the same as for the SAT competitions).

The performance of our solvers is evaluated using the following success metrics: penalized average runtime (PAR-2) sums the execution time of a solver and penalizes the executions that exceed the timeout with a factor 2; solution-count ranking (SCR) counts the number of problems solved by a solver; cumulative time of the intersection (CTI) sums the execution time of a solver on the problems solved by all the solvers.

Table 1 presents the results of our experiments, where each solver is compared to its counterpart (with a *Reducer* component). The shaded cells indicate which one of the two solvers has the best results. We observe that in all metrics, but two cases, the versions with a *Reducer* are better: more instances are solved and better PAR-2 values are obtained in all cases. Only CTI of the DC version is not as good as the other values. Also, the gains in the number of instances solved appears to be greater in the UNSATcategory, but the number of SATinstances also improves.

To go further in our evaluation, we measured the minimisation capabilities of the *Reducer* on instances that each solver could actually solve, while discarding those where the *Reducer* did not receive any clause (problem solved too quickly): (1) P-MCOMSPS-L4-REDUCE (255 instances), 44.21% of the clauses treated by the *Reducer* are actually shortened. The mean size of these clauses after strengthening is 25.45% less than the mean of their original size; (2) P-MCOMSPS-L2-REDUCE (257 instances), treated 32.59% of the clauses and it lower their size by 23.67%; (3) P-MCOMSPS-AI-REDUCE (258 instances) treated 34.79% clauses and reduced by 27.75%; (4) DC-MCOMSPS-L4-REDUCE (245 instances) reduced 28.80% clauses by 18.86%. In conclusion, the *Reducer* succeeded to reduce 1/3 of the clauses it receives by 1/4 of their size.

---

[4] http://sat2018.forsyte.tuwien.ac.at/benchmarks/Main.zip.

6   Conclusion

This paper presents an implementation of clause strengthening [17] which has been integrated into Painless [9]. Thanks to the modularity of Painless, we were able to test the efficiency of strengthening within different configurations of parallel SAT solvers.

In this study, we used several sharing strategies and different parallelisation paradigms (*i.e.*,portfolio and divide-and-conquer). Our experiments show that having a core dedicated to strengthening improves the performance of our parallel solvers whatever the configuration is (including the winner configuration from the SAT competition 2018).

References

1. Audemard, G., Simon, L.: Predicting learnt clauses quality in modern sat solvers. In: Proceedings of the 21st International Joint Conferences on Artificial Intelligence (IJCAI), pp. 399–404. AAAI Press (2009)
2. Balyo, T., Sanders, P., Sinz, C.: HordeSat: a massively parallel portfolio SAT solver. In: Heule, M., Weaver, S. (eds.) SAT 2015. LNCS, vol. 9340, pp. 156–172. Springer, Cham (2015). https://doi.org/10.1007/978-3-319-24318-4_12
3. Balyo, T., Sinz, C.: Parallel satisfiability. Handbook of Parallel Constraint Reasoning, pp. 3–29. Springer, Cham (2018). https://doi.org/10.1007/978-3-319-63516-3_1
4. Biere, A., Cimatti, A., Clarke, E., Zhu, Y.: Symbolic model checking without BDDs. In: Cleaveland, W.R. (ed.) TACAS 1999. LNCS, vol. 1579, pp. 193–207. Springer, Heidelberg (1999). https://doi.org/10.1007/3-540-49059-0_14 ·
5. Davis, M., Logemann, G., Loveland, D.: A machine program for theorem-proving. Communun. ACM 5(7), 394–397 (1962)
6. Hamadi, Y., Jabbour, S., Sais, L.: ManySAT: a parallel SAT solver. J. Satisf. Boolean Model. Comput. 6(4), 245–262 (2009)
7. Han, H., Somenzi, F.: Alembic: an efficient algorithm for CNF preprocessing. In: Proceedings of the 44th Annual Design Automation Conference. DAC 2007, pp. 582–587. Association for Computing Machinery, New York (2007). https://doi.org/10.1145/1278480.1278628
8. Heule, M.J.H., Järvisalo, M., Biere, A.: Efficient CNF simplification based on binary implication graphs. In: Sakallah, K.A., Simon, L. (eds.) SAT 2011. LNCS, vol. 6695, pp. 201–215. Springer, Heidelberg (2011). https://doi.org/10.1007/978-3-642-21581-0_17
9. Le Frioux, L., Baarir, S., Sopena, J., Kordon, F.: PaInleSS: a framework for parallel SAT solving. In: Gaspers, S., Walsh, T. (eds.) SAT 2017. LNCS, vol. 10491, pp. 233–250. Springer, Cham (2017). https://doi.org/10.1007/978-3-319-66263-3_15
10. Le Frioux, L., Baarir, S., Sopena, J., Kordon, F.: Modular and efficient divide-and-conquer SAT solver on top of the painless framework. In: Vojnar, T., Zhang, L. (eds.) TACAS 2019. LNCS, vol. 11427, pp. 135–151. Springer, Cham (2019). https://doi.org/10.1007/978-3-030-17462-0_8
11. Le Frioux, L., Metin, H., Baarir, S., Colange, M., Sopena, J., Kordon, F.: painless-mcomsps and painless-mcomsps-sym. In: Proceedings of SAT Competition 2018: Solver and Benchmark Descriptions, pp. 33–34. Department of Computer Science, University of Helsinki, Finland (2018)

12. Liang, J.H., Ganesh, V., Poupart, P., Czarnecki, K.: Learning rate based branching heuristic for SAT solvers. In: Creignou, N., Le Berre, D. (eds.) SAT 2016. LNCS, vol. 9710, pp. 123–140. Springer, Cham (2016). https://doi.org/10.1007/978-3-319-40970-2_9

13. Liang, J.H., Oh, C., Ganesh, V., Czarnecki, K., Poupart, P.: MapleCOMSPS, MapleCOMSPS LRB, MapleCOMSPS CHB. In: Proceedings of SAT Competition 2016: Solver and Benchmark Descriptions, p. 52. Department of Computer Science, University of Helsinki, Finland (2016)

14. Marques-Silva, J.P., Sakallah, K.: GRASP: a search algorithm for propositional satisfiability. IEEE Trans. Comput. 48(5), 506–521 (1999)

15. Piette, C., Hamadi, Y., Saïs, L.: Vivifying propositional clausal formulae. In: Proceedings of the 2008 Conference on ECAI 2008: 18th European Conference on Artificial Intelligence, pp. 525–529. IOS Press, NLD (2008)

16. Sörensson, N., Biere, A.: Minimizing learned clauses. In: Kullmann, O. (ed.) SAT 2009. LNCS, vol. 5584, pp. 237–243. Springer, Heidelberg (2009). https://doi.org/10.1007/978-3-642-02777-2_23

17. Wieringa, S., Heljanko, K.: Concurrent clause strengthening. In: Järvisalo, M., Van Gelder, A. (eds.) SAT 2013. LNCS, vol. 7962, pp. 116–132. Springer, Heidelberg (2013). https://doi.org/10.1007/978-3-642-39071-5_10

18. Zhang, L., Madigan, C.F., Moskewicz, M.H., Malik, S.: Efficient conflict driven learning in a Boolean satisfiability solver. In: Proceedings of the 20th IEEE/ACM International Conference on Computer-Aided Design (ICCAD), pp. 279–285. IEEE (2001)

Solvers and Program Analysis

Verifying a Solver for Linear Mixed Integer Arithmetic in Isabelle/HOL

Ralph Bottesch[1]([✉]), Max W. Haslbeck[1][iD], Alban Reynaud[2],
and René Thiemann[1][iD]

[1] University of Innsbruck, Innsbruck, Austria
ralph.bottesch@uibk.ac.at
[2] ENS Lyon, Lyon, France

Abstract. We implement a decision procedure for linear mixed integer arithmetic and formally verify its soundness in Isabelle/HOL. We further integrate this procedure into one application, namely into CeTA, a formally verified certifier to check untrusted termination proofs. This checking involves assertions of unsatisfiability of linear integer inequalities; previously, only a sufficient criterion for such checks was supported. To verify the soundness of the decision procedure, we first formalize the proof that every satisfiable set of linear integer inequalities also has a small solution, and give explicit upper bounds. To this end we mechanize several important theorems on linear programming, including statements on integrality and bounds. The procedure itself is then implemented as a branch-and-bound algorithm, and is available in several languages via Isabelle's code generator. It internally relies upon an adapted version of an existing verified incremental simplex algorithm.

Keywords: Branch-and-bound · Isabelle/HOL · Linear programming · Polyhedra · Simplex algorithm

1 Introduction

The computational problem of deciding whether a system of linear inequalities with integer coefficients has an integral solution arises in many practical situations. Since it is NP-complete, no currently known algorithm can in general avoid searches of exponential length. Furthermore, while satisfiable instances always have short solutions that can be efficiently checked, there need not be short, efficiently-checkable proofs for the fact that an instance is unsatisfiable, unless NP = co-NP. (Contrast this with the related problem of deciding whether a system of linear inequalities with integer coefficients has a *rational* solution – this problem is in P, and Farkas' lemma provides a short and efficiently checkable certificate that an unsatisfiable instance indeed has no solution.) Thus, if a

This research was supported by the Austrian Science Fund (FWF) project Y757. The authors are listed in alphabetical order regardless of individual contributions or seniority.

© The Author(s) 2020, corrected publication 2020
R. Lee et al. (Eds.): NFM 2020, LNCS 12229, pp. 233–250, 2020.
https://doi.org/10.1007/978-3-030-55754-6_14

solver declares that a given instance is unsatisfiable over the integers, the length of any proof for this fact may be exponential in the size of the input instance, in which case the computational effort required to check such a proof would be exponential as well.

Instead of repeatedly performing certification tasks that require immense amounts of data and computational effort, it may be more fruitful to formally verify the soundness of a solver *once*, so that it can then be trusted without instance-by-instance certification of its output. The implementation of such a solver, together with a formal proof of its soundness, is the goal of the present work. Specifically, we use Isabelle/HOL [19] to implement and prove the correctness of a branch-and-bound algorithm [21, Chapter 24.1], and then use Isabelle's code generator [11] to obtain verified executable code. Along the way, we also give the first formalized proofs for several important results on integer programming.

A concrete example of an application for our solver comes from *termination analysis*, where a program is given as input to a termination tool that tries to determine whether the given program terminates on all inputs. Since termination tools get patched and improved repeatedly, maintaining an up-to-date formal proof of soundness would be extremely difficult. Therefore, the approach that is typically used is to have the (unverified) termination tool output a certificate for its analysis, which can then be checked by a verified certificate checker. One such certificate checker is CeTA [5,24]. It has been verified in Isabelle/HOL, so that whenever it accepts a proof of termination for some program, the formal proof of CeTA's soundness ensures that the program does indeed terminate.

As an example, consider a program to compute the binary logarithm.

```
int log2(int x) {
  int n := 0;
  while (x > 0) {
    x := x div 2;
    n := n + 1;
  }
  return n;
}
```

This program can be translated into an integer transition system and termination can be proved by showing that the value of x is decreased by at least 1 in every loop iteration. This property can be expressed in linear integer arithmetic (LIA): it is equivalent to the validity of formula (1), where x' and n' represent the new values of x and n, respectively, after an iteration of the loop.

$$x > 0 \land 2x' \leqslant x \land x \leqslant 2x' + 1 \land n' = n + 1 \longrightarrow x \geqslant x' + 1 \qquad (1)$$

Validity of (1) is equivalent to unsatisfiability of the negated formula, which is simply a conjunction of linear inequalities:

$$x > 0 \land 2x' \leqslant x \land x \leqslant 2x' + 1 \land n' = n + 1 \land x < x' + 1 \qquad (2)$$

A *sufficient* condition for the unsatisfiability of (2) over the integers (LIA) is the unsatisfiability of the same system over the rationals (LRA); the latter can be shown, for instance, via the simplex algorithm [9]. Indeed, a verified implementation [23] of the simplex algorithm is currently integrated into CeTA [5]. However, whereas (2) is unsatisfiable over the integers, it has a rational solution $x = n' = 1$, $x' = \frac{1}{2}$, $n = 0$. For such examples, considering the problem over the rationals may prohibit CeTA from detecting unsatisfiability over the integers.

Therefore, in this paper we develop a verified theory solver for LIA (in fact, for linear *mixed* integer arithmetic, where only a user-specified part of the solution is required to be integral). The verified solver takes a conjunction of strict and non-strict linear inequalities as input, and decides whether they are simultaneously solvable. We fully integrate the LIA solver into CeTA, so that the new version can handle all instances that are unsatisfiable over the integers and not only those that are unsatisfiable over the rationals as well. Of course, the LIA solver can also be used as a stand-alone theory solver, e.g., to perform verified SMT solving.

We verify our LIA solver in two major steps.

1. First, we show that for every set of LIA constraints it suffices to search for small solutions. To this end, we formally verify an a priori bound in the style of Papadimitriou [20]: If there is an integer solution to a set of LIA constraints, then there is also one that is bounded by $b := n(ma)^{2m+1}$, where n is the number of variables, m the number of inequalities, and a the largest absolute value of any number occurring in the inequalities. To be more precise, the small solution satisfies $|x| \leq b$ for each variable x.

   Our verified upper bound matches the one given in a textbook [21, Thm. 17.1] (which is considerably lower than the one by Papadimitriou).[1] Specifically, we establish a bound of $(n + 1)!a^n$ (with no dependence on m). To prove this bound in Isabelle/HOL we mostly follow the textbook proofs and formalize several important results from linear programming, often with additional statements on bounds and integrality. These results include: the fundamental theorem of linear inequalities, the Farkas–Minkowski–Weyl theorem, Carathéodory's theorem, and the decomposition theorem for polyhedra. Note that the bound on the size of solutions also implies the fact that the problem of deciding satisfiability for linear integer inequalities is in NP.

2. Using the upper bound, we can decide satisfiability via a finite search. For instance, for formula (2) we have $n = 4$, $a = 2$ and $m = 6$ (the equality counts as two inequalities), and we know that if (2) is satisfiable, then there is an integer solution with absolute values at most 1920.

   To perform this search, we implement and verify a basic branch-and-bound algorithm. It is based on an incremental version of the simplex algorithm by Dutertre and de Moura [10], which is used to deliver candidate solutions and to prune the search tree by detecting unsatisfiability in LRA. Although the incremental simplex algorithm has recently been verified in Isabelle/HOL [3],

---

[1] The textbook bound is somewhat more precise than ours, as it is phrased in terms of sub-determinants, whereas we use a generic bound on sub-determinants.

its integration into the branch-and-bound algorithm is not immediate: the branch-and-bound algorithm requires frequent updates of bounds on variables, and this operation is not supported by the existing verified incremental simplex algorithm.

Note that our verified LIA solver is missing several possible optimizations [6,7,14], some of which might be integrated in future work. Therefore, it clearly cannot compete with state-of-the-art (unverified) solvers. Still, our experimental results show that there are some examples from SMT-LIB where our solver is successful, but both CVC4 [2] and Z3 [16] fail.

Structure. We give some preliminaries on linear (integer) programming and Isabelle in Sect. 2. Afterwards, we present our formalization of linear programming and the mentioned bound in Sect. 3. The branch-and-bound algorithm with the adaptation of the incremental simplex algorithm are covered in Sect. 4. We provide experimental results in Sect. 5 and conclude in Sect. 6.

The collection of theorems on polyhedra and small solutions is available as part of the archive of formal proofs (AFP) in the entry on linear inequalities [4], and the branch-and-bound algorithm is part of IsaFoR/CeTA [24]. All of the theorems of this paper are linked to the formalization on an accompanying website. It also provides details on the experiments.

http://cl-informatik.uibk.ac.at/software/ceta/experiments/lia/

Related Work. Allamigeon and Katz [1] have implemented the simplex algorithm in Coq and used it to give constructive proofs of a number of important theorems about convex polyhedra. The overlap between our work and [1] consists of formalizations of basic facts concerning cones and polyhedra, the fundamental theorem of linear inequalities, and Farkas' lemma. However, whereas in [1] a simplex algorithm for optimization problems is implemented in order to be used in constructive mathematical proofs, we formalize theorems concerning integer programming, including bounds on the size of solutions, and use these together with the previously Isabelle-verified simplex algorithm to obtain formally verified, yet efficient, software.

There is also a formalization of theorems about polyhedra in HOL Light, due to Harrison [12], but it contains neither a formalization of the simplex algorithm nor does it cover integer programming.

Cooper's algorithm has been formalized by Nipkow [18] in Isabelle/HOL. Although this algorithm also solves linear integer arithmetic, it internally works completely differently and its formalization requires different proofs; therefore, we do not see any overlap between the two works. We nevertheless consider the verified version of Cooper's algorithm in our experiments.

Finally, we mention two general-purpose verified solvers. Carlier *et al.* [8] used Coq to implement and verify an algorithm for solving constraint satisfaction problems over finite domains. As with [1], the resulting implementation can be used in principle, but is not efficient enough to compete with unverified implementations of the same algorithm. Narkawicz and Muñoz [17] used

PVS to verify a general branch-and-bound algorithm; a C++ implementation of this algorithm is described in [22]. In contrast to our work, this implementation was not automatically generated from a formal, verified algorithm specification, but was coded separately. Furthermore, in order to use the general branch-and-bound algorithm, one must first tailor it to an application domain by specifying a number of functions that must respect certain specifications, whereas every part of our LIA solver (both branch-and-bound and simplex) has been formally verified. Thus, while the algorithm we verify lacks the generality of the one in [17], our implementation retains a higher degree of reliability than the one in [22], due to being entirely generated from a formally verified algorithm, and it is nevertheless reasonably efficient.

2 Preliminaries

We briefly review some linear programming and Isabelle background.

2.1 Linear Programming

We assume familiarity with vector spaces. Although our Isabelle theorems use a more general type, here we present our results in the context of Euclidean spaces ($\mathbb{R}^n$). We denote the usual inner product in $\mathbb{R}^n$ by '$\cdot$'.

A *(non-strict) linear inequality* is an inequality of the form $a \cdot x \leq b$, where $a, x \in \mathbb{R}^n$ (a a row vector, x a column vector) and $b \in \mathbb{R}$. A system of linear inequalities can therefore be written as $Ax \leq b$, with $A \in \mathbb{R}^{m \times n}$ and $b \in \mathbb{R}^m$ a column vector. A system of linear inequalities is a *mixed integer system* if, for some $I \subseteq \{1, \ldots, n\}$, it is required that $x_i \in \mathbb{Z}$ for all $i \in I$. We also define *strict linear inequalities* to be inequalities of the form $ax < b$, with a, x and b as before.

In this work we consider mixed integer systems of linear inequalities containing both non-strict and strict inequalities.

For reference, we collect below the definitions of several important concepts from linear algebra that are needed in order to state the theorems that we formalize. These definitions can be found in textbooks on linear programming such as [21, Chapters 7.1–2 and 16.2].

Definition 1 (Half-spaces, hyperplanes, polyhedra). *For $c \in \mathbb{R}^n \setminus \{0_n\}$ (a row vector) and $d \in \mathbb{R}$, we say that the set $H = \{x \mid c \cdot x \leq d\}$ is an* affine half-space, *and that c is its* normal vector. *If $d = 0$, then H is called a* linear half-space *(or just a* half-space*). The set $\{x \mid c \cdot x = 0\}$ is called a* hyperplane *(of which c is a* normal vector*).*

A set $P \subseteq \mathbb{R}^n$ is called a (convex) polyhedron *if $P = \{x \mid Ax \leq b\}$, for some matrix $A \in \mathbb{R}^{m \times n}$ and $b \in \mathbb{R}^m$. In words, a polyhedron is the intersection of a finite collection of affine half-spaces.*

Definition 2 (Cones). *A non-empty set $C \subseteq \mathbb{R}^n$ is a* cone *if, for all $x, y \in C$ and $\lambda, \mu \geq 0$, we have $\lambda x + \mu y \in C$. A cone C is* generated *by the set of vectors X if $C = \{\lambda_1 v_1 + \ldots + \lambda_m v_m \mid \lambda_1, \ldots, \lambda_m \geq 0, \{v_1, \ldots, v_m\} \subseteq X\}$, and*

C is finitely generated *if it is generated by a finite set of vectors. A cone is* polyhedral *if it is the intersection of finitely many (linear) half-spaces.*

Definition 3 (Convex hull, polytopes, integer hull). *The* convex hull *of a vector set X is the set of all convex linear combinations of vectors from X. More precisely,*

$$conv.hull\ X = \{\lambda_1 v_1 + ... + \lambda_m v_m \mid \lambda_1, ..., \lambda_m \geq 0, \sum \lambda_i = 1, \{v_1, ..., v_m\} \subseteq X\}$$

The convex hull of a finite set of vectors is called a (convex) polytope.

Finally, if P is a polyhedron, then the integer hull *of P, denoted P_I, is the convex hull of the set of integral vectors of P. (Integral vectors are vectors whose coordinates with respect to the standard basis are integers.)*

2.2 Isabelle

For our formalization work we use the theorem prover Isabelle. Knowledge of Isabelle will be helpful, but is not necessary in order to read the paper, as we have tried to make the formal source listings accessible even to a reader with a purely mathematical background.

Nevertheless, we briefly explain the meaning of some important notation here. First, we have `carrier_vec n` $= \mathbb{R}^n$, `carrier_mat m n` $= \mathbb{R}^{m \times n}$, and denote the zero-vector of dimension n by 0_n. Often, the statement that a vector or a matrix has a certain property will be expressed as membership in the set of all vectors or matrices with that property: `Bounded_vec bnd` is the set of vectors (of finite dimension) with entries bounded in absolute value by `bnd` (similarly `Bounded_mat bnd`), `indexed_Ints_vec I` is the set of vectors v with $v_i \in \mathbb{Z}$ for all $i \in I$, and, finally, $\mathbb{Z}_v$ is the set of vectors (of finite dimension) with integer entries (similarly, $\mathbb{Z}_m$ is a set of matrices). We also have a notation for sets defined by some set of vectors or by a matrix: `finite_cone X` denotes the cone generated by the finite set X; other examples are `cone X`, `polyhedral_cone A` and `polyhedron A b`, all with the obvious meanings.

3   Mixed-Integer Linear Problems

3.1   The Main Formalized Theorems

We discuss our formalization of several results that are needed in order to formally prove the soundness of a branch-and-bound-based solver for mixed-integer linear systems of inequalities. The main theorem for this purpose states that if a mixed integer system of linear inequalities can be described using only integers, then it has a solution if and only if it also has a solution involving only numbers of bounded size.

Theorem 4. `small_mixed_integer_solution`:
   assumes $A_1 \in$ `carrier_mat` nr_1 n and $A_2 \in$ ... and ...

and $Bnd \geq 0$

and $\{A_1, A_2\} \subseteq \mathbb{Z}_m \cap Bounded\_mat\ Bnd$

and $\{b_1, b_2\} \subseteq \mathbb{Z}_v \cap Bounded\_vec\ Bnd$

and $x \in indexed\_Ints\_vec\ I$

and $A_1 x \leq b_1$ and $A_2 x < b_2$

shows $\exists x.\ x \in carrier\_vec\ n \wedge x \in indexed\_Ints\_vec\ I$

$\wedge\ A_1 x \leq b_1 \wedge A_2 x < b_2 \wedge x \in Bounded\_vec\ (fact\ (n{+}1) * Bnd\hat{}\,n)$

In order to derive this result, we require formalizations of several results from the theory of linear inequalities, beginning with the fundamental theorem of linear inequalities. This theorem states that for any finite set of vectors A and vector b, either b is in the cone generated by a subset of A, or there exists a hyperplane $\{x \mid c \cdot x = 0\}$ separating b from A and containing some number of vectors of A.

Theorem 5. fundamental_theorem_of_linear_inequalities:[2]

assumes $A \subseteq carrier\_vec\ n$ and finite A and $b \in carrier\_vec\ n$

shows $(\exists B.\ B \subseteq A \wedge b \in finite\_cone\ B \wedge lin\_indpt\ B) \longleftrightarrow$

$\neg\ (\exists c\ B.\ c \in carrier\_vec\ n \wedge B \subseteq A \wedge |B|{+}1 = dim\_span\ (A \cup \{b\}) \wedge$

$lin\_indpt\ B \wedge (\forall a \in B.\ c \cdot a = 0) \wedge (\forall a \in A.\ c \cdot a \geq 0) \wedge c \cdot b < 0)$

To prove the theorem, one first considers an algorithm that iteratively applies a procedure that takes a subset of vectors from A and produces either the cone containing b from the theorem statement, or the separating hyperplane, or a new set of vectors from A. In case of the third outcome, the output set is used as the input for the next iteration. Thus, starting from some valid set of vectors, the above algorithm either never terminates (if the third outcome occurs in every iteration), or it produces an object satisfying the theorem statement. The proof is completed by showing that an infinite execution cannot occur.

The above argument could in principle be formalized in Isabelle by defining a function that incorporates the algorithm, and then proving that the function is well-defined (which implies the termination of the algorithm on all inputs). However, we are really only interested in the algorithm's termination; the fact that some input is mapped to a certain output is irrelevant for the proof of the theorem. Furthermore, we only need that the algorithm terminates when the set of input vectors is valid (i.e., of the right cardinality and linearly independent), but, due to the limitations of the Isabelle function-package [13], the domain of a function cannot be restricted in this manner. Consequently, we formalize the proof without modeling the algorithm as an Isabelle function. Instead, we define a relation on pairs of valid subsets of A: The pair (J', J) is in the relation if and only if, starting with J as input, one iteration of the algorithm produces output J'. In other words, the relation encodes all iterations of the algorithm where the third outcome occurs. Since A is finite, termination is equivalent to the fact that the above relation has no cycles. The latter fact is established by

---

[2] The Isabelle statement given here matches the presentation of the theorem in [21]; in our formalization, the equivalence is written as an equality of sets.

a proof by contradiction (here, our formalization closely follows the textbook proof [21, Chapter 7.1]).

We also need to formalize three corollaries of Theorem 5. First, we have the theorem of Carathéodory, which follows directly.

Theorem 6. `Caratheodory_theorem:` `assumes A ⊆ carrier_vec n`
  `shows cone A = ∪ {finite_cone B | B. B ⊆ A ∧ lin_indpt B}`

Next, we have the Farkas-Minkowski-Weyl theorem, which states that a cone is polyhedral if and only if it is finitely generated.

Theorem 7. `farkas_minkowsky_weyl_theorem:`
  `(∃X. X ⊆ carrier_vec n ∧ finite X ∧ P = cone X) ⟷`
  `(∃A nr. A ∈ carrier_mat nr n ∧ P = polyhedral_cone A)`

The proofs of Theorems 7 and 5 in [21] contain some simplifying assumptions that can be made without loss of generality. Of course, in Isabelle we must provide the full details of every proof, which often entails a non-trivial amount of additional formalization work. For example, the textbook proof of the "⟶"-implication of Theorem 7 only covers the case where X spans $\mathbb{R}^n$. One way to recover this part of the theorem in full generality is to identify the span of X with $\mathbb{R}^m$ for some $m < n$, apply the "⟶"-implication for dimension m, and then extend the half-spaces (of span X) that define the polyhedral cone, into $\mathbb{R}^n$. In fact, this argument is essentially the justification for the *wlog* that is given in the book. Unfortunately, the Isabelle vector/matrix library we use does not support identifying an arbitrary proper subspace of $\mathbb{R}^n$ with a Euclidean subspace of lower dimension: Even if we prove some statement for `carrier_vec` `m`, we cannot apply it to some arbitrary m-dimensional subspace of $\mathbb{R}^n$. Instead, our formalization of the general case involves adding suitable dummy vectors to X until the set spans all of $\mathbb{R}^n$, so that we can apply the full-dimension implication for `carrier_vec n`. This is one of several situations where filling in the "obvious" steps of a proof in a way that can be formally expressed in Isabelle requires some creativity.

The third corollary is the decomposition theorem for polyhedra, stating that every polyhedron can be written as the sum of a polytope and a polyhedral cone:

Theorem 8. `decomposition_theorem_polyhedra:`
  `(∃A b nr. A ∈ carrier_mat nr n ∧`
  `b ∈ carrier_vec nr ∧ P = polyhedron A b)`
  `⟷ (∃Q X. Q ∪ X ⊆ carrier_vec n ∧ finite (Q ∪ X) ∧`
  `P = convex_hull Q + cone X)`

For both Farkas-Minkowski-Weyl (Theorem 7) and the decomposition theorem, the fact that we used a set-based matrix/vector library proved to be beneficial. To show the "⟶"-implication of Theorem 7, one defines a matrix, the dimension of which is a function of X (and can therefore not be independently fixed just by the type of X). Constructing matrices of dimensions that depend on the value of some variable is easy when using `carrier_mat`, but would be very difficult with matrix libraries which utilize Harrison's encoding of dimensions in types [12]. In the case of the decomposition theorem for polyhedra, the proof involves adding a new component to each vector from a set of n-dimensional vectors and then reasoning about the resulting set of $(n + 1)$-dimensional vectors, while maintaining the correspondence between the two sets. Here, the use of `carrier_vec` makes it possible to easily switch between dimensions and reason about objects such as "the vector formed of the first n components of some $(n + 1)$-dimensional vector".

Since the set of (real) solutions of a system of linear inequalities is a polyhedron, the decomposition theorem for polyhedra allows us to write any solution vector x as $y + z$, with y an element of a polytope (and therefore bounded), and z an element of a finitely generated cone. This suggests the following approach to proving Theorem 4 (`small_mixed_integer_solution`): If x is such that $x_i \in \mathbb{Z}$ for all $i \in I$, we may try to replace z with a vector z' of the same cone, with bounded entries, such that $(y + z')_i \in \mathbb{Z}$ for all $i \in I$ (thus, $y + z'$ would be the desired bounded solution). This approach does in fact work, but it clearly requires a more powerful version of the decomposition theorem, since the one we have shown so far says nothing about bounds or integrality. The proof of the new decomposition theorem also requires a bounded integer version of Theorem 7. This latter theorem in turn is based on a modified version of Theorem 5 which describes more precisely how separating hyperplanes can be computed so that the normal vectors are integral and with components of bounded size.

Theorem 9. `decomposition_theorem_polyhedra_1`:
  assumes $A \in$ `carrier_mat nr n`
    and $b \in$ `carrier_vec nr` and $P =$ `polyhedron A b`
  shows $\exists Q\ X.\ X \subseteq$ `carrier_vec n` $\land\ Q \subseteq$ `carrier_vec n` $\land$ `finite` $(X \cup Q)$
    $\land\ P =$ `convex_hull` $Q +$ `cone` $X\ \land$
    $(A \in \mathbb{Z}_m\ \cap$ `Bounded_mat Bnd` $\longrightarrow b \in \mathbb{Z}_v\ \cap$ `Bounded_vec Bnd` $\longrightarrow$
    $X \subseteq \mathbb{Z}_v\ \cap$ `Bounded_vec` $(...) \land Q \subseteq$ `Bounded_vec` $(...))$

The '$\longrightarrow$'-implication of this stronger version of the decomposition theorem for polyhedra states that if A and b have bounded integer entries, then the finite sets Q and X can be chosen such that they contain only bounded vectors and, furthermore, such that X contains only integral vectors. The integrality of the vectors in X is the crucial ingredient necessary for constructing the vector z' as required and completing the proof of Theorem 4.

In [21], only a weaker version of Theorem 4 is proved; it covers only the case of non-strict linear inequalities with integral solutions. Although our result trivially implies this weaker form, we have formalized the proof from the textbook as well, for the sake of completeness.

This proof relies on a decomposition theorem for the integer hull of a polyhedron, which also requires bounded integer versions of Theorem 7 and the decomposition theorem for polyhedra. Only a rough sketch is given in the book as to how the bounded integer versions of these theorems can be obtained. When formalizing this part, however, we encounter the following issue: In the course of a proof, it will be necessary to add new vectors to a set until it has a certain property, or to add half-spaces to a collection until its intersection coincides with some polyhedron. This suffices if we only wish to prove the *existence* of a set of vectors with some property, or of a specific representation of a polyhedron, but if we also need to prove bounds on the numbers needed to describe these objects, it becomes crucial *which* vectors or half-spaces are chosen, because some choices, while valid, will lead to results that do not respect the desired bounds.

For a concrete example, we return to the "⟶"-implication of Theorem 7 (Farkas-Minkowski-Weyl), this time in its bounded integer version:

Theorem 10. `farkas_minkowsky_weyl_theorem_1`:

assumes $X \subseteq$ `carrier_vec` n and finite X

shows $\exists nr\ A.\ A \in$ `carrier_mat` $nr\ n \land$ `cone` $X =$ `polyhedral_cone` $A\ \land$

$(X \subseteq \mathbb{Z}_v \cap$ `Bounded_vec` $Bnd \longrightarrow A \in \mathbb{Z}_m \cap$ `Bounded_mat` $(\ldots))$

As mentioned earlier in this section, this implication is proved for the case where the span of X is $\mathbb{R}^n$, which is then used to prove the general implication, but the switch from the special to the general case involves adding vectors to X until the set spans the entire space, and then applying the full-dimension statement to obtain the half-spaces that define the polyhedral cone. Now, the vectors that are added to X can affect the size of the entries of the resulting matrix A, and the fact that these vectors can also be chosen in such a way that the entries of A are bounded in terms of only Bnd and n, is not obvious, and in fact requires a careful construction. Whereas such matters are simply glossed over in the textbook, resolving the *wlogs* in the proof of the bounded version of Theorem 5 and of Theorem 7 resulted in Isabelle proofs of 176 lines and 110 lines, respectively.

In the end, we achieve the following formalized version of the textbook theorem [21, Thm. 17.1].

Theorem 11. `small_integer_solution_nonstrict_via_decomp`:

assumes $A \in$ `carrier_mat` $nr\ n \cap \mathbb{Z}_m \cap$ `Bounded_mat` Bnd

and $b \in$ `carrier_vec` $nr \cap \mathbb{Z}_v \cap$ `Bounded_vec` Bnd

and $x \in$ `carrier_vec` $n \cap \mathbb{Z}_v$ and $Ax \leq b$

shows $\exists y.\ y \in$ `carrier_vec` $n \cap \mathbb{Z}_v \land Ay \leq b$

$\land\ y \in$ `Bounded_vec` $(\text{fact } (n{+}1) * (\max 1\ Bnd)\hat{\ }n)$

3.2 Additional Formalized Theorems

In order to formalize the proofs of the main theorems, we collect a number of basic lemmas concerning cones, convex hulls, integer hulls, normal vectors and bases of vector spaces. On the one hand, these lemmas include very basic statements that would not normally require separate proofs, but were needed for the formalization, such as the fact that a set of vectors is a subset of the cone it generates, or that a convex combination of two vectors of a cone belongs to the cone. On the other hand, our supporting lemmas include statements that appear in standard mathematical texts, such as the fact stated in Lemma 12 that any linearly independent set of vectors can be extended to a basis of the vector space. We mention that we have proved all of these facts only for Euclidean vector spaces, making heavy use of the fact that the dimension is finite, because this case suffices for our application.

Lemma 12. `expand_to_basis`: assumes `lin_indpt_list xs`
  shows ∃ys. `set ys ⊆ set (unit_vecs n) ∧ lin_indpt_list (xs @ ys)`
  ∧ `length (xs @ ys) = n`

We note that in Lemma 12, `@` is list concatenation and `unit_vecs n` refers to the standard basis of $\mathbb{R}^n$. Of course, a linearly independent set can be extended in many other ways, but we use vectors from the standard basis because they allow us to obtain the same number bounds as for the original linearly independent set. Adding the standard basis vectors is also the reason for using `max 1 Bnd` instead of `Bnd` in many theorems that mention upper bounds. Indeed, the "`max 1`"-operation often cannot be dropped. For instance, consider the "⟵"-implication of Theorem 7 and the degenerate case where the matrix A is empty or just contains zeros. Then the entries of A are bounded by 0 and the cone is the whole space. Thus, for generating this cone one needs at least n non-zero vectors, e.g., the unit vectors. And these do not have all their entries bounded by 0, but by `max 1 0`.

A notable exception, without "`max 1`", is our main Theorem 4 (`small_mixed_integer_solution`). This result is first proved with the "`max 1`" expression in the bounds. The version without the `max`-operation is then established by proving that the theorem also holds in all degenerate cases (where the bound is 0).

Aside from the main theorems and supporting lemmas, we also formally prove two variants of Farkas' lemma. We do not need these for our work on the verified linear arithmetic solver, but obtaining them did not entail a prohibitively large additional effort, and they may be useful for other formalizations.

Although there already exists an entry for Farkas' lemma in the AFP, its proof there is based not on the fundamental theorem of linear inequalities (Theorem 5), but on a separate formalization of the simplex algorithm (one that has been formalized solely for rational numbers). Since here we use Theorem 5, we obtain a version of a lemma that allows for the use of a more general type than just the rationals. (In Isabelle, type annotation is denoted by `::`. Below, `'a` is a type variable that stands for the type of the entries of a matrix/vector; it can be any type with the suitable algebraic properties.)

Lemma 13. `Farkas_Lemma`: fixes `A :: 'a mat` and `b :: 'a vec`
  assumes `A ∈ carrier_mat n nr` and `b ∈ carrier_vec n`
  shows $(\exists x.\ x \geq 0_{nr} \wedge Ax = b) \longleftrightarrow$
    $(\forall y.\ y \in carrier\_vec\ n \wedge A^T y \geq 0_{nr} \longrightarrow yb \geq 0)$

Lemma 14. `Farkas_Lemma'`: fixes `A :: 'a mat` and `b :: 'a vec`
  assumes `A ∈ carrier_mat nr nc` and `b ∈ carrier_vec nr`

shows $(\exists x.\ x \in \mathit{carrier\_vec}\ nc \wedge Ax \le b) \longleftrightarrow$
$\quad (\forall y.\ y \ge 0_{nr} \wedge A^T y = 0_{nc} \longrightarrow yb \ge 0)$

Finally, we remark that, while the first of the two variants of Farkas' lemma follows easily from Theorem 5, the second variant (which, in [21], has a three-line proof that is based on the first variant) is somewhat more difficult to formalize. This is because its proof involves concatenating matrices and deducing inequalities involving the resulting matrix from facts about its components. Such operations require laborious low-level manipulations of vector inequalities, turning a three-line textbook proof into 102 lines of Isabelle code.

4 A Verified Branch-and-Bound Algorithm

4.1 The Branch-and-Bound Algorithm

Algorithm 1 shows the Isabelle/HOL function bnb, which is our implementation of a branch-and-bound algorithm for solving LIA problems. It takes as parameters a list of constraints cs, the list of variables Is that should get an integer assignment and (total) functions lb and ub that map the variables in Is to their lower and upper integer bounds. bnb returns either a satisfying assignment which maps variables to rational numbers and all variables in Is to integers, or $None$, if the mixed integer problem is unsatisfiable within the bounds lb and ub. bnb first uses the simplex algorithm to find a rational solution of the constraints within the bounds. If the constraints are already unsatisfiable in the rational numbers or if the solution is already integral for all values in Is, then bnb terminates accordingly. Otherwise, there exists an $x \in Is$ where $v\ x$ (the value assigned to x in the rational solution v) is not an integer. We update the bounds on x once in lb and once in ub and branch by running bnb with the new upper bound and then with the new lower bound.

To verify bnb in Isabelle/HOL we have to show that it always terminates. Note that in every recursive call, we either decrease one of the upper bounds ub or increase one of the lower bounds lb. This fact is used to show that in every

```
function bnb :: constraint list ⇒ var list ⇒ (var⇒int) ⇒ (var⇒int)
                ⇒ (var⇒rat) option where
  bnb cs Is lb ub =
    case simplex (bounds_to_constraints Is lb ub @ cs) of
      Unsat _ ⇒ None
    | Sat v ⇒ case find (λx. v x ∉ ℤ) Is of
        None ⇒ Some v
      | Some x ⇒ case bnb cs Is lb (ub(x := ⌊v x⌋)) of
          Some sol ⇒ Some sol
        | None ⇒ bnb cs Is (lb(x := ⌈v x⌉)) ub
```

Algorithm 1: A simple implementation of a branch-and-bound algorithm

recursive call, the range of possible values decreases for *some* x, and, hence, so does the search space. Thus, we use the following measure (of the size of the search space) to prove termination in Isabelle/HOL:

$$\max \left(0, \sum_{x_i \in \text{Is}} (\text{ub}(x_i) - \text{lb}(x_i)) \right)$$

We then prove two theorems about `bnb`: any detected solution is valid, and whenever `bnb` delivers `None`, no solution exists within the range that is specified by the lower- and upper-bounds. The expression $v \models_{mcs}$ (`set cs, set Is`) means that the solution v satisfies all of the constraints in `cs` and that all $x \in$ `Is` are assigned integer values by v.

lemma branch_and_bound_sat:
  assumes bnb cs Is lb ub = Some v
  shows v $\models_{mcs}$ (set cs, set Is)

lemma branch_and_bound_unsat:
  assumes bnb c Is lb ub = None
    and $\forall\ i \in$ set Is. lb i $\leq$ v i $\wedge$ v i $\leq$ ub i
  shows v $\not\models_{mcs}$ (set cs, set Is)

At this point we connect the branch-and-bound algorithm with the bounds from Sect. 3 to obtain a decision procedure for linear (mixed) integer arithmetic:

definition branch_and_bound cs Is = (let B = compute_bound cs
                in bnb cs Is (λ_. $-B$) (λ_. B))

Here, `compute_bound` is an algorithm that extracts the relevant parameters (number of variables, maximal absolute value in constraints) and then calculates the upper bound as in Sect. 3. One complication comes from the fact that there are two different representations of constraints: the statements regarding bounds have been proved for constraints given in matrix-vector form, $Ax \leq b$ or $Ax < b$ with integral matrix A and integral vector b, whereas the input to the branch-and-bound algorithm is a set of constraints, where each constraint is represented via a (sparse) linear polynomial with rational entries, e.g., $x_5 + \frac{1}{10}x_{1041} \leq \frac{7}{3}$. Hence, `compute_bound` internally also normalizes the constraints, e.g., by canceling fractions, and by renaming the variables so that the indices of variables with non-zero coefficients form a contiguous block: $x_0, \ldots, x_{n-1}$. The normalized constraints can then easily be translated into matrix-vector-form, which enables a lifting of Theorem 4 (`small_mixed_integer_solution`) to constraints that are represented via sparse polynomials.

lemma compute_bound:
  assumes v $\models_{mcs}$ (set cs, Is)
  shows $\exists$ v. v $\models_{mcs}$ (set cs, Is) $\wedge$ ($\forall\ i \in$ Is. $|v\ i| \leq$ compute_bound cs)

At this point, it is easy to combine the results of `bnb` with `compute_bound` to finally show that `branch_and_bound` is a complete and sound decision procedure.

Either it returns some assignment, which is then a solution to the mixed integer problem; or it returns *None*, and the mixed integer problem is unsatisfiable.

```
lemma branch_and_bound:
  branch_and_bound cs Is = Some v ⟹ v ⊨mcs (set cs, set Is)
  branch_and_bound cs Is = None ⟹ ∄v. v ⊨mcs (set cs, set Is)
```

4.2 Using the Incremental Version of Simplex

One problem of the branch-and-bound algorithm from the previous section is in the way it invokes the simplex algorithm: although in every iteration only a single constraint changes, the simplex algorithm is always started from scratch.

Therefore, in this section we optimize the branch-and-bound algorithm to use an already existing verified *incremental* version of the simplex algorithm [3,15], which returns a state instead of only returning a satisfying assignment or stating unsatisfiability. The state contains for instance a tableau, i.e., a list of equations which is essential for the simplex algorithm. By reusing the state, expensive operations like creating the tableau can be avoided, making the incremental simplex very attractive to be used within the branch-and-bound algorithm.

A complication arises, since the verified incremental simplex algorithm was developed to be used in a DPLL(T)-solver, where all constraints are known beforehand and the constraints are not changed throughout one DPLL(T) run. Therefore, the incremental interface does not allow for changing constraints or adding new ones. As a consequence, an integration of the incremental simplex into the branch-and-bound algorithm is not immediate, since there the bounds are changed in every iteration.

Our solution is a slight extension of the incremental simplex algorithm. To be more precise, we write a function which changes exactly one constraint in the state in a way that the relevant invariants of the incremental interface still hold. This extension allows us to reuse all the existing soundness properties and proofs of the incremental simplex algorithm without modifications. It is specifically tailored for running the branch-and-bound algorithm. We choose this approach instead of adding a feature to change arbitrary constraints in the incremental simplex interface, since such a feature would require a major rewrite.

Since the algorithmic structure and the soundness statement of the modified branch-and-bound algorithm is completely identical to the one of Sect. 4.1, we just refer to the formalization for further details.

5 Benchmarking

We tested two versions of our solver (based on incremental/non-incremental simplex) by comparing them with two well-established SMT-solvers, Z3 and CVC4. Testing was done on a subset of the non-incremental[3] QF_LIA (quantifier-free

---

[3] Here, "non-incremental" means that the tests are simply sets of constraints, as opposed to constraints together with an assert/check script that a solver must execute.

linear integer arithmetic)[4] benchmark set from SMT-LIB. For this experiment we had two goals in mind: 1. to see whether it is worthwhile to use the non-incremental version of simplex as a sub-routine in the branch-and-bound algorithm, and 2. to get an idea about the extent to which our verified, non-optimized solver can handle practical examples.

We did not go through the effort of making our solver compliant with the language of SMT-LIB, as we felt that for the above two goals, it would suffice to write a simple converter that could handle a reasonable portion of the QF_LIA benchmarks. Thus, we obtained a dataset of 1192 benchmarks, comprising 18% of the 6489 benchmarks in QF_LIA. (More specifically, the following sub-folders were fully converted to a format that is readable by our solver: 20180326-Bromberger, miplib2003, pb2010, pidgeons, prime-cone, and slacks.) All solvers were tested on this dataset, on the same hardware, with a 60s-timeout per benchmark. Z3 version 4.4.0pre-2, CVC4 version 1.5-4, and the 2019-05-09 release of SMT-LIB were used.

The only other verified LIA solver that we are aware of is an Isabelle formalization of Cooper's algorithm in the AFP. This algorithm solves a more general problem than linear integer arithmetic (namely linear arithmetic with arbitrary quantifiers over integer variables). We obtained an implementation with minimal changes to make code generation possible (just as we produced executables for our own solver).

Table 1. Experimental results

	Sat	Unsat	Total
Non-incremental bnb	245	131	376
Incremental bnb	314	131	445
CVC4	470	158	628
Z3	570	164	734
Verified Cooper	2	0	2

Evaluation. Our branch-and-bound implementation solves 37% of the dataset with incremental simplex as a sub-routine, and 31% with non-incremental simplex (Table 1). Since we have only implemented a naive branch-and-bound algorithm, without any additional heuristics for pruning the search space, it is unsurprising that its performance cannot match that of more mature solvers. Somewhat surprising is the fact that some benchmarks are solved by our solvers but not by Z3 or CVC4: of the benchmarks solved by incremental bnb, 28 are not solved by Z3, 29 are not solved by CVC4, and 8 are solved by neither Z3 nor CVC4.

---

[4] QF_LIRA (quantifier-free mixed integer real arithmetic) contains only 8 tests.

Interestingly, the non-incremental simplex-based solver can handle a few instances that the incremental simplex-based solver does not. Although using an incremental simplex leads to better overall results, it appears that reusing valuations from previous simplex runs can sometimes lead the search astray in such a way that simple solutions are missed. The phenomenon of a search proceeding in the wrong direction and missing a simple solution may also be the reason why some instances cannot be handled by either Z3 or CVC4, despite being solved by our solver.

Cooper's algorithm is known to have a very high asymptotic complexity, which means that its performance is not a matter of optimizing an implementation. As such, the outcome of our experiments with regards to Cooper's algorithm is as expected, showing that this algorithm is not usable on medium-sized examples in practice.

6   Conclusion and Future Work

We have developed a verified solver for linear mixed integer arithmetic, and have formalized important results on linear integer programming that were needed in order to prove the soundness of the solver. To the extent of our knowledge, the main mathematical theorems of which we formalized proofs had not been previously verified in any formal system, and our solver is the first verified LIA solver that is also usable in practice. The two parts of our formalization amount to 9813 lines of Isabelle code and took roughly 10 person-months to implement.

Currently, our solver is essentially "proof of concept" software, and there are a number of known optimizations that could improve it, e.g., preprocessing of constraints, integration of cutting planes, unit-cube-tests, etc. [6,7,14]. We have also used run-time profiling in order to establish which sub-routines our solver spends most time on, and have identified parts of the incremental simplex algorithm that we could further modify in order to improve running times.

References

1. Allamigeon, X., Katz, R.D.: A formalization of convex polyhedra based on the simplex method. In: Ayala-Rincón, M., Muñoz, C.A. (eds.) ITP 2017. LNCS, vol. 10499, pp. 28–45. Springer, Cham (2017). https://doi.org/10.1007/978-3-319-66107-0_3
2. Barrett, C., et al.: CVC4. In: Gopalakrishnan, G., Qadeer, S. (eds.) CAV 2011. LNCS, vol. 6806, pp. 171–177. Springer, Heidelberg (2011). https://doi.org/10.1007/978-3-642-22110-1_14
3. Bottesch, R., Haslbeck, M.W., Thiemann, R.: Verifying an incremental theory solver for linear arithmetic in Isabelle/HOL. In: Herzig, A., Popescu, A. (eds.) FroCoS 2019. LNCS (LNAI), vol. 11715, pp. 223–239. Springer, Cham (2019). https://doi.org/10.1007/978-3-030-29007-8_13
4. Bottesch, R., Reynaud, A., Thiemann, R.: Linear inequalities. Archive of Formal Proofs, June 2019. http://isa-afp.org/entries/Linear_Inequalities.html. Formal proof development

5. Brockschmidt, M., Joosten, S.J.C., Thiemann, R., Yamada, A.: Certifying safety and termination proofs for integer transition systems. In: de Moura, L. (ed.) CADE 2017. LNCS (LNAI), vol. 10395, pp. 454–471. Springer, Cham (2017). https://doi.org/10.1007/978-3-319-63046-5_28

6. Bromberger, M.: A reduction from unbounded linear mixed arithmetic problems into bounded problems. In: Galmiche, D., Schulz, S., Sebastiani, R. (eds.) IJCAR 2018. LNCS (LNAI), vol. 10900, pp. 329–345. Springer, Cham (2018). https://doi.org/10.1007/978-3-319-94205-6_22

7. Bromberger, M., Weidenbach, C.: New techniques for linear arithmetic: cubes and equalities. Form. Methods Syst. Des. 51(3), 433–461 (2017). https://doi.org/10.1007/s10703-017-0278-7

8. Carlier, M., Dubois, C., Gotlieb, A.: A certified constraint solver over finite domains. In: Giannakopoulou, D., Méry, D. (eds.) FM 2012. LNCS, vol. 7436, pp. 116–131. Springer, Heidelberg (2012). https://doi.org/10.1007/978-3-642-32759-9_12

9. Dantzig, G.B.: Linear Programming and Extensions. Princeton University Press, Princeton (1963)

10. Dutertre, B., de Moura, L.: A fast linear-arithmetic solver for DPLL(T). In: Ball, T., Jones, R.B. (eds.) CAV 2006. LNCS, vol. 4144, pp. 81–94. Springer, Heidelberg (2006). https://doi.org/10.1007/11817963_11

11. Haftmann, F., Nipkow, T.: Code generation via higher-order rewrite systems. In: Blume, M., Kobayashi, N., Vidal, G. (eds.) FLOPS 2010. LNCS, vol. 6009, pp. 103–117. Springer, Heidelberg (2010). https://doi.org/10.1007/978-3-642-12251-4_9

12. Harrison, J.: The HOL light theory of Euclidean space. J. Autom. Reasoning 50, 173–190 (2013). https://doi.org/10.1007/s10817-012-9250-9

13. Krauss, A.: Partial and nested recursive function definitions in higher-order logic. J. Autom. Reasoning 44(4), 303–336 (2010). https://doi.org/10.1007/s10817-009-9157-2

14. Marchand, H., Martin, A., Weismantel, R., Wolsey, L.A.: Cutting planes in integer and mixed integer programming. Discrete Appl. Math. 123(1–3), 397–446 (2002). https://doi.org/10.1016/S0166-218X(01)00348-1

15. Marić, F., Spasić, M., Thiemann, R.: An incremental simplex algorithm with unsatisfiable core generation. Archive of Formal Proofs, August 2018. http://isa-afp.org/entries/Simplex.html. Formal proof development

16. de Moura, L., Bjørner, N.: Z3: an efficient SMT solver. In: Ramakrishnan, C.R., Rehof, J. (eds.) TACAS 2008. LNCS, vol. 4963, pp. 337–340. Springer, Heidelberg (2008). https://doi.org/10.1007/978-3-540-78800-3_24

17. Narkawicz, A., Muñoz, C.: A formally verified generic branching algorithm for global optimization. In: Cohen, E., Rybalchenko, A. (eds.) VSTTE 2013. LNCS, vol. 8164, pp. 326–343. Springer, Heidelberg (2014). https://doi.org/10.1007/978-3-642-54108-7_17

18. Nipkow, T.: Linear quantifier elimination. J. Autom. Reasoning 45(2), 189–212 (2010). https://doi.org/10.1007/s10817-010-9183-0

19. Nipkow, T., Wenzel, M., Paulson, L.C. (eds.): Isabelle/HOL – A Proof Assistant for Higher-Order Logic. LNCS, vol. 2283. Springer, Heidelberg (2002). https://doi.org/10.1007/3-540-45949-9

20. Papadimitriou, C.H.: On the complexity of integer programming. J. ACM 28(4), 765–768 (1981). https://doi.org/10.1145/322276.322287

21. Schrijver, A.: Theory of Linear and Integer Programming. Wiley, Hoboken (1999)

22. Smith, A., Muñoz, C., Narkawicz, A., Markevicius, M.: A rigorous generic branch and bound solver for nonlinear problems. In: 2015 17th International Symposium on Symbolic and Numeric Algorithms for Scientific Computing (SYNASC), pp. 71–78. IEEE (2015). https://doi.org/10.1109/SYNASC.2015.20

23. Spasić, M., Marić, F.: Formalization of incremental simplex algorithm by stepwise refinement. In: Giannakopoulou, D., Méry, D. (eds.) FM 2012. LNCS, vol. 7436, pp. 434–449. Springer, Heidelberg (2012). https://doi.org/10.1007/978-3-642-32759-9_35

24. Thiemann, R., Sternagel, C.: Certification of termination proofs using CeTA. In: Berghofer, S., Nipkow, T., Urban, C., Wenzel, M. (eds.) TPHOLs 2009. LNCS, vol. 5674, pp. 452–468. Springer, Heidelberg (2009). https://doi.org/10.1007/978-3-642-03359-9_31

Constraint Caching Revisited

Jan Taljaard, Jaco Geldenhuys$^{(\boxtimes)}$, and Willem Visser

Stellenbosch University, Stellenbosch, South Africa
johannes.h.taljaard@gmail.com, {geld,visserw}@sun.ac.za

Abstract. Satisfiability Modulo Theories (SMT) solvers play a major role in the success of symbolic execution as program analysis technique. However, often they are still the main performance bottleneck. One approach to improve SMT performance is to use caching. The key question we consider here is whether caching strategies are still worthwhile given the performance improvements in SMT solvers. Two main caching strategies exist: either simple *sat/unsat* results are stored, or entire solutions (=models) are stored for later reuse. We implement both approaches in the Green framework and compare them with the popular Z3 constraint solver. We focus on linear integer arithmetic constraints; this is typical for symbolic execution, and both caching strategies and constraint solvers work well in this domain. We use both classic symbolic and concolic execution to see whether caching behaves differently in these settings. We consider only time consumption; memory use is typically negligible. Our results suggest that (1) the key to caching performance is factoring constraints into independent parts, and this by itself is often sufficient, (2) Z3's incremental mode often outperforms caching; and (3) reusing models fares better for concolic than for classic symbolic execution.

Keywords: SMT · Caching · Symbolic execution · Concolic execution

1 Introduction

Many program verification techniques produce propositional logic formulas with linear integer arithmetic. Questions like whether a given formula is satisfiable, what variable assignments (=*models*) satisfy it, and how many such models exist [14], are typically generated. Many symbolic and concolic program analysis techniques use Satisfiability Modulo Theories (SMT) solvers to verify properties of programs. In recent years, the performance of SMT solvers have improved dramatically, but more advances are needed to handle ever-increasing targets. Although SMT solvers are powerful, large inputs still require long running times.

One way of tackling scalability is *caching*. SMT solvers can provide solutions more quickly if they store their results. The logic behind caching is simple: expensive solver invocations can potentially be avoided, as long as the overhead of storing and retrieving results is low enough. To overcome the performance issue of SMT solvers, different caching strategies have been developed. One of the first

© Springer Nature Switzerland AG 2020
R. Lee et al. (Eds.): NFM 2020, LNCS 12229, pp. 251–266, 2020.
https://doi.org/10.1007/978-3-030-55754-6_15

general libraries for such caching is the Green framework [16]. It allows extensive customisation, but basically it factorizes formulas into independent parts, performs a canonisation step (e.g., renaming and reordering of variables) and looks up results in a store. Recently an alternative approach [4,5] was proposed: rather than storing *sat/unsat* results, it caches satisfying models and unsatisfiable cores. Stored results are reused to compute the result of new queries.

This paper evaluates various approaches for caching in the context of symbolic and concolic execution. Reuse rates are high for many of the caching strategies, but how fast are the strategies really? High reuse is of no use if the strategies perform poorly. Our results shed new light on the true benefits and weaknesses of the two respective approaches for caching (reusing models versus reusing satisfiability results). This work makes the following contributions:

- A model-core reuse strategy implementation within the Green framework.
- An investigation of the performance of caching versus a simpler approach: factorising constraints without any caching whatsoever.
- A comparison between caching during symbolic and concolic execution.

The rest of this paper provides background on the main technologies and frameworks (Sect. 2), presents and interprets experimental results (Sect. 3), describes related work (Sect. 4), and concludes with observations (Sect. 5).

2   Background

King [12] was one of the first to propose the use of symbolic execution for test generation. The basic approach executes a program with symbolic rather than concrete inputs. Path conditions that describe the constraints on the inputs are collected from branching conditions during execution. Whenever a constraint is added to the path condition, the result is checked for feasibility. If not feasible, the path is terminated and not analysed further. The feasibility check is performed by external constraint solvers.

One can think of the analysis performed during symbolic execution as a search for feasible execution paths in a tree where edges represent path conditions. At any point during this search the current path condition must be feasible, and a solution to the path condition will represent inputs that when used during execution will reach this location in the code. For example, if an assertion violated is reached during analysis, any solution to the current path condition constitute concrete inputs that produces an execution that leads to the violation.

2.1   Concolic Execution

Concolic is a portmanteau of *concrete* and symb*olic*. Concolic execution is broadly similar to symbolic execution: the program is executed with concrete inputs, but the analysis keeps track of the corresponding symbolic constraints along the concrete path that is executed. When the end of a path is reached, the path condition for this executed path is then manipulated and passed to an SMT to generate new concrete inputs to explore a different path. This manipulation is typically to negate the last constraint obtained to mimic a depth-first traversal of the symbolic execution tree of the program. Unlike the classic symbolic execution approach (above), concolic execution does not make a solver call for each encountered edge of the execution tree, but rather calls the solver only once at the end of a path. Concolic execution typically starts with a single run of the program with user-specified values of the variables.

2.2 Green

Green [2,16] is an open source project that provides a framework for users to construct "pipelines" for a variety of constraint solving queries, such as constraint simplification, satisfiability queries, finding satisfying models, and counting the number of satisfying models. Each pipeline comprises a series of "services" that processes a query sequentially. In addition to a standard set of services, the framework allows users to easily add services of their own. The Green architecture also supports the automatic concurrent execution of services and pipelines.

An important feature of Green is a store where the results of services are recorded. By caching these results, it is possible to avoid expensive operations and to thus improve the performance of query resolution. The store itself can be configured in different ways: it can use combinations of in-memory and on-disk databases, provide various levels of persistence, and various levels of sharing among users. Results can be reused within a single run, across separate runs and users and different type of applications (analyses).

A common pipeline targets linear integer arithmetic (LIA) constraints in conjunctive normal form (CNF). This is shown on the left of Fig. 3:

Factorise: Breaks the input into independent sub-constraints. Two constraints are independent if none of the variables in one constraint affects the solution of the other. For CNF inputs, all factors must be satisfiable for the whole to be satisfiable. Example: $(a > 5) \wedge (b < 7)$ is factorised as $a > 5$ and $b < 7$.

Canonise: Converts the input to semi-canonical form [16]. This includes renaming variables, rearranging inequalities, sorting clauses in lexicographic order, and applying basic simplification rules. Example: $(a > 5) \wedge (a = b)$ becomes $(-v_0 + 6 \leq 0) \wedge (v_0 - v_1 = 0)$.

Reuse: Checks if the now-canonised input constraint is already cached. If so, the stored result is returned immediately.

Z3Translator: Converts the constraint from Green's data structure to Z3's format and passes the query to the external solver. The result is stored and then returned to the client.

Green uses Microsoft's Z3 [9], released in 2007, and still regularly updated and improved. Its settings include an incremental solving mode where constraints are constructed clause by clause. This mirrors how symbolic execution works, and many consider incremental solving to be most efficient for symbolic execution.

2.3   Grulia

A novel approach to SMT caching was proposed by Aquino et al. [4,5]. Figure 1 shows the intuition behind the approach. The grey area represents all possible variable assignments, or models. Constraints ϕ_1, ϕ_2, and ϕ_3 are each satisfied by a subset of models, and ϕ_1 and ϕ_2 happen to share some models. Instead of invoking a potentially expensive SMT solver, a constraint can be shown to be satisfiable if a satisfying model can be found quickly. To check if ϕ_2 is satisfiable, it suffices to check if models of "nearby" constraints happen to also satisfy ϕ_2.

The pivotal trick is how distances between constraints are computed. A constraint is given a score known as its *sat-delta* value, by triangulating with respect to reference models; in Fig. 1 the reference models are $M = \{M_1, M_2, M_3\}$. (The number and identities of the reference models are customizable but remain fixed across a run.) The details of scoring is explained below, but in essence it captures aspects of the "behaviour" of constraints so that similar constraints that are likely to share models are given similar scores. If the satisfiability of a constraint cannot be resolved, it is passed to an external SMT solver, which generates a model if possible, which is then stored for future use.

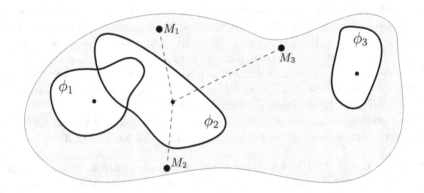

Fig. 1. Intuition behind the idea of *sat-delta* calculation

SAT-Delta. It is important that *sat-delta* score calculation is fast and that it reflects the notion of proximity between constraints. Fortunately, both criteria are satisfied by the proposed approached. The *sat-delta* score of constraint ϕ is computed as the average of its scores with respect to each reference model:

$$\texttt{sat-delta}(\phi) = \frac{1}{|M|} \sum_i \texttt{sat-delta}'(\phi, M_i)$$

Assuming that the constraint is in CNF, this second function is the sum of the scores for each clause with respect to the reference model:

$$\texttt{sat-delta}'(\phi = \psi_1 \wedge \psi_2 \wedge \ldots, M) = \sum_i \texttt{sat-delta}''(\psi_i, M)$$

Lastly, given a clause $\psi = a \sim b$, its score is calculated as

$$\texttt{sat-delta}''(a \sim b, M) = \begin{cases} 0 & \text{if } a_M \sim b_M \\ |a_M - b_M| & \text{if } \sim \in \{\leq, =, \geq\} \\ |a_M - b_M| + 1 & \text{if } \sim \in \{<, \neq, >\} \end{cases}$$

where x_M is expression x evaluated with the variable assignments of model M.

Example: Suppose that $M_1 \colon (x = 0, y = 0)$ and $M_2 \colon (x = 1, y = 1)$ and that $\phi = (x > 5) \wedge (x = y - 1) \wedge (y \leq 7)$. Then (sat-delta abbreviated as sd):

$$\textsf{sd}''(x > 5, M_1) = |0 - 5| + 1 = 6 \qquad \textsf{sd}''(x > 5, M_2) = |1 - 5| + 1 = 5$$
$$\textsf{sd}''(x = y - 1, M_1) = |0 + 1| + 1 = 2 \qquad \textsf{sd}''(x = y - 1, M_2) = |1 - 0| + 1 = 2$$
$$\textsf{sd}''(y \leq 7, M_1) = 0 \qquad \textsf{sd}''(y \leq 7, M_2) = 0$$

$$\textsf{sd}'(\phi, M_1) = 6 + 2 + 0 = 8 \qquad \textsf{sd}'(\phi, M_2) = 5 + 2 + 0 = 7$$

$$\textsf{sd}(\phi) = (8 + 7)/2 = 7.5$$

Note that $\texttt{sat-delta}''(\psi, M)$ is either positive or zero (if M satisfies ψ), and $\texttt{sat-delta}'(\phi, M)$ is exactly zero if and only if reference model M satisfies the entire constraint ϕ. GRULIA detects this and returns the result immediately.

Otherwise, the *sat-delta* score is used as the key in the model cache. The reference models must therefore be chosen carefully to avoid too many constraints from mapping to the same *sat-delta* score, but to also guarantee that similar constraints are mapped to similar scores. In the experiments we use the reference models $M_1 \colon (v_i = -10000)$, $M_2 \colon (v_i = 0)$, and $M_3 \colon (v_i = 100)$. All three models assign a constant value to all the variables in an expression.

In this paper, the *sat-delta* calculation is used only for LIA constraints, but the concept are easy to extend to other theories.

UNSAT-Cores. What about unsatisfiable constraints that do not have models? In this case, a infeasible subset of clauses (known as an unsatisfiable core or just "unsat-core") is computed and cached, just as above. The idea of computing unsat-cores has been investigated under various formulations; it was long considered too expensive to be practical, but recent advances has changed this [6,8,10,13]. For example, the unsat-cores of $(x < y) \wedge (x = y) \wedge (x > y)$ include

$$(x < y) \wedge (x = y), \quad (x > y) \wedge (x = y), \quad \text{and} \quad (x > y) \wedge (x < y).$$

Small subconstraints are preferable because they are faster to match against new constraints and more likely to match a greater number of constraints. Within the basic Green pipeline, the constraint is stored as the key and the value as false, will produce only a store hit if a constraint with the exact same syntax is queried. The unsat-core can be obtained from a solver such as Z3.

Implementation. The explanation of GRULIA's strategy is done with the assistance of Fig. 2.

sat-delta: The approach starts by calculating the *sat-delta* value sd of the input constraint with respect to a fixed set of reference models M (lines 6–10). The value gives the average distance from satisfiability of the input constraint from the models in M. If the calculated *sat-delta* for a constraint is 0, the function can return that the constraint is satisfiable (a reference model satisfies the constraint).

SATstore.extract: Next, a fixed number of K models are retrieved from the sat store (line 12). The value of K, just as M, is predetermined by the user, and stays constant throughout the computation. The models are selected for their proximity to sd.

satisfies: If any of the models satisfy the constraint, the function returns true immediately (lines 13–14).

UNSATstore.extract: The same procedure is followed for the unsat-cores from the unsat store (line 16).

sharesUnsatCore: If constraint contains any unsat-core, false is returned immediately (lines 17–18).

SMTsolver: Once the algorithm reaches line 21, the answer has not been found in the stores. An SMT solver is invoked to compute the result, and the answer is stored and returned (lines 21–23).

Figure 3 represents in summary the two different caching tools that perform pre-processing of constraints and provides a speed up to present solutions for the analysis. For Green the pre-processing is factorisation and canonisation of the constraints. Whereas GRULIA executes factorisation and a simple renaming of the variables in the constraints. For simplicity the second factor (ψ) is ignored in Fig. 3. Green's caching layer checks for exact matches, whereupon sat/unsat solutions are stored. The solutions are stored in a key-value store, with the constraint as key and solution as value. GRULIA's caching layer conducts an approximate matching with *sat-delta*, where it gets the K closest matches to the target's *sat-delta*.

Then those matches are picked one at a time, and tested to see if a model satisfies the constraints (in the sat case) or implicitly proves that the constraint is unsat with an unsat-core (in the unsat case). GRULIA's solving layer produces a model or unsat-core for the target constraint. The solutions are stored in two separate stores, with an entry having the *sat-delta* value as identifier and another parameter referencing the solution. In Green's solving layer, the sat/unsat is computed. Z3 is an SMT solver, used in the solver layer by most solution caching frameworks, to compute solutions for constraints.

The GRULIA pipeline is similar to that of Green, except that the Canoniser component is replaced by a Renamer, and the basic reuse component is replaced with the model-core reuse strategy (which the GRULIA service implements). Having GRULIA as a service in Green, makes it helpful and more suitable to compare the classic Green pipeline for satisfiability, with one that shares some of the exact same components but also includes the GRULIA approach. For the Green

```
1    // M = a set of reference models
2    // K = bound on number of models/cores to extract
3
4    boolean solve(constraint):
5        total = 0
6        for m in M:
7            sdc = sat-delta(constraint, m)
8            if sdc == 0: return sat
9            else: total += sdc
10       sd = total / |M|
11
12       models = SATstore.extract(sd, K)
13       for m in models:
14           if satisfies(constraint, m): return true
15
16       cores = UNSATstore.extract(sd, K)
17       for c in cores:
18           if sharesUnsatCore(constraint, c): return false
19
20       sat = SMTsolver(constraint)
21       if sat: SATstore.store(sd, constraint.getModel())
22       else: UNSATstore.store(sd, constraint.getCore())
23       return sat
```

Fig. 2. Summary of the GRULIA strategy.

pipeline the Factoriser is first followed by the Canoniser and then the solver (Z3). GRULIA's pipeline consists of the Factoriser, Renamer then the GRULIA service and lastly Z3. The Renamer service is a stripped down version of the Canoniser service, with only the renaming feature. It is a light-weight service to accomplish the renaming of variables in lexicographic order for constraints. The renaming functionality is still needed for the model assignments (value substitution) for the GRULIA service. Note that the Renamer and the *sat-delta* calculations in GRULIA serve as an approximation for the canonisation step in Green, and one of the important aspects of an evaluation of GRULIA is to see how well this works.

3   Evaluation

Taljaard showed that reuse rates are generally high for the Green and GRU-LIA strategies [15]. Reuse rate refer to the fraction of cases where a result is found in the cache. The questions addressed in this section is whether the overhead of caching is greater than the cost of resolving constraints for repeated queries. Consequently, all experiments focus on running time, not reuse rates. Each experiment is repeated ten times and outliers (minimum and maximum running times) are discarded before the average is computed. Sects. 3.2 and 3.3 discuss the results for symbolic and concolic execution, respectively.

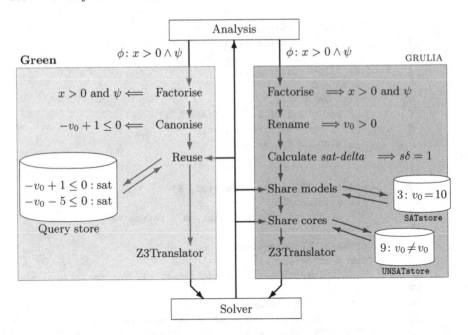

Fig. 3. Green vs. GRULIA caching

3.1 Experimental Setting

Experiments run inside a Docker container based on Ubuntu 18.04 LTS with 16 Gb memory. The containers run on a server with 4 Intel Xeon(R) E5-2640v2 2.00 GHz CPUs, each with 8 cores and 16 threads.

The following configurations are used to run the programs in the experiments:

	Z3Inc	Z3	Green	GRULIA	Z3Fact	Z3Cached	Z3Model
Factoriser			✓	✓	✓		
Canoniser			✓				
Renamer				✓			
Store			✓	✓		✓	
Incremental	✓						
SAT queries	✓	✓	✓			✓	✓
Model queries				✓			✓

Both SPF and COASTAL use the Java library distributed with Z3 to pass queries and answers to and from the solver. The environment is set up with Java 8, Z3 4.8.4, Jedis 2.9.0, and Redis 5.3.0.

3.2   Symbolic Execution Experiments

Caching for symbolic execution is evaluated with SPF and the following configurations: Z3Inc, Z3, Green, GRULIA, Z3Fact, anf Z3Cached. The 23 programs are taken from the SPF distribution (marked with a *) and from GitHub. Together, these programs generate ~3.9 million constraints.

Table 1 shows the results of the experimental runs. Column "#c" gives the number of constraints for the program and column "#f/#c" reflects the effect of factorization as the ratio of factors to constraints. The higher this ratio, the greater the number of independent subconstraints. The rest of the columns show running times. Those in column "Z3Inc" are measured in milliseconds; the other times are given as ratios to the Z3Inc time. In other words, ratios below (above) 1.0 indicate that the configuration was faster (slower) than Z3Inc.

One of the core advantages of caching comes when results can be reused from one analysis to the next. In order to evaluate this we focused on the absolute best case, where an identical second run is executed. This might seem overly optimistic, but it gives us a baseline, since if caching doesn't help in this setting then it is truly a waste of time. Note also that this setting is more realistic than it might sound, since symbolic execution are nowadays run in continuous integration settings where little or no changes are made to the constraints being solved. We therefore enable a secondary persistent store and show the times in the Run 2 columns.

Table 1 shows the number of input constraints per example under the column #cstrs and the effect of the factorizing step in the #factors/#cstrs column. For the latter, the higher the ratio the more independent sub-constraints were found by the factorizer. The rest of the columns shows the ratio of time of that tool taken over Z3Inc on its own (Z3 with incremental mode). The last two columns are a sanity check, with Z3Cache and its persistent storage and second run. Z3Cache doesn't do any processing of the constraints and just passes it to Z3, so it can only show a benefit in the second run. Note that the best timings (i.e. lower ratios) of Green, GRULIA, Z3Fact and Z3Cache are highlighted in a darker shade. Table 1 is sorted into three categories:

Intra-run: First eight examples where first run of one of the tools beats Z3Inc.
Across-runs: Next nine examples where only the second run beats Z3Inc.
Misc: Last six examples where none of the tools beat Z3Inc.

Each category is sorted from most to least number of constraints obtained from the analysis. Keep in mind that the rest of the table show normalised values, even though a large number of constraints are evaluated and the running time is quite long, the normalised value can be small, for example in the case of *Jadx*.

The **Intra-run** grouping focuses on the first runs from the caching tools that were the fastest. The second run being faster in this grouping should be a given although a few outliers are present which will be discussed later. Z3Fact is the fastest in all examples of this run, except for *FlapController* which achieved similar reuse to Z3Cache yet is slower due to the overhead of the factoriser. Note the interesting scenario where *Jadx* gives many constraints for evaluation

Table 1. Normalized SPF running times (Z3Inc in msec, rest of columns as ratios to Z3Inc)

Program	#c	#f/#c	Z3Inc	Z3	Green		GRULIA		Z3Fact		Z3Cached	
NanoXML	871580	5.9	185186	4.920	0.893	0.898	1.251	1.236	0.422	0.416	—	
Jadx	658475	3.0	496531	1.519	0.413	0.412	0.490	0.487	0.229	0.224	—	
Strings	557838	14.4	117000	4.262	0.548	0.547	0.567	0.573	0.275	0.266	6.866	0.564
*SortedListInt	340114	3.9	76804	3.883	0.588	0.518	7.458	10.605	0.312	0.251	6.190	0.473
ObjectRec	282088	10.5	31247	5.359	1.080	1.078	0.992	1.011	0.617	0.601	9.493	1.417
*Stack	131070	11.3	30718	3.234	0.444	0.452	0.414	0.403	0.231	0.222	5.349	0.483
*WBS	27646	8.2	6231	2.971	0.547	0.544	0.528	0.503	0.324	0.316	5.049	0.608
*FlapController	14860	2.0	3722	1.593	0.271	0.266	0.307	0.259	0.173	0.162	0.110	0.114
*TreeMap	151944	6.9	42804	3.328	1.253	0.582	11.367	11.988	1.021	0.338	5.171	0.413
Median	103950	1.0	19968	3.788	6.723	1.161	30.242	31.066	5.820	0.784	5.609	0.595
BubbleSort	103950	1.0	20049	3.702	6.596	1.147	30.274	30.024	5.880	0.767	5.606	0.592
Sorting	80638	1.0	20867	3.288	6.483	1.005	21.877	21.552	4.945	0.597	4.785	0.445
BinomialHeap	47460	7.7	7864	4.043	1.721	1.001	8.813	8.688	3.530	0.934	7.161	0.804
*BinTree	15226	5.9	3250	3.290	1.634	0.932	14.884	15.643	2.496	0.820	4.859	0.741
Dijkstra	12512	1.0	3820	3.173	5.231	1.293	8.695	4.994	4.485	0.854	4.422	0.605
MagicIndex	7200	9.9	2157	3.378	2.235	1.235	2.975	0.610	1.736	0.834	4.012	0.688
TCAS	4390	9.6	796	4.505	1.494	1.456	4.165	2.795	1.030	0.954	6.574	1.366
CLI	364492	4.9	47967	6.668	2.440	2.441	3.509	3.403	1.568	1.461	—	
CoinChange	160302	3.8	8632	7.787	2.536	2.403	9.469	7.424	3.057	1.839	18.788	2.591
Operations	15618	2.0	3689	10.605	6.822	6.150	12.154	9.857	6.074	5.166	16.421	2.150
Triangle	2206	1.0	434	4.627	1.776	1.475	6.657	8.145	1.399	1.184	4.604	1.530
Flink	1020	7.1	779	16.116	7.356	7.433	8.552	7.651	5.633	4.755	—	
Remainder	956	1.0	718	6.019	55.901	52.567	67.848	58.479	58.242	51.156	10.794	3.708

whereupon Green and GRULIA is faster than Z3Inc, but a smaller example like *BubbleSort* they are significantly slower than Z3Inc. This is due to the fact that the factoriser had no effect in this case, or any case where the ratio in the second column is 1.0. **Whenever the factoriser has no effect then Z3Inc is always fastest.** Further inspection for *Jadx* shows that 26% of the GRULIA service running time is spent waiting for the solver solutions, 20% (30 s) is the *sat-delta* computation, 35% is checking shared models and 12% of the time is checking for shared unsat-cores. The breakdown is noted because in other examples the other components take negligible time and most of the running time is spent waiting for the solver solutions. Another outlier is *SortedListInt* where GRULIA is much slower than Green in the first run, since the store is populated with many solutions (with *sat-delta* values in close proximity) but reusable solutions are not found. Note also that the second run here is much slower than the first, this is due to the overhead of reloading the store for the second run in GRULIA. With *Jadx* and *ObjectRec* Green performs quite close to the second run, which is ascribed to the few solver calls that are made in the first run and the rest of the running time is spent on the store especially the communication with the persistent store in the second run. Recall that Green follows the greedy approach with the persistent store, meaning in the worst-case a call is made to Redis for each constraint to obtain the solution. This grouping shows that reuse helps in 8 of 23 examples. Note that **there are very few cases where grulia is faster than Green** in any of the examples.

In the **Across-runs** grouping encapsulate programs that produce constraints that are structurally similar, resolving to high reuse and fast analysis upon a second run. Furthermore cases like *Dijkstra* and *BubbleSort* obtained no or little reuse, yet the analysis ran faster with Green compared to GRULIA. The outliers of GRULIA and large ratios such as *TreeMap* and *BubbleSort* will be discussed later, because it is a greater overarching phenomenon. The grouping shows that reuse across runs helps in 17 of 23 examples.

In the **Misc** grouping Z3Fact is still the fastest in the second run among the caching tools, although significantly slower than Z3Inc. *CLI* is an example where GRULIA spends 50% of the service running time waiting for solver solutions, and the other significant time consuming components are checking for shared models and unsat-cores. With *CoinChange* both Z3Fact and Z3Cache runs slower than Green in the first run but have a close running time in the second run. Green runs faster than Z3Fact and Z3Cache in the first run of *CoinChange*, which makes sense since it got better unsat reuse on an example that has majority unsat constraints. *Remainder* is an example where pre-processing of constraints are a hindrance and it can be better simply ignoring it and rather use a store only. The group portrays, with 6 of 23, examples that sometimes caching and reuse do not help and can simply run the solver alone.

Overarching Observations: Z3Cache shows that pre-processing might be unnecessary if one works with constraint reuse across runs. Z3Cache is always slower than the other tools in the first run over all examples except for *Remain-*

der. In the first two groupings Z3Cache comes close to Z3Fact in the second run, and in the last grouping it is faster than Green in the second run. Z3 is in most cases slower than Z3Inc, except for small examples, yet in some cases basic Z3 is still faster than some of the tools in a few cases for example *BubbleSort*, *CoinChange* and *Remainder*. Again the column with average number of factors server as a predictor, hinting that with an average greater than 3.0 Z3Fact will perform well. An example constraint, from the one data sample, that explains how the phenomenon of sharing models performs better than identical factors, works as follows. Consider the following where the first constraint encountered is $\phi_1 : [v_0 \leq 349]$, followed later by $\phi_2 : [v_0 \leq 348]$. Green will consider both these as different and will not be able to get any reuse, whereas the other tools will reuse a solution, for example $v_0 = 0$. This phenomenon indicates cases, such as sorting where numerous comparisons (in the form of $v \leq k$, where v is a variable and k is a constant) are performed, where the model caching strategy can be better suited for the analysis of a program. The effect is that for example the model $v = 0$ continues to satisfy the constraints as k increases, whereas Green will not find any matches. Conversely Green will excel in constraints of the form $v = k$, since it does less computation compared to the model caching strategy.

3.3   Concolic Execution Experiments

For these experiments a subset of 13 of the examples from the previous section is taken. The reason for the reduction is that COASTAL is not as mature as SPF and cannot yet handle the bytecode instructions required for the additional cases. Initially we also had the goal to compare runtimes for SPF and COASTAL, but COASTAL was too slow. Unfortunately, it meant we had to reduce the input domains for the COASTAL examples and thus in this set of experiments we only had 37516 constraints. We hope to have resolved COASTAL's performance issues by the time of the final version to allow us to run larger experiments. Also note that the running times, both in this section and the previous only pertains to the time spent in the solving component and not in the actual running of SPF and COASTAL.

The baseline for the COASTAL analysis is set using Z3 interfaced through Green. Note that here we are not evaluating the performance of a second run, hence there is no need to have a Z3Cache option.

In Table 2 the rows are grouped by the fastest tool (GRULIA, Green, Z3Fact, and Z3, in this order). Within each grouping, the rows are sorted by increasing running time. As in the previous table, the running time for Z3 is given in milliseconds, while the other running times are normalized with respect to Z3.

The first thing to note is that **grulia now outperforms Green in a number of cases**. The main reason for this is that in the symbolic execution experiments, in the case of Green, Z3 only had to answer sat/unsat queries, whereas for GRULIA it had to answer the more expensive model queries. In the concolic execution case, all the solver calls (for both Green and GRULIA) are model calls, in other words, equally expensive. The difference in runtime between the solver

Table 2. Running times (normalised) of COASTAL analysis on programs

Program	#c	$\frac{\#f}{\#c}$	Z3Model	Green	GRULIA	Z3Fact
Stack	1023	6.8	7712	0.092	0.063	0.077
SortedListInt	347	2.6	2656	0.300	0.185	0.296
CoinChange	108	5.6	744	0.456	0.366	1.176
Sorting	719	1.0	5460	1.161	0.686	1.029
MagicIndex	200	5.8	1324	1.649	0.707	1.218
BinomialHeap	4982	6.5	21246	0.202	0.406	0.458
BinTree	7613	5.9	38631	0.429	0.859	0.957
ObjectRec	827	5.6	7131	0.072	0.164	0.053
WBS	1150	5.2	4444	0.117	0.209	0.103
Triangle	1103	1.0	5694	0.229	1.162	0.219
Operations	7809	2.0	62209	0.396	0.899	0.362
BubbleSort	11631	1.0	40884	0.967	1.554	0.694
Remainder	573	1.0	8514	1.152	3.015	1.202

timings can be seen by comparing the Z3 running time in Table 2 with Z3Inc running time in Table 1.

Another observation is that, as before, Z3Fact competes with the other tools in performance, displaying the strength of factorisation.

Maybe most importantly, for all but one of these concolic experiments we see that one of the two caching strategies (Green or GRULIA) outperforms the solver. **As the cost of solver queries increases the better the caching strategies perform.** The exception is *Remainder*, that as in the symbolic cache seems immune to factorisation and thus caching is slower than just calling the solver directly. This example requires further investigation.

4   Related Work

Yang et al. [17] have performed initial work on memoised symbolic execution using Tries. Recal is a caching tool [3] where a target constraint is simplified based on a set of rules and is transformed into a matrix where the information can be converted into a canonical form for better matching to previous solutions. The tool is further improved with the version Recal+ where the tool looks at the structural composition of the constraint for implied logical satisfiability with solution reuse. GreenTrie [11] which is similar to Recal+, is an extension to Green. Optimising constraint solving by introducing an assertion stack has been tried by [18]. The aim here is to maintain a stack of formulas and declarations, which is provided by the symbolic executor. Zou et al. [18] store each query result of the stack for further reuse and avoiding redundant queries. Brennan et al. [7] developed Cashew [1] which is built on top of Green, and is designed to process and store constraint solutions in the theory of linear integers and strings.

A comparative study [4,5] is done, where Green, GreenTrie, Recal, Recal+ and Julia (a caching framework that also implements the model-core reuse strategy) are compared, and in which it is shown that Julia outperforms the other caching tools.

5   Conclusion and Future Work

To the best of our knowledge this is the largest study to evaluate whether caching is worth it, given the advances in solver technology. It not only considers standard sat/unsat approaches as used in Green, but also considers the more recent approach of caching models. In addition it also explores whether doing the caching during symbolic or concolic execution makes a difference.

Some of the core results we found are summarised below:

- During symbolic execution rather do incremental solving (this is a well known result, but here we show ample data to support it).
- Factorisation is fairly cheap and well worth doing in both the symbolic and concolic case.
- The more advanced pre-processing steps in Green, most notably finding a canonical form for LIA formulas, seems to not pay off in most cases.
- Model reuse starts to become viable for concolic execution, but is not worth doing for the symbolic case. This is mostly due to the model queries being slow in the solver.
- Caching becomes useful when the queries take longer to finish. This is obvious, and is even more pronounced when one performs model counting (as supported by Green).

There are a number of weaknesses in our current study that we would like to address in future work.

We focused on LIA constraints here, since they are the sweet-spot for symbolic/concolic execution, but the picture will change considerably when more complex domains are treated, for example floating point operations and operations over strings (where solving will be slower). However we are confident that the observation that factorisation is the important step in caching, will still hold.

Even though this might be a large study, we should have even larger examples. For instance we do need COASTAL to become more robust so that it can handle all the examples that SPF can handle. It is unlikely that COASTAL will ever be faster than SPF on a single path, but COASTAL can also run in a multi-threaded mode where it should be much more competitive. Note, as an aside, it is hard to parallelize a symbolic execution, but it is comparatively easy to do for concolic since each run is completely independent. We will report on these results in a final version.

The use of a persistent (across runs) store for GRULIA that doesn't require being loaded in upfront in the second run would make the reuse of models across runs more efficient. This is just engineering, and it is not completely obvious it is worth doing. What is worth doing, is incorporating an approach similar to Z3Cache for all techniques, i.e. cache constraints results (sat/unsat) at the highest level (i.e. before factorisation). This will have the drawback of using more storage, but a hashing approach can be tried that will make the approach more probabilistic (but with very small chance of a hash collision and thus an incorrect sat/unsat result).

Symbolic analysis displayed the sweet spot for the solver, where the constraints are in the quantifier free integer domain and only produce a single value solution (sat/unsat). The experiments showed that the caching tools have difficulty to keep up with performance when the incremental solver is involved. The difficulty of concolic execution is that it is not that obvious how to implement an incremental solver for the analysis. The solver in its basic mode performed immensely slow, therefore the caching tools display a greater relevancy. The model-core reuse strategy shows advantage over the sat/unsat alternative. For concolic analysis a model is required for the constraint, which is more expensive to compute, therefore the caching strategies (and more so the model-core approach) improved the analysis run time.

Take-Home Message. If you plan to do a single analysis (with symbolic execution), it can be faster to just run Z3 incremental mode. If you want to analyse a program or different programs multiple times, it will definitely still be useful to run a persistent storage. Regarding concolic execution, model/solution caching offers benefit and it is up to the user to decide whether classical caching is the approach or model reuse will be better suited for the analysis. Despite all that said, at the very least, the recommendation will be to have a factorisation step to reduce the constraint size – this gives the best trade-off between effective reuse and not too much extra computation and time consumption.

Acknowledgements. Jan Taljaard's work was supported in part by NRF (National Research Foundation) of South Africa.

References

1. Cashew. https://cashew.vlab.cs.ucsb.edu/. Accessed Feb 2020
2. Green. https://github.com/GreenSolver/green/. Accessed Feb 2020
3. Aquino, A., Bianchi, F.A., Chen, M., Denaro, G., Pezzè, M.: Reusing constraint proofs in program analysis. In: ISSTA 2015, pp. 305–315. ACM (2015). https://doi.org/10.1145/2771783.2771802
4. Aquino, A., Denaro, G., Pezzè, M.: Heuristically matching solution spaces of arithmetic formulas to efficiently reuse solutions. In: ICSE 2017, pp. 427–437. IEEE/ACM (2017). https://doi.org/10.1109/ICSE.2017.46
5. Aquino, A., Denaro, G., Pezzè, M.: Reusing solutions modulo theories. IEEE Trans. Softw. Eng. (Early access), 385–394 (2019). https://doi.org/10.1109/TSE.2019.2898199
6. Bailey, J., Stuckey, P.J.: Discovery of minimal unsatisfiable subsets of constraints using hitting set dualization. In: Hermenegildo, M.V., Cabeza, D. (eds.) PADL 2005. LNCS, vol. 3350, pp. 174–186. Springer, Heidelberg (2005). https://doi.org/10.1007/978-3-540-30557-6_14

7. Brennan, T., Tsiskaridze, N., Rosner, N., Aydin, A., Bultan, T.: Constraint normalization and parameterized caching for quantitative program analysis. In: FSE 2017, pp. 535–546. ACM (2017). https://doi.org/10.1145/3106237.3106303
8. De la Banda, M.J.G., Stuckey, P.J., Wazny, J.: Finding all minimal unsatisfiable subsets. In: PPDP 2003, pp. 32–43. ACM (2003). https://doi.org/10.1145/888251.888256
9. de Moura, L., Bjørner, N.: Z3: an efficient SMT solver. In: Ramakrishnan, C.R., Rehof, J. (eds.) TACAS 2008. LNCS, vol. 4963, pp. 337–340. Springer, Heidelberg (2008). https://doi.org/10.1007/978-3-540-78800-3_24
10. Gleeson, J., Ryan, J.: Identifying minimally infeasible subsystems of inequalities. INFORMS J. Comput. 2(1), 61–63 (1990). https://doi.org/10.1287/ijoc.2.1.61
11. Jia, X., Ghezzi, C., Ying, S.: Enhancing reuse of constraint solutions to improve symbolic execution. In: ISSTA 2015, pp. 177–187. ACM (2015). https://doi.org/10.1145/2771783.2771806
12. King, J.C.: Symbolic execution and program testing. Commun. ACM 19(7), 385–394 (1976). https://doi.org/10.1145/360248.360252
13. Liffiton, M.H., Malik, A.: Enumerating infeasibility: finding multiple MUSes quickly. In: Gomes, C., Sellmann, M. (eds.) CPAIOR 2013. LNCS, vol. 7874, pp. 160–175. Springer, Heidelberg (2013). https://doi.org/10.1007/978-3-642-38171-3_11
14. Morgado, A., Matos, P., Manquinho, V., Marques-Silva, J.: Counting models in integer domains. In: Biere, A., Gomes, C.P. (eds.) SAT 2006. LNCS, vol. 4121, pp. 410–423. Springer, Heidelberg (2006). https://doi.org/10.1007/11814948_37
15. Taljaard, J.H.: Optimised constraint solving for real-world problems. Master's thesis, Stellenbosch University (2019). https://doi.org/10019.1/107292
16. Visser, W., Geldenhuys, J., Dwyer, M.B.: Green: reducing, reusing and recycling constraints in program analysis. In: FSE 2012, pp. 1–11. ACM (2012). https://doi.org/10.1145/2393596.2393665
17. Yang, G., Păsăreanu, C.S., Khurshid, S.: Memoized symbolic execution. In: ISSTA 2012, pp. 144–154. ACM (2012). https://doi.org/10.1145/2338965.2336771
18. Zou, Q., An, J., Huang, W., Fan, W.: Integrating assertion stack and caching to optimize constraint solving. In: ICCSNT 2015, pp. 397–401. IEEE (2015). https://doi.org/10.1109/ICCSNT.2015.7490777

Per-Location Simulation

Liyi Li[(✉)] and Elsa L. Gunter[(✉)]

Department of Computer Science, University of Illinois at Urbana-Champaign,
Champaign, USA
{liyili2,egunter}@illinois.edu

Abstract. Simulation/bisimulation is one of the most widely used frameworks for proving program equivalence/semantic preservation. In this paper, we propose a new per-location simulation (PLS) relation that is simple and suitable for proving that a compiled program semantically preserves its original program under a CFG-based language with a real-world, C/C++ like, weak memory model. To the best of our knowledge, PLS is the first simulation framework weaker than the CompCert [26]/CompCertTSO [47] one that is used for proving compiler correctness. With a combination of PLS, the compiler proof-framework Morpheus [34], and a language semantics with a weak memory model, we are able to prove that programs are semantically preserved through a transformation. All the definitions and proofs have been implemented in Isabelle/HOL.

1 Introduction

When the preservation of concurrency behavior was being verified in the CompCert compiler [26], the researchers found that it is not enough to tell the whole story just to use a traditional bisimulation framework to prove the program equivalence between a compiled program and its original one, so they designed a new bisimulation framework by treating safe programs and programs that might reach error states differently. CompCert's concurrency model was sequential consistency. The extent to which traditional bisimulation is inappropriate is even clearer when dealing with weak concurrency models. Weak concurrency models have been studied broadly for real world imperative programming languages (C/C++/LLVM) [1,3,5,9,10,14,18,19,21–24,37,38,40,41,45]. When using these models to prove compiler correctness, a problem arises. Historically, the semantics of these languages has been determined by the behavior of their compilers, so the behavioral effects of compiler optimizations also need to be considered in the concurrency models. For example, in the program piece (b) in Fig. 1, variables a and b can both read 1 if we consider the fact that a simple optimization removes the Boolean guards in (b), transforming it as the program piece (a). The well-known confusion about out-of-thin-air behaviors [8] is a typical consequence of the problem.

Researchers [19,21,40,41] have tried to solve the thin-air problems by merging the extra behaviors caused by compiler optimizations into their concurrency

© Springer Nature Switzerland AG 2020
R. Lee et al. (Eds.): NFM 2020, LNCS 12229, pp. 267–287, 2020.
https://doi.org/10.1007/978-3-030-55754-6_16

/* number after the blue "//" along with a read restricts the value of the read to be the number */
/* initially, x = 0 and y = 0 */

$$
\begin{array}{ccc}
\text{(a)} & \text{(b)} & \text{(c)} \\
\begin{array}{l|l}
a :=_{\mathrm{rlx}} y//1 & b :=_{\mathrm{rlx}} x//1 \\
x :=_{\mathrm{rlx}} 1 & y :=_{\mathrm{rlx}} 1
\end{array} &
\begin{array}{l|l}
a :=_{\mathrm{rlx}} y//1 & b :=_{\mathrm{rlx}} x//1 \\
\text{if } (a{=}a) & \text{if } (b{=}b) \\
\quad x :=_{\mathrm{rlx}} 1 & \quad y :=_{\mathrm{rlx}} 1
\end{array} &
\begin{array}{l|l}
a :=_{\mathrm{rlx}} y//1 & b :=_{\mathrm{rlx}} x//1 \\
\text{if } (a{=}1) & y :=_{\mathrm{rlx}} 1 \\
\quad x :=_{\mathrm{rlx}} 1 &
\end{array}
\end{array}
$$

$$
\text{(d)}
\begin{array}{l}
x :=_{\mathrm{rlx}} 1 \\
y :=_{\mathrm{rlx}} 1 \\
a :=_{\mathrm{rlx}} y \\
b :=_{\mathrm{rlx}} x
\end{array}
\quad
\text{(e)}
\begin{array}{l|l}
a :=_{\mathrm{rlx}} y//1 & b :=_{\mathrm{rlx}} x//1 \\
\text{if } (a{=}1) & \text{if } (b{=}1) \\
\quad x :=_{\mathrm{rlx}} 1 & \quad y :=_{\mathrm{rlx}} 1
\end{array}
\quad
\text{(f)}
\begin{array}{l|l|l}
a :=_{\mathrm{rlx}} y//z & b :=_{\mathrm{rlx}} x//z & \text{if } (\text{ram}()) \\
\text{if } (a{=}a) & \text{if } (b{=}b) & \quad z :=_{\mathrm{rlx}} 1 \\
\quad x :=_{\mathrm{rlx}} z & \quad y :=_{\mathrm{rlx}} z & \text{else} \\
& & \quad z :=_{\mathrm{rlx}} 2
\end{array}
$$

Fig. 1. Motivating examples

models. These models have several problems. Vafeiadis *et al.* [42] has shown that most of the compiler optimizations are invalid in these weak models. Moreover, Batty *et al.* [4] proved that it does not exists a candidate execution style axiomatic C++ concurrency model to incooperate the thin-air problems raised by (b) (Fig. 1). Additionally, these models are built upon a very limited set of memory actions or language pieces, and provide correct compiler schemes generated from the models based on the limited set. It requires a great effort to extend the schemes to prove a real-world compiler optimization preserving the multi-threaded program semantics for a real-world language under a real-world concurrency model. In some cases, even if the underlying language is extended a little, these models failed to show all supposedly allowed behaviors. For example, the promising model [21] is designed specifically to prove that the two reads in (d) (Fig. 1) can both read 1, but it fails to prove that the variables a and b in (f) can read any possible value from location z because z does not have a fixed value in all possible executions. The IMM model [41] is able to prove that the two reads in (a) can both read 1, but it fails to prove the two reads in (b) (Fig. 1) can both read 1. PLS is able to handle all these cases.

In this paper, we propose a simulation framework, named Per-Location Simulation (PLS), that is able to prove semantic preservation between compiled programs and their original programs under a language semantics with a weak concurrency model. We focus on safe traces (traces not going wrong) here, and assume that there is an outer layer on top of PLS to deal with reaching-error-state traces the same as the forward simulation framework in defined by CompCert [26]. As a main example, we provide a clear border for acceptable behaviors and out-of-thin-air behaviors in a CFG-based language with a weak concurrency model by using PLS to prove the semantic preservation of a simple optimization. The border is summarized by the examples in Fig. 1, which can be divided into two parts. The first is the PLS core part (Sect. 2.1). By the traditional simulation framework, the example (c) cannot be proven to simulate (a) (meaning that (a) semantically preserves (c)), because the memory trace (d) can be generated by (a), but it cannot be observed from (c). By analyzing closely the output of the two reads and two writes in both (a) and (c), all values that can be observed in these reads and writes of (c) can also be observed in (a). Thus, we should have a kind of similarity between (a) and (c). The PLS core produces such kind. It filters traces of programs into sub-traces based on locations. Instead of comparing the whole traces (as (d)), the PLS core compares the sub-traces of location x (and y) in (a) and (c) to determine if (c) per-location simulates (a). The second part is the full PLS definition (Sect. 2.3), which addresses the focal point of thin-air problems. (b) (Fig. 1) is supposed to be proved to be semantically preserved by (a), but (e) is not; because the two Boolean guards in (d) can be compiled away, but such guards in (e) cannot be removed. There are traces appearing in (a) but not appearing in (e). To validate the proof, we augment the PLS core with additional equations that capture some very simple compiler optimization syntactic dependencies. Instead of proving the simulation from (d) to (a), we prove the simulation from an equivalent representative of (d) to (a). To the best of our knowledge, PLS is the first simulation framework weaker than the one in CompCert/CompCertTSO [47], and to be used to prove compiler correctness under a CFG-based imperative language with a weak memory model, and is able to correctly distinguish thin-air and correct behaviors.

2   The Per-Location Simulation Definition

This section provides an introduction of PLS. We first introduce PLS core, then we provide an example language, and then we introduce the full PLS definition.

2.1   PLS Core

Transition System

States: $\sigma \in \Sigma$ Labels: $\alpha \in A$ Labeled Transition Systems (LTS): $(\Sigma, A, \xrightarrow{\alpha})$
Locations: Loc Label's Value: $\text{val}(\alpha)$ Label's Type: $\text{type}(\alpha)$ Label's Location: $\text{loc}(\alpha) \in Loc$
Transition System Property: $(\forall \alpha.\ \text{type}(\alpha) = \tau \Rightarrow \text{val}(\alpha) = \bot \wedge \text{loc}(\alpha) = \bot) \wedge (\bot \notin Loc)$
Transition System Syntactic Sugar

$\sigma \xrightarrow{\tau} \sigma' \triangleq \exists \alpha.\ \sigma \xrightarrow{\alpha} \sigma' \wedge \text{type}(\alpha) = \tau$ $\sigma \rightarrow_{\text{not}(x)} \sigma' \triangleq \exists \alpha.\ \sigma \xrightarrow{\alpha} \sigma' \wedge \text{loc}(\alpha) \neq x$

$\sigma \xrightarrow{\alpha}_x \sigma' \triangleq \exists \sigma_n\ \alpha.\ \sigma \rightarrow^*_{\text{not}(x)} \sigma_n \xrightarrow{\alpha} \sigma' \wedge \text{type}(\alpha) \neq \tau \wedge \text{loc}(\alpha) = x$

PLS Definition

Label Equivalence: $\alpha \equiv \beta \triangleq \text{val}(\alpha) = \text{val}(\beta) \wedge \text{type}(\alpha) = \text{type}(\beta) \wedge \text{loc}(\alpha) = \text{loc}(\beta)$

$\text{LTS}_\Xi \colon (\Xi, A, \xrightarrow{\alpha}^\Xi)$ $\text{LTS}_\Sigma \colon (\Sigma, B, \xrightarrow{\beta}^\Sigma)$

$\sqsubseteq_x$ is a PLS_x relation on two transition systems LTS_Ξ and LTS_Σ:
a.k.a. $\text{PLS}_x(\sqsubseteq_x) \triangleq$

$\forall \xi\ \xi_1 \in \Xi.\ (\forall \sigma \in \Sigma\ (\forall \alpha \in A.\ \xi \sqsubseteq_x \sigma \wedge \xi \xrightarrow{\alpha}^\Xi_x \xi_1 \Rightarrow (\exists \beta\ \sigma_1.\ \sigma \xrightarrow{\beta}^\Sigma_x \sigma_1 \wedge \alpha \equiv \beta \wedge \xi_1 \sqsubseteq_x \sigma_1)))$

$\text{PLS}_{Loc}(\sqsubseteq) \triangleq \forall x \in Loc.\ \text{PLS}_x(\sqsubseteq_x)$

Fig. 2. Per-location simulation core definition

Here, we introduce the PLS core definition and utility examples. Figure 2 includes the PLS core definition. We assume that there is a labeled transition system (LTS) $(\Sigma, A, \xrightarrow{\alpha})$, including a set of states (Σ), a set of labels (A), and a labeled transition function $(\xrightarrow{\alpha})$. The transition system is parameterized by a set of locations Loc. Every label in the transition system has three properties: its value (accessed by val), its type (at least having a τ type and normally having additional read and write types), and its memory location (be in the set Loc). For simplicity, we assume that if the type of a label is τ, then the value and location of the label are $\bot$ in a given transition system. To best describe the PLS core definition, we define some syntactic sugar on top of the transition system $\overset{\alpha}{\rightarrow}$ in Fig. 2. We first describe a predicate PLS_x defining PLS core on a single location x. A relation $\sqsubseteq_x$ is a PLS core relation on x over two labeled transition systems (LTS_Ξ and LTS_Σ in Fig. 2), if for any two states ($\xi \in \Xi$ and $\sigma \in \Sigma$) in the relation ($\xi \sqsubseteq_x \sigma$), ξ can transition by an x step (defined by $\overset{\alpha}{\rightarrow}_x$), then σ can also transition by an x step, where the two labels are equivalent ($\equiv$) and the resulting states are again related by $\sqsubseteq_x$. A family of relations ($\sqsubseteq$), one for each location in Loc, is a PLS core relation if each indexed relation ($\sqsubseteq_x$) satisfies PLS_x for each x in Loc, where Loc is a finite set of memory locations.

$$(\mathrm{wr\_a}) \begin{array}{l} x :=_{\mathrm{rlx}} 1 \\ y :=_{\mathrm{rlx}} 1 \\ z :=_{\mathrm{rlx}} 1 \end{array} \qquad (\mathrm{wr\_b}) \begin{array}{l} y :=_{\mathrm{rlx}} 1 \\ x :=_{\mathrm{rlx}} 1 \\ z :=_{\mathrm{rlx}} 1 \end{array} \qquad (\mathrm{prop})\ x :=_{\mathrm{rlx}} 1 \wedge y :=_{\mathrm{rlx}} 1 \wedge z :=_{\mathrm{rlx}} 1$$

We first discuss the single-threaded cases. The program pieces above (($\mathrm{wr\_a}$) and ($\mathrm{wr\_b}$)) describe two sequences of memory writes. Regarding the underlying memory concurrency model, the outputs of the two program pieces should be the same, i.e. to write 1 to the locations x, y, and z. However, ($\mathrm{wr\_a}$) and ($\mathrm{wr\_b}$) cannot be proved to be similar with each other using the traditional simulation framework under the assumption of sequential consistency. Only if we assume a relaxed concurrency model can we prove that ($\mathrm{wr\_a}$) and ($\mathrm{wr\_b}$) are similar. In PLS, both ($\mathrm{wr\_a}$) and ($\mathrm{wr\_b}$) are viewed as three sub-traces as shown in (prop) (for simplicity, in each sub-trace, we only show instructions without mentioning other state environments), each of which describes a write for a location; so that we are able to prove that ($\mathrm{wr\_a}$) and ($\mathrm{wr\_b}$) are per-loc similar to each other.

$$(\mathrm{a\_dd}) \begin{array}{cc} R_y & R_x \\ \ulcorner & \urcorner \\ \mathrm{rf} & \mathrm{rf} \\ W_x & W_y \end{array} \qquad (\mathrm{b\_dd}) \begin{array}{cc} R_y & R_x \\ \mathrm{ctrl}\ \ulcorner & \mathrm{rf}\ \urcorner\ \mathrm{rf} \\ W_x & W_y \end{array} \qquad (\mathrm{prop\_a}) \begin{array}{l} x :=_{\mathrm{rlx}} 1 \\ b :=_{\mathrm{rlx}} x \end{array} \wedge \begin{array}{l} y :=_{\mathrm{rlx}} 1 \\ a :=_{\mathrm{rlx}} y \end{array}$$

We now discuss multi-threaded cases under a weak relaxed memory model [24]. One of the example per-loc simulation relations that PLS enables is the one between programs (a) and (c) in Fig. 1, whose execution diagrams are listed as ($\mathrm{a\_dd}$) and ($\mathrm{b\_dd}$) above. An execution diagram is a graph representation of the execution of a program (only listing memory instructions), with arrows representing the memory instruction order that the execution must obey. In ($\mathrm{a\_dd}$), W (or R) represents a write (or a read) instruction with the subscripts (x or y) representing the memory locations (details are the $\mathcal{A}ct$ type in Fig. 3). The rf arrow between R_y and W_y in ($\mathrm{a\_dd}$) means that the read from y reads the value written by the write, so the read must happen after the write. The ctrl arrow in ($\mathrm{b\_dd}$) is a control dependency so that R_y must happen before W_x in any valid execution of (c) (Fig. 1). This is the reason that program (c) does not simulate program (a) by traditional simulation methods, i.e. because the execution ((d) in Fig. 1) happens in (a) but never happens in (c). On the other hand, PLS deals the two programs by first splitting all executions in both programs into a sub-trace per-location like the one in (prop_a). Thus, (c) per-loc simulates (a) ((a) semantically preserves (c)).

2.2   Example Language Syntax

Before we describe the full PLS definition, we first provide the example language that we will use in the paper. We focus on the syntax here, and the operational semantics in Sect. 3. The language is described in Fig. 3. In the figure, every name in *Chancery* font is a type defined for a language component; everything in tt font is a constructor or terminal in the language; and everything in *Italics* is a variable representing a term. The figure also introduces ranging conventions that will be employed throughout the paper.

Domains and Syntax

$a, b \in \mathcal{V}ar \triangleq \mathcal{N}ame$ Variables $x, y \in \mathcal{L}oc \triangleq \mathbb{N}$ Memory Locations

$v \in \mathcal{V}al \triangleq \mathbb{Z}$ Integer Values $O_r \ni o_r \triangleq \mathtt{rlx} \mid \mathtt{acq}$ Read Orderings

$O_w \ni o_w \triangleq \mathtt{rlx} \mid \mathtt{rel}$ Write Orderings

Expressions: $\mathcal{E}xp \ni e \triangleq v \mid a \mid e + e \mid e * e \mid e = e \mid e < e$

Instructions: $\mathit{Inst} \ni in \triangleq a := e \mid a := \&x \mid a :=_{o_r} (b \mid x) \mid (a \mid x) :=_{o_w} b \mid \mathtt{skip}$

Terminations: $\mathit{CInst} \ni c \triangleq \mathtt{if}\ e \mid \mathtt{br} \mid \mathtt{exit}$

CFG Labels: $L \ni l \triangleq \mathtt{seq} \mid \mathtt{yes} \mid \mathtt{no}$ CFG Nodes: $\pi \in N \subseteq \mathbb{N}$

CFG Basic Block: $B \in \mathcal{B} \triangleq \mathit{Inst\ List} \times \mathit{CInst}$ CFG Edges: $E \subseteq N \times L \times N$

CFG Label Function: $\lambda : N \to (\mathit{Inst\ List} \times \mathit{CInst})$

Control Flow Graph (CFG): $\mathcal{CFG} \ni C \triangleq (N, \pi_0, \lambda, E)$ Thread IDs: $tid \in \mathit{Tid} \subseteq \mathit{Tid} \triangleq \mathcal{N}ame$

Memory Actions: $\mathcal{A}ct \ni ac \triangleq \tau \mid \mathtt{R}^x_{v,o_r} \mid \mathtt{W}^x_{v,o_w}$ Programs: $\mathcal{P}rog \ni \mu \triangleq \mathit{Tid} \to \mathcal{CFG}$

Fig. 3. Example language syntax

The language contains a set of variables ($\mathcal{V}ar$), integer values ($\mathcal{V}al$), and memory locations ($\mathcal{L}oc$). There are two kinds of memory orderings: one for read instructions (O_r), and the other for write instructions (O_w). The memory orderings are similar to the C++ memory orderings [24], but we only describe the relaxed (rlx), acquire (acq), and release (rel) orderings in this paper. There are two kinds of instructions: normal instructions and terminations. Normal instructions are in the LLVM style, where every instruction can produce no more than one assignment definition. For example, the purpose of the instruction $a := \&x$ is to get the address of location x and put it in the variable a as an integer. Terminations include a binary branching instruction (if), an unconditional branching (br), and a control flow graph (CFG, type: $\mathcal{CFG}$) exit instruction (exit). A **control flow graph** (CFG) is a tuple (N, π_0, λ, E) where N is a finite set of nodes, π_0 is the start node, λ is a labeling of each node having a basic block that comprises a list of sequential instructions ended by a termination, and E is a set of edges labeled seq, yes, or no such that, if $\mathsf{snd}(\lambda(n)) = \mathtt{br}$ then there is a unique out-edge from n labeled seq; if $\mathsf{snd}(\lambda(n)) = \mathtt{exit}$ then there are no out-edges from n; and otherwise there are exactly two out-edges, one labeled yes and one labeled **no**. In a **basic block** ($\mathcal{B}$), we assign each instruction a **position number** (i), the sequential instructions their position in the list (starting from 0), and the termination the length of the list of sequential instructions, which is one greater than the position number of the last instruction in the list. Programs (*Prog*) is a function from a set of thread-IDs (*Tid*) to CFGs. All program piece examples appearing in the paper are syntactic sugars of the programs in Fig. 3. Memory actions (*Act*) are the core parts of the labels in the transition system described in the beginning of the section, and are viewed as a way for threads to communicate with the main memory.

2.3 Full PLS

The PLS core definition is suitable for building the **per-loc** simulation between (a) and (c) in Fig. 2, but the relation between (a) and (b) (Fig. 2) cannot be handled by the PLS core. To enhance the usability of PLS, we associate a reflexive relation **eq** with the PLS core definition as the Full PLS definition (Fig. 4).

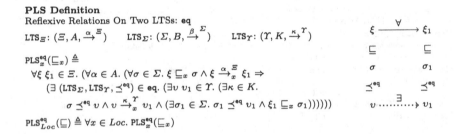

Fig. 4. Full per-location simulation definition

The **eq** relation is at least a reflexive relation describing program transformations and capturing the syntactic dependencies of program instructions that are hard to be discovered by only the program concurrency semantics, such as the example (b) in Fig. 1. **eq** including the identity relation (as $\preceq^{eq}$) relates two systems LTS_Σ and LTS_Υ, such as the tuple $(\mathrm{LTS}_\Sigma, \mathrm{LTS}_\Upsilon, \preceq^{eq})$ in Fig. 4. PLS_x^{eq} can be understood by the right diagram in Fig. 4. Assume that we have two systems LTS_Ξ and LTS_Σ. We want to show the **per-loc** simulation ($\sqsubseteq_x$) from LTS_Ξ to LTS_Σ by showing that for every transition ξ to ξ_1, there exists a transition σ to σ_1, such that the two transition labels are equivalent ($\equiv$). However, we cannot directly have a transition from σ to σ_1 in some cases. Instead, through the **eq** set, we find a relation $\preceq^{eq}$ that relates LTS_Σ with another system LTS_Υ; and the transition from υ to υ_1 is found in LTS_Υ, where υ and υ_1 are related to σ and σ_1 through $\preceq^{eq}$, respectively, and ξ_1 and σ_1 are also related by $\sqsubseteq_x$. PLS_x^{eq} is a generalization of the PLS_x predicate in Fig. 2, if we just select the tuple in **eq** as $(\mathrm{LTS}_\Sigma, \mathrm{LTS}_\Sigma, =)$. By selecting such tuple, the two systems LTS_Σ and LTS_Υ are the same. Finally, PLS_{Loc}^{eq} includes the functionality as PLS_{Loc}, but it builds a family of relations over the predicate PLS_x^{eq}.

$$eq \triangleq \ldots$$

$(N, \pi_0, \lambda \cup \{\pi \mapsto (ins, \text{if } e)\}, E' \cup \{(\pi, \text{ yes}, \pi_1), (\pi, \text{ no}, \pi_2)\})$
$\cong_{eq} (N, \pi_0, \lambda \cup \{\pi \mapsto (ins, \text{br})\}, E' \cup \{(\pi, \text{ seq}, \pi_1)\})$
  IF $eval(e) = \text{true}$;
$(N, \pi_0, \lambda \cup \{\pi \mapsto (ins, \text{if } e)\}, E' \cup \{(\pi, \text{ yes}, \pi_1), (\pi, \text{ no}, \pi_2)\})$
$\cong_{eq} (N, \pi_0, \lambda \cup \{\pi \mapsto (ins, \text{br})\}, E' \cup \{(\pi, \text{ seq}, \pi_2)\})$
  IF $eval(e) = \text{false}$;
$(N, \pi_0, \lambda \cup \{\pi \mapsto (ins, \text{if } e)\}, E' \cup \{(\pi, \text{ yes}, \pi_1), (\pi, \text{ no}, \pi_2)\})$
$\cong_{eq} (N, \pi_0, \lambda \cup \{\pi \mapsto (ins, \text{br})\}, E' \cup \{(\pi, \text{ seq}, \pi_1)\})$
  IF $\lambda(\pi_1) = \lambda(\pi_2) \wedge (\forall l\ \pi'.(\pi_1, l, \pi') \in E \Leftrightarrow (\pi_2, l, \pi') \in E)$;
  $\ldots$

(a) Example eq Relation

(b) Roach Model on Acquire/Release Atomics

Fig. 5. Example and Roach model

Figure 5a provides a partial definition of an example eq set. The set contains equations to relate two labeled transition systems LTS_Ξ and LTS_Σ by relating the two program texts in any two states ξ and σ from the systems. The conditional equations shown in Fig. 5a is to equate two CFGs for a thread in any two program texts, i.e. two program texts μ and μ' are equivalent, if for any thread tid in the domain of μ/μ', $\mu(tid) \cong_{eq} \mu'(tid)$ ($\cong_{eq}$ means equivalence closed under the conditional equations in Fig. 5a). The first two conditional equations in Fig. 5a describe the equivalence relation that if a Boolean guard of a binary branching is always evaluated to true or false statically (by the eval function), then the CFG is related to the version formed by transforming the branching operation to a unconditional branching operation. The third rule describes the relation that if the outgoing edges of a branching block have the same target, then the CFG can be rewritten as a version only going through one branch.

The following single-threaded programs ((pa_a), (pa_b), and (pa_c)) are examples for which traditional simulation frameworks cannot provide satisfactory explanations. Using a sequential consistency model, a traditional simulation framework enables the proof of similarity between programs (pa_a) and (pa_b) (let's assume that the executions of a program generate an LTS), because an execution of (pa_a) always executes a write to x, then a read from y, and then a write to z, which is the same sequence as the one produced by (pa_b). The problem is that we also want to show that (pa_a) and (pa_c) are similar, which the traditional framework cannot enable.

(pa_a)
$x :=_{rlx} c$
if $(a=b \wedge b=c)$
$\quad a :=_{rlx} y$
else
$\quad a :=_{rlx} y$
$z :=_{rlx} b$

(pa_b)
$x :=_{rlx} c$
$a :=_{rlx} y$
$z :=_{rlx} b$

(pa_c)
$a :=_{rlx} y$
$z :=_{rlx} b$
$x :=_{rlx} c$

(prop_pa) $x :=_{rlx} c \wedge a :=_{rlx} y \wedge z :=_{rlx} b$

Under a weak memory model, like RC11 [24], a transitional simulation method enables the proof that (pa_c) simulates (pa_a) but not the opposite, because the Boolean guard in (pa_a) contains the variables a and b, so it has data dependency on the later instructions (read from y and write to z). Thus, they cannot move to execute before the Boolean guard as well as the write to x. Clearly, by using the full PLS, to prove that (pa_a) simulates (pa_c), we can first find an equivalent program of (pa_a), which is exactly the one in (pa_b). Then we prove that (pa_a) per-loc simulates (pa_c) by showing that (pa_b) per-loc simulates (pa_c).

$$
\text{(a\_dd)} \quad
\begin{array}{cc}
\mathbf{R}_y & \mathbf{R}_x \\
\ulcorner \quad \urcorner \\
\mathtt{rf} \quad \mathtt{rf} \\
\downarrow \quad \downarrow \\
\mathbf{W}_x & \mathbf{W}_y
\end{array}
\qquad
\text{(d\_dd)} \quad
\begin{array}{cc}
\mathbf{R}_y & \mathbf{R}_x \\
\ulcorner \\
\mathtt{ctrl} \; \mathtt{rf} \quad \mathtt{rf} \; \mathtt{ctrl} \\
\downarrow \quad \downarrow \\
\mathbf{W}_x & \mathbf{W}_y
\end{array}
\qquad
\text{(prop\_a)} \quad
\begin{array}{l}
x :=_{\mathtt{rlx}} 1 \\
b :=_{\mathtt{rlx}} x
\end{array} \wedge
\begin{array}{l}
y :=_{\mathtt{rlx}} 1 \\
a :=_{\mathtt{rlx}} y
\end{array}
$$

The simulation from (pa_a) to (pa_c) can also be proved by the PLS core definition in Sect. 2.1. To understand the additional proving ability that the full PLS brings us, the simulation from (b) to (a) in Fig. 1 provides a better hint. The execution diagram of (a) is shown as (a_dd) above, while the diagram of (b) is shown as (d_dd). In (d_dd), for every single thread, a control dependency (ctrl) exists from the read to the write. If we observe that the two reads both read 1, we have exactly two reads-from edges (rf) from writes to reads. Thus, the diagram contains a cycle, which means that the execution of reading both as 1 is impossible if no optimization is applied to (b) (Fig. 1). Like the traditional simulation frameworks, PLS core is unable to prove the per-loc simulation from (b) to (a), which is the correct behavior in the sense that no optimization is applied. the desired simulation between (b) and (a) must take into account some resulting behaviors caused by optimizations. It is clear that the two ctrl edges in (d_dd) can be removed by some very simple optimizations, so that (b) becomes (a); and its execution diagram is the same as that of (a_dd). Then we can use the PLS core to build the simulation relation as the one in Sect. 2.1. This is the main content of the full PLS definition, which includes the optimization effects as the equivalence relation eq, then proves the per-loc similarity from an equivalence representative of (b) to (a) by using the PLS core.

$$
\text{(par)} \quad
\begin{array}{l}
a :=_{\mathtt{rlx}} y//1 \\
\text{if } (a{=}1) \\
\quad x :=_{\mathtt{rlx}} 1
\end{array}
\Bigg\|
\begin{array}{l}
b :=_{\mathtt{rlx}} x//1 \\
\text{if } (b{=}1) \\
\quad y :=_{\mathtt{rlx}} 1 \\
\text{else} \\
\quad y :=_{\mathtt{rlx}} 1
\end{array}
\qquad
\text{(par')} \quad
\begin{array}{l}
a :=_{\mathtt{rlx}} y \\
\text{if } (a{=}1) \\
\quad x :=_{\mathtt{rlx}} 1
\end{array}
\Bigg\|
\begin{array}{l}
b :=_{\mathtt{rlx}} x \\
y :=_{\mathtt{rlx}} 1
\end{array}
\qquad
\text{(par'\_dd)} \quad
\begin{array}{cc}
\mathbf{R}_y & \mathbf{R}_x \\
\ulcorner \quad \urcorner \\
\mathtt{ctrl} \; \mathtt{rf} \quad \mathtt{rf} \\
\downarrow \\
\mathbf{W}_x & \mathbf{W}_y
\end{array}
$$

If a traditional simulation framework would be parameterized with the eq relation, it could prove the simulation from (b) to (a) in Fig. 1, but it is inadequate for the simulation from the (par) above to (a) (Fig. 1). For that, the full power of PLS is required. To prove such a per-loc simulation, we first select an equivalence representative of program (par) to be the program (par'). Then, we prove the per-loc simulation from (par') to (a) by the strategy for proving the relation from (c) to (a) (Sect. 2.1).

We then need to answer the question: what kind of equations are allowed in eq? The principle is described in the Roach Model of Manson et al. [35], and systematically explained by Vafeiadis et al. [43]: the short answer is any equation that can preserve program meaning, especially, the meaning of the critical section created by the acquire (acq) and release (rel) atomic memory operations. Essentially, the acquire/release atomics are C++ memory devices that implement a weak version of the memory locking mechanism. Moving a memory operation before an acquire atomic operation or after a release atomic operation violates the Roach Model principle that states: "shared memory accesses can be moved in critical regions but not out of them" (Fig. 5b). In the paper of Vafeiadis *et al.*, several cases are mentioned of an optimization violating this principle; each of them involves the removal or addition of read/write memory operations. For simplicity in this paper, we provide the following observation about a conservative construction of eq to preserve the Roach Model principle. In it, $\text{LTS}|_{tid}$ means chopping the LTS to only execute single-threaded CFGs in the thread tid.

Observation 1. Assume that we have a transition system LTS_Σ, and a singleton relation set $\text{eq} = \{(\text{LTS}_\Sigma, \text{LTS}_\Xi, \sim)\}$. We assume that for every thread tid, we derive two single-threaded systems from LTS_Σ and LTS_Ξ as $\text{LTS}_\Sigma|_{tid}$ and $\text{LTS}_\Xi|_{tid}$, the $\sim$ relation ($\text{LTS}_\sigma|_{tid} \sim \text{LTS}_\sigma|_{tid}$) has the property that $\text{LTS}_\sigma|_{tid}$ is bisimilar to $\text{LTS}_\sigma|_{tid}$. Then, for any relation $\sqsubseteq$, such that $\text{PLS}^{\text{eq}}_{Loc}(\sqsubseteq)$, and any state ξ in LTS_Ξ that does not transition (in LTS_Ξ) to a Roach-Model-violating state (Fig. 5b), if $\sigma \sqsubseteq \xi$, then σ does not transition (in LTS_Σ) to a Roach-Model-violating state.

3   Program Meaning Preservation

Morpheus is a a domain-specific language for formal specification of program transformations. In previous papers about Morpheus [32,34], it was shown how to combine a sequential memory model, the Morpheus framework, and an underlying instruction semantics for a programming language to prove the correctness of a traditional compiler optimization (PRE). This section introduces a combination of PLS, Morpheus, and the program semantics for the language in Fig. 3 (based on a weak memory model) to prove an optimization semantically preserving the program meaning. We first introduce the Morpheus specification language and examples of optimizations specified in Morpheus. Then, we introduce the program semantics of the language in Fig. 3, which combines the instruction semantics with a weak memory model. Given an optimization ζ and program μ, we rewrite μ to μ' by ζ. The proof is to build a PLS relation from a LTS, whose states have the form (μ', ω) for any environment state ω with a fixed format (Fig. 8), to another LTS, whose states have the form (μ, ω).

3.1   Morpheus and Example Optimization Specifications

The Morpheus specification language [34] is enlightened by the Trans language of Kalvala *et al.* [20]. Morpheus specifies an optimization as conditional compositions of rewrites on CFGs. Morpheus is split into three components: core graph transformations, conditions given in First Order Computation Tree Logic

(FOCTL), and a strategy language for building complex transformations out of component transformations and conditions. The details of the Morpheus syntax are in the work [34] (and in the report [28]). Conceptually, for an optimization specified in Morpheus, the rewrite portion expresses the local transformation to be made, the condition characterizes the situations in which the optimization should be applied, and the strategy language allows us to build a combination of transformations out of collections of local ones. Morpheus is a special-purpose language for the transformation of CFGs, and as such is parameterized by aspects of CFGs, namely node names (π in Fig. 3), node contents (program basic block B in Sect. 3), and edge labels marking control flow (l in Fig. 3). Transformation specifications may mention aspects of CFGs concretely, but more generally, they use pattern variables that will be instantiated with control flow graph components in each specific application. We will use the term "expressions" to refer to patterns built from both concrete entities and metavariables (which will be instantiated with concrete entities when the transformation is applied). We use the term **metavariable** (range: a and b) to refer to the variables in the patterns and expressions in Morpheus transformations, as opposed to the concrete programming variables and memory locations that will be found in Fig. 3.

Fig. 6. Examples of simple code motion optimizations

In this paper, we use two kinds of simple code motion (SCM) optimizations as examples. The general strategies for them are shown as graphs in Fig. 6. Given a CFG C for a thread in a program μ, the left optimization in Fig. 6 locates (by a Morpheus condition expression) a basic block B of C, whose termination is a binary branching instruction and the two outgoing edges pointing to the two basic blocks B_1 and B_2 that have the same content and same outgoing edges. Then the left optimization changes the binary branching instruction in B to a non-conditional one, and also changes the edges of B to a single outgoing edge with a label **seq**. This is done by a strategy code in Morpheus with a sequence of graph transformations. Similarly, the right optimization first locates a basic block B of C whose termination is a binary branching instruction whose Boolean guard is always evaluated as **true** (by static rewriting). Then the optimization changes the binary branching instruction to an unconditional branching one **br**, and makes all of the outgoing edges of B point to the basic block indicated by the **true** branching of B.

$$\texttt{sameOutEdge}(a,b) \triangleq \texttt{stmt}(a) = \texttt{stmt}(b) \wedge \texttt{sameEdges}(a,b)$$
$$\vee \texttt{stmt}(a) = \texttt{stmt}(b) \wedge \neg\texttt{sameEdges}(a,b) \wedge \texttt{sameOutEdge}(\texttt{next}(a),\texttt{next}(b))$$

$$\texttt{leftOpt}(\pi) \triangleq \texttt{EXISTS } \pi_1 \ \pi_2.\texttt{SATISFIED\_AT } \pi.\texttt{sameOutEdge}(\texttt{next}(\texttt{yes},\pi),\texttt{next}(\texttt{no},\pi))$$
$$;\texttt{relabel\_node}(\pi,(\texttt{insts}(\pi),\texttt{br}));\texttt{move\_edge}((\pi,\texttt{no},\pi_2),(\texttt{seq},\pi_1))$$
$$;\texttt{move\_edge}((\pi,\texttt{yes},\pi_1),(\texttt{seq},\pi_1))$$

$$\texttt{rightOpt}(\pi) \triangleq \texttt{EXISTS } a \ \pi_1 \ \pi_2.\texttt{SATISFIED\_AT } \pi.\texttt{tem\_inst}(\pi) = a \wedge \texttt{eval}(a) = \texttt{true}$$
$$;\texttt{relabel\_node}(\pi,(\texttt{insts}(\pi),\texttt{br}));\texttt{move\_edge}((\pi,\texttt{no},\pi_2),(\texttt{seq},\pi_1))$$
$$;\texttt{move\_edge}((\pi,\texttt{yes},\pi_1),(\texttt{seq},\pi_1))$$

Fig. 7. Simple code motion transformations in Morpheus

Figure 7 contains the Morpheus formulas `leftOpt` and `rightOpt` defining the left and right compiler optimizations from Fig. 6. The `sameOutEdge` formula defines the predicate for checking if two statements are the same; and their children have the same outgoing edges or statements. a and b are two metavariables representing two nodes; the `stmt`(π) function gets the basic block represented by node π, and the `sameEdges` predicate checks if a and b have the same out going edges. `leftOpt` represents the left optimization in Fig. 6. It first searches a node π that has a binary branching instruction with two out going edges (defined by the `SATISFIED_AT` Morpheus strategy operation). The `next` function gets the outgoing node of π with a fixed edge label (`yes` or `no` in `leftOpt`). It does three actions: first, it replaces the termination of π with `br` (by the Morpheus `relabel_node` action); second, it changes the `no` edge of π to π_1 with the label `seq` (by the Morpheus `move_edge` action), and finally it exchanges the `yes` edge of π with the label `seq` (also by the Morpheus `move_edge` action). The `insts` function gets the instruction list in the basic block of π. The `rightOpt` formula implements the right optimization in Fig. 6. It is similar to `leftOpt`. The only difference is that it checks if the binary branching instruction in the basic block of node π has a Boolean guard that is always evaluated as `true` (by the `eval` function). The termination is retrieved by the `tem_inst` function, and the metavariable a represents the termination of π.

The semantics of Morpheus [32,34] is basically the implementation of a graph rewrite algorithm over the FOCTL style conditions. Given an optimization formula (like Fig. 7) and a program μ, for every CFG C for a thread in μ, the algorithm generates a set of new CFGs. It first locates a basic block node satisfying the condition φ defined in a `SATISFIED_AT` strategy operation; and then it does a series of actions that change the structure of the CFG based on the node, as with the `relabel_node` and `move_edge` actions in `leftOpt`.

Here, we have briefly introduced Morpheus and given examples of optimizations defined therein. We will introduce program semantics in the next section.

3.2 Example Language Semantics Under a Weak Memory Model

Here we discuss the operational program semantics for the language in Fig. 3 to support the proof in this section. The semantics is a bridge connecting single instruction semantics and a multi-threaded weak memory model. Figure 8 provides a taste of the instruction semantics, memory concurrency model, and

Domain

Time Points: $s, t \in T \subseteq \mathbb{N}$　　Registers: $\varphi \subseteq (\mathit{Var} \to \mathit{Val})$　　Heap Snapshots: $\gamma \subseteq (\mathit{Loc} \to (T \times \mathit{Val}))$

Thread-IDs: $\mathit{tid} \in \mathit{Tid} \subseteq \mathit{Tid}$　　　　　　　　　Dyanmic Block Number: $\mathit{Bn} \ni \overline{\pi} \triangleq (N \times N)$

Dyanmic Block Family: $\overline{\Pi} \subseteq \mathit{Tid} \to (N \times N)$　　　Action-IDs: $\mathit{Aid} \ni d \triangleq (\mathit{Bn} \times N)$

Semantic Function Types

Expression Semantics: $\mathtt{eval} \subseteq (\mathit{Exp} \times \varphi) \to \mathit{Val}$　　Inst Semantics: $\psi \subseteq (\mathit{Inst} \times \varphi \times \gamma) \to (\varphi \times \mathit{Act})$

Termination Semantics: $\eta \subseteq (\mathit{CInst} \times (\mathit{Var} \to \mathit{Val})) \to \mathcal{L}$

Example Instruction Semantics

$\psi(a := e, \varphi, \gamma) \triangleq (\varphi[a \leftarrow \mathtt{eval}(\varphi, e)], \tau)$　　　　　　　　Assignment Semantics

$\psi(a :=_{o_r} x, \varphi, \gamma) \triangleq (\varphi[a \leftarrow \mathtt{snd}(\gamma(x))], \mathtt{R}^x_{\mathtt{snd}(\gamma(x)), o_r})$　　　Read Semantics

$\psi(x :=_{o_w} a, \varphi, \gamma) \triangleq (\varphi, \mathtt{W}^x_{\mathtt{eval}(\varphi, a), o_w})$　　　　　　　　Write Semantics

$\eta(\mathtt{if}\ e\ \mathtt{then}\ \pi_1\ \mathtt{else}\ \pi_2, \varphi) \triangleq \mathtt{IF}\ \eta(\varphi, e) = 0\ \mathtt{THEN}\ \mathtt{yes}\ \mathtt{ELSE}\ \mathtt{no}$　　Binary Branching Semantics

Single-Threaded Memory Concurrency Model

Events: $\mathit{Ev} \ni ev \triangleq \mathit{Tid} \times \mathit{Aid} \times \mathit{Act}$　　　Execution Map: $\rho \subseteq T \to \mathit{Ev}$

Data Dependency: $\mathtt{dd} \subseteq T \times T$　　　　　　Data Dependency Family: $\mathtt{dds} \subseteq \mathit{Tid} \to (T \times T)$

Sequenced-Before Relation: $\mathtt{sb} \subseteq T \times T$　　Sequenced-Before Family: $\mathtt{sbs} \subseteq \mathit{Tid} \to (T \times T)$

Acquire Dependency: $\mathtt{acq}(T, \rho, \mathtt{sb}) \triangleq \{(s, t) \in T^2 \mid (s, t) \in \mathtt{sb} \wedge \mathtt{is\_read}(\rho(s)) \wedge \mathtt{is\_acq}(\rho(s))\}$

Release Dependency: $\mathtt{rel}(T, \rho, \mathtt{sb}) \triangleq \{(s, t) \in T^2 \mid (s, t) \in \mathtt{sb} \wedge \mathtt{is\_rel}(\rho(t)) \wedge \mathtt{is\_write}(\rho(t))\}$

True Program Order: $\mathtt{po}(T, \rho, \mathtt{sb}, \mathtt{dd}) \triangleq \mathtt{dd} \cup \mathtt{acq}(T, \rho, \mathtt{sb}) \cup \mathtt{rel}(T, \rho, \mathtt{sb})$

$\mathtt{single\_prop}(\mathit{Tid}, T, \rho, \mathtt{sbs}, \mathtt{dds}, \mathtt{rf}) \triangleq \forall (s, t) \in (\mathtt{rf} \cup \bigcup_{\mathit{tid} \in \mathit{Tid}} \mathtt{po}(T, \rho, \mathtt{sbs}(\mathit{tid}), \mathtt{dds}(\mathit{tid}))).\ s < t$

$\mathtt{sat}(\mathit{Tid}, T, \rho, \mathtt{sbs}, \mathtt{dds}, \mathtt{rf}) \triangleq \mathtt{single\_prop}(\mathit{Tid}, T, \rho, \mathtt{sbs}, \mathtt{dds}, \mathtt{rf}) \wedge \ldots$

Operational Program Semantics

Program Order Family: $\mathtt{pos} \subseteq \mathit{Tid} \to \mathtt{po}$　　Current Program Pointer: $\theta \subseteq \mathit{In\ Set} \times \mathit{In\ Set}$

Registers Family: $\Phi \subseteq \mathit{Tid} \to \varphi$　　　　　Heap Family: $\Gamma \subseteq \mathit{Tid} \to \gamma$

Program Pointer Family: $\Theta \subseteq \mathit{Tid} \to \theta$

Single Step Transition Function:

$\mathtt{trans} \subseteq (C, \mathit{Tid}, \overline{\pi}, \mathtt{po}, \mathtt{sb}, \mathtt{dd}, T, \rho, \varphi, \Gamma, \theta) \to (\overline{\pi}, \mathtt{po}, \mathtt{sb}, \mathtt{dd}, T, \rho, \varphi, \Gamma, \theta, \mathtt{rf})$

State Environment: $\omega \triangleq (\mathit{Tid\ Set}, \mathtt{pos}, \mathtt{sbs}, \mathtt{dds}, \overline{\Pi}, \Phi, \Gamma, \Theta, T, \rho, \mathtt{rf})$

State: (μ, ω)　　　Transition System: $(\mu, \omega) \xrightarrow{ev} (\mu, \omega)$

One Example Transition Rule:

$\mathit{tid} \in \mathit{Tid} \wedge \mathtt{pos}' = \mathtt{pos}[\mathit{tid} \mapsto \mathtt{po}'] \wedge \mathtt{sbs}' = \mathtt{sbs}[\mathit{tid} \mapsto \mathtt{sb}']\wedge \mathtt{dds}' = \mathtt{dds}[\mathit{tid} \mapsto \mathtt{dd}']$

$\wedge \overline{\Pi}' = \overline{\Pi}[\mathit{tid} \mapsto \overline{\pi}] \wedge \Phi' = \Phi[\mathit{tid} \mapsto \varphi'] \wedge \Theta' = \Theta[\mathit{tid} \mapsto \theta'] \wedge \mathtt{sat}(\mathit{Tid}, T', \rho, \mathtt{sbs}', \mathtt{dds}', \mathtt{rf} \cup \mathtt{rf}')$

$\wedge \mathtt{trans}(\mu(\mathit{tid}), \mathit{tid}, \overline{\Pi}(\mathit{tid}), \mathtt{pos}(\mathit{tid}), \mathtt{sbs}(\mathit{tid}), \mathtt{dds}(\mathit{tid}), T, \rho, \Phi(\mathit{tid}), \Gamma, \Theta(\mathit{tid}))$

$= (\overline{\pi}', \mathtt{po}', \mathtt{sb}', \mathtt{dd}', T', \rho', \varphi', \Gamma', \theta', \mathtt{rf}')$

$$\frac{}{(\mu, \mathit{Tid}, \mathtt{pos}, \mathtt{sbs}, \mathtt{dds}, \overline{\Pi}, \Phi, \Theta, \Gamma, T, \rho, \mathtt{rf})}$$
$$\xrightarrow{\rho'(\max(T'))} (\mu, \mathit{Tid}, \mathtt{pos}', \mathtt{sbs}', \mathtt{dds}', \overline{\Pi}', \Phi', \Theta', \Gamma', T', \rho', \mathtt{rf} \cup \mathtt{rf}')$$

Fig. 8. Language semantics with a weak memory model

operational semantics based on the language in Fig. 3. In Fig. 8, T is a downward closed natural number set of **time points** without 0, each of whose elements represent a "time" when an instruction executes in a program. We implement a heap snapshot (γ) as a function from a location to a pair: the pair is the time point of the most recent write to the location and the value in the location. In Fig. 3, we introduced the concept of basic blocks, nodes are numbers identifying basic blocks. We use a pair of natural numbers as a **dynamic basic block number** (Bn); the pair uniquely identify an executing basic block in a thread during an execution. For a program $\mu : \mathit{Tid} \to \mathit{CFG}$, we have a family of dynamic basic block numbers ($\overline{\Pi}$), one for each thread. In Sect. 2.2, we introduced an instruction number for each instruction in a basic block; it is represented by a natural number. Here, we name an **action-ID** as the combination of a dynamic block number $\overline{\pi}$ and an instruction number in the basic block indexed by the second argument of $\overline{\pi}$. Hence, it is clear that an **action-ID** can uniquely define an executing instruction in a thread.

At the instruction level, there are three semantic functions. The eval function (Fig. 8) is for evaluating an expression (*Exp*) in Fig. 3. It is a straight evaluation of each term of the expression, so we omit the detailed implementation here. The function ψ implements the semantics of an instruction (*Inst* in Fig. 3). It takes an instruction, a register map (φ), and a heap snapshot (γ), and produces a resulted register map and a memory action (*Act*) indicating the type of memory communication the instruction could bring. We show three cases for ψ in Fig. 8: the case when a normal assignment happens and ψ returns a τ action, the case when a read happens and ψ returns a read action, and the case when a write happens and ψ returns a write action. The function η implements the semantics of terminations. It takes a termination and registers, and returns an edge label. In Fig. 8, we show the semantics of a binary branching instruction.

The memory concurrency model is in the format of an axiomatic candidate execution model [1]. Here, we use a subset of the ATRCM model [27], which has been proved to be sound with respect to the C/C++ memory model defined by Lahav *et al.* [24] and the IMM model [41]. The basis of the model is an execution with a pair of time points T and a function ρ mapping T to memory events. By defining a set of binary relations and predicates on top of the pair, the model selects a valid set of memory executions from a set of candidate executions. If there is a pair (s, t) in one of the relations, the memory event $\rho(s)$ must happen before the event $\rho(t)$ in the execution. In Fig. 3, we also introduced actions (*Act*). A memory instruction produces a read/write action, while other instructions/terminations produce a τ action. Here we combine an action, thread-ID and action-ID, making a memory event (*Ev*). In the model in Fig. 8, for an execution, we assume that a family (sbs) of sequenced-before relations (sb) is given, one sb for each thread; and a family (dds) of data dependency relations (dd) is also given, one dd for each thread. A straight-forward algorithm for generating a sequenced-before relation for executing a CFG can be taken from the program text order of the CFG; also, a data dependency relation for a CFG execution can be produced by the traditional data-flow, alias, and control dependency analysis algorithms. Here we omit the details of these algorithms. In Fig. 8, we mainly introduce the single-threaded relations and predicates for the model. More details are in the report [28]. In a single thread, we assume that instructions can be executed out-of-order. We define a single-threaded program order relation (po) for each thread to restrict the out-of-order execution, to respect the program meaning. po is the union of the single-threaded data dependency (dd) relation, acq relation for acquire (acq) reads, and rel relation for release (rel) writes. In the definition of the relation for the acquire read instruction, we require no instruction sequenced-after the acquire read can be executed before the read; while in the relation for a release write instruction, no instruction sequenced-before the release write can be executed after it. These two relations can be better understood by the Roach Model in Fig. 5b. The single_prop predicate represents all single-threaded behaviors that an execution must satisfy. The predicate requires that any single-threaded po relation and the reads-from relation (rf) in an execution must not have a pair of time points (s,t), for which t happens before s. The sat predicate is the collection of all predicates that a valid execution must satisfy. It is detailed in the report [28], and includes the single_prop predicate.

The operational transition semantics in Fig. 8 is a combination of the instruction level semantics and memory concurrency model. It is represented as a labeled transition system whose states are pairs of programs (μ) and the state environment (ω), and whose labels are memory events. A state environment is a long tuple of a set of thread-IDs (Tid), a program order family (pos, one for each thread), a sequenced-before relation family (sbs), a data dependency family (dds), a current dynamic block number family ($\overline{\Pi}$), a registers family (Φ), a heap snapshot family (Γ) representing different views of the threads of the main memory, a program pointer family (Θ) representing the current executing instruction of each thread, a time point set (T), a ρ mapping, and a reads-from relation (rf). We show the top-most rule of the transition system in Fig. 8. This rule selects a thread tid, applies the one-step transition function trans to the state environment of tid, checks the result of the one-step transition to see if the accumulated result satisfies the predicate of the memory model (sat), and then moves forward to a new step via the memory event label $\rho'(\max(T'))$. The function max produces the maximum number in T'. We can retrieve the memory event by the max function because the trans function always creates a map entry in ρ from the maximum time point plus 1 to the current memory event. The detailed implementation of the trans function is found in the report [28]. It needs to finish several tasks as a one step evaluation for a thread tid with a CFG C. First, if its program pointer $\Theta(tid)$ points to the end of a basic block (no instructions left for execution), it selects a new basic block according to the edge information in C (applying function η to it with registers ($\Phi(tid)$) to get the edge label), and assigns a new dynamic basic block number with a new program pointer pointing to the top of the new block. In this case, trans also adds new relations of program order, sequenced-before, and data dependency to the existing relation sets inside the new basic block. Second, if $\Theta(tid)$ indicates that there are instructions in the basic block waiting for execution, an instruction is non-deterministically selected for execution (applying function ψ to it with registers ($\Phi(tid)$) and heap snapshot ($\Gamma(tid)$)) if the instruction satisfies the program order relation on the basic block. Third, for a step, trans also picks a new time point (the maximum number of the time point set T plus 1) to add to the set T, and assigns the new time point to a new memory event. The creation of the event is to combine the thread-ID tid, a newly generated action-ID (the action-ID is calculated by combining the dynamic block number with the instruction number), and a memory action calculated from the function ψ (if the instruction is a termination, we assume that the action is τ). Fourth, trans also generates a new rf pair if the action is a read, and modifies the memory snapshot by inserting the current time point and write value if the action is a write.

3.3   The PLS Proof over Morpheus Optimizations

We utilize the optimizations and the program semantics defined in the last two sections to prove the correctness of a simple code motion optimization (SCM) as a utility of PLS. We want to show that any compiler-optimized (by SCM) program in the language (Fig. 3) per-loc simulates its original unoptimized program.

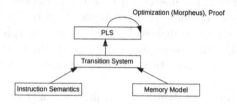

Fig. 9. Optimization proof with PLS

Figure 9 provides the structure of the optimization proof. In Sect. 2.1, we described how the PLS framework is parameterized by transition systems. Here we instantiate these systems with the same program transition system in Sect. 3.2. We then instantiate the states (ξ, σ and v in Fig. 4) as the form (μ, ω) (Fig. 8). For any two states in a LTS (LTS$_\Xi$, LTS$_\Sigma$, or LTS$_\Upsilon$), they have the same program μ. We also map the labels (α, β, and κ) to memory events ($\mathcal{E}v$). Given a label event ev, the property val is implemented as getting the value of the action in ev only if the action is a read or write; if it is a τ event, then the val answers $\perp$. type is implemented as a read for a read action in the event, as a write for a write action, and as τ for a τ action. loc is implemented as getting the memory location in the action of the event (if it is a τ event, then loc answers $\perp$). We keep the relation set eq the same as the one in Fig. 5a. Assume that a program μ is given, by applying the Morpheus optimization algorithm of SCM, we can rewrite μ as an optimized program μ'. For a fixed initial state ω, the PLS proof is to show that the LTS (LTS$_\Xi$) with the initial state (μ', ω) per-loc simulates the LTS (LTS$_\Sigma$) with the initial state (μ, ω), where there exists a per-loc simulation relation $\sqsubseteq$ for a finite set of locations Loc, such that (μ', ω) $\sqsubseteq$ (μ, ω). We formalize this result as Theorem 2, and the proof is done in Isabelle. The approach of the proof is first to prove a lemma with a similar structure but for only a single-threaded program with one CFG, and then prove Theorem 2 by using induction on the number of threads in the domain of the program.

Theorem 2. Let (μ, ω)(x) ($\xi(x)$ or $\sigma(x)$) be the value of location x at the ω's heap snapshot (Γ in Fig. 8) that belongs to the thread tid such that $\rho(\max(T)) = (tid, aid, ac)$ (ρ and T are the elements in ω in Fig. 8). For any program μ in the language in Fig. 3 with a finite domain (Tid has size n), for any π and any $tid \in Tid$, let $\mu'(tid) \in \text{leftOpt}(\pi)(\mu(tid))$ (or $\mu'(tid) \in \text{rightOpt}(\pi)(\mu(tid))$).

Given a non-empty finite set of memory locations Loc and a given state environment ω, there exists a per-loc simulation $\sqsubseteq$ that satisfies $\text{PLS}^{\text{eq}}_{Loc}(\sqsubseteq)$ and

$(\mu', \omega) \sqsubseteq_x (\mu, \omega)$ for all location x, and for all ξ and σ such that $\xi \sqsubseteq_x \sigma$ for a location x, $\xi(x) = \sigma(x)$.

Isabelle Formalization. The PLS framework, the combination of PLS and Morpheus, and the proof of the semantic preservation of a particular optimization on a specific language are achieved through an elegant combination of different **locale** structures [2] in Isabelle. An Isabelle locale structure is a polymorphic theorem structure that is parameterized by a list of Isabelle terms with proper types and a list of assumptions for these terms. Through a locale structure, a collection of theorems can be defined for a list of polymorphic terms, provided that the terms satisfies the assumptions defined for the terms. Users can later instantiate the locale structure to a specific instance of terms by proving the assumptions.

In the Isabelle Morpheus definition, we first define the syntax for the Morpheus specification language. We then define a polymorphic CFG locale structure, named Flow_graph, with all necessary elements in a CFG, such as a set of nodes, a set of edges, the start node and the exit node for the CFG with several assumptions on the CFG well-formedness. The Morpheus specification language semantics is also defined as a locale structure, named Morpheus_sem, which is built on top of the Flow_graph locale. Based on the CFG structure and assumptions provided by flow_graph, Morpheus_sem defines an inductive relation capturing the graph rewriting semantics of Morpheus based on the polymorphic CFG structure (flow_graph).

Before we define PLS in Isabelle, we define an LTS locale for a polymorphic labeled transition system (LTS) with four properties with some well-formedness assumptions. Three of them are listed in Fig. 2. The other one is the program text of the LTS described in Sect. 2.3. PLS is defined as a locale, named PLS, with two LTSs and an equation set eq as the input terms. The two LTSs are based on the LTS locale. In the PLS locale, we define a predicate as the one in Fig. 4, which defines the full PLS. When using PLS to prove language properties, one might be more interested in finding a PLS relation. To do that, we combine the Morpheus_sem and the PLS locales, as a new locale Morpheus_com, to build a PLS relation on top of the Morpheus semantics. In Morpheus_com, we build a new predicate sim_x^{eq} μ μ' steprel n, where μ and μ' are two programs (with the same thread domain), and μ' is the transformed program of μ through a specific optimization defined as an input term of Morpheus_com. steprel is a polymorphic function (defined as a term in a locale) to produce an LTS based on a program by omitting the implementation details of the LTS but only producing the four properties above. It takes in a program μ and a state ω, and outputs a label ev and a new state ω' transitioned from ω. The sim_x^{eq} predicate is valid if and only if the LTS with the program text μ, and an initial state ω (μ, ω), per-loc simulates (with the equation set eq) the LTS with the program text μ, and an initial state ω (μ, ω) in n steps.

As an example (in Isabelle) of defining the optimization in Fig. 7 and proving Theorem 2 on a language in Fig. 3, we first define its instruction and CFG syntax with a definition capturing the instruction level semantics of the language. We also define a memory model as a locale structure capturing the relaxed concurrency behaviors described in Fig. 8 (and the report [28]). We then define the program semantics as the LTS ($\rightarrow$) in Fig. 8 by instantiating the memory model locale with the language (Fig. 3) and adding more structures (like the program pointer family). Now, we instantiate the Morpheus_sem locale by the CFG syntax in the language, the Steprel locale (for instantiating the function steprel) by the LTS ($\rightarrow$), and the eq set as the one in Fig. 5a, and the compiler optimization term in Morpheus_sem as the one in Fig. 7. The proof of Theorem 2 is then turned to show that the predicate $\mathsf{sim}_x^{\mathsf{eq}}\ \mu\ \mu'$ steprel n is valid for arbitrary x in a location set Loc. We first show the case when $n = 1$ by proving for any one-step transition defined by the LTS ($\rightarrow$) for arbitrary x; then, we lift the proof inductively to arbitrary n step based on the one-step proof result.

4   Related Work

The PLS framework is a combination of three pieces of work: a simulation framework, a compiler-verification framework, and a weak memory model. Simulation/bisimulation were first introduced by Park [39]. Subsequently, much work was published that defined and proved properties about simulations [6,11–13,46]. Verifying compilers is one of the top problems in computer science since the work of McCarthy and Painter [36]. A good survey can be found in Dave's work [17]. Recently, one of the most significant achievements in verifying large-language compilers is Leroy's CompCert compiler [7,26]. Chlipala built verified compilers in Coq from λ-calculus to an idealized machine language [15] and from a small functional language to the language [16]. Lochbihler verified a whole-program compiler for multi-threaded Java [31]. Sevcik et al. built CompCertTSO [47], which adapted CompCert's correctness proofs to x86TSO to consider the compilation of racy C code. Our domain-specific language for specifying compiler optimizations in Sect. 3 is from Mansky and Gunter's [33,34].

Defining weaker memory models for multi-threaded programs than sequential consistency started with Lamport [25]. Batty et al. formalized the C11 model in the axiomatic candidate-execution model format, which was described in depth by Alglave et al. [1]. Vafeiadis et al. [44] found many other problems in Batty et al.'s model and proposed fixes. Lahav et al. [22,24] defined a comprehensive C++ model (RC11) based on all previous models, with extra fixes on Batty et al.'s model. Many previous papers [19,21,40] also proposed solutions for out-of-thin-air problems, while Podkopaev et al. [41] proposed a weaker model than C/C++ concurrency model including these solutions for out-of-thin-air problems. As we mentioned in Sect. 1, the distinguishing of out-of-thin-air behaviors in a program is essentially discovering syntactic similarities between programs that are semantically different. The solutions for out-of-thin-air problems can and should be attained through a well-engineered simulation framework like PLS because merging syntactically similar programs into a semantic memory model building results in incompleteness. Moreover, these models provide correct compilation schemes for a regular and small memory action and language set. It is non-trivial to extend their work to prove a compiler optimization in a large language with a weak concurrency model. Sometimes, extending their work to a little more features is problematic, such as the failing in proving examples about the promising memory model [21] and IMM memory model [41]; not to mention that some of the work has been found to contain problems in their model [41].

The first framework to combine a sequential consistency memory model, compiler proof framework, and bisimulation was CompCert [26]. There are two kinds of simulations in CompCert: the forward and backward simulations, which together describe the simulation relations between a program and its compiled/optimized program. It assumes that any execution of a program is classified into either an execution reaching an error state or a normal execution, and defines simulation relations differently for these two cases. In a normal execution, every element of the execution sequence is either a memory event or a program finishing point. In the framework, an execution sequence is neither split into different sub-traces nor distinguished based on memory location information. Moreover, CompCert's simulation framework does not recognize syntactic dependency on programs just like what PLS does with the eq set (Sect. 2.3). CompCertTSO [47] inherited CompCert's bisimulation framework. With minor extensions, they use the framework to prove program semantic preservations in a total store order memory model. Several studies proposed fixes to the bisimulation framework on different topics, such as divergence preservation [30] and creating a program-logic bisimulation framework for the termination-preserving refinement of concurrent programs [29]. All these works enlighten our development of PLS. PLS introduced in this paper is assumed to deal with the normal executions described in CompCert's simulation framework, and the error-state-reaching executions are assumed to be dealt with by the same mechanism as CompCert's framework. The main development and advantage of PLS in proving program semantic preservation properties in weak memory model has been introduced in Sect. 1 and 2.

5   Conclusion and Future Work

In this paper, we propose a new per-location simulation (PLS) relation that is simple and suitable for proving a compiled program preserves its original program semantics under a CFG-based programming language with a real-world, C/C++ like, weak memory model. PLS can be divided into two parts (Sect. 2.1 and 2.3). Based on the small language in Fig. 3, the concurrency model (a subset of weak memory model from C/C++ [22,24]) and program semantics in Sect. 3.2, we have shown the utility of PLS by proving that program semantics is preserved for a simple code motion optimization (defined in Sect. 3.1) for all possible programs. In the future we will use the PLS framework to prove program semantic preservation for complicated compiler optimizations with a complete weak memory model and a large real-world programming language like C/C++/LLVM.

References

1. Alglave, J., Maranget, L., Tautschnig, M.: Herding cats: modelling, simulation, testing, and data mining for weak memory. ACM Trans. Program. Lang. Syst. **36**(2), 7:1–7:74 (2014). https://doi.org/10.1145/2627752. http://doi.acm.org/10.1145/2627752

2. Ballarin, C.: Tutorial to locales and locale interpretation. In: Contribuciones cientíÂficas en honor de Mirian Andrés Gómez, 1 Januray 2010, pp. 123–140 (2010). ISBN 978-84-96487-50-5

3. Batty, M., Donaldson, A.F., Wickerson, J.: Overhauling SC atomics in C11 and OpenCL. SIGPLAN Not. **51**(1), 634–648 (2016)

4. Batty, M., Memarian, K., Nienhuis, K., Pichon-Pharabod, J., Sewell, P.: The problem of programming language concurrency semantics. In: Vitek, J. (ed.) ESOP 2015. LNCS, vol. 9032, pp. 283–307. Springer, Heidelberg (2015). https://doi.org/10.1007/978-3-662-46669-8_12

5. Batty, M., Owens, S., Sarkar, S., Sewell, P., Weber, T.: Mathematizing C++ concurrency. SIGPLAN Not. **46**(1), 55–66 (2011). https://doi.org/10.1145/1925844.1926394. http://doi.acm.org/10.1145/1925844.1926394

6. van Benthem, J.: Exploring Logical Dynamics. Center for the Study of Language and Information, Stanford, CA, USA (1997)

7. Blazy, S., Leroy, X.: Mechanized semantics for the Clight subset of the C language. J. Autom. Reason. **43**(3), 263–288 (2009). https://doi.org/10.1007/s10817-009-9148-3

8. Boehm, H.J.: Memory Model Rationales. http://www.open-std.org/jtc1/sc22/wg21/docs/papers/2007/n2176.html. Accessed 9 Mar 2007

9. Boehm, H.J., Adve, S.V.: Foundations of the C++ concurrency memory model. SIGPLAN Not. **43**(6), 68–78 (2008)

10. Boehm, H.J., Demsky, B.: Outlawing ghosts: avoiding out-of-thin-air results. In: Proceedings of the Workshop on Memory Systems Performance and Correctness, MSPC 2014, pp. 7:1–7:6. ACM, New York, NY, USA (2014)

11. Burkart, O., Caucal, D., Steffen, B.: Bisimulation collapse and the process taxonomy. In: Montanari, U., Sassone, V. (eds.) CONCUR 1996. LNCS, vol. 1119, pp. 247–262. Springer, Heidelberg (1996). https://doi.org/10.1007/3-540-61604-7_59

12. Caucal, D.: On the regular structure of prefix rewriting. In: Arnold, A. (ed.) CAAP 1990. LNCS, vol. 431, pp. 87–102. Springer, Heidelberg (1990). https://doi.org/10.1007/3-540-52590-4_42

13. Caucal, D.: On infinite transition graphs having a decidable monadic theory. In: Meyer, F., Monien, B. (eds.) ICALP 1996. LNCS, vol. 1099, pp. 194–205. Springer, Heidelberg (1996). https://doi.org/10.1007/3-540-61440-0_128

14. Chakraborty, S., Vafeiadis, V.: Formalizing the concurrency semantics of an LLVM fragment. In: Proceedings of the 2017 International Symposium on Code Generation and Optimization, CGO 2017, pp. 100–110. IEEE Press, Piscataway, NJ, USA (2017). http://dl.acm.org/citation.cfm?id=3049832.3049844

15. Chlipala, A.: A certified type-preserving compiler from lambda calculus to assembly language. SIGPLAN Not. **42**(6), 54–65 (2007)

16. Chlipala, A.: A verified compiler for an impure functional language. SIGPLAN Not. **45**(1), 93–106 (2010)

17. Dave, M.A.: Compiler verification: a bibliography. SIGSOFT Softw. Eng. Notes **28**(6), 2–2 (2003)

18. Dodds, M., Batty, M., Gotsman, A.: C/C++ causal cycles confound composition-ality. TinyToCS **2** (2013). http://tinytocs.org/vol2/papers/tinytocs2-dodds.pdf

19. Jeffrey, A., Riely, J.: On thin air reads towards an event structures model of relaxed memory. In: Proceedings of the 31st Annual ACM/IEEE Sympo-sium on Logic in Computer Science, LICS 2016, pp. 759–767. ACM, New York, NY, USA (2016). https://doi.org/10.1145/2933575.2934536. http://doi.acm.org/10.1145/2933575.2934536

20. Kalvala, S., Warburton, R., Lacey, D.: Program transformations using temporal logic side conditions. ACM Trans. Program. Lang. Syst. **31**, 1–48 (2009). https://doi.org/10.1145/1516507.1516509

21. Kang, J., Hur, C.K., Lahav, O., Vafeiadis, V., Dreyer, D.: A promising semantics for relaxed-memory concurrency. SIGPLAN Not. **52**(1), 175–189 (2017). https://doi.org/10.1145/3093333.3009850. http://doi.acm.org/10.1145/3093333.3009850

22. Lahav, O., Giannarakis, N., Vafeiadis, V.: Taming release-acquire consistency. SIGPLAN Not. **51**(1), 649–662 (2016). https://doi.org/10.1145/2914770.2837643. http://doi.acm.org/10.1145/2914770.2837643

23. Lahav, O., Vafeiadis, V.: Owicki-Gries reasoning for weak memory models. In: Halldórsson, M.M., Iwama, K., Kobayashi, N., Speckmann, B. (eds.) ICALP 2015. LNCS, vol. 9135, pp. 311–323. Springer, Heidelberg (2015). https://doi.org/10.1007/978-3-662-47666-6_25

24. Lahav, O., Vafeiadis, V., Kang, J., Hur, C.K., Dreyer, D.: Repairing sequential consistency in C/C++ 11. SIGPLAN Not. **52**(6), 618–632 (2017). https://doi.org/10.1145/3140587.3062352. http://doi.acm.org/10.1145/3140587.3062352

25. Lamport, L.: How to make a multiprocessor computer that correctly executes mul-tiprocess programs. IEEE Trans. Comput. **28**(9), 690–691 (1979)

26. Leroy, X.: A formally verified compiler back-end. J. Autom. Reason. **43**(4), 363–446 (2009). https://doi.org/10.1007/s10817-009-9155-4

27. Li, L., Gunter, E.: The axiomatic timed relaxed memory model (2019).https://github.com/liyili2/timed-relaxed-memory-model

28. Li, L., Gunter, E.L.: Per-location simulation – appendix. Technical report, Depart-ment of Computer Science, University of Illinois at Urbana-Champaign (2020). https://github.com/liyili2/timed-relaxed-memory-model/PLS

29. Liang, H., Feng, X., Shao, Z.: Compositional verification of termination-preserving refinement of concurrent programs. In: Proceedings of the Joint Meeting of the Twenty-Third EACSL Annual Conference on Computer Science Logic (CSL) and the Twenty-Ninth Annual ACM/IEEE Symposium on Logic in Computer Science (LICS), CSL-LICS '14, pp. 65:1–65:10. ACM, New York, NY, USA (2014). https://doi.org/10.1145/2603088.2603123. http://doi.acm.org/10.1145/2603088.2603123

30. Liu, X., Yu, T., Zhang, W.: Analyzing divergence in bisimulation semantics. SIGPLAN Not. **52**(1), 735–747 (2017). https://doi.org/10.1145/3093333.3009870. http://doi.acm.org/10.1145/3093333.3009870

31. Lochbihler, A.: Mechanising a type-safe model of multithreaded java with a verified compiler. J. Autom. Reason. **61**(1), 243–332 (2018)

32. Mansky, W., Garbuzov, D., Zdancewic, S.: An axiomatic specification for sequen-tial memory models. In: Kroening, D., Păsăreanu, C.S. (eds.) CAV 2015. LNCS, vol. 9207, pp. 413–428. Springer, Cham (2015). https://doi.org/10.1007/978-3-319-21668-3_24

33. Mansky, W., Gunter, E.: A framework for formal verification of compiler optimiza-tions. In: Kaufmann, M., Paulson, L.C. (eds.) ITP 2010. LNCS, vol. 6172, pp. 371–386. Springer, Heidelberg (2010). https://doi.org/10.1007/978-3-642-14052-5_26

34. Mansky, W., Gunter, E.L., Griffith, D., Adams, M.D.: Specifying and executing optimizations for generalized control flow graphs. Sci. Comput. Program. **130**, 2–23 (2016). https://doi.org/10.1016/j.scico.2016.06.003

35. Manson, J., Pugh, W., Adve, S.V.: The java memory model. SIGPLAN Not. **40**(1), 378–391 (2005). https://doi.org/10.1145/1047659.1040336

36. Mccarthy, J., Painter, J.: Correctness of a compiler for arithmetic expressions, pp. 33–41. American Mathematical Society (1967)

37. Meshman, Y., Rinetzky, N., Yahav, E.: Pattern-based synthesis of synchronization for the C++ memory model. In: Proceedings of the 15th Conference on Formal Methods in Computer-Aided Design. FMCAD 2015, pp. 120–127. FMCAD Inc., Austin, TX (2015)

38. Norris, B., Demsky, B.: Cdschecker: checking concurrent data structures written with C/C++ atomics. SIGPLAN Not. **48**(10), 131–150 (2013)

39. Park, D.: Concurrency and automata on infinite sequences. In: Deussen, P. (ed.) GI-TCS 1981. LNCS, vol. 104, pp. 167–183. Springer, Heidelberg (1981). https://doi.org/10.1007/BFb0017309

40. Pichon-Pharabod, J., Sewell, P.: A concurrency semantics for relaxed atomics that permits optimisation and avoids thin-air executions. SIGPLAN Not. **51**(1), 622–633 (2016)

41. Podkopaev, A., Lahav, O., Vafeiadis, V.: Bridging the gap between programming languages and hardware weak memory models. Proc. ACM Program. Lang. **3**(POPL), 69:1–69:31 (2019). https://doi.org/10.1145/3290382. http://doi.acm.org/10.1145/3290382

42. Vafeiadis, V., Balabonski, T., Chakraborty, S., Morisset, R., Nardelli, F.Z.: Common compiler optimisations are invalid in the C11 memory model and what we can do about it. In: Rajamani, S.K., Walker, D. (eds.) Proceedings of the 42nd Annual ACM SIGPLAN-SIGACT Symposium on Principles of Programming Languages, POPL 2015, Mumbai, India, 15–17 January 2015, pp. 209–220. ACM (2015). https://doi.org/10.1145/2676726.2676995

43. Vafeiadis, V., Balabonski, T., Chakraborty, S., Morisset, R., Zappa Nardelli, F.: Common compiler optimisations are invalid in the C11 memory model and what we can do about it. SIGPLAN Not. **50**(1), 209–220 (2015). https://doi.org/10.1145/2775051.2676995. http://doi.acm.org/10.1145/2775051.2676995

44. Vafeiadis, V., Balabonski, T., Chakraborty, S., Morisset, R., Zappa Nardelli, F.: Common compiler optimisations are invalid in the C11 memory model and what we can do about it. SIGPLAN Not. **50**(1), 209–220 (2015)

45. Vafeiadis, V., Narayan, C.: Relaxed separation logic: a program logic for C11 concurrency. SIGPLAN Not. **48**(10), 867–884 (2013). https://doi.org/10.1145/2544173.2509532. http://doi.acm.org/10.1145/2544173.2509532

46. Van Benthem, J.: Correspondence Theory, pp. 197–247. Springer, Netherlands (1984). https://doi.org/10.1007/978-94-009-6259-0_4

47. Ševčík, J., Vafeiadis, V., Zappa Nardelli, F., Jagannathan, S., Sewell, P.: CompCertTSO: A Verified Compiler for Relaxed-Memory Concurrency. J. ACM **60**(3), 22:1–22:50 (2013). https://doi.org/10.1145/2487241.2487248. http://doi.acm.org/10.1145/2487241.2487248

Verification and Timed Systems

Sampling Distributed Schedulers
for Resilient Space Communication

Pedro R. D'Argenio[1,2,3], Juan A. Fraire[1,2,3], and Arnd Hartmanns[4(✉)]

^{1} CONICET, Córdoba, Argentina
^{2} Saarland University, Saarbrücken, Germany
^{3} Universidad Nacional de Córdoba, Córdoba, Argentina
^{4} University of Twente, Enschede, The Netherlands
a.hartmanns@utwente.nl

Abstract. We consider routing in delay-tolerant networks like satellite constellations with known but intermittent contacts, random message loss, and resource-constrained nodes. Using a Markov decision process model, we seek a forwarding strategy that maximises the probability of delivering a message given a bound on the network-wide number of message copies. Standard probabilistic model checking would compute strategies that use global information, which are not implementable since nodes can only act on local data. In this paper, we propose notions of distributed schedulers and good-for-distributed-scheduling models to formally describe an implementable and practically desirable class of strategies. The schedulers consist of one sub-scheduler per node whose input is limited to local information; good models additionally render the ordering of independent steps irrelevant. We adapt the lightweight scheduler sampling technique in statistical model checking to work for distributed schedulers and evaluate the approach, implemented in the MODEST TOOLSET, on a realistic satellite constellation and contact plan.

1 Introduction

There is an increasing commercial and scientific interest in deploying large-scale satellite networks in low-Earth orbit (LEO) to collect and distribute information [4]. Real-time access to data is, however, only feasible when many satellites align to form a chain of links between a (remote) destination source or destination and a ground station. This vision favours mega-constellations; e.g. SpaceX's Starlink is composed of 12,000 satellites [26]. A different and more sustainable approach is to relax the real-time constraint and leverage the store-carry-and-forward principle where nodes store received messages for later forwarding to other nodes in the network, once a communication window—a contact—appears. This gives rise to a *delay-tolerant network* (DTN) [19]. Originally intended for

---

The authors are listed alphabetically. This work was supported by ANPCyT PICT-2017-3894 (RAFTSys), ERC grant 695614 (POWVER), NWO VENI grant no. 639.021.754, and SeCyT project 33620180100354CB (ARES).

R. Lee et al. (Eds.): NFM 2020, LNCS 12229, pp. 291–310, 2020.
https://doi.org/10.1007/978-3-030-55754-6_17

interplanetary networks [16], the DTN architecture has been identified as a disruptive approach for LEO constellations which allows for a better utilisation of communication opportunities [17]. In DTN, there is no upper bound on the propagation delay, and no expectation of continuous or bi-directional end-to-end connectivity. While DTN satellite constellations do not work for e.g. voice services, they can network Earth observation and high-latency data service missions. In particular, they can utilise slower inter-satellite links by advance forwarding [28], adapt transmission schedules to limited battery conditions [31], work with constrained spacecraft antennas and subsystem architectures [32], and tailor communication resources to fit mission traffic and routes [33,34]. Ultimately, the DTN approach enables sparse topologies of fewer and cheaper satellites [30].

A *contact* is the opportunity to establish a temporal communication link. As a DTN node's network state information may be inaccurate or obsolete, traditional Internet routing schemes cannot be used. Space DTN routing approaches (both near-Earth and deep-space) thus seek to exploit the *a priori* knowledge of contacts: inter-satellite and satellite-to-ground contacts can be precomputed based on the orbital elements and communication parameters. The result is a *contact plan* [27]. We visualise a simple plan for four satellites—nodes N_1 through N_4—

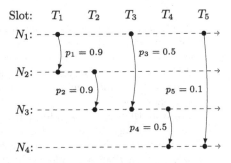

Fig. 1. Abstract uncertain contact plan

in Fig. 1. A bent vertical arrow indicates a contact from the arrow's origin to its target node. We abstract real time into discrete time slots T_1 through T_5; actual contact plans would show actual time intervals of varying durations (and potentially overlapping) with up to sub-second precision. Contact plans describe the expected network connectivity over time. They are the input for centralised or distributed DTN routing procedures. Existing solutions turn contact plans into e.g. time-expanded graphs [53] or contact graphs [5] on which routing calculations can be performed efficiently. Contact graphs have notably been validated by technological demonstrations in orbit [45,54].

In practice, the actual contacts may differ from the original plan due to failures or incomplete/inaccurate knowledge at the time the plan was computed. Space DTN in particular face fault-prone nodes [29], interference-sensitive communication links [52], and inaccurate orbit determination and station keeping procedures [39]. We thus need *uncertain contact plans* where contacts may fail for various reasons. Based on statistical data, we can annotate every contact with its success probability. In Fig. 1, we use probabilities p_1 through p_5 for illustration. Given an uncertain contact plan, we would then like to find a routing strategy that maximises the probability that the message is delivered to its destination. To increase that probability, we can allow *copies* of the message that propagate along different paths. However, as typical DTN satellites have limited resources, we also want to bound the number of copies. Existing routing schemes only perform well under perfectly known or fully unknown contact plans [29,49], leaving significant room for improvement for uncertain contact plan routing.

The routing problem in uncertain contact graphs with bounded copies matches very well with the modelling capabilities of Markov decision processes (MDP) [50]. They combine discrete probabilistic choices as in discrete-time Markov chains, which can represent contact failures, with nondeterministic choices as in Kripke structures [7], which can represent the routing options. Given an MDP model, we can use probabilistic model checking (PMC) [6] to determine the routing strategy (corresponding to the *scheduler* in PMC) with the highest probability for eventual message delivery. Raverta et al. [51] recently used this approach with optimisations that exploit the structure of the DTN routing models. However, PMC computes *global-information* schedulers, which take the local states of *all* nodes into account to make the optimal decision; they are thus *unimplementable*.

Example 1. In the contact plan of Fig. 1, assume we can send one message per slot. The highest-probability route from N_1 to N_4 is N_1-N_2-N_3-N_4 (in slots T_1, T_2, and T_4, with probability 0.405). The second-best is N_1-N_3-N_4 (in T_3 and T_4, $p = 0.25$). Sending directly from N_1 to N_4 is least reliable. If N_1 starts with two copies of the message, then the first should be sent to N_2 in T_1. In slot T_3, N_1 can then either try to send the remaining copy to N_3, or keep it for slot T_5. We will show in Sect. 2 that the best choice for <u>node N_1</u> computed by PMC is to send in T_3 iff <u>node N_3</u> does not already have a copy of the message, i.e. if communication in slot T_1 or T_2 failed. In a space DTN, N_1 *cannot know this!*

PMC is thus not well suited for space DTN routing. The underlying problem of applying PMC to distributed systems was recognised almost 20 years ago [3,21,35], and led to the development of the notion of *(strongly) distributed schedulers* [35,36] that only act on locally observable information. However, depending on the exact formalism and definition used, PMC for these schedulers is undecidable [35] in general, and NP-hard in the memoryless case [2,36].

In this paper, we propose to use statistical model checking (SMC) [44,56] with lightweight scheduler sampling (LSS) [48] in place of PMC to obtain routing strategies with a high probability for message delivery. Our contributions are (1) a modern and practical definition of distributed schedulers and models (in Sect. 3) appropriate for the space DTN setting that matches the compositional state-based modelling approach with undirected synchronisation common to today's probabilistic modelling languages [9,14,40,46] and tools [24,41,43,46]; (2) an adaptation and implementation of SMC with LSS for distributed schedulers (in Sect. 4), and (3) a modelling pattern and SMC-based analysis toolchain for routing in space DTN with uncertain contact plans (in Sect. 5). We start (in Sect. 2) with a simplified but complete definition of the compositional MDP formalism that underpins our approach, introducing a detailed model for Fig. 1 along the way. We end (in Sect. 5) with an experimental evaluation of our new technique on a realistic satellite constellation model and contact plan.

2   Scheduling in Markov Decision Processes

Preliminaries. $\mathbb{Z}$ is the set of integer numbers. We write $[a, b]$ for the real interval $\{x \in \mathbb{R} \mid a \leq x \leq b\}$. Given a set S, its powerset is 2^S. A probability distribution over S is a function $\mu\colon S \to [0, 1]$ with countable support $spt(\mu) \overset{\text{def}}{=} \{s \in S \mid \mu(s) > 0\}$ and $\sum_{s \in spt(\mu)} \mu(s) = 1$. $Dist(S)$ is the set of all probability distributions over S. We write $\{x_1 \mapsto y_1, \dots\}$ for the function that maps each x_i to y_i, and if necessary implicitly maps to 0 all other x. Thus we can e.g. write $\{s \mapsto 1\}$ for the *Dirac distribution* that assigns probability 1 to s. For a tuple $t = \langle y_1, \dots, y_n \rangle$, $t[i] \overset{\text{def}}{=} y_i$ is its i-th component.

Definition 1. *A* Markov decision process *(MDP) is a tuple* $M = \langle S, s_I, A, T \rangle$ *where S is a finite set of* states *with initial state $s_I \in S$, A is a finite set of* actions, *and $T\colon S \to 2^{A \times Dist(S)}$ is the transition* function *with $T(s) \neq \varnothing$ for all $s \in S$. The set of all* transitions *is $Tr(M) \overset{\text{def}}{=} \cup_{s \in S} T(s)$; it must be finite.*

We also write $s \xrightarrow{a}_T \mu$ for $\langle a, \mu \rangle \in T(s)$, and may omit the $_T$ subscript. An element of $spt(\mu)$ is a *branch* of transition $s \xrightarrow{a}_T \mu$. To leave a state, we first choose a transition, then select the next state probabilistically among its branches. An MDP with $\forall s\colon |T(s)| = 1$ is a *discrete-time Markov chain* (DTMC). We draw MDP as shown above on the right: this MDP has three states

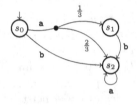

with $s_I = s_0$, four transitions, and five branches. For transitions with a single branch, we omit the dot and probability 1. We have $s_0 \xrightarrow{a} \{s_1 \mapsto \frac{1}{3}, s_2 \mapsto \frac{2}{3}\}$.

Modelling with MDP directly is cumbersome; we instead use a higher-level modelling language like MODEST [9, 40] that extends MDP with discrete variables and parallel composition. Given a set of (integer-valued) *variables* X, let $Val_X \overset{\text{def}}{=} X \to \mathbb{Z}$ be their *valuations*. Let Bxp_X and Ixp_X contain all Boolean and integer *expressions* over the variables in X, respectively. We omit $_X$ subscripts if clear from the context. For $e \in Bxp$ ($e \in Ixp$), let $v(e) \in \{true, false\}$ ($v(e) \in \mathbb{Z}$) be the value of e in $v \in Val$. Finally, let $Upd \overset{\text{def}}{=} X \mapsto Ixp$ be the set of *updates* that map each variable to an expression determining the value assigned to it.

Definition 2. *An* MDP with variables *(VMDP) is a tuple* $M = \langle Loc, \ell_I, A, X, x_I, E \rangle$ *where Loc is a set of* locations *with initial location $\ell_I \in Loc$, A is a set of* actions, *X is a set of* variables *with initial values given by $x_I \in Val$, and $E\colon Loc \to 2^{Bxp \times A \times Dist(Upd \times Loc)}$ is the edge* function. *All sets must be finite.*

We write $s \xrightarrow{g,a}_E \nu$ for $\langle g, a, \nu \rangle \in E(\ell)$, and may omit the $_E$ subscript. An edge in a VMDP has a *guard* g that determines whether the edge is *enabled*. A branch of an edge carries an update u that changes the variables' values. Formally:

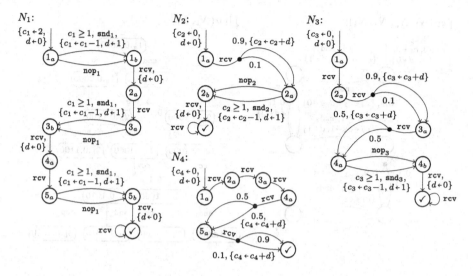

Fig. 2. Four VMDP modelling the nodes of the example contact plan

Definition 3. *Given a VMDP* $M = \langle Loc, \ell_I, A, X, x_I, E \rangle$, *its semantics is the MDP* $[\![M]\!] \stackrel{\text{def}}{=} \langle Loc \times Val, \langle \ell_I, x_I \rangle, A, T \rangle$ *with* T *the smallest function satisfying*

$$\frac{\ell \xrightarrow{g,a}_E \nu \wedge v(g)}{\langle \ell, v \rangle \xrightarrow{a}_T \{ \langle \ell', v' \rangle \mapsto \sum_{\{u | u \in Upd \wedge v' = \{x \mapsto v(u(x))\}\}} \nu(\langle u, \ell' \rangle) \mid \ell' \in Loc, v' \in Val \}}$$

We must restrict to VMDP whose semantics is finite and deadlock-free.

Example 2. Figure 2 shows four VMDP N_1 through N_4 that model the nodes of Fig. 1. Every node has a variable c_i to track the number of message copies it owns. We write $x \leftarrow e$ for the mapping of variable x to value or expression e. In every slot where a node N_i can send, it has a choice between two transitions labelled $\mathbf{nop}_i$ (do not send) and $\mathbf{snd}_i$ (send one copy: decrement c_i, set d to 1). In a slot T_j where N_i can receive, it always tries to do so via action $\mathbf{rcv}$; this succeeds with probability p_j as given in Fig. 1. If the sender decided not to send, then a successful receive has no effect on c_i because d is zero. The *parallel composition* of these four VMDP models the entire contact plan, with the nodes synchronising on shared action $\mathbf{rcv}$ and exchanging data via shared variable d.

Definition 4. *Given two VMDP* $M_i = \langle Loc_i, \ell_{I_i}, A_i, X_i, x_{I_i}, E_i \rangle$, $i \in \{1, 2\}$, *a finite set* A *of actions, and a synchronisation relation*

$$sync \subseteq (A_1 \uplus \{\bot\}) \times (A_2 \uplus \{\bot\}) \times A,$$

their parallel composition *is*

$$M_1 \parallel_{sync} M_2 \stackrel{\text{def}}{=} \langle Loc_1 \times Loc_2, \langle \ell_{I_1}, \ell_{I_2} \rangle, A, X_1 \cup X_2, x_{I_1} \cup x_{I_2}, E \rangle$$

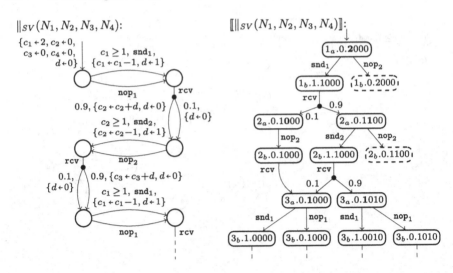

Fig. 3. Excerpt of the network of the node VMDP (left) and its semantics (right)

where E is the smallest function that satisfies the inference rules

$$\frac{\ell_1 \xrightarrow{g_1, a_1}_{E_1} \nu_1 \qquad \langle a_1, \bot, a \rangle \in sync}{\langle \ell_1, \ell_2 \rangle \xrightarrow{g_1, a}_E \{\langle\langle \ell'_1, \ell_2\rangle, u_1\rangle \mapsto \nu_1(\langle \ell'_1, u_1\rangle) \mid \langle \ell'_1, u_1\rangle \in spt(\nu_1)\}} \quad (ind_1),$$

$$\frac{\ell_1 \xrightarrow{g_1, a_1}_{E_1} \nu_1 \qquad \ell_2 \xrightarrow{g_2, a_2}_{E_2} \nu_2 \qquad \langle a_1, a_2, a\rangle \in sync}{\langle \ell_1, \ell_2\rangle \xrightarrow{g_1 \wedge g_2, a}_E \{\langle\langle \ell'_1, \ell'_2\rangle, u_1 \cup u_2\rangle \mapsto \nu_1(\langle \ell'_1, u_1\rangle) \cdot \nu_2(\langle \ell'_2, u_2\rangle) \mid \dots\}} \quad (syn),$$

plus a rule ind_2 for M_2 that is symmetric to ind_1, with $\dots$ in syn replaced by

$$\langle \ell'_1, u_1\rangle \in spt(\nu_1) \wedge \langle \ell'_2, u_2\rangle \in spt(\nu_2) \wedge u_1 \cup u_2 \text{ is a function.}$$

Inference rules ind_1 and ind_2 allow the individual VMDP to proceed <u>indepen</u>dently if allowed by *sync*; rule *syn* covers the case where they <u>synchronise</u> on a pair of actions. An element of *sync* is called a *synchronisation vector*; we also write $\langle a_1, a_2\rangle \mapsto a$ for vector $\langle a_1, a_2, a\rangle$. This flexible form of parallel composition can be generalised to more than two VMDP with longer synchronisation vectors. We refer to such a general parallel composition as a *network* of VMDP and write e.g. $\|_{SV}(M_1, M_2, M_3)$ for the network of M_1, M_2, and M_3, with the set of synchronisation vectors SV. The case in *syn* where $\nu_1(\langle \ell'_1, u_1\rangle) \cdot \nu_2(\langle \ell'_2, u_2\rangle) \neq 0$ but u_1 and u_2 assign different expressions to a shared variable (s.t. $u_1 \cup u_2$ is not a function) is a modelling error, and we do not consider networks of VMDP with such inconsistent assignments, or with inconsistent initial valuations x_{I_1} and x_{I_2}.

Example 3. Figure 3 shows an initial fragment of the network of the node VMDP N_1 through N_4 on the left. We omit location labels. Synchronisation vectors are

$$SV = \{\langle \mathtt{rcv}, \mathtt{rcv}, \mathtt{rcv}, \mathtt{rcv}\rangle \mapsto \mathtt{rcv}, \langle \mathtt{snd}_1, \bot, \bot, \bot\rangle \mapsto \mathtt{snd}_1, \dots\}:$$

In every slot, the nodes first independently make their choices of whether to send or not ($\mathtt{snd}_i$ vs. $\mathtt{nop}_i$); then they synchronise on $\mathtt{rcv}$ to perform their receive actions simultaneously. Updates are atomic, i.e. all right-hand sides are evaluated first, thus there is no order dependency in e.g. $\{c_3 \leftarrow c_3+d, d \leftarrow 0\}$. On the right of Fig. 3, we show a fragment of the network's MDP semantics. We write $\ell.v_d.v_{c_1}v_{c_2}v_{c_3}v_{c_4}$ for state $\langle\langle \ldots, \ell, \ldots\rangle, \{d \mapsto v_d, c_1 \mapsto v_{c_1}, \ldots\}\rangle$.

A *path* defines the behaviour of an MDP by resolving all nondeterminism and probabilistic choices. A *scheduler* resolves the nondeterminism only.

Definition 5. *Let M be an MDP as in Definition 1. A path π of M is an infinite sequence $\pi = s_0\, tr_0\, s_1 \ldots \in (S \times Tr(M))^{\omega}$ such that, for all $i \in \{0, \ldots\}$, we have $tr_i = \langle a, \mu\rangle \in T(s_i)$ and $\mu(s_{i+1}) > 0$. $\Pi(M)$ is the set of all paths of M. We write $\Pi_{fin}(M)$ for the set of all* path prefixes π_{fin} *ending in a state. The last state of π_{fin} is denoted $last(\pi_{fin})$.*

Definition 6. *Let M be an MDP as above. A (randomised, history-dependent) scheduler is a function $\sigma \colon \Pi_{fin}(M) \to Dist(Tr(M))$ such that $\forall s \in S\colon \sigma(s) = tr \Rightarrow tr \in T(s)$. We write $\mathfrak{S}(M)$ for the set of all schedulers of M. A deterministic scheduler is in $\Pi_{fin}(M) \to Tr(M)$; a (deterministic) memoryless scheduler is in $S \to Tr(M)$. A memoryless scheduler σ_{ml} defines a corresponding deterministic scheduler σ_{det} by $\sigma_{det}(\pi_{fin}) = \sigma_{ml}(last(\pi_{fin}))$ and a deterministic scheduler σ_{det} defines a scheduler σ by $\sigma(\pi_{fin}) = \{\sigma_{det}(\pi_{fin}) \mapsto 1\}$.*

If we "apply" a scheduler σ to an MDP M, it removes all nondeterminism and we obtain a DTMC $M|_{\sigma}$, whose paths can be measured and assigned probabilities according to the transitions' distributions. Formally, these probability measures over sets of paths are built via cylinder sets; we refer the interested reader to e.g. [25] for details. Given a set of goal states $G \subseteq S$ and a scheduler σ, we are interested in the probability of the measurable subset of paths of $\Pi(M|_{\sigma})$ including a state in G. We call the supremum (infimum) when ranging over all schedulers $\sigma \in \mathfrak{S}(M)$ the *maximum (minimum) reachability probability*. There is always a memoryless scheduler that achieves the supremum respectively infimum [8].

Example 4. For our example contact plan, we are interested in the maximum probability to reach a state where N_4 has at least one copy, and the corresponding scheduler. Expanding the MDP of Example 3, we can calculate that probability to be 0.493. The optimal choices are to send in slots T_1 and T_2; then in slot T_3,

- if we are in state $3_a.0.1000$ (i.e. if the first copy was lost on the way from N_1 via N_2 to N_3): send from N_1 to N_3, and send from N_3 to N_4 in T_4;
- if we are in state $3_a.0.1010$ (i.e. the first copy made it to N_3), do not send from N_1 to N_3 (since N_3 already has a copy and can only send to N_4 once), then send in both T_4 and T_5.

Thus the optimal choice of node N_1 in slot T_3 depends on whether node N_3 has a copy of the message or not. In a real distributed setting, N_1 cannot know this.

3 Distributed Scheduling

Example 4 showed that a scheduler that maximises the probability for eventual message delivery may need complete *global* information. In a distributed system like a satellite constellation, such a scheduler cannot be implemented; the satellites must decide whether to send based on their local state (here: their number of message copies c_i) only. This problem was initially studied with a focus on aspects of compositionality [21], ignoring algorithms except for a simple partial-information setting [2]. Giro et al. [35] defined *distributed schedulers*, for which computing and approximating optimal probabilities is in general impossible [35]. The formalisms of [2] and [35] do not provide for scheduling the interleaving of parallel components, i.e. deciding which component acts first in case both of them have an enabled edge in the same state. This gap was filled in [36] along with the introduction of *strongly distributed* schedulers. Though model checking remains undecidable in general, [36] proved that for memoryless schedulers it is "only" NP-hard. Consequently, no model checker as of today supports (strongly) distributed schedulers. The only prototype [18] was restricted to time-bounded reachability and suffered from exponential explosion in intermediate model sizes. Other prototype tools only provide overapproximations [37,38]. Our formalism of Sect. 2 is more expressive than those previously considered by allowing interleaving and information exchange via both synchronisation and (shared) variables.

In this paper, we restrict to a memoryless deterministic variant of distributed schedulers adapted to our formalism (Sect. 3.1), and we define a desirable characteristic of models that makes scheduling decisions about interleavings irrelevant (Sect. 3.2). We prefer memoryless distributed schedulers because history-dependent ones need infinite memory (which is again unimplementable), and using randomised schedulers would add additional unpredictability to the behaviour of the system, which is undesirable from the practitioner's point of view.

3.1 Simple Distributed Schedulers

Definition 7. *Given a network of VMDP $M = \parallel_{SV}(M_1, \dots, M_n)$ and $i \in \{1, \dots, n\}$, let $read(M_i)$ be the set of all variables that occur in the guards of edges of M_i or on the right-hand sides of assignments in the updates in M_i. A state in $[\![M]\!] = \langle S, s_I, A, T \rangle$ has the form $s = \langle \langle \ell_i, \dots, \ell_n \rangle, v \rangle$ where ℓ_i is the current location of M_i and $v \in Val_{\cup_i X_i}$. Then the M_i-projection of s is $s{\downarrow}_{M_i} \stackrel{\text{def}}{=} \langle \ell_i, v{\downarrow}_{read(M_i)} \rangle$ with $v{\downarrow}_{read(M_i)} \stackrel{\text{def}}{=} \{x \mapsto v(x) \mid x \in read(M_i)\} \in Val_{read(M_i)}$. Let $S{\downarrow}_{M_i} \stackrel{\text{def}}{=} \{s{\downarrow}_{M_i} \mid s \in S\}$ be the set of all projected states. Every transition $tr = s \xrightarrow{a} s'$ in $[\![M]\!]$ can be traced back to a unique (generalised) synchronisation vector $sv \in SV$ through the rules of Definitions 3 and 4. We say that M_i is involved in tr if $sv[i] \neq \perp$. We write $I_t(M_i)$ for the set of all transitions M_i is involved in. For a transition tr, $I_c(tr) \stackrel{\text{def}}{=} \{M_i \mid tr \in I_t(M_i)\}$ is the set of all components involved in tr, and for a set of transitions TR, $I_c(TR) \stackrel{\text{def}}{=} \bigcup_{tr \in TR} I_c(tr)$.*

Simple distributed schedulers now consist of an interleaving scheduler (to select the component to perform the next transition) plus a local scheduler per component that only sees the component's projection of the current state:

Definition 8. *A simple distributed scheduler for M as above is a tuple $\sigma_{sd} = \langle \sigma_I, \sigma_1, \ldots, \sigma_n \rangle$ of an interleaving scheduler $\sigma_I \colon S \to \mathbb{N}$ and n local schedulers $\sigma_i \colon S \to I_t(M_i) \cup \{\bot\}$ for $i \in \{1, \ldots, n\}$ s.t. $\sigma_I(s) \in \{i \mid T(s) \cap I_t(M_i) \neq \emptyset\}$, $\sigma_{\sigma_I(s)}(s) \in T(s) \cap I_t(M_i)$, and $s\!\downarrow_{M_i} = s'\!\downarrow_{M_i} \Rightarrow \sigma_i(s) = \sigma_i(s')$ for all $s, s' \in S$, $i \in \{1, \ldots n\}$. It defines a memoryless scheduler σ for $[\![M]\!]$ by $\sigma(s) = \sigma_{\sigma_I(s)}(s)$.*

Simple distributed schedulers differ from the partial-information setting of [2], and from hidden Markov models or partially-observable MDP, by combining multiple projections in one scheduler. They also differ from the (strongly) distributed schedulers of [35, 36] by hiding information in states but not admitting information disclosure via synchronisation (by virtue of being memoryless). As such, they match the nowadays standard state-based approach to probabilistic verification where transition labels are only used for synchronisation, as embedded in e.g. the JANI [14], MODEST [9, 40], and PRISM languages [46], and implemented in e.g. EPMC [41], the MODEST TOOLSET [43], PRISM [46], and STORM [24].

Unlike [18, 36], our formalism does not partition actions into inputs and outputs; thus every component involved in one of our (undirected) transitions can be chosen by the interleaving scheduler. Interleaving schedulers are problematic: They may disclose global information by scheduling transitions in certain orders (see [36]), the nondeterminism they deal with is in fact uncontrollable, and they would again be unimplementable in fully distributed systems.

3.2   Good-for-Distribution Models

In [36], the problem of information disclosure by the interleaving scheduler was solved by restricting to *strongly* distributed schedulers which do not reveal information in this way *by definition*. Since this is not a constructive approach, and since we cannot implement an interleaving scheduler anyway, we only create models where the interleaving scheduler is by construction irrelevant.

Definition 9. *A network of VMDP $M = \|_{SV}(M_1, \ldots, M_n)$ is good for distributed scheduling w.r.t. reachability of goal set G if in all states $s \in S$ of $[\![M]\!] = \langle S, s_I, A, T \rangle$ where $|T(s)| > 1 \wedge |\{i \mid T(s) \cap I(M_i) \neq 0\}| > 1$ we have*

$$\forall s \xrightarrow{a} s' \colon s \in G \Leftrightarrow s' \in G \ \vee \ \forall s \xrightarrow{a} s' \colon s \in G \Leftrightarrow s' \notin G, \tag{1}$$

$$\forall i \in \{1, \ldots, n\} \colon |I_t(M_i) \cap T(s)| > 1 \ \Rightarrow \ I_c(I_t(M_i) \cap T(s)) = \{M_i\}, \tag{2}$$

and $\quad s \xrightarrow{a} s' \ \Rightarrow \ \forall M_c \in \{M_1, \ldots, M_n\} \setminus I_c(s \xrightarrow{a} s') \colon s'\!\downarrow_{M_c} = s'\!\downarrow_{M_c}. \tag{3}$

In words, a network is good if in all states where the interleaving scheduler has a nontrivial choice among multiple components, (1) it cannot influence whether we directly move to a goal state, (2) no component has a local choice involving at least one synchronising transition, and (3) no transition can change variables that are visible to a component not involved in the transition.

Lemma 1. *For a good-for-distributed-scheduling network of VMDP M, fair interleaving schedulers σ_{I_1} and σ_{I_2}, and a set G of goal states, the maximum (minimum) probability to reach a state in G under σ_{I_1} is the same as under σ_{I_2}.*

An interleaving scheduler is *fair* if, on every cycle in $[\![M]\!]$, it chooses every available component at least once. This is a reasonable assumption in practice.

Proof Sketch. The conditions of Definition 9 only apply to states where the interleaving scheduler actually has a choice; in all others, σ_{I_1} and σ_{I_2} must coincide. So let s be a state where $\sigma_{I_1}(s) \neq \sigma_{I_2}(s)$ and let $TR_i = T(s) \cap I_t(M_{\sigma_{I_i}(s)})$ with $tr_i = s \xrightarrow{a_i} s_i' \in TR_i$ for $i \in \{1, 2\}$. Then $T(s_1') \supseteq T(s) \setminus TR_i$ and $T(s_2') \supseteq T(s) \setminus TR_i$, i.e. the choice of the interleaving scheduler cannot disable a non-local transition. This is because (a) condition 3 prevents the tr_i from changing the values of guards in non-involved components, and (b) condition 2 requires that, if more than one component is involved in tr_i, then $TR_i = \{tr_i\}$. The latter ensures that taking a synchronising transition cannot disable another synchronising transition by taking away a needed "synchronisation partner" (a transition with the same label as needed by the synchronisation vectors). Thus the restriction of $[\![M]\!]$ induced by an interleaving scheduler together with condition 1 and the fairness requirement is a (stronger) variant of a partial order reduction using ample sets as in [37] (with condition **A5'**).

The fairness requirement is trivially satisfied for acyclic models (modulo self-loops in leaf states) like our running example, or if we replace σ_I by σ_{uni}, the randomised scheduler that picks a component uniformly at random every time.

Example 5. Our running example from Examples 2 and 3 is good for distributed scheduling: in every state, either a single node internally decides between snd_i and nop_i or all nodes synchronise on rcv. In the former states, the interleaving scheduler has no choice, thus no conditions apply. In the latter states, conditions 2 and 3 are directly satisfied. The only way to move into a goal state is from a state of the latter kind, thus condition 1 also holds.

While simple distributed schedulers restrict local schedulers from *reading* certain variables, a good-for-distributed-scheduling model restricts component edges from *writing* to certain variables. A model checker can easily determine whether a model is good, but a precise syntactic check on the network-of-VMDP level is not possible. We can still use syntactic overapproximations, e.g. by requiring that locations with multiple outgoing edges have only internal edges not writing to shared variables, and that a shared variable may only be updated by synchronising edges involving all components that read the variable. Our running example does not satisfy this syntactic restriction due to the writes to d on snd_i-labelled edges. We solve this (in Sect. 5.1) by using a feature of MODEST and JANI that allows to specify *sequences* of atomic updates, moving the d-write assignments onto the rcv transitions and executing them before the d-read assignments.

4 Lightweight Distributed Scheduler Sampling

Since PMC for distributed schedulers is undecidable or computationally infeasible, we propose a different approach to find useful high-probability strategies: we combine statistical model checking (SMC) [44,56] with a new variant of lightweight scheduler sampling (LSS) [48] that samples only simple distributed schedulers. As our models are good for distributed scheduling by construction (see Sect. 5.1), only the satellites' local choices are relevant and we can replace the interleaving scheduler by uniformly random choices.

SMC with LSS. SMC is Monte Carlo simulation with formal models: perform several *simulation runs* using a pseudo-random number generator (PRNG) to resolve probabilistic choices according to the model's distributions, then return a statistical estimate and confidence for the probability of interest. As-is, SMC does not consider the optimisation problem over nondeterminism posed by MDP. LSS is to date the only extension of SMC that takes scheduling into account (in contrast to e.g. PRISM or UPPAAL SMC [23], which always use the uniformly random scheduler) and also preserves SMC's constant memory usage (in contrast to learning-based approaches like [11]). The basic idea of LSS is as follows:

1. Randomly select m 32-bit integers. Each of them is a *scheduler identifier* σ.
2. For each σ, perform standard SMC under the scheduler identified by σ.
3. Return the maximum (or minimum) result and the corresponding σ.

Due to the multiple tests, we need to adjust SMC's statistical evaluation [22,48]. Within step 2, when there is a choice between n transitions from state s, LSS concatenates the bit-vector representations of s and σ into $s.\sigma$, hashes the result into a 32-bit number $h = \mathcal{H}(s.\sigma)$, and picks the h mod n-th transition. $\mathcal{H}$ is deterministic so that σ defines a fixed memoryless scheduler. If $\mathcal{H}$ is also uniform (w.r.t. all bits of $s.\sigma$), then LSS uniformly samples memoryless schedulers.

The result of SMC with LSS is an *under*approximation (overapproximation) of the maximum (minimum) probability. It can thus e.g. disprove safety, or show schedulability—which is what we are interested in. Its efficiency—how large an m we need to get a good approximation—is determined by the probability of sampling a near-optimal scheduler, and thus strongly depends on the model at hand.

LSS for Distributed Schedulers. In contrast to PMC, LSS is easy to adapt to different classes of schedulers by changing the input to $\mathcal{H}$. In Algorithm 1, we show pseudocode for our adaptation to simple deterministic schedulers for MDP. We write $\mathcal{U}(\mu)$ for the pseudo-random selection by PRNG $\mathcal{U}$ of a value from $spt(\mu)$ according to the probabilities of μ. Line 5 implements the interleaving scheduler; we assume good-for-distributed-scheduling models and thus use uniform random resolution here, but could equally replace the line by $i := \mathcal{H}(\sigma.s) \bmod |T_i|$. Line 7 implements the local scheduler, whose input is restricted to the chosen component's projection of the current state. In line 8, we use $\mathcal{U}_{\mathrm{pr}}$ to pseudo-randomly

Input: Network of VMDP $M = \|_{SV}(M_1, \ldots, M_n)$ with $[\![M]\!] = \langle S, s_I, A, T \rangle$,
　　　　 goal set $G \subseteq S$, $\sigma \in \mathbb{Z}_{32}$, $\mathcal{H}$ uniform deterministic, PRNG $\mathcal{U}_{\mathrm{pr}}$.

1　$s := s_I$
2　**while** $s \notin G$ **do**　　　　　　　　　　　　　　　　// break on goal state
3　　**if** $\forall s \xrightarrow{a} \mu \colon \mu = \{\, s \mapsto 1 \,\}$ **then break**　　　// break on self-loops
4　　$C := \{\, j \mid T(s) \cap I_t(M_j) \neq \emptyset \,\}$　　　　// get active components
5　　$i := \mathcal{U}_{\mathrm{pr}}(\{\, j \mapsto \frac{1}{|C|} \mid j \in C \,\})$　　　　// select component uniformly
6　　$T_i := T(s) \cap I_t(M_i)$　　　　　　　　// get component's transitions
7　　$\langle a, \mu \rangle := (\mathcal{H}(\sigma.s{\downarrow}_{M_i}) \bmod |T_i|)$-th element of T_i　// schedule local transition
8　　$s := \mathcal{U}_{\mathrm{pr}}(\mu)$　　　　　　　　　// select next state according to μ
9　**return** $s \in G$

Algorithm 1. Lightweight simple distributed scheduler sampling

select the successor state according to the distribution determined by the scheduled transition. Line 3 terminates the simulation negatively if we find a state that only has deterministic self-loop transitions; this suffices for our space DTN models, but could be replaced by smarter loop detection or methods like [47,55].

We have implemented Algorithm 1 in MODES [12], the statistical model checker of the MODEST TOOLSET [43]. MODES is implemented in C#, freely available at modestchecker.net, runs on 64-bit Linux, macOS, and Windows, and is faster than other current general-purpose SMC tools [13, Section 7.1]. Its input languages are MODEST [9,40] and the tool-independent JANI model exchange format [14]. It provides both variants of line 5 discussed above, and implements corrected statistical tests as well as two-phase and smart sampling.

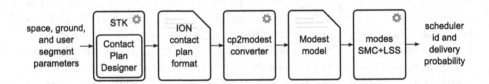

Fig. 4. Satellite DTN routing scheduling toolchain

5　Scheduling Satellite Communication

To apply our new LSS method of Sect. 4 to space DTN, we created the toolchain shown in Fig. 4. We use the STK tool by AGI [1] and the Contact Plan Designer plugin [27] to model the scenario and export the contact plan to a file in Interplanetary Overlay Network format (ION) [15]. This plan contains the precise real-time communication windows; we developed the Python CP2MODEST tool that, given such a plan, message source and destinations, and a bound on the number of copies, (1) abstracts the plan into the form of Fig. 1 with discrete non-overlapping slots,[1] and (2) creates a MODEST model representing a network of VMDP of the same structure as Example 2. We then run MODES with LSS for simple distributed schedulers to obtain a good scheduler and its probability. Compared to the previous PMC-based work [51], we not only generate guaranteed implementable schedules, but also support multiple message copies.

5.1 Modelling Satellite DTN

The model of Fig. 1 given in Example 2 uses unidirectional unreliable communication: for every contact, one node is predetermined as sender; if communication fails, the copy is lost. We also assumed that there is at most one contact and we transmit at most one copy per slot. The models generated by CP2MODEST keep the same structure, but assume bidirectional half-duplex communication, support multiple contacts per slot (including one node having a contact with multiple others; it then needs to choose with whom to communicate), allow sending multiple copies (to one node in one slot), and use either unreliable or acknowledgment-based communication. The latter allows the sender to determine whether a message was successfully received, thus in such models it will keep the sent copies in case of failure. Unreliable communication is a natural choice in deep-space networks, the original application of DTN, while acknowledgment mechanisms are possible and typical in LEO constellations.

```
1  process Node1(int(0..COPIES) copies) {
2    alt {                                      // slot 1: contact with node 2
3    :: nop1; rcv                                 // do nothing in this slot
4    :: when(copies >= 1) snd1to2_1;           // send one copy to node 2
5       rcv palt {
6       :0.9: {= data1 = 1, dest1 = 2, 2: copies -= ack2==1 ? 1 : 0 =}
7       :0.1: {= /* lost */ =} }
8    :: when(copies >= 2) snd1to2_2;          // send two copies to node 2
9       rcv palt {
10      :0.9: {= data1 = 2, dest1 = 2, 2: copies -= ack2==1 ? 2 : 0 =}
11      :0.1: {= /* lost */ =} }
12   :: rcv2to1;                                // listen for communication from node 2
13      rcv {= 1: copies += dest2==1 ? data2 : 0, 1: ack1 = 2 =}
14   };
15   rcv;                                       // slot 2: no contact
16   ... }                                      // three more slots of the same pattern
```

Listing 1. Excerpt of the MODEST code for node N_1 with a bound of 2 copies

The models created by CP2MODEST consist of one *process* definition per node. Listing 1 shows an excerpt of node N_1 in the plan of Fig. 1, but with acknowledgments and all mechanisms to support multiple contacts per slot in place. Like in the VMDP of Example 2, in every slot in which a node has a contact, we have a choice of action followed by a global synchronisation on action rcv. Here, in T_1, the choices are to (a) do nothing (line 3), (b) try to send one (line 4) or two

---

[1] The abstraction underapproximates contacts (it may only remove or shorten communication opportunities), so a strategy for the abstract plan is always implementable.

copies (line 8) to N_2, or (c) listen to N_2 (line 12). We use distinct actions for every choice to make it easier to trace the best scheduler's decisions later on. Global variable data1 takes the role of d of Example 2, but only for messages sent by N_1, and dest1 indicates the intended receiver—both of this is to support multiple contacts per slot. As mentioned at the end of Sect. 3.2, we moved these assignments onto the rcv edge to make the model syntactically good for distributed scheduling; assignments prefixed 2: are executed after prefix 1: which follow those with no prefix. The acknowledgment mechanism uses global variables like ack2 indicating from whom node N_2 successfully received a message. The sending node then reduces its copies count by that number. In slots without a contact, like slot T_2 for N_1, we just move to the next slot by a rcv together with the other nodes (line 15). Note that nodes cannot *create* copies; this is because they cannot know how many copies there are at other nodes and must not violate the global bound; we can let the initial node create as many copies as allowed w.l.o.g. since any number of copies can be transmitted in a slot.

5.2   The Walker Constellation

As a realistic case study, we propose a LEO satellite constellation in a Walker formation of three orbital planes each with four equally separated satellites. The constellation is thought to provide high-latency data service to ten isolated ground nodes randomly distributed around the globe. A ground station located in Córdoba, Argentina, provides an Internet gateway that the nodes access using DTN protocols. The ranges from ground station to satellites are set to 2000 km at a minimal elevation angle of 20° (mimicking a constrained antenna at the satellite). In turn, satellites can reach ground terminals at a distance of 1500 km at the same elevation angle. Figure 5 shows the ground track and a 3D visualisation of the constellation. Ground nodes (user terminals) are shown in red, the ground station in green, and satellites in cyan. The domes and cones over the ground nodes and under the satellites illustrate the communication ranges. The contact plan runs for 24 h from 01 Jul 2020 00:00:00.

5.3   Experiments

We applied our toolchain to the example contact plan of Fig. 1 and the Walker constellation described above, both with at most 2 message copies in the network. For the example contact plan with unreliable communication, we can easily determine the best simple distributed scheduler and its transmission probability by again expanding the MDP semantics of Fig. 3; the probability is 0.4645. Recall from Example 4 that global-information schedulers achieve probability 0.493. We can thus compare the probabilities computed by LSS with the actual values for distributed schedulers on this example. The state space of our model of the Walker constellation is still small enough for PMC, so we can compare the values obtained via PMC and LSS for global-information schedulers at least, but not for distributed schedulers due to the infeasibility of PMC in this case. Since the effectiveness of LSS depends on the rarity of near-optimal schedulers, we expect

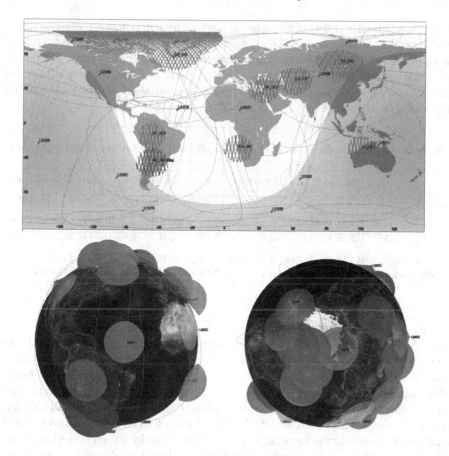

Fig. 5. Visualisation of the Walker constellation

to see a tradeoff between LSS for global-information and LSS for distributed schedulers: There are many more global-information schedulers than distributed ones. So even though the former may realise higher probabilities, LSS might only rarely find any good global-information scheduler, whereas it may often find a good distributed scheduler due to their more limited choices.

Our experiments ran on an Intel Core i7-4790 workstation (3.6–4.0 GHz, 4 cores) with 64-bit Ubuntu Linux 18.04. We used smart sampling [22] with a fixed number of initial schedulers m_0 equal to the per-iteration budget n_0. In iteration i, smart sampling performs $\lceil \frac{n_i}{m_i} \rceil$ simulation runs for each of the m_i schedulers, discards the "worst" half of the schedulers according to their current probability estimate, and moves to iteration $i + 1$ with $m_{i+1} = \lfloor \frac{m_i}{2} \rfloor$. We can thus cover a large number of schedulers with only $\approx \log_2(m_0) \cdot n_0$ simulation runs in total. We show the results in Table 1. We used the MODEST TOOLSET's MCSTA model checker for PMC and MODES as described in Sect. 4 for the SMC-LSS-m_0 runs. Due to the randomised nature of the experiments, we repeated each three times and report the average and highest maximum probability over the repetitions. Runtimes were at most 5 min, for the $m_0 = 100000$ setting, with distributed scheduler runs taking around 10% longer that those for global-information schedulers. We use the adaptive method of [20, Section III] for the statistical evaluation and request the probability for absolute error <0.0025 on the example and <0.005 on the Walker case to be 95%.

Table 1. Experimental results: average (highest) max. probabilities over 3 repetitions

model	PMC	SMC-LSS-1000		SMC-LSS-10000		SMC-LSS-100000	
	global	global	distrib.	global	distrib.	global	distrib.
example/unrel.	0.493	0.48 (0.49)	0.46 (0.47)	0.49 (0.49)	0.46 (0.47)	0.49 (0.49)	0.46 (0.46)
example/acks	0.505	0.49 (0.50)	0.46 (0.48)	0.50 (0.50)	0.50 (0.50)	0.50 (0.50)	0.50 (0.51)
walker/unrel.	0.438	0.03 (0.06)	0.21 (0.30)	0.10 (0.16)	0.30 (0.37)	0.26 (0.33)	0.37 (0.38)
walker/acks	0.734	0.36 (0.38)	0.47 (0.48)	0.38 (0.40)	0.54 (0.60)	0.45 (0.47)	0.54 (0.56)

We see that, on the example, both variants of LSS find respective optimal schedulers easily. With acknowledgment-based communication ("acks"), the optimal distributed scheduler curiously realises the same probability as the global one. We asked MODES to print traces under this scheduler identifier, and found that nodes N_1 and N_3 can collaborate to implement a strategy similar to the one of Example 4: In slot T_3, N_1 *always* tries to send to N_3. However, if N_3 already has a copy, it chooses nop3 in this slot; then N_1 does not receive an acknowledgment and gets to keep its copy for sending in T_5. While "sneaky", such behaviour could clearly be implemented in satellites, and it being found validates the correctness and applicability of our distributed LSS approach. On the Walker case study, the tradeoff described earlier comes into play: distributed-scheduler LSS consistently finds better schedulers, and more reliably finds them even for lower values of m_0, despite global-information schedulers being able to realise higher probabilities in principle. In particular, our new version of LSS consistently finds schedulers not too far from the maximum achievable with global information according to PMC—but its schedulers are guaranteed implementable.

6   Conclusion

We have developed new theory and tools to tackle the challenge of computing good and implementable routing strategies for satellite DTNs under uncertain contact plans, using formal methods technology. We have proposed a new, modern notion of distributed schedulers appropriate for the application, extended the LSS technique to work with this new notion, created a toolchain incorporating the new theory and technology, and applied it to a realistic case study. While LSS may be limited (e.g. by not being able to prove safety) in a general setting, we showed that it works very well for this application—which particularly benefits from the flexibility of LSS w.r.t. handling different scheduler classes. Once we found a good scheduler, it can be implemented in a satellite by a program that feeds its identifier, the current slot offset, and the number of local copies into a reimplementation of MODES' hash function. We plan to adapt other methods (e.g. [10]) to extract compact human-readable descriptions of the scheduler, too.

Data Availability.   All data generated in our experimental evaluation plus instructions to replicate the experiments are available at DOI 10.4121/uuid:6aa24e1a-3551-4073-b533-4ba6e408212d [42].

References

1. AGI Systems Tool Kit (STK). http://www.agi.com/STK
2. de Alfaro, L.: The verification of probabilistic systems under memory less partial information policies is hard. In: 2nd International Workshop on Probabilistic Methods in Verification, pp. 19–32. Technical report CSR-99-8, University of Birmingham (1999)
3. de Alfaro, L., Henzinger, T.A., Jhala, R.: Compositional methods for probabilistic systems. In: Larsen, K.G., Nielsen, M. (eds.) CONCUR 2001. LNCS, vol. 2154, pp. 351–365. Springer, Heidelberg (2001). https://doi.org/10.1007/3-540-44685-0_24
4. Alvarez, J., Walls, B.: Constellations, clusters, and communication technology: expanding small satellite access to space. In: 2016 IEEE Aerospace Conference, pp. 1–11 (2016). https://doi.org/10.1109/AERO.2016.7500896
5. Araniti, G., et al.: Contact graph routing in DTN space networks: overview, enhancements and performance. IEEE Commun. Mag. **53**(3), 38–46 (2015). https://doi.org/10.1109/MCOM.2015.7060480
6. Baier, C., de Alfaro, L., Forejt, V., Kwiatkowska, M.: Model checking probabilistic systems. Handbook of Model Checking, pp. 963–999. Springer, Cham (2018). https://doi.org/10.1007/978-3-319-10575-8_28
7. Baier, C., Katoen, J.P.: Principles of Model Checking. MIT Press, Cambridge (2008)
8. Bianco, A., de Alfaro, L.: Model checking of probabilistic and nondeterministic systems. In: Thiagarajan, P.S. (ed.) FSTTCS 1995. LNCS, vol. 1026, pp. 499–513. Springer, Heidelberg (1995). https://doi.org/10.1007/3-540-60692-0_70
9. Bohnenkamp, H.C., D'Argenio, P.R., Hermanns, H., Katoen, J.P.: MoDeST: a compositional modeling formalism for hard and softly timed systems. IEEE Trans. Soft. Eng. **32**(10), 812–830 (2006). https://doi.org/10.1109/TSE.2006.104
10. Brázdil, T., Chatterjee, K., Chmelík, M., Fellner, A., Křetínský, J.: Counterexample explanation by learning small strategies in Markov decision processes. In: Kroening, D., Păsăreanu, C.S. (eds.) CAV 2015. LNCS, vol. 9206, pp. 158–177. Springer, Cham (2015). https://doi.org/10.1007/978-3-319-21690-4_10
11. Brázdil, T.: Verification of Markov decision processes using learning algorithms. In: Cassez, F., Raskin, J.-F. (eds.) ATVA 2014. LNCS, vol. 8837, pp. 98–114. Springer, Cham (2014). https://doi.org/10.1007/978-3-319-11936-6_8
12. Budde, C.E., D'Argenio, P.R., Hartmanns, A., Sedwards, S.: A statistical model checker for nondeterminism and rare events. In: Beyer, D., Huisman, M. (eds.) TACAS 2018. LNCS, vol. 10806, pp. 340–358. Springer, Cham (2018). https://doi.org/10.1007/978-3-319-89963-3_20

13. Budde, C.E., D'Argenio, P.R., Hartmanns, A., Sedwards, S.: An efficient statistical model checker for nondeterminism and rare events. STTT (2020, under review). http://www.modestchecker.net/Publications/PDF/BDHS20-prelim.pdf
14. Budde, C.E.: JANI: quantitative model and tool interaction. In: Legay, A., Margaria, T. (eds.) TACAS 2017. LNCS, vol. 10206, pp. 151–168. Springer, Heidelberg (2017). https://doi.org/10.1007/978-3-662-54580-5_9
15. Burleigh, S.: Interplanetary overlay network: an implementation of the DTN bundle protocol. In: 4th IEEE Consumer Communications and Networking Conference, pp. 222–226 (2007). https://doi.org/10.1109/CCNC.2007.51
16. Burleigh, S.: Delay-tolerant networking: an approach to interplanetary Internet. IEEE Commun. Mag. **41**(6), 128–136 (2003). https://doi.org/10.1109/MCOM.2003.1204759
17. Caini, C., Firrincieli, R.: Application of contact graph routing to LEO satellite DTN communications. In: 2012 IEEE International Conference on Communications (ICC), pp. 3301–3305 (2012). https://doi.org/10.1109/ICC.2012.6363686
18. Calin, G., Crouzen, P., D'Argenio, P.R., Hahn, E.M., Zhang, L.: Time-bounded reachability in distributed input/output interactive probabilistic chains. In: van de Pol, J., Weber, M. (eds.) SPIN 2010. LNCS, vol. 6349, pp. 193–211. Springer, Heidelberg (2010). https://doi.org/10.1007/978-3-642-16164-3_15
19. Cerf, V., et al.: Delay-tolerant networking architecture. RFC 4838, RFC Editor (April 2007). http://www.rfc-editor.org/rfc/rfc4838.txt
20. Chen, J., Xu, J.: Sampling adaptively using the Massart inequality for scalable learning. In: 12th International Conference on Machine Learning and Applications (ICMLA), pp. 362–367. IEEE (2013). https://doi.org/10.1109/ICMLA.2013.149
21. Cheung, L., Lynch, N., Segala, R., Vaandrager, F.: Switched probabilistic i/o automata. In: Liu, Z., Araki, K. (eds.) ICTAC 2004. LNCS, vol. 3407, pp. 494–510. Springer, Heidelberg (2005). https://doi.org/10.1007/978-3-540-31862-0_35
22. D'Argenio, P., Legay, A., Sedwards, S., Traonouez, L.M.: Smart sampling for lightweight verification of Markov decision processes. STTT **17**(4), 469–484 (2015). https://doi.org/10.1007/s10009-015-0383-0
23. David, A., Larsen, K.G., Legay, A., Mikucionis, M., Poulsen, D.B.: Uppaal SMC tutorial. STTT **17**(4), 397–415 (2015). https://doi.org/10.1007/s10009-014-0361-y
24. Dehnert, C., Junges, S., Katoen, J.-P., Volk, M.: A Storm is coming: a modern probabilistic model checker. In: Majumdar, R., Kunčak, V. (eds.) CAV 2017. LNCS, vol. 10427, pp. 592–600. Springer, Cham (2017). https://doi.org/10.1007/978-3-319-63390-9_31
25. Forejt, V., Kwiatkowska, M., Norman, G., Parker, D.: Automated verification techniques for probabilistic systems. In: Bernardo, M., Issarny, V. (eds.) SFM 2011. LNCS, vol. 6659, pp. 53–113. Springer, Heidelberg (2011). https://doi.org/10.1007/978-3-642-21455-4_3
26. Foust, J.: SpaceX's space-Internet woes: despite technical glitches, the company plans to launch the first of nearly 12,000 satellites in 2019. IEEE Spectr. **56**(1), 50–51 (2019). https://doi.org/10.1109/MSPEC.2019.8594798
27. Fraire, J.A.: Introducing contact plan designer: a planning tool for DTN-based space-terrestrial networks. In: 6th International Conference on Space Mission Challenges for Information Technology (SMC-IT), pp. 124–127 (2017). https://doi.org/10.1109/SMC-IT.2017.28
28. Fraire, J.A., Burleigh, S., Finochietto, J.M.: Disruption-Tolerant Satellite Networks. ArtechHouse (2017)

29. Fraire, J.A., et al.: Assessing contact graph routing performance and reliability in distributed satellite constellations. Hindawi J. Comput. Netw. Commun. 2017, 18 p. (2017). Article ID 2830542. https://doi.org/10.1155/2017/2830542

30. Fraire, J.A., Madoery, P.G., Finochietto, J.M.: On the design and analysis of fair contact plans in predictable delay-tolerant networks. IEEE Sens. J. **14**(11), 3874–3882 (2014). https://doi.org/10.1109/JSEN.2014.2348917

31. Fraire, J.A., Nies, G., Gerstacker, C., Hermanns, H., Bay, K., Bisgaard, M.: Battery-aware contact plan design for LEO satellite constellations: the Ulloriaq case study. IEEE Trans. Green Commun. Netw. (2019). https://doi.org/10.1109/TGCN.2019.2954166

32. Fraire, J.A., Finochietto, J.M.: Design challenges in contact plans for disruption-tolerant satellite networks. IEEE Commun. Mag. **53**(5), 163–169 (2015). https://doi.org/10.1109/MCOM.2015.7105656

33. Fraire, J.A., Finochietto, J.M.: Routing-aware fair contact plan design for predictable delay tolerant networks. Ad Hoc Netw. **25**, 303–313 (2015). New Research Challenges in Mobile, Opportunistic and Delay-Tolerant Networks Energy-Aware Data Centers: Architecture, Infrastructure, and Communication. https://doi.org/10.1016/j.adhoc.2014.07.006

34. Fraire, J.A., Madoery, P.G., Finochietto, J.M., Leguizamón, G.: An evolutionary approach towards contact plan design for disruption-tolerant satellite networks. Appl. Soft Comput. **52**, 446–456 (2017). https://doi.org/10.1016/j.asoc.2016.10.023

35. Giro, S., D'Argenio, P.R.: Quantitative model checking revisited: neither decidable nor approximable. In: Raskin, J.-F., Thiagarajan, P.S. (eds.) FORMATS 2007. LNCS, vol. 4763, pp. 179–194. Springer, Heidelberg (2007). https://doi.org/10.1007/978-3-540-75454-1_14

36. Giro, S., D'Argenio, P.R.: On the expressive power of schedulers in distributed probabilistic systems. Electr. Notes Theor. Comput. Sci. **253**(3), 45–71 (2009). https://doi.org/10.1016/j.entcs.2009.10.005

37. Giro, S., D'Argenio, P.R., Ferrer Fioriti, L.M.: Partial order reduction for probabilistic systems: a revision for distributed schedulers. In: Bravetti, M., Zavattaro, G. (eds.) CONCUR 2009. LNCS, vol. 5710, pp. 338–353. Springer, Heidelberg (2009). https://doi.org/10.1007/978-3-642-04081-8_23

38. Giro, S., Rabe, M.N.: Verification of partial-information probabilistic systems using counterexample-guided refinements. In: Chakraborty, S., Mukund, M. (eds.) ATVA 2012. LNCS, pp. 333–348. Springer, Heidelberg (2012). https://doi.org/10.1007/978-3-642-33386-6_26

39. Gottzein, E.: Challenges in the control and autonomy of communications satellites. Control Eng. Pract. **8**(4), 409–427 (2000). https://doi.org/10.1016/S0967-0661(99)00171-9

40. Hahn, E.M., Hartmanns, A., Hermanns, H., Katoen, J.P.: A compositional modelling and analysis framework for stochastic hybrid systems. Formal Meth. Syst. Des. **43**(2), 191–232 (2013). https://doi.org/10.1007/s10703-012-0167-z

41. Hahn, E.M., Li, Y., Schewe, S., Turrini, A., Zhang, L.: iscasMc: a web-based probabilistic model checker. In: Jones, C., Pihlajasaari, P., Sun, J. (eds.) FM 2014. LNCS, vol. 8442, pp. 312–317. Springer, Cham (2014). https://doi.org/10.1007/978-3-319-06410-9_22

42. Hartmanns, A.: Sampling distributed schedulers for resilient space communication (artifact). 4TU.Centre for Research Data (2020). https://doi.org/10.4121/uuid:6aa24e1a-3551-4073-b533-4ba6e408212d

43. Hartmanns, A., Hermanns, H.: The Modest Toolset: an integrated environment for quantitative modelling and verification. In: Ábrahám, E., Havelund, K. (eds.) TACAS 2014. LNCS, vol. 8413, pp. 593–598. Springer, Heidelberg (2014). https://doi.org/10.1007/978-3-642-54862-8_51

44. Hérault, T., Lassaigne, R., Magniette, F., Peyronnet, S.: Approximate probabilistic model checking. In: Steffen, B., Levi, G. (eds.) VMCAI 2004. LNCS, vol. 2937, pp. 73–84. Springer, Heidelberg (2004). https://doi.org/10.1007/978-3-540-24622-0_8

45. Jenkins, A., Kuzminsky, S., Gifford, K.K., Pitts, R.L., Nichols, K.: DTN: flight test results from the international space station. In: 2010 IEEE Aerospace Conference, pp. 1–8 (2010)

46. Kwiatkowska, M., Norman, G., Parker, D.: PRISM 4.0: verification of probabilistic real-time systems. In: Gopalakrishnan, G., Qadeer, S. (eds.) CAV 2011. LNCS, vol. 6806, pp. 585–591. Springer, Heidelberg (2011). https://doi.org/10.1007/978-3-642-22110-1_47

47. Lassaigne, R., Peyronnet, S.: Probabilistic verification and approximation. Ann. Pure Appl. Logic 152(1–3), 122–131 (2008). https://doi.org/10.1016/j.apal.2007.11.006

48. Legay, A., Sedwards, S., Traonouez, L.-M.: Scalable verification of Markov decision processes. In: Canal, C., Idani, A. (eds.) SEFM 2014. LNCS, vol. 8938, pp. 350–362. Springer, Cham (2015). https://doi.org/10.1007/978-3-319-15201-1_23

49. Madoery, P.G., Raverta, F.D., Fraire, J.A., Finochietto, J.M.: Routing in space delay tolerant networks under uncertain contact plans. In: 2018 IEEE International Conference on Communications (ICC), May 2018, pp. 1–6 (2018). https://doi.org/10.1109/ICC.2018.8422917

50. Puterman, M.L.: Markov Decision Processes: Discrete Stochastic Dynamic Programming. Wiley Series in Probability and Mathematical Statistics: Applied Probability and Statistics. Wiley, Hoboken (1994)

51. Raverta, F.D., Demasi, R., Madoery, P.G., Fraire, J.A., Finochietto, J.M., D'Argenio, P.R.: A Markov decision process for routing in space DTNs with uncertain contact plans. In: 6th IEEE International Conference on Wireless for Space and Extreme Environments (WiSEE), pp. 189–194. IEEE (2018). https://doi.org/10.1109/WiSEE.2018.8637330

52. Sahai, A., Tandra, R., Mishra, S.M., Hoven, N.: Fundamental design tradeoffs in cognitive radio systems. In: Proceedings of the 1st International Workshop on Technology and Policy for Accessing Spectrum, p. 2. ACM (2006)

53. Sheng, M., Xu, G., Fang, X.: The routing of interplanetary Internet. China Commun. 3(6), 63–73 (2006)

54. Wyatt, J., Burleigh, S., Jones, R., Torgerson, L., Wissler, S.: Disruption tolerant networking flight validation experiment on NASA's EPOXI mission. In: First International Conference on Advances in Satellite and Space Communications (SPACOMM), pp. 187–196 (2009). https://doi.org/10.1109/SPACOMM.2009.39

55. Younes, H.L.S., Clarke, E.M., Zuliani, P.: Statistical verification of probabilistic properties with unbounded until. In: Davies, J., Silva, L., Simao, A. (eds.) SBMF 2010. LNCS, vol. 6527, pp. 144–160. Springer, Heidelberg (2011). https://doi.org/10.1007/978-3-642-19829-8_10

56. Younes, H.L.S., Simmons, R.G.: Probabilistic verification of discrete event systems using acceptance sampling. In: Brinksma, E., Larsen, K.G. (eds.) CAV 2002. LNCS, vol. 2404, pp. 223–235. Springer, Heidelberg (2002). https://doi.org/10.1007/3-540-45657-0_17

Model Checking Timed Hyperproperties in Discrete-Time Systems

Borzoo Bonakdarpour[1($\boxtimes$)], Pavithra Prabhakar[2], and César Sánchez[3]

[1] Iowa State University, Ames, USA
borzoo@iastate.edu
[2] Kansas State University, Manhattan, USA
pprabhakar@ksu.edu
[3] IMDEA Software Institute, Pozuelo de Alarcón, Spain
cesar.sanchez@imdea.org

Abstract. Many important timed requirements of computing systems cannot be described by the behavior of individual execution traces. Examples include countermeasures to deal with side-channel timing attacks and service-level agreements, which are examples of *timed hyperproperties*. In this paper, we propose the temporal logic HyperMTL, that extends MTL by allowing explicit and simultaneous quantification over multiple timed traces in the point-wise semantics. We demonstrate the application of HyperMTL in expressing important properties in information-flow security and cyber-physical systems. We also introduce a model checking algorithm for a nontrivial fragment of HyperMTL by reducing the problem to model checking untimed hyperproperties.

1 Introduction

There has been tremendous progress in automated reasoning about *trace properties* in the past three decades. These properties were classified by Alpern and Schneider [3] into *safety* and *liveness* properties. Temporal logics like LTL [31] and CTL [11] were crafted to give formal syntax and semantics of trace properties, and many verification algorithms and tools were developed to reason about these logics (see [4,5,9–12,29,34]). However, many interesting requirements are not trace properties. For example, information-flow security policies such as *noninterference* [25] and *observational determinism* [35] cannot be expressed as properties of individual execution traces. Also, service level agreement requirements (e.g., mean response time and percentage uptime) that use statistics across all executions of a system are not trace properties. Rather, they are properties of sets of execution traces. These requirements are *hyperproperties* [14]. Temporal logics, like HyperLTL and HyperCTL* [13], and probabilistic variants, like HyperPCTL [1], have been proposed to reason about temporal hyperproperties.

This research has been partially supported by the United States NSF SaTC Award 1813388, NSF CAREER Award 1552668, ONR YIP Award N000141712577, and by the Madrid Regional Government under project "S2018/TCS-4339 (BLOQUES-CM)" by Spanish National Project "BOSCO (PGC2018-102210-B-100)".

© Springer Nature Switzerland AG 2020
R. Lee et al. (Eds.): NFM 2020, LNCS 12229, pp. 311–328, 2020.
https://doi.org/10.1007/978-3-030-55754-6_18

Hyperproperties can also be timed, i.e., they explicitly stipulate the timing relation of independent executions. An example of a timed hyperproperty is countermeasures against *timing channels*. A timing channel is

```
L := 1;
for (i := 1 to H) {do something};
L := 2;
```

Fig. 1. Timing leak.

one through which an attacker learns sensitive information by observing the time at which publicly observable events occur. A *timing leak* is an information leak through a timing channel. For instance, consider the program in Fig. 1, where H and L denote "high" (i.e., secret) and "low" (i.e., public) security variables or channels confidentiality. By observing the timing of the public channel L, an adversary can infer information about H. In order to prevent an attacker to infer the value of H, a countermeasure is to make sure that in any given system, the for-loop takes equal time for any two distinct values of H. This policy to defend against timing leaks is a *system property* (as opposed to the property of individual executions) and constitutes a *timed* hyperproperty. We propose here the temporal logic HyperMTL to express timed hyperproperties. Designing a temporal logic for timed hyperproperties has multiple challenges, and a trivial extension of HyperLTL to a timed logic or lifting MTL to a hyper logic result in a flawed or impractical framework. We discuss these issues next.

Dealing with Multiple Timed Traces. Timed traces of the same system may not *align.* Consider the following timed traces σ_1 and σ_2 shown on the left:

$\sigma_1 = (\{a\}, 2)(\{b\}, 5)(\{a, b\}, 8) \cdots$ $\sigma_1' = (\{a\}, 1)(\{a\}, 3)(\{a\}, 5) \cdots$

$\sigma_2 = (\{b\}, 3)(\{a, b\}, 4)(\{a\}, \quad 7) \cdots$ $\sigma_2' = (\{a\}, 1)(\{a\}, 2)(\{a\}, 3)(\{a\}, 4)(\{a\}, 5) \cdots$

These traces have no matching time stamps, which makes reasoning about them simultaneously challenging. Another challenge is the speed of time progress in different traces. Consider traces σ_1' and σ_2' above on the right, where σ_1' reaches time 5 in fewer steps than σ_2', which has to be taken into account when reasoning about σ_1' and σ_2' simultaneously. These two examples show why HyperLTL cannot be trivially extended to a timed version, as the semantics of HyperLTL evaluates a set of traces *synchronously*, that is, positions advance in a lock-step manner (see Fig. 2 (left) for an example, where evaluation occurs at identical positions of both traces).

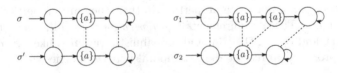

Fig. 2. Synchronous semantics (left) vs asynchronous semantics (right).

Decidability of Verification. In order to allow reasoning about traces with different speeds, one has to allow *asynchronous* semantics, where one trace may make progress while another stutters (see Fig. 2 (right)). However, the computation power needed to reason about such a model of computation rises to the level required to solve the *post correspondance problem* (PCP) [32], which is known to be undecidable (the formal proof is out of the scope of this paper).

Our first contribution is the temporal logic HyperMTL with the following features:

– *Timed Temporal Operators.* HyperMTL generalizes HyperLTL by allowing explicit timing constraints over temporal operators. For example, formula $\varphi = \forall \pi. \forall \pi'. \Box_{[2,5]} (a_\pi \leftrightarrow a_{\pi'})$ means that any pair of traces π and π' should agree on the position of proposition a in all events within time period $[2,5]$. In addition to explicit timing constraints, we augment the temporal operators with features to express bounds on the difference in time elapse between traces. This is essential to realistically capture policies such as countermeasures to timing side-channels. For example, we enrich temporal operators to express properties like $\Diamond_{[0,\infty),[0,1]}(r_\pi \wedge r_{\pi'})$ which requires that proposition r should hold in events in trace π and π' that are at most one time unit of each other.

– *Two-Layered Design.* In order to obtain a decidable model-checking problem, HyperMTL is divided into two layers. The outer layer is interpreted with synchronous semantics, that is, the operators are evaluated position by position in a lock-step manner similar to HyperLTL (see Fig. 2 (left)). The inner layer allows temporal operators to be interpreted by the *asynchronous* semantics, where evaluation of traces can be asynchronous (see Fig. 2 (right)). For example, formula $\varphi = \forall \pi. \exists \pi'. \Box_{[0,\infty)} \mathsf{A}.(\Diamond_{[3,6],[1,2]}(r_\pi \wedge r_{\pi'}))$ means that for every trace π, there is another trace π', where it is (synchronously) always the case that eventually (asynchronously) within interval $[3,6]$ proposition r is observed in the two traces within interval $[1,2]$ of each other.

– *Framing.* Finally, the synchronous semantics can suffer from anomalies because evaluation points of a formula may depend on its context. We fix this problem by introducing the notion of formula *framing*. For instance, formulas *true* and $p_\pi \vee \neg p_\pi$ are only equivalent when *true* is evaluated at the ticking instants of π and therefore cannot be substituted as in an arbitrary context. Our solution allows to "frame" *true* and $p_\pi \vee \neg p_\pi$ forcing their evaluation to consider π (and only π) to regain substitutivity.

Our second contribution is to show the application of HyperMTL in different areas of computing. We demonstrate how HyperMTL can express important (1) security policies such as countermeasures to side-channel timing attacks and insecure composition, (2) service level agreements, and (3) properties of cyber-physical systems such as robustness, sensitivity, and overshoot observability.

Our third contribution is a model-checking algorithm for a fragment of Hyper-MTL. We show that the fragment with bounded intervals for the asynchronous operators and unrestricted synchronous operators the logic is decidable. This fragment covers all interesting examples listed above. We obtain the decidability result by reducing the model-checking problem for this fragment of HyperMTL to the model-checking of HyperLTL [13,24].

Organization. The rest of the paper is organized as follows. In Sect. 2, we review the preliminary concepts. Then, we present the syntax and semantics of Hyper-MTL in Sect. 3, while its applications are discussed in Sect. 4. Our model checking algorithm is presented in Sect. 5. We discuss related work in Sect. 6 and finally conclude in Sect. 7.

2   Preliminaries

Let AP be a set of *atomic propositions* and $\Sigma = 2^{\mathsf{AP}}$ be the *alphabet*. We call each element of Σ a *letter*. A *trace* is an infinite sequence $\sigma = a_0 a_1 \cdots$ of letters from Σ. We use $\sigma(i)$ for a_i and σ^i for the suffix $a_i a_{i+1} \cdots$. An *indexed trace* is a pair (σ, p), where $p \in \mathbb{N}$ is a natural number (called the *pointer*). Indexed traces are used to traverse a trace by moving the pointer. Given an indexed trace (σ, p) and $n > 0$, we use $(\sigma, p) + n$ to denote the resulting indexed trace $(\sigma, p + n)$.

We fix the time domain to be non-negative integers $\mathbb{Z}_{\geq 0}$. An *event* is a pair (a, t), where $a \in \Sigma$ and $t \in \mathbb{Z}_{\geq 0}$. Given an event $e = (a, t)$, we use *label*(e) for a and *time*(e) for t. A *timed trace* is an infinite sequence $\sigma = (a_0, t_0)(a_1, t_1)(a_2, t_2) \ldots$, over $(\Sigma \times \mathbb{Z}_{\geq 0})$, such that for all $i \geq 0$, we have $t_i < t_{i+1}$. Given an indexed timed trace (σ, p), we use *time*(σ, p) to denote *time*$(\sigma(p))$.

2.1   HyperLTL

HyperLTL [13] is a temporal logic for hyperproperties, which allows reasoning about multiple execution traces simultaneously. The syntax of HyperLTL is:

$$\alpha ::= \exists \pi. \alpha \mid \forall \pi. \alpha \mid \varphi \qquad\qquad \varphi ::= a_\pi \mid \varphi \vee \varphi \mid \neg \varphi \mid \bigcirc \varphi \mid \varphi \, \mathcal{U} \, \varphi$$

where π is a *trace variable* from an infinite supply of trace variables. The intended meaning of a_π is that proposition $a \in \Sigma$ holds in the current time in trace π. Trace quantifiers $\exists \pi$ and $\forall \pi$ allow reasoning simultaneously about different traces of the computation. Atomic predicates a_π refer to a single trace π, and can be combined with Boolean operators to build relational tests as well as with temporal operators to construct temporal relational formulas. Informally, HyperLTL allows to reason about properties of systems that require to reason about the whole set of traces of the system at once, and not about each individual trace at a time.

Given a HyperLTL formula φ, we use $Var(\alpha)$ for the set of trace variables quantified in α. A formula α is well-formed if for all atoms a_π in α, π is quantified in α (i.e., $\pi \in Var(\alpha)$) and if no trace variable is quantified twice in α.

Given a set of traces W, the semantics of a HyperLTL formula α is defined in terms of trace assignments, which is a (partial) map from trace variables to indexed traces $\Pi : Var(\alpha) \rightharpoonup (W \times \mathbb{N})$. We use $Dom(\Pi)$ for the subset of $Var(\alpha)$ for which Π is defined. Given a trace assignment Π, a trace variable π, a trace σ and a pointer p, we denote by $\Pi[\pi \mapsto (\sigma, p)]$ the assignment that coincides with Π for every path variable except for π, which is mapped to (σ, p). Also, we use $\Pi + n$ to denote trace assignment Π' such that $\Pi'(\pi) = \Pi(\pi) + n$ for all $\pi \in Dom(\Pi) = Dom(\Pi')$. The semantics of HyperLTL is as follows:

$$
\begin{array}{llll}
(W, \Pi) \models \exists \pi.\alpha & \text{iff} & \text{for some } \sigma \in W, (W, \Pi[\pi \mapsto (\sigma, 0)]) \models \alpha \\
(W, \Pi) \models \forall \pi.\alpha & \text{iff} & \text{for all } \sigma \in W, (W, \Pi[\pi \mapsto (\sigma, 0)]) \models \alpha \\
(W, \Pi) \models \varphi & \text{iff} & \Pi \models \varphi \\
\Pi \models a_\pi & \text{iff} & a \in \sigma(p), \text{ where } (\sigma, p) = \Pi(\pi) \\
\Pi \models \varphi_1 \vee \varphi_2 & \text{iff} & \Pi \models \varphi_1 \text{ or } \Pi \models \varphi_2
\end{array}
$$

$$
\begin{array}{llll}
\Pi \models \neg \varphi & \text{iff} & \Pi \not\models \varphi \\
\Pi \models \bigcirc \varphi & \text{iff} & (\Pi + 1) \models \varphi \\
\Pi \models \varphi_1 \, \mathcal{U} \, \varphi_2 & \text{iff} & \text{for some } j \geq 0 \; (\Pi + j) \models \varphi_2 \\
& & \text{and for all } 0 \leq i < j, (\Pi + i) \models \varphi_1
\end{array}
$$

Note that quantifiers assign traces to trace variables and set the pointer to the initial position 0. Also, the pointer in all trace assignments move in lock-step (at the same speed) within the semantics of $\mathcal{U}$ (that is, like in Fig. 2 (left), all pointers for different traces have the same value). Given a HyperLTL formula α and a Kripke structure that can generate a set of traces W, the model-checking problem for HyperLTL consists of deciding whether $(W, \Pi_\emptyset) \models \alpha$, where $\Pi_\emptyset$ is the trace assignment with $Dom(\Pi_\emptyset) = \emptyset$.

Example 1. The meaning of HyperLTL formula $\alpha = \forall \pi.\forall \pi'. \Box (a_\pi \leftrightarrow a_{\pi'})$ is that any pair of traces should agree on the value of a at every position.

In Sect. 5, we will use a timed version of the $\mathcal{U}$ operator, so we define a derived temporal operator $\mathcal{U}_I$ that requires the satisfaction of the second argument in the interval I, using repeated applications of the next operator. The operator $\mathcal{U}_I$ is formally defined as follows ($\bigcirc^i$ refers $\bigcirc$ operator applied i times on the argument):

$$
\varphi_1 \, \mathcal{U}_{[a,b]} \, \varphi_2 \overset{\text{def}}{=} \bigvee_{a \leq i \leq b} (\bigcirc^i \varphi_2 \wedge \bigwedge_{0 \leq j < i} \bigcirc^j \varphi_1), \quad \varphi_1 \, \mathcal{U}_{[a,\infty)} \, \varphi_2 \overset{\text{def}}{=} \bigwedge_{0 \leq i < a} \bigcirc^i \varphi_1 \wedge \bigcirc^a \varphi_1 \, \mathcal{U} \, \varphi_2
$$

2.2 Kripke Structures

We model timed systems as *timed Kripke structures* with time elapse in the arcs.

Definition 1. *A Kripke structure (KS) is a tuple* $\mathcal{M} = (S, S^0, \rightarrow, \mathsf{AP}, L)$, *where*

- *S is a set of states, and $S^0 \subseteq S$ is a set of initial states;*
- *$\rightarrow \subseteq S \times \mathbb{Z}_{\geq 0} \times S$ is a set of transitions;*
- *AP is the set of atomic propostions; and*
- *$L : S \rightarrow 2^{\mathsf{AP}}$ is a labeling function that assigns a set of atomic propositions to each state.*

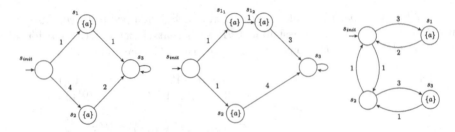

Fig. 3. Three timed Kripke structures: $\mathcal{K}_1$ (left) $\mathcal{K}_2$ (middle) and $\mathcal{K}_3$ (right).

We assume that every state has a successor, so each sink state s is equipped with a self-loop of the form $(s, 1, s)$. Note that untimed Kripke structures are simply Kripke structures for which all edges are of the form $(s, 1, s')$.

A *run* of a Kripke structure $(S, S^0, \to, \mathsf{AP}, L)$ from a state $s \in S$ is an infinite sequence of the form $\gamma_s = s_0 d_0 s_1 d_1 s_2 d_2 \cdots$, where $s_0 = s$ and for each $i \geq 0$, we have $(s_i, d_i, s_{i+1}) \in \to$, for some $d_i \in \mathbb{Z}_{\geq 0}$. A *trace* of a run γ_s is a timed trace of the form $(L(s_0), t_0)(L(s_1), t_1)(L(s_2), t_2) \cdots$, such that $t_0 = 0$ and for every $i > 0$, $t_{i+1} = t_i + d_i$, that is, we encode the delays from the actions of the Kripke structure into time-stamps on the letters of the timed trace. The *language* of a Kripke structure $\mathcal{M}$ (denoted $\mathcal{L}(\mathcal{M})$) is the set of all traces corresponding to runs of $\mathcal{M}$.

Example 2. The untimed interpretation of the Kripke structure $\mathcal{K}_1$ shown in Fig. 3 (left) satisfies HyperLTL formula $\alpha = \forall \pi. \forall \pi'. \Box (a_\pi \leftrightarrow a_{\pi'})$, whereas $\mathcal{K}_2$, in Fig. 3 (middle), does not.

3   The Temporal Logic HyperMTL

In this section, we present the syntax and semantics of HyperMTL. In HyperMTL, formulas are constructed in two *layers* using two kinds of temporal operators, *synchronous* and *asynchronous*. This layering enables the construction of both synchronous and asynchronous formulas, and a limited combination that still guarantees decidability. Synchronous operators allow comparing traces at the same point in time and reason about the time elapses. The evaluating time instants are those where at least one of the traces involved contains an event. If a trace σ does not contain an event at an evaluation time t then the closest previous event is used (we assume all traces contain an event at the initial time 0). Consider for example, traces σ and σ' shown on the right.

The evaluation of $\{\sigma, \sigma'\}$ at time $t = 3$ considers event $(a_1, 1)$ for σ and $(b_2, 3)$ for σ'. On the other

$$\sigma = (a_0, 0)\,(a_1, 1)\,(a_2 4)\,(a_3, 5) \cdots$$
$$\sigma' = (b_0, 0)\,(b_1, 1)\,(b_2, 3)\,(b_3, 5) \cdots$$

hand, asynchronous operators allow traces to proceed at different speeds and also allow to reason about the difference in elapsing times between two traces.

We first present the syntax and then the semantics of each layer. Finally, we show how the choice of the evaluation point in the synchronous semantics can lead to unexpected logical cases and propose a simple *framing* mechanism to fix these anomalies.

3.1 Syntax

As with HyperLTL, the outermost layer (α formulas) introduces the trace quantifiers that bind trace variables; then the *synchronous layer* (φ formulas) introduces the synchronous temporal operators and the *asynchronous layer* (ψ formulas) introduce the asynchronous temporal constructs:

$$\alpha ::= \exists \pi.\alpha \mid \forall \pi.\alpha \mid \varphi$$

$$\varphi ::= true \mid a_\pi \mid \varphi \vee \varphi \mid \neg \varphi \mid \varphi \, \mathcal{U}_I \, \varphi \mid \mathsf{A}.\psi$$

$$\psi ::= true \mid a_\pi \mid \psi \vee \psi \mid \neg \psi \mid \psi \, \mathcal{U}_{I,J} \, \psi$$

Here, $a \in \mathsf{AP}$ is an atomic proposition, and I and J are intervals of the form $[l, u]$ with $l, u \in \mathbb{Z}_{\geq 0} \cup \{\infty\}$ and $l \leq u$. As for HyperLTL, the meaning of a_π is that a holds in the trace assigned to trace variable π. The intended meaning of $\varphi_1 \mathcal{U}_I \varphi_2$ is that there is an event at time t within an interval I, such that φ_2 holds at t and that φ_1 holds at all events before t. The meaning of interval $J = [l, u]$ is that the difference in time elapse between any two traces must be between l and u, when the obligation φ_2 is fulfilled. As usual, we use the syntactic sugar $\Diamond_I \varphi \overset{\text{def}}{=} true \, \mathcal{U}_I \, \varphi$ and $\Box_I \varphi \overset{\text{def}}{=} \neg(\Diamond_I \neg \varphi)$, and $\Diamond_{I,J} \varphi \overset{\text{def}}{=} true \, \mathcal{U}_{I,J} \, \varphi$, etc.

Temporal operators in synchronous formulas allow time to flow according to a global clock. The evolution of time in the evaluation of a formula proceeds according to the time-stamps of events in any of the traces in the formula. In case a_π is evaluated at a given time t, and the trace σ assigned to π does not contain an event at t, then the most recent past event in σ is used. The operator A (for (A)synchronous) denotes the evaluation of the subformula asynchronously, and allows to reuse temporal and propositional symbols. The asynchronous layer considers the possibility that traces proceed at different speeds which is captured by the notion of trajectory, also called a time-flow, defined below.

3.2 Semantics

The Quantifier Layer. To define the semantics of synchronous HyperMTL, we use pointed-timed trace assignments, that is, partial mappings $\Pi \colon Var(\alpha) \rightharpoonup (\Sigma \times \mathbb{Z}_{\geq 0})^\omega \times \mathbb{N}$, which are pointed assignments over timed traces. The intended meaning of $\Pi(\pi) = (\sigma, p)$ is that the event from timed trace σ at position p is currently used in the evaluation of trace π. Given a subset of trace variables $\overline{\pi} \subseteq Var(\alpha)$, we use $\Pi \setminus \overline{\pi}$ for the map that removes from the domain of Π all $\pi \in \overline{\pi}$. As in the untimed case, $\Pi[\pi \mapsto (\sigma, p)]$ is the assignment that coincides with Π for every trace variable except for π, which is mapped to (σ, p). The satisfaction of a HyperMTL formula φ over a timed word assignment Π, and a set W of timed words, denoted by $(W, \Pi) \models \varphi$, is defined as for HyperLTL:

$$(W, \Pi) \models \exists \pi.\alpha \qquad \text{iff} \qquad (W, \Pi[\pi \mapsto (\sigma, 0)]) \models \alpha \text{ for some } \sigma \in W$$
$$(W, \Pi) \models \forall \pi.\alpha \qquad \text{iff} \qquad (W, \Pi[\pi \mapsto (\sigma, 0)]) \models \alpha \text{ for all } \sigma \in W$$
$$(W, \Pi) \models \varphi \qquad \text{iff} \qquad \Pi \models_s \varphi$$

where $\models_s$ is the semantics of the synchronous layer defined next.

The Synchronous Layer. We present first some preliminary definitions to capture the passage of time, by defining the sequence of *time ticks* for a given collection of traces. Intuitively speaking, this sequence contains the instants of the events in the union of events in the traces. We start by defining the position of trace σ at time t as the index of the latest event in σ whose time does not surpass t:

$$pos(\sigma, t) \stackrel{\text{def}}{=} i, \text{ such that } time(\sigma(i)) \leq t < time(\sigma(i+1))$$

Recall that $time(\sigma(i))$ is the time-stamp of the i-th event in σ. The position adjustment $\Pi|_t$ is an assignment (with $Dom(\Pi|_t) = Dom(\Pi)$), which moves the pointer to the position denoted by t. That is, for $\pi \in Dom(\Pi)$, $\Pi|_t(\pi) = (\sigma, pos(\sigma, t))$ for $(\sigma, p) = \Pi(\pi)$. Then, given Π, we define the current instant and the next instant as follows:

$$now(\Pi) = \max_{\pi \in Dom(\Pi)} \left\{ time(\sigma(p)) \quad | \text{ for } (\sigma, p) = \Pi(\pi) \right\}$$
$$next(\Pi) = \min_{\pi \in Dom(\Pi)} \left\{ time(\sigma(p+1)) \mid \text{ for } (\sigma, p) = \Pi(\pi) \right\}$$

Finally, the synchronous successor of Π is $\mathbf{succ}(\Pi) = \Pi|_{next(\Pi)}$. This can be extended to $\mathbf{succ}^{j+1}(\Pi) = \mathbf{succ}^j(\mathbf{succ}(\Pi))$. Note that, starting at time 0, $\mathbf{succ}$ follows the union of the time-stamps of $Dom(\Pi)$ in increasing order. We use $\Pi^{(j)}$ as short for $\mathbf{succ}^j(\Pi)$. We are now ready to define the semantics $\models_s$:

$$\Pi \models_s true \qquad \text{iff} \qquad \text{always holds}$$
$$\Pi \models_s a_\pi \qquad \text{iff} \qquad a \in label(\sigma(p)) \text{ for } (\sigma, p) = \Pi(\pi)$$
$$\Pi \models_s \varphi_1 \vee \varphi_2 \qquad \text{iff} \qquad \Pi \models_s \varphi_1 \text{ or } \Pi \models_s \varphi_2$$
$$\Pi \models_s \neg\varphi \qquad \text{iff} \qquad \Pi \not\models_s \varphi$$
$$\Pi \models_s \varphi_1 \, \mathcal{U}_I \, \varphi_2 \qquad \text{iff} \qquad \text{for some } i \geq 0,$$
$$\Pi^{(i)} \models_s \varphi_2 \text{ and } (now(\Pi^{(i)}) - now(\Pi)) \in I$$
$$\text{and for all } j < i, \ \Pi^{(j)} \models_s \varphi_1$$
$$\Pi \models_s A.\psi \qquad \text{iff} \qquad \text{for some trajectory } \tau, \ (\Pi, \tau) \models_a \psi$$

The notion of a *trajectory* is related to the asynchronous layer, defined next.

Example 3. Consider the following HyperMTL formula with only synchronous temporal operator $\alpha = \forall \pi.\forall.\pi'. \, \Box_{[1,2]} (a_\pi \leftrightarrow a_{\pi'})$. The Kripke structure $\mathcal{K}_1$ in Fig. 3 (left) does not satisfy this formula, whereas $\mathcal{K}_2$ in Fig. 3 (middle) does.

The Asynchronous Layer. The asynchronous layer allows traces to proceed at different speeds. We start by the asynchronous semantics of intervals. Let α be a formula, $[l, u]$ be a time interval and Δ be a map from $Var(\alpha) \rightharpoonup \mathbb{Z}_{\geq 0}$ that gives a time duration for each π in $Dom(\Delta)$. We write $\Delta \models_I [l, u]$ whenever for all π in $Dom(\Delta)$, $\Delta(\pi) \in [l, u]$. We write $\Delta \models_J [l, u]$ whenever for all distinct $\pi, \pi' \in Dom(\Delta)$, $|\Delta(\pi) - \Delta(\pi')| \in [l, u]$.

A *trajectory* encodes which traces move and which traces stay at a given instant.

Definition 2. *Let V be a set of trace variables. A trajectory is an infinite sequence $\tau_0 \tau_1 \tau_2 \cdots$ of subsets of V, such that for every $\pi \in V$, there are infinitely many $i \in \mathbb{Z}_{\geq 0}$ for which $\pi \in \tau_i$.*

For example, the trajectory depicted in Fig. 2 (right) is $\{\sigma_1, \sigma_2\}\{\sigma_1\}\{\sigma_1, \sigma_2\} \cdots$. Similar to timed traces, by τ^i, we mean the suffix $\tau_i \tau_{i+1} \ldots$. The asynchronous successor of a pointed time trace assignment Π with respect to a trajectory τ, denoted $\mathbf{succ}_a(\Pi, \tau)$, is the pair (Π', τ^1), where Π' is defined as follows. First, $Dom(\Pi') = Dom(\Pi)$; then for $\pi \in Dom(\pi')$, $\Pi'(\pi) = \Pi(\pi) + 1$ if $\pi \in \tau_0$, and $\Pi'(\pi) = \Pi(\pi)$ otherwise. Again, this definition can be extended to the j-th successor by defining $\mathbf{succ}_a^j$ to be the function that applies j times the function $\mathbf{succ}_a$. We use $(\Pi, \tau)^{(j)}$ as a short for $\mathbf{succ}_a^j(\Pi, \tau)$.

Given two pointed time trace assignments Π and Π' with the same domain $Dom(\Pi) = Dom(\Pi')$ (as it is the case with successors) the passage of time is defined as a map from $Var(\alpha) \rightharpoonup \mathbb{Z}_{\geq 0}$ that returns the passage of time for each assignment as follows:

$$\Delta(\Pi, \Pi')(\pi) \overset{\text{def}}{=} time(\Pi'(\pi)) - time(\Pi(\pi))$$

Finally, we define the time passage in j steps $\Delta^j(\Pi, \tau)$ as the time passage between the current evaluation instant and the evaluation instant obtained after j steps, that is, $\Delta^j(\Pi, \tau) = \Delta(\Pi, \Pi')$, where $(\Pi', \tau') = (\Pi, \tau)^{(j)}$. We are finally ready to define the semantics of the asynchronous layer:

$$
\begin{array}{lll}
(\Pi, \tau) \models_a true & \text{iff} & \text{always holds} \\
(\Pi, \tau) \models_a a_\pi & \text{iff} & a \in label(\sigma(p)) \text{ for } (\sigma, p) = \Pi(\pi) \\
(\Pi, \tau) \models_a \psi_1 \vee \psi_2 & \text{iff} & (\Pi, \tau) \models_a \psi_1 \text{ or } (\Pi, \tau) \models_a \psi_2 \\
(\Pi, \tau) \models_a \neg\psi & \text{iff} & (\Pi, \tau) \not\models_a \psi \\
(\Pi, \tau) \models_a \psi_1 \, \mathcal{U}_{I,J} \, \psi_2 & \text{iff} & \text{for some } i > 0, (\Pi, \tau)^{(i)} \models_a \psi_2, \\
& & \quad \Delta^i(\Pi, \tau) \models_I I \text{ and } \Delta^i(\Pi, \tau) \models_J J, \text{ and} \\
& & \quad \text{for all } j < i, (\Pi, \tau)^{(j)} \models_a \psi_1
\end{array}
$$

Essentially, the asynchronous until operator $\mathcal{U}_{I,J}$ checks whether following the trajectory τ the attempt ψ_2 is met (also satisfying the temporal constraints I and J) and the obligation ψ_1 is fulfilled at all previous evaluation instants.

Example 4. The meaning of formula $\alpha = \forall\pi.\exists\pi'.\square_{[0,\infty)} \mathsf{A}.(\diamondsuit_{[0,\infty),[0,1]}(a_\pi \wedge a_{\pi'}))$ is that for every trace, there exists another one, such that it is (synchronously) always the case that proposition a is (asynchronously) observed in both traces within one time unit of each other. For example, $\mathcal{K}_3$ in Fig. 3 (right) satisfies this formula.

3.3   Framing

Unfortunately, the semantics defined above has some unexpected drawbacks, which we fix here with the notion of framing. Consider a formula α that contains a synchronous sub-formula φ. The set of time instants at which φ is evaluated depends on the events of all traces in $Var(\alpha)$ (which is a super-set of the traces that actually appear as trace variables in φ). For example, consider the formula $\forall \pi.\exists \pi'.(\Diamond_{[5,10]} a_\pi \leftrightarrow \Diamond_{[4,10]} a_{\pi'})$. The sub-formula $\varphi_1 = \Diamond_{[5,10]} a_\pi$ only refers to π while its enclosing formula refers to π and π'. Let σ and σ' be the traces assigned to π and π'. The semantics of the synchronous layer of HyperMTL evaluates φ_1 at the points at which either σ or σ' contain an event and not only at the points at which σ does. This evaluation causes semantic anomalies, illustrated in the following examples.

Example 5. Consider $\varphi = \Diamond_{[1,3]} true$ and $W = \{\sigma\}$ for $\sigma = (a,0)(a,2)(a,4)\ldots$. In this case $(W, \Pi_\emptyset) \not\models \varphi$ but $(W, \Pi_\emptyset) \models \exists \pi.\varphi$ and $(W, \Pi_\emptyset) \models \forall \pi.\varphi$ even though $\pi \notin Var(\varphi)$.

In first-order logic, if a variable x does not appear in a formula P, P is equivalent to $\exists x.P$ and to $\forall x.P$, but the previous example illustrates that this is not the case for HyperMTL. It is true in the asynchronous semantics, but not necessarily for synchronous formulas due to the additional ticking instants.

Example 6. Consider formulas $\varphi_1 = \Diamond_{[1,2]} a_{\pi_1}$ and $\varphi_2 = \Diamond_{[3,4]} a_{\pi_2}$ and consider timed words $\sigma_1 = (a,0)(a,4)(a,8)\ldots$ and $\sigma_2 = (a,0)(a,2)(a,12)\ldots$ In this case $(\sigma_1, 0) \not\models \varphi_1$ and $(\sigma_2, 0) \not\models \varphi_2$, but $((\sigma_1, \sigma_2), 0) \models \varphi_1 \wedge \varphi_2$. Even though σ_1 is the trace assigned to π_1, the ticks in σ_1 make φ_2 true (even though φ_2 does not refer to π_1 and hence "should not be affected" by the trace assigned to π_1).

To fix these anomalies, we enrich the synchronous layer with a *framing* operator $[\varphi]_{\overline{\pi}}$ that restricts the time-words that the semantics use, resulting in the following syntax:

$$\varphi ::= true \mid a_\pi \mid \varphi \vee \varphi \mid \neg \varphi \mid \varphi \, \mathcal{U}_I \, \varphi \mid \mathsf{A}.\psi \mid [\varphi]_{\overline{\pi}}$$

To be well-formed we require that every sub-formula of the form $[\varphi]_{\overline{\pi}}$ satisfies that $Var(\varphi) \subseteq \overline{\pi}$. We assume that every formula is well-formed. The semantics for the synchronous layer is now extended so $\Pi \models_s [\varphi]_{\overline{\pi}}$ whenever $\Pi[\overline{\pi}] \models_s \varphi$. Using this new definition we can prove that $[true]_\pi$ and $[p_\pi \vee \neg p_\pi]_\pi$ are equivalent, and can be substituted in every context (that includes π as a path).

4   HyperMTL in Action

We first note that in all the applications explored in this section, explicit framing was not necessary as the context of every sub-formula guarantee that it was evaluated when necessary.

Side-Channel Timing Attacks. A timing attack is one that exploits the time-dependent behavioral characteristics of the implementation of an algorithm rather than other "functional" properties of the algorithm. For example, the execution time for the square-and-multiply algorithm used in modular exponentiation in encryption algorithms depends linearly on the number of '1' bits in the encryption key. While the number of '1' bits alone is not nearly enough information to make finding the key easily, repeated executions with the same key and different inputs can be used to perform statistical correlation analysis of timing information to recover the key completely, even by a passive attacker. This is a practical attack against a number of encryption algorithms, including RSA and ElGamal. In order to design a countermeasure against this attack, one can require that in any given system, for any pairs of executions, it should always be the case that, if the function is invoked in both executions, they both return within close enough times. The corresponding HyperMTL formula is $\varphi_{\mathsf{timing}}$ in Fig. 4, where inv and ret denote invocation and return of a function, interval $[0, 10]$ is an upper bound on the execution time of the function, and interval $[0, 1]$ specifies how close the execution times should be in π and π'.

$$\varphi_{\mathsf{timing}} = \forall \pi. \forall \pi'. \Box_{[0,\infty)} \mathsf{A}. \left((\mathsf{inv}_\pi \wedge \mathsf{inv}_{\pi'}) \;\rightarrow\; \Diamond_{[0,10),[0,1]} (\mathsf{ret}_\pi \wedge \mathsf{ret}_{\pi'}) \right)$$

$$\varphi_{\mathsf{compose}} = \forall \pi. \forall \pi'. \Box_{[0,\infty)} \mathsf{A}. \left((\mathsf{inv}_\pi^H \wedge \mathsf{inv}_{\pi'}^H) \;\rightarrow\; \Box_{[0,5],[0,2]} (\mathsf{hcopy}_\pi \wedge \mathsf{hcopy}_{\pi'}) \right)$$

$$\varphi_{\mathsf{sla}} = \forall \pi. \exists \pi'. \Box_{[0,\infty)} \mathsf{A}. \left((\mathsf{req}_\pi \wedge \mathsf{req}_{\pi'}) \;\rightarrow\; \Diamond_{[0,100),[0,1]} (\mathsf{res}_\pi \wedge \mathsf{res}_{\pi'}) \right)$$

$$\varphi_{\mathsf{robust}} = \forall \pi. \forall \pi'. \Box_{[0,\infty)} \mathsf{A}. \left(\Box_{I,[0,\infty)} \left(d(x_\pi, x_{\pi'}) \leq c \right) \;\rightarrow\; \Box_{I',[0,\infty)} \left(d(y_\pi, y_{\pi'}) \leq c' \right) \right)$$

$$\varphi_{\mathsf{overshoot}} = \forall \pi. \forall \pi'. \Box_{[0,\infty)} \mathsf{A}. \left[step_\pi \;\rightarrow\; \Box_{I,[0,\infty)} (x_\pi < c) \right] \;\rightarrow$$
$$\Box_{[0,\infty)} \mathsf{A}. \left[(step_{\pi'} \wedge \Diamond_{I,[0,\infty)} (x_{\pi'} > c)) \;\rightarrow\; \Diamond_{I,[0,\infty)} d(y_\pi, y_{\pi'}) > \epsilon \right]$$

Fig. 4. Examples of properties expressed in HyperMTL.

Another example of timing leaks is related to composing secure components. For example, secure multi-execution (SME) [16] removes insecurities (including timing leaks) in any given process. To this end, it runs two copies, H (for secrets) and L (for public channels), of a given program; feeding (a copy of) H and L input to the H-copy, and dropping its L output; and feeding only L input to the L-copy, and dropping its H output. Since the L-copy receives no H input, no information can be leaked. In some implementations of SME inputs enter a queue, which is serviced by first running the L-copy on the L projection of the next input, then running the H-copy on the input. While this approach prevents leaks to output values, the time at which the L-copy processes the next input depends on how long it takes for the H-copy to finish processing previous inputs, which in turn, opens a timing channel. In other words, a correct composition of two secure components should satisfy φ_{compose} in Fig. 4. where inv^H denotes invocation of the H-copy and hcopy denotes that the execution is in the H-copy. Again, intervals $[0, 5]$ and $[0, 2]$ are arbitrary.

Service Level Agreements. A *service level agreement* (SLA) specifies acceptable performance of a system. These agreements often use statistics such as mean response time, the mean time that elapses between a request and a response. Other examples include time service factor, and percentage uptime. If these statistics are used to define policies across all executions of a system, then they are timed hyperproperties. Here, we consider a simple *fair* SLA policy, where no execution can be discriminated. More specifically, we require that for any execution with a particular response time, there has to exists another one with a similar timing behavior, as show in φ_{sla} in Fig. 4, where req and res denote request and response propositions, respectively, and intervals $[0, 100]$ and $[0, 1]$ are arbitrary.

Cyber-Physical Systems. In cyber-physical systems, *robustness* is the ability of a computer system to cope with errors during execution and cope with erroneous input. More specifically, we require that if the distance between two different input values is bounded by some value c within some time interval I, then the distance between outputs is also bounded by some value c' within time interval I', as shown in φ_{robust} in Fig. 4, where x and y are input and output variables, respectively. Note that by abuse of notation x and y refer to the value of variables rather than atomic propositions.

Another feature in cyber-physical systems is *overshoot observability*. Here, we require that (1) in one execution, if a signal steps, then for some time interval I the input is bounded, (2) in another execution the signal steps and the input overshoots, then (3) the distance between the output signals is greater than some bound (i.e., the overshoot is observed in the output). This is shown in $\varphi_{\text{overshoot}}$ in Fig. 4.

5   Model Checking

The model-checking problem is the following: Given a Kripke structure $\mathcal{K}$, whose language is W, and a HyperMTL formula α decide whether $(W, \Pi) \models \alpha$. In this section, we show that the model-checking problem for HyperMTL is decidable for a fragment of HyperMTL, where the intervals in the asynchronous until operator $\mathcal{U}_{I,J}$ are bounded. We will refer to this fragment as "bounded HyperMTL". Another fragment we will consider are formulas without the asynchronous subformulas (those starting with A). We will refer to the fragment as the "synchronous HyperMTL". Our approach to show decidability consists of the following:

- Step 1: Reduce the model-checking problem of bounded HyperMTL to that of synchronous HyperMTL.
- Step 2: Reduce the model-checking problem of synchronous HyperMTL to that of HyperLTL, which is known to be decidable [13].

We provide the details of these steps separately.

Bounded HyperMTL to Synchronous HyperMTL. Given a bounded HyperMTL formula α, we provide an algorithm to construct an equivalent synchronous HyperMTL formula $\hat{\alpha}$. The intuition is that an asynchronous formula A.ψ with bounded until operators only depends on a finite interval of a timed trace. Hence, the asynchronous formula can be replaced by a synchronous formula that encodes all finite interval patterns satisfied by A.ψ.

First, we formalize when two timed traces σ and σ' agree on certain intervals. Given two timed traces σ and σ', and natural numbers r, r' and s, we say that σ and σ' are (r, r', s)-*conformant*, if the timed trace σ starting from r and the timed trace σ' starting from r' are the same for a duration of s, that is, for every i such that $r \leq time(\sigma(i)) \leq r + s$, there is a j such that $time(\sigma'(j)) - r' = time(\sigma(i)) - r$ and $label(\sigma(i)) = label(\sigma'(j))$ (and vice-versa for σ' and σ). The first time of an assignment defined as $first(\Pi) = \min\limits_{\pi \in Dom(\Pi)} \Big\{ time(\sigma(p)) \mid$
for $(\sigma, p) = \Pi(\pi) \Big\}$. This allows us to define conformance between assignments. Two assignments Π and Π' are s-*conformant*, if $Dom(\Pi) = Dom(\Pi')$ and for all $\pi \in Dom(\Pi)$, $label(\sigma(p)) = label(\sigma'(p'))$ and σ and σ' are $(first(\Pi), first(\Pi'), s)$-conformant, where $\Pi(\pi) = (\sigma, p)$ and $\Pi'(\pi) = (\sigma', p')$.

Next, given a bounded asynchronous formula ψ we define the future time period T_ψ of a timed trace which has an effect on the satisfaction of ψ. Let $ub(I)$ be the least upper-bound of an interval I. T_ψ is defined inductively as: $T_{true} = 0$; $T_{a_\pi} = 0$; $T_{\psi_1 \vee \psi_2} = \max\{T_{\psi_1}, T_{\psi_2}\}$; $T_{\neg\psi} = T_\psi$; $T_{\psi_1 \mathcal{U}_{I,J} \psi_2} = ub(I) + ub(J) + \max\{T_{\psi_1}, T_{\psi_2}\}$.

The next proposition formalizes the intuition that the satisfaction of a bounded asynchronous formula depends on only a finite interval of an assignment starting from the first time of the assignment.

Proposition 1. *Let ψ be bounded asynchronous, and let Π and Π' be two T_ψ-conformant assignments. Then, for any τ, $\Pi, \tau \models_a \psi$ if and only if $\Pi', \tau \models_a \psi$.*

The proof proceeds by induction on the structure of ψ. For the case $\psi = a_\pi$ the result follows because labels match at the pointer indices in the two assignments. For the until operator, $\psi_1 \mathcal{U}_{I,J} \psi_2$, a witness for ψ_2 happens at pointer values that satisfy I and J, hence, the latest pointer values corresponding to the witness are within $ub(I) + ub(J)$ from the $first(\Pi)$ and $first(\Pi')$, respectively.

Next, we provide a construction for a synchronous formula that encodes all the assignments that are conformant to a given assignment in a given interval. Let $\varphi_{\sigma,r}^{s,\pi}$ encode the pattern of σ in the interval $[r,s]$. More precisely, if $\sigma = (a_0,t_0)(a_1,t_1)\cdots$, then

$$\varphi_{\sigma,r}^{s,\pi} = \bigwedge_{i:r\leq time(\sigma(i))\leq r+s, a=label(\sigma(i))} true\, \mathcal{U}_{[t_i,t_i]}\, a_\pi$$

Given any assignment Π and a natural number s, we construct a synchronous formula φ_Π^s such that $\Pi' \models_s \varphi_\Pi^s$ for every Π' that is s-conformant with Π.

$$\varphi_\Pi^s = \bigwedge_{\pi\in Dom(\Pi),\Pi(\pi)=(\sigma,p)} \left[\varphi_{\sigma,time(\sigma(p))}^{s-(time(\sigma(p))-first\Pi),\pi}\right]_\pi.$$

Finally, we are ready to construct a synchronous formula $\hat{\psi}$ that is equivalent to a bounded synchronous formula A.ψ. From Proposition 1, the satisfaction of ψ by an assignment Π only depends on the values in the interval $I = [first(\Pi), first(\Pi) + T_\psi]$. Given the values of an assignment Π in the interval I, one can algorithmically check if $\Pi \models_s$ A.ψ. More precisely, there are only finitely many τ's that are relevant within I, hence, by iterating over these τ's, and using the semantics of $\models_a$, one can effectively check $\Pi, \tau \models_a \psi$. Given a natural number s, let Π_s be the set of all assignments that are s-conformant with Π. Note that s-conformance is an equivalence relation on the set of assignments with finite index. Let $Rep(\Pi, s)$ denote a finite set of representative assignments for each equivalence class. Further, let $Sat(\psi, \Pi, s)$ denote those elements of $Rep(\Pi, s)$ that correspond to satisfying assignments for ψ. Then $\hat{\psi}$ is given by the disjunction of φ_Π^s for all $\Pi \in Sat(\psi, \Pi, s)$. Note that $Sat(\psi, \Pi, s)$ is computable, and hence, $\hat{\psi}$ (which does not contain asynchronous sub-formulas) is effectively constructible.

Lemma 1. *Given a bounded asynchronous formula ψ and an assignment Π, the $\Pi \models_s$ A.ψ if and only if $\Pi \models_s \hat{\psi}$.*

Synchronous HyperMTL to HyperLTL. We show now how to transform a synchronous HyperMTL formula α to a HyperLTL formula $\hat{\alpha}$ such that the set of timed traces and timed assignments satisfying α is the same as the set of the corresponding untimed traces and assignments satisfying $\hat{\alpha}$. Then we reduce the model-checking problem of α with respect to a (timed) Kripke structure to that of $\hat{\alpha}$ with respect to an untimed Kripke structure.

Given a timed trace, its untiming refers to a sequence that contains an event at every time instant obtained by repeating an actual event until the next actual event in the time trace. Given a letter $a \in \Sigma$, let $\bar{a}$ be a fresh letter (not in Σ), used in the filled events between two actual occurrences. We also use the fresh special symbol $\epsilon \notin \Sigma$. Given a timed trace $\sigma = (a_0,t_0)(a_1,t_1)\cdots$, we define

$untime(\sigma)$ to be the trace $b_0 b_1 \cdots$, where for each $j \geq 0$, $b_j = a_i$ if $j = t_i$ for some i, and $b_j = \bar{a}_i$ if $t_i < j < t_{i+1}$, and $b_j = \epsilon$ if $0 \leq j < t_0$. For instance, if $\sigma = (a, 2)(b, 5)(b, 7)(a, 9) \cdots$, $untime(\sigma) = \epsilon\epsilon a\bar{a}\bar{a}b\bar{b}\bar{b}a \cdots$. For a Π, we define $untime(\Pi)$ to be the trace assignment, where $Dom(\Pi) = Dom(untime(\Pi))$ and for every $\pi \in Dom(\Pi)$, $untime(\Pi)(\pi) = (untime(\sigma), now(\Pi))$, where $\Pi(\pi) = (\sigma, p)$.

Next, given a synchronous HyperMTL formula φ, we define a transformed formula $U(\varphi)$ inductively as follows. Here, $Event^\varphi$ corresponds to the occurrence of an event, and is defined as $Event^\varphi = \bigvee_{\pi \in Var(\varphi), a \in AP} a_\pi$.

$$U(true) = true \qquad\qquad\qquad\qquad U(a_\pi) = a_\pi \vee \bar{a}_\pi$$
$$U(\varphi_1 \vee \varphi_2) = U(\varphi_1) \vee U(\varphi_2) \qquad\qquad U(\neg\varphi) = \neg U(\varphi)$$
$$U(\varphi_1 \, \mathcal{U}_I \, \varphi_2) = (Event \to U(\varphi_1)) \, \mathcal{U}_I \, (Event \wedge U(\varphi_2)) \qquad U(Q.\alpha) = Q.U(\alpha)$$

Lemma 2. *Given a synchronous formula α, a set of timed traces W and an assignment Π, $(W, \Pi) \models \alpha$ if and only if $(untime(W), untime(\Pi)) \models U(\alpha)$.*

The above lemma can be proved by induction on the structure of α.

Given a Kripke structure $\mathcal{M}$ and a synchronous HyperMTL formula α, our objective is to check if $\mathcal{L}(\mathcal{M}), \Pi_\emptyset \models \alpha$. Lemma 2 states that it is equivalent to checking $untime(\mathcal{L}(\mathcal{M})), untime(\Pi_\emptyset) \models U(\alpha)$. It is straightforward to construct an $\hat{\mathcal{M}}$ that generates $untime(\mathcal{M})$ from $\mathcal{M}$ by replacing transitions in $\mathcal{M}$, say, from a state s to a state s' with delay d, by sequence of $d - 1$ intermediate states whose labels are $\bar{a}$, where a is the label of s.

6 Related Work

There has been a lot of recent progress in automatically verifying [15,22–24] and monitoring [2,7,8,20,21,26,33] HyperLTL specifications, including a growing set of tools, like the model checker MCHyper [15,24], the satisfiability checkers EAHyper [19] and MGHyper [17], and the runtime monitoring tool RVHyper [20]. Synthesis techniques for HyperLTL has been studied in [18] and in [6].

Comparatively, much less attention has been put to timed hyperproperties. The work in [30] introduces HyperSTL, which extends STL by allowing quantification over real-valued signals, and proposes a monitoring algorithm for HyperSTL formulas. The work in [27] introduces the temporal logic timed HyperLTL, which adds one type of timing constraint to the until operator in the synchronous semantics of HyperLTL. This covers some timed hyperproperties, but it falls short in expressing requirements such as timing side-channels as presented in Sect. 4. Our formulation allows the execution times in different traces to be *similar* (i.e., $\Diamond_{[0,\infty),[0,1]}(r_\pi \wedge r_{\pi'})$), rather than just within a prescribed time bound as in [27]). Also, the proposed logic operates only in the HyperLTL synchronous semantics, meaning that all evaluations are conducted in the same trace positions.

Another recent work on timed hyperproperties is [28], which proposes an alternative definition to HyperMTL also distinguishing synchronous and asynchronous semantics, but there are fundamental differences. The synchronous semantics is similar to that of the one proposed in [27], and forces all traces to include events at the same instants, with the global time-stamp as an additional value. The asynchronous semantics in [27] is similar to our synchronous semantics, which keeps a global clock in the evaluation and proceeds in a total order. In comparison, our asynchronous semantics is based on the existence of a trajectory and allows to compare traces that evolve at different speeds, which cannot be captured in [28]. Additionally, most of the fragments of the logic in [28] are undecidable. Finally, the logic in [28] does not incorporate framing and suffers from many logical anomalies. For example, $\forall \pi_b.(p_{\pi_b} \, \mathcal{U} \, q_{\pi_b})$ is not equivalent to $\forall \pi_a.\forall \pi_b.(p_{\pi_b} \, \mathcal{U} \, q_{\pi_b})$ in spite of π_a not occurring in the inner formula (see [28] p. 16:6). Also, it is possible in the logic in [28] that for a given model M and formula φ, neither $M \models \varphi$ nor $M \models \neg\varphi$. All these anomalies are fixed by framing introduced here, but the formal proof is out of the scope of this paper.

7   Conclusion and Future Work

We introduced the temporal logic HyperMTL for *timed hyperproperties*. Even though our logic can be easily extended to richer models of time, we described here a discrete-time domain that guarantees a decidable model-checking problem. We showed that HyperMTL can elegantly express important properties such as countermeasures to a rich class of side-channel timing attacks, SLA, and properties of CPS such as robustness and overshoot detectability. To automate the verification task, we proposed a model checking algorithm by reducing the problem to model checking HyperLTL. As future work, we plan to implement our algorithm, build tools, and conduct case studies in the areas mentioned in Sect. 4. Other important research directions include foundational problems such as satisfiability, verification, monitoring, and synthesis for different fragments of HyperMTL, as well as extensions to richer time domains.

References

1. Ábrahám, E., Bonakdarpour, B.: HyperPCTL: a temporal logic for probabilistic hyperproperties. In: Proceedings of the 15th International Conference on Quantitative Evaluation of Systems (QEST), pp. 20–35 (2018)

2. Agrawal, S., Bonakdarpour, B.: Runtime verification of k-safety hyperproperties in HyperLTL. In: Proceedings of the IEEE 29th Computer Security Foundations (CSF), pp. 239–252 (2016)

3. Alpern, B., Schneider, F.B.: Defining liveness. Inf. Process. Lett. **21**, 181–185 (1985)

4. Alur, R., Dill, D.: A theory of timed automata. Theor. Comput. Sci. **126**(2), 183–235 (1994)

5. Biere, A., Cimatti, A., Clarke, E., Zhu, Y.: Symbolic model checking without BDDs. In: Cleaveland, W.R. (ed.) TACAS 1999. LNCS, vol. 1579, pp. 193–207. Springer, Heidelberg (1999). https://doi.org/10.1007/3-540-49059-0_14

6. Bonakdarpour, B., Finkbeiner, B.: Program repair for hyperproperties. In: Chen, Y.-F., Cheng, C.-H., Esparza, J. (eds.) ATVA 2019. LNCS, vol. 11781, pp. 423–441. Springer, Cham (2019). https://doi.org/10.1007/978-3-030-31784-3_25

7. Bonakdarpour, B., Sanchez, C., Schneider, G.: Monitoring hyperproperties by combining static analysis and runtime verification. In: Margaria, T., Steffen, B. (eds.) ISoLA 2018. LNCS, vol. 11245, pp. 8–27. Springer, Cham (2018). https://doi.org/10.1007/978-3-030-03421-4_2

8. Brett, N., Siddique, U., Bonakdarpour, B.: Rewriting-based runtime verification for alternation-free HyperLTL. In: Legay, A., Margaria, T. (eds.) TACAS 2017. LNCS, vol. 10206, pp. 77–93. Springer, Heidelberg (2017). https://doi.org/10.1007/978-3-662-54580-5_5

9. Burch, J.R., Clarke, E.M., McMillan, K.L., Dill, D.L., Hwang, L.J.: Symbolic model checking: 10^{20} states and beyond. Inf. Comput. **98**(2), 142–170 (1992)

10. Cimatti, A., Clarke, E.M., Giunchiglia, F., Roveri, M.: NUSMV: a new symbolic model checker. Soft. Tools Technol. Transf. (STTT) **2**(4), 410–425 (2000)

11. Clarke, E.M., Emerson, E.A.: Design and synthesis of synchronization skeletons using branching time temporal logic. In: Kozen, D. (ed.) Logic of Programs 1981. LNCS, vol. 131, pp. 52–71. Springer, Heidelberg (1982). https://doi.org/10.1007/BFb0025774

12. Clarke, E.M., Filkorn, T., Jha, S.: Exploiting symmetry in temporal logic model checking. In: Courcoubetis, C. (ed.) CAV 1993. LNCS, vol. 697, pp. 450–462. Springer, Heidelberg (1993). https://doi.org/10.1007/3-540-56922-7_37

13. Clarkson, M.R., Finkbeiner, B., Koleini, M., Micinski, K.K., Rabe, M.N., Sánchez, C.: Temporal logics for hyperproperties. In: Abadi, M., Kremer, S. (eds.) POST 2014. LNCS, vol. 8414, pp. 265–284. Springer, Heidelberg (2014). https://doi.org/10.1007/978-3-642-54792-8_15

14. Clarkson, M.R., Schneider, F.B.: Hyperproperties. J. Comput. Secur. **18**(6), 1157–1210 (2010)

15. Coenen, N., Finkbeiner, B., Sánchez, C., Tentrup, L.: Verifying hyperliveness. In: Dillig, I., Tasiran, S. (eds.) CAV 2019. LNCS, vol. 11561, pp. 121–139. Springer, Cham (2019). https://doi.org/10.1007/978-3-030-25540-4_7

16. Devriese, D., Piessens, F.: Noninterference through secure multi-execution. In: Proceedings of the 31st IEEE Symposium on Security and Privacy, S&P, pp. 109–124 (2010)

17. Finkbeiner, B., Hahn, C., Hans, T.: MGHYPER: checking satisfiability of HyperLTL formulas beyond the $\exists^*\forall^*$ fragment. In: Lahiri, S.K., Wang, C. (eds.) ATVA 2018. LNCS, vol. 11138, pp. 521–527. Springer, Cham (2018). https://doi.org/10.1007/978-3-030-01090-4_31

18. Finkbeiner, B., Hahn, C., Lukert, P., Stenger, M., Tentrup, L.: Synthesizing reactive systems from hyperproperties. In: Chockler, H., Weissenbacher, G. (eds.) CAV 2018. LNCS, vol. 10981, pp. 289–306. Springer, Cham (2018). https://doi.org/10.1007/978-3-319-96145-3_16

19. Finkbeiner, B., Hahn, C., Stenger, M.: EAHyper: satisfiability, implication, and equivalence checking of hyperproperties. In: Majumdar, R., Kunčak, V. (eds.) CAV 2017. LNCS, vol. 10427, pp. 564–570. Springer, Cham (2017). https://doi.org/10.1007/978-3-319-63390-9_29

20. Finkbeiner, B., Hahn, C., Stenger, M., Tentrup, L.: RVHyper: a runtime verification tool for temporal hyperproperties. In: Beyer, D., Huisman, M. (eds.) TACAS 2018. LNCS, vol. 10806, pp. 194–200. Springer, Cham (2018). https://doi.org/10.1007/978-3-319-89963-3_11

21. Finkbeiner, B., Hahn, C., Stenger, M., Tentrup, L.: Monitoring hyperproperties. Formal Meth. Syst. Des. **54**(3), 336–363 (2019). https://doi.org/10.1007/s10703-019-00334-z

22. Finkbeiner, B., Hahn, C., Torfah, H.: Model checking quantitative hyperproperties. In: Chockler, H., Weissenbacher, G. (eds.) CAV 2018. LNCS, vol. 10981, pp. 144–163. Springer, Cham (2018). https://doi.org/10.1007/978-3-319-96145-3_8

23. Finkbeiner, B., Müller, Ch., Seidl, H., Zalinescu, E.: Verifying security policies in multi-agent workflows with loops. In: Proceedings of the 15th ACM Conference on Computer and Communications Security (CCS) (2017)

24. Finkbeiner, B., Rabe, M.N., Sánchez, C.: Algorithms for model checking Hyper-LTL and HyperCTL*. In: Kroening, D., Păsăreanu, C.S. (eds.) CAV 2015. LNCS, vol. 9206, pp. 30–48. Springer, Cham (2015). https://doi.org/10.1007/978-3-319-21690-4_3

25. Goguen, J.A., Meseguer, J.: Security policies and security models. In: IEEE Symposium on Security and Privacy, pp. 11–20 (1982)

26. Hahn, C., Stenger, M., Tentrup, L.: Constraint-based monitoring of hyperproperties. In: Vojnar, T., Zhang, L. (eds.) TACAS 2019. LNCS, vol. 11428, pp. 115–131. Springer, Cham (2019). https://doi.org/10.1007/978-3-030-17465-1_7

27. Heinen, J.: Model checking timed hyperproperties. Master's thesis. Saarland University (2018)

28. Ho, H.-M., Zhou, R., Jones, T.M.: On verifying timed hyperproperties. In: Proceedings of the 26th International Symposium on Temporal Representation and Reasoning (TIME), pp. 20:1–20:18 (2019)

29. Holzmann, G.: The model checker spin. IEEE Trans. Soft. Eng. 23(5), 279–295 (1997)

30. Nguyen, L.V., Kapinski, J., Jin, X., Deshmukh, J.V., Johnson, T.T.: Hyperproperties of real-valued signals. In: Proceedings of the 15th ACM-IEEE International Conference on Formal Methods and Models for System Design (MEMOCODE), pp. 104–113 (2017)

31. Pnueli, A.: The temporal logic of programs. In: Symposium on Foundations of Computer Science (FOCS), pp. 46–57 (1977)

32. Sipser, M.: Introduction to the Theory of Computation, 3rd edn. Cengage Learning (2012)

33. Stucki, S., Sánchez, C., Schneider, G., Bonakdarpour, B.: Gray-box monitoring of hyperproperties. In: ter Beek, M.H., McIver, A., Oliveira, J.N. (eds.) FM 2019. LNCS, vol. 11800, pp. 406–424. Springer, Cham (2019). https://doi.org/10.1007/978-3-030-30942-8_25

34. Vardi, M.Y., Wolper, P.: Automata theoretic techniques for modal logic of programs. J. Comput. Syst. Sci. 32, 183–221 (1986)

35. Zdancewic, S., Myers, A.C.: Observational determinism for concurrent program security. In: Proceedings of the 16th IEEE Computer Security Foundations Workshop (CSFW), p. 29 (2003)

Verifying Band Convergence for Sampled Control Systems

P. Ezudheen[1], Zahra Rahimi Afzal[2], Pavithra Prabhakar[2],
Deepak D'Souza[1(✉)], and Meenakshi D'Souza[3]

[1] Indian Institute of Science, Bangalore, India
deepakd@iisc.ac.in
[2] Kansas State University, Manhattan, USA
[3] International Institute of Information Technology, Bangalore, India

Abstract. We present a method to verify transient and settling time properties, called band convergence properties, of digitally controlled continuous systems, wherein we consider a linear dynamical system model for a plant and a PID controller. We consider the discrete-time sampled behavior of the closed loop system, and verify band convergence for the discrete-time behavior. The basic idea is to look for a box-shaped invariant for the system which is adequate to ensure that the system stays within the given band. We first give a technique to handle a general discrete-time system, but with determinate matrix entries. We then give a technique to handle discrete-time systems with matrices that lie in a range which over-approximate the matrix exponentials (which arise when we consider the discrete-time version of a continuous system), using the notion of an abstract discrete-time system. We have implemented the verification approach, and evaluate its efficacy on some popular Simulink models.

1 Introduction

Modern control systems are deployed in safety critical environments with rigorous real-time constraints. For instance, autonomous vehicles consist of controllers that are required to respond in real-time to environmental uncertainties including detection of pedestrians and changing weather and lighting conditions. Hence, there is an increasing demand for rigorous analysis methods that can guarantee that these control systems meet the real-time requirements. In this paper, we focus on a fundamental real-time property expected of any control system design, namely, that the controller drives the system output to a set-point. We refer to the property as the band convergence property. More precisely, the property specifies that the closed loop system behavior remains within some bound of a set point between the rise time and settling time and remains close to the set-point after the settling time, where rise time refers to the time required for the output signal to reach from 10% to 90% of the set-point, and settling time refers to time it takes the output signal to reach within 2% of the set-point. See Fig. 1 for an illustration.

© Springer Nature Switzerland AG 2020
R. Lee et al. (Eds.): NFM 2020, LNCS 12229, pp. 329–349, 2020.
https://doi.org/10.1007/978-3-030-55754-6_19

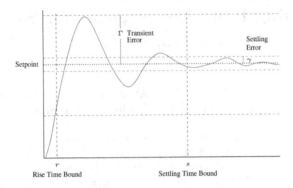

Fig. 1. The band convergence property

The band convergence property can be conveniently modeled in Signal Temporal Logic (STL) [1,2], that extends the classical linear temporal logic (LTL), with predicates capturing properties about the system states and real-time constraints. While there has been extensive work on monitoring [3,4], trace generation [5], and model-checking over reach sequences [6], for STL properties, the verification problem for STL properties is undecidable for most system models, including discrete systems. To verify continuous and hybrid system models for STL properties, standard abstraction based approaches such as predicate abstraction can be used that reduce the problem to LTL verification problem on a finite state system. However, such an approach will quickly lead to a statespace explosion as the number of predicates increases. In this paper, we focus on a specific class of hybrid system models, namely, a linear dynamical system model of a plant controlled by a digital proportional, integral and derivative controller. This is a widely used class of systems and controllers. We consider a specific, albeit important, subclass of STL properties, namely, band convergence properties.

We first consider a discrete version of the problem, wherein we discretize the continuous plant by observing the states at only certain sample times. While exactly computing the discrete-time behavior at periodic sample times is computationally infeasible due to the matrix exponential computations involved, we consider an "approximate" discrete time problem for which we verify the band convergence property.

Next we consider an abstract version of the problem. We define an abstract system by providing two sets of system matrices capturing the lower and upper bounds on the actual system matrices. We briefly sketch how to compute such an abstract system for a continuous plant and a PID controller, such that all the sampled behaviors of the original closed loop system are captured by this abstract system.

Our solutions to these two problems are based on box invariants, that are efficiently checkable. Initially, we present a sufficient condition to check that the abstract system satisfies the band convergence property, by searching for a box invariant. Finally, we show that the solution for the abstract version of the problem can be efficiently customized/tuned to solve the discrete version of the band convergence problem.

2 Models of Control Systems and Band Convergence Property

In this section we present various models of a control system comprising of a plant and a controller, and define the band convergence property verification problem. We begin with a continuous-time linear dynamical system model of a plant that is controlled by a sampled-data PID (proportional, integral, derivative) controller. We then focus on the behavior of the closed loop system at periodic sample times, and model it as a discrete-time linear dynamical system and verify this system against the band convergence property.

In the sequel we use $\mathbb{N}$ and $\mathbb{R}$ to denote the set of natural numbers and real numbers respectively. For a matrix M, the matrix exponential e^M denotes the sum of the series $1 + M + \frac{M^2}{2!} + \frac{M^3}{3!} \cdots$. We denote by $T_k(M)$ the sum of the first k terms of this series: i.e. $T_k(M) = \sum_{j=0}^{k} M^j/j!$. For a real value α and $m \times n$ matrix M we denote by αM the $m \times n$ matrix M' given by $M'(i,j) = \alpha(M(i,j))$.

2.1 Linear Dynamical System

A continuous-time linear dynamical system can be represented by a system of equations as follows:

$$\dot{x}(t) = A_c x(t) + B_c u(t) \qquad\qquad x(0) = x_0 \qquad\qquad (1)$$
$$y(t) = C_c x(t) \qquad\qquad\qquad\qquad (2)$$

where $A_c \in \mathbb{R}^{n \times n}$, $B_c \in \mathbb{R}^{n \times d}$, and $C_c \in \mathbb{R}^{m \times n}$ are system matrices, and for every t, $x(t) \in \mathbb{R}^n$, $y(t) \in \mathbb{R}^m$ and $u(t) \in \mathbb{R}^d$, are the state, output and input at time t, respectively, and x_0 is the initial state of the system.

Given an input signal $u(t)$, the solution of System (1) is unique and is given by:

$$x(t) = e^{A_c t}[x_0 + \int_0^t e^{-A_c \tau} B_c u(\tau) d\tau] \qquad\qquad (3)$$

A controller for the system provides the value of input $u(t)$ at all times t.

2.2 Sampled-Data Control System

We consider a digital controller that senses the value of the state/output periodically at intervals of size h, that is, at times $0, h, 2h, \ldots$, and computes a corresponding input based on the values of the state/output at these points, and applies the computed input in the interval $[ih, (i+1)h)$. That is, $u(t) = g(y(ih))$, where ih represents the last sample time before t, and g is a state feedback controller. Let us denote by x_i, y_i and u_i the state, output and the input respectively, at the i-th sample time ih, that is, $x_i = x(ih), y_i = y(ih)$ and $u_i = u(ih)$ (in fact, $u_i = u(t)$ for all $t \in [ih, (i+1)h)$). By considering a constant input u_i, and the initial state x_0 and state x_i, and assuming A_c to be an invertible matrix, we can rewrite Eqs. (3) and (2) as follows:

$$x_i = e^{A_c h} x_{i-1} + A_c^{-1}(e^{A_c h} - I)B_c u_{i-1} \qquad (4)$$
$$y_i = C_c x_i \qquad (5)$$

2.3   Sampled-Data PID Control System

In this paper we focus on a state-feedback PID controller whose objective is to drive the system output close to a set point y^*. A PID controller computes the input u_i based on the error e_i between the observed output y_i and the set point y^*, an integral value ι_i that accumulates the error, and a derivative value d_i that measures the difference between successive errors. Hence, a PID controller is specified as follows:

$$u_i = K_P e_i + K_I \iota_i + K_D d_i \qquad (6)$$

where K_P, K_I and K_D are scalar matrices referred to as the proportional, integral and derivative gains respectively, and e_i, ι_i and d_i are vectors corresponding to the error, integral and derivative terms respectively, are defined as:

$$e_i = y^* - y_i \qquad (7)$$
$$\iota_i = \iota_{i-1} + e_i \qquad (8)$$
$$d_i = e_i - e_{i-1} \qquad (9)$$

Initial values e_0, d_0 and ι_0 are taken to be 0. Note that once the initial state x_0 is provided, all values of the variables $x_i, y_i, u_i, e_i, \iota_i$ and d_i, for $i = 0, 1, \ldots$ are uniquely defined. We refer to the system defined by Eqs. 4, 5, 6, 7, 8, and 9 as a *closed loop system* $S_c = (A_c, B_c, C_c, K_P, K_I, K_D, y^*, x_0)$, whose *execution* is the sequence $\{x_i\}_{i \in \mathbb{N}}$, and whose *trace* is the sequence $\{y_i\}_{i \in \mathbb{N}}$. We refer to $\{\iota_i\}_{i \in \mathbb{N}}$ and $\{d_i\}_{i \in \mathbb{N}}$ as the integral and derivative sequence of S_c respectively.

2.4   Discrete-Time Linear System

The behavior (execution and trace) of a closed loop system S_c can also be generated by a discrete-time linear system, which we present next.

Definition 1. *A discrete-time system is of the form $S = (A, B, C, y^*, z_0)$. The execution of the system S is the sequence $\{z_i\}_{i \in \mathbb{N}}$, where for $i \geq 0$, z_i is inductively defined as $z_i = A z_{i-1} + B y^*$. The trace of the system S is the sequence $\{C z_i\}_{i \in \mathbb{N}}$.*

The following proposition defines the discrete-time system $S = (A, B, C, y^*, z_0)$ corresponding to the closed loop system S_c given by Eqs. 4, 5, 6, 7, 8, and 9.

Proposition 1. *Consider a closed loop system* $S_c = (A_c, B_c, C_c, K_P, K_I, K_D, y^*, x_0)$, *and a discrete-time system* $S = (A, B, C, y^*, z_0)$, *where:*

$$A = \begin{bmatrix} A' - B'(K_P + K_D)C_c & B'K_I & -B'K_D \\ C_c(B'(K_P + K_D)C_c - A') & I - C_cB'K_I & C_cB'K_D \\ -C_c & 0 & 0 \end{bmatrix}, \quad B = \begin{bmatrix} B'(K_P + K_D) \\ I - C_cB'(K_P + K_D) \\ I \end{bmatrix},$$

$$C = \begin{bmatrix} C_c & 0 & 0 \end{bmatrix}, \quad z_0 = \begin{bmatrix} x_0 \\ 0 \\ 0 \end{bmatrix}, \quad A' = e^{A_ch} \quad and \quad B' = A_c^{-1}(e^{A_ch} - I)B_c.$$

Let $\{x_i\}_{i \in \mathbb{N}}$, $\{\iota_i\}_{i \in \mathbb{N}}$, *and* $\{e_{i-1}\}_{i \in \mathbb{N}}$ *be the execution, integral and error sequences of* S_c, *and* $\{z_i\}_{i \in \mathbb{N}}$ *the execution of* S. *Then the following hold:*

- $z_i = \begin{bmatrix} x_i & \iota_i & e_{i-1} \end{bmatrix}$,
- *The traces of* S_c *and* S *are the same; that is,* $C_c x_i = C z_i$ *for all* i.

Proof. The following derivation proves Proposition 1.

$$x_i = A'x_{i-1} + B'u_{i-1} \tag{10}$$

$$= A'x_{i-1} + B'(K_P e_{i-1} + K_I \iota_{i-1} + K_D d_{i-1}) \tag{11}$$

$$= A'x_{i-1} + B'(K_P(y^* - y_{i-1}) + K_I \iota_{i-1} + K_D(y^* - y_{i-1} - e_{i-2})) \tag{12}$$

$$= A'x_{i-1} + B'(-K_P y_{i-1} - K_D y_{i-1} + K_I \iota_{i-1} - K_D e_{i-2} + K_P y^* + K_D y^*) \tag{13}$$

$$= A'x_{i-1} + B'(-(K_P + K_D)y_{i-1} + K_I \iota_{i-1} - K_D e_{i-2} + (K_P + K_D)y^*) \tag{14}$$

$$= A'x_{i-1} - B'(K_P + K_D)y_{i-1} + B'K_I \iota_{i-1} - B'K_D e_{i-2} + B'(K_P + K_D)y^* \tag{15}$$

$$= (A' - B'(K_P + K_D)C_c)x_{i-1} + B'K_I \iota_{i-1} - B'K_D e_{i-2} + B'(K_P + K_D)y^* \tag{16}$$

$$\iota_i = e_i + \iota_{i-1} \tag{17}$$

$$= -C_c x_i + y^* + \iota_{i-1} \tag{18}$$

$$= -C_c((A' - B'(K_P + K_D)C_c)x_{i-1} + B'K_I \iota_{i-1} - B'K_D e_{i-2} + B'(K_P + K_D)y^*) + y^* + \iota_{i-1} \tag{19}$$

$$= -C_c(A' - B'(K_P + K_D)C_c)x_{i-1} - C_cB'K_I \iota_{i-1} + C_cB'K_D e_{i-2} - C_cB'(K_P + K_D)y^* + y^* + \iota_{i-1} \tag{20}$$

$$= C_c(B'(K_P + K_D)C_c - A')x_{i-1} + (I - C_cB'K_I)\iota_{i-1} + C_cB'K_D e_{i-2} + (I - C_cB'(K_P + K_D))y^* \tag{21}$$

$$e_{i-1} = -C_c x_{i-1} + y^* \tag{22}$$

Equations (16), (21) and (22) essentially imply that $z_i = Az_{i-1} + By^*$, where $z_i = \begin{bmatrix} x_i & \iota_i & e_{i-1} \end{bmatrix}$.

Proposition 1 states that the trace of the closed loop system S_c is captured exactly by the trace of the discrete system S, and the execution of S_c is captured by the first component of the execution of S. Since S has fewer components than S_c, we consider S for our analysis instead of S_c.

2.5 Band Convergence Property

We are interested in verifying a fundamental property of control systems, namely, that the closed loop system "converges" to a given set-point, and remains close to the set-point in an initial transient phase. We call this a "band convergence" property. More precisely, we require that (1) the output of the system remains within a Γ distance (called the *transient error*) from the set-point between the rise time bound and the settling time bound, and (2) the output remains within a smaller γ distance (called the *settling error*) from the set-point after the settling time bound. Formally, a band convergence property is given by a tuple (Γ, γ, r, s), where $\Gamma > 0$ denotes the transient error, $\gamma > 0$ the settling error, $r \in \mathbb{N}$ the rise time, and $s \in \mathbb{N}$ the settling time. For $\epsilon > 0$, let $\mathbb{B}_\epsilon(x)$ denote the set $\{x' \mid \|x-x'\| \le \epsilon\}$, where $\|x''\|$ is the Euclidean norm of x''. We say a discrete-time system $S = (A, B, C, y^*, z_0)$ *satisfies* a band convergence property (Γ, γ, r, s) if $y_i \in \mathbb{B}_\Gamma(y^*) \; \forall i \in [r, s]$, and $y_i \in \mathbb{B}_\gamma(y^*) \; \forall i \in (s, \infty)$, where $\{y_i\}_{i \in \mathbb{N}}$ is the trace of S.

Problem 1. Given a discrete-time system $S = (A, B, C, y^*, z_0)$ and a band convergence property (Γ, γ, r, s), check whether S satisfies band convergence with respect to (Γ, γ, r, s).

2.6 Abstract System

Computing the execution and trace of a discrete system S obtained from the given closed loop system S_c as given by Proposition 1 involves matrix exponentials which are infeasible to compute exactly. Hence we cannot guarantee exact computation of the matrices of S always. We propose the notion of an abstract system that is intended to capture a "parameterized set" of linear systems and define the corresponding band convergence problem. In the next subsection, we show how to compute an abstract system $\hat{S}$ from S_c (or equivalently S) such that the set of executions and traces of S are contained in the set of executions and traces of $\hat{S}$ respectively.

For a matrix A, we use $A(i, j)$ to refer to the entry at the i-th row and j-th column of A. We write $A > 0$ to mean every element of A has a positive value, and $A \le B$ to mean $A(i, j) \le B(i, j)$ for every i, j. For a given set of matrices $A_1, A_2, ..., A_n$, the matrix operations min and max are defined as $min(A_1, A_2, ..., A_n)(i, j) = min(A_1(i, j), A_2(i, j), ..., A_n(i, j))$ and $max(A_1, A_2, ..., A_n)(i, j) = max(A_1(i, j), A_2(i, j), ..., A_n(i, j))$ for every i, j. For a real value α, we use $\alpha_{m \times n}$ to denote a two dimension matrix such that every element of this matrix is α, and we use I_m to denote an identity matrix of rank m.

Definition 2. *An abstract system is of the form $\hat{S} = (A_l, A_u, B_l, B_u, C, y^*, z_0)$, where C, y^* and z_0 are as in Definition 1, A_l and A_u are matrices of similar dimension to matrix A, and B_l and B_u are matrices of similar dimension to matrix B of Definition 1. The execution of $\hat{S}$ is a sequence of sets of states $\{Z_i\}_{i \in \mathbb{N}}$ given by $Z_0 = \{z_0\}$, and $Z_i = \{Az + By^* \mid z \in Z_{i-1}, A_l \le A \le A_u, B_l \le B \le B_u\}$. The trace of $\hat{S}$ is given by $\{Y_i\}$, where $Y_i = \{Cz \mid z \in Z_i\}$.*

Note that when $A_l = A_u$ and $B_l = B_u$, $\hat{S}$ in fact represents a standard discrete system, and the execution and trace will be a sequence of singleton sets, representing the execution and trace, respectively, of the discrete system.

We say an abstract system $\hat{S} = (A_l, A_u, B_l, B_u, C, y^*, z_0)$ with trace $\{Y_i\}_{i \in \mathbb{N}}$ *satisfies* and a band convergence property (Γ, γ, r, s), if $Y_i \subseteq \mathbb{B}_r(y^*) \; \forall i \in [r, s]$, and $Y_i \subseteq \mathbb{B}_\gamma(y^*) \; \forall i \in (s, \infty)$. Problem 1 can now be phrased analogously over an abstract system as follows:

Problem 2. Given an abstract system $\hat{S}$ and a band convergence property (Γ, γ, r, s), check whether $\hat{S}$ satisfies (Γ, γ, r, s).

We now formalize when an abstract system over-approximates a discrete system, and how it preserves the band convergence property.

Proposition 2. *Let $S = (A, B, C, y^*, z_0)$ be a discrete-time system and $\hat{S} = (A_l, A_u, B_l, B_u, C, y^*, z_0)$ be an abstract system such that $A_l \leq A \leq A_u$ and $B_l \leq B \leq B_u$. Let (Γ, γ, r, s) be the parameters of a band convergence property. If $\hat{S}$ satisfies (Γ, γ, r, s), then S satisfies (Γ, γ, r, s).*

If $A_l \leq A \leq A_u$ and $B_l \leq B \leq B_u$, then we say that $\hat{S}$ over-approximates S. The above proposition states that if the abstract system $\hat{S}$ over-approximates S and the band convergence property is satisfied in the abstract system, then it holds in the discrete system too. The proof follows from the fact that $z_i \in Z_i$, for every i, where $\{z_i\}_{i \in \mathbb{N}}$ and $\{Z_i\}_{i \in \mathbb{N}}$ are the executions of S and $\hat{S}$, respectively.

2.7 Computation of the Abstract System

Our objective in this section is to compute an abstract system $\hat{S} = (A_l, A_u, B_l, B_u, C_c, y^*, z_0)$, which over-approximates the discrete system $S = (A, B, C, y^*, z_0)$ which, in turn, is a simplified representation of the closed loop system S_c as defined in Proposition 1. We essentially need to compute A_l, A_u, B_l and B_u such that $A_l \leq A \leq A_u$ and $B_l \leq B \leq B_u$. Proposition 2 then ensures that if $\hat{S}$ satisfies the band convergence property (Γ, γ, r, s), then S satisfies it as well. However, note that while we intend to over-approximate S, S is only specified indirectly using S_c whose elements we assume are all rational.

In the rest of the section, we discuss the computation of $\hat{S}$ from S_c. We observe from Proposition 1 that the matrices A, B and C are computed from the matrices of S_c by computing matrix exponentials and inverses (at the base) and then performing multiplications, additions and subtractions. While inverses, multiplications, additions and subtractions of matrices with rational elements can be computed precisely, the same is not true for exponentials. Our strategy is to over-approximate a matrix exponential e^M with two matrices M_l and M_u such that $M_l \leq e^M \leq M_u$. Though matrix exponentials are performed only on A_c in Proposition 1, it is then used in the computation of A and B. Hence, we need to provide a method to carry over the over-approximation of matrix exponentials through addition, subtraction and multiplication to compute upper and lower bounds on A and B. Proposition 3 shows how we can compute lower and upper approximations of a matrix exponential, while Proposition 4 states how to carry over the over-approximation through addition, subtraction and multiplication operations.

Proposition 3 *[7]. Let M be an $m \times n$ matrix. Suppose k is a positive integer and ϵ a positive real number such that $\|M\|/(k + 2) < 1$ and*

$$\left(\frac{\|M\|^{k+1}}{(k+1)!} \right) \left(\frac{1}{1 - \|M\|/(k+2)} \right) \leq \epsilon. \text{ Then}$$

$$T_k(M) - \epsilon_{m \times n} \leq e^M \leq T_k(M) + \epsilon_{m \times n}.$$

Using this proposition we can obtain lower and upper approximations N_l and N_u for $e^{A_c h}$ by choosing k such that $\|A_c h\|/(k + 2) < 1$ and $\epsilon = \left(\frac{\|A_c h\|^{k+1}}{(k+1)!} \right) \left(\frac{1}{1 - \|A_c h\|/(k+2)} \right)$, and taking $N_l = T_k(A_c h) - \epsilon_{n \times n}$ and $N_u = T_k(A_c h) + \epsilon_{n \times n}$.

Our next objective is to over-approximate $A + B$, $A - B$ and AB given over-approximations of A and B. Broadly, the upper and lower bounds correspond to performing the corresponding interval arithmetic operations on interval matrices. More precisely, given intervals $[a, b]$ and $[c, d]$, the interval arithmetic operations corresponding to addition, subtraction and multiplication are given by $[a, b] + [c, d] = [a + c, b + d]$, $[a, b] - [c, d] = [a - d, b - c]$ and $[a, b] * [c, d] = [min(a * c, a * d, b * c, b * d), max(a * c, a * d, b * c, b * d)]$. Given two matrices A' and B', where each element is an interval, $A' + B'$, $A' - B'$ and $A'B'$ are defined analogous to that of real matrices, where the addition, subtraction and multiplication are now replaced by the corresponding interval arithmetic operations as defined above. Given matrices $M_l \leq M_u$, let $\langle M_l, M_u \rangle$ denote the matrix whose (i, j)-th element is the interval $[M_l(i, j), M_u(i, j)]$. Given a matrix M' with bounded interval entries, $[M']_L$ and $[M']_U$ are matrices whose entries correspond to the left and the right end points of the corresponding intervals in M'.

Proposition 4. *Given matrices A_l, A, A_u and B_l, B, B_u, if $A_l \leq A \leq A_u$ and $B_l \leq B \leq B_u$ then*

(a) $[\langle A_l, A_u \rangle \langle B_l, B_u \rangle]_L \leq AB \leq [\langle A_l, A_u \rangle \langle B_l, B_u \rangle]_U$
(b) $[\langle A_l, A_u \rangle + \langle B_l, B_u \rangle]_L \leq A + B \leq [\langle A_l, A_u \rangle + \langle B_l, B_u \rangle]_U$
(c) $[\langle A_l, A_u \rangle - \langle B_l, B_u \rangle]_L \leq A - B \leq [\langle A_l, A_u \rangle - \langle B_l, B_u \rangle]_U$

We observe that the last two inequalities simplify to $A_l + B_l \leq A + B \leq A_u + B_u$ and $A_l - B_u \leq A - B \leq A_u - B_l$.

Proposition 5. *Given $m \times n$ matrices A_l, A, A_u and $n \times r$ matrices B_l, B, B_u such that $A_l \leq A \leq A_u$ and $B_l \leq B \leq B_u$, we can compute $m \times r$ matrices $[\langle A_l, A_u \rangle \langle B_l, B_u \rangle]_L$ and $[\langle A_l, A_u \rangle \langle B_l, B_u \rangle]_U$ as follows.*

1. $[\langle A_l, A_u \rangle \langle B_l, B_u \rangle]_L(i, j) = \sum_{k=1}^{n} min(A_l(i, k) * B_l(k, j), A_l(i, k) * B_u(k, j), A_u(i, k) * B_l(k, j), A_u(i, k) * B_u(k, j))$

2. $[\langle A_l, A_u \rangle \langle B_l, B_u \rangle]_U(i,j) = \sum_{k=1}^{n} \max(A_l(i,k) * B_l(k,j), A_l(i,k) * B_u(k,j),$
$A_u(i,k) * B_l(k,j), A_u(i,k) * B_u(k,j)).$

Using the approximations N_l and N_u for $e^{A_c h}$ we can use Propositions 4 and 5 to compute lower and upper approximations A_l and A_u for A, and B_l and B_u for B.

3   Example: Cruise Control System

We illustrate our problem using a cruise control in Fig. 2, listed as one of the examples of control systems in [8]. Other examples are used as benchmarks in Sect. 6. The plant here is the car along with its rolling resistance and air drag which are proportional to the speed of the car. A PI controller periodically senses the speed of the car and controls the throttle angle in order to maintain the desired speed.

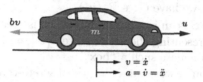

Fig. 2. Cruise control system

The dynamic behavior of the plant is represented using the following equations.

$$[\dot{v}] = \left[\tfrac{-b}{m}\right][v] + \left[\tfrac{1}{m}\right][u], v_0 = 0 \tag{23}$$

$$[y] = [1][v] \tag{24}$$

The control input to the plant is computed using the equation

$$[u] = [K_P][e] + [K_I][\iota] \tag{25}$$

where $m = 1000$ is the mass of the car, $b = 50$ is the friction constant, $K_P = 800$, $K_I = 40$ and v is the speed of the car. The parameters corresponding to Problem 1 are $y^* = 120$, $r = 5$, $s = 20$, $\gamma = 2.4$ and $\Gamma = 12$.

The components of the corresponding discrete-time system, $S = (A, B, C, y^*, z_0)$ are given below. We have taken a truncated value of $e^{A_c h}$.

$$A = \begin{bmatrix} 0.1709 & 0.0390165 & 0 \\ -0.1709 & 0.960984 & 0 \\ -1 & 0 & 0 \end{bmatrix}, \quad B = \begin{bmatrix} 0.780329 \\ 0.219671 \\ 1 \end{bmatrix}, \quad C = \begin{bmatrix} 1 \\ 0 \\ 0 \end{bmatrix} \quad \text{and} \quad z_0 = \begin{bmatrix} 0 \\ 0 \\ 0 \end{bmatrix}$$

4   Box Invariants

An invariant for a system is a set of states of the system such that the next step successor of every state in the set is also inside the set. It ensures that if a system starts within an invariant then all future states of the execution starting from that state also remain within the invariant. The approach we will propose for verifying that a system satisfies a band convergence property essentially looks for a "box-shaped" invariant for the system whose outputs are within the allowed γ-band of the set-point, and to see if the system eventually gets into this invariant while satisfying the transient requirements upto this point. More formally, we define an invariant for an abstract system as follows.

Definition 3. *Let $\hat{S} = (A_l, A_u, B_l, B_u, C, y^*, z_0)$ be an abstract system. A set of states Z is an* invariant *for $\hat{S}$ if for every z, A, B such that $z \in Z$, $A_l \leq A \leq A_u$ and $B_l \leq B \leq B_u$, we have $Az + By^* \in Z$.*

We say an invariant Z for $\hat{S}$ is an *adequate* invariant for $\hat{S}$ with respect to a settling error γ, if the output of the states in Z are contained in the set $\mathbb{B}_\gamma(y^*)$; that is for each $z \in Z$, we have $Cz \in \mathbb{B}_\gamma(y^*)$.

A *box* invariant for $\hat{S}$ is an invariant for $\hat{S}$ which is specified by a pair of state vectors z_l and z_u, representing the set of states $\{z \mid z_l \leq z \leq z_u\}$. We will use the notation $[z_l, z_u]$ to denote such a "box".

In the rest of this paper we assume that the discrete-time system has a unique equilibrium point, which corresponds to $(I - A)$ being an invertible matrix, where I is the identity matrix. An equilibrium point is a state of the system such that the execution of the system from that state remains in that state. In particular, if a system is in an equilibrium state, the next state of the system is the same as the current state.

Definition 4. *Let $S = (A, B, C, y^*, z_0)$ be a discrete-time system. Then z_e is an equilibrium point of S if $Az_e + By^* = z_e$. If $(I - A)$ is invertible, then the unique equilibrium point is $z_e = (I - A)^{-1}By^*$.*

Next we introduce a theorem which gives a necessary and sufficient condition for a box to be an invariant of an abstract system. The theorem reduces the invariant checking problem to checking the satisfiability of a logical formula.

Theorem 1. *Let $\hat{S} = (A_l, A_u, B_l, B_u, C, y^*, z_0)$ be an abstract system, and z_l, z_u be state vectors. Consider the conditions C1 and C2 below:*

$$C1 : [\langle A_l, A_u \rangle \langle z_l, z_u \rangle]_U + [\langle B_l, B_u \rangle \langle y^*, y^* \rangle]_U \leq z_u$$
$$C2 : z_l \leq [\langle A_l, A_u \rangle \langle z_l, z_u \rangle]_L + [\langle B_l, B_u \rangle \langle y^*, y^* \rangle]_L.$$

Then $[z_l, z_u]$ is an invariant for $\hat{S}$ iff the conditions C1 and C2 hold.   □

In a discrete system, where essentially $A_l = A_u$ and $B_l = B_u$, Theorem 1 provides an efficient way to check if some box centered around the equilibrium point is an invariant for the system. In the corollary below, for a vector p we use the notation $-p$ to mean the vector p' of the same dimension as p with $p'[i] = -p[i]$.

Corollary 1. *Let $S = (A, B, C, y^*, z_0)$ be a discrete-time system with dimensions as in Definition 1, such that $(I - A)$ is invertible. Then for any $n \times 1$ vector $p > 0$ the following conditions are equivalent:*

(a) $-p \leq [\langle A, A \rangle \langle -p, p \rangle]_L$ *and* $[\langle A, A \rangle \langle -p, p \rangle]_U \leq p$
(b) $[z_e - p, z_e + p]$ *is an invariant of S.*

Let A be an $m \times n$ matrix. The *infinity norm* of A, denoted $\|A\|_\infty$, is defined to be the maximum of the sums of the absolute values of the rows of A. More precisely, $\|A\|_\infty = \max_{i=1}^m \sum_{j=1}^n |A(i,j)|$. Note that when $\|A\|_\infty \leq 1$ the condition $-p \leq [\langle A, A \rangle \langle -p, p \rangle]_L$ and $[\langle A, A \rangle \langle -p, p \rangle]_U \leq p$ introduced in Corollary 1 will be satisfied by any $p > 0$.

4.1 Computation of an Adequate Box Invariant

Theorem 1 gives us a necessary and sufficient condition for a box $[z_l, z_u]$ to be an invariant of an abstract system $\hat{S}$. This constraint is of the form

$$[\langle A_l, A_u \rangle \langle z_l, z_u \rangle]_U + [\langle B_l, B_u \rangle \langle y^*, y^* \rangle]_U \leq z_u) \wedge (z_l \leq [\langle A_l, A_u \rangle \langle z_l, z_u \rangle]_L + [\langle B_l, B_u \rangle \langle y^*, y^* \rangle]_L,$$

where z_l, z_u are free variables (more precisely vectors of variables). One can add a conjunct

$$y^* - \gamma \leq [\langle C, C \rangle \langle z_l, z_u \rangle]_L \wedge [\langle C, C \rangle \langle z_l, z_u \rangle]_U \leq y^* + \gamma$$

which asks for the invariant to be adequate w.r.t. a given tolerance γ. One can now ask a solver like Z3 to find satisfying valuations for z_l and z_u. We note here that we would like to *maximize* the size of the box $[z_l, z_u]$ to reduce the number of iterations in the final verification algorithm (Algorithm 2 in the next section). Hence we could also ask the solver to optimize the values of z_l and z_u accordingly. As we report in our experimental results, this approach does reasonably well on small dimension systems, but does not scale well for systems with larger dimension.

In order to improve scalability we investigate a fixed point computation based algorithm, which uses a combination of bounded-precision numerical computation and precise constraint solving. The general fixed point algorithm is described in Algorithm 1. The algorithm takes three arguments: an abstract system $\hat{S}$, an initial box $[z_{l0}, z_{u0}]$, and a settling error (γ). The algorithm returns a structure comprising a status bit (successfully computed the invariant or not) and an adequate box invariant (if successfully computed).

The algorithm begins with the initial box, and iteratively computes the "closure" of this set of states under a single step of the abstract system. Lines 5 and 6 compute the lower and upper bounds respectively, of a single closure step. The algorithm will terminate successfully (status bit $b = \textit{True}$) if the lower and upper bounds remain unchanged (Line 13). The algorithm will terminate unsuccessfully (status bit $b = \textit{False}$) if the number of iterations exceed the time-out (TO) or the lower or upper bounds exceed the settling error (Line 8).

Algorithm 1. Computation of an adequate invariant for an abstract system

---

Require: $\hat{S} = (A_l, A_u, B_l, B_u, C, y^*, z_0), [z_{l0}, z_{u0}], \gamma$
Ensure: Return status bit b and box $[z_l, z_u]$. Whenever $b = $ *True*, $[z_l, z_u]$ is an adequate invariant for $\hat{S}$.

1:   $count \leftarrow 0$
2:   $z_l, w_l \leftarrow z_{l0}$
3:   $z_u, w_u \leftarrow z_{u0}$
4:   **repeat**
5:       $z_l \leftarrow \min(z_l, w_l)$
6:       $z_u \leftarrow \max(z_u, w_u)$
7:       **if** $[\langle C, C \rangle \langle z_l, z_u \rangle]_L < y^* - \gamma$ OR $y^* + \gamma < [\langle C, C \rangle \langle z_l, z_u \rangle]_U$ OR $count > TO$
    then
8:          return *False*, $[z_l, z_u]$
9:       $w_u \leftarrow [\langle A_l, A_u \rangle \langle z_l, z_u \rangle]_U + [\langle B_l, B_u \rangle \langle y^*, y^* \rangle]_U$
10:     $w_l \leftarrow [\langle A_l, A_u \rangle \langle z_l, z_u \rangle]_L + [\langle B_l, B_u \rangle \langle y^*, y^* \rangle]_L$
11:     $count \leftarrow count + 1$
12: **until** $z_l \leq w_l$ AND $w_u \leq z_u$
13: return *True*, $[z_l, z_u]$

We would ideally like to implement Algorithm 1 with *precise* numerical computation. A naive implementation in a programming language like C++ would use bounded precision floating point numbers. While efficient, with such an implementation the results of the algorithm may not be valid. We get around this problem by storing the values of the variables like w_l and w_u as symbolic *expressions* rather than evaluated values, and using a solver to evaluate conditions over these expressions. We call this a *symbolic* implementation of the algorithm.

However, as one may expect, such a symbolic execution leads to expressions whose size increases exponentially with the number of iterations of the loop, and at some point the solver will not be able to handle the queries. In order to alleviate this problem, we first run a numerical implementation of the algorithm in C++ to come up with a (potentially invalid) box invariant. We then run the symbolic version of the algorithm, using this invariant as the initial box. This two-phase approach, by combining the speed of numerical evaluation with the precision of symbolic evaluation speeds up the invariant computation without compromising on numerical correctness.

For the cruise control example we were able to compute an adequate box invariant

$$[[117.6 \; 139.488 \; -2.4]^T, \; [122.4 \; 160.512 \; 2.4]^T]$$

using this algorithm, with an initial box of the form $[[120, \; 150, \; 0]^T, \; [120, \; 150, \; 0]^T]$, obtained as described in Sect. 6.

5   Verification of Band Convergence Using Box Invariants

We now describe our main verification algorithm, Algorithm 2, for checking band convergence of an abstract system (Problem 2). The algorithm is given an abstract system and an adequate box invariant for it, and all it does is to "execute" the system one step at a time, till it finds the abstract state is contained in the given invariant, while ensuring that until this point the system state does not violate the transient band requirements.

Algorithm 2. Algorithm for checking band convergence for an abstract system

---

Require: Abstract system $\hat{S} = (A_l, A_u, B_l, B_u, C, y^*, z_0)$, band convergence property (γ, Γ, r, s), adequate invariant $[z_l, z_u]$ for $\hat{S}$ w.r.t. γ.
Ensure: Whenever the algorithm returns True, $\hat{S}$ satisfies the property (γ, Γ, r, s).

1:   $i \leftarrow 0$
2:   $w_l \leftarrow z_0$
3:   $w_u \leftarrow z_0$
4:   **while** True **do**
5:      $y_l \leftarrow [\langle C, C \rangle \langle w_l, w_u \rangle]_L$
6:      $y_u \leftarrow [\langle C, C \rangle \langle w_l, w_u \rangle]_U$
7:      **if** $r \leq i \leq s$ AND $(\|y_l - y^*\| > \Gamma$ OR $\|y_u - y^*\| > \Gamma)$ **then**
8:          return Unknown
9:      **if** $i > s$ AND $(\|y_l - y^*\| > \gamma$ OR $\|y_u - y^*\| > \gamma)$ **then**
10:       return Unknown
11:      **if** $i > s$ AND $[w_l, w_u] \subseteq [z_l, z_u]$ **then**
12:        return True
13:      $v_l \leftarrow [\langle A_l, A_u \rangle \langle w_l, w_u \rangle]_L + [\langle B_l, B_u \rangle \langle y^*, y^* \rangle]_L$
14:      $v_u \leftarrow [\langle A_l, A_u \rangle \langle w_l, w_u \rangle]_U + [\langle B_l, B_u \rangle \langle y^*, y^* \rangle]_U$
15:      $w_l \leftarrow v_l$
16:      $w_u \leftarrow v_u$
17:      $i \leftarrow i + 1$

The algorithm takes three arguments; an abstract system $\hat{S}$, an *adequate* invariant $[z_l, z_u]$, and a band convergence property (γ, Γ, r, s). Whenever the algorithm returns *True*, the system $\hat{S}$ satisfies the given band convergence property. The algorithm executes the abstract system from the initial state z_0 onwards and verifies three logical formulas corresponding to the band convergence properties. We note that similar to Algorithm 1, this algorithm must be implemented symbolically using an SMT solver, to ensure precision.

For a discrete-time system, where essentially $A_l = A_u$ and $B_l = B_u$, we can take an adequate box invariant of the form $[z_e - p, z_e + p]$ (where z_e is the equilibrium point of the system), and Algorithm 2 will provide an efficient solution for Problem 1. We note that there are many sampled-data PID control systems which can be encoded into linear discrete-time systems without matrix exponentials and the need for representation in the form of abstract systems. For this specific subclass of systems, this version of Algorithm 2 can be useful.

6 Implementation and Results

We have implemented the entire verification procedure discussed in the sections above. Our implementation has two different modes of operations. In the first mode of operation, the tool verifies a closed loop system S_c. In the second mode of operation it verifies a discrete-time system S. As discussed in the Sect. 5 there are a few Simulink models which can be encoded into discrete-time systems without need for abstraction. The second mode of operation is used to verify these models.

As shown in the Fig. 3 our verification tool has five major components. The first component named *Generate Abstract System* when given a closed loop system S_c generates an abstract system $\hat{S}$ using the procedure outlined in Sect. 2.7. We chose a uniform value of $k = 20$ for all our benchmarks.

The second component named *Generate Approximate System* when given S_c, generates an *approximate* discrete-time system $S = (A, B, C, y^*, z_0)$ using the procedure introduced in the Sect. 2.4 and a truncated value of $e^{A_c h}$. The third component named *Compute Equilibrium Point*; computes an equilibrium point z_e for the approximate discrete-time system, which can be used as an initial box for Algorithm 1.

The fourth component named *Compute Adequate Box Invariant* has two sub-components. The first sub component implementats the constraint solving approach for finding a maximal adequate box invariant for an abstract system, using the Z3 solver, and we call this sub-component "Symbolic". The second sub-component is implementation of the Algorithm 1 which computes an adequate box invariant for an abstract system, and we it "Numerical+Symbolic". A note about the initial box we use for Algorithm 1: We use the equilibrium point z_e corresponding to *approximate* discrete-time system (generated by the second and third components above) to generate an initial box $[z_e, z_e]$ for Algorithm 1. In case both the sub components successfully compute adequate box invariants, we choose the maximal adequate box invariant.

Finally, the fifth component *Verification of Abstract System* implements Algorithm 2. In the *second* mode of operation this component will be configured to verify a discrete-time system.

6.1 Benchmarks

Our benchmark suite consists of six linear dynamical systems with varying dimensions and system properties, listed in the Simulink Examples website maintained by University of Michigan [8].

A few of the examples have *singular* state matrices and a naive implementation cannot verify these systems. In order to overcome this we have alternatively encoded few of the examples with non-singular matrices. For example the dynamics of the *Aircraft Pitch* with singular state matrix is given as:

$$\dot{x} = A_c x + B_c u \quad and \quad y = C_c x \quad where,$$

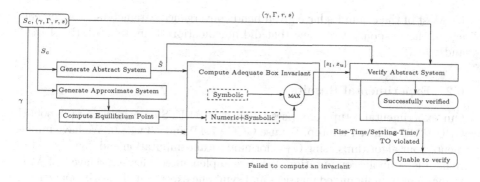

Fig. 3. Architecture of the verification tool

$$x = \begin{bmatrix} \alpha \\ q \\ \theta \end{bmatrix}, \; A_c = \begin{bmatrix} -0.313 & 56.7 & 0 \\ -0.0139 & -0.426 & 0 \\ 0 & 56.7 & 0 \end{bmatrix}, \; B_c = \begin{bmatrix} 0.232 \\ 0.0203 \\ 0 \end{bmatrix} \; \text{and} \; C_c = \begin{bmatrix} 0 & 0 & 1 \end{bmatrix}$$

We have encoded this dynamics without singular state matrices, while preserving the behaviour, as follows:

$$\dot{x} = A_c x + B_c u \quad and \quad \dot{y} = C_c x \quad where,$$

$$x = \begin{bmatrix} \alpha \\ q \end{bmatrix}, \; A_c = \begin{bmatrix} -0.313 & 56.7 \\ -0.0139 & -0.426 \end{bmatrix}, \; B_c = \begin{bmatrix} 0.232 \\ 0.0203 \end{bmatrix} \; \text{and} \; C_c = \begin{bmatrix} 0 & 56.7 \end{bmatrix}$$

Three of the models (DC Motor Position, Inverted Pendulum, Aircraft Pitch) have been encoded similarly. Two of the models (Cruise Control, DC Motor Speed) have non-singular state matrices. One of the models (Ball & Beam) has a singular and sparse state matrix and its dynamics is given as:

$$\dot{x} = A_c x + B_c u \quad and \quad y = C_c x \quad where,$$

$$x = \begin{bmatrix} \gamma \\ \dot{\gamma} \\ \alpha \\ \dot{\alpha} \end{bmatrix}, \; A_c = \begin{bmatrix} 0 & 1 & 0 & 0 \\ 0 & 0 & 7 & 0 \\ 0 & 0 & 0 & 1 \\ 0 & 0 & 0 & 0 \end{bmatrix}, \; B_c = \begin{bmatrix} 0 \\ 0 \\ 0 \\ 1 \end{bmatrix} \; \text{and} \; C_c = \begin{bmatrix} 1 & 0 & 0 & 0 \end{bmatrix}$$

We have manually computed the discrete-time representation corresponding to this model as follows:

$$x_i = A' x_{i-1} + B' u_{i-1} \quad and \quad y_i = C_c x_i \quad where,$$

$$x_i = \begin{bmatrix} \gamma_i \\ \alpha_i \end{bmatrix}, \; A' = \begin{bmatrix} 0 & 0 \\ 0 & 0 \end{bmatrix}, \; B' = \begin{bmatrix} 0.005 \\ 0.0000291666667 \end{bmatrix}, \; C_c = \begin{bmatrix} 1 & 0 \end{bmatrix} \; \text{and} \; h = \begin{bmatrix} 0.1 & 0 \\ 0 & 0.1 \end{bmatrix}$$

We note that this discretization process does not introduce any matrix exponential, and we can use the second mode of our implementation to verify this system.

Most of the examples have given band convergence parameters, as a percentage of the set-point. For a few that did not mention them, we took $\Gamma = 10\%y^*$ and $\gamma = 2\%y^*$.

6.2 Experimental Results

Our experimental setup comprises Ubuntu 18.04 LTS on a Intel Core i3-6006U CPU @2.00 GHz × 4 Laptop. We use GCC v7.4.0 and Z3 v4.8.0. We have implemented our algorithms using C++ for numerical computation and Z3:C++ APIs to handle symbolic computation. We have implemented a few extra layers of APIs to incorporate unbounded matrices and symbolic execution of matrix operations.

Table 1. Experimental Results. Times shown are in seconds.

Simulink model	Symbolic			Numerical+Symbolic		
	Invariant computation (Z3 optimization)	Verification (Algo 2)	Total	Invariant computation (Num+Symbolic Algo 1)	Verification (Algo 2)	Total
Cruise control	0.85	5.65	6.50	0.19	96.94	97.13
DC motor speed	25.04	1.21	26.25	0.19	3.36	3.55
Ball & beam	Error	-	-	0.25	0.23	0.48
DC motor position	93.73	TO	-	TO	-	-
Inverted pendulum	No box inv exists	-	-	Unknown	-	-
Aircraft pitch	40.37	TO	-	0.46	TO	-
3D	538.61	9.35	547.96	0.26	20.96	21.22
4D	TO	-	-	0.30	0.42	0.72

A summary of our analysis is given in Table 1. The first column shows the list of benchmark programs. The first six are the Simulink models from [8] mentioned above. The last two are synthetic examples we came up with to evaluate our algorithms on larger dimension systems. The next three columns show the performance of our "Symbolic" approach which uses the constraint solving and optimization approach to find an adequate box invariant. The first of these columns shows the time taken for the solver to come up with such an invariant, the second shows the time taken by Algorithm 2 with this invariant as input, and the third column shows the sum of the the two times. The next set of three columns shows similar details, but with using the "Numerical+Symbolic" version of Algorithm 1. In the table, "Error" means that the solver was unable to come up with a valid invariant. "No box inv exists" means that the solver was able to conclude that no solution exists for the given constraints. "TO" represents a time out after 600 s. A "-" entry indicates that time taken is not applicable in the absence of an adequate invariant in the first step. "Unknown" means that Algorithm 2 terminates unsuccessfully before time out.

Observations. We note that while we could verify only 50% of the Simulink models, we could find adequate *box* invariants for 5 out of the 6 models. The repeated symbolic execution till we reach the invariant in the verification algorithm consumes the majority of the verification time, and speeding up this step using other techniques will be helpful. We also note that the invariant computation step using Algorithm 1 is faster than Z3 in most cases. We guess that Algorithm 1 benefits from knowledge about the shape of the invariant and the symmetry of the invariant around the approximate equilibrium point. Finally, since the Symbolic approach computes the maximal box invariant, the verification algorithm runs faster than with an invariant computed using the Algorithm 1 which may not be maximal. Symbolic execution in the verification algorithm takes more number of steps to reach a narrow invariant than a wider one.

7 Related Work

We group related work according to two closely related properties, namely temporal logics and stability, and verification of sampled control systems using relational abstractions. Our problem is also related to bounded model-checking and invariant generation. We discuss all of these briefly.

Temporal Logic. Settling time properties can be naturally expressed in Signal Temporal Logic (STL) [1,2]. While there has been extensive work on monitoring [3,4], trace generation [5], and model-checking over reach sequences [6], for STL properties, the verification problem for STL properties is undecidable for most system models, including discrete systems. Belta, Yordanov and others [9,10] address the problem of model-checking and controller synthesis for classical LTL specifications. They use quotienting techniques to first obtain a finite discrete system and then use standard LTL model-checking. However, in general such quotienting techniques are not guaranteed to terminate.

Stability. Blondel et al. [11,12] study decidability of the problem of global convergence properties like stability for discrete dynamical systems. In particular the stability problem for saturated linear discrete dynamical systems is shown to be undecidable. There is a great deal of work on using Lyapunov functions for proving stability of systems and we refer the reader to the surveys [13–15]. Duggirala et al. [16,17] and Prabhakar et al. [18,19] consider abstraction refinement and model-checking based techniques for proving Lyapunov and asymptotic stability of hybrid systems. Band convergence properties cannot directly be phrased in terms of stability, though this is an interesting future direction to investigate. Podelski and Wagner study region-based stability [20–22] where one requires that trajectories starting from an initial state eventually enter a target region.

However settling time properties cannot readily be phrased in terms of region stability due to the multiple bands and the bounded times to enter the bands. Moreover their techniques rely on a sufficient condition involving the target region being a *strong attractor* which does not necessarily hold in our case.

Sampled Data Control System Verification. In closely related work, Zutshi, Sankarnarayanan and Tiwari [23] address the problem of verifying safety properties of sampled data control systems. The last two authors also study relational invariants for dynamical and hybrid systems [24], with the aim of verifying safety properties. Both these works use relational abstractions to construct discrete transition systems which are then analyzed using model-checkers like SAL [25]. Our work differs from theirs in a couple of ways. To begin with the properties we consider require time-varying safety regions rather than a single safety invariant. Secondly, while the above approach is limited to using techniques like k-induction to check safety with respect to the given property, we focus on finding adequate invariants to prove band convergence. Finally, there is work on checking stability of digital controller implementations. For instance Bessa et al. [26] consider issues like finite word length (FWL), uncertainty in sampling, delay etc, where the controller is assumed to be asymptotically stable, and they use bounded model-checking to verify that the implementation is internally stable. In contrast we are addressing the correctness of the mathematical model of the closed loop system.

Bounded Model-Checking and Invariant Generation. Our approach to band convergence essentially consists of two steps, synthesizing an invariant and checking that certain conditions hold until the invariant is reached. The latter can be checked by a solving a series of bounded-model checking problems, which can solve the problem of whether a set is reach within a given number of steps. Bounded model-checking [27–29] has been investigated for dynamical and hybrid systems using bounded error approximation techniques and reducing to delta-decision procedures of SMT solver *dReach, dReal, gao2013dreal*. Soonho et al. [30] introduced a bounded reachability analysis tool for nonlinear hybrid systems named, *dReach*. It encodes bounded reachability problems of hybrid systems to first-order formulas over real numbers, which are solved using the delta-decision procedures of the SMT solver *dReal* [31]. However, repeated calls to a BMC algorithm is inefficient compared to iterative reach computation proposed in the paper.

8   Conclusion

In this paper we have investigated an approach based on finding adequate inductive invariants to verify important band convergence properties, like transient and settling time properties, of control systems. We also showed how to account for numerical errors in the discretization procedure, by providing a sufficient condition for verification of an abstract system that over-approximates all the exact behaviors of the closed loop system.

In future work we plan to explore the use of Lyapunov functions that are traditionally used for proving stability properties, for the band convergence problem. We also intend to explore methods for incorporating inter-sample behaviors as well as more general dynamics of digitally controlled systems.

Acknowledgements. The authors acknowledge support from the Royal Academy of Engineering, UK, and the Robert Bosch Center for Cyber-Physical Systems, India. Pavithra Prabhakar was partially supported by NSF CAREER Award No. 1552668 and ONR YIP Award No. N000141712577.

References

1. Maler, O., Nickovic, D.: Monitoring temporal properties of continuous signals. In: Lakhnech, Y., Yovine, S. (eds.) FORMATS/FTRTFT -2004. LNCS, vol. 3253, pp. 152–166. Springer, Heidelberg (2004). https://doi.org/10.1007/978-3-540-30206-3_12

2. Donzé, A., Maler, O., Bartocci, E., Nickovic, D., Grosu, R., Smolka, S.: On temporal logic and signal processing. In: Chakraborty, S., Mukund, M. (eds.) ATVA 2012. LNCS, pp. 92–106. Springer, Heidelberg (2012). https://doi.org/10.1007/978-3-642-33386-6_9

3. Fainekos, G.E., Pappas, G.J.: Robustness of temporal logic specifications for continuous-time signals. Theor. Comput. Sci. **410**(42), 4262–4291 (2009)

4. Deshmukh, J.V., Donzé, A., Ghosh, S., Jin, X., Juniwal, G., Seshia, S.A.: Robust online monitoring of signal temporal logic. Formal Meth. Syst. Des. **51**(1), 5–30 (2017). https://doi.org/10.1007/s10703-017-0286-7

5. Prabhakar, P., Lal, R., Kapinski, J.: Automatic trace generation for signal temporal logic. In: Proceedings of the IEEE Real-Time Systems Symposium (RTSS), Nashville, USA, December 2018, pp. 208–217. IEEE Computer Society (2018)

6. Roehm, H., Oehlerking, J., Heinz, T., Althoff, M.: STL model checking of continuous and hybrid systems. In: Artho, C., Legay, A., Peled, D. (eds.) ATVA 2016. LNCS, vol. 9938, pp. 412–427. Springer, Cham (2016). https://doi.org/10.1007/978-3-319-46520-3_26

7. Moler, C., Van Loan, C.: Nineteen dubious ways to compute the exponential of a matrix, twenty-five years later. SIAM Rev. **45**(1), 3–49 (2003)

8. Control Tutorials for MATLAB and Simulink. http://ctms.engin.umich.edu/CTMS/

9. Yordanov, B., Belta, C.: Formal analysis of discrete-time piecewise affine systems. IEEE Trans. Automat. Contr. **55**(12), 2834–2840 (2010)

10. Yordanov, B., Tumova, J., Cerna, I., Barnat, J., Belta, C.: Temporal logic control of discrete-time piecewise affine systems. IEEE Trans. Automat. Contr. **57**(6), 1491–1504 (2012)

11. Blondel, V.D., Tsitsiklis, J.N.: Complexity of stability and controllability of elementary hybrid systems. Automatica **35**(3), 479–489 (1999)

12. Blondel, V.D., Bournez, O., Koiran, P., Tsitsiklis, J.N.: The stability of saturated linear dynamical systems is undecidable. J. Comput. Syst. Sci. **62**(3), 442–462 (2001)

13. Branicky, M.S.: Multiple Lyapunov functions and other analysis tools for switched and hybrid systems. IEEE Trans. Automat. Contr. **43**(4), 3–17 (1998)

14. Davrazos, G., Koussoulas, N.T.: A review of stability results for switched and hybrid systems. In: Proceedings of the Mediterranean Conference on Control (2001)
15. Lin, H., Antsaklis, P.J.: Stability and stabilizability of switched linear systems: a survey of recent results. IEEE Trans. Automat. Contr. **54**(2), 308–322 (2009)
16. Duggirala, P.S., Mitra, S.: Abstraction refinement for stability. In: Proceedings of the IEEE/ACM Conference on Cyber-Physical Systems (ICCPS), Chicago, USA, April 2011, pp. 22–31. IEEE Computer Society (2011)
17. Duggirala, P.S., Mitra, S.: Lyapunov abstractions for inevitability of hybrid systems. In: Proceedings of the 15th Conference on Hybrid Systems: Computation and Control (HSCC), Beijing, China, April 2012, pp. 115–124. ACM (2012)
18. Prabhakar, P., Garcia Soto, M.: Abstraction based model-checking of stability of hybrid systems. In: Sharygina, N., Veith, H. (eds.) CAV 2013. LNCS, vol. 8044, pp. 280–295. Springer, Heidelberg (2013). https://doi.org/10.1007/978-3-642-39799-8_20
19. Prabhakar, P., Soto, M.G.: Counterexample guided abstraction refinement for stability analysis. In: Chaudhuri, S., Farzan, A. (eds.) CAV 2016. LNCS, vol. 9779, pp. 495–512. Springer, Cham (2016). https://doi.org/10.1007/978-3-319-41528-4_27
20. Podelski, A., Wagner, S.: Model checking of hybrid systems: from reachability towards stability. In: Hespanha, J.P., Tiwari, A. (eds.) HSCC 2006. LNCS, vol. 3927, pp. 507–521. Springer, Heidelberg (2006). https://doi.org/10.1007/11730637_38
21. Podelski, A., Wagner, S.: Region stability proofs for hybrid systems. In: Raskin, J.-F., Thiagarajan, P.S. (eds.) FORMATS 2007. LNCS, vol. 4763, pp. 320–335. Springer, Heidelberg (2007). https://doi.org/10.1007/978-3-540-75454-1_23
22. Podelski, A., Wagner, S.: A sound and complete proof rule for region stability of hybrid systems. In: Bemporad, A., Bicchi, A., Buttazzo, G. (eds.) HSCC 2007. LNCS, vol. 4416, pp. 750–753. Springer, Heidelberg (2007). https://doi.org/10.1007/978-3-540-71493-4_76
23. Zutshi, A., Sankaranarayanan, S., Tiwari, A.: Timed relational abstractions for sampled data control systems. In: Madhusudan, P., Seshia, S.A. (eds.) CAV 2012. LNCS, vol. 7358, pp. 343–361. Springer, Heidelberg (2012). https://doi.org/10.1007/978-3-642-31424-7_27
24. Sankaranarayanan, S., Tiwari, A.: Relational abstractions for continuous and hybrid systems. In: Gopalakrishnan, G., Qadeer, S. (eds.) CAV 2011. LNCS, vol. 6806, pp. 686–702. Springer, Heidelberg (2011). https://doi.org/10.1007/978-3-642-22110-1_56
25. Rushby, J., Lincoln, P., Owre, S., Shankar, N., Tiwari, A.: Symbolic Analysis Laboratory (SAL), SRI, California. http://www.csl.sri.com/projects/sal/
26. Bessa, I., Ismail, H., Palhares, R.M., Cordeiro, L.C., Filho, J.E.C.: Formal non-fragile stability verification of digital control systems with uncertainty. IEEE Trans. Comput. **66**(3), 545–552 (2017)
27. Lal, R., Prabhakar, P.: Bounded error flowpipe computation of parameterized linear systems. In: 13th International Conference on Embedded Software (EMSOFT) (2015)
28. Lal, R., Prabhakar, P.: Safety analysis using compositional bounded error approximations of communicating hybrid systems. In: Proceedings of the 56th IEEE Conference on Decision and Control (CDC) (2017)

29. Lal, R., Prabhakar, P.: Compositional construction of bounded error over-approximations of acyclic interconnected continuous dynamical systems. In: Proceedings of the 17th ACM-IEEE International Conference on Formal Methods and Models for System Design, MEMOCODE 2019, La Jolla, CA, USA, 9–11 October 2019, pp. 12:1–12:5 (2019)

30. Kong, S., Gao, S., Chen, W., Clarke, E.: dReach: δ-reachability analysis for hybrid systems. In: Baier, C., Tinelli, C. (eds.) TACAS 2015. LNCS, vol. 9035, pp. 200–205. Springer, Heidelberg (2015). https://doi.org/10.1007/978-3-662-46681-0_15

31. Gao, S., Kong, S., Clarke, E.M.: dReal: an SMT solver for nonlinear theories over the reals. In: Bonacina, M.P. (ed.) CADE 2013. LNCS (LNAI), vol. 7898, pp. 208–214. Springer, Heidelberg (2013). https://doi.org/10.1007/978-3-642-38574-2_14

Autonomy and Other Applications

Heterogeneous Verification of an Autonomous Curiosity Rover

Rafael C. Cardoso[⊠], Marie Farrell, Matt Luckcuck, Angelo Ferrando,
and Michael Fisher

Department of Computer Science, University of Liverpool, Liverpool L69 3BX, UK
{rafael.cardoso,marie.farrell,m.luckcuck,
angelo.ferrando,mfisher}@liverpool.ac.uk

Abstract. The Curiosity rover is one of the most complex systems successfully deployed in a planetary exploration mission to date. It was sent by NASA to explore the surface of Mars and to identify potential signs of life. Even though it has limited autonomy on-board, most of its decisions are made by the ground control team. This hinders the speed at which the Curiosity reacts to its environment, due to the communication delays between Earth and Mars. Depending on the orbital position of both planets, it can take 4–24 min for a message to be transmitted between Earth and Mars. If the Curiosity were controlled autonomously, it would be able to perform its activities much faster and more flexibly. However, one of the major barriers to increased use of autonomy in such scenarios is the lack of assurances that the autonomous behaviour will work as expected. In this paper, we use a Robot Operating System (ROS) model of the Curiosity that is simulated in Gazebo and add an autonomous agent that is responsible for high-level decision-making. Then, we use a mixture of formal and non-formal techniques to verify the distinct system components (ROS nodes). This use of heterogeneous verification techniques is essential to provide guarantees about the nodes at different abstraction levels, and allows us to bring together relevant verification evidence to provide overall assurance.

1 Introduction

We present a case study with a simulation of the Curiosity rover undertaking an exploration mission. Crucially, we have equipped the rover with decision-making capabilities so that it does not rely on human teleoperation. As a result of the added autonomous behaviour, it is important to provide safety assurances about critical components in the system. Usually, components in such systems are modular and each individual component often requires a different verification technique(s) [6,9,13]. We have applied distinct verification techniques to various

Work supported by UK Research and Innovation, and EPSRC Hubs for "Robotics and AI in Hazardous Environments": EP/R026092 (FAIR-SPACE) and EP/R026084 (RAIN).

R. Lee et al. (Eds.): NFM 2020, LNCS 12229, pp. 353–360, 2020.
https://doi.org/10.1007/978-3-030-55754-6_20

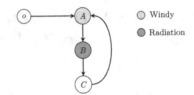

Fig. 1. The Curiosity begins at the origin, o, and then visits the waypoints A, B and C in whichever order is safe. We indicate waypoints with high levels of wind (grey) and radiation (yellow) (Color figure online).

critical components and at different abstraction levels to ensure the correctness of the overall system. All of the artefacts (source code, videos, etc.) discussed in this paper are available in our online repository.[1]

2   Mission Description, Simulation and Autonomy

Mission Description: We simulate an inspection mission, where the Curiosity patrols a topological map of the surface of Mars. We assume that the map is known prior to this mission, and in this paper we only consider a small subset of the map (i.e. the agent has map coordinates for each waypoint in the map). Specifically, we consider four different waypoints (o, A, B, and C) that are spread across the Martian terrain. Low-level movement is achieved through a dead reckoning or feedback control.

We begin with the deployment of the Curiosity and a startup period where it initialises all three of its control modules (wheels, arms, and mast). After the agent receives confirmation that the modules are ready, it autonomously controls the Curiosity to move between the waypoints in the following order: ($o \rightarrow A \rightarrow B \rightarrow C \rightarrow A \rightarrow \ldots$), as shown in Fig. 1. This is the ideal scenario, however, if one of the waypoints is experiencing high levels of radiation then the rover should skip it until the radiation has reduced to a safe level. For data collection, the mast and arm should be open, however, it is unsafe to do so in windy conditions. We do not model battery power. Instead, we assume that the rover has sufficient battery power to traverse the waypoints and operate the equipment.

Simulation: We obtained a Robot Operating System (ROS) [10] version of the Curiosity from a ROS teaching website[2] which uses official data and 3D models of the Curiosity and Martian terrain which have been made public by NASA. This ROS simulation runs in Gazebo,[3] a 3D simulator.

Most of the Curiosity's effectors are included in the simulation. It has the complete chassis of the rover with all six wheels and the suspension system, a

---

[1] https://github.com/autonomy-and-verification-uol/curiosity-NFM2020.
[2] https://bitbucket.org/theconstructcore/curiosity_mars_rover/src/master/.
[3] http://gazebosim.org/.

retractable arm with four joints, and a retractable mast with two joints and a camera (Mastcam) on top. Some of the sensors are missing, e.g. MAHLI (Mars Hand Lens Imager), as these would require simulated sensor data.

In the original configuration, the standard control method of the Curiosity was implemented using ROS services and it was controlled via teleoperation. ROS services are defined as a pair of request and reply messages that are provided by ROS nodes. In our simulation, we re-implemented the control method through action libraries, which follow a client-server model that is similar to ROS services. Both can receive a request to perform some task and then generate a reply. The difference in using action libraries is that the client can cancel the action, as well as receive feedback about the task execution. Thus, action libraries are more suited for use with decision-making agents since they allow more fine-grained control.

We developed three action libraries: one each for the wheels, arm, and mast. The wheels client receives high-level action commands to move forward, backward, left, and right; or a waypoint from the topological map (using the move base library for path planning). Based on the command received, the server controls each of the six wheels and publishes speed commands to the appropriate wheels depending on the direction or topological waypoint requested in the action. If a direction command is given, then the server expects three parameters: direction of movement, speed, and distance. After a movement action, the server always calls a stop action that sets the speed of all wheels to zero. The arm and mast action libraries control the joints of their respective effectors so that they can be positioned correctly for use.

Enabling Autonomous Decision-Making: We use the GWENDOLEN [4] agent programming language to implement the high-level control and autonomous decision-making behaviour of the Curiosity. Agent programming languages abstract the environment and other external sources, focusing on high-level autonomous control, resulting in smaller and more modular code than other languages. Due to the agent's reasoning cycle an execution trace can clearly show how the agent came to a decision, thus providing us with explainability. Using GWENDOLEN allows us to verify properties of the agent's reasoning, allowing the safeguard of critical behaviours.

GWENDOLEN agents follow the Belief-Desire-Intention (BDI) model [11]. Beliefs, desires, and intentions represent respectively the information, motivational, and deliberative states of the agent. We developed a GWENDOLEN environment that communicates with ROS through the *rosbridge* library. When the agent executes an action in the environment, the action is processed and published to the action's associated ROS topic. The environment creates subscribers that listen to specific topics so that necessary perceptions are created and sent to the agent.

In the Curiosity simulation, the GWENDOLEN agent has four high-level actions. The action *control_wheels* has three parameters: direction of movement (forward, backward, left, or right), speed (an integer with sign to indicate direction), and distance (in seconds). The *move_to_waypoint* action contains one

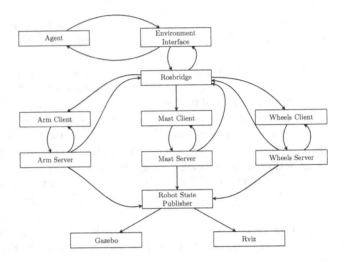

Fig. 2. Overview of the system. Arrows indicate data flow between the nodes.

parameter with a waypoint from the topological map. The actions, *control_arm* and *control_mast*, both have one parameter whose possible values are either *open* or *close*.

Figure 2 illustrates a high-level system diagram with the communication paths between the nodes in the simulation. We have verified distinct components of this simulation using different methods. Specifically, we verify the autonomous agent using the AJPF program model checker; the interface that this agent has with the environment using Dafny; a CSP specification of the action library nodes using FDR4; and we use each of these formal models to guide the generation of runtime monitors. This combination of simulation-based testing, and the use of multiple formal methods at different levels of abstraction, gives us a basis for providing assurances about the use of autonomous decision-making in this extreme environment mission scenario, and could be transferred and applied to other similar case studies as shown in [6,9,13].

3   Verification

This section describes our verification of four critical areas of our simulation of an autonomous Curiosity rover. We verify properties of this system at different levels of abstraction. We begin by describing how we verify that the agent, which is fundamentally controlling the system, makes the correct decisions about which waypoint to visit next.

Next, we discuss our use of an automated theorem prover to verify that the information that the agent receives from the environment sensors is interpreted and acted upon correctly. Then, we outline how we verified that the communication between the *client* and *server* action library nodes (as shown in Fig. 2) functions correctly. Finally, we outline our runtime verification of design-time assumptions about the environment. Interestingly, we used the preceding formal models as a way to focus these runtime checks on appropriate properties.

Verifying the Agent using AJPF: Model-checking [2] exhaustively examines the state space to check if some desired property holds. This can be applied to either a formal model of the system, encoded in some specification language, or directly to the implementation. The property to be verified is usually specified in a logic-based language. For example, we may want to verify that the Curiosity will not move its arm while collecting soil and rock data, in order to protect the sample.

Agent Java PathFinder (AJPF) [5], an extension of Java PathFinder (JPF) [12], is a model-checker that works directly on Java program code. This extension facilitates formal verification of BDI-based agent programs by providing a property specification language based on Linear-time Temporal Logic (LTL) that supports the description of terms usually found in BDI agents.

For example, some of the properties that we verified of the implementation of our agent were as follows:

$$\Box(A_{\text{rover}}move\_to\_waypoint(A) \rightarrow \Diamond \mathcal{B}_{\text{rover}}(at(A)))$$
$$\Box(A_{\text{rover}}move\_to\_waypoint(B) \rightarrow \Diamond \mathcal{B}_{\text{rover}}(at(B)))$$
$$\Box(A_{\text{rover}}move\_to\_waypoint(C) \rightarrow \Diamond \mathcal{B}_{\text{rover}}(at(C))$$

These properties state that it is always the case ($\Box$) that if the *rover* agent executes the action *move_to_waypoint* (to either A, B, or C), then eventually ($\Diamond$) the *rover* agent will believe that it is currently located in that waypoint.

The syntax of the AJPF specification language is limited to expressing agent related properties, such as beliefs, goals, actions, and intentions of a specific agent that was written in GWENDOLEN. Moreover, properties specified in AJPF must be ground (i.e. cannot be parameterised). For verifying the interface between the agent and the environment, we employ the Dafny program verifier.

Verifying the Agent-Environment Interface: Dafny facilitates the use of specification constructs e.g. pre-/post-conditions, loop invariants and variants [8]. Dafny is used in the static verification of functional program correctness. Programs are translated into the Boogie intermediate verification language [1] and then the Z3 automated theorem prover discharges the associated proof obligations [3].

Our Dafny model centres on the decisions made by the agent in response to the input that it receives from the environment. In this simple model, we verify an important safety property that the rover will not select any actions if the arm, mast or wheels have not been initialised yet. This is specified as follows:
`ensures (wheelsready && armready && mastready) == false ==> actions ==[];`
Here, `wheelsready`, `armready` and `mastready` are boolean flags that are toggled by the associated modules, and `actions` is the sequence of returned actions.

Our Dafny model has functions for accessing the environmental conditions at a given waypoint e.g. `getEnvironment()` and `getWind()`. This allows us to verify properties about the how the environmental conditions affect where the rover goes. The `getEnvironment()` method then checks the wind and radiation at a particular waypoint and we verify that the following condition is met where e is a variable that represents the current status of the environment:

```
ensures windspeed < 5 && radiation < 5 ==> e == Fine;
```

In this way, our Dafny model allows us to verify conditions about the safety of the agent and also that the information coming from the environment is interpreted correctly by the agent. We provide other verified methods including `getRad()` which is a high-level implementation of how the radiation at waypoint B decays over time. Our loop invariant in the `CuriosityAgent()` also ensures that the rover can't be at waypoint B when the radiation is too high:

```
invariant !(current == B && env == Radiation);
```

We included radiation at B in the Dafny implementation to examine how the rover reacts to radiation at a particular waypoint, as per the mission description (Sect. 2). Next, we verify the action library client and server nodes using CSP.

Verifying Action Library Communication: We verify the communication between the pairs of action library client–server nodes that interface between the software and hardware (arm, mast, and wheels). Each client accepts instructions from the agent (via *rosbridge*) which it then sends to the relevant server node as a goal (task to complete). Since the AJPF model checker can only check agent-programs, we decided to use Communicating Sequential Processes (CSP) to verify this critical link. CSP processes describe sequences of events; $a \Rightarrow b \Rightarrow Skip$ is the process where events a and b occur sequentially, then terminates ($Skip$).

The CSP model is constructed from the Curiosity ROS code, capturing both the program-specific and the generic action library behaviour. Each of the client–server pairs is modelled by one CSP file, with one further file modelling the generic behaviour of an action library server. We use the FDR4 model-checker [7] to check three properties: (1) when a client sends a goal, it will begin execution on the correct server, (2) when a client sends a goal, eventually it receives a result from the server, and (3) when the agent instructs a client node to perform an action, the server informs the agent that it is ready and then eventually the agent receives a result. Here we give an example of (2), where we check that if the arm client sends a goal then eventually it will receive a result:

$$send\_goal\_arm?\_ \rightarrow executeGoal.arm \rightarrow SKIP$$

Runtime Verification: It is achieved by examining the current execution of the system at runtime against a formal specification. Since runtime monitors only observe the current system execution, the resulting approach is not exhaustive in the sense that model-checking is (which examines the entire state space). However, monitor implementations are usually extremely efficient since they do not consider all possible system executions and they can remain as safeguards after deployment. In this way, a monitor helps to ensure correct system behaviour.

ROSMonitoring[4] (ROSMon) is a flexible and formalism-agnostic Runtime Verification (RV) framework for ROS. ROSMon creates gaps in the communication between nodes in the system. These gaps are then filled by monitors which

---

[4] https://github.com/autonomy-and-verification-uol/ROSMonitoring.

are automatically synthesised by ROSMon. In this way, the messages of interest are forced to pass through the monitors and are checked against a corresponding formal specification. We applied ROSMon to our simulation to check properties at runtime. For example, using Dafny, we verify the agent-environment interface; ROSMon bridges the gap between the Dafny model and the real environment by checking at runtime if the assumptions used in the Dafny model are satisfied by the real system.

We used a property, written in Runtime Monitoring Language (RML), to synthesise a monitor to check the constraint used in the Dafny `getEnvironment` method. Here, we check that the wind speed and radiation are always positive, and if the wind speed and radiation are less than 5 each, then the environment is "Fine". This is (partially) written as follows:

```
Main = (GetEnvironmentConstraints /\ (wind_speed(_) >> wind_speed_at_least(0)*) /\
        (radiation_units(_) >> radiation_units_at_least(0)*));
GetEnvironmentConstraints =
  wind_speed_up_to(4) GetEnvironmentConstraints1
  \/ radiation_units_up_to(4) GetEnvironmentConstraints2
  \/ any GetEnvironmentConstraints;
...
```

In this way, we used abstract formal system models to guide the development of corresponding runtime monitors to examine these properties at runtime.

4 Discussion

This paper has reported on our case study of using multiple verification techniques to provide assurance for an autonomous Curiosity rover undertaking an exploration/sampling mission. We used the GWENDOLEN agent programming language to implement an autonomous agent in a ROS-based simulation of the Curiosity. We verified this agent using AJPF, how it responds to discrete input from its environment using Dafny, the message passing between the action library nodes using CSP, and we synthesised runtime monitors using ROSMon.

We employed a myriad of verification techniques to verify the behaviour of distinct aspect(s) of the system. Our aim was to streamline the process of verifying the system by verifying each system component using a suitable technique, rather than attempting to verify everything using only one technique. For example, we use an agent programming language for the agent and CSP for message passing. The tool used to verify the agent program is not appropriate (and would generally not work) to verify message passing.

Our use of RV is of particular interest here since the system is implemented in C++ or Python for which formal verification at code level is not currently feasible/possible. However, the tools and techniques that were chosen are not necessarily the only ones that were suitable for any specific component and certainly other choices could have been made. Future work includes investigating these alternatives.

Our use of heterogeneous techniques for various critical components of the system was motivated by the work done in [6,9,13]. Our case study exhibits how heterogeneous verification techniques can be applied to various components of an autonomous robotic system at different levels of abstraction. Future work seeks to link the results of these heterogeneous techniques in a holistic framework so that they might inform one another.

References

1. Barnett, M., Chang, B.-Y.E., DeLine, R., Jacobs, B., Leino, K.R.M.: Boogie: a modular reusable verifier for object-oriented programs. In: de Boer, F.S., Bonsangue, M.M., Graf, S., de Roever, W.-P. (eds.) FMCO 2005. LNCS, vol. 4111, pp. 364–387. Springer, Heidelberg (2006). https://doi.org/10.1007/11804192_17
2. Clarke, E.M., Grumberg, O., Peled, D.: Model Checking. MIT Press, Cambridge (1999)
3. de Moura, L., Bjørner, N.: Z3: an efficient SMT solver. In: Ramakrishnan, C.R., Rehof, J. (eds.) TACAS 2008. LNCS, vol. 4963, pp. 337–340. Springer, Heidelberg (2008). https://doi.org/10.1007/978-3-540-78800-3_24
4. Dennis, L.A., Farwer, B.: Gwendolen: A BDI language for verifiable agents. In: Logic and the Simulation of Interaction and Reasoning. AISB, Aberdeen (2008)
5. Dennis, L.A., Fisher, M., Webster, M.P., Bordini, R.H.: Model checking agent programming languages. Autom. Soft. Eng. 19(1), 5–63 (2012)
6. Farrell, M., Luckcuck, M., Fisher, M.: Robotics and integrated formal methods: necessity meets opportunity. In: Furia, C.A., Winter, K. (eds.) IFM 2018. LNCS, vol. 11023, pp. 161–171. Springer, Cham (2018). https://doi.org/10.1007/978-3-319-98938-9_10
7. Gibson-Robinson, T., Armstrong, P., Boulgakov, A., Roscoe, A.W.: FDR3 — a modern refinement checker for CSP. In: Ábrahám, E., Havelund, K. (eds.) TACAS 2014. LNCS, vol. 8413, pp. 187–201. Springer, Heidelberg (2014). https://doi.org/10.1007/978-3-642-54862-8_13
8. Leino, K.R.M.: Dafny: an automatic program verifier for functional correctness. In: Clarke, E.M., Voronkov, A. (eds.) LPAR 2010. LNCS (LNAI), vol. 6355, pp. 348–370. Springer, Heidelberg (2010). https://doi.org/10.1007/978-3-642-17511-4_20
9. Luckcuck, M., Farrell, M., Dennis, L.A., Dixon, C., Fisher, M.: Formal specification and verification of autonomous robotic systems: a survey. ACM Comput. Surv. (CSUR) 52(5), 100 (2019)
10. Quigley, M., et al.: ROS: an open-source robot operating system. In: Workshop on Open Source Software at the International Conference on Robotics and Automation. IEEE, Japan (2009)
11. Rao, A.S., Georgeff, M.: BDI agents: from theory to practice. In: International Conference on Multi-agent Systems, pp. 312–319. AAAI (1995)
12. Visser, W., Havelund, K., Brat, G., Park, S.J., Lerda, F.: Model checking programs. Autom. Soft. Eng. 10(2), 3–11 (2002)
13. Webster, M., et al.: A corroborative approach to verification and validation of human-robot teams. Int. J. Robot. Res. 39(1), 73–99 (2020)

Run-Time Assurance
for Learning-Enabled Systems

Darren Cofer[1]([⊠]), Isaac Amundson[1], Ramachandra Sattigeri[1], Arjun Passi[1],
Christopher Boggs[1], Eric Smith[2], Limei Gilham[2], Taejoon Byun[3],
and Sanjai Rayadurgam[3]

[1] Collins Aerospace, Minneapolis, MN, USA
darren.cofer@collins.com
[2] Kestrel Institute, Palo Alto, CA, USA
[3] Department of Computer Science, University of Minnesota, Minneapolis, MN, USA

Abstract. There has been much publicity surrounding the use of
machine learning technologies in self-driving cars and the challenges this
presents for guaranteeing safety. These technologies are also being investigated for use in manned and unmanned aircraft. However, systems
that include "learning-enabled components" (LECs) and their software
implementations are not amenable to verification and certification using
current methods. We have produced a demonstration of a run-time assurance architecture based on a neural network aircraft taxiing application
that shows how several advanced technologies could be used to ensure
safe operation. The demonstration system includes a safety architecture
based on the ASTM F3269-17 standard for bounded behavior of complex systems, diverse run-time monitors of system safety, and formal
synthesis of critical high-assurance components. The enhanced system
demonstrates the ability of the run-time assurance architecture to maintain system safety in the presence of defects in the underlying LEC.

1 Introduction

Significant advances are being made in the development of autonomous systems that employ learning and adaptation algorithms. It is therefore inevitable
that *learning-enabled components* (LEC) will begin to find their way into safety-
critical applications, including manned and unmanned vehicles. However, the
technologies being applied – machine learning, deep neural networks, probabilistic languages – are not amenable to verification using traditional methods. This
essentially precludes use of these technologies in many safety-critical aerospace
applications. Our team is developing technologies to overcome these limitations,
thus expanding opportunities for autonomous systems to be safely deployed in
critical environments.

Aircraft systems have legal requirements for airworthiness certification that
present barriers to the use of LECs. In a typical LEC, much of the complexity
and design information resides in its training data rather than in the actual code
produced. For example, one of the key principles of avionics software certification

© Springer Nature Switzerland AG 2020
R. Lee et al. (Eds.): NFM 2020, LNCS 12229, pp. 361–368, 2020.
https://doi.org/10.1007/978-3-030-55754-6_21

(covered in DO-178C [9]) is the use of requirements-based testing along with structural coverage metrics. These objectives not only demonstrate compliance with functional requirements, but are intended to show the absence of unintended functionality. However, complete structural coverage can be achieved for a typical neural network with a single test case, providing almost no confidence in its correctness. Showing that a component or system is correct *and* does no harm through behaviors that were unintended by designers or unexpected by operators is a critical aspect of the certification process.

Since it is difficult to demonstrate assurance by examining the LEC itself (as is assumed by existing certification processes) other approaches are needed. In this paper we report on the use of a run-time assurance architecture based on the ASTM F3269-17 standard for bounded behavior of complex systems [1], also known as a simplex architecture [10]. The standard provides guidance for mitigating unintended functionality (such as may be present in a LEC) through the use of run-time monitors. When a violation of system safety properties or an unsafe LEC output is detected, the architecture switches to a verified backup controller to continue safe operation. The main idea is that system performance is provided by the complex system or LEC while system safety is guaranteed by high-assurance components (though with lower performance). Our implementation of the standard includes:

- System architecture modeled using the *Architecture Analysis and Design Language* (AADL) [6]
- Formal verification of system behaviors using the *Assume Guarantee Reasoning Environment* (AGREE) [11]
- Architecture-based assurance case for showing correct implementation using Resolute [5]
- Diverse run-time monitors for system safety, integrity, and availability
- Synthesis from formal specifications with proof of correctness for critical high-assurance components

The purpose of this paper is to show the effectiveness of a run-time assurance architecture for bounding the behavior of an autonomous system to maintain its safety requirements. In this example, surface movement of a general aviation class aircraft is controlled during taxi based on a position estimate computed by an LEC. Our work illustrates the general effectiveness of the run-time assurance approach and demonstrates some of the tools and methods that can be applied in a real system. However, each specific application will require different monitors and backup safety functions, depending on requirements and variables that can be monitored. We discuss some of the challenges and limitations in Sect. 4.

2   Demonstration

The "TaxiNet" demonstration system is shown in Fig. 1. The bottom row of boxes in the figure show the baseline system, consisting of the aircraft (or simulation), the guidance LEC, a controller for steering the aircraft, and the Vehicle Management System (VMS) which manages actuators on the aircraft and

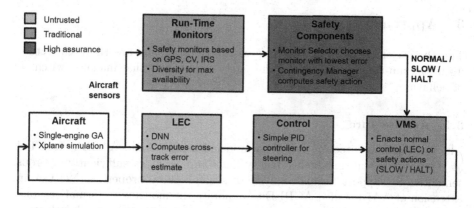

Fig. 1. TaxiNet demonstration system with run-time assurance architecture

integrates other autonomy functionality. The LEC is implemented as a deep neural network (DNN) trained to estimate the cross-track error (CTE) of the aircraft (position left or right of the runway centerline) based on images from a forward-looking camera on the aircraft. An equivalent high-fidelity simulation environment is also available for testing and demonstrations. Six different LECs trained in various lighting and weather conditions are available. This allows faulty behaviors to be simulated by operating an LEC in conditions other than those for which it was trained. This autonomy framework was developed by the Boeing Research and Technology (BR&T) organization and is being used as a demonstration platform in DARPA's Assured Autonomy program [3].

The run-time assurance architecture adds components in the top row of Fig. 1. This includes four different run-time monitors (three for system safety, one for LEC confidence), a Monitor Selector for choosing which monitor to use at any time, and a Contingency Manager that determines when intervention is needed to maintain safety and what action should be taken. In this example, the safety actions available (via the VMS) are to reduce the commanded aircraft speed or to use the brakes to halt the aircraft.

The goal of the run-time assurance architecture is to ensure that the LEC does not result in violation of aircraft safety requirements. While the LEC is responsible for performance (tracking the center line), the safety requirements for this application are to ensure that 1) the aircraft does not deviate too far from the center line and leave the runway and 2) unnecessary stopping on the runway is minimized. In the baseline system, the LEC cannot be verified using traditional means and is considered the complex or untrusted component in the architecture. The run-time safety monitors, PID controller, and the VMS are either based on existing verified algorithms or have been developed using traditional methods compatible with DO-178C. The Monitor Selector and Contingency Manager are high-assurance components that are synthesized and verified using formal methods.

3   Approach

The three elements of our run-time assurance approach are the architecture itself, the run-time monitors, and the safety components that manage switching of behaviors.

3.1   Architecture

The assurance architecture has been modeled using AADL. AADL is targeted at distributed, real-time-embedded systems and provides sufficiently rigorous semantics to support formal analysis of system safety properties. We use an extension of AADL called AGREE to annotate the model with formal assume-guarantee contracts for components and subsystems. AGREE uses k-induction model checking to verify the top-level contracts of the system using a compositional approach [11]. Verification of the safety property in our demonstration system relies on the correctness of the monitors and other safety components, and establishes system safety for each state of the architecture.

The AADL model also includes an assurance case embedded in the architecture using the Resolute language [5]. Resolute assurance cases are linked to architectural components and formal evidence produced by other tools, and can be continuously re-evaluated during system development to check for errors. We have used Resolute to produce an assurance case showing that the run-time assurance architecture has been used correctly and has not been compromised by other elements of the system design. It also addresses the goal of minimizing unnecessary stopping through the use of independent monitors to maximize availability.

In other projects we have demonstrated how the implementation can be built from the verified AADL model for execution on the formally verified seL4 kernel [2]. While outside the scope of the current project, the isolation provided by seL4 adds assurance that a malfunctioning LEC does not have any computational side effects (memory or execution time) on the rest of the system.

3.2   Run-Time Monitors

The assurance architecture includes three independent monitors of system safety and one monitor that assesses confidence in the current operation of the LEC.

The first monitor uses global positioning system (GPS) signals to compute the aircraft position relative to a virtual runway centerline. This provides the primary estimate of CTE (with an error bound) to assess aircraft safety. Starting from a known position, the monitor integrates GPS velocity signals (delta range) to estimate the current position. It executes with low overhead and makes use of existing code and verification techniques.

The second monitor processes camera images and detects the runway centerline using traditional computer vision (CV) algorithms. It provides a secondary estimate of CTE in case the GPS monitor becomes unavailable or its error bound grows too large. The CV monitor can also be used to reset the GPS initial position when it has a lower error bound. It uses an edge detection algorithm to identify the strongest lines in the image. It also uses a pattern identification algorithm to detect the dashed center-line. Finally, the detected center-line is transformed to the aircraft frame of reference to compute CTE. This monitor makes use of existing algorithms, but requires fairly large computing overhead, making full use of two CPU cores.

The third monitor uses high-integrity inertial reference system (IRS) measurements to compute aircraft position. It provides coverage when both the GPS and CV monitors are unavailable. This monitor uses acceleration data from IRS to propagate the last CTE estimate and error bound from the GPS or CV monitors. It also make use of existing code and traditional verification techniques, and executes with low overhead.

The final monitor is used to determine if the LEC is operating in a region of competence relative to its training data. It is not a trusted component and is therefore not used to enforce system safety, but only as an additional check on LEC performance. It uses a Variational Autoencoder (VAE), a pair of neural networks that are learned in an unsupervised way to capture the complicated distribution of the training dataset in a compact representation space. The pair of neural networks—an encoder and a decoder—maps the input data to and from the representation. When an input deviates from the training data distribution, the encoder cannot find an accurate representation, and the decoder consequently fails to reconstruct the input faithfully. The monitor then captures the magnitude of reconstruction error as a signal for a lack of confidence [4]. We used this monitor to allow the Contingency Manager to recover from a transient SLOW or HALT action if the current safety monitor output returns to normal and the LEC appears to be in its region of competence. The monitor is relatively expensive, requiring time from both the CPU and GPU.

3.3   Safety Components

The Monitor Selector and Contingency Manager are critical for safe operation (single instance, no backup) and so have been implemented as high-assurance components using formal synthesis. They provide inputs to the VMS that determine the control action to be taken to guarantee system safety.

The Monitor Selector must choose which of the three safety monitors should be used at each time step. If GPS and CV are both available, it chooses the one with the smallest error bound (subject to minimum switching time). If neither GPS nor CV is available, it uses the IRS monitor. If no monitor is available, this will cause the Contingency Manager to trigger a halt.

The Contingency Manager determines whether control should be based on LEC outputs (NORMAL) or one of the contingency actions (SLOW or HALT). SLOW is selected if the current CTE exceeds the 'slow' threshold or the predicted stopping position based on the current speed is too close to the runway edge. HALT is selected if the current CTE exceeds 'halt' threshold or the predicted stopping position is too close to runway edge. Recovery from SLOW or HALT is allowed if the LEC confidence monitor output is above its threshold and a specified time limit has not been exceeded.

Both the Monitor Selector and the Contingency Manager are synthesized with proof of correctness from formal tabular specifications in ACL2 using the Automated Program Transformations (APT) toolkit [7]. A table specifies the behavior of a component declaratively as a set of cases corresponding to the columns of the table. Each case specifies the outputs and next state as a function of the inputs and current state. Proofs checked by ACL2 ensure that each table is complete and unambiguous (in every input scenario, exactly one case applies). A generic function to apply the table is specialized by the APT `simplify` transformation to create by partial evaluation a large, provably-equivalent set of if-then-else expressions. These conditional expressions are quite fast to execute but would be tedious and error prone to define by hand. The proofs done by the `simplify` transformation ensure that it correctly encodes the decision logic specified declaratively in the table.

4   Results

To evaluate performance of the run-time assurance architecture, testing was performed using all six LEC variants in a variety of environmental conditions with and without the assurance architecture components. Faulty LECs were simulated by operating in conditions outside of the LEC training data set. In all we evaluated 46 different scenarios. This allowed us to assess baseline performance, intervention of the assurance architecture in the presence of LEC errors, and absence of unnecessary intervention (false alarms). A screenshot of the demonstration video including the synoptic display of the monitor outputs is shown in Fig. 2.

We found that the architecture performed in accordance with expectations in all scenarios. In every case where the faulty LEC caused the aircraft to deviate from the required center-line tracking performance, the assurance architecture detected the condition and slowed or halted the aircraft. At no time was the aircraft allowed to depart from the paved runway. Furthermore, the architecture never intervened when the aircraft was performing within requirements.

For example, in one scenario the LEC trained with morning-only data is tested in clear conditions at 1600. This leads to the aircraft departing from the runway after approximately two minutes. When the scenario is repeated with the run-time assurance architecture active, the aircraft is first slowed when it begins to deviate from the centerline, then briefly halted, and then allowed to resume normal operation using the LEC guidance. Later, at a runway crossing, the aircraft deviates more severely and is halted to prevent it from leaving the runway. AADL models for the run-time assurance architecture, the Resolute assurance case, and videos of the demonstration are available at the project website [8].

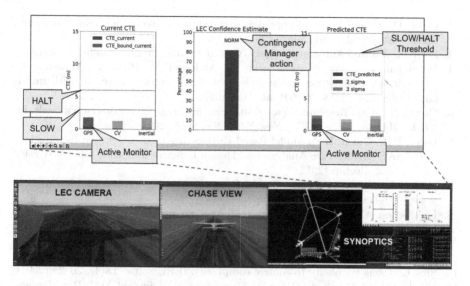

Fig. 2. Simulation results and display

5   Conclusion

In this project we have explored run-time monitors that observe LEC inputs, outputs, and internal state, and also monitors that directly observe system safety (as shown here in the TaxiNet demo). The run-time assurance approach works best when it is possible to clearly distinguish requirements for system safety and performance, and the functions responsible for each. For example, a complex planning system may be used to compute a desired vehicle trajectory, but if safety is defined by staying within a prescribed geofence, this is simple to monitor using GPS. However, it is not always possible to monitor the variables or conditions needed to detect safety violations. And in some cases it is not obvious how to create a safe backup function that is less complex (and easier to verify) than the complex function to be bounded. But where the necessary conditions are satisfied, run-time assurance architectures based on ASTM F3269-17 can be a useful means for safely bounding LEC behavior.

Acknowledgments. The authors wish to thank our colleagues James Paunicka, Matthew Moser, Alex Chen, and Dragos Margineantu for their support during integration and testing on the BR&T autonomy platform. This work was funded by DARPA contract FA8750-18-C-0099. The views, opinions and/or findings expressed are those of the author and should not be interpreted as representing the official views or policies of the Department of Defense or the U.S. Government.

References

1. ASTM F3269–17: Standard practice for methods to safely bound flight behavior of unmanned aircraft systems containing complex functions (2017)

2. Cofer, D., et al.: A formal approach to constructing secure air vehicle software. IEEE Comput. Mag. **51**, 14–23 (2018)
3. DARPA: Assured Autonomy. https://www.darpa.mil/program/assured-autonomy
4. Denouden, T., Salay, R., Czarnecki, K., Abdelzad, V., Phan, B., Vernekar, S.: Improving reconstruction autoencoder out-of-distribution detection with mahalanobis distance (2018). CoRR, abs/1812.02765
5. Gacek, A., et al.: Resolute: an assurance case language for architecture models. In: HILT 2014, pp. 19–28. ACM, New York, NY, USA (2014)
6. Feiler, P.H., Gluch, D.P.: Model-Based Engineering with AADL: An Introduction to the SAE Architecture Analysis and Design Language, 1st edn. Addison-Wesley Professional, Boston (2012)
7. Kestrel Institute: APT: Automated Program Transformations (2019). https://www.kestrel.edu/home/projects/apt/
8. Loonwerks: AAHAA: Architecture and Analysis for High-Assurance Autonomy. http://loonwerks.com/projects/aahaa.html
9. RTCA DO-178C: Software considerations in airborne systems and equipment certification (2011)
10. Sha, L.: Using simplicity to control complexity. IEEE Softw. **18**(4), 20–28 (2001)
11. Whalen, M.W., Gacek, A., Cofer, D., Murugesan, A., Heimdahl, M.P., Rayadurgam, S.: Your "what" is my "how": iteration and hierarchy in system design. IEEE Softw. **30**(2), 54–60 (2013)

hpnmg: A C++ Tool for Model Checking Hybrid Petri Nets with General Transitions

Jannik Hüls, Henner Niehaus, and Anne Remke[(✉)]

Westfälische Wilhelms-Universität, 48149 Münster, Germany
{jannik.huels,henner.niehaus,anne.remke}@uni-muenster.de

Abstract. hpnmg is a tool for model checking Hybrid Petri nets with an arbitrary but finite number of general transition firings against specifications formulated in STL. The tool efficiently implements and combines algorithms for state space creation, transformation to a geometric representation, model checking a potentially nested STL formula and integrating over the resulting satisfaction set to yield the probability that the specification holds at a specific time.

Keywords: Stochastic hybrid systems · Model checking · C++ tool

1 Introduction

We present the tool hpnmg for the automated verification of *Hybrid Petri nets with general transitions* (HPnG) [15]. HPnGs extend Hybrid Petri nets [1] by adding general transitions with a randomly distributed delay. They provide a high-level formalism for a restricted class of stochastic hybrid systems, where the continuous behaviour is piece-wise linear without resets and the inherent non-determinism is resolved probabilistically. Hybrid Petri nets have shown to be useful for evaluating e.g. the *survivability* of critical infrastructures [14,23] via model checking properties specified using Stochastic Time Logic (STL), which closely resembles MITL [2] or the temporal layer of STL/PSL [25].

The evolution of the state space over time of a HPnG can be partitioned into sets of states with similar behavior. This is done by conditioning their evolution on the firing times of the general transitions, either as *locations*, organized in a Parametric Location Tree (PLT) [19] or using a geometric representation as convex polytopes (so-called regions) [21]. The idea of a polyhedra based representation has been explored before, e.g., for (flowpipe) approximations [11,12] and to abstract uncountable-state stochastic processes [30,31]. Our approach includes the stochastic behaviour over time symbolically into the state representation; every stochastic firing adds a dimension to the state space. Model checking then identifies all realizations of the random variables, which satisfy a given STL formula. Based on the computed satisfaction sets, multi-dimensional

© Springer Nature Switzerland AG 2020
R. Lee et al. (Eds.): NFM 2020, LNCS 12229, pp. 369–378, 2020.
https://doi.org/10.1007/978-3-030-55754-6_22

integration computes the probability that the STL formula holds, using the joint probability distribution of all stochastic firings.

The development of efficient and automated model checking techniques for HPnGs has been limited in the number of stochastic firings mainly due to the lack of libraries that can solve the hyperplane arrangement problem in arbitrary dimensions. Recently vertex enumeration was proposed [29] to circumvent this problem by first constructing the tree-based representation, which can then be turned into a geometric representation for model checking. The current implementation of hpnmg features the library HyPRO [29], which offers efficient implementations for operations on convex polytopes [33] in higher dimensions. The advantage of HyPro e.g. with respect to [3,32], is the clean interface and the options to directly import their flowpipe construction. Technically, hpnmg is a complete redevelopment, integrating new and existing implementations into a fully coherent tool, which also allows model checking in parallel. The satisfaction sets are returned by the model checker as arbitrary convex polytopes and their representation is then adapted for the computation of the corresponding probabilities using multi-dimensional integration.

Many different tools exist for the simulation and analysis of (stochastic) timed and hybrid systems. Oris [4] is a tool for modeling and analysis of reactive timed systems, based on various classes of Petri nets. CPN Tools [22] is a toolset for simulating and analysing Colored Petri nets, for which extensions to stochastic and dynamic CPNs exist [9]. Both tools implement quantitative evaluation and qualitative verification for systems with a discrete notion of state. StocHy[6] is a simulator for the quantitative evaluation of discrete-time stochastic hybrid systems. Formal abstractions of possibly possibly non-deterministic discrete-time Markov processes over a continuous state space into finite-state Markov chains or Markov decision processes are provided by the tool FAUST[2] [31]. Möbius [8] supports modeling formalisms like Stochastic Petri Nets (SPNs), Stochastic Automata Networks (SANs) and Markov Chains and mainly implements discrete-event simulation. The Modest toolset [17] provides an extensible and comprehensive toolset for analytical and statistical model checking. It allows numerous model formalisms and in contrast to hpnmg can also deal with nondeterminsm. Möbius and modes [5] rely on simulation for stochastic hybrid models. A limited overapproximating model checker for stochastic hybrid automata has also been released as part of Modest [16]. SpaceX [13] and Flow* [7] provide reachability analysis for non-linear hybrid automata without stochasticity. Also constraint solvers have been proposed for the automated analysis of probabilistic hybrid automata [10]. HYPEG [27] implements statistical model checking with various confidence intervals and hypothesis tests for HPnGs.

The paper is further organized as follows: Sect. 2 presents the architecture and implementation details of hpnmg, Sect. 3 shows results for a feasibility study and Sect. 4 concludes the paper.

2 Architecture and Implementation

The tool **hpnmg** is implemented in C++ and runs on Linux and Mac OS X. The architecture of **hpnmg** follows the unix philosophy on minimalist, modular software development [28] and builds on a set of other libraries. An extensive test suite has been created using the C++ googletest framework[1]. The Boost[2] program options are used to provide a user friendly command line interface. The tool **hpnmg** allows to create HPnG models in both a graphical user interface and an xml-based language and to specify corresponding STL formulas for automated model checking. The presented tool unifies implementations of previous contributions on the following aspects of model checking HPnGs:

- Automated generation of the state-space of a given HPnG as PLT, as in [19].
- Efficient conversion of locations into convex polytopes, as proposed in [21].
- Efficient and full-fledged STL model checking, as in [20], which has additionally been parallelized for better performance.
- Triangulation of convex polytopes and transformation to standard simplices.
- Multi-dimensional Monte-Carlo integration over these standard simplices to compute probabilities corresponding to the satisfaction sets [19,20].

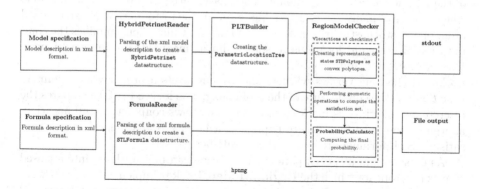

Fig. 1. Tasks of the tool **hpnmg** to analyse a formal model w.r.t. a property of interest.

Figure 1 depicts a high-level overview of the different parts of the tool. **hpnmg** takes as input a HPnG model and an STL formula as XML file and transforms them into the appropriate data structures HybridPetrinet and STLFormula using the **HybridPetrinetReader** and **FormulaReader** classes which implement the Xerces-C++ XML Parser[3].

A HPnG is defined as a tuple $\mathcal{H} = (\mathcal{P}, \mathcal{T}, \mathcal{A}, \mathbf{M}_0, \Phi)$. The set of *places* $\mathcal{P}$, contains discrete and continuous places. The initial marking $\mathbf{M}_0$ describes the

---

[1] https://github.com/google/googletest.

[2] https://www.boost.org/.

[3] https://xerces.apache.org/xerces-c/.

initial number of tokens in each discrete place and the amount of fluid in each continuous place. *Transitions* change the content of places upon firing. The set of transitions T holds immediate, deterministic, general and continuous transitions. All but continuous transitions are denoted discrete transitions. *Arcs* $\mathcal{A}$ connect places and transitions. Discrete transitions change the discrete marking of connected places upon firing. A deterministic transition fires after being enabled for a predefined amount of time. Immediate transitions fire after zero time. The random firing delay of a general transition is distributed according to an arbitrary unique cumulative distribution function (CDF). A general transition may fire at any point in time, if enabled. Continuous transitions change the fluid level of continuous places with a constant nominal rate. Φ is a vector of parameter functions such as priorities of transitions e.g. used to resolve conflicts between transitions of equal type.

The evolution of a HPnG results in uncountably many states, when considering a state to contain the marking, information on the general transition firings, as well the evolution time. Hence, we use a symbolic representation of states called *Parametric Location Tree* (PLT) [19]. Nodes are parametric locations and symbolically represent a state. Branching to new locations happens by the occurrence of events, e.g. a continuous place reaching its boundary or an enabled discrete transition fires. The **PLTBuilder** implements the generation of the PLT for an arbitrary amount of stochastic firings up to a maximum time. The presence of many random variables requires the introduction of a strict total order on the stochastic firings, as proposed in [19], which then simplifies the computation of the child locations to solving linear inequalities using a variant of Fourier-Motzkin elimination.

Model checking verifies whether the system meets a property at a point in time t' and is the core feature of the tool hpnmg. The logic STL [20] compares the discrete and continuous marking to constants, allows conjunction and negation, as well as the until operator to express reachability over time. All states that satisfy a STL formula are collected in a satisfaction set.

As presented in [21] each parametric location can be translated into a closed convex polytope for which the **RegionModelChecker** implements model checking using geometric operations. The transformation into convex polytopes and the geometric operations for model checking are implemented using the library HYPRO [29]. First all locations in which the system can be at t' are identified. Model checking is then performed on a STDPolytope along the parse tree of the STLFormula and the satisfaction set $Sat^R(\Phi)$ is returned as a set of polytopes.

Since the representation in terms of polytopes is not closed under negation, the current implementation may result in a set of not necessarily disjoint polytopes. We implement *inclusion-exclusion* to integrate overlapping areas exactly once. As described in [20], the overall complexity of the model checking routine is $O(|R|^2 \times |L| \times |H_P|^3)$ with the number of regions in the PLT $|R|$, the number of operators in the STL formula $|L|$ and the number of halfspaces $|H_P|$. Since the PLT is independent of the STL specification, model checking is performed

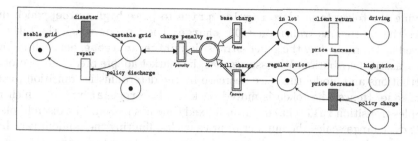

Fig. 2. Model of a plug-in electric vehicle charging process.

for each location separately, allowing for parallel execution via the OpenMP application programming interface, thereby improving the computation time [26].

Integrating the joint probability distribution of all stochastic firings over the convex polytopes of $Sat^R(\Phi)$ results in the probability that the STL formula Φ is satisfied in R. Each random variable $s \in \mathbf{s}$ is assigned a unique probability density function and together with the previously defined order on the stochastic firings, the **ProbabilityCalculator** implements the d-dimensional Delauney Triangulation of the library CGAL [18] to create simplices of random polytopes. The ordered integration bounds are then obtained from an affine transformation of these simplices. To calculate the actual value of the integral, for now, Monte Carlo methods [24] of the GSL library[4] by GNU are used. This approximate method could also be used on arbitrary polytopes, however the ordered sequence of intervals also allows to substitute the concrete integration method.

3 Experimental Results

We compute results for a HPnG model of a plug-in electric vehicle (pev) charging station, as shown in Fig. 2. The model has a continuous part modeling the battery and its (dis-)charging process, as well as a discrete part, which models the status of the power grid and whether a car is available for charging. The continuous place ev models the battery, where the level x_{ev} represents the current state of charge. The continuous transition base charge defines the baseline charging rate r_{base} for the pev. The discrete place in lot initially contains one token modeling the presence of the pev. The guard arc between place ev and transition base charge ensures that the pev is only charged if connected. The client retrieves the vehicle after a random delay defined by the general transition client return, whose firing removes the token from place in lot.

The pev is initially charged with full rate, as indicated by a token in place regular price which enables the continuous transition full charge. Whenever the energy price increases, the operators decrease the charging rate to reduce the operating cost of the charging station. This is represented in the model by

---

[4] https://www.gnu.org/software/gsl/doc/html/montecarlo.html.

moving the token from place `regular price` to place `high price`, which disables the continuous transition `full charge`. The time at which the token is moved is determined by the general transition `price increase`, hence, it follows a stochastic distribution. We assume that the market adapts predictably to price fluctuations and model the price decrease by the deterministic transition `price decrease`. Hence, the token is moved back to place `regular price`, which re-enables transition `full charge`, after a fixed time has passed. The discrete place `policy charge` scales the number of price cycles, limiting the random variables present in the system. The deterministic transition `disaster` brings the model into a state where the grid suddenly has to support a high load, represented by a token in place `unstable grid`. By deterministically chosing the point in time at which the grid fails allows us to verify the influence of failure at different points in time. A disaster decreases the rate at which the battery is charged by enabling the continuous transition `charge penalty`. The token is moved back to place `stable grid`, which again disables the transition `charge penalty`, when firing the general transition `repair`. Hence, the repair time follows a stochastic distribution. Also the place `policy discharge` is used to determine the number of time the general transition `repair` may fire. Note that, in the current marking of the model, i.e. one token in place `policy discharge` and zero token in place `policy charge`, every general transition can fire at most once.

All experiments were conducted on an Intel Core i7 with 2.5 GHz and 16 GB RAM running Mac OS X. An artefact to reproduce the following experiments is available online.[5] The general transitions are all set to a folded normal distribution, with values $\mu = 9$ and $\sigma = 1$ for client return, $\mu = 4$, $\sigma = 2$ for price increase and $\mu = 0.25$ and $\sigma = 0.5$ for repair. We evaluate the following STL properties: **(a)** $\Phi_1 := x_{ev} \geq 30$, **(b)** $\Phi_2 := (m_{in \, lot} = 1) \vee (x_{ev} \geq 30)$ and **(c)** $\Phi_3 := (m_{in \, lot} = 1) \, \mathcal{U}^{[t', t'+20]} ((m_{in \, lot} = 0) \wedge (x_{ev} \geq 30))$. Φ_1 compares the state of charge to a constant, Φ_2 states that either the state of charge is larger or equal to thirty, or the pev should currently be connected. Φ_3 ensures that the pev is connected until the state of charge reaches at least thirty.

Recall that model checking requires first converting parametric locations into convex polytopes, then computes the satisfaction sets for each region and finally integrates the joint probability density over these sets. The current implementation of the tool allows for model checking in parallel and Fig. 3 compares the serial and parallel computation times for the STL properties Φ_1, Φ_2 and Φ_3.

Serial model checking requires between 2 and 120 s, depending on the formula and the chosen time point. The execution in four parallel threads achieved a speedup factor of two. For later time points the number of candidate locations grows with the depth of the tree. Only for property **(c)** computation times decrease with later time points, since goal states are reached more quickly. Integration forms the bottleneck of the current implementation (cf. Fig. 3). However, the computation times seem reasonable, especially when considering that the results are computed without approximation or abstraction.

---

[5] https://uni-muenster.sciebo.de/s/IFEzCBfiY4ItIu8.

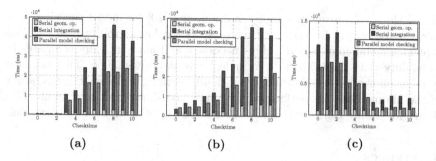

Fig. 3. Serial and parallel model checking **(a)** $\Phi_1 := x_{ev} \geq 30$, **(b)** $\Phi_2 := (m_{in\ lot} = 1) \vee (x_{ev} \geq 30)$ and **(c)** $\Phi_3 := (m_{in\ lot} = 1)\,\mathcal{U}^{[t',t'+20]}\,((m_{in\ lot} = 0) \wedge (x_{ev} \geq 30))$.

Table 1. Robustness computed for different values of (esoc) by HYPEG and hpnmg. The confidence interval (CI) in HYPEG is computed for a confidence level of 0.99.

esoc		40	50	60	70	80	90
HYPEG	Probability	0.9999	0.8884	0.6897	0.4254	0.1896	0.0569
	CI	±0.0003					
	Comp. time	10 s	663 s	1397 s	1646 s	1066 s	378 s
hpnmg	Probability	0.9999	0.8883	0.6890	0.4258	0.1901	0.0563
	Error		±3.09e−4	±3.09e−4	±3.09e−4	±3.07e−4	±3.00e−4	2.90e−4
	Time	35 s	45 s	46 s	46 s	85 s	97 s

In the following we evaluate the robustness of the presented system. Robustness is defined as the probability that the plug-in electric vehicle is charged, at least up to an expected state of charge (esoc), upon the return of the client:

$$\text{robustness} = (m_{in\ lot} = 1)\,\mathcal{U}^{[0,15]}\,((m_{in\ lot} = 0) \wedge (x_{ev} \geq \text{esoc})),$$

The robustness computed by hpnmg for different values of esoc is compared to results obtained from the statistical model checker HYPEG [27] for validation purposes. Table 1 shows that the results match nicely. Note that the computation times strongly depend on the number of simulation runs required for HYPEG and the number of polytopes handled by hpnmg and especially the required accuracy of the integration. The computation times above have mainly been included to indicate that hpnmg is competitive. We refer to [19] and [20] for further more detailed studies of computation times for state space creation and model checking, respectively.

4 Conclusion

We present a tool for model checking HPnGs with an arbitrary but finite number of stochastic firings against the logic STL. Different algorithms necessary for the procedure have been published before: [19] for state space generation, [21] for switching to a geometric representation, and [20] for model checking. However, the tool hpnmg for the first time presents a coherent tool, which efficiently implements and combines the steps necessary and automatically computes the probability that a specific STL formula holds at a given time. The tool heavily relies on the library HyPro for efficiently performing geometric operations, on the library CGAL for performing Delauney transformation, and on the GNU library for Monte Carlo integration. OpenMP has been used for parallelization.

References

1. Alla, H., David, R.: Continuous and hybrid Petri nets. J. Circuits Syst. Comput. **8**(01), 159–188 (1998)
2. Alur, R., Feder, T., Henzinger, T.A.: The benefits of relaxing punctuality. Technical report, Cornell University (1994)
3. Bagnara, R., Hill, P.M., Zaffanella, E.: The Parma Polyhedra library: toward a complete set of numerical abstractions for the analysis and verification of hardware and software systems. Sci. Comput. Program. **72**(1–2), 3–21 (2008)
4. Bucci, G., Carnevali, L., Ridi, L., Vicario, E.: Oris: a tool for modeling, verification and evaluation of real-time systems. Int. J. Softw. Tools Technol. Transfer **12**(5), 391–403 (2010)
5. Budde, C.E., D'Argenio, P.R., Hartmanns, A., Sedwards, S.: A statistical model checker for nondeterminism and rare events. In: Beyer, D., Huisman, M. (eds.) TACAS 2018. LNCS, vol. 10806, pp. 340–358. Springer, Cham (2018). https://doi.org/10.1007/978-3-319-89963-3_20
6. Cauchi, N., Abate, A.: StocHy: automated verification and synthesis of stochastic processes. In: Vojnar, T., Zhang, L. (eds.) TACAS 2019. LNCS, vol. 11428, pp. 247–264. Springer, Cham (2019). https://doi.org/10.1007/978-3-030-17465-1_14
7. Chen, X., Ábrahám, E., Sankaranarayanan, S.: Flow*: an analyzer for non-linear hybrid systems. In: Sharygina, N., Veith, H. (eds.) CAV 2013. LNCS, vol. 8044, pp. 258–263. Springer, Heidelberg (2013). https://doi.org/10.1007/978-3-642-39799-8_18
8. Deavours, D.D., et al.: The Mobius framework and its implementation. IEEE Trans. Softw. Eng. **28**(10), 956–969 (2002)
9. Everdij, M.H., Blom, H.A.: Hybrid state Petri nets which have the analysis power of stochastic hybrid systems and the formal verification power of automata. In: Petri Nets, chapter 12. IntechOpen (2010)
10. Fränzle, M., Teige, T., Eggers, A.: Engineering constraint solvers for automatic analysis of probabilistic hybrid automata. J. Logic Algebraic Program. **79**(7), 436–466 (2010)
11. Frehse, G., Han, Z., Krogh, B.: Assume-guarantee reasoning for hybrid I/O-automata by over-approximation of continuous interaction. In: 43rd IEEE Conference on Decision and Control, pp. 479–484 (2004)
12. Frehse, G., Kateja, R., Le Guernic, C.: Flowpipe approximation and clustering in space-time. In: 16th International Conference on Hybrid Systems: Computation and Control, pp. 203–212. ACM (2013)
13. Frehse, G., et al.: SpaceEx: scalable verification of hybrid systems. In: Gopalakrishnan, G., Qadeer, S. (eds.) CAV 2011. LNCS, vol. 6806, pp. 379–395. Springer, Heidelberg (2011). https://doi.org/10.1007/978-3-642-22110-1_30

14. Ghasemieh, H., Remke, A., Haverkort, B.: Analysis of a sewage treatment facility using hybrid Petri nets. In: 7th EAI International Conference on Performance Evaluation Methodologies and Tools, pp. 165–174. ACM (2013)

15. Gribaudo, M., Remke, A.: Hybrid Petri nets with general one-shot transitions. Perform. Eval. **105**, 22–50 (2016)

16. Hahn, E.M., Hartmanns, A., Hermanns, H., Katoen, J.P.: A compositional modelling and analysis framework for stochastic hybrid systems. Formal Methods Syst. Des. **43**(2), 191–232 (2013)

17. Hartmanns, A., Hermanns, H.: The modest toolset: an integrated environment for quantitative modelling and verification. In: Ábrahám, E., Havelund, K. (eds.) TACAS 2014. LNCS, vol. 8413, pp. 593–598. Springer, Heidelberg (2014). https://doi.org/10.1007/978-3-642-54862-8_51

18. Hert, S., Seel, M.: dD convex hulls and delaunay triangulations. In: CGAL User and Reference Manual. CGAL Editorial Board, 4.14 edn. (2019)

19. Hüls, J., Pilch, C., Schinke, P., Delicaris, J., Remke, A.: State-space construction of hybrid petri nets with multiple stochastic firings. In: Parker, D., Wolf, V. (eds.) QEST 2019. LNCS, vol. 11785, pp. 182–199. Springer, Cham (2019). https://doi.org/10.1007/978-3-030-30281-8_11

20. Hüls, J., Remke, A.: Model checking HPnGs in multiple dimensions: representing state sets as convex polytopes. In: Pérez, J.A., Yoshida, N. (eds.) FORTE 2019. LNCS, vol. 11535, pp. 148–166. Springer, Cham (2019). https://doi.org/10.1007/978-3-030-21759-4_9

21. Hüls, J., Schupp, S., Remke, A., Ábrahám, E.: Analyzing hybrid Petri nets with multiple stochastic firings using HyPro. In: 11th EAI International Confrence on Performance Evaluation Methodologies and Tools, pp. 178–185. ACM (2017)

22. Jensen, K., Kristensen, L.M.: Coloured Petri Nets: Modelling and Validation of Concurrent Systems. Springer, Heidelberg (2009). https://doi.org/10.1007/b95112

23. Jongerden, M.R., Hüls, J., Remke, A., Haverkort, B.R.: Does your domestic photovoltaic energy system survive grid outages? Energies **9**(9), 736 (2016)

24. Lepage, G.P.: A new algorithm for adaptive multidimensional integration. J. Comput. Phys. **27**(2), 192–203 (1978)

25. Maler, O., Nickovic, D.: Monitoring temporal properties of continuous signals. In: Lakhnech, Y., Yovine, S. (eds.) FORMATS/FTRTFT -2004. LNCS, vol. 3253, pp. 152–166. Springer, Heidelberg (2004). https://doi.org/10.1007/978-3-540-30206-3_12

26. OpenMP Architecture Review Board: OpenMP Application Program Interface Version 5.0, May 2018

27. Pilch, C., Edenfeld, F., Remke, A.: HYPEG: statistical model checking for hybrid Petri nets: tool paper. In: Proceedings of the 11th EAI International Conference on Performance Evaluation Methodologies and Tools, pp. 186–191. ACM (2017)

28. Raymond, E.S.: The Art of Unix Programming. Addison-Wesley Professional, Boston (2003)

29. Schupp, S., Ábrahám, E., Makhlouf, I.B., Kowalewski, S.: HYPRO: A C++ library of state set representations for hybrid systems reachability analysis. In: Barrett, C., Davies, M., Kahsai, T. (eds.) NFM 2017. LNCS, vol. 10227, pp. 288–294. Springer, Cham (2017). https://doi.org/10.1007/978-3-319-57288-8_20

30. Soudjani, S.E.Z., Abate, A.: Adaptive and sequential gridding procedures for the abstraction and verification of stochastic processes. SIAM J. Appl. Dyn. Syst. **12**(2), 921–956 (2013)

31. Soudjani, S.E.Z., Gevaerts, C., Abate, A.: FAUST^2: formal abstractions of uncountable-STate STochastic processes. In: Baier, C., Tinelli, C. (eds.) TACAS 2015. LNCS, vol. 9035, pp. 272–286. Springer, Heidelberg (2015). https://doi.org/10.1007/978-3-662-46681-0_23

32. The CGAL Project: CGAL user and reference manual. In: CGAL Editorial Board, 4.10 edn. (2017)

33. Ziegler, G.M.: Lectures on Polytopes, vol. 152. Springer, New York (2012). https://doi.org/10.1007/978-1-4613-8431-1

Hybrid and Cyber-Physical Systems

A Transformation of Hybrid Petri Nets with Stochastic Firings into a Subclass of Stochastic Hybrid Automata

Carina Pilch[1($\boxtimes$)], Maurice Krause[1], Anne Remke[1], and Erika Ábrahám[2]

[1] Westfälische Wilhelms-Universität, Münster, Germany
{carina.pilch,maurice.krause,anne.remke}@uni-muenster.de
[2] RWTH Aachen University,Aachen, Germany
abraham@informatik.rwth-aachen.de

Abstract. We present a transformation of Hybrid Petri nets extended with stochastic firings (HPnGs) into a subclass of Stochastic Hybrid Automata (SHA), thereby making HPnGs amenable to techniques from that domain. While (non-stochastic) Hybrid Petri nets have previously been transformed into Hybrid Automata, we consider also stochastic aspects and transform HPnGs into Singular Automata, which are Hybrid Automata restricted to piecewise constant derivatives for continuous variables, extended by random clocks. We implemented our transformation and show its usefulness by comparing results for time-bounded reachability for HPnGs extended with non-determinism on the one hand, and for the transformed SHAs using the *ProHVer* tool on the other hand.

1 Introduction

Hybrid Petri nets, as proposed by David and Alla [7], have been extended by stochastic firings to *Hybrid Petri nets with general transitions (HPnGs)* [13]. The construct of *general transitions* supports the modeling of random time delays, like time-to-repair or time-to-failure, in dependability models of critical infrastructures such as water sewage systems and smart homes [12,20].

Previous works [1,7] have shown that Hybrid Petri nets can be transformed to Hybrid Automata (HA), allowing the usage of HA analysis tools for the analysis of Hybrid Petri nets. In contrast, recent work on analysis techniques for HPnGs rather focused on the development of dedicated techniques for state-space construction and model checking [18,19]. Instead of dedicated analysis techniques for HPnGs, in this paper we propose a *transformation of HPnGs into a subclass of Stochastic Hybrid Automata* for which tool support is available for their analysis. Using the transformation presented in this work allows to use existing analysis tools for Stochastic Hybrid Automata also for Hybrid Petri nets.

The main restrictions in the modeling power of HPnGs lie in the piecewise-constant derivatives of continuous variables, conditions that must not compare continuous variables to each other, and the exclusion of non-determinism as an explicit modeling feature. Note that there is an intrinsic non-determinism in

© Springer Nature Switzerland AG 2020
R. Lee et al. (Eds.): NFM 2020, LNCS 12229, pp. 381–400, 2020.
https://doi.org/10.1007/978-3-030-55754-6_23

Hybrid Petri nets, which is traditionally resolved probabilistically, but which can also be resolved by a (non-)prophetic scheduler, as proposed in [25].

Due to these syntactical restrictions, we can transform HPnGs into so-called Singular Automata extended with random clocks. Singular Automata are Hybrid Automata with only constant derivatives and rectangular sets for conditions and resets. To cover the stochastic aspects of HPnGs, we extend Singular Automata with random clocks [6] to model the firings of general transitions. Whenever a general transition in the HPnG is freshly enabled (for the first time or after a previous firing), the corresponding random clock in the Singular Automaton is sampled from the probability distribution assigned to the general transition. The transformation is based on the construction of a symbolic computation tree for a given HPnG, which we can compute only for a given time horizon, therefore the above transformation is exact only up to this time bound. We discuss the details of the transformation, however a formal correctness proof exceeds the scope of this paper. The feasibility of our transformation is demonstrated in a small case study on a battery (dis-)charging model, which we also use as a running example throughout this work. We compute time-bounded reachability, using the approach presented in [15] which discretizes probability distributions for the Singular Automaton.

Related Work. For Generalised Stochastic Petri nets (GSPNs), which do not include continuous variables and whose stochastic variables are restricted to negative exponential distributions, a Markov Automata semantics has been defined in [9], maintaining their intrinsic non-determinism. In the presence of continuous variables, David and Alla presented a transformation of Hybrid Petri nets into HA in [7]. They do not further discuss the resulting subclass of HA and do not include stochastic extensions in the transformation. The expressivity of (non-stochastic) multisingular Hybrid Petri nets has been compared to HA in [24].

Hybrid Automata are so expressive that reachability is undecidable in general [16]. Only for certain strongly restricted subclasses, like initialized rectangular automata, unbounded reachability is still decidable [17]. Reachability by a bounded number of discrete steps is decidable for rectangular automata also without initialization [2,10]. Different approaches extend HA e.g. with probabilistic jumps or random delays. Timed Automata have been extended by *probabilistic discrete jumps* [22,23] and by continuous probability distributions [3,14].

Other formalisms, e.g., Piecewise Deterministic Markov Processes [8], allow *initialized jumps* to take place at *random times*. For (restricted) extensions of decidable classes of HA, reachability is decidable [29]. For more general classes, incomplete approximative approaches are available [21,27]. CEGAR-style abstraction allows the application of model checking methods for HA [30].

The tool Faust[2] generates abstractions for uncountable-state discrete-time stochastic processes for verifying reachability. It supports Stochastic Hybrid Systems (SHS) with a single mode and finite actions [28]. A recent extension [5] features formal abstraction to interval Markov Decision Processes. Different approaches exist for overapproximating reachability probabilities for SHS: [11] present a safe overapproximation for SHS with non-determinism and continuous probability distributions in discrete jumps, and [15] discretize the support of random variables and present a reduction to Markov Decision Processes.

Outline. Section 2 defines HPnGs and their evolution. Section 3 presents Singular Automata with random clocks as the SHA subclass that we use for the transformation. A semantics for HPnGs in terms of Singular Automata with random clocks is introduced in Sect. 4. Section 5 presents the corresponding transformation algorithm. Section 6 reports on a feasibility experiment for a battery case study, before Sect. 7 concludes the paper.

2 Hybrid Petri Nets with General Transitions

First we introduce HPnGs in Sect. 2.1, before capturing their evolution by Parametric Location Trees (PLTs) in Sect. 2.2.

2.1 Hybrid Petri Nets with General Transitions

HPnGs, as defined in [13], extend traditional Petri nets with continuous variables, which have piecewise-linear evolution, and stochastic variables that follow arbitrary probability distributions.

Definition 1. *A* Hybrid Petri net with general transitions *(HPnG) is a tuple* $\mathcal{H} = (\mathcal{P}, \mathcal{T}, \mathcal{A}, \mathbf{M}_0, \Phi)$ *with the following components:*

- $\mathcal{P} = \mathcal{P}^{disc} \cup \mathcal{P}^{cont}$ *is a finite set of* places, *partitioned into disjoint sets of* discrete *and* continuous *places.*
- $\mathcal{T} = \mathcal{T}^{imm} \cup \mathcal{T}^{det} \cup \mathcal{T}^{gen} \cup \mathcal{T}^{cont}$ *is a finite set of* transitions, *partitioned into disjoint sets of* immediate, deterministic, general *and* continuous *transitions.*
- $\mathcal{A} = \mathcal{A}^{disc} \cup \mathcal{A}^{cont} \cup \mathcal{A}^{test} \cup \mathcal{A}^{inh}$ *is a finite set of* arcs, *partitioned into disjoint sets of* discrete, continuous, test *and* inhibitor *arcs. Every arc connects one place and one transition. Discrete arcs in* $\mathcal{A}^{disc} \subseteq (\mathcal{P}^{disc} \times (\mathcal{T} \setminus \mathcal{T}^{cont})) \cup ((\mathcal{T} \setminus \mathcal{T}^{cont}) \times \mathcal{P}^{disc})$ *connect discrete places and non-continuous transitions. Continuous arcs in* $\mathcal{A}^{cont} \subseteq (\mathcal{P}^{cont} \times \mathcal{T}^{cont}) \cup (\mathcal{T}^{cont} \times \mathcal{P}^{cont})$ *connect continuous places and continuous transitions. Test and inhibitor arcs in* $\mathcal{A}^{test}, \mathcal{A}^{inh} \subseteq (\mathcal{P}^{disc} \times \mathcal{T}) \cup (\mathcal{P}^{cont} \times (\mathcal{T} \setminus \mathcal{T}^{cont}))$ *connect places to transitions, excluding the combination of continuous places and continuous transitions.*
- $\mathbf{M}_0 = (\mathbf{m}_0, \mathbf{x}_0)$ *is an initial marking with* $\mathbf{m}_0 = (m_1, \ldots, m_{|\mathcal{P}^{disc}|}) \in \mathbb{N}_0^{|\mathcal{P}^{disc}|}$ *and* $\mathbf{x}_0 = (x_1, \ldots, x_{|\mathcal{P}^{cont}|}) \in \mathcal{R}_{\geq 0}^{|\mathcal{P}^{cont}|}$.
- $\Phi = (\Phi_b^{\mathcal{P}}, \Phi_d^{\mathcal{T}}, \Phi_g^{\mathcal{T}}, \Phi_c^{\mathcal{T}}, \Phi_w^{\mathcal{A}}, \Phi_s^{\mathcal{A}}, \Phi_p^{\mathcal{A}})$ *is a tuple of* parameter functions *with:* $\Phi_b^{\mathcal{P}} : \mathcal{P}^{cont} \to (\mathcal{R}_{>0} \cup \infty)$, $\Phi_d^{\mathcal{T}} : \mathcal{T}^{det} \to \mathcal{R}_{>0}$, $\Phi_g^{\mathcal{T}} : \mathcal{T}^{gen} \to (f : \mathcal{R}_{>0} \to [0,1])$, $\Phi_c^{\mathcal{T}} : \mathcal{T}^{cont} \to \mathcal{R}_{>0}$, $\Phi_w^{\mathcal{A}} : \mathcal{A} \to \mathcal{R}_{>0}$, $\Phi_s^{\mathcal{A}} : \mathcal{A}^{cont} \to \mathcal{R}_{>0}$, $\Phi_p^{\mathcal{A}} : \mathcal{A}^{cont} \to \mathbb{N}$.

Let in the following $\mathcal{H} = (\mathcal{P}, \mathcal{T}, \mathcal{A}, \mathbf{M}_0, \Phi)$ be an HPnG as defined above. In each state of $\mathcal{H}$, discrete places hold a number of *tokens* and continuous places hold an amount of *fluid*. The initial marking $\mathbf{M}_0 = (\mathbf{m}_0, \mathbf{x}_0)$ defines the initial

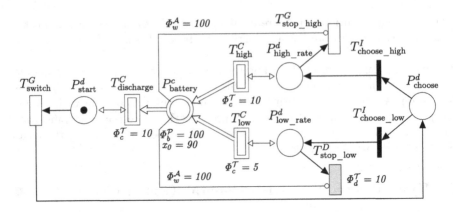

Fig. 1. HPnG of a battery (dis-)charging process with non-deterministic choice.

number of tokens $\mathbf{m}_0$ and fluid levels $\mathbf{x}_0$. Continuous places have upper bounds defined by Φ_b^P; lower bounds for all places are zero.

Markings can be changed by the *firing* of transitions. Immediate transitions in $\mathcal{T}^{imm}$ fire as soon as they get *enabled*. Deterministic transitions in $\mathcal{T}^{det}$ fire after being enabled for a deterministic time period defined by Φ_d^T; the firing times are *preemptive resume*, meaning that the transition needs to be enabled for this amount of time since its last firing in total, but not necessarily continuously. For general transitions in $\mathcal{T}^{gen}$, the firing time is a random variable, which follows a continuous probability distribution function defined by Φ_g^T.

Non-continuous transitions are enabled when their input places match the weight Φ_w^A of their connecting arcs. Whenever multiple non-continuous transitions are supposed to fire at the same time, there is naturally a non-deterministic choice between those transitions in *conflict*. Continuous transitions in $\mathcal{T}^{cont}$ have an inflow and an outflow and fire continuously if enabled, i.e. all connected input places hold fluid. The nominal firing rates of continuous transitions are defined by Φ_c^T and adapted in case a boundary is reached according to *share* (Φ_s^A) and *priority* (Φ_p^A). Note that test and inhibitor arcs further control the enabling of transitions, requiring that the marking of the connected place exceeds Φ_w^A.

Running Example. Fig. 1 presents the HPnG of a (dis-)charging process of a (linear) battery model, which non-deterministically chooses between two charging rates, after the battery has been drained to a random state of charge. Note that all weights, priorities and shares that are not shown in the figure equal 1. The battery is modeled by the continuous place $P_{battery}^c$ (depicted as double-outline circle), which has a capacity of 100 and an initial charge of 90. It is discharged by the transition $T_{discharge}^C$ (double-outline bar) with a rate of 10 per hour as long as the discrete place P_{start}^d (solid circle) holds a token (connected via a test arc, double arrow). This token is moved to place P_{choose}^d when the general transition T_{switch}^G (single-outline bar) fires after a uniformly distributed amount of time. After this firing, the two immediate transitions $T^I_{\text{choose\_high}}$ and $T^I_{\text{choose\_low}}$ (solid black bars) become enabled, such that a non-deterministic conflict arises. If $T^I_{\text{choose\_low}}$ fires, the continuous transition T^C_{low} becomes enabled (via place $P^d_{\text{low\_rate}}$) and charges P^c_{battery} with a rate of 5 per hour. The token in $P^d_{\text{low\_rate}}$ is removed after 10 hours by the firing of the deterministic transition $T^D_{\text{stop\_low}}$ (grey filled bar). If instead $T^I_{\text{choose\_high}}$ fires, P^c_{battery} is charged with a rate of 10 per hour, until the token in $P^d_{\text{high\_rate}}$ is removed by the firing of the general transition $T^G_{\text{stop\_high}}$. Note that the inhibitor arcs (circle arrows) between P^c_{battery} and $T^G_{\text{stop\_low}}$ resp. $T^G_{\text{stop\_high}}$ prevent the transitions from firing when the battery has reached its capacity. This is done only to reduce the size of the state space and transformed automaton by eliminating unnecessary additional events.

Next we define the notion of a state for HPnGs, following [26].

Definition 2. *A* state *of $\mathcal{H}$ is a tuple $\Gamma = (\mathbf{m}, \mathbf{x}, \mathbf{c}, \mathbf{d}, \mathbf{g}, \mathbf{e})$ with discrete markings $\mathbf{m} \in \mathbb{N}_0^{|\mathcal{P}^{disc}|}$, continuous markings $\mathbf{x} \in \mathcal{R}_{\geq 0}^{|\mathcal{P}^{cont}|}$, enabling times $\mathbf{c} \in \mathcal{R}_{\geq 0}^{|\mathcal{T}^{det}|}$ (clocks) for deterministic transitions, drifts $\mathbf{d} \in \mathbb{R}^{|\mathcal{P}^{cont}|}$ for the current change of fluid level per time unit in continuous places, enabling times $\mathbf{g} \in \mathcal{R}_{\geq 0}^{|\mathcal{T}^{gen}|}$ for general transitions and enabling status $\mathbf{e} \in \{0,1\}^{|\mathcal{T}|}$ for all transitions.*

The set of all states is denoted S, the initial state $\Gamma_0 = (\mathbf{m}_0, \mathbf{x}_0, \mathbf{0}, \mathbf{d}_0, \mathbf{0}, \mathbf{e}_0)$. By $\Gamma.\mathbf{m}$ we refer to the component $\mathbf{m}$ of Γ, and similarly for other components and tuples. During evolution, *events* may change a state if either a fluid marking boundary is reached, or a transition fires, or an arc condition changes [26]. We adopt concession and enabling rules, the definition of the evolution of continuous variables, clocks and enabling times as well as the concept for fluid share and rate adaption from [13] and do not explicitly state them in this work. The behavior of general transitions is additionally adopted from [26].

Definition 3. *An* event *$(\Gamma, \Delta\tau, \varepsilon, \Gamma')$ in $\mathcal{H}$ changes the state Γ to another state Γ' at time $\Delta\tau \in \mathcal{R}_{\geq 0}$ after entering the state Γ, caused by $\varepsilon \in \mathcal{P}^{cont} \cup (\mathcal{T} \setminus \mathcal{T}^{cont}) \cup \mathcal{A}^{test} \cup \mathcal{A}^{inh}$.*

We use $\mathcal{E}$ to denote the set of all events, $\mathcal{E}(\Gamma)$ those starting in state Γ, and $\mathcal{E}(\Gamma, \Gamma')$ for those that start in Γ and end in Γ'. We write $(\Gamma, \Gamma') \in \mathcal{E}$ if there exists some $\Delta\tau$ and ε such that $(\Gamma, \Delta\tau, \varepsilon, \Gamma') \in \mathcal{E}$.

Definition 4. *We define the* set of events with minimum remaining time *in state Γ as $\mathcal{E}^{min}(\Gamma) = \{(\Gamma, \Delta\tau', \varepsilon', \Gamma') \in \mathcal{E}(\Gamma) \mid \forall (\Gamma, \Delta\tau'', \varepsilon'', \Gamma'') \in \mathcal{E}(\Gamma). \Delta\tau' \leq \Delta\tau''\}$. Having $(\Gamma, \Delta\tau', \varepsilon', \Gamma') \in \mathcal{E}^{min}(\Gamma)$, the continuous evolution from Γ to Γ' visits the states $S(\Gamma, \Gamma') = \{\Gamma'' \in S \mid \exists \Delta\tau'' \in \mathcal{R}_{\geq 0}. \ 0 \leq \Delta\tau'' < \Delta\tau' \wedge \Gamma''.\mathbf{m} = \Gamma.\mathbf{m} \wedge \Gamma''.\mathbf{x} = \Gamma.\mathbf{x} + \Gamma.\mathbf{d} \cdot \Delta\tau'' \wedge \Gamma''.\mathbf{c} = \Gamma.\mathbf{c} + \Delta\tau'' \wedge \Gamma''.\mathbf{d} = \Gamma.\mathbf{d} \wedge \Gamma''.\mathbf{g} = \Gamma.\mathbf{g} + \Delta\tau'' \wedge \Gamma''.\mathbf{e} = \Gamma.\mathbf{e}\}$.*

Note that the set of events with minimum remaining time is always finite. The definition of finite paths is based on events [26], where cycles of instantaneous immediate or general transition firings are prohibited to prevent Zeno-behavior.

Definition 5. *A (finite) path of the HPnG* $\mathcal{H}$ *is a sequence* $\sigma = \Gamma_0 \xrightarrow{(\Delta\tau_0,\varepsilon_0)}$ $\Gamma_1 \xrightarrow{(\Delta\tau_1,\varepsilon_1)} \dots \Gamma_n$ *with* $(\Gamma_i, \Delta\tau_i, \varepsilon_i, \Gamma_{i+1}) \in \mathcal{E}^{min}(\Gamma_i)$ *for every* $i \in \mathbb{N}_0, i < n$, *and* $\Delta\tau_i$ *is the time spent in states from* $S(\Gamma_i, \Gamma_{i+1})$ *before the event occurs. We denote by* $\gamma(\sigma, t)$ *the state that the path* σ *reaches at time point* t, *which is a state from* $S(\Gamma_i, \Gamma_{i+1})$ *with* $i = \min\{j \in \mathbb{N} \mid t \leq \sum_{0 \leq l \leq j} \Delta\tau_l\}$, *and define* $\Delta\tau(\gamma(\sigma, t)) = t - \sum_{0 \leq l \leq i-1} \Delta\tau_l$.

Let further Paths(Γ_0) denote the set of all paths which start from the initial state Γ_0, *and let its subset of paths up to time* t *(starting from* Γ_0*) be denoted by* $Paths(\Gamma_0, t) = \{\sigma = \Gamma_0 \xrightarrow{(\Delta\tau_0,\varepsilon_0)} \Gamma_1 \xrightarrow{(\Delta\tau_1,\varepsilon_1)} \dots \Gamma_k \mid \exists\sigma \xrightarrow{(\Delta\tau_k,\varepsilon_k)} \Gamma_{k+1} \in Paths(\Gamma_0). \sum_{i=0}^{k-1} \Delta\tau_i \leq t < \sum_{i=0}^{k} \Delta\tau_i\}$.

Let $Confl(\Gamma_n) \subset \mathcal{T} \backslash \mathcal{T}^{cont}$ consist of those transitions of $\mathcal{H}$ that are in conflict in state Γ_n. One way to resolve non-determinism is using priorities and weights as in [13]. Here we follow [25] for a more general approach using *schedulers*. We will need the notion of a *discrete probability distribution* over a set D, which is a function $\mu : D \to [0,1] \subseteq \mathbb{R}$ such that $support(\mu) = \{d \in D \mid \mu(d) > 0\}$ is countable and $\sum_{d \in support(\mu)} \mu(d) = 1$. Let $Dist(D)$ be the set of discrete probability distributions over D.

Definition 6. *A scheduler for the HPnG* $\mathcal{H}$ *with initial state* Γ_0 *is a function* $\mathfrak{s} : Paths(\Gamma_0) \to Dist(\mathcal{T} \backslash \mathcal{T}^{cont})$ *that assigns to every path* σ *starting in* Γ_0 *and ending in* Γ_n *a distribution with* $support(\mathfrak{s}(\sigma)) \subseteq Confl(\Gamma_n)$. *We denote the set of all schedulers for* $\mathcal{H}$ *as* $\mathfrak{S}$.

We are interested in *time-bounded reachability*, which is the problem to determine the probability of entering certain states within a certain time limit t_{max} in an HPnG $\mathcal{H}$. As the solution depends on the resolution of non-deterministic conflicts, every scheduler induces a fully stochastic version of $\mathcal{H}$. For a formal definition of time-bounded reachability under a given scheduler, we refer to [25].

2.2 The Parametric Location Tree

Previous work has defined an evolution graph for Hybrid Petri nets to describe their behaviour over time [1,7]. Similarly, previous work has defined the (time-bounded) evolution of HPnGs in terms of *parametric location trees* (PLTs), which abstract from concrete probabilities [13,18].

Every node in a PLT, called parametric location, symbolically represents a set of states with common discrete marking, drift and enabling status. The discrete state is changed due to a *source event* that leads to a child node in the PLT. The evolution of the continuous variables might depend on the firing times of the general transition, such that different firing times may lead to different successor nodes in the PLT. Recall that every firing time of a general transition is a random variable which is distributed according to its continuous probability distribution. The PLT symbolically describes the stochastic behaviour of an HPnG in terms of random variables $s_1, s_2, \dots, s_n$, where n equals the number of already occurred general transition firings plus the number of currently enabled general transitions [19]. The deterministic evolution is described by *linear functions* in those random variables that correspond to past firings. This allows a symbolic representation that is independent of the probability distributions.

The definition of a PLT in [18] includes so-called potential domains in each parametric location, which collect all values of random variables that can lead to this location. Since these are not required for the proposed transformation, we provide a simplified definition as follows.

Definition 7. *Let* $\mathcal{H} = (\mathcal{P}, \mathcal{T}, \mathcal{A}, \mathbf{M}_0, \Phi)$ *be an HPnG and* $t_{max} \in \mathcal{R}_{\geq 0}$ *a time bound. The parametric location tree (PLT) of* $\mathcal{H}$ *is a tree* $(\mathbf{V}, \mathbf{E}, \mathsf{v}_0)$ *with nodes* $\mathbf{V}$ *and edges* $\mathbf{E}$. *Every node* $\mathsf{v}_i \in \mathbf{V}$ *is related to a parametric location* $\Lambda_i = (ID_i, t_i, \Gamma_i)$ *with unique identifier* ID_i, *a state* Γ_i *of* $\mathcal{H}$, *and an entry time* t_i *that is either a constant from* $\mathcal{R}_{\geq 0}$ *or a linear function* $a_0 + a_1 \cdot s_1 + a_2 \cdot s_2 + \cdots + a_n \cdot s_n$ *of the random variables* $s_1, s_2, \ldots, s_n$ *which are present in the HPnG with coefficients* $a_j \in \mathbb{R}$ *for* $j = 0, \ldots, n$. *An edge* $(\mathsf{v}_j, \mathsf{v}_k) \in \mathbf{E}$ *exists for* $\mathsf{v}_j, \mathsf{v}_k \in \mathbf{V}$ *if an event from state* Γ_j *to state* Γ_k *exists. The root node of the PLT is* v_0 *whose state component is the initial state of* $\mathcal{H}$.

For HPnGs with n stochastic firings, the resulting PLT up to time t_{max} is finite due to Definition 4, defining the set of next events, and can be constructed in $\mathcal{O}(n^2 \times |\bigcup_{\Lambda_i \in \Lambda} \mathcal{E}^{\min}(\Lambda_i.\Gamma)|)$ according to [18]. We denote the corresponding set of parametric locations as $\Lambda = \{\Lambda_i \mid \exists \mathsf{v}_i \in \mathbf{V}\}$.

The PLT of the example model in Fig. 1 is made available in the appendix of this paper, including a description.

3   Related Hybrid Automata Formalisms

The following definition of Hybrid Automata follows [2], however ommitting labels of automata, as they are not required in the context of this work.

Definition 8. *A Hybrid Automaton is a tuple* $(Loc, Var, Edg, Act, Inv, Init)$. *Loc is the finite set of* locations *(drawn as circles) and Var is a set of real-valued variables. A valuation* $v : Var \rightarrow \mathbb{R}$ *assigns a real-value to each variable and we denote the set of all valuations as* V.

The set $Edg \subseteq Loc \times 2^{V^2} \times Loc$ *is the finite set of* transitions *(drawn as arrows). Every transition* $(l, \mu, l') \in Edg$ *consists of a source location* $l \in Loc$, *a transition relation* $\mu \subseteq V^2$ *and a target location* $l' \in Loc$.

The function $Act : Loc \rightarrow (f : \mathcal{R}_{\geq 0} \rightarrow V)$ *assigns a set of activities to each location. Activities are time-invariant functions, which means that for* $l \in Loc$, $f \in Act(l)$ *implies* $(f + t) \in Act(l)$, *where* $(f + t)(t') = f(t + t')$ *for all* $t' \in \mathcal{R}_{\geq 0}$. *The function* $Inv : Loc \rightarrow 2^V$ *assigns an invariant* $Inv(l) \subseteq V$ *to each location* $l \in Loc$. *A state is a tuple* (l, v) *which consists of a location* $l \in Loc$ *and valuation* $v \in V$. *Init* $\subseteq Loc \times V$ *is the set of initial states.*

The state of a Hybrid Automaton can change in two ways: Either time passes or a transition is taken. A time delay only changes the values of the variables, but not the location. The values evolve according to the activities, i.e. in a state (l, v), $Act(l)$ assigns a new valuation to every time delay $t \in \mathcal{R}_{\geq 0}$. In particular, $Act(l)(0) = v$ and $Act(l)(t') \in Inv(l)$ have to hold for all $0 \leq t' \leq t$. Hence, the system can only be in states (l, v), in which the values of the variables satisfy the invariant of the location. A transition $(l, \mu, l') \in Edg$ can only be taken in a state (l, v) if $(v, v') \in \mu$ for some valuation $v' \in V$ and further $v \in Inv(l)$ and $v' \in Inv(l')$. Taking this transitions then leads to the new state (l', v'). For the complete semantics of Hybrid Automata, we refer to [2].

In this work, we mainly consider a subclass of Hybrid Automata, which is called Singular Automata, defined according to [16,17].

Definition 9. *Let $\mathcal{R}$ be the set of all intervals in $\mathbb{R}$ with rational or infinite endpoints and let $d \in \mathbb{N}$. A subset of $\mathbb{R}^d$ is* rectangular *if it is a Cartesian product of intervals, i.e. if it is from $\mathcal{R}^d$. A rectangular set is a* singleton *if each of its intervals is a singleton, i.e. a set with exactly one element.*

A Hybrid Automaton, in which the activities, initial states, invariants and the transition relations are restricted to rectangular sets, is called a Rectangular Automaton. A Singular Automaton is however a Rectangular Automaton, in which the activities are further restricted to a singleton.

Definition 10. *A Singular Automaton is a HA $(Loc, Var, Edg, Act, Inv, Init)$ where the set of transitions is restricted to $Edg \subseteq Loc \times (\mathcal{R}^{|Var|} \times \mathcal{R}^{|Var|} \times 2^{\{1,...,|Var|\}}) \times Loc$, the invariant function is $Inv: Loc \to \mathcal{R}^{|Var|}$, the initital states are in $Init \subseteq Loc \times \mathcal{R}^{|Var|}$ and the activities are singletons $Act: Loc \to \mathbb{R}^{|Var|}$.*

The derivatives of all variables in a location $l \in Loc$ are deterministically given by $Act(l)$. A transition $(l, (pre, post, jump), l') \in Edg$ in a Singular Automaton may only be taken in a state (l, v) if the valuation $v \in V$ lies in pre. When the transition is taken, the value of every variable $y_i \in Var$ is updated as follows: If $i \notin jump$, y_i is not changed and must lie in $post_i$ and if $i \in jump$, y_i is non-deterministically set to a new value in $post_i$.

Definition 11. *A Singular Automaton with random clocks $(Loc, Var, Edg, Act, Inv, Init, F)$ is a Singular Automaton extended by a set $\mathcal{C} \subset Var$ and a function $F: \mathcal{C} \to (f: \mathbb{R}^+ \to [0, 1])$, which associates a continuous probability distribution function to each clock in $\mathcal{C}$, such that the following holds:*

1. *$\forall l \in Loc: x_i \in \mathcal{C} \Rightarrow Act(l)_i \in \{0, -1\}$,*
2. *For each $(l, (pre, post, jump), l') \in Edg$ and for all $x_i \in \mathcal{C}$ holds that if $i \in jump$, then $v(x_i)$ is set to a random value, for which we write $v(x_i) = F(x_i)$.*

4   Singular Automaton Semantics for HPnGs

The deterministic evolution of an HPnG can be described by means of a Hybrid Automaton, as will be explained in the following: A parametric location in the

PLT of an HPnG represents a set of states with the same discrete marking. The evolution of the continuous state in a parametric location can be described by an automaton location. Consequently, transitions between locations in the automaton correspond to events between parametric locations in the PLT. The continuous variables (i.e. the fluid level of the continuous places) in an HPnG further relate to continuous variables in the corresponding automata.

The PLT describes the stochastic behavior of an HPnG only symbolically in terms of random variables that are added for every (potential) firing of a general transition in the PLT, modeling the firing time. Each random variable is translated to a random clock, such that the firing of the general transition corresponds to the expiration of the random clock in the automaton.

The piecewise linear evolution of continuous variables in HPnGs translates to locations with constant derivatives for continuous variables, i.e. singletons. Further test and inhibitor arcs only compare continuous variables to constants and not to each other, which again results in rectangular sets. The capacities of continuous places translate to rectangular invariant sets. The clocks of deterministic transitions are translated to continuous variables which are reset to the constant firing time of the transition and evolve with derivative -1 if enabled and 0 otherwise. Their expiration also leads to constant invariant and pre-guard bounds for the corresponding clocks. Hence, the transformation of HPnGs leads to a Singular Automaton with random clocks.

Let $\mathcal{H} = (\mathcal{P}, \mathcal{T}, \mathcal{A}, \mathbf{M}_0, \Phi)$ be an HPnG and $(\mathbf{V}, \mathbf{E}, \mathbf{v}_0)$ the corresponding parametric location tree up to a time bound $t_{\max}$, with the set of parametric locations Λ and n general transition firings. Let $T_k^G \in \mathcal{T}^{gen}$ denote the general transition whose firing corresponds to random variable s_k.

Definition 12. *The set $\Lambda_{im} \subset \Lambda$ is the set of parametric locations, where at least one immediate transition is enabled, i.e. $\forall \Lambda_i \in \Lambda_{im} \colon \exists T_j \in \mathcal{T}^{imm} \colon \Lambda_i.\Gamma.e_j = 1$. For every parametric location $\Lambda_p \in \Lambda$, we define the set of child locations $\Lambda_c(\Lambda_p) = \{\Lambda_c \in \Lambda \mid \exists (\Lambda_p.\Gamma, \cdot, \cdot, \Lambda_c.\Gamma) \in \mathcal{E}^{min}(\Lambda_p.\Gamma)\}$ and further the set of next-delayed locations $\Lambda_d(\Lambda_p)$ as:*

$$\Lambda_d(\Lambda_p) = \begin{cases} \{\Lambda_p\} & \text{if } \Lambda_p \notin \Lambda_{im} \\ \bigcup_{\Lambda_c \in \Lambda_c(\Lambda_p)} \Lambda_d(\Lambda_c) & \text{otherwise.} \end{cases}$$

The set of next-delayed locations is defined recursively and contains the location itself if it is delayed, i.e. no immediate transition is enabled, and otherwise recursively collects all delayed children. Note that Λ_{im} is called the set of vanishing parametric locations. Definition 13 provides the core of our transformation approach as it gives the basic Singular Automaton semantics for HPnGs including random clocks.

Definition 13. *For an HPnG $\mathcal{H}$, the corresponding Singular Automaton with random clocks up to time t_{max} is given by $(Loc, Var, Edg, Act, Inv, Init, F)$, where*

a) $Loc = \Lambda \backslash \Lambda_{im}$ is the set of parametric locations, excluding vanishing locations,

b) $Var = X \cup D \cup G$ unites the sets of variables describing (i) the continuous marking $X = \{x_k \in \mathbb{R}_0^+ \mid k \in \mathbb{N} \wedge 0 \leq k \leq |\mathcal{P}^{cont}|\}$, (ii) the remaining time to fire of the deterministic transitions $D = \{c_k \in \mathbb{R}_0^+ \mid k \in \mathbb{N} \wedge 0 \leq k \leq |\mathcal{T}^{det}|\}$ and (iii) of general transition firings $G = \{s_k \in \mathbb{R}_0^+ \mid k \in \mathbb{N} \wedge 0 \leq k \leq n\}$, which equals the set of random clocks. The function $m : Var \rightarrow \mathcal{P}^{cont} \cup \mathcal{T}^{det} \cup \mathcal{T}^{gen}$ maps every variable to the corresponding place or transition.

c) Edg collects transitions $(\Lambda_i, (pre, post, jump), \Lambda_j)$ for every (delayed) event $(\Lambda_i.\Gamma, \Delta\tau_i, \varepsilon_i, \Lambda_{i+1}.\Gamma)$ where $\Lambda_i \in Loc$, and $\Lambda_j \in \Lambda_d(\Lambda_{i+1})$. For every $y_k \in Var$, we define pre_k and $post_k$:

(i)
$$pre_k = \begin{cases} 0 & \text{if } \left(\varepsilon_i = m(y_k) = T \in \mathcal{T}^{det} \cup \mathcal{T}^{gen}\right) \\ & \quad \vee \left(\varepsilon_i = m(y_k) = P_j^c \in \mathcal{P}^{cont} \wedge \Lambda_i.\Gamma.d_j < 0\right), \\ \Phi_b^P(P_j^c) & \text{if } \varepsilon_i = m(y_k) = P_j^c \in \mathcal{P}^{cont} \wedge \Lambda_i.\Gamma.d_j > 0, \\ \Phi_w^A(\langle P_j^c, T \rangle) & \text{if } \varepsilon_i = \langle P_j^c, T \rangle \in \mathcal{A}^{test} \cup \mathcal{A}^{inh} \wedge m(y_k) = P_j^c \in \mathcal{P}^{cont}, \\ [-\infty, \infty] & \text{otherwise}, \end{cases}$$

(ii) $k \in jump$, only if $\left(m(y_k) = T_j^D \in \mathcal{T}^{det} \wedge \Lambda_i.\Gamma.c_j = 0 \wedge \Lambda_{i+1}.\Gamma.e_j = 1\right)$
$\vee \left(m(y_k) = T_j^G \in \mathcal{T}^{gen} \wedge \Lambda_i.\Gamma.g_j = 0 \wedge \Lambda_{i+1}.\Gamma.e_j = 1\right)$, and

$$post_k = \begin{cases} \Phi_d^T(T_j^D) & \text{if } k \in jump \wedge m(y_k) = T_j^D \in \mathcal{T}^{det}, \\ F(y_k)) & \text{if } k \in jump \wedge m(y_k) \in \mathcal{T}^{gen}, \\ [-\infty, \infty] & \text{otherwise}, \end{cases}$$

d) $Act: Loc \rightarrow \mathbb{R}^{|Var|}$ defines the derivatives for every location $\Lambda_i \in Loc$ and for every variable $y_k \in Var$:

$$Act(\Lambda_i)_k = \begin{cases} \Lambda_i.\Gamma.d_j & \text{if } m(y_k) = P_j^c \in \mathcal{P}^{cont}, \\ -1 & \text{if } m(y_k) = T_j \in \mathcal{T} \wedge \Lambda_i.\Gamma.e_j = 1, \\ 0 & \text{otherwise}, \end{cases}$$

e) $Inv: Loc \rightarrow \mathcal{R}^{|Var|}$ defines invariants for every location $\Lambda_i \in Loc$, such that for every event $(\Lambda_i.\Gamma, \Lambda_{i+1}.\Gamma, \Delta\tau_i, \varepsilon_i) \in \mathcal{E}^{min}(\Lambda_i.\Gamma)$ and for every variable $y_k \in Var$ holds:

$$Inv(\Lambda_i)_k = \begin{cases} [0, \infty] & \text{if } \left(\varepsilon_i = m(y_k) = T \in \mathcal{T}^{det} \cup \mathcal{T}^{gen}\right) \\ & \quad \vee \left(\varepsilon_i = m(y_k) = P_j^c \in \mathcal{P}^{cont} \wedge \Lambda_i.\Gamma.d_j < 0\right), \\ [-\infty, \Phi_b^P(P_j^c)] & \text{if } \varepsilon_i = m(y_k) = P_j^c \in \mathcal{P}^{cont} \wedge \Lambda_i.\Gamma.d_j > 0, \\ [-\infty, \Phi_w^A(\langle P_j^c, T \rangle)] & \text{if } \varepsilon_i = \langle P_j^c, T \rangle \in \mathcal{A}^{test} \cup \mathcal{A}^{inh} \wedge m(y_k) = P_j^c \\ & \quad \in \mathcal{P}^{cont} \wedge \Lambda_i.\Gamma.x_j < \Phi_w^A(\langle P_j^c, T \rangle) \\ [\Phi_w^A(\langle P_j^c, T \rangle), \infty] & \text{if } \varepsilon_i = \langle P_j^c, T \rangle \in \mathcal{A}^{test} \cup \mathcal{A}^{inh} \wedge m(y_k) = P_j^c \\ & \quad \in \mathcal{P}^{cont} \wedge \Lambda_i.\Gamma.x_j > \Phi_w^A(\langle P_j^c, T \rangle) \\ [-\infty, \infty] & \text{otherwise}, \end{cases}$$

f) Init $\subseteq$ Loc $\times$ V collects each initial state (Λ_i, v) with $\Lambda_i \in$ Loc and $v \in V$, for which holds that $\Lambda_i.t = 0$ and $\forall y_k \in$ Var :

$$v(y_k) = \begin{cases} \Lambda_i.\Gamma.x_j & \text{if } m(y_k) = P_j^c \in \mathcal{P}^{cont}, \\ \Phi_d^T(T_k^D) & \text{if } m(y_k) = T_j^D \in \mathcal{T}^{det} \wedge \Lambda_{i+1}.\Gamma.e_j = 1, \\ F(y_k) & \text{if } m(y_k) = T_j^G \in \mathcal{T}^{gen} \wedge \Lambda_{i+1}.\Gamma.e_j = 1, \\ 0 & \text{otherwise,} \end{cases}$$

g) F assigns a probability distribution to every random clock y_k with $m(y_k) = T_j^G \in \mathcal{T}^{gen}$, such that $F(y_k) = \Phi_g^T(T_j^G)$.

According to Definition 13 *a)*, the set of automaton locations *Loc* relates to the set of non-vanishing parametric locations in the PLT, by directly moving to the next-delayed location in case of a vanishing location. The set of variables contains one variable for each continuous place describing its marking, one variable for each deterministic transition describing its clock and one random clock for each general transition firing describing the remaining time to fire (Definition 13 *b)*). To ease notation, we introduce a mapping m from variables to corresponding places and transitions.

For the sake of clarity we first describe Definition 13 *d)*: all continuous variables evolve with a constant flow per location. For variables related to continuous places, the derivative equals the drift of the place. For variables describing the clocks of deterministic or general transitions, the derivative equals -1 if the corresponding transition is enabled and 0 otherwise.

Part *c)* defines transitions for every delayed event: the automaton contains one transition for delayed target location, and potentially multiple transitions, otherwise, depending on the size of the set of next-delayed parametric locations.

Parts *c)* and *e)* combine pre-guards with invariants of source locations, such that transitions are *urgent*, i.e., they have to be taken as soon as the guard is satisfied. The firing of a deterministic or general transition relates to the expiration of the corresponding clock. The resulting automaton transition hence contains the pre-guard, which compares the value of the clock to zero. The invariant of the source location is chosen accordingly. For guard arcs connected to continuous places, the value of the corresponding continuous variable is compared to the weight of the arc in a similar way. Upper and lower place boundaries are also translated into invariants and pre-guards, which compare the continuous variable to the upper boundary or to zero (depending on the sign of its current derivative). Note that rate adaption, as included in the PLT, prevents time locks in the automaton by recomputing adapted rates whenever a boundary is hit.

Part *c)(ii)* defines the jump set and post-guards for transitions in *Edg*. Variables that relate to transition clocks are reset whenever the transition is freshly enabled (for the first time or after a previous firing). Clocks of deterministic transitions are set to their firing time and random clocks are set according to their probability distribution. As their derivative is set to zero when disabled, the preemptive resume policy is preserved for all clocks, as in the PLT.

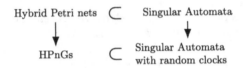

Fig. 2. Relations between Hybrid Petri nets and Singular Automata classes

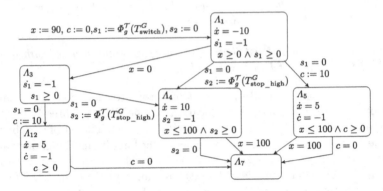

Fig. 3. Singular Automaton with random clocks modeling battery (dis-)charging.

Initially, the continuous variables equal the initial marking. Clocks are initialized to firing time if the transition is initially enabled. Random clocks for initially enabled general transitions are set according to their probability distribution (Part g)). All disabled clocks and random clocks are set to zero (Part f)). In case that multiple immediate transitions are initially enabled and hence, in conflict, the automaton has multiple initial locations (Part f)). Accordingly, nondeterminism from transition conflicts in the HPnG is maintained in the semantic.

Note that the PLT is built only up to time t_{max}. As the semantics of Definition 13 is based on the PLT, the evolution of the corresponding Singular Automaton may exceed this time bound. However, the evolution of the automaton beyond t_{max} can possibly differ from the evolution of the HPnG. Hence, we can only guarantee that the given semantics holds up to t_{max}. Recall that Zeno behavior has been excluded in the PLT by prohibiting cycles of (immediate and general) transition firings and hence does also not arise in the automaton.

Figure 2 illustrates the relations between those four model classes, where the arrows demonstrate extending a class by stochastic variables and the inclusions indicate proper sub-class relations. The resulting automaton from Definition 13 only contains singular sets for pre-guards, invariants, post-guards and initial values, where Singular Automata usually allow rectangular sets. Hence, we obtain a strict subclass of Singular automaton with random clocks and urgent transitions.

Example (continued). Fig. 3 presents the resulting Singular Automaton with random clocks for the running example. Note that all derivatives that are not shown in the model equal zero. The resulting Singular Automaton only has six locations (after merging identical ones), while the PLT has fifteen parametric locations (see appendix). The variable x with derivative $\dot{x}$ models the fluid level of P^c_{battery}. Since clocks are running backwards, c models the remaining time for $T^D_{\text{stop\_low}}$ to fire. Similarly, s_1 and s_2 represent the remaining time until firing for the general transitions T^G_{switch} resp. $T^G_{\text{stop\_high}}$.

5   Transformation of HPnGs into SHA

We now present an algorithm which transforms HPnGs into Singular Automata with random clocks, according to the semantics introduced above. First, the PLT needs to be constructed, as described in [18] and is then processed by pre-order depth-first traversal. For every parametric location, a new location is added to the automaton and its source event is turned into a transition that connects the new location to the location that corresponds to its parent node in the PLT. However, in case that the event is the firing of an immediate transition, the latter is instead removed and all affected transitions are updated to bypass the removed location, according to Definition 13.

Due to its tree structure, the PLT cannot contain cycles. In contrast, automata allow a cyclic structure and hence, identical locations with identical outgoing transitions can be merged in the resulting automaton without changing system behaviour. Note that this is possible as the automaton locations have no restrictions on the values of continuous variables, clocks, random clocks or on the time, in contrast to parametric locations in the PLT. To obtain automata without redundant locations, we therefore perform cycle detection and merge identical locations after translating the PLT into the Singular Automaton.

Algorithm 1 describes the transformation of an HPnG into a Singular Automaton with random clocks. The PLT is constructed first by the function `constructParametricLocationTree()`, as described in [18] (Line 1). The automaton is created afterwards with a set of variables and function F, as defined in Definition 13b) and g), but with empty sets for locations, labels and transitions (Line 2). Next, all initial and delayed parametric locations are determined according to Definition 13f) by the function `determineInitialLocations()` (Line 3). Each of these locations is translated into an automaton location

---

Algorithm 1. `transformIntoSingularAutomaton`($hpng, t_{max}$)

```
 1: plt = constructParametricLocationTree(hpng, t_max);
 2: automaton = new Automaton(plt);
 3: initialParametricLocations = determineInitialLocations(plt);
 4: for (initialPL : InitialParametricLocations) do
 5:    initialLocation = generateLocation(initialPL);
 6:    automaton.add(initialLocation);
 7:    traverseChildren(plt, automaton, initialPL, initialLocation);
 8: end for
 9: mergeIdenticalLocations(automaton);
10: return (automaton);
```

Algorithm 2. traverseChildren($plt, automaton, parentPL, sourceLocation$)

```
1: delete = false;
2: for (childPL : parentPL.children) do
3:     childLocation = generateLocation(childPL);
4:     automaton.add(childLocation);
5:     event = childLocation.sourceEvent;
6:     if (isImmediateTransitionFiring(event)) then
7:         delete = true;
8:     else
9:         transition = generateTransition(event, sourceLocation, childLocation);
10:        automaton.add(transition);
11:        sourceLocation.addInvariants(event);
12:    end if
13:    traverseChildren(plt, automaton, childPL, childLocation);
14: end for
15: if (delete == true) then
16:    automaton.adaptAllTransitions(sourceLocation, parentPL);
17:    automaton.remove(sourceLocation)
18: end if
```

---

by generateLocation(), which takes any parametric location and creates an automaton location with activities as defined in Definition 13$e)$ and $f)$ (Line 5). Note that also vanishing parametric locations are processed, but removed later, when the next delayed parametric location is processed, as discussed in the following. The location is then added to the automaton (Line 6). Finally all child locations are traversed recursively by the function traverseChildren() (Line 7). After all initial locations have been processed, identical locations are merged by mergeIdenticalLocations() (Line 9), before the transformed automaton is returned (Line 11).

Algorithm 2 recursively traverses over all parametric locations in the PLT (Lines 2–14) and adds automaton locations for each of them (Lines 3–4). If the source event of a child parametric location is the firing of an immediate transition, a boolean *delete* is set to true (Lines 6–7). Otherwise, a transition is generated by the function generateTransition(), according to Definition 13$d)$, and invariants of the source locations are updated (Line 11), according to Definition 13$f)$. Next, traverseChildren() is recursively called for the currently considered child location (Line 13). Afterwards, all child locations have been traversed. If *delete* equals true, all incoming and outgoing transitions are adapted to bypass the source location, which is then removed from the automaton (Lines 15–18),

Concluding, Algorithm 1 iterates through all initial parametric locations and recursively traverses all child nodes. We assume that generateLocation() and generateTransition() create automaton locations and transitions according to Definition 13 $b)$-$e)$, assigning probability distributions according to Definition 13 $g)$. Since vanishing locations are removed from the automaton in Algorithm 2, the resulting set of locations corresponds to Definition 13 $a)$ and $f)$.

Table 1. Feasibility study results

Scenario			ProHVer $\Delta p = 0.01$		ProHVer $\Delta p = 0.005$		hpnmg		
no.	$\Phi_g^T(T_{\text{switch}}^G)$	$\Phi_g^T(T_{\text{stop\_high}}^{gen})$	$p_{\max}$	time	$p_{\max}$	time	$p_{\max}$	error	time
1	u[1h,7h]	u[0h,8h]	0.597502	336.1 s	0.595700	7236.3 s	0.593743	$\pm 5.75E^{-6}$	859.4 s
2	u[1h,7h]	n(4h,1h)	0.517995	359.4 s	0.515875	6756.4 s	0.513885	$\pm 9.31E^{-8}$	649.6 s
3	u[1h,7h]	n(6h,4h)	0.709199	382.6 s	0.707403	6531.7 s	0.704827	$\pm 1.40E^{-6}$	640.0 s
4	n(6h,1h)	u[0h,8h]	0.158263	358.1 s	0.152848	5875.4 s	0.148484	$\pm 1.37E^{-5}$	492.7 s
5	n(6h,1h)	n(4h,1h)	0.047712	371.4 s	0.039319	6006.4 s	0.033465	$\pm 6.85E^{-8}$	662.5 s
6	n(6h,1h)	n(6h,4h)	0.343163	359.2 s	0.337639	5683.9 s	0.327344	$\pm 5.12E^{-6}$	572.3 s

The worst case complexity of the transformation, including the construction of the PLT, is in $\mathcal{O}\left(\left(|\mathcal{P}^{cont}| + |\mathcal{T}^{det}| + n^2\right) \times |\bigcup_{\Lambda_i \in \Lambda} \mathcal{E}^{\min}(\Lambda_i.\Gamma)|\right)$ for n stochastic variables.

6 Feasibility Study

We implemented the transformation of HPnGs into Singular Automata as an addition to our existing analysis tool $hpnmg$[1][18] where the resulting automaton is saved in the JANI file format for stochastic hybrid systems [4]. JANI files can be loaded into the tool $ProHVer$[15], which is part of the $Modest\ Toolset$[2]. $ProHVer$ discretizes the probability distributions of an SHA to obtain a Probabilistic Hybrid Automaton, transforms it into a non-probabilistic HA and then uses $PHAVER$[3] to overapproximate the maximum probability for time bounded reachability by reduction on a Markov Decision Process [15]. The obtained results are compared to time-bounded reachability under a prophetic scheduler computed by the $hpnmg$ tool, as proposed in [25].

We investigate the (dis-)charging process of a (linear) battery model of Fig. 1. Charging at the higher rate terminates after a random time delay, while charging at the lower rate continues for a deterministic amount of time. We evaluate the model for different probability distributions for the time periods of (i) discharging and (ii) charging at high rate and compute the probability that the battery is fully recharged within 24 h.

We present results for six scenarios where the general transitions follow different probability distributions. In the first three scenarios, the firing time of T_{switch}^G is uniformly distribution between 1 h and 7 h. In Scenario 4 to 6, the firing time of T_{switch}^G is normally distributed with a mean of 6 h and a variance of 1 h. The firing time of $T_{\text{stop\_high}}^G$ follows a uniform distribution with bounds 0 h and 8 h in Scenario 1 and 4 and it follows normal distributions in the remaining scenarios: with a mean of 4 h and a variance of 1 h in Scenario 2 and 5, and with a mean of 6 h and a variance of 4 h in Scenario 3 and 6.

---

[1] https://github.com/jannikhuels/hpnmg.
[2] http://www.modestchecker.net.
[3] http://www-verimag.imag.fr/%7Efrehse/phaver_web/index.html.

The *ProHVer* flags `no-cheap-contain-return-others` and `no-partition-check-time-relevance-during` have been set to false and all given probability distributions have been discretized into intervals, such that every interval covers a probability mass Δp of either 0.01 or 0.005. For the *hpnmg* tool, we run the computation of the prophetic scheduler, as described in [25]. Building the PLT took 5.63 ms, the transformation took 16.77 ms and writing the JANI output another 0.72 ms. All computations have been performed on a *macOS Mojave* system (2.7 GHz Intel Core i5, 8 GB RAM), with *ProHVer* executed on a VirtualBox running Ubuntu 18.04.

Table 1 presents the probability that the battery is fully recharged within 24 h for different scenarios. The error estimate stems from the numerical integration method used to compute probabilities [25]. The maximum probabilities of *ProHVer* lie slightly above the probabilities computed by the *hpnmg* tool, which is due to the discretization and overapproximation performed by *ProHVer*.

Comparing the probabilities computed by *ProHVer* for different discretizations, the approximation error is mostly bounded by the value of $2 \cdot \Delta p$: For both, $\Delta p = 0.01$ and $\Delta p = 0.005$, one can see that the difference between the results obtained by *ProHVer* and by *hpnmg* exceeds $2 \cdot \Delta p$ only slightly in Scenario 6 for $\Delta p = 0.005$. We assume that the factor 2 results from the number of general transition firings, whose probability distributions both require separate discretizations. *ProHVer* consistently overapproximates the *hpnmg* results for prophetic scheduling. *ProHVer* discretizes the support of the random variables before *PHAVER* optimizes the MDP reachability for a fixed (interval) value of the random variables, which implies prophetic scheduling. Reachability probabilities for the HPnG battery model could hence be matched by *ProHVer* for a Singular Automaton with random clocks, after transformation with the algorithm proposed in this paper. Depending on the discretization factor, *ProHVer* takes more time than *hpnmg*. This is due to the fact that the *hpnmg* tool has been developed for this restricted class of models, whereas *ProHVer* is able to deal with more general stochastic hybrid models. Hence, the presented transformation can also be used to enrich Hybrid Petri net with more modeling features.

7　Conclusion

We introduced a semantics for HPnGs in terms of Singular Automata extended with random clocks and presented an algorithm for their transformation. This allows making use of existing techniques for the reachability analysis of Stochastic Hybrid Automata. The feasability of this transformation was demonstrated for a battery (dis-) charging process, for which we were able to compute matching results using the tools *ProHVer* and *hpnmg*. The size of the approximation error in *ProHVer* is consistent with the chosen discretization, however *hpnmg* was able to compute more accurate results in shorter time for this model.

Future work will investigate how e.g. flow-pipe construction can be efficiently used for the analysis of Singular Automata with random clocks. Furthermore, we will investigate the approximation error of *ProHVer* in the context of subclasses of Stochastic Hybrid Automata.

Appendix

Parametric Location Tree

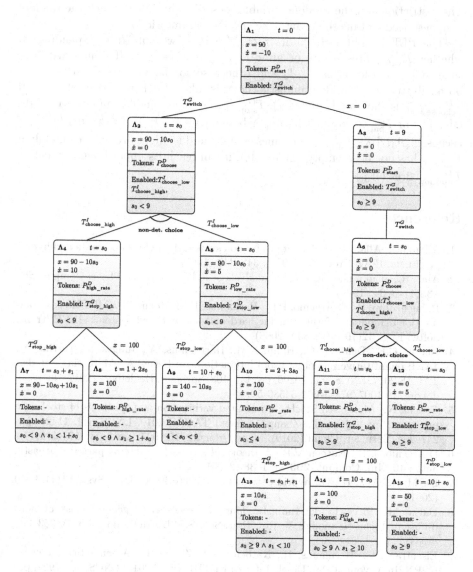

Fig. 4. Parametric location tree for the feasibility study example

Figure 4 shows the Parametric Location Tree for the model of the feasibility study (r.t. Sect. 6). t is the entry time into each parametric location, x denotes the fluid level of the continuous place P^c_{battery} and $\dot{x}$ its drift upon entry. Further s_0 denotes the random variable, which describes the firing of T^G_{switch}, and similarly s_1 denotes the one of $T^G_{\text{stop\_high}}$. Every node shows how many discrete places contain one token each and which non-continuous transitions are enabled. The restrictions on the random variables describe the values which the random variables need to take to get into the specific parametric location.

The PLT is split right at its root (Λ_1) into two sub-trees, depending on whether T^G_{switch} fires before or after P^c_{battery} reaches zero. If it fires within 9 time units, this leads us to Λ_2 and otherwise to Λ_6, via Λ_3. From there, in both sub-trees the non-deterministic choice is taken, further splitting the tree. If $T^I_{\text{choose\_high}}$ is chosen (Λ_4 and Λ_{11}), $T^G_{\text{stop\_high}}$ becomes enabled and either it fires (Λ_7, Λ_{13}) or P^c_{battery} reaches its upper boundary (Λ_8, Λ_{14}). If instead $T^I_{\text{choose\_low}}$ is chosen (Λ_5, Λ_{12}), $T^D_{\text{stop\_low}}$ becomes enabled and is might fire (Λ_9, Λ_{15}). Only if P^c_{battery} has not been empty before (Λ_5), it can reach its upper boundary before $T^D_{\text{stop\_low}}$ fires (Λ_{10}).

References

1. Allam, M., Alla, H.: Modelling production systems by hybrid automata and hybrid petri nets. IFAC Proc. Vol. **30**(6), 343–348 (1997)
2. Alur, R., et al.: The algorithmic analysis of hybrid systems. Theor. Comput. Sci. **138**(1), 3–34 (1995)
3. Bohnenkamp, H., D'Argenio, P.R., Hermanns, H., Katoen, J.P.: MODEST: a compositional modeling formalism for hard and softly timed systems. IEEE Trans. Softw. Eng. **32**(10), 812–830 (2006)
4. Budde, C.E., Dehnert, C., Hahn, E.M., Hartmanns, A., Junges, S., Turrini, A.: JANI: quantitative model and tool interaction. In: Legay, A., Margaria, T. (eds.) TACAS 2017. LNCS, vol. 10206, pp. 151–168. Springer, Heidelberg (2017). https://doi.org/10.1007/978-3-662-54580-5_9
5. Cauchi, N., Abate, A.: StocHy: automated verification and synthesis of stochastic processes. In: Vojnar, T., Zhang, L. (eds.) TACAS 2019. LNCS, vol. 11428, pp. 247–264. Springer, Cham (2019). https://doi.org/10.1007/978-3-030-17465-1_14
6. D'Argenio, P.R., Katoen, J.P.: A theory of stochastic systems part I: stochastic automata. Inf. Comput. **203**(1), 1–38 (2005)
7. David, R., Alla, H.: On hybrid petri nets. Discrete Event Dyn. Syst. **11**(1), 9–40 (2001)
8. Davis, M.: Piecewise-deterministic Markov processes: a general class of non-diffusion stochastic models. J. Roy. Stat. Soc. Ser. B (Methodol.) **46**(3), 353–388 (1984)
9. Eisentraut, C., Hermanns, H., Katoen, J.-P., Zhang, L.: A semantics for every GSPN. In: Colom, J.-M., Desel, J. (eds.) PETRI NETS 2013. LNCS, vol. 7927, pp. 90–109. Springer, Heidelberg (2013). https://doi.org/10.1007/978-3-642-38697-8_6
10. Frehse, G.: PHAVer: algorithmic verification of hybrid systems past HyTech. In: Morari, M., Thiele, L. (eds.) HSCC 2005. LNCS, vol. 3414, pp. 258–273. Springer, Heidelberg (2005). https://doi.org/10.1007/978-3-540-31954-2_17

11. Fränzle, M., Hahn, E.M., Hermanns, H., Wolovick, N., Zhang, L.: Measurability and safety verification for stochastic hybrid systems. In: 14th ACM International Conference on Hybrid Systems: Computation and Control. HSCC 2011, pp. 43–52. ACM, New York (2011)

12. Ghasemieh, H., Remke, A., Haverkort, B.: Analysis of a sewage treatment facility using hybrid petri nets. In: 7th EAI International Conference on Performance Evaluation Methodologies and Tools, VALUETOOLS 2013. pp. 165–174. ICST (2013)

13. Gribaudo, M., Remke, A.: Hybrid Petri nets with general one-shot transitions. Perform. Eval. **105**, 22–50 (2016)

14. Hahn, E.M., Hartmanns, A., Hermanns, H.: Reachability and reward checking for stochastic timed automata. ECEASST **70** (2014)

15. Hahn, E.M., Hartmanns, A., Hermanns, H., Katoen, J.P.: A compositional modelling and analysis framework for stochastic hybrid systems. Formal Meth. Syst. Des. **43**(2), 191–232 (2013)

16. Henzinger, T.A.: The theory of hybrid automata. In: Inan, M.K., Kurshan, R.P. (eds.) Verification of Digital and Hybrid systems, NATO ASI Series, vol. 170, pp. 265–292. Springer, Berlin, Heidelberg (2000)

17. Henzinger, T.A., Kopke, P.W., Puri, A., Varaiya, P.: What's decidable about hybrid automata? J. Comput. Syst. Sci. **57**(1), 94–124 (1998)

18. Hüls, J., Pilch, C., Schinke, P., Delicaris, J., Remke, A.: State-space construction of hybrid petri nets with multiple stochastic firings. In: Parker, D., Wolf, V. (eds.) QEST 2019. LNCS, vol. 11785, pp. 182–199. Springer, Cham (2019). https://doi.org/10.1007/978-3-030-30281-8_11

19. Hüls, J., Remke, A.: Model checking HPnGs in multiple dimensions: representing state sets as convex polytopes. In: Pérez, J.A., Yoshida, N. (eds.) FORTE 2019. LNCS, vol. 11535, pp. 148–166. Springer, Cham (2019). https://doi.org/10.1007/978-3-030-21759-4_9

20. Jongerden, M., Hüls, J., Haverkort, B., Remke, A.: Assessing the cost of energy independence. In: 2016 IEEE International Energy Conference, ENERGYCON, pp. 1–6. IEEE (2016)

21. Koutsoukos, X.D., Riley, D.: Computational methods for verification of stochastic hybrid systems. IEEE Trans. Syst. Man Cybern. Part A Syst. Humans **38**(2), 385–396 (2008)

22. Kwiatkowska, M., Norman, G., Segala, R., Sproston, J.: Automatic verification of real-time systems with discrete probability distributions. Theor. Comput. Sci. **282**(1), 101–150 (2002)

23. Kwiatkowska, M.Z., Norman, G., Parker, D., Sproston, J.: Performance analysis of probabilistic timed automata using digital clocks. Formal Meth. Syst. Des. **29**(1), 33–78 (2006)

24. Motallebi, H., Azgomi, M.A.: Modeling and verification of hybrid dynamic systems using multisingular hybrid Petri nets. Theor. Comput. Sci. **446**, 48–74 (2012)

25. Pilch, C., Hartmanns, A., Remke, A.: Classic and non-prophetic model checking for hybrid petri nets with stochastic firings. In: 23rd ACM International Conference on Hybrid Systems: Computation and Control, HSCC 2020. ACM, New York (2020)

26. Pilch, C., Remke, A.: Statistical model checking for hybrid petri nets with multiple general transitions. In: 47th Annual IEEE/IFIP International Conference on Dependable Systems and Networks, DSN 2017, pp. 475–486. IEEE (2017)

27. Prandini, M., Hu, J.: A stochastic approximation method for reachability compu-
    tations. In: Blom, H., Lygeros, J. (eds.) Stochastic Hybrid Systems: Theory and
    Safety Critical Applications, LNCIS, vol. 337, pp. 107–139. Springer, Berlin, Hei-
    delberg (2006). https://doi.org/10.1007/11587392_4
28. Soudjani, S.E.Z., Gevaerts, C., Abate, A.: FAUST2: Formal Abstractions of
    Uncountable-STate STochastic processes. In: Baier, C., Tinelli, C. (eds.) TACAS
    2015. LNCS, vol. 9035, pp. 272–286. Springer, Heidelberg (2015). https://doi.org/
    10.1007/978-3-662-46681-0_23
29. Sproston, J.: Decidable model checking of probabilistic hybrid automata. In:
    Joseph, M. (ed.) FTRTFT 2000. LNCS, vol. 1926, pp. 31–45. Springer, Heidel-
    berg (2000). https://doi.org/10.1007/3-540-45352-0_5
30. Zhang, L., She, Z., Ratschan, S., Hermanns, H., Hahn, E.M.: Safety verification
    for probabilistic hybrid systems. Eur. J. Control 18(6), 572–587 (2012)

Constraining Counterexamples in Hybrid System Falsification: Penalty-Based Approaches

Zhenya Zhang[1,2,3](✉) [iD], Paolo Arcaini[1] [iD], and Ichiro Hasuo[1,2] [iD]

[1] National Institute of Informatics, Tokyo, Japan
{zhangzy,arcaini,hasuo}@nii.ac.jp
[2] SOKENDAI (The Graduate University for Advanced Studies), Hayama, Japan
[3] JSPS Research Fellow, Tokyo, Japan

Abstract. *Falsification* of hybrid systems is attracting ever-growing attention in quality assurance of Cyber-Physical Systems (CPS) as a practical alternative to exhaustive formal verification. In falsification, one searches for a falsifying input that drives a given black-box model to output an undesired signal. In this paper, we identify *input constraints*—such as the constraint "the throttle and brake pedals should not be pressed simultaneously" for an automotive powertrain model—as a key factor for the practical value of falsification methods. We propose three approaches for systematically addressing input constraints in optimization-based falsification, two among which come from the lexicographic method studied in the context of constrained multi-objective optimization. Our experiments show the approaches' effectiveness.

Keywords: Hybrid system falsification · Signal temporal logic · Constraints · Penalty · Lexicographic methods

1 Introduction

Cyber-physical systems (CPS) combine physical systems with digital controllers: while the former are characterized by continuous dynamics, the latter are inherently discrete. Such a combination is usually named as *hybrid systems*. The continuous dynamics of hybrid systems leads to infinite search spaces, and this makes their formal verification—especially automated methods—almost impossible. Therefore, research has followed a more pragmatic approach by pursuing the *falsification* of the system: since checking whether all inputs satisfy the specification is not feasible, falsification considers the opposite problem and looks for an input that violates it. Formally, given a *model* $\mathcal{M}$ that takes an input signal $\mathbf{u}$ and outputs a signal $\mathcal{M}(\mathbf{u})$, and a *specification* φ (a temporal formula), the

The authors are supported by ERATO HASUO Metamathematics for Systems Design Project (No. JPMJER1603), JST; Zhenya Zhang is supported by Grant-in-Aid for JSPS Fellows No. 19J15218.

© Springer Nature Switzerland AG 2020
R. Lee et al. (Eds.): NFM 2020, LNCS 12229, pp. 401–419, 2020.
https://doi.org/10.1007/978-3-030-55754-6_24

falsification problem consists in finding a *falsifying input*, i.e., an input signal **u** such that the corresponding output $\mathcal{M}(\mathbf{u})$ violates φ.

State-of-the-art falsification approaches see the falsification problem as an optimization problem. This is possible thanks to the *robust semantics* of temporal formulas [16, 22]; instead of the classical Boolean satisfaction relation $\mathbf{v} \models \varphi$, robust semantics assigns a value $[\![\mathbf{v}, \varphi]\!] \in \mathbb{R} \cup \{\infty, -\infty\}$ that assesses not only whether φ is satisfied or violated (by the sign), but also *how robustly* the formula is satisfied or violated. Falsification algorithms exploit this fact by iteratively generating inputs in the direction of decreasing robustness, with the aim of finding an input with negative robustness (i.e., a falsifying input). Different optimization-based falsification algorithms have been developed [2,5,6,13,15–17,21,22,29,33–36]. See [27] for a survey. Moreover, also tools have been developed, as BREACH [15], S-TALIRO [6], and FALSTAR [34], that work with Simulink models.

In real scenarios, there usually exist some *(input) constraints* ψ over input signals. For example, in an automotive system, one usually assumes that *throttle* and *brake* should not be positive at the same time. Descriptions of CPS sometimes report constraints on the system inputs, e.g., [11, 26]. Therefore, when generating inputs for the falsification problem, we should also guarantee that those inputs respect the constraints; otherwise, there is the risk that the resulting falsifying input is unrealistic and thus useless. However, not too many research efforts have been spent on this problem in the falsification community. To the best of our knowledge, explicit attempts to consider input constraints in falsification have been made only in [10]. In [10], constraints are represented in terms of a timed automaton, and inputs to be used for falsification are sampled from the accepted words of the automaton. The main drawback of this approach is that it can only rely on sampling for falsification, and cannot take advantage of more efficient optimization-based techniques.

Contribution. In this paper we propose three approaches in which input constraints are addressed explicitly in the falsification problem, and that still benefit from optimization-based techniques. The general idea of the three approaches is to add a penalty factor to the objective function for the inputs that do not satisfy the input constraints.

The first proposed approach consists in modifying the specification under falsification in $\psi \rightarrow \varphi$: the only way to falsify the whole formula is to satisfy the input constraint ψ and falsify the specification φ. The penalty factor for the violation of the input constraints is directly given by the STL robustness.

Our second approach employs the *lexicographic method*, a method developed in multi-objective optimization [12]. In our adaptation of the method, the satisfaction of the input constraints is embedded in a *global cost function* that must be minimized: if the input constraints are not satisfied, the cost function is principally determined by the *degree of violation* of the input constraints. In contrast, if the input constraints are satisfied, the cost function value is only determined by the robustness of the specification (as in the classical unconstrained falsification setting). The advantage of the approach is that the satisfaction of the input constraints is prioritized w.r.t. the falsification of the specification: indeed, it is useless to find a falsifying input that does not respect the constraints.

The third approach tries to improve the second approach by simulating the model only when the input constraints are satisfied. Although this can reduce the accuracy of the search, it can also speed up the falsification process.

The three approaches have been experimented over 3 Simulink models and 17 specifications that are used in falsification competitions [20]; for each model, we experimented the approaches using several input constraints of different complexity. Experimental results show that the approaches can effectively handle the constraints. In terms of falsification capability, no approach is strictly better than the others, although lexicographic methods seem better on average.

Paper structure. Section 2 introduces some necessary background on the kind of models, specifications, and algorithms used in falsification. Then, Sect. 3 presents our proposed approach, and Sect. 4 describes some experiments we performed to evaluate it. Finally, Sect. 5 reviews some related work, and Sect. 6 concludes the paper.

2   Background

In this section, we review the widely-accepted method of hill-climbing optimization-based falsification. The core of making use of hill-climbing optimization is the introduction of *robust semantics* of temporal formulas.

2.1   Robust Semantics for STL

Our definitions here are taken from [16,22].

Definition 1 ((Time-bounded) signal). Let $T \in \mathbb{R}_+$ be a positive real. An M-*dimensional signal* with a time horizon T is a function $\mathbf{w} \colon [0, T] \to \mathbb{R}^M$.

Let $\mathbf{w} \colon [0, T] \to \mathbb{R}^M$ and $\mathbf{w}' \colon [0, T'] \to \mathbb{R}^M$ be M-dimensional signals. Their *concatenation* $\mathbf{w} \cdot \mathbf{w}' \colon [0, T + T'] \to \mathbb{R}^M$ is the M-dimensional signal defined by $(\mathbf{w} \cdot \mathbf{w}')(t) = \mathbf{w}(t)$ if $t \in [0, T]$, and $(\mathbf{w} \cdot \mathbf{w}')(t) = \mathbf{w}'(t - T)$ if $t \in (T, T + T']$.

Let $0 < T_1 < T_2 \leq T$. The *restriction* $\mathbf{w}|_{[T_1, T_2]} \colon [0, T_2 - T_1] \to \mathbb{R}^M$ of $\mathbf{w} \colon [0, T] \to \mathbb{R}^M$ to the interval $[T_1, T_2]$ is defined by $(\mathbf{w}|_{[T_1, T_2]})(t) = \mathbf{w}(T_1 + t)$.

We treat the system model as a black box, i.e., the system behaviors are only observed from inputs and their corresponding outputs. We therefore simply define the system model as a function.

Definition 2 (System model $\mathcal{M}$). A *system model*, with M-dimensional input and N-dimensional output, is a function $\mathcal{M}$ that takes an input signal $\mathbf{u} \colon [0, T] \to \mathbb{R}^M$ and returns a signal $\mathcal{M}(\mathbf{u}) \colon [0, T] \to \mathbb{R}^N$. Here the common time horizon $T \in \mathbb{R}_+$ is arbitrary. Furthermore, we impose the following *causality* condition on $\mathcal{M}$: for any time-bounded signals $\mathbf{u} \colon [0, T] \to \mathbb{R}^M$ and $\mathbf{u}' \colon [0, T'] \to \mathbb{R}^M$, we require that $\mathcal{M}(\mathbf{u} \cdot \mathbf{u}')\big|_{[0,T]} = \mathcal{M}(\mathbf{u})$.

Definition 3 (STL syntax). We fix a set **Var** of variables. In STL, *atomic propositions* and *formulas* are defined as follows, respectively: $\alpha ::\equiv f(x_1, \ldots, x_N) > 0$, and $\varphi ::\equiv \alpha \mid \perp \mid \neg\varphi \mid \varphi \wedge \varphi \mid \varphi \vee \varphi \mid \varphi \, \mathcal{U}_I \, \varphi$. Here f is an N-ary function $f \colon \mathbb{R}^N \to \mathbb{R}$, $x_1, \ldots, x_N \in$ **Var**, and I is a closed non-singular interval in $\mathbb{R}_{\geq 0}$, i.e. $I = [a, b]$ or $[a, \infty)$ where $a, b \in \mathbb{R}$ and $a < b$.

We omit subscripts I for temporal operators if $I = [0, \infty)$. Other common connectives such as $\to$, $\top$, $\Box_I$ (always) and $\Diamond_I$ (eventually), are introduced as abbreviations: $\varphi_1 \to \varphi_2 \equiv \neg\varphi_1 \vee \varphi_2$, $\Diamond_I \varphi \equiv \top \, \mathcal{U}_I \, \varphi$ and $\Box_I \varphi \equiv \neg\Diamond_I \neg\varphi$. An atomic formula $f(\boldsymbol{x}) \leq c$, where $c \in \mathbb{R}$, is accommodated using $\neg$ and the function $f'(\boldsymbol{x}) := f(\boldsymbol{x}) - c$.

Definition 4 (Robust semantics [16]). Let $\mathbf{w} \colon [0, T] \to \mathbb{R}^N$ be an N-dimensional signal, and $t \in [0, T)$. The *t-shift* of $\mathbf{w}$, denoted by $\mathbf{w}^t$, is the time-bounded signal $\mathbf{w}^t \colon [0, T - t] \to \mathbb{R}^N$ defined by $\mathbf{w}^t(t') := \mathbf{w}(t + t')$.

Let $\mathbf{w} \colon [0, T] \to \mathbb{R}^{|\mathbf{Var}|}$ be a signal, and φ be an STL formula. We define the *robustness* $[\![\mathbf{w}, \varphi]\!] \in \mathbb{R} \cup \{\infty, -\infty\}$ as follows, by induction on the construction of formulas. Here $\bigsqcap$ and $\bigsqcup$ denote infimums and supremums of real numbers, respectively. Their binary version $\sqcap$ and $\sqcup$ denote minimum and maximum.

$$[\![\mathbf{w}, f(x_1, \cdots, x_n) > 0]\!] := f\big(\mathbf{w}(0)(x_1), \cdots, \mathbf{w}(0)(x_n)\big)$$

$$[\![\mathbf{w}, \perp]\!] := -\infty \qquad [\![\mathbf{w}, \neg\varphi]\!] := -[\![\mathbf{w}, \varphi]\!]$$

$$[\![\mathbf{w}, \varphi_1 \wedge \varphi_2]\!] := [\![\mathbf{w}, \varphi_1]\!] \sqcap [\![\mathbf{w}, \varphi_2]\!] \qquad [\![\mathbf{w}, \varphi_1 \vee \varphi_2]\!] := [\![\mathbf{w}, \varphi_1]\!] \sqcup [\![\mathbf{w}, \varphi_2]\!]$$

$$[\![\mathbf{w}, \varphi_1 \, \mathcal{U}_I \, \varphi_2]\!] := \bigsqcup_{t \in I \cap [0,T]} \big([\![\mathbf{w}^t, \varphi_2]\!] \sqcap \bigsqcap_{t' \in [0,t)} [\![\mathbf{w}^{t'}, \varphi_1]\!] \big)$$

For atomic formulas, $[\![\mathbf{w}, f(\boldsymbol{x}) > c]\!]$ stands for the vertical margin $f(\boldsymbol{x}) - c$ for the signal $\mathbf{w}$ at time 0. A negative robustness value indicates how far the formula is from being true. It follows from the definition that the robustness for the eventually modality is given by $[\![\mathbf{w}, \Diamond_{[a,b]}(x > 0)]\!] = \bigsqcup_{t \in [a,b] \cap [0,T]} \mathbf{w}(t)(x)$.

The above robustness notion taken from [16] is therefore *spatial*. Other robustness notions take *temporal* aspects into account, too, such as "how long before the deadline the required event occurs." See e.g. [3,16]. Our choice of spatial robustness in this paper is for the sake of simplicity, and is thus not essential.

The original semantics of STL is Boolean, given as usual by a binary relation $\models$ between signals and formulas. The robust semantics refines the Boolean one in the following sense: $[\![\mathbf{w}, \varphi]\!] > 0$ implies $\mathbf{w} \models \varphi$, and $[\![\mathbf{w}, \varphi]\!] < 0$ implies $\mathbf{w} \not\models \varphi$, see [22, Proposition 16]. Optimization-based falsification via robust semantics hinges on this refinement.

2.2 Hill Climbing-Guided Falsification

For the falsification problem, hill-climbing optimization is the main applied technique [2,4,6,13,15–18,27,29,33,35], and different tools exist, as BREACH [15], S-TALIRO [6], and FALSTAR [34]. We here formulate the falsification problem.

Definition 5 (Falsifying input). Let $\mathcal{M}$ be a system model, and φ be an STL formula. A signal $\mathbf{u}: [0, T] \to \mathbb{R}^{|\mathbf{Var}|}$ is a *falsifying input* if $[\![\mathcal{M}(\mathbf{u}), \varphi]\!] < 0$; the latter implies $\mathcal{M}(\mathbf{u}) \not\models \varphi$.

Definition 6 (Unconstrained falsification problem). The technique for solving a falsification problem is via transforming it into an optimization problem, shown as follows:

$$\begin{aligned}
&\underset{\mathbf{u}}{\text{minimize}} \quad [\![\mathcal{M}(\mathbf{u}), \varphi]\!] \\
&\text{subject to} \quad \mathbf{u} \in \Omega
\end{aligned} \tag{1}$$

In practice, the system input signal $\mathbf{u}$ is represented with a finite set of variables defined over the search space Ω (a hyperrectangle)[1]. The use of quantitative robust semantics $[\![\mathcal{M}(\mathbf{u}), \varphi]\!] \in \mathbb{R} \cup \{\infty, -\infty\}$ in the above problem enables the use of hill-climbing optimization. Hill climbing is a family of metaheuristics-based optimization algorithms, which is usually used for handling black-box optimization. The hill-climbing optimization scheme is shown in Fig. 1.

The algorithm is iterative: in every loop, it takes some samplings and computes the fitness of them. Globally, the sampling process is divided into two stages: random initial samplings and the sequent samplings based on the observation of sampling history in order to minimize the objective function. The most expensive step in each loop is given by the computation of the fitness that requires to simulate the system. Hill-climbing includes various implementations of stochastic optimization algorithms. Examples are CMA-ES [8] (used in our experiments), SA, and GNM [30].

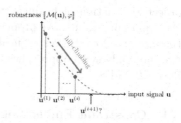

Fig. 1. Hill-climbing optimization

3 Penalty-Based Approaches for Handling Input Constraints

The problem setting of falsification introduced in Definition 6 does not take into consideration possible constraints over the input signals, which limits the

---

[1] Although the problem has a simple form of constraints, we prefer to name it *unconstrained* to distinguish it from the constrained setting we introduce later.

practicality of the falsification techniques in real contexts. Indeed, some works [11,26] report that input constraints do exist in CPS.

In this paper, we tackle the problem of handling input constraints in optimization-based falsification.

Definition 7 (Constrained falsification problem). The constrained falsification problem can be stated as follows, where ψ are input constraints, expressed in STL, over the input signals **u**.

$$\begin{aligned} \underset{\mathbf{u}}{\text{minimize}} \quad & [\![\mathcal{M}(\mathbf{u}), \varphi]\!] \\ \text{subject to} \quad & \mathbf{u} \models \psi \\ & \mathbf{u} \in \Omega \end{aligned}$$

In our approach, input constraints ψ are assumed to be expressible in STL.

More generally, constraints in optimization solutions have been studied in the field of optimization: see [23] for an overview. For example, the *death penalty* method [9] discards all the solutions that violate the constraints; while this method can work well when the feasible search space is convex, it does not work well in general, and particularly in our context where the constraints can be arbitrarily complex. Other more advanced methods (static penalty, dynamic penalty, and adaptive penalty) add a penalty factor to the objective function [23], so that solutions violating the constraints are penalized during the search.

In this work, we follow this second line of research in which we add, to the objective function of falsification, a penalty related to the non-satisfaction of the input constraints. We propose three approaches: a simple approach based on the modification of the specification under study is presented in Sect. 3.1, while two more advanced approaches based on lexicographic methods are proposed in Sect. 3.2 and Sect. 3.3.

3.1 Constraint Embedding Approach

A straightforward penalty-based approach to the constrained falsification problem consists in embedding the input constraints ψ as a prerequisite of the system specification φ. In this way, we obtain the STL formula $\psi \rightarrow \varphi$ as a new falsification goal.

The constrained problem of Definition 7 can be stated as the following unconstrained problem.

$$\begin{aligned} \underset{\mathbf{u}}{\text{minimize}} \quad & [\![\langle \mathbf{u}, \mathcal{M}(\mathbf{u}) \rangle, \psi \rightarrow \varphi]\!] \\ & \mathbf{u} \in \Omega \end{aligned}$$

The falsification approach must now evaluate the robustness of a formula that predicates both over the input and output signals, formally denoted as $\langle \mathbf{u}, \mathcal{M}(\mathbf{u}) \rangle$.

The soundness of the approach is given by Theorem 1.

Theorem 1 (Soundness and completeness of the Constraint Embedding Approach). *For all input signals* $\mathbf{u}$, $[\![\langle \mathbf{u}, \mathcal{M}(\mathbf{u}) \rangle, \psi \to \varphi]\!] < 0$ *if and only if the input constraints* ψ *are satisfied and the specification* φ *is falsified.*

The proof directly comes from the robustness definition of STL and the semantics of the implication.

3.2 Lexicographic Method Approach

While the constraint embedding approach can be effective in some cases, it does not dictate a search algorithm to first satisfy input constraints ψ and then falsify the specification φ. We here propose a method that imposes a strict prioritization between the satisfaction of the input constraints and the optimization of the objective function for falsification. This method is based on the use of a *lexicographic method* [12] for defining the fitness function of the optimization problem.

A lexicographic method [12] can be applied for a multi-objective optimization problem that aims at minimizing objective functions $f_1, \ldots, f_N$, and for which there exists a preference order in the optimization of the objective functions, i.e., functions with higher priorities must be optimized first. Formally, there exists a total order of priorities $p_1, \ldots, p_N$, where $p_k = N - k$ for each $k \in \{1, \ldots, N\}$; the larger p_k is, the higher priority f_k has.

$$\underset{\mathbf{x}}{\text{minimize}} \qquad f_1(\mathbf{x}), \ldots, f_N(\mathbf{x})$$
$$\text{subject to} \qquad \mathbf{x} \in \Omega \tag{2}$$

The method defines a global cost function GCF in the following way:

$$GCF(\mathbf{x}) = \sum_{k=1}^{N} B^{p_k} \lceil (B-1) T_k(f_k(\mathbf{x})) \rceil \tag{3}$$

where $B \in \mathbb{R}_+$ with $B > 1$ is a base number, $\lceil \rceil$ is the regular ceiling operator, and each T_k is a transformation function. Note that $\lceil (B-1) T_k(f_k(\mathbf{x})) \rceil$ is needed to map the transformed value of the objective function f_k in B quantization levels. Such a quantization is required by the lexicographic method to maintain the total order of the inputs [19] w.r.t. the priorities of the objective functions, i.e., the fitness value of a unachieved function with higher priority always dominates the fitness values of functions of lower priority. Note that the value of B can have an effect on the efficiency of the search [19], as also noted during the application of the lexicographic methods in other contexts [32]. In the experiments, we will evaluate such effect using different values for B.

The definition of a T_k is specific to the type of optimization problem; for example, we will see later how to define it for the constraint satisfaction problem and the falsification problem. In any case, the definition of a T_k must at least satisfy the monotonicity property, i.e., given two values $v_1 \leq v_2$, then $T_k(v_1) \leq T_k(v_2)$. Usually, a transformation function T_k is implemented as a normalization function between [0,1]: in such a case, the values of f_k that are mapped to 0 are those that *achieve* the objective.[2]

We apply the lexicographic method to the constrained falsification problem introduced in Definition 7. To do this, we first turn the constrained falsification problem in a unconstrained multi-objective problem as follows.

$$\underset{\mathbf{u}}{\text{minimize}} \qquad [\![\mathbf{u}, \neg\psi]\!] \qquad (4)$$

$$\underset{\mathbf{u}}{\text{minimize}} \qquad [\![\mathcal{M}(\mathbf{u}), \varphi]\!] \qquad (5)$$

$$\text{subject to} \qquad \mathbf{u} \in \Omega$$

The constraint satisfaction problem has been turned into an optimization problem by exploiting the robust semantics of STL (recall that also the input constraints are expressed in STL). Since in a lexicographic method all objective functions must be minimized (see Eq. 2), we consider the negation of the input constraints (negative robustness of $\neg\psi$ corresponds to positive robustness of ψ).

We can now combine the two objectives (Eq. 4 and Eq. 5) into a single global cost function, following Eq. 3. Since we want to prioritize the satisfaction of the input constraints, we take $[\![\mathbf{u}, \neg\psi]\!]$ as f_1, and $[\![\mathcal{M}(\mathbf{u}), \varphi]\!]$ as f_2. The definition of the global cost function is as follows.

Definition 8 (Lexicographic fitness function GCF_{fal} for falsification). Let $f_1(\mathbf{u}) := [\![\mathbf{u}, \neg\psi]\!]$, and $f_2(\mathbf{u}) := [\![\mathcal{M}(\mathbf{u}), \varphi]\!]$. The definition of the global cost function for the constrained falsification problem is as follows:

$$GCF_{\mathsf{fal}}(\mathbf{u}) = B\lceil (B-1)\,T_1(f_1(\mathbf{u}))\rceil + (B-1)\,T_2(f_2(\mathbf{u}))$$

As explained before, the definition of a transformation function T_k is specific to the kind of optimization problem. In our context, the transformation function T_1 considers values r given by the robustness evaluation of the input constraints: for any negative value of the robustness, the input constraints are satisfied, while positive values indicate the degree of violation of the input constraints ψ. Therefore, T_1 is defined as a normalization function as follows:

$$T_1(r) = \begin{cases} 0 & r < 0 \\ \dfrac{r}{R_{max}^{\psi}} & \text{otherwise} \end{cases} \qquad (6)$$

where R_{max}^{ψ} is the possible maximum value of r. The identification of a correct R_{max}^{ψ} requires minimum effort by sampling the input space. We will present how we come up with R_{max}^{ψ} later in Sect. 4.

The transformation function T_2, instead, considers values r given by the robustness evaluation of the specification φ. Also in this case, negative values of the robustness mean that the objective is achieved (i.e., the specification is

---

[2] Note that, in general, it is not always possible to specify when an objective function is "achieved". However, the lexicographic methods require that for functions $f_1, \ldots, f_{N-1}$, this is possible, and this is applicable in our context.

falsified). Therefore, the definition of the transformation function for T_2 is as follows:

$$T_2(r) = \begin{cases} 0 & r < 0 \\ \epsilon & r = 0 \\ \dfrac{r}{R_{max}^{\varphi}} & \text{otherwise} \end{cases} \tag{7}$$

where R_{max}^{φ} is the possible maximum value of r, and ϵ is an arbitarily small positive number[3]. We will also explain later in Sect. 4 how we select a proper R_{max}^{φ}.

Considering the definitions of the two transformation functions, we can now analyse the behaviour of function GCF_{fal} (see Definition 8). Given an input signal $\mathbf{u}$, if the input constraints ψ are satisfied, the first operand of the sum will be 0 (due to the transformation function T_1 in Eq. 6), and therefore the value of GCF_{fal} will only depend on the robustness value of the temporal specification (i.e., the second operand). On the other hand, if the input constraints are not satisfied, the first operand will be positive and guaranteed to be larger than the second one (so driving the search towards the satisfaction of the input constraints).

Note that in the definition of GCF_{fal}, we do not apply the ceiling operator to the robustness evaluation of the specification φ (i.e., f_2). It is indeed known that the ceiling operator is not really needed by the lexicographic method for the last operand of the sum [12,32], and we take advantage of this. Therefore, since f_2 corresponds to the falsification algorithm, we prefer to remove the ceiling in order to preserve as much information as possible regarding the specification robustness that could be helpful for driving the search. Indeed, removing the ceiling avoids the quantization effect that in general is adversarial for the hill-climbing search.

Theorem 2 (Soundness of the GCF_{fal} fitness function). *If there exists an input signal $\mathbf{u}$ such that $GCF_{fal}(\mathbf{u}) = 0$, then the input constraints ψ are satisfied and the specification φ is falsified.*

The proof directly comes from the definitions of GCF_{fal}, T_1, and T_2, and the robustness definition of STL.

3.3 Partially Simulation Free Lexicographic Method Approach

In this section, we present a variation of the plain application of the lexicographic method presented in Sect. 3.2. The current technique takes into account a particular feature of our problem: regarding the two objective functions in Eq. 4 and Eq. 5, the computation of $[\![\mathbf{u}, \neg\psi]\!]$ does not need system simulation, while computation of $[\![\mathcal{M}(\mathbf{u}), \varphi]\!]$ does. Since system simulation is the most time-consuming process (as we have already observed in Sect. 2.2), we adapt the GCF_{fal} function into a *partially simulation free* version GCF_{fal_sf} that avoids running simulations when ψ is not satisfied, so saving time.

---

[3] Note that this is needed to distinguish inputs having robustness 0 (not falsifying) from those having negative robustness (falsifying).

Definition 9 (Lexicographic fitness function $GCF_{\mathsf{fal\_sf}}$ for falsification).
Let $f_1(\mathbf{u}) := [\![\mathbf{u}, \neg\psi]\!]$, and $f_2(\mathbf{u}) := [\![\mathcal{M}(\mathbf{u}), \varphi]\!]$. The definition of the *partially simulation free* global cost function for the constrained falsification problem is as follows:

$$
GCF_{\mathsf{fal\_sf}}(\mathbf{u}) = \begin{cases} B\lceil (B-1)\,T_1(f_1(\mathbf{u}))\rceil & \text{if } f_1(\mathbf{u}) > 0 \\ (B-1)\,T_2(f_2(\mathbf{u})) & \text{otherwise} \end{cases}
$$

Note that the only difference between Definition 8 and Definition 9 is when the input constraints ψ are not satisfied (first case): in this case, Definition 9 ignores the system specification in Eq. 5 (so, no system simulation is performed), and thus $GCF_{\mathsf{fal\_sf}}(\mathbf{u})$ is only decided by the robustness of the input constraints, i.e., $[\![\mathbf{u}, \neg\psi]\!]$; otherwise, it is the same as Definition 8. In the second case, we do not report the first operand of the sum that is 0 because the input constraints are satisfied.

Note that the definition of $GCF_{\mathsf{fal\_sf}}$ still guarantees the priorities between the two objective functions, i.e., inputs violating the input constraints still have higher fitness values than those satisfying them.

The soundness of the approach still holds, as stated in Theorem 3.

Theorem 3 (Soundness of the $GCF_{\mathsf{fal\_sf}}$ fitness function). *If there exists an input signal $\mathbf{u}$ such that $GCF_{\mathsf{fal\_sf}}(\mathbf{u}) = 0$, then the input constraints ψ are satisfied and the specification φ is falsified.*

The proof is similar to that of Theorem 2.

4   Experimental Evaluation

In order to evaluate the proposed techniques, we show their application to the benchmarks commonly used in the falsification community [20]. Specifically, we experimented them on 3 Simulink models, and 17 specifications to achieve comprehensive and reliable evaluation results. Note that the documents reporting the original Simulink models and temporal specifications do not provide any input constraints. Therefore, for each model, we identified some input constraints of different kinds, by using different logical and relational operators, and considering different input signals. The 3 Simulink models and their specifications are reported in Table 1a. The input constraints are reported in Table 1b.

In the following, we provide a detailed description of the benchmarks.

The *Automatic Transmission* (AT) model [25] is a typical benchmark model in falsification. It has two input signals, *throttle* $\in [0, 100]$ and *brake* $\in [0, 325]$, and several output signals including *speed*, *rpm*, *gear*, etc. Specifications AT1, ..., AT13 mainly concern safety of the system in different aspects. In the experiments, we consider 5 different input constraints, by considering both *throttle* and *brake*, or only *throttle*.

The *Abstract Fuel Control* (AFC) model [26] takes two input signals, *Pedal_Angle* and *Engine_Speed*, and outputs the controller mode subject to

Table 1. Benchmarks of temporal specifications and input constraints in STL. Here, $\mathbf{w}^t$ represents the *t-shift* of $\mathbf{w}$ (see Definition 4) and $\Delta_t(\mathbf{w})$ represents $\mathbf{w}^t - \mathbf{w}$

(a) Temporal specifications φ

Model	Spec. ID	Temporal specification in STL
AT	AT1	$\square_{[0,30]}\,(speed < 120)$
	AT2	$\square_{[0,30]}\,(gear = 3 \rightarrow speed \geq 19)$
	AT3	$\square_{[0,30]}\,(gear = 4 \rightarrow speed \geq 35)$
	AT4	$\neg(\square_{[10,30]}((50 < speed) \wedge (speed < 60)))$
	AT5	$\neg(\square_{[10,30]}((53 < speed) \wedge (speed < 57)))$
	AT6	$\square_{[0,29]}(speed < 100) \vee \square_{[29,30]}(speed > 75)$
	AT7	$\square_{[0,29]}(speed < 100) \vee \square_{[29,30]}(speed > 70)$
	AT8	$\square_{[0,30]}(rpm < 4770 \vee \square_{[0,1]}(rpm > 1000))$
	AT9	$\square_{[0,30]}(rpm < 4770 \vee \square_{[0,1]}(rpm > 700))$
	AT10	$\square_{[0,30]}(rpm < 3000) \rightarrow \square_{[0,20]}(speed < 65)$
	AT11	$\square_{[0,10]}\,(speed < 50) \vee \Diamond_{[0,30]}\,(rpm > 2520)$
	AT12	$\square_{[0,26]}(\Delta_4(speed) > 40 \rightarrow \Delta_4(gear) > 0)$
	AT13	$\square_{[0,27]}(\Delta_3(speed) > 30 \rightarrow \Delta_3(gear) > 0)$
AFC	AFC1	$\square_{[11,50]}(\mu < 0.22)$
	AFC2	$\square_{[11,50]}(\Diamond_{[0,10]}(|\mu| < 0.05))$
NN		$NN\_req \equiv \square_{[0,16]}(\neg close\_ref \rightarrow reach\_ref\_in\_tau)$
		$close\_ref \equiv |Pos - Ref| \leq \alpha_1 + \alpha_2 \cdot |Ref|$
		$reach\_ref\_in\_tau \equiv \Diamond_{[0,2]}(\square_{[0,1]}(close\_ref))$
	NN1	NN_req with $\alpha_1 = 0.003, \alpha_2 = 0.04$
	NN2	NN_req with $\alpha_1 = 0.01, \alpha_2 = 0.03$

(b) Input Constraints ψ

Model	Constr. ID	Constraint in STL
AT	AT_con1	$\square_{[0,30]}(throttle = 0 \vee brake = 0)$
	AT_con2	$\square_{[0,30]}(throttle \leq 20 \vee brake \leq 50)$
	AT_con3	$\square_{[0,30]}(throttle > 3 \cdot brake \vee brake > 3 \cdot throttle)$
	AT_con4	$\square_{[0,24]}(throttle > 70 \rightarrow throttle^6 < 10)$
	AT_con5	$\square_{[6,30]}(throttle = 0 \vee brake = 0) \wedge \square_{[0,6]}(brake = 0)$
AFC	AFC_con1	$\square_{[0,50]}(Pedal\_Angle \geq 50 \rightarrow Engine\_Speed > 1000)$
	AFC_con2	$\square_{[0,20]}(\Delta_{10}(Pedal\_Angle) \geq 0)$
NN	NN_con1	$\square_{[0,12]}(\Delta_6(Ref) \geq 0)$
	NN_con2	$\Diamond_{[0,18]}(Ref > 2.5)$

Pedal_Angle, and a ratio μ reflecting the deviation of *air-fuel-ratio* from its reference value. In our experiment, we set the range of *Pedal_Angle* $\in [8.8, 70]$ to keep the model in a *normal* mode, and *Engine_Speed* $\in [900, 1100]$ consistent with [26]. Specifications AFC1 and AFC2 reason about the related safety properties. We created two different input constraints, one constraining the value *Engine_Speed* w.r.t. the value of *Pedal_Angle*, and another one constraining the value of *Pedal_Angle* over time.

The third benchmark model is based on MathWork's *Neural Network controller* (NN) for a magnet system. Specifications NN1 and NN2 formalize the safety requirement about the position *Pos* of the magnet w.r.t. its reference value *Ref*, which ranges over $[1, 3]$. Since *Ref* is the only input signal, we cannot reason about input constraints over different signals. Therefore, we just specified two input constraints over *Ref*: the first one requiring *Ref* to be non-decreasing, and the second one requiring *Ref* to be larger of 2.5 in at least one time point.

In the lexicographic method-based approaches proposed in Sect. 3.2 and Sect. 3.3, we need to choose a proper base number B and transformation functions T_1 and T_2 for the global cost function. Regarding B, we performed a preliminary experiment by comparing the performance of the approaches using different values of B: from the experiment described in RQ3, $B = 10$ resulted to be one of two best settings (see Table 4). Therefore, for the main experiments of the paper reported in Table 3, we used 10 as base number B. As for transformation functions T_1 and T_2, we need to determine R_{max}^{ψ} and R_{max}^{φ} in each case (see Sect. 3.2). We handle this problem as follows. We take a small set of samplings of the input space and compute their robustness values (both for the input constraint and the specification). Then, for the input constraints, we determine R_{max}^{ψ} by multiplying the maximum value of the obtained robustness values by a reasonable factor, namely 1.5. For the specification, we determine R_{max}^{φ} in a similar way.

In our experiments we use CMA-ES [8], one of the state-of-the-art stochastic optimization algorithms for black box, as an implementation of hill-climbing optimization.

The experiments use Breach version 1.2.13 on an Amazon EC2 c4.2xlarge instance (2.9 GHz Intel Xeon E5-2666 v3 Processor, 15 GB main memory).

4.1   Evaluation

In order to evaluate our proposed approaches, we first check the performances of a state-of-the-art falsification tool (BREACH) that does not consider input constraints during falsification; we name such unconstrained approach as *Baseline Approach* (BA). We run falsification using BA over all the specifications reported in Table 1 with a timeout budget of 600 secs. In order to account for random variation of the approach, each experiment has been performed 30 times, by following guidelines of reporting results for randomized algorithms [7]. Table 2 reports the experimental results. For each specification, it reports the *falsification rate* (FR) as the number of experiments for which a falsifying input has been found, and the average execution *time* over the successful executions. Moreover, for each input constraint ψ reported in Table 1b, we also check whether the found falsifying input satisfies (by chance) ψ: the Constraint Satisfaction Rate (CSR) reports the number and percentage of falsifying inputs that also satisfy

Table 2. Results of falsification without considering the input constraints (FR: Falsification Rate (out of 30) – CSR: Constraint Satisfaction Rate (out of falsifying inputs))

(a) Automatic Transmission

	FR (/30)	time (s)	CSR									
			AT_con1		AT_con2		AT_con3		AT_con4		AT_con5	
			#	%	#	%	#	%	#	%	#	%
AT1	30	27.06	1	3.3%	1	3.3%	1	3.3%	0	0	0	0
AT2	20	29.3	1	5%	7	35%	0	0	20	100%	0	0
AT3	12	25.36	0	0	2	16.7%	1	8.3%	10	83.3%	0	0
AT4	30	41.06	1	3.3%	3	10%	1	3.3%	26	86.7%	1	3.3%
AT5	28	157.09	0	0	2	7.1%	2	7.1%	25	89.3%	0	0
AT6	20	96.3	0	0	0	0	0	0	0	0	0	0
AT7	18	87.09	0	0	0	0	0	0	0	0	0	0
AT8	13	58.88	0	0	1	7.6%	0	0	0	0	0	0
AT9	13	131.27	0	0	0	0	0	0	0	0	0	0
AT10	30	46.04	0	0	3	10%	1	3.3%	30	100%	0	0
AT11	23	227.32	0	0	0	0	0	0	23	100%	0	0
AT12	6	50.6	0	0	1	16.7%	0	0	0	0	0	0
AT13	21	23.15	0	0	1	4.8%	0	0	0	0	0	0

(b) Abstract Fuel Control

	FR (/30)	time (s)	CSR			
			AFC_con1		AFC_con2	
			#	%	#	%
AFC1	30	44.79	8	26.7%	1	3.3%
AFC2	6	211.82	0	0	0	0

(c) Neural Network controller

	FR (/30)	time (s)	CSR			
			NN_con1		NN_con2	
			#	%	#	%
NN1	20	163.57	0	0	8	40%
NN2	27	26.43	1	3.7%	7	25.9%

the input constraints. FR informs us about the complexity of the falsification problem, and we will use it later in the experiments to see how handling the input constraints affects the falsification problem. Regarding CSR, we observe that, most of the times, the falsifying input violates the input constraint: in such a case, the *falsifying area* of the input space is not strictly contained in the *feasible area* satisfying the input constraints. In few cases, the input constraints are satisfied with a high percentage, meaning that there is a big overlap (if not proper inclusion in case of 100%) between the falsifiable area and the feasible area.

Then, we run the three approaches proposed in the paper over all the benchmarks.[4] We name as CE the Constraint Embedding approach presented in Sect. 3.1, as LM the approach based on Lexicographic Method presented in Sect. 3.2, and as LM_{sf} its modification presented in Sect. 3.3. Also in this case, all the experiments have been performed 30 times.

---

[4] Technically, we modified the fitness evaluation of BREACH to use the 3 new fitness functions.

Table 3. Experimental results (FR: Falsification Rate)

(a) Automatic Transmission

		AT_con1		AT_con2		AT_con3		AT_con4		AT_con5	
		FR (/30)	time (s)	FR (/30)	time (s)	FR (/30)	time (s)	FR (/30)	time (s)	FR (/30)	time (s)
AT1	CE	18	78.62	26	64.05	14	88.43	13	367.26	15	114.72
	LM	2	378.25	19	138.01	3	178.62	14	350.78	16	303.89
	LM$_{sf}$	0	-	15	89.22	3	169.69	19	316.92	9	125.93
AT2	CE	5	85.19	18	44.91	23	62.21	22	24.7	10	59.57
	LM	10	33.75	10	56.63	25	49.82	21	47.47	0	-
	LM$_{sf}$	10	9.29	11	17.71	21	19.53	26	25.7	0	-
AT3	CE	2	126.5	6	34.38	11	60.46	17	28.28	9	64.35
	LM	6	38.05	5	49.92	11	83.93	16	15.81	0	-
	LM$_{sf}$	6	26.49	7	24.72	14	29	17	27.24	0	-
AT4	CE	23	136.14	30	73.7	9	80.81	30	35.37	23	143.71
	LM	11	273.27	28	70.69	28	137.06	30	42.73	30	183.5
	LM$_{sf}$	12	132.63	28	175.28	26	86.96	30	42.98	23	74.72
AT5	CE	21	260.97	28	195.83	8	278.95	30	156.36	13	259.86
	LM	3	332.99	28	173.75	21	286.24	30	174.9	14	326.72
	LM$_{sf}$	5	239.26	28	175.28	25	180.69	30	134.08	17	243.24
AT6	CE	5	406.83	13	263.15	4	203.02	1	421.7	4	470.8
	LM	1	594.79	5	405.46	5	317.91	1	395.75	0	-
	LM$_{sf}$	0	-	5	229.01	5	197.38	0	-	0	-
AT7	CE	0	-	0	-	0	-	4	465.65	0	-
	LM	0	-	0	-	5	351.57	2	528.73	0	-
	LM$_{sf}$	0	-	0	-	2	203.09	2	395.26	0	-
AT8	CE	7	362.45	8	241.13	1	450.03	0	-	10	372.02
	LM	7	184.5	6	86.59	1	176.33	0	-	4	211.28
	LM$_{sf}$	5	99.62	9	72.49	1	26.84	0	-	3	103.04
AT9	CE	7	401.25	6	356.97	0	-	0	-	7	385.24
	LM	10	182.46	9	70.64	1	105.46	0	-	4	172.34
	LM$_{sf}$	3	75.76	12	72.27	0	-	0	-	5	108.18
AT10	CE	15	186.41	29	117.35	18	201.62	30	36.56	24	167.23
	LM	7	133.63	25	149.34	25	182.6	30	28.28	17	81.18
	LM$_{sf}$	8	63.62	27	97.33	24	147.82	30	32.67	19	155.15
AT11	CE	10	234.12	22	223.15	3	307.46	26	264.61	13	261.85
	LM	2	184.39	22	220.04	1	554.55	21	260.33	1	51.71
	LM$_{sf}$	2	404.31	25	178.26	4	203.27	21	253.18	13	261.84
AT12	CE	8	103.62	7	62.48	4	141.61	2	190.71	2	159.95
	LM	9	147.38	15	89.01	11	118.55	1	166.02	8	149.39
	LM$_{sf}$	4	87.93	12	63.96	13	80.96	1	183.14	4	120.75
AT13	CE	8	97.34	15	37.02	8	67.82	5	149.97	8	123.05
	LM	16	147	15	61.32	15	116.86	10	74.4	7	108.82
	LM$_{sf}$	16	45.97	15	49.92	13	53.4	7	63.53	7	30.95

(b) Abstract Fuel Control

		AFC_con1		AFC_con2	
		FR (/30)	time (s)	FR (/30)	time (s)
AFC1	CE	25	120.17	23	356.78
	LM	29	56.32	29	53.55
	LM$_{sf}$	29	49.03	29	46.89
AFC2	CE	10	312.48	5	284.98
	LM	11	350.47	10	139.01
	LM$_{sf}$	9	160.95	11	197.00

(c) Neural Network controller

		NN_con1		NN_con2	
		FR (/30)	time (s)	FR (/30)	time (s)
NN1	CE	11	152.26	26	192.28
	LM	16	181.65	24	139.79
	LM$_{sf}$	15	210.55	19	217.30
NN2	CE	23	82.01	29	84.09
	LM	19	66.45	30	67.99
	LM$_{sf}$	17	51.73	22	68.35

Table 3 reports the experimental results. Note that, by definition, all the approaches return falsifying inputs that respect the input constraints, i.e., CSR is always 100% and so it is not reported. The table only reports FR and time. We analyse the results using 3 research questions.

RQ1. *Does constraint handling affect the falsifiability rate?*

First of all, we want to observe that, in most of the cases, FR of the three approaches is diminished w.r.t. that of BA (i.e., BREACH without constraint handling). This is expected, because almost all the falsifying inputs found by BA do not satisfy the input constraints, and so our approaches correctly focus only on the feasible area. Note that, in the few cases in which also BA had 100% CSR (e.g., AT2 with input constraint AT_con4), the falsification rate of the proposed approaches is the same as that of BA, and sometimes even better. This holds also for cases in which CSR was high but not 100% for BA (e.g., AT3 with input constraint AT_con4).

RQ2. *How do the three proposed approaches perform?*

We are here interested in comparing the performance of the three proposed approaches. Regarding FR, in 11 out of 73 cases, the performances of the three approaches are the same. For the remaining 62 experiments, in 28 cases CE is strictly better or equal than the other two approaches. Although quite simple, CE can be effective in some cases. However, the lexicographic methods seem to be better on average.

Regarding LM and LM$_{sf}$, in 28 cases they have the same FR, while in 24 cases LM is better than LM$_{sf}$, and in 21 cases the other way round. This means that the optimization implemented by LM$_{sf}$ of not simulating the inputs that violate the input constraint, has a positive effect in some cases; however, when simulation is skipped, the objective function does not receive any contribution related to the robustness of the specification, and this may weaken the falsification ability of the approach.

Regarding the computation time when a falsifying input is found, LM$_{sf}$ is faster than LM in 47 cases out 61 (in which both approaches find a falsifying input). This confirms that LM$_{sf}$ does indeed speed up the process. However, there are some notable exceptions. For AT11 with input constraint AT_con5, LM$_{sf}$ is much slower, but it has a much better falsification rate: this may be due to the fact that the time saved is used for exploring other inputs that turned out to be falsifiable and feasible (while LM, in 29/30 cases, timeouts without finding any falsifying input).

RQ3. *Is there any influence in using different values for the base parameter in the lexicographic methods?*

In Sect. 3.2, we have described that the global cost function of a lexicographic method requires to define a base number B, that it is only required to be larger than 1. However, literature shows that different values of B can affect the performance of the underlying optimization problems [12,32]. In this RQ, we investigate which is the effect of the choice of B in our approaches. We selected 3 specifications of the AT benchmark (AT2, AT5, and AT13), and 2 input constraints (AT_con2 and AT_con3). For the six combinations, we run the two lexicographic methods LM and LM$_{sf}$ using 4 values for B, namely 5, 10, 100, and 1000. Results are reported in Table 4. We observe that there seems to be an effect on the falsification results. The two extreme cases of B equal to 5 and to 1000 almost

Table 4. Comparison of different values for base B (FR: falsification rate)

	base	AT_con2 FR (/30)	time (s)	AT_con3 FR (/30)	time (s)		base	AT_con2 FR (/30)	time (s)	AT_con3 FR (/30)	time (s)		base	AT_con2 FR (/30)	time (s)	AT_con3 FR (/30)	time (s)
AT2 LM	5	9	45.44	26	41.04	AT5 LM	5	25	247.24	23	257.94	AT13 LM	5	13	63.51	14	68.09
	10	10	56.63	25	49.82		10	28	173.75	21	286.24		10	15	61.32	15	116.86
	100	15	34.78	22	43.22		100	26	180.92	27	252.89		100	16	53.73	10	133.94
	1000	13	33.33	20	46.38		1000	25	261.10	25	267.52		1000	11	90.65	6	182.43
LM_st	5	9	16.16	24	13.49	LM_st	5	28	189.06	14	241.07	LM_st	5	11	34.06	13	51.13
	10	11	17.71	21	19.53		10	28	175.28	25	180.69		10	15	49.92	13	53.40
	100	16	26.07	25	20.80		100	24	181.10	24	199.52		100	14	46.60	12	84.43
	1000	13	30.07	24	26.53		1000	26	174.37	28	191.11		1000	10	72.59	10	117.91

always produce the worst results, while the best results are distributed between the cases in which B is 10 or 100. This is expected, as low values of B produce more areas having flat robustness values (due to the combined use of the ceiling operator and B) for the input constraints and the specification: therefore, in this case, the search may not find the right direction. On the other hand, high values of B generate a global cost function that prioritizes "too much" the first objective related to the input constraints, and a modification of the robustness of the specification has less effect on the global cost function (given a same value for the robustness of the input constraints).

5   Related Work

Stochastic optimization-based falsification technique has drawn great many research attentions in recent years [2,5,6,13,15–17,21,22,28,29,31,33–35], and becomes one of the most effective approaches to quality assurance of CPS products. Most of research efforts focus on developing or improving search techniques, and a lot of techniques were proposed to handle the "exploration and exploitation" trade-off, which is a core problem in search-based testing. Notably some recent works [5,14,34] introduce advanced machine learning techniques into falsification, improving the effectiveness and efficiency substantially. A comparison of the state-of-the-art tools is given in [20].

Our work bridges the gap between effectiveness and practicality of falsification, as few works consider the meaningfulness of falsifying results. This problem was studied in [10], where they use timed automata to formalize the input constraints and generate meaningful samplings. However, the proposed framework cannot be integrated into the state-of-the-art hill-climbing optimization-based falsification framework. Other examples include [26], in which they mentioned an approach similar to our Constraint Embedding approach to handle an *input profile*. Earlier works [31] use sampling techniques so they can handle input constraints more complicated than bound constraints.

The constrained optimization problem is one of the major research directions in the optimization community. However, a large amount of the research is based on white-box model. Techniques on black-box models are more challenging as no derivative information is given. Genetic algorithm (GA) (or more generally, evolutionary algorithm (EA)) is a big branch of such techniques. A comprehensive list of literatures on handling constraints in GA is maintained [1].

The constraint embedding approach builds a specification that predicates over both input and output signals. The approach in [24] is tailored for handling safety properties having this combination of signals. However, that approach is not applicable to the constraint embedding approach which considers a different class of properties.

6 Conclusion and Future Work

The paper presented three approaches for handling the input constraints in optimization-based falsification of hybrid systems. They implement, in different ways, a penalty method that adds a penalty factor to the fitness function that penalizes inputs that violate the input constraints. Experiments showed that each of the three approaches performs better in some cases. We believe that this depends on the relationship between the feasible area and the falsifying area of the input space. As future work, we plan to perform more detailed experiments in this direction to better characterize the strengths and weaknesses of the three approaches. In particular, we want to identify which constraints and/or specifications are better handled by a given method.

References

1. List of references on constraint-handling techniques used with evolutionary algorithms. https://www.cs.cinvestav.mx/~constraint/
2. Adimoolam, A., Dang, T., Donzé, A., Kapinski, J., Jin, X.: Classification and coverage-based falsification for embedded control systems. In: Majumdar, R., Kunčak, V. (eds.) CAV 2017. LNCS, vol. 10426, pp. 483–503. Springer, Cham (2017). https://doi.org/10.1007/978-3-319-63387-9_24
3. Akazaki, T., Hasuo, I.: Time robustness in MTL and expressivity in hybrid system falsification. In: Kroening, D., Păsăreanu, C.S. (eds.) CAV 2015. LNCS, vol. 9207, pp. 356–374. Springer, Cham (2015). https://doi.org/10.1007/978-3-319-21668-3_21
4. Akazaki, T., Kumazawa, Y., Hasuo, I.: Causality-aided falsification. In: Proceedings First Workshop on Formal Verification of Autonomous Vehicles, FVAV@iFM 2017, Turin, Italy, 19th September 2017, vol. 257, pp. 3–18. EPTCS (2017)
5. Akazaki, T., Liu, S., Yamagata, Y., Duan, Y., Hao, J.: Falsification of cyber-physical systems using deep reinforcement learning. In: Havelund, K., Peleska, J., Roscoe, B., de Vink, E. (eds.) FM 2018. LNCS, vol. 10951, pp. 456–465. Springer, Cham (2018). https://doi.org/10.1007/978-3-319-95582-7_27
6. Annapureddy, Y., Liu, C., Fainekos, G., Sankaranarayanan, S.: S-Taliro: a tool for temporal logic falsification for hybrid systems. In: Abdulla, P.A., Leino, K., Rustan, M. (eds.) TACAS 2011/ETAPS 2011, pp. 254–257. Springer-Verlag, Berlin, Heidelberg (2011)
7. Arcuri, A., Briand, L.: A practical guide for using statistical tests to assess randomized algorithms in software engineering. In: Proceedings of the 33rd International Conference on Software Engineering, ICSE 2011, New York, NY, USA, pp. 1–10. ACM (2011)
8. Auger, A., Hansen, N.: A restart CMA evolution strategy with increasing population size. In: Proceedings of the IEEE Congress on Evolutionary Computation, CEC 2005, pp. 1769–1776. IEEE (2005)

9. Bäck, T., Hoffmeister, F., Schwefel, H.: A survey of evolution strategies. In: Belew, R.K., Booker, L.B., (eds.) Proceedings of the 4th International Conference on Genetic Algorithms, San Diego, CA, USA, July 1991, pp. 2–9 (1991)

10. Barbot, B., Basset, N., Dang, T.: Generation of signals under temporal constraints for CPS testing. In: Badger, J.M., Rozier, K.Y. (eds.) NASA Formal Methods. pp, pp. 54–70. Springer International Publishing, Cham (2019)

11. Ben Abdessalem, R., Nejati, S., Briand, L.C., Stifter, T.: Testing vision-based control systems using learnable evolutionary algorithms. In: Proceedings of the 40th International Conference on Software Engineering, ICSE 2018, New York, NY, USA, pp. 1016–1026. ACM (2018)

12. Chang, K.-H.: Chapter 19 - multiobjective optimization and advanced topics. In: Chang, K.-H. (ed.) e-Design, pp. 1105–1173. Academic Press, Boston (2015)

13. Deshmukh, J., Jin, X., Kapinski, J., Maler, O.: Stochastic local search for falsification of hybrid systems. In: Finkbeiner, B., Pu, G., Zhang, L. (eds.) ATVA 2015. LNCS, vol. 9364, pp. 500–517. Springer, Cham (2015). https://doi.org/10.1007/978-3-319-24953-7_35

14. Deshmukh, J.V., Horvat, M., Jin, X., Majumdar, R., Prabhu, V.S.: Testing cyber-physical systems through Bayesian optimization. ACM Trans. Embed. Comput. Syst. **16**(5), 170:1–170:18 (2017)

15. Donzé, A.: Breach, a toolbox for verification and parameter synthesis of hybrid systems. In: Touili, T., Cook, B., Jackson, P. (eds.) CAV 2010. LNCS, vol. 6174, pp. 167–170. Springer, Heidelberg (2010). https://doi.org/10.1007/978-3-642-14295-6_17

16. Donzé, A., Maler, O.: Robust satisfaction of temporal logic over real-valued signals. In: Chatterjee, K., Henzinger, T.A. (eds.) FORMATS 2010. LNCS, vol. 6246, pp. 92–106. Springer, Heidelberg (2010). https://doi.org/10.1007/978-3-642-15297-9_9

17. Dreossi, T., Dang, T., Donzé, A., Kapinski, J., Jin, X., Deshmukh, J.V.: Efficient guiding strategies for testing of temporal properties of hybrid systems. In: Havelund, K., Holzmann, G., Joshi, R. (eds.) NFM 2015. LNCS, vol. 9058, pp. 127–142. Springer, Cham (2015). https://doi.org/10.1007/978-3-319-17524-9_10

18. Dreossi, T., Donzé, A., Seshia, S.A.: Compositional falsification of cyber-physical systems with machine learning components. In: Bobaru, M., Havelund, K., Holzmann, G.J., Joshi, R. (eds.) NFM 2011. LNCS, vol. 6617. Springer, Heidelberg (2011). https://doi.org/10.1007/978-3-642-20398-5

19. Ehrgott, M.: Multicriteria Optimization. Springer-Verlag, Berlin (2005)

20. Ernst, G., Arcaini, P., Donzé, A., Fainekos, G., Mathesen, L., Pedrielli, G., Yaghoubi, S., Yamagata, Y., Zhang, Z.: ARCH-COMP 2019 category report: falsification. In: Frehse, G., Althoff, M., (eds.) ARCH19. 6th International Workshop on Applied Verification of Continuous and Hybrid Systems. EPiC Series in Computing, vol. 61, pp. 129–140. EasyChair (2019)

21. Ernst, G., Sedwards, S., Zhang, Z., Hasuo, I.: Fast falsification of hybrid systems using probabilistically adaptive input. In: Parker, D., Wolf, V. (eds.) Quantitative Evaluation of Systems. pp, pp. 165–181. Springer International Publishing, Cham (2019)

22. Fainekos, G.E., Pappas, G.J.: Robustness of temporal logic specifications for continuous-time signals. Theor. Comput. Sci. **410**(42), 4262–4291 (2009)

23. Fan, Z., Fang, Y., Li, W., Lu, J., Cai, X., Wei, C.: A comparative study of constrained multi-objective evolutionary algorithms on constrained multi-objective optimization problems. In: 2017 IEEE Congress on Evolutionary Computation, CEC 2017, pp. 209–216. IEEE (2017)

24. Ferrère, T., Nickovic, D., Donzé, A., Ito, H., Kapinski, J.: Interface-aware signal temporal logic. In: Ozay, N., Prabhakar, P., (eds.) Proceedings of the 22nd ACM International Conference on Hybrid Systems: Computation and Control, HSCC 2019, Montreal, QC, Canada, 16–18 April 2019, pp. 57–66. ACM (2019)

25. Hoxha, B., Abbas, H., Fainekos, G.E.: Benchmarks for temporal logic requirements for automotive systems. In: Frehse, G., Althoff, M., (eds.) 1st and 2nd International Workshop on Applied veRification for Continuous and Hybrid Systems, ARCH@CPSWeek 2014, Berlin, Germany, 14 April 2014/ARCH@CPSWeek 2015, Seattle, USA, 13 April 2015. EPiC Series in Computing, vol. 34, pp. 25–30. EasyChair (2014)

26. Jin, X., Deshmukh, J.V., Kapinski, J., Ueda, K., Butts, K.: Powertrain control verification benchmark. In: Proceedings of the 17th International Conference on Hybrid Systems: Computation and Control, HSCC 2014, NY, USA, pp. 253–262. ACM (2014)

27. Kapinski, J., Deshmukh, J.V., Jin, X., Ito, H., Butts, K.: Simulation-based approaches for verification of embedded control systems: an overview of traditional and advanced modeling, testing, and verification techniques. IEEE Control Syst. 36(6), 45–64 (2016)

28. Kato, K., Ishikawa, F.: Learning-based falsification for model families of cyber-physical systems. In: 2019 IEEE 24th Pacific Rim International Symposium on Dependable Computing (PRDC), pp. 236–245, December 2019

29. Kuřátko, J., Ratschan, S.: Combined global and local search for the falsification of hybrid systems. In: Legay, A., Bozga, M. (eds.) FORMATS 2014. LNCS, vol. 8711, pp. 146–160. Springer, Cham (2014). https://doi.org/10.1007/978-3-319-10512-3_11

30. Luersen, M.A., Le Riche, R.: Globalized Nelder-Mead method for engineering optimization. Comput. Struct. 82(23), 2251–2260 (2004)

31. Nghiem, T., Sankaranarayanan, S., Fainekos, G., Ivancić, F., Gupta, A., Pappas, G.J.: Monte-carlo techniques for falsification of temporal properties of non-linear hybrid systems. In: Proceedings of the 13th ACM International Conference on Hybrid Systems: Computation and Control, HSCC 2010, NY, USA, pp. 211–220. ACM (2010)

32. Pinchera, D., Perna, S., Migliore, M.D.: A lexicographic approach for multi-objective optimization in antenna array design. Prog. Electromagn. Res. 59, 85–102 (2017)

33. Silvetti, S., Policriti, A., Bortolussi, L.: An active learning approach to the falsification of black box cyber-physical systems. In: Polikarpova, N., Schneider, S. (eds.) IFM 2017. LNCS, vol. 10510, pp. 3–17. Springer, Cham (2017). https://doi.org/10.1007/978-3-319-66845-1_1

34. Zhang, Z., Ernst, G., Sedwards, S., Arcaini, P., Hasuo, I.: Two-layered falsification of hybrid systems guided by monte carlo tree search. IEEE Trans. Comput. Aided Des. Integr. Circuits Syst. 37(11), 2894–2905 (2018)

35. Zutshi, A., Deshmukh, J.V., Sankaranarayanan, S., Kapinski, J.: Multiple shooting, cegar-based falsification for hybrid systems. In: 2014 International Conference on Embedded Software, EMSOFT 2014, New Delhi, India, 12–17 October 2014, pp. 5:1–5:10. ACM (2014)

36. Zutshi, A., Sankaranarayanan, S., Deshmukh, J.V., Kapinski, J., Jin, X.: Falsification of safety properties for closed loop control systems. In: Proceedings of the 18th International Conference on Hybrid Systems: Computation and Control, HSCC 2015, Seattle, WA, USA, 14–16 April 2015, pp. 299–300 (2015)

Falsification of Cyber-Physical Systems with Constrained Signal Spaces

Benoît Barbot[1], Nicolas Basset[2], Thao Dang[2(✉)], Alexandre Donzé[3],
James Kapinski[5], and Tomoya Yamaguchi[4]

[1] Univ Paris Est Creteil, LACL, 94010 Creteil, France
[2] VERIMAG/CNRS, Université Grenoble Alpes, Grenoble, France
thao.dang@univ-grenoble-alpes.fr
[3] Decyphir SAS, Moirans, France
[4] Toyota Motors North America R&D, Saline, USA
[5] Gardena, USA

Falsification has garnered much interest recently as a way to validate complex CPS designs with respect to a specification expressed via temporal logics. Using their quantitative semantics, the falsification problem can be formulated as a robustness minimization problem. To make this infinite-dimensional problem tractable, a common approach is to restrict to classes of signals that can be defined using a finite number of parameters, such as piecewise-constant or piecewise-linear signals with fixed time intervals. A drawback of this approach is that when the input signals must satisfy non-trivial temporal constraints, encoding these constraints into bounded domains for parameters can be difficult. In this work, to better capture temporal constraints on the input signal space, we use timed automata (TA) and make use of a transformation that allows sampling TA traces by sampling points in the unit box. We exploit this transformation to efficiently encode constrained CPS signals in the robustness minimization problem. This transformation also allows us to define an effective coverage measure for the constrained signal space so as to provide quantitative guarantees when no falsifying behaviour is found. Additionally, the coverage measure is used to improve the black-box optimisation performance by detecting situations where the search is stuck near a local optimum. The approach is demonstrated on a $\Delta\Sigma$ modulator and a model of a car automatic transmission subject to constraints that describe usual driving patterns.

1 Introduction

Cyber-physical systems (CPS) are found in many safety-critical applications, like aircraft, medical devices, and automobiles, hence it is vital that they behave in a manner consistent with their design expectations. CPS models are growing rapidly in complexity and size and are often beyond the scalability of formal verification techniques. As of today, industrial validation is carried out mostly by sampling a finite number of input stimuli and checking the corresponding behaviors obtained by model simulation or system execution.

Another approach to CPS validation is requirement falsification using black-box optimization. Falsification can be thought of as testing where requirements

© Springer Nature Switzerland AG 2020
R. Lee et al. (Eds.): NFM 2020, LNCS 12229, pp. 420–439, 2020.
https://doi.org/10.1007/978-3-030-55754-6_25

are expressed in a formal specification language such as metric temporal logic (MTL) or signal temporal logic (STL) [32,35], which are appropriate for specifying behaviors defined using real-valued signals over dense time. A key feature of such logics is that they are equipped with *quantitative* semantics, and for a given behavior, a real value, called the *robustness*, quantifies the property satisfaction level of the behavior [20,24]. Using such semantics, the falsification problem can be formulated as a robustness minimization problem, so as to automatically find behaviors that violate (falsify) the property. Falsification techniques have been applied to many CPS systems and are finding applications in industry (see a recent survey [10]), by way of tools like S-TaLiRo and Breach [4,18].

The *optimization-based approach* is faced with several challenges. First, existing optimization solvers expect decision variables in a space of finite dimension, whereas the search space for CPS falsification problems can be of infinite dimension, as they include continuous-time input signals. This gives rise to the problem of encoding CPS signal spaces. To address this, a common practice (initiated in [18,37]) is to restrict to classes of signals that can be defined using a finite number of parameters. A second challenge is that, for cases where the inputs must satisfy non-trivial temporal constraints, encoding these constraints into bounded domains for parameters can be difficult. Ad hoc rejection sampling methods become inefficient when the portion of signals satisfying the constraints is small. Lastly, it is difficult to define meaningful coverage measures for CPS falsification problems. When the input signals are subject to complex temporal constraints, the resulting constrained signal space may be difficult to encode and measure.

In this paper we address the above challenges by introducing the following into the optimization-based falsification framework: (1) a new encoding of input signal spaces that are subject to temporal constraints specified using timed automata [3]; (2) a new coverage measure for constrained signal spaces that is based on this encoding, which we use to improve the efficiency of an iterative black-box optimization procedure. For clarity of explanation, before describing our contributions and comparing them with the current state of the art, we provide an overview of the existing approaches and their limitations.

2   Requirement Falsification Problem

CPS Models and Specification. We model the behaviors of a CPS using the following input-output mapping:

$$y = \mathcal{F}(u), \tag{1}$$

where $u \in \mathcal{U}$ is a function of time that represents the input signals to the system, that is $u : \mathcal{I} \to U$, where $\mathcal{I}$ is an interval of the form $[0, T]$ with $T \in \mathbb{R}_{>0}$, and U is some metric space of finite dimension. Note that initial conditions as well as other parameters (some finite set of variables influencing the system's behavior) can be captured as constant input signals. Similarly, we assume that each output signal $y \in \mathcal{Y}$ is a function $\mathcal{I} \to Y$, where Y is some metric space of finite dimension. To specify the correct or expected behaviors for the system (1) in an unambiguous form that can be efficiently measured and quantified, we use the Signal Temporal Logic (STL) language [35].

Overview of STL. An STL formula φ consists of atomic predicates along with logical and temporal connectives. Atomic predicates are defined over signal values and have the form $f(y(t)) \sim 0$, where f is a scalar-valued function over the signal y evaluated at time t, and $\sim \in \{<, \leq, >, \geq, =, \neq\}$. Temporal operators "always" ($\square$), "eventually" ($\Diamond$), and "until" ($\mathcal{U}$) have the usual meaning and are scoped using intervals of the form (a, b), $(a, b]$, $[a, b)$, $[a, b]$, or (a, ∞), where $a, b \in \mathbb{R}_{\geq 0}$ and $a < b$. If I is a time interval, the following grammar defines the STL language.

$$\varphi := \top \mid f(y(t)) \sim 0 \mid \neg\varphi \mid \varphi_1 \wedge \varphi_2 \mid \varphi_1 \mathcal{U}_I \varphi_2 : \quad \sim \in \{<, \leq, >, \geq, =, \neq\} \quad (2)$$

The $\Diamond$ operator is defined as $\Diamond_I \varphi \triangleq \top \mathcal{U}_I \varphi$, and the $\square$ operator is defined as $\square_I \varphi \triangleq \neg(\Diamond_I \neg\varphi)$. When omitted, the interval I is taken to be $[0, \infty)$. Given a signal y and an STL formula φ, we use the quantitative semantics for STL, which is defined formally in [20]. The quantitative semantics defines a function ρ such that when $\rho(\varphi, y, t)$ is positive it indicates that (y, t) satisfies φ, and its absolute value estimates the *robustness* of this satisfaction. If φ is an inequality of the form $f(y) > b$, then its robustness is $\rho(\varphi, y, t) = f(y(t)) - b$. When t is omitted, we assume $t = 0$ (i.e., $\rho(\varphi, y) = \rho(\varphi, y, 0)$). For the conjunction of two formulas $\varphi := \varphi_1 \wedge \varphi_2$, we have $\rho(\varphi, y) = \min(\rho(\varphi_1, y), \rho(\varphi_2, y))$, while for the disjunction $\varphi := \varphi_1 \vee \varphi_2$, we have $\rho(\varphi, y) = \max(\rho(\varphi_1, y), \rho(\varphi_2, y))$. For a formula with until operator as $\varphi := \varphi_1 \mathcal{U}_I \varphi_2$, the robustness is computed as $\rho(\varphi, y, t) = \max_{t' \in I} \left(\min \left(\rho(\varphi_2, y, t'), \min_{t'' \in [t, t']} (\rho(\varphi_1, y, t'')) \right) \right)$.

Falsification Problem. Given a system model such as (1) and a requirement φ specified as an STL formula, we want to find an input $u \in \mathcal{U}$ such that $y = \mathcal{F}(u)$ does not satisfy φ, denoted $y \not\models \varphi$. Such a behavior y is called a counter-example, which is identified when $\rho(\varphi, y) < 0$. This is usually solved by formulating the following optimization problem:

$$\min_{u \in \mathcal{U}} \rho(\varphi, y) \; s.t. \; y = \mathcal{F}(u) \quad (3)$$

This formulation has been the focus of numerous research efforts [10]. We next discuss the challenges in solving this optimization problem and some existing approaches.

Input Signal Encoding. The input signals are taken from an infinite-dimensional space (*i.e.*, they can be a partial function over a continuous time-domain); one thus needs a finite encoding of the signals. As mentioned earlier, most of the existing approaches restrict to classes of input signals that are *finitely parameterizable*—that is, input signals u can be uniquely characterized by a finite set of parameters. Therefore, the infinite-dimensional optimization problem (3) becomes finite-dimensional. For example, a right-continuous piecewise constant input signal u with discontinuities occurring at monotonically increasing instants $t_1, \ldots, t_m$ where $0 = t_1 < t_m < T$, can be uniquely characterised by m values $v_i = u(t_i)$. By fixing the number m of time intervals, the time points $t_1, \ldots, t_m$ and the corresponding signal values are the decision variables for the search.

Minimizing the Robustness. Fixing an input signal parametrization, the optimization problem (3) becomes finite-dimensional but is still challenging for a number of reasons. First, the input-output mapping $\mathcal{F}$ is not specified explicitly; rather, it enforces that y is the output signal of the dynamical system model $\mathcal{F}$, given the input signal u. For cases where $\mathcal{F}$ is a nonlinear hybrid system modelled using heterogenous formalisms (such as Simulink®/Stateflow®), the output y can only be determined approximately using numerical simulation. This also gives rise to the hard problem of determining the gradients of the cost function, often required by traditional continuous optimization techniques. Additionally, the cost function ρ is often non-convex and contains discontinuities. For such problems, in general there are no algorithms that can guarantee to find a global optimum [26]. Hence, the robustness minimization step is often done using a black-box optimization approach because it does not require derivative information [38]. This approach relies on search techniques called metaheuristics [21], which aim to combine the strengths of existing algorithms for discrete and continuous domains. Such a search consists of a sequence of moves from one candidate solution to another. In each move if the candidate satisfies the falsification goal, a counter-example is found, otherwise, the candidate is updated. The updating heuristics in general perform well for simple search spaces, for instance, multidimensional boxes, or linear algebraic constraints [38]. This is one reason why in practice the input signal parametrization is often chosen such that the search space is essentially a box. The essential ideas related to black-box optimization using a metaheuristic are summarized by the following abstract algorithm.

Algorithm 1. Optimization-based Falsification Algorithm

$k = 1$, $\rho_m = +\infty$
Select a set $\mathcal{U}_s \subset \mathcal{U}$ of input signals
repeat
  $\rho_m = \min\{\rho_m, \min_{u \in \mathcal{U}_s}\{\rho(\varphi, y) \mid y = \mathcal{F}(u)\}\}$
  if $\rho_m < 0$ **then**
    Report the falsifying behavior. Exit
  end if
  $k = k + 1$
  $\mathcal{U}_s = Update(\mathcal{U}_s)$ ▷ (using black-box optimization)
until $k = K_{max}$
No falsifying behavior found.

Quantitative Guarantees. When no falsifying behavior is found, it is of great interest to provide a quantitative guarantee expressed by a measure of the set of behaviors that was tested. Such a 'coverage' measure was proposed only for point spaces (see related work on coverage measures in Sect. 5), which are appropriate only for properties defined over the system states (such as, safety). It is thus useful to use a more general notion of signal/function space coverage, which is a problem we address in this work.

Limitations of the Existing Solutions and Our Approach. Concerning signal encoding: using fixed parametrizations restricts the searchable space, and the falsification performance depends on the selected parametrizations, which requires validation engineers to use intuition to select the number of intervals and their duration. Furthermore, as mentioned in the introduction, input signals in practical applications are often subject to constraints imposed by their generators. Examples of such signals include noises from specific environments or controls from under-actuated controllers. In these cases the input signals must satisfy non-trivial temporal constraints, and encoding these constraints in forms that can be efficiently handled by existing optimizers can be difficult; the optimizers often treat such constraints using ad hoc methods, such as using rejection sampling. Little attention has been given to these considerations in the falsification-related literature, but [17,39] propose some strategies that involve incrementally increasing the number of time intervals. If these constraints are not taken into account, there are two consequences. First the optimizers can come up with trivial non-realistic solutions, such as Zeno behaviors switching between extreme values. Second, the unconstrained search space may be too conservative compared to the valid search space, which makes rejection sampling inefficient, as we will show in an example involving a rather intuitive temporal constraint.

In this work, to capture temporal constraints on the input signal space, we use timed automata (TA) [3]. Such constraints are previously considered in a procedure to uniformly generate random signals [7], which relies on the calculation of a transformation from the unit box to timed polytopes (allowing sampling timed words of a TA by sampling points in the unit box) [6]. We extend this transformation to encode constrained input signal spaces, which constitutes a crucial ingredient in the optimization process. Unlike the work [7] where the falsification process is based on a given set of uniformly sampled timed words, in this work we perform optimization in a search space that satisfies both signal timed pattern and value constraints. In other words, this encoding allows us not only to consider signals uniformly but also to perform best-case search strategies according to an objective function, which enhances the falsification performance as shown by the experimental results. This transformation also allows us to define an effective coverage measure of the constrained signal space in order to provide quantitative guarantees. In addition, this coverage will be used to improve the black-box optimization performance by detecting situations where the search is trapped near a local optimum and to make online decisions about when and how to switch from one optimization strategy to another.

The remainder of the paper is organized as follows. In Sect. 3 we briefly recall timed automata [3] and the transformation from the unit box to timed polytopes [6,7]. We then show how this transformation can be used to encode constrained signals and to define coverage measures for the space of such signals. Section 5 describes the falsification algorithm and Sect. 6 presents our experimental results. Section 7 concludes and Sect. 8 describe with more technical details the transformation from the unit box to timed polytopes and the sampling.

3   Preliminaries on Timed Automata and Timed Word Generation

3.1   Timed Automata

A *timed automaton* $\mathcal{A} = (Q, X, \Sigma, \Delta, Inv, i_0)$ is a tuple where Q is a finite set of locations with i_0 as initial location; X is a finite set of clocks which values are assumed bounded by a constant $M \in \mathbb{N}$; Δ is a finite set of transitions. Each transition is the form $\delta = (q, \psi, a, r, q')$ where $q, q' \in Q$ are the source and destination locations; ψ is the guard, which is a conjunction of clock constraints of the form $x_i \sim c$ or $x_i \sim x_j + c$ with $x_i, x_j \in X$, $\sim \in \{<, \leq, =, \geq, >\}$; c an integer in $[-M; M]$ and $a \in \Sigma$ is a label; r is the reset map; Inv associates with each location q a conjunction of clock constraints, called the invariant of q. A state of $\mathcal{A}$ is a pair $(q, \boldsymbol{x})$ where $q \in Q$ and $\boldsymbol{x}$ is a clock valuation[1]. The transitions of the automaton are of two types: timed transitions and discrete transitions. Timed transitions correspond to the evolution of the clocks within a location as long as the clock valuation satisfies the invariant of the location. Concerning discrete transitions, if the transition $\delta = (q, \psi, a, r, q')$ is enabled at the state $(q, \boldsymbol{x})$ (that is $\boldsymbol{x}$ satisfies the guard ψ), the discrete transition from q to q' can take place (if the clock valuation after applying the reset map r satisfies the invariant $Inv_{q'}$ of q'). The *reset* map r is determined by a subset of clocks $B \subseteq X$ and this transition resets to 0 all the clocks in B and does not modify the other clocks. The initial state of $\mathcal{A}$ is $(i_0, \boldsymbol{0})$. A *trace* is an alternating sequence $(i_0, \boldsymbol{x}_0) \xrightarrow{a_1, \tau_1} (q_1, \boldsymbol{x}_1) \ldots \xrightarrow{a_n, \tau_m} (q_m, \boldsymbol{x}_m)$ of states and timed transitions with the following updating rules: q_i is the successors of q_{i-1} by transition $\delta_i = (q_{i-1}, \psi_i, a_i, r_i, q_i)$, the vector $(\boldsymbol{x}_{i-1} + (\tau_i, \ldots, \tau_i))$ must satisfy the guard ψ_i and applying the reset map r_i to it gives $\boldsymbol{x}_i$. This trace is *labelled* by the *timed word* $\gamma = (\tau_1, a_1), \ldots, (\tau_m, a_m)$ where a_i are transition labels and τ_i are *time delays* between two consecutive transitions, $(\tau_1, \ldots, \tau_m)$ is called a *timed vector* and $(a_1, \ldots, a_m)$ a *discrete pattern*. Given a discrete path $\alpha = \delta_1, \ldots, \delta_n$ of $\mathcal{A}$ the set of timed vectors $(t_1, \ldots, t_n) \in [0, M]^n$ such that $(i_0, \boldsymbol{0}) \xrightarrow{t_1, \delta_1} (q_1, t_1) \ldots \xrightarrow{t_n, \delta_n} (q_n, t_n)$ is called the *timed polytope* associated with the path α. The set of timed words that label all the traces from the initial state is called the *timed language* of $\mathcal{A}$. As an example, we consider the TA in Fig. 1, which will be used in our experiments. This automaton models a quasi-periodic pattern of signals with uncertain period ranging between 8 and 12. It has the property that after entering the cycle the time lapse between 4 consecutive transitions is contained in the interval $[8, 12]$. Intuitively, the traces of this automaton are loosely periodic as transitions cannot be taken too early or too late. Moreover the global invariant condition $x < 4$ (not depicted in Fig. 1) ensures that each duration is bounded from above by 4. An example of timed word in the timed language is $(3.4, b)(3.6, c)(1.1, d)(2.3, a)(3.3, b)$.

---

[1] A clock valuation, denoted by the letter $\boldsymbol{x}$ in bold, is a vector of clock values, while x_i denotes the ith clock of the automaton, as in Fig. 1.

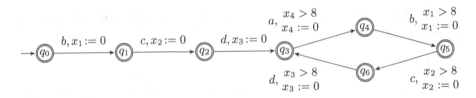

Fig. 1. A timed automaton used in our experiments. To avoid overloading the figure, a global clock x (reset to 0 at each transition) and the global invariants $x_1, x_2, x_3, x_4 < 12$ and $x < 4$ hold for each guard and are not depicted.

3.2   Transformation from the Unit Box to a Timed Polytope

We want that the exploration within the domains of optimization variables reflects the exploration within the timed language, in terms of coverage. To this end, we will use a volume-preserving transformation developed in [6,7], which we summarize in the Appendix (Sect. 8).

From a timed automaton $\mathcal{A}$, we can define inductively volume functions v_n so that $v_n(q, x)$ is the volume of the language of words of length n starting from the state (q, x) accepted by $\mathcal{A}$ [5,6]. Based on such volume functions we define cumulative distribution functions (CDFs) that we use to sequentially sample each transition and time delay via the inverse sampling method. These CDFs give us a transformation from the unit box $[0, 1]^{2n}$ to the set of timed words of length n recognized by the automaton.

In previous work [7] three tools were used to perform the sampling: Prism [34] for computing the zone graph, SageMath [42] for computing distributions and Cosmos [8] for the sampling. In the present work, the tool WordGen [9] combining the three steps has been developed, which greatly increases the usability of the method.

4   Encoding Constrained Signal Space in the Optimization Problem

A timed automaton can naturally provide a qualitative description, annotated with timing information, for a class of CPS signals of interest. In addition, we can consider quantitative constraints on signal values by associating them with the transition labels of the automaton. More concretely, each transition label a is associated with a predicate of the form $\pi_a(v) \leq 0$ where $v \in \mathbb{R}$ is the signal value.

To perform optimization over the space of such signals, we need an efficient representation of this space. For simplicity of explanation, we focus only on the signals corresponding to the timed words of $\mathcal{A}$ having a single discrete pattern $\alpha = (a_1, \cdots, a_m)$. The timed polytope $\mathcal{P}_\tau$, defined by the delays τ between the transitions that are subject to the clock constraints (imposed by the guards, resets and invariants along the transition sequence), is the search space for timed words with the fixed pattern α. To couple it with the search space for signal values, we couple $\mathcal{P}_\tau$ with the set of signal values satisfying the associated predicates: $\mathcal{P}_v = \{v \mid \forall i \in \{1, \ldots, m\}, \ \pi_{a_i}(v) \leq 0\}$. In this work, we assume that each π_{a_i} is an interval predicate[2], and the set $\mathcal{P}_v$ is thus a box, called a *valued box*. Hence, this coupling of time and value constraints leads to a polytope in $\mathbb{R}^{2m}$: $\Pi = \{(\tau, v) \mid \tau \in \mathcal{P}_\tau \wedge v \in \mathcal{P}_v\}$, called a *timed-valued polytope*. The signal constructed from any point (τ, v) in Π is guaranteed to satisfy the constraints specified by the timed automaton $\mathcal{A}$ and its associated predicates. Thus the constrained signal space in question is encoded by this *timed-valued polytope*.

To generate candidate solutions from a timed-valued polytope, as mentioned earlier, we make use of the transformation that maps the unit box to this timed polytope and extend it to a timed-valued polytope, in order to reduce the search space to a box domain (instead of complex polytopic domains). Indeed, since a timed-valued polytope Π is the product of a timed polytope $\mathcal{P}_\tau$ and a valued box $\mathcal{P}_v$, it is not hard to see that the transformation for Π, denoted by $\mathcal{S}$, is composed of $\mathcal{S}_\tau$ for the timed polytope $\mathcal{P}_\tau$ and $\mathcal{S}_v$ for the valued box $\mathcal{P}_v$. Note that $\mathcal{S}_v$ is simply an affine function transforming $\mathcal{P}_v$ to the unit box $[0,1]^m$. In short, using the transformation $\mathcal{S}$, the initial search domain, which is a timed-valued polytope, becomes the unit box $[0,1]^{2m}$. We consider this the product of two unit boxes, $\mathcal{B}_\tau \times \mathcal{B}_v$.

This transformation was implemented in the tool WordGen to generate a timed word from a point in the unit box $\mathcal{B}_\tau$. Then, to construct CPS signals corresponding to a given timed word, we use the tool Breach [19]. This tool is also used to simulate the system behaviours and evaluate their robustness. To recap, the input signal construction is done as follows:

1. Pick a point p_τ in the unit box $\mathcal{B}_\tau$. Pick a point p_v in the unit box $\mathcal{B}_v$.
2. Use WordGen to generate a timed word w from p_τ.
3. Use Breach to generate a signal u from w and p_v.

Note that the above first step is done by the procedure of updating candidate input signals. This procedure is based on a combination of metaheuristics that we discuss in the sequel.

5   Guided Combination of Metaheuristics

One natural strategy for updating candidate solutions is to use methods related to gradient descent, wherein new points are selected based on some estimate of the gradient of the cost function near promising previously evaluated points. Such a descent strategy may not lead to a global optimum, leaving the search stuck around a local optimum. When this occurs, it is possible to restart the search from a new set of candidate solutions, but this can become expensive when there are many local optima. Metaheuristics [21] are one way to go about this problem, by accepting from time to time candidates that do not improve the

---

[2] Using more general predicates, such as linear predicates, leads to a more complicated problem of defining the transformation from the unit box, which we plan to consider in future work. This is indeed related to the problem of uniform sampling within a convex polytope.

cost function value. In this work we propose a method for combining a number of well-known metaheuristics. The method switches between two different types of solvers or search algorithms that, borrowing the terminology from [12,21], are called exploitation-driven and exploration-driven.

The exploitation-driven algorithms try to make greedy changes (often small) around the current candidate. We make use of a number of well-known solvers in this type[3], namely Simulated Annealing [31], Global Nelder-Mead algorithms [2,36], and CMAES (Covariance Matrix Adaptation Evolution Strategy) [28]. This type of solver is used to explore locally around promising candidates. On the other hand, the exploration-driven solvers explore the parameter space widely, and thus quickly enlarge the exploration space. Such solvers are particularly useful to help the search escape a local optimum, where the cost value has stagnated. The exploration-driven solver we use in this work is based on the low-discrepancy and uniform sampling method in [7].

It is of great interest to be able to synergize exploration and exploitation by adaptive switching between the two strategies using appropriate measures for exploitation and exploration performance. The trade-offs between exploitation and exploration have been explored for the purposes of falsification for CPS [33]. Exploitation performance can be measured by the reduction in the cost value (that is the robustness value). Exploration performance can be measured using the notion of search space coverage. For our framework, we introduce in the subsequent section a *signal space coverage measure*.

5.1   Signal Space Coverage Measure

We define a signal space coverage measure based on a partition of the variable domains, called *cell occupancy*. A similar measure was already used in our previous work [1] but was restricted to the parameter space corresponding to the space of signal values over fixed time parameterizations. Equipped with the transformation from the unit box, we can now extend it to a more general class of signals. Let G be a partition of the unit box $[0, 1]^{2m}$ into N_t rectangular cells with equal side length. Cell occupancy is based on the ratio between the number N_o of cells occupied by points and the total number N_t of cells. Then, the cell occupancy measure is given as $\dfrac{\log N_o}{\log N_t}$. Logarithm functions are used because the total number of cells could be very large as compared to the number of occupied cells. A major advantage of the cell-occupancy measure is that it is easy to compute; however, it is clear that when the cell size is large this measure does not reflect levels of uniformity or equi-distributivity, as provided by the Kolmogorov-Smirnov statistic [7].

Related Work on Coverage Measures. In the context of CPS, a signal space coverage measure should be defined over continuous-time signals, such as the input signal space or the system behaviour space. The latter option is more difficult

---

[3] The exploitation-driven and exploration-driven characterization refers only to the behaviors of the solvers seen on a global level, since the above-mentioned metaheuristics contain both exploitation-driven and exploration-driven aspects.

because the space of all possible system behaviours is in general unknown. When an input signal space is finitely parameterized, a point coverage measure can be defined on its associated parameter space. Measures like *dispersion* try to capture the size of the empty space between points that have been explored [23]. A related and simple measure, partitions the search space into cells and measures the proportion of cells that are occupied by explored points [41]. This method is related to the combinatorial entropy notion from the domain of physics to measure the degree of randomness in a distribution of points [27]. The *star discrepancy* measure is a measure of the degree to which a set of points are equidistributed [29]; it was also used for measuring the coverage of reachable states [1,16,22]. In this work, where the specification imposes on the input signals complex temporal constraints, the resulting parameter space is difficult to define; however, using the above-described volume preserving transformation, any point coverage can be defined over the unit box and carried over to the signal space. Hence, we can use in principle any existing point coverage. In this work, we choose to use the cell occupancy measure, since it can be efficiently computed for the high dimensional search spaces encountered in our case studies.

5.2 Algorithm for Guided Combination of Metaheuristics

We describe our algorithm for guided combination of metaheuristics, summarized in Algorithm 2. The search strategy is based on the robustness and coverage measures.

Algorithm 2. Abstract Algorithm for Combining Metaheuristics

▷ s: solver index; $\mathcal{S}_\rho$: set of exploitation-driven solvers; G: set of visited states; ρ^* and c: sequences such that $\rho^*[k]$ and $c[k]$ are respectively the best robustness value and the coverage value up to iteration k

$k = 1$
while $k \leq k_{max}$ **do**
    $\{\rho^*, G\} = Exploitation(\mathcal{S}_\rho, G)$ ▷ run all the exploitation-driven solvers
    $c = updateCoverage(c, G)$
    $blocking = DetectBlocking(c, \rho^*)$ ▷ based on coverage and robustness
    if $(blocking)$ **then**
        $s = Rand$
        $(\rho^*, G) = Run(s, T_s)$ ▷ run a sampling-based solver for T_s time
    end if
    $k + +$
end while

The algorithm is organized in iterations, and in each iteration the solvers (or metaheuristics) are sequentially called, based on the current search results. Throughout the search process, we maintain a set G of *intermediate visited states*. By 'visited state', we mean the pair (p, ρ) where p is a candidate point—in the search domain, which is the unit box—and ρ is its associated cost value, and by 'intermediate' we mean the points successively computed by the solver scheme. The procedure starts with *Exploitation*, which runs each of the exploitation-driven solvers and updates the set G of visited states. Then *updateCoverage* updates the coverage c of G (using the cell-occupancy measure). Next, the procedure *DetectBlocking* determines whether the search has entered a blocking situation. If it has, the exploration-based search *Rand*, using quasi-random (that is, low-discrepancy) or uniform methods, is run for T_s seconds.

Switching to Exploration to Escape a Local Minimum. The search is said to be *blocking*, if it does not improve the cost value after some execution time limit, without increasing the coverage. Such a blocking situation often indicates a local optimum, and an exploration-driven solver, either the uniform or low-discrepancy sampling methods, is used to escape it. We monitor the coverage and robustness evolution, to detect if they do not increase and decrease respectively by some predefined amounts, for a predefined number of iterations. Due to the monotonicity of the coverage and robustness evolution with respect to the number of visited points, the detection can be done by comparing the coverage and the robustness values of the current iteration to those of the previous iteration.

Exploitation to Improve Best Candidates. An exploitation-driven solver with index s runs from a set P of initial points for T_s time (see Algorithm 2). The corresponding best cost value is stored in ρ^*. The reason we store the visited states is that they can reflect the relation between the cost function and the decision variables and can thus indicate promising regions, so as to derive good initializations for subsequent solvers.

Solver Initialization. We select initial points for a solver using the following heuristics:

- Select an initial point or a population of initial points from the best points obtained from previous iterations.
- Pick initial points according to a distribution that is dynamically updated based on the previous results, as inspired by the population based methods such as the CMAES. As described above, after each iteration we keep the points visited in the previous iterations. We select a set of best points, the robustness values of which are below some threshold, and use them to define the sampling distribution for new candidates. Let p be a parameter point and p_i denote its ith coordinate. For any point p in G, let $[\underline{p}_i, \overline{p}_i]$ be the bounding interval such that each coordinate $p_i \in [\underline{p}_i, \overline{p}_i]$. In the kth iteration, the sampling distribution of p_i can be a normal distribution $\mathcal{N}(\overline{p}_i^k, \sigma_i^k)$, where the mean $\overline{p}_i^k$ is one of the most promising candidates from the previous iteration, selected based on the robustness value. The standard deviation σ_i^k in the kth iteration can be determined by $\sigma_i^k = (\overline{p}_i - \underline{p}_i)(\frac{1}{N^k})^{k/n}$, which decreases iteration after iteration. The number N^k of candidates can vary, being large at the beginning and decreasing gradually. In the first iteration where no information is available, we can sample candidate points according to the uniform distribution.

6 Experimentation

We use two case studies to evaluate our algorithms: a model of a $\Delta\Sigma$ modulator and an automatic transmission control system. We demonstrate the efficiency gained by encoding the constrained signal spaces and evaluate the advantage of combining different metaheuristics. The combination algorithm is implemented in MATLAB® and uses 4 metaheuristics (integrated in Breach [19]): Simulated Annealing (SA) [31], CMAES [28], a globalized version of the Nelder Mead algorithm proposed by Luersen and Le Richec [2] abbreaviated by LRNM, and another globalized version of the Nelder Mead algorithm combining the classical Nelder Mead algorithm [36] with some corner searches, abbreaviated by GNM. The tool Breach [19] also provides robustness evaluation and signal construction from timed words. The generation of timed words from points in the unit box is done by the tool WordGen. Our experiments were performed on a computer with a 1.4 GHz processor with 4GB RAM, running MATLAB® R2015a 64-bit version.

$\Delta\Sigma$ **Modulator.** We illustrate the application of our method of encoding constrained signal space with a $\Delta\Sigma$ modulator, which is an important component of analog-to-digital converters. Practical quantizers have limited input and output ranges, which may lead them to saturation, and we want to check whether the output ever saturates. We use a behavioral model of a second-order modulator specified using Simulink®, which takes into account most non-idealities [13], including sampling jitter, integrator noise, and op-amp parameters (finite gain, finite bandwidth, slew-rate and saturation voltages). There exist simplified discrete-time $\Delta\Sigma$ modulator models without non-idealities, for which it is possible to derive its dynamic equations and thus can be analyzed using optimization [15] and statistical model-checking [14]; however, this Simulink model is heterogeneous, including embedded MATLAB code and a mix of discrete-time and continuous-time components. Therefore, it is too complex for existing formal verification tools. We consider the falsification of the absence of saturation of some quantizer signal Out under a certain class of nearly oscillatory inputs In. Formally In and Out must satisfy for some $t_s \geq 0$ and $\forall t \geq 0$,

$$|Out(t)| < 2 \tag{4}$$

$$\exists T \in [8t_s, 12t_s] \text{ such that } In(t + T) = In(T) \tag{5}$$

Encoding (4) as an STL formula is trivial: $\varphi_{\neg\text{sat}} = \Box |Out| < p_{sat}$. However, enforcing that In satisfies (5) is not so simple. For instance, unbounded periodic properties are known to be beyond STL expressivity [35], and this is before considering that periods may be uncertain. We consider two approaches: one based on the above-described TA framework and another using only STL formulas. In both approaches, we use a signal generator interpolating the signal values between points of a periodic discrete sequence of the form:
$u_0 \; \tau_0 \; u_1 \; \tau_1 \; u_2 \; \tau_2 \; u_3 \; \tau_3 \; u_0 \; \tau_4 \; u_1 \; \tau_5 \; u_2 \; \tau_6 \; u_3 \; \tau_7 \; u_0 \; \tau_N \; u_{\hat{N}} \ldots$
The value $In(t)$ is obtained by finding k such that $\sum_0^k \tau_i \leq t < \sum_0^{k+1} \tau_i$ and interpolating between $u_{\overline{k}}$ and $u_{\overline{k}+1}$ where $\overline{k}$ is the remainder of $k/4$. Since the discrete sequence u_i is periodic, the resulting signal satisfies (5) iff

$\forall i$, $8t_s \leq \tau_i + \tau_{i+1} + \tau_{i+2} + \tau_{i+3} \leq 12t_s$. Note that this constraint is satisfied by the delays of the timed words of our TA of Fig. 1. Hence by using WordGen to generate timed words and mapping labels a, b, c, d to values u_0, u_1, u_2, u_3 we obtain the desired signals. To cross-validate this approach, we used a simple formula: $\varphi_{per} = \Diamond_{[0,t_{end}]}(up \rightarrow upnext) \wedge \Diamond_{[0,t_{end}]}(down \rightarrow downnext)$, where $up = In1[t] > 1.9$ and $upnext = \Box_{[7.5*ts,12.5*ts]}(up)$, and $down$ and $downnext$ are defined similarly. We then defined the falsification problem as

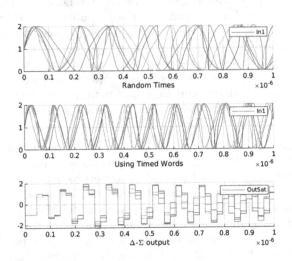

Fig. 2. Example traces for the $\Delta\Sigma$ modulator output (bottom) using inputs signals with random timings (top) and timings based on timed words from the TA of Fig. 1 (middle).

$$\min_{v} \rho(\varphi_{\neg\text{sat}}, Out(v)) \tag{6}$$

$$\text{s.t. } In(v) \models \varphi_{\text{per}}. \tag{7}$$

where v is a parameter vector. In the TA based approach, $v \in \mathcal{P}_v$ (as described in Sect. 4); whereas in the TA-free approach, v encodes directly delays between the specified signal values: $v \in \{(\tau_0, \ldots, \tau_N) \mid \tau_i \in [0, 4t_s]\}$. In the latter case, the solver is responsible for the satisfaction of constraint (7). Breach implements a simple "optimized rejection" strategy where the constrained optimization problem (6–7) is basically replaced by an unconstrained $\min_v(J(v))$ where $J(v) = \rho(\varphi_{\neg\text{sat}}, Out(v))$ if φ_{per} is satisfied and $J(v) = -\rho(\varphi_{\text{per}}, In(v))$ otherwise. In other words, when in an infeasible region, Breach actively tries to satisfy φ_{per} with the current optimization strategy. This is a *rejection* strategy in the sense that when φ_{per} is not satisfied, v is not used, meaning $Out(v)$ is not computed to avoid useless simulations. With these settings, we could confirm that the TA-based approach indeed generated only inputs satisfying φ_{per}, for arbitrarily long inputs. In addition, the optimized rejection approach only works for short horizons. For instance, we considered simulations of duration $1e{-}6$ s with

$t_s = 1e{-}8\,$s. To be able to satisfy φ_{per} we had to set the horizon t_{end} to $3e{-}7\,$s, which considers only about 3 periods. Longer horizons would result in the solver rejecting most of considered inputs, which can be explained by a small ratio of the volume of the language of valid inputs w.r.t. that of the language of all inputs (Fig. 2).

For the saturation threshold $p_{sat} = 2$ used in the model [13], the property $\varphi_{\neg\mathrm{sat}}$ was easily falsified in our optimization setting. In addition, we could compare the performance of different metaheuristics by continuing the optimization after falsification. Using our previous algorithm [7] based purely on a set of 10,000 uniformly generated signals, the highest absolute output value is 2.32032. However, using the combined metaheuristics after exploring only 826 signals, a higher value, 2.322586, is found. More concretely, we fixed the saturation threshold p_{sat} to be 2.325 in $\varphi_{\neg\mathrm{sat}}$ and ran the metaheuristics with the option of stopping at the first falsifying trace that is found. With some fixed seed[4] (100 in this case), all the stand-alone metaheuristics could not falsify the property, but the combined metaheuristics could (see Table 1). The combined metaheuristics first used Simulated Annealing and then LR Nelder Mead, which got stuck in a blocking situation where the robustness is not improved and the coverage does not increase significantly. It then switched to the CMAES metaheuristics but used the points explored by the previous metaheuristics to estimate a good initial distribution for this CMAES solver, which could then falsify the property. The CMAES method seemed to have the best performance for this example, among the stand-alone metaheuristics; we thus compared it with the combined metaheuristics using different seeds. The comparison results are summarized in Table 2, which indicates that the combined metaheuristics algorithm outperformed the stand-alone CMAES for seeds 1,000 and 10,000, but the results were mixed for seed 5,000. This shows how initializations can affect the performance of the metaheuristics, and the combination guided by coverage and robustness can be thought of as a heuristic (on top of the metaheuristics) that tries to use the information gained through the search to lead it towards promising initializations.

Table 1. Using the different methods on the $\Delta\Sigma$ model with seed 100.

Search method	Min robustness; Max $(\lvert Out \rvert)$	Nb fct eval	Comp time (s)
CMAES	0.003746; 2.321254	10,000	6,103.282974
SA	0.027244; 2.297756	10,000	8,036.702422
GNM	0.031889; 2.293111	10,000	6,763.065164
Uniform Rand	0.00338031; 2.32161969	10,000	4,539.560286
LRNM	0.07562901; 2.24937099	10,000	4,854.569456
Combined Meta	−0.002414; 2.327414	826	431.434701

---

[4] The seed here refers to the index for a sequence of random numbers in MATLAB.

Table 2. Comparing the combined metaheuristics and the CMAES with different seeds.

Search method	Seed	Min robustness; Max ($|Out|$)	Nb fct eval	Comp time (s)
CMAES	1,000	0.002282; 2.322718	10,000	6,430.215422
Combined Meta	1,000	-0.00323532; 2.32823532	936	489.150343
CMAES	5,000	-0.00164623; 2.32664623	1,081	463.796410
Combined Meta	5,000	-0.00201822; 2.32701822	1,100	536.904802
CMAES	10,000	0.00226337; 2.32273663	10,000	7,747.896409
Combined Meta	10,000	-0.000305395; 2.324694605	766	310.282428

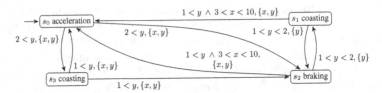

Fig. 3. timed automaton describing the driving patterns of interest. A global invariant $y < 15$ (meaning that the location changes within at most 15 s) is not depicted.

Automatic Transmission Control. This model [30] has been used as a bench-mark for evaluating hybrid systems validation techniques[5]. Here we extend it to capture constraints on the input signals that reflect usual driving patterns, based on the data from the study in [40]. The system has two inputs: throttle α and brake β, and two outputs: the engine speed w (RPM) and the vehicle speed v (mph). We consider the input signals that satisfy the constraints of the timed automaton with two clocks x and y in Fig. 3. 'Coasting' means that both the brake and acceleration pedals are not pressed, that is the two inputs are 0. The loop consisting of locations s_0, s_3 describes accelerating behaviors with coasting. At the location 'acceleration', braking can happen after accelerating for at least 2 and not more than 19 s, indicated by the transition from 'acceleration' to 'braking'. The loop between 'braking' and 'coasting' models the fact that the driver can push and release the brake pedal successively a number of times to adjust the vehicle speed. The clock x, which is not reset in the transitions between 'braking' and 'coasting', measures the time the system remains in this loop before returning to 'acceleration' by one of the two transitions both guarded by $x > 3$. In other words, the driver must stay in the braking-coasting (s_1–s_2) loop for at least 3 s. The transition labels are associated with the following range constraints on the input signal values: s_0 to s_3 (acceleration to coasting), $\alpha = 0, \beta = 0$; s_3 to s_2 (coasting to brake) $\alpha = 0$, $\beta = [100, 325]$; s_3 to s_0 (coasting to acceleration) $\alpha = (0, 500]$, $\beta = [100, 325]$; s_0 to s_2 (acceleration to braking) $\alpha = 0, \beta = 0$; s_1 to s_2 (coasting to brake) $\alpha = 0$, $\beta = [100, 325]$; s_2 to s_1 (brake to coasting) $\alpha = 0$, $\beta = 0$; s_2 to s_0 (brake to acceleration) $\alpha = (0, 500]$, $\beta = 0$; s_1 to s_0 (coasting to

---

[5] See http://cps-vo.org/node/12116.

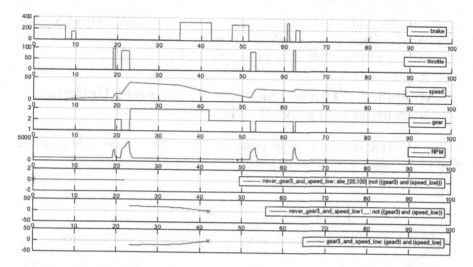

Fig. 4. A falsifying trace of the automatic transmission control system found by the combined metaheuristics algorithm. The (red) cross on the last plots indicates the instant of worst violation as computed by the diagnostics algorithm of [25] which allows ignoring quantitative information from the gear signal to focus on the speed signal only, which explains why robustness is not plotted in certain intervals. (Color figure online)

acceleration) $\alpha = (0, 500]$, $\beta = 0$. In terms of values, we use piece-wise constant signals satisfying the ranges associated to the transition labels. The property to check states that if the gear is 3 the vehicle speed should not be too slow, which is described by a STL formula: $\phi = \Box_{[20,100]} \neg ((gear = 3) \wedge (v < v_{min}))$. We seek a driving behavior (that is the input signals of throttle and brake) that leads to a violation of this property. For $v_{min} = 19.76$ (mph) the combined metaheuristics algorithm falsified it after 326 s, while GNM alone took 974 s and CMAES took 650 s to falsify. This experiment shows that these metaheuristics, when used alone, spent much time around local optima (Figs. 3 and 4).

7   Conclusion

We presented a new falsification algorithm based on a method for encoding input signals subject to timed automaton constraints. We defined a coverage measure for such constrained signal spaces. We also proposed a combination of different metaheuristics to exploit their complementary properties. Switching between the metaheuristics, based on the coverage information, allows escaping local optimum situations. We successfully demonstrated the efficacy and advantage of the new algorithms through two case studies. Ongoing work includes considering the usage of other coverage measures, such as combinatorial entropy. Furthermore, the metaheuristic switching currently depends on global coverage and robustness improvement thresholds determining blocking situations, and a biased switching can be defined using local coverage measures based on multi-resolution partitions. We also plan to use ideas from the racing algorithms [11] for identifying and dropping inferior candidates during the search.

8   Appendix – Timed Language Volume and Uniform Generation of Timed Words

From a timed automaton $\mathcal{A}$ we can define inductively the volume of the language of words of length n accepted by the automaton from the state $(q, \boldsymbol{x})$:

$$v_0(\_) = 1;$$

$$v_n^{(q,\psi,a,r,q')}(\boldsymbol{x}) = \int_{t=0}^{+\infty} \mathbb{1}_{\boldsymbol{x}+(t,\ldots,t)\models\psi}\ v_{n-1}\left(q', r(\boldsymbol{x}+(t,\ldots,t),r)\right) dt; \tag{8}$$

$$v_n(q,\boldsymbol{x}) = \sum_{\delta\in\Delta_q} v_n^{\delta}(\boldsymbol{x}) \text{ where } \Delta_q \text{ is the set of transitions starting from } q.$$

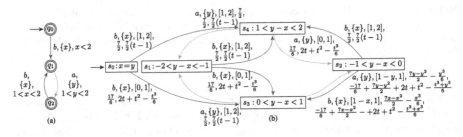

Fig. 5. On the left (a) a simple quasi-periodic automaton, and on the right (b) the stochastic process used for sampling its timed words. The states are labelled by the invariants on the clocks. To explain the labels associated to the transitions, let us consider the transition from location s_0 to s_3. This transition is labelled by b (action name), $\{x\}$ (set of clocks to reset), $[0,1]$ (guard on the delay τ (waiting time)); $\frac{17}{6}$ (weight to define the probability of taking the transition); $2t + t^2 - \frac{t^3}{6}$ (cumulative probability distribution for sampling the delay τ).

The function r produces a new clock valuation by setting to 0 the values of the clocks to be reset and keeping the others unchanged. The function $v_n^{(q,\psi,a,r,q')}(\boldsymbol{x})$ is the volume of the set of timed words starting at $\boldsymbol{x}$ which are generated by the transition (q, ψ, a, r, q'). The function $v_n(q, \boldsymbol{x})$ is the volume of the set of timed words starting at $(q, \boldsymbol{x})$ that are generated by all possible transitions from q. Note that the above volume definition is not operational in this form, since the integral bounds contain max/min functions. We show in [6] that by decomposing the automaton into a zone graph with additional constraints to ensure that the resulting bounds are linear so that the integrals can be effectively computed. Using this decomposition, the volume v_n can be computed efficiently in polynomial time and can be written as polynomials functions of clock valuations. Next the transformation is defined as the cumulative probability distributions (CDF) for sequentially sampling each transition and time delay as follows: in state (q, x) the next transition δ is chosen with probability $p_{trans}(\delta|q, x) = v_n^\delta(q, x)/v_n(q, x)$. Once the transition is chosen, the delay t is distributed according to the following cumulative probability distribution: $p_{delay}(t|\delta, q, x) = 1 - v_n^\delta(x + (t, \ldots, t))/v_n^\delta(x)$. In other words, these distributions define the inverse of the transformation from the timed polytope of a given discrete pattern to the unit box. Indeed, to generate a timed word of length n, one starts with a sequence $(u_i)_{i=1}^{2n} \in [0, 1]$ of real values, which corresponds to a point in the unit box of dimension $2n$. Starting from the initial state of the automaton and the clock valuation equal to $\mathbf{0}$, the transition and the delay at step i are chosen using the inverse transform method applied to the distribution p_{trans} and p_{delay} with the reals u_{2i} and u_{2i+1}.

References

1. Adimoolam, A., Dang, T., Donzé, A., Kapinski, J., Jin, X.: Classification and coverage-based falsification for embedded control systems. In: Majumdar, R., Kunčak, V. (eds.) CAV 2017. LNCS, vol. 10426, pp. 483–503. Springer, Cham (2017). https://doi.org/10.1007/978-3-319-63387-9_24
2. Luersen, M.A., Le Richec, R.: Globalized Nelder-mead method for engineering optimization. Comput. Struct. **82**(23), 2251–2260 (2004)
3. Alur, R., Dill, D.L.: A theory of timed automata. Theor. Comput. Sci. **126**(2), 183–235 (1994)
4. Annapureddy, Y., Liu, C., Fainekos, G.E., Sankaranarayanan, S.: S-TaLiRo: a tool for temporal logic falsification for hybrid systems. In: TACAS, pp. 254–257 (2011)
5. Asarin, E., Basset, N., Degorre, A.: Entropy of regular timed languages. Inf. Comput. **241**, 142–176 (2015)
6. Barbot, B., Basset, N., Beunardeau, M., Kwiatkowska, M.: Uniform sampling for timed automata with application to language inclusion measurement. In: Agha, G., Van Houdt, B. (eds.) QEST 2016. LNCS, vol. 9826, pp. 175–190. Springer, Cham (2016). https://doi.org/10.1007/978-3-319-43425-4_13
7. Barbot, B., Basset, N., Dang, T.: Generation of signals under temporal constraints for CPS testing. In: Badger, J.M., Rozier, K.Y. (eds.) NFM 2019. LNCS, vol. 11460, pp. 54–70. Springer, Cham (2019). https://doi.org/10.1007/978-3-030-20652-9_4
8. Barbot, B., Bérard, B., Duplouy, Y., Haddad, S.: Integrating simulink models into the model checker cosmos. In: Khomenko, V., Roux, O.H. (eds.) PETRI NETS 2018. LNCS, vol. 10877, pp. 363–373. Springer, Cham (2018). https://doi.org/10.1007/978-3-319-91268-4_19
9. Benoît Barbot. WordGen (2019). https://git.lacl.fr/barbot/wordgen
10. Bartocci, E., Deshmukh, J., Donzé, A., Fainekos, G., Maler, O., Ničković, D., Sankaranarayanan, S.: Specification-based monitoring of cyber-physical systems: a survey on theory, tools and applications. In: Bartocci, E., Falcone, Y. (eds.) Lectures on Runtime Verification. LNCS, vol. 10457, pp. 135–175. Springer, Cham (2018). https://doi.org/10.1007/978-3-319-75632-5_5
11. Birattari, M., Stützle, T., Paquete, L., Varrentrapp, K.: A racing algorithm for configuring metaheuristics. In: Proceedings of the 4th Annual Conference on Genetic and Evolutionary Computation, GECCO 2002, San Francisco, CA, USA, pp. 11–18. Morgan Kaufmann Publishers Inc. (2002)

12. Blum, C., Roli, A.: Metaheuristics in combinatorial optimization: overview and conceptual comparison. ACM Comput. Surv. **35**(3), 268–308 (2003)

13. Brigati, S., Francesconi, F., Malcovati, P., Tonietto, D., Baschirotto, A., Maloberti, F.: Modeling sigma-delta modulator non-idealities in simulink. In: ISCAS 1999. Proceedings of the 1999 IEEE International Symposium on Circuits and Systems VLSI, May 1999, vol. 2, pp. 384–387 (1999)

14. Clarke, E.M., Donzé, A., Legay, A.: On simulation-based probabilistic model checking of mixed-analog circuits. Formal Method Syst. Des. **36**(2), 97–113 (2010)

15. Dang, T., Donzé, A., Maler, O.: Verification of analog and mixed-signal circuits using hybrid system techniques. In: Hu, A.J., Martin, A.K. (eds.) FMCAD 2004. LNCS, vol. 3312, pp. 21–36. Springer, Heidelberg (2004). https://doi.org/10.1007/978-3-540-30494-4_3

16. Dang, T., Nahhal, T.: Coverage-guided test generation for continuous and hybrid systems. Formal Method Syst. Des. **34**(2), 183–213 (2009)

17. Deshmukh, J., Jin, X., Kapinski, J., Maler, O.: Stochastic local search for falsification of hybrid systems. In: Finkbeiner, B., Pu, G., Zhang, L. (eds.) ATVA 2015. LNCS, vol. 9364, pp. 500–517. Springer, Cham (2015). https://doi.org/10.1007/978-3-319-24953-7_35

18. Donzé, A.: Breach, a toolbox for verification and parameter synthesis of hybrid systems. In: CAV, pp. 167–170 (2010)

19. Donzé, A.: Breach, a toolbox for verification and parameter synthesis of hybrid systems. In: Touili, T., Cook, B., Jackson, P. (eds.) CAV 2010. LNCS, vol. 6174, pp. 167–170. Springer, Heidelberg (2010). https://doi.org/10.1007/978-3-642-14295-6_17

20. Donzé, A., Maler, O.: Robust satisfaction of temporal logic over real-valued signals. In: Chatterjee, K., Henzinger, T.A. (eds.) FORMATS 2010. LNCS, vol. 6246, pp. 92–106. Springer, Heidelberg (2010). https://doi.org/10.1007/978-3-642-15297-9_9

21. Dreo, J., Siarry, P., Petrowski, A., Taillard, E.: Metaheuristics for Hard Optimization: Methods and Case Studies. Springer, Berlin (2006). https://doi.org/10.1007/3-540-30966-7

22. Dreossi, T., Dang, T., Donzé, A., Kapinski, J., Jin, X., Deshmukh, J.V.: Efficient guiding strategies for testing of temporal properties of hybrid systems. In: Havelund, K., Holzmann, G., Joshi, R. (eds.) NFM 2015. LNCS, vol. 9058, pp. 127–142. Springer, Cham (2015). https://doi.org/10.1007/978-3-319-17524-9_10

23. Esposito, J.M., Kim, J., Kumar, V.: Adaptive RRTs for validating hybrid robotic control systems. In: WAFR (2004)

24. Fainekos, G.E., Pappas, G.J.: Robustness of temporal logic specifications. In: Havelund, K., Núñez, M., Roşu, G., Wolff, B. (eds.) FATES/RV -2006. LNCS, vol. 4262, pp. 178–192. Springer, Heidelberg (2006). https://doi.org/10.1007/11940197_12

25. Ferrère, T., Nickovic, D., Donzé, A., Ito, H., Kapinski, J.: Interface-aware signal temporal logic. In: HSCC, pp. 57–66. ACM (2019)

26. Floudas, C.A., Pardalos, P.M. (eds.): Encyclopedia of Optimization, 2nd edn. Springer, New York (2009)

27. Gabbay, D.M., Thagard, P., Woods, J., Butterfield, J., Earman, J.: Philosophy of Physics: Handbook of the Philosophy of Science. Elsevier Science, Amsterdam (2006)

28. Hansen, N.: The CMA evolution strategy: a comparing review. In: Lozano, J.A., Larranaga, P., Inza, I., Bengoetxea, E. (eds.) Towards a New Evolutionary Computation. Studies in Fuzziness and Soft Computing, vol. 192, pp. 75–102. Springer, Heidelberg (2006). https://doi.org/10.1007/3-540-32494-1_4

29. Heinrich, S.: Some open problems concerning the star-discrepancy. J. Complex. **19**(3), 416–419 (2003). Oberwolfach Special Issue

30. Hoxha, B., Abbas, H., Fainekos, G.E.: Benchmarks for temporal logic requirements for automotive systems. In: 1st and 2nd International Workshop on Applied veRification for Continuous and Hybrid Systems, ARCH@CPSWeek 2014, Berlin, Germany, 14 April 2014/ARCH@CPSWeek 2015, Seattle, WA, USA, 13 April 2015, pp. 25–30 (2014)

31. Kirkpatrick, S., Gelatt, C.D., Vecchi, M.P.: Optimization by simulated annealing. Science **220**(4598), 671–680 (1983)

32. Koymans, R.: Specifying real-time properties with metric temporal logic. Real Time Syst. **2**(4), 255–299 (1990)

33. Kuřátko, J., Ratschan, S.: Combined global and local search for the falsification of hybrid systems. In: Legay, A., Bozga, M. (eds.) FORMATS 2014. LNCS, vol. 8711, pp. 146–160. Springer, Cham (2014). https://doi.org/10.1007/978-3-319-10512-3_11

34. Kwiatkowska, M., Norman, G., Parker, D.: PRISM 4.0: verification of probabilistic real-time systems. In: Proceedings of CAV 2011 (2011)

35. Maler, O., Nickovic, D.: Monitoring temporal properties of continuous signals. In: FORMATS/FTRTFT, pp. 152–166 (2004)

36. Nelder, J.A., Mead, R.: A simplex method for function minimization. Comput. J. **7**, 308–313 (1965)

37. Nghiem, T., Sankaranarayanan, S., Fainekos, G., Ivanciec, F., Gupta, A., Pappas, G.J.: Monte-Carlo techniques for falsification of temporal properties of non-linear hybrid systems. In: HSCC 2010 - Proceedings of the 13th ACM International Conference on Hybrid Systems: Computation and Control, pp. 211–220 (2010)

38. Rios, L.M., Sahinidis, N.V.: Derivative-free optimization: a review of algorithms and comparison of software implementations. J. Global Optim. **56**(3), 1247–1293 (2013)

39. Silvetti, S., Policriti, A., Bortolussi, L.: An active learning approach to the falsification of black box cyber-physical systems. In: Polikarpova, N., Schneider, S. (eds.) IFM 2017. LNCS, vol. 10510, pp. 3–17. Springer, Cham (2017). https://doi.org/10.1007/978-3-319-66845-1_1

40. Sim, G., Ahn, S., Park, I., Youn, J., Yoo, S., Min, k.: Automatic longitudinal regenerative control of EVS based on a driver characteristics-oriented deceleration model. World Electr. Veh. J. **10**, 58 (2019)

41. Skruch, P.: A coverage metric to evaluate tests for continuous-time dynamic systems. Central Eur. J. Eng. **1**(2), 174–180 (2011)

42. Stein, W.A., et al.: Sage Mathematics Software (Version 6.9). The Sage Development Team (2015). http://www.sagemath.org

Correction to: NASA Formal Methods

Ritchie Lee, Susmit Jha, Anastasia Mavridou,
and Dimitra Giannakopoulou

Correction to:
R. Lee et al. (Eds.): *NASA Formal Methods*, **LNCS 12229,**
https://doi.org/10.1007/978-3-030-55754-6

The original versions of this book and Chapter 14 were revised. The following was corrected:

Dimitra Giannakopoulou, the General Chair of the NFM 2020 conference, was inadvertently forgotten and, therefore, added as a volume editor.

Chapter 14 was retrospectively made available open access under a CC BY 4.0 license at link.springer.com.

The updated version of the book can be found at
https://doi.org/10.1007/978-3-030-55754-6_14
https://doi.org/10.1007/978-3-030-55754-6

R. Lee et al. (Eds.): NFM 2020, LNCS 12229, p. C1, 2020.
https://doi.org/10.1007/978-3-030-55754-6_26

Author Index